BUDGETING
FORMULATION *And* EXECUTION

BUDGETING
FORMULATION and EXECUTION

EDITED BY

Jack Rabin
Professor of Public Administration and Public Policy
School of Public Affairs
The Pennsylvania State University–Harrisburg
Middletown, Pennsylvania

W. Bartley Hildreth
Regents Distinguished Professor of Public Finance
Hugo Wall School of Urban & Public Affairs
Wichita State University
Wichita, Kansas

Gerald J. Miller
Associate Professor of Public Administration
Graduate Department of Public Administration
Rutgers–The State University of New Jersey
Newark, New Jersey

CARL VINSON INSTITUTE OF GOVERNMENT
THE UNIVERSITY OF GEORGIA

Budgeting: Formulation and Execution

Editorial coordination: Inge Whittle

Design: Reid McCallister

Digital composition: Lisa Carson

Proofreading: Norma Pettigrew, Charlotte Eberhard

Publications editor: Emily Honigberg

Copyright © 1996 by the Carl Vinson Institute of Government, The University of Georgia. Printed in the United States of America. All rights reserved. No part of this publication may be used or reproduced in any manner whatsoever without written permission except in the case of brief quotations embodied in critical articles and reviews. For information, write Publications Program, Carl Vinson Institute of Government, 201 North Milledge Avenue, University of Georgia, Athens, Georgia 30602-5482.

Fourth printing

Library of Congress Cataloging-in-Publication Data

Budgeting : formulation and execution / edited by Jack Rabin, W. Bartley Hildreth, Gerald J. Miller.
    p. cm.
   Rev. ed. of: Budget management. c1983.
   Includes bibliographical references.
   ISBN 0-89854-180-8. — ISBN 0-89854-181-6 (pbk.)
    1. Local budgets. 2. Local budgets—United States. I. Rabin, Jack, 1945-   .
II. Hildreth, W. Bartley, 1949-   . III. Miller, Gerald. IV. Budget management.
HJ9111.B83   1996
352.1′2—dc20
                                                   95–39776
                                                   CIP

Foreword

Budgeting: Formulation and Execution is a comprehensive collection of articles concerning local government budget management by authors from academic, business, and public sector backgrounds. It is one component of the *Public Budgeting Laboratory,* a simulation designed to offer participants experience in local government budgeting. *Laboratory* participants learn how to analyze data relevant to budget decisions, including revenue forecasting, expenditure estimation, and budget balancing. In total, the simulation includes this volume, a student workbook, a data sourcebook, and an instructor's manual.

Budgeting: Formulation and Execution is an extensive revision of *Budget Management: A Reader in Local Government Financial Management* which was published with the original edition of the *Laboratory*. Besides meshing with the *Laboratory* simulation, *Budgeting* can be used alone, as a sourcebook for people involved in making local government budget decisions, and for public administration students and instructors.

The *Laboratory,* first published in the 1980s, is the result of a collaborative effort begun by the authors while they were associated with the Vinson Institute. Jack Rabin is professor of public administration and public policy, School of Public Affairs, The Pennsylvania State University–Harrisburg; W. Bartley Hildreth is Regents Distinguished Professor of Public Finance, Hugo Wall School of Urban & Public Affairs, Wichita State University; and Gerald J. Miller is associate professor of public administration, Graduate Department of Public Administration, Rutgers–The State University of New Jersey, at Newark.

                                                         Melvin B. Hill, Jr.
                                                         Director
                                                         Carl Vinson Institute of Government

Contents

Preface xi

Overview 3

PART 1: FORMULATION 5

1 Introduction 7

Political Economy

2 Local Government Structure 12
David R. Morgan

3 States and Their Local Governments 21
Advisory Commission on Intergovernmental Relations

4 Principles of Fiscal Federalism 28
Department of the Treasury

5 Local Public Economies: Provision, Production, and Governance 49
Ronald J. Oakerson

6 Government as Competitor: Alternatives to Privatization 57
Marc Holzer and Arie Halachmi

7 The Three Policy Arenas 63
Paul E. Peterson

8 Economic Base: What Our Jobs Are Tied To 79
Eva C. Galambos and Arthur F. Schreiber

Budget Setting

9 Productivity and the Budget Process 91
Gerald J. Miller

10 Mandates: Cases in State-Local Relations 110
Advisory Commission on Intergovernmental Relations

11 Financial Indicators for Local Government   119
Sanford M. Groves, W. Maureen Godsey, and Martha A. Shulman

12 Cutback Management in an Era of Scarcity: Hard Questions for Hard Times   130
Charles H. Levine

13 Six Steps for Communities in Crisis   134
Allen J. Proctor

14 How to Read a Budget   140
James D. Carney and Stanley Schoenfeld

Revenues

15 Criteria for Evaluating a Tax (Revenue) System   154
The District of Columbia Tax Revision Commission

16 Evaluating Alternative Revenue Sources   159
Ian J. Allan

17 Property Tax and Assessment   168
International Association of Assessing Officers

18 Pricing Public Services   172
Kevin Neels and Michael Caggiano

19 Projecting Local Government Revenue   183
Charles D. Liner

20 Adjusting for Inflation When Comparing Revenues or Expenditures   192
David N. Ammons

Expenditures

21 Evaluating Public Expenditures: A Guide for Local Officials   196
Therese A. Freeman, Ernest G. Niemi, and Peter M. Wilson

22 Cost-Benefit Analysis   211
Gerald J. Miller

23 Local Government Financial and Budgetary Analysis   231
Kenneth D. Sanders and Charlie Tyer

24 Monitoring Performance   248
State of Rhode Island

25 Service Efforts and Accomplishments: The Case of Road Maintenance   257
William A. Hyman and Joan A. Allen

26 Calculating Compensation Costs   265
Marvin Friedman

27 Budgeting Capital Outlays and Improvements   276
A. John Vogt

28 Capital Financing: A New Look at an Old Idea   292
Ronald Chapman

PART 2: EXECUTION   297

29 Introduction   299

Budget Implementation

30 Rebudgeting: The Serial Nature of Municipal Budgetary Processes   304
John P. Forrester and Daniel R. Mullins

31 Cash Management: Basic Principles and Guidelines   313
Aman Khan

Debt Management

32 The Development of a Planned Debt Policy   323
Michael Zino

33 State and Local Governments as Borrowers:
Strategic Choices and the Capital Market   329
W. Bartley Hildreth

34 Municipal Finance Criteria   341
Standard and Poor's

35 The Fundamentals of Revenue Bond Credit Analysis   361
Moody's Investors Service

36 Competitive versus Negotiated Sale of Debt   375
California Debt Advisory Commission

37 Understanding the Underwriting Spread   381
California Debt Advisory Commission

38 Techniques to Lower Municipal Borrowing Costs   387
Manly W. Mumford

39 Types and Purposes of Lease Financing   399
California Debt Advisory Commission

Operations

40 Government Purchasing: The State of the Practice   409
Charles K. Coe

41 Life-Cycle Costing   420
Roderick C. Lee

42 Advantages of a Risk Management Program   424
Gerald J. Miller and W. Bartley Hildreth

43 Pension Policy, Management, and Analysis   431
W. Bartley Hildreth and Gerald J. Miller

Accounting

44 Fund Accounting: An Introduction for Public and
Nonprofit Organization Managers   438
Gloria A. Grizzle

45 Managerial Accounting   452
James E. Sorensen, Glyn W. Hanbery, and A. Ronald Kucic

46 Identifying Full Costs of a Program   462
David N. Ammons

Reporting

47 Unreserved Fund Balance and Local Government Finance   469
Ian J. Allan

48 Understanding Local Government Financial Statements   479
Price Waterhouse

49 The 10-Point Test of Financial Condition:
Toward an Easy-to-Use Assessment Tool for Smaller Cities   492
Ken W. Brown

50 Proposed Financial Ratios for Use in Analysis of
Municipal Annual Financial Reports   500
Karl M. Zehms

Accountability

51 Government Auditing Standards   508
U.S. General Accounting Office

52 The Municipal Audit: Choice and Opportunity   521
State of Massachusetts

53 Local Government Accountability and the Need for Audit Follow-Up   525
Richard C. Brooks and David B. Pariser

Preface

This collection of discussions deals with local government budget management. Designed as a basic source on the formulation and execution of the annual budget, it addresses the needs of three target user groups.

The first target group consists of participants in the *Public Budgeting Laboratory* simulation (also published by the Vinson Institute, at the University of Georgia). As an experiential learning exercise in budget making, the *Public Budgeting Laboratory* guides participants in the development of a local government budget and the structuring of a budget analysis. In teaching the lab, we found that participants needed ready access to additional materials. This reader provides such information.

A second target group is practicing public financial managers. We believe that our view of the state of the art, as reflected by the selected articles presented here, is consistent with the direction that financial executives are taking with their practice.

In addition, the book addresses the needs of public administration students and instructors. Public budgeting remains an expression of politics, but there is more to formulating and executing budgets. It is important for a student's educational experience to reflect that diverse knowledge base. This collection of essays seeks to help instructors translate best practice discussions into a classroom setting.

Budgeting: Formulation and Execution is presented in two parts: budget formulation and budget execution. Part 1 focuses on budget development, opening with readings designed to place budgeting in the context of political economy. The section then offers a review of budget setting, revenues, and expenditures. Part 2 discusses budget execution, including management options (e.g., cash and debt management), controls (i.e., accounting), reporting practices, and accountability devices (i.e., auditing). Combined, the two parts introduce the reader to the variety of skills, perspectives, and concepts critical to budget management.

Jack Rabin
W. Bartley Hildreth
Gerald J. Miller

BUDGETING

FORMULATION
And
EXECUTION

Overview

Once a year, every local government adopts the most important statement about its purpose or existence: the *budget,* which includes decisions concerning the allocation of community resources to meet goals of civic improvement. The effort to decide on these goals and execute the resulting policies represents *budget management.* The readings in the following sections—the formulation of a budget and its execution—describe and apply available techniques for making and implementing the civic will.

This publication is intended to contribute to a full understanding of the relationships within and between budget formulation and execution. Budget participants, as the accompanying readings suggest, must devote attention to questions involving *budget formulation,* such as these:

- What is the role of government in the local economy?
- What preconditions, or settings, structure budget making?
- What are the various types of revenues and how are they projected?
- How does one analyze expenditures for services, compensation costs, and capital outlays?

and those involving *budget execution*, including the following:

- In implementing the budget, how does the budget change to meet emerging needs and cash flows?
- What is involved in debt issuance and the management of long-term liabilities?
- How does government acquire and protect assets?
- How can management controls—the accounting system—meet the needs of decision makers?
- What purpose does financial reporting serve?
- How can evaluation and auditing be of use to managers?

These questions illustrate the range and scope of issues facing budget makers. Each question frames the discussion contained in each unit of this collection of readings. Thus, Part 1 focuses on budget formulation and its four subdivisions—political economy, definition and budget setting, revenues, and expenditures. Part 2 reviews the budget execution process, using six subdivisions—implementation, debt management, operations, accounting, reporting, and accountability.

PART 1
FORMULATION

Introduction

Budget management describes a structure for making and enforcing fiscal choices. The first half of the budgeting process, formulation, covers decisions about what community resources are allocated to meet what goals of civic improvement. A public budget reflects a view of the political economy. This flows from political institutions adapting to a dynamic marketplace of individuals making hundreds of economic decisions each and every day. Private firms and other governments enrich this environment, requiring attention by public managers.

Part 1 of *Budgeting: Formulation and Execution* examines the productivity-oriented pressures on budgeting and the constraints imposed by mandates. Budgeting in an era of scarcity reaffirms the need for assessing government's financial condition.

Because local governments must adopt balanced budgets, attention generally focuses quickly on the simplistic balancing equation of local government budgeting: projected revenues equal authorized expenditures. To deal with the left side of the equation, the opening readings examine the criteria for evaluating revenue sources and the particulars of various key sources, including the pricing of public services. These discussions include methods for making revenue projections and adjusting for inflation. A subsequent set of articles presents expenditure analysis, with attention given to identifying the costs and benefits of services, establishing service efforts and accomplishments, analyzing the costs of compensation, and improving the planning and scheduling of large capital outlay purchases.

POLITICAL ECONOMY

Governance of local political jurisdictions can be accomplished through one of several forms, a diversity befitting the more than 80,000 units of local government in America. David Morgan provides a concise review of the two basic forms of local government—mayor-council and council-manager—and describes their common variations. While he focuses on cities, the same forms are increasingly found in county government too, as the commission form falls from favor. He concludes that despite its limitations, the strong-mayor variation of the mayor-council form "is especially suitable to large cities with diverse populations, where strong political leadership is required to arrange compromises and arbitrate struggles for power among contending interests." According to Morgan, the council-manager form of government "has achieved considerable success among those places with little community diversity, where a high degree of consensus exists over the proper scope and function of city government." As to his discussion of the election of office holders, Morgan adds flavor by surveying the nature of partisan ballots and district elections.

The U.S. Constitution is silent on the matter of local governments, leaving it to the states to decide how to handle such internal affairs, which they have done by deciding the nature and condition for local self-governance. City governments are incorporated with certain taxing powers to deliver a range of services to their residents. Counties are subdivisions of the state with a history of administrative and judicial duties strictly delegated by the state, but this is changing due to suburban growth and citizen demands for more city-type services. As the Advisory Commission on Intergovernmental Relations concludes after exploring these rich linkages: "state governments hold the key to many matters determining (the) well-being and success (of local governments)."

What is the proper role of government and what are its responsibilities? American federal, state, and local governments combine to form a major share of this nation's income. Yet federalism emerges from a political philosophy premised on protecting individual liberty from abuse by government power and preserving national unity in a pluralistic society. Economic theory helps interpret this legacy, as outlined in the selection, "Principles of Fiscal Federalism." This special report, presented to the president of the United States, offers a balanced review of the key fiscal principles for evaluating the relationships between citizens and their government, and among federal, state, and local governments.

Even if a local government decides to provide a service, public employees are not necessarily the ones who must deliver it. In "Local Public Economies: Provision, Production, and Governance," Ronald Oakerson shows that "multiple local governments constitute a 'local public economy' consisting of a provision side and a production side that can be organized in quite different ways." Provision relates to big decisions: when (and if) government should intervene in the economy; what mix of taxing, regulation and spending is appropriate; and how accountability is maintained and quality promoted. In contrast, production involves the delivery of the chosen goods and services. For example, the local government can contract with a private firm to fix the streets, pick up the garbage, manage the sewer plant, or fight fires. Empowering parents with a funded school voucher so a child has the option of attending a public or a private school is an alternative to the traditional pattern of public production of public schools.

Caution against strict adoption of the privatization option is offered by Marc Holzer and Arie Halachmi, founders of the National Center for Public Productivity. In "Government as Competitor: Alternatives to Privatization," they call for governments to develop internal capacities in order to compete effectively against private sector options. This selection, as well as that of Oakerson, clarifies the distinctions between provision and production decisions.

Local governments vary in their economic policies. Paul Peterson, in "The Three Policy Arenas," sees three policy types:

> *Developmental* policies enhance the economic position of the city. *Redistributive* policies benefit low-income residents but at the same time negatively affect the local economy. *Allocational* policies are more or less neutral in their economic effects.

Peterson not only defines the features of each policy area, he examines the relationships between these policies and expenditures. He finds redistributive policies in communities with stronger fiscal capacity where, ironically, they are needed less. Developmental policies, in contrast, flow more from need than fiscal condition. If there is a need, even the less prosperous community will find a way to fulfill it, thereby enhancing its economic position. Differences in local political characteristics and history have little sway, yielding instead to external economic forces. Peterson concludes that local officials must vigilantly focus on the "long-term economic welfare of their community."

Budgets are premised on the strength of the local economy. It does not take a Ph.D in economics to analyze the economic base. The steps for preparing a simple analysis are outlined in "Economic Base: What Our Jobs Are Tied To." In this selection, Eva Galambos and Arthur Schreiber offer specific guidance on data acquisition, computation, and analysis.

BUDGET SETTING

What is a budget? A budget can be viewed as a spending plan for a particular period of time, usually a 12-month fiscal year. Implicit is the need for controls to ensure that actual results conform to the plan.

Budget choices reflect both the process by which decisions are made and the outcomes revealed by the numbers. Several important questions arise: Who is involved in making budget choices, and to what extent? How are these choices framed? What service-related questions can a lay reader answer after reviewing the budget? How is a desired end result enhanced by a specific budget item?

The format of budgeting offers structure to these concerns. The budget serves as a signal of the intentions of the chief executive. In "Productivity and the Budget Process," Gerald Miller notes that a budget "helps unite the organization members in a purpose; it both decentralizes decision making and integrates activities from lowest to highest levels."

Local choices are limited by requirements imposed from both the state and federal levels of government. Taking form as either obligations to perform or prohibitions on performance, mandates have always been a part of life at the local level. As the Advisory Commission on Intergovernmental Relations study points out, "mandates arise from statutes, constitutional provisions, court decisions, and administrative regulations, or orders that demand action from 'subordinate' governments under pain of civil or criminal sanctions." The ACIR study also focuses on the more fundamental problem: the imposition of new mandates without added financial flexibility.

Budgeting for an upcoming 12 months assumes some state of financial capability, which in turn is based on fiscal history. A local government's financial health is measurable, but also subject to interpretation. Unfortunately, for purposes of simplification there is not a single measure like "increasing shareholder wealth," the all-purpose indicator enjoyed by corporate finance. In "Financial Indicators for Local Government," authors Sanford Groves, W. Maureen Godsey, and Martha Shulman note: "(n)ot only are there a large number of factors to evaluate, but many of them are difficult to isolate and quantify."

A local government's financial condition is determined by the interplay of numerous factors, including past budget decisions, economic uncertainty, resource scarcity, taxpayer revolts, and legal mandates, many of which subtly escape the attention of decision makers until unexpected fiscal stress rivets attention on them and creates unwanted surprises. To help monitor a government's financial condition, fiscal indicators have evolved which permit the tracking of changes in the social, economic, and financial characteristics of the governmental unit. Budget makers can employ such indicators to help uncover favorable or unfavorable trends deserving further analysis. A financial trend monitoring system provides a comprehensive tool for assessing the financial condition of local governments.

Local governments face compelling problems in matching resources to needs, especially at times of economic uncertainty. In such situations, services or programs have to be reduced or taxes have to be raised, or both. Citizens generally express disapproval of the idea of new taxes, but at the same time expect better, if not expanded, services.

Managers continually must cope with demands to reduce or limit government activities—the concept of cutback management. Attention turns to doing more with less. Charles Levine, an authority on cutback management in government, addressed the issue, defining cutback management as

> managing organizational change toward lower levels of resource consumption and organizational activity. Cutting back an organization involves making hard decisions about who will be asked to make sacrifices.

Levine's article also outlines the sources of resistance and problems one encounters while managing fiscally stressed governments.

Once a crisis occurs, however, financial managers have to take steps "designed to enhance the ability to maintain budget balance and to begin a process of restoring stability to government policymaking and service delivery." Allen Proctor specifies six remedial steps to establish fiscal control with the aim of emerging in a stronger position for the next financial period.

Moreover, a public budget can be quite imposing, both in size and complexity. Professional norms* now expect public budget documents to serve as a policy document, an operations guide, a financial plan, and—as a communications medium—to be more "user friendly." Along these lines, James Carney and Stanley Schoenfeld offer a guide to reading and understanding the budget.

REVENUES

A budget links projected revenues with expected expenditures. In arriving at projected revenues, a budget maker should first examine the economics of taxation. In "Criteria for Evaluating a Tax (Revenue) System," the fundamental principles of tax policy are

---

*As embodied in the "Distinguished Budget Presentation Awards Program" of the Government Finance Officers Association.

outlined. Emerging from a need for revenue, a particular tax policy can have unintended economic effects and place a burden where it was not expected. Furthermore, a given tax scheme can lead to overly complex administrative and compliance duties. While policy trade-offs are inevitable, tax policy should address these basic principles.

Local governments generally use variations of the same revenue types. Ian Allan explores the basic features of major local government revenue sources. A selection by the International Association of Assessing Officers then explores the basics of the property tax, the major source of local taxation.

Local governments also must contend with citizens who resist increasing local taxes (and, in fact, push for taxes to be lower) at the same time that pressures mount on state and federal government budgets to fund their own programs—and not local ones. This requires local governments to assume a more entrepreneurial orientation, as in benefit-based financing. The article "Pricing Public Services," by Kevin Neels and Michael Caggiano, reveals how such an approach can work in a city.

Locally imposed user fees are direct charges for services provided. For example, citizens may pay a fee for the use of public swimming pools and tennis courts, and a city's garbage collection service can be financed through direct charges for services rendered, not out of a general levy.

One reason for the growth of benefit-based revenue strategies is equity: the user fee contrasts with the ability-to-pay principle underlying taxes—one may accept or refuse the service and pay accordingly. Supporters of user fees argue that charges and fees can reduce the cost of government services. Critics suggest, in part, that user fees place public services out of reach of the poor and economically distressed segments of the population. Likewise, many argue that government services are, simply, "priceless."

In preparing a budget, collections under all current and any new proposed revenue sources also must be projected. How can this be accomplished? Charles Liner elaborates two basic projection methods: time series and trend-line analysis. Each technique can be employed in even the smallest unit of government. (A further discussion of revenue will occur in the next section where "Local Government Financial and Budgetary Analysis" presents the foundations of revenue and expenditure analysis together.)

When comparing a time series of revenues or expenditures, it is misleading to assume that the buying power of each period is the same. In fact, prices change and a dollar can buy more (or less) from year to year. Thus, it is important to adjust nominal dollars into the real dollar equivalent (a price-adjusted basis). To do so requires a measure of constant prices, as is offered by the Consumer Price Index (CPI) and the Implicit Price Deflator (IPD). The CPI is a measure of a common "basket" of goods purchased by individual consumers, including such staples as an 8-ounce bottle of name-brand ketchup and a car tune-up. The IPD is an alternative measure, but it captures the prices paid by producers (such as local governments). David Ammons provides a step-by-step guide on "Adjusting for Inflation When Comparing Revenues or Expenditures."

EXPENDITURES

Governmental entities provide direct services to citizens (e.g., line activities, such as fire suppression, police protection, street repair, and building inspection) and perform activities to support the line agencies (e.g., staff activities, such as personnel and finance). Each service component expends money, but the exact costs and benefits defy easy measurement. Because of these problems, performance improvement efforts face enormous difficulties in government.

New and expanded services present special difficulties for the budget maker. For example, are all service expansions worthwhile? If not, how can managers differentiate among and between alternatives? Analysis could help. Research on the costs and benefits of projects can help guide the preferences of policymakers and prevent arbitrary service changes.

Perceived or artificial political pressure may be weighed against study of the actual problems and gains from service improvement. In "Evaluating Public Expenditures: A Guide for Local Officials," Therese Freeman, Ernest Niemi, and Peter Wilson offer practical steps, as employed in Massachusetts, for public expenditure analysis. Emphasizing ways to determine calculated project costs and benefits, Gerald Miller presents a more detailed examination in "Cost-Benefit Analysis."

Tools of the craft include financial and budgetary analysis. Kenneth Sanders and Charlie Tyer give a practical introduction to these critical skills in "Local Government Financial and Budgetary Analysis." Their attention is both on revenues and expenditures. This work demonstrates the value gained by teasing information from the numbers in the budget.

If analysis and management of the costs and benefits of additional services come only with great difficulty, measurement of improvements in current services—especially through productivity-oriented evaluations—faces intractable problems. For example, public sector performance budgeting, which relies upon measures of productivity, is elusive for most governments. A difficult and frustrating offshoot of private sector cost accounting, this type of productivity evaluation requires personnel skills, large amounts of calculative detail, and much analytical time, making it hard to adapt in government.

Nevertheless, progress may come through trial and error, as indicated in a report issued by the state of Rhode Island, "Monitoring Performance." Measurement efforts do promote a clearer understanding of the city's program and services, and "the process of improving services relies heavily on effective evaluation of existing services." In fact, the Governmental Accounting Standards Board has embarked on efforts to promote reporting of service efforts and accomplishments (SEA). An example of the application of SEA reporting is presented in "Service Efforts and Accomplishments: The Case of Road Maintenance" by William Hyman and Joan Allen.

Salaries and employee benefits account for an estimated 60 to 75 percent of most local governments' annual operating expenditures. Unfortunately, many governments have little idea of their total compensation costs. This lack of information complicates both budgeting and collective bargaining. Marvin Friedman presents an exercise showing how to "cost out" compensation agreements. If costs are known and understood by both management and union, bargaining can begin on a firmer financial basis resulting in settlements tied to their full costs. In terms of budgeting, such compensation calculators offer managers and citizens alike a more accurate picture of the full cost of government services.

Another major problem area for government managers is budgeting for costly, long-life capital improvements such as new fire trucks and waste treatment facilities. Typically, these expenditures are impossible to fund out of one year's revenue collections, especially in small local governments. Most governments seek external funding either from debt issues or federal or state aid, a complex procedure of both planning and purchasing. In order to deal with these capital item purchases and their funding in a more orderly fashion, a specialized budget process has evolved called capital budgeting.

The capital budget helps in systematic planning and in scheduling the purchase of expensive, physical improvements that will serve the community for several years. In "Budgeting Capital Outlays and Improvements," A. John Vogt outlines procedures employed in this budgeting procedure. He shows how the capital budget process can be integrated with the annual operating budget and outlines methods for constructing the various parts of a capital budget. A companion piece by Ronald Chapman, "Capital Financing: A New Look at an Old Idea," shows how capital investments can rely on simple payback methods or more complicated, yet more appropriate, cost-benefit analysis (requiring the calculation of discounted time value of money).

Following a matching of resources with expenditures through the budgeting process, the local government must formally adopt the budget for the upcoming fiscal year. Usually, the chief executive—the mayor or manager—presents the proposed budget to the legislative body—the council—which has the responsibility of approving the budget plan officially, either with or without modification. Once formally adopted, budgeted expenditures and planned revenue serve as the basis for decisions within the fiscal year. While service provisions reflect the actual end result of the budget preparation and adoption phase, financial efforts continue throughout the year.

Political Economy

Local Government Structure

David R. Morgan

FORMS OF CITY GOVERNMENT

This article examines two basic forms of municipal government, the electoral systems that accompany them, and municipal home rule.

Mayor–Council Government

We can identify two variations of mayor-council government: the weak-mayor and strong-mayor forms. Essentially the two types differ in degree only, and few cities reflect the extremes of either.

The mayor-council form of government preserves the basic separation of powers between the legislative and executive branches. Historically, owing to widespread suspicion of concentrated executive power, councils were the dominant force in city government. Gradually, as cities grew and government became increasingly complex, more concentrated authority was put in the hands of the chief executive. Now most authorities favor the strong-mayor variation as a way of providing the political leadership thought to be so crucial, especially for larger cities. For smaller communities the weak-mayor form still remains popular.

Weak-Mayor Form

The weak-mayor form was characterized by Charles Adrian and Charles Press:

Excerpted from "Urban Political Structure," in *Managing Urban America,* 3d ed. (Pacific Grove, Calif.: Brooks/Cole Publishing Co., 1989), 48-64. By permission of the publisher. (Notes have been renumbered.)

The weak-mayor plan is a product of Jacksonian democracy....It grew out of a time when the functions of city government were few, when the need for a single executive was not recognized, and when people were afraid to give powers to a single executive. Implicit in the weak-mayor plan are the beliefs that if politicians have few powers and many checks upon them, they can do relatively little damage and that if one politician becomes corrupt, he or she will not necessarily corrupt the whole city government.[1]

A number of features distinguish the weak-mayor form:

- The council possesses both legislative and executive authority. The council may appoint several important administrative officials itself and invariably must approve the mayor's appointees.
- The mayor's appointive powers are restricted.
- A long ballot may dictate the direct election of certain key administrative officials.
- The council exercises primary control over the municipal budget, perhaps through the operation of a budget or finance committee.

Figure 1 illustrates the essence of the weak-mayor form. Notice that the voters elect not only the mayor and the council, but also several other administrative officials. Moreover, the council has considerable appointive power itself and, of course, must consent to the mayor's choice of department heads and appointees to various boards and commissions. Clearly no single administrative head of city govern-

Figure 1: *Hypothetical Weak-Mayor Form*

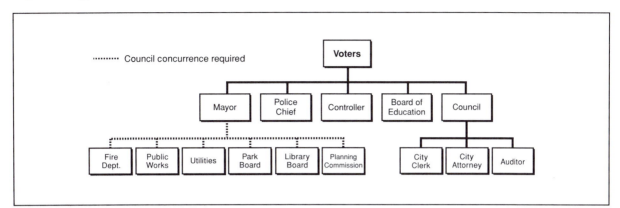

ment exists under this arrangement. Power is fragmented, and the mayor is severely hemmed in. Adrian and Press note, however, that the "mayors are not 'weak' because they lack policy-making power—they normally have a veto, can recommend legislation, and may even preside over the council. They are 'weak' because they lack administrative power."[2]

The weak-mayor plan was designed for an earlier era, when cities were smaller and government simpler. Today, it seems especially ill suited for large cities in which political and administrative leadership is vital. Many of the nineteenth-century machines evolved under the weak-mayor structure because its lack of administrative centralization was an open invitation for external direction and control. Fragmented authority at the top also encourages greater bureaucratic independence. The effect of autonomy is to make city government into a series of many little governments rather than a single coordinated one. For a number of reasons, then, larger cities have searched for ways to bring about more central control of administrative activities.

Strong-Mayor Form

The strong-mayor government represents a significant departure from the fragmented executive office of the weak-mayor plan. It includes the following features:

- The mayor has almost total administrative authority, with the power to appoint and dismiss virtually all department heads without council approval.
- The mayor prepares and administers the budget.
- A short ballot restricts the number of elected administrative officials.
- Policy making is a joint enterprise between mayor and council.

Strong mayors also have a veto power that usually can be overridden only by a two-thirds or three-fourths majority of the council. Because of this strong legal position, the mayor becomes the dominant force in city government, as Figure 2 illustrates.

The strong-mayor form is subject to criticism. First, it requires that the mayor be both a good political leader and a competent administrator, two traits not always found in mayoral candidates. In addition, much as in national government, conflict can erupt periodically between a strong, politically ambitious mayor and a recalcitrant council. A legislative-executive deadlock remains a continual threat.

In some large strong-mayor cities, a new development is working to rectify the first potential shortcoming of the plan—the need to combine a good administrator and a good politician in the same office. Here, a chief administrative officer (CAO) is appointed by the mayor to serve at his or her pleasure. The CAO might supervise department heads, prepare the budget (under the mayor's direction), coordinate various departments in the performance of day-to-day activities, and give technical advice to the mayor. By assigning these more mundane responsibilities to the CAO, the mayor frees time for two other major jobs—serving as ceremonial head of

Figure 2: *Hypothetical Strong-Mayor Form*

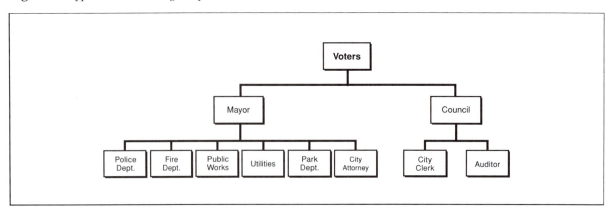

the city and providing broad policy leadership. The CAO remains the mayor's person because he or she is responsible only to the mayor, not to the council. It is this mayoral control that distinguishes the job of the CAO from that of the city manager.

With or without the CAO, the strong-mayor form is especially suitable to large cities with diverse populations, where strong political leadership is required to arrange compromises and arbitrate struggles for power among contending interests.

Council–Manager Government

In 1913 Dayton, Ohio, became the first city of any size to successfully adopt the council-manager form of government. Since then, with the approval and ardent commitment of reform groups, the plan has spread rapidly. Today a majority of cities with population over 25,000 use the form. The basic characteristics of the council-manager plan include:

- A small city council—usually five to seven people—often elected at large on a nonpartisan ballot.
- Council responsibility for making policy, passing ordinances, voting appropriations, and supervising in an overall sense the administration of city government.
- A full-time professionally trained city administrator to serve at the pleasure of the council with full responsibility for day-to-day city operations (including hiring and firing department heads without council approval).
- An executive budget prepared and administered by the city manager.
- A mayor who performs strictly ceremonial duties and has no involvement in the city's administrative affairs.

This description represents the plan as ideally conceived, and usually only slight deviations are found in actual practice. The form is shown schematically in Figure 3. The council-manager plan departs most drastically from historical American government practice in its abandonment of the doctrines of separation of powers and checks and balances. All executive and legislative authority resides in the council alone. The manager is essentially the council's hired hand and has no direct responsibility to the citizenry. Originally, reformers feared the mayor might be tempted to interfere in the administrative affairs of city government unless mayoral powers were circumscribed strictly. The solution was to make the mayor responsible to the council rather than to the people. Over time, this view has undergone modification, so that today more than half of council-manager cities provide for direct popular election of the mayor.[3]

The council-manager plan's main attribute is its businesslike approach to city government, which presumably maximizes efficiency and technical expertise. In fact, in many places manager government has been supported by business groups, which perhaps excessively tout its capacity to save taxpayers' money. These groups argue that professional administration reduces waste and inefficiency and thereby effects great savings. As we noted earlier, council-

Figure 3: *Hypothetical Council-Manager Plan*

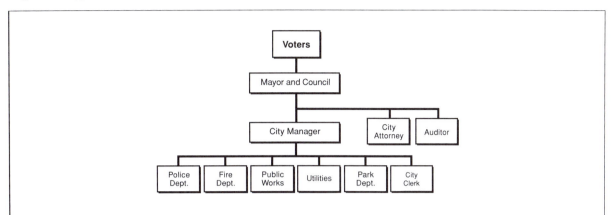

manager governments *do* tend to tax and spend less, but how much of this can be attributed to business-like methods is debatable. In any event, the plan's reputation for efficiency makes it appealing to the upper- and middle-class suburbs that so many business people call home. And, unmistakably, manager government has achieved considerable success among those places with little community diversity, where a high degree of consensus exists over the proper scope and function of city government.

Limitations on the Form

Despite its obvious popularity there are potential shortcomings to the council-manager form. The sharp distinction between policy making and administration is unrealistic. We should stress that the full-time professional manager inevitably will provide considerable policy advice to the part-time amateur council. Yet council members may not be certain just what the policy relationship should be between themselves and the manager. Citizens also may wonder who is really in charge of city affairs. Should administrative problems be brought to the mayor or to individual council members? And if a council merely rubber-stamps a manager's recommendations, then the manager—who is not directly accountable to the people—may seem to have too much power. Obviously, this confusion cannot improve a government's responsiveness.

But the major potential limitation of the council-manager plan is its lack of formal provision for strong policy leadership. The council is a group of equals, the mayor is limited to a ceremonial role, and the manager presumably serves only in an advisory role. Sometimes the mayor or one of the council members emerges as a policy leader, but "more likely, the council will flounder about or turn to the manager."[4] An argument can be made, of course, that the experienced professional manager is in a better position than the council to interpret the needs of the community and thus should take the lead in policy formulation. But what does this do to the idealized role of the council? The issue is not an easy one to resolve.

The Commission Form

Born at the turn of the century in response to a major hurricane in Galveston, Texas, the commission plan was an early reform favorite. In the wake of the hurricane's destruction, the state legislature appointed a group of five businessmen to conduct city affairs. The scheme worked well and began to attract attention as a way of changing mayor-council government. Initially pushed by reformers as a businesslike approach to local government, the plan spread quickly. But its popularity was short-lived once council-manager government caught the fancy of reform groups. Today, only about 4 percent of all cities with a population of over 10,000 use the commission form.

The commission plan provides for no separation of powers. The commissioners individually serve as elected heads of specific departments and collectively sit as the legislative body of the city. The commission is a small group (usually no more than five people) elected at large, ordinarily on nonpartisan ballots. The mayor normally has no more authority than other commissioners, all of whom are expected to serve as full-time officials. One of the fairly large cities that continues to operate under the commission form is Tulsa, Oklahoma. Here, the five-member commission consists of a directly elected mayor and commissioners for water, public safety, streets, and finance.

The commission plan has several serious weaknesses. First, no provision exists for a chief executive. Because the commission is a group of equals collectively responsible for administration, there is no way to ensure administrative coordination or policy leadership. This makes it difficult for the public to fix responsibility. In addition, the commission form lacks internal checks and balances. Instead, it seems to encourage mutual accommodation on the part of commissioners: "If you stay out of my department, I will stay out of yours."[5] These inherent shortcomings have led to the gradual decline of the form.

LOCAL ELECTORAL SYSTEMS

Reformers overwhelmingly won one battle: The vast majority of American cities of all sizes now use nonpartisan ballots. But formal nonpartisanship does not necessarily eliminate the influence of the political party in local elections. In one survey of 110 cities, highly or moderately active partisan organizations were found in 32 of the 69 cities that had officially banned party labels.[6] Nonpartisan elections were most susceptible to partisan forces in the Midwest; southern and western cities were the least likely to reflect party influences. However, partisan activity is limited in most cities, even those with party labels on the ballot.[7]

Partisan versus Nonpartisan Ballots

As often happens with any reform, unanticipated side effects developed. Reform groups wanted to get the party out of municipal government as a way of destroying bosses and machine politics. Moreover, parties were considered irrelevant, if not harmful, to providing services; experts and professionals should determine the service needs of the populace. But evidence now reveals that nonpartisanship had other effects, some of which are of dubious value. Before examining the consequences of removing party labels in municipal elections, we should mention that much of the research done on nonpartisan elections focuses on cities that also have other reform features, namely the council-manager plan and citywide elections. Therefore, in some instances, it is difficult to separate the effects of nonpartisan ballots from other influences.

Some research suggests that nonpartisan ballots give a slight edge to Republicans.[8] Recent evidence, however, indicates that this relationship is not clearcut. Relying on surveys from city council members from around the nation, political scientists Susan Welch and Timothy Bledsoe report that a significant Republican bias appears only in communities that have *both* nonpartisan elections and at-large balloting.[9] Nonpartisanship also tends to produce elected officials more representative of the upper socioeconomic strata than of the general populace. Examining six California cities, the following portrait of a nonpartisan council member was developed:

> The "California councilman" is a man of 45 to 50 years of age, engaged in some professional, managerial, or sales activity and living in the "better" part of town. He belongs to a service club, is probably a Mason, a member of a veterans group and of the Chamber of Commerce. He is a Protestant but not necessarily affiliated with any church. He had no previous official city experience, although he was active in Community Chest, Red Cross, or related activities. He is a registered Republican, but has not taken a very extensive part in partisan politics. He has lived in the city for a considerable length of time.[10]

Some suggest the nonpartisan ballot gives incumbent council members a reelection advantage, but the data do not confirm this. In a comprehensive survey of cities around the country it was found that council incumbents were reelected at the rate of between 70 and 80 percent, but no particular advantage was noted by ballot type.[11]

Finally, it seems nonpartisanship may have policy consequences. In a study of 88 San Francisco Bay Area cities, political scientist Willis Hawley discovered that nonpartisan elections, because of their tendency to slightly overrepresent Republicans and conservative Democrats, "seem to reduce the priorities placed on the solution of social problems and the propensity of local governments to exploit more thoroughly the full public power that might be employed in solving the problems their citizens face."[12]

But an argument can be made that communities with partisan elections are no more effective in mobilizing city governments to deal with policy issues than are nonpartisan governments. Murray Stedman, Jr., for example, contends that urban parties cannot govern.[13] Historically, perhaps it was possible, but Stedman maintains that the conditions for successful brokerage politics no longer exist in American cities. He suggests that parties no longer seem able to establish clear priorities, and even where those priorities are delineated, city governments find it increasingly difficult to implement them. Although Stedman does not discuss the urban bureaucracy by name, his reasoning obviously parallels that of others regarding the intractability of autonomous bureaucrats.

At-Large versus Ward Elections

Citywide or district elections—which should a city have? Again, there is no simple answer. Proponents of at-large elections argue:

- Council members in an at-large system can rise above the limited perspective of the ward and concern themselves with the problems of the whole community.
- Vote trading and logrolling are minimized.
- The chance of domination by a machine is lessened.
- Better-qualified individuals are elected to council.

Arguments in behalf of district elections are just the opposite. In particular, those advocating ward elections insist:

- District elections give all legitimate groups, especially those with a geographic base, a better chance of being represented on the city council.
- Ward council members are more sensitive to the small but frequently important little problems that people have (unfixed chuckholes, needed stop signs).
- Ward elections reduce voter alienation by bringing city government closer to the people.

Because of the apparent strengths and shortcomings of both electoral systems, certain combinations of the two have developed. In one combination, council members are nominated by district and then elected citywide. This arrangement ensures geographic representation but also forces elected officials to think about the needs of the whole city. This combination guarantees as well that the larger community will have the dominant voice in choosing representatives from each district. Blacks sometimes object to the arrangement, however, claiming it can be confusing and potentially divisive for the minority community.[14]

A second combination requires that a certain number of the council members be elected from wards, while others run at large. For example, a city might be divided into four wards with one council member elected from each ward. Then three or four additional council members would be voted on by the entire city. This combination, too, is open to criticism. Those officials elected at large may think they are more important than the others and in some cases may see themselves as potential rivals of the mayor.[15]

The method of choosing council members—ward or at-large—does affect who is elected. As noted above, citywide elections tend to disadvantage blacks and other geographically concentrated minority groups. Additional evidence indicates that ward elections provide a greater opportunity for people of lower income and education levels to be elected, regardless of race.[16] The importance of electoral structure is demonstrated by a series of recent legal battles over equal representation, many of which involve ward and at-large elections. The U.S. Supreme Court has found the issue of fair representation for minorities to be a slippery one. By a 6-to-3 vote, the Court in *Mobile v. Bolden* (1980) overturned a lower court opinion that had forced the city of Mobile to abandon its historic three-member commission form mandating at-large elections, which had never produced a black commissioner. In effect, the decision forced protesting groups to prove that at-large elections were *designed* to discriminate against minorities. Despite this ruling, 1982 amendments to the Voting Rights Act, subsequent interpretations by the Justice Department, and lower court rulings have forced some cities to abandon at-large voting on the grounds that the *results* of such electoral schemes dilute minority voting strength.

Even where a court case is not at issue, blacks continue to try to force cities away from at-large elections. The court cases and the debate continue. A trend toward ward or mixed systems is clear.[17]

The Initiative, the Referendum, and the Recall

During the heyday of machine politics, reformers searched for various ways to circumvent boss-dominated local legislatures and return control of government to the people. One means of doing this was to allow citizens to employ petitions to force a communitywide vote on various local propositions.

The *initiative* enables a legally determined number of electors, through use of a petition, to have a charter amendment or city ordinance put on the ballot for a vote by the people. The city council is not involved in the process and cannot prevent the vote except by challenging the validity of the petition in court. The *referendum* allows a prescribed number or percentage of qualified voters, by means of a petition, to force a vote on a legislative measure after it has passed the council. If no emergency clause is attached (attesting to the urgent need to protect the public health, safety, or welfare), city ordinances often do not take effect immediately. This gives a disenchanted group an opportunity to collect signatures and bring the ordinance to a popular vote. *Recall* provides a mechanism for voters to remove an unsatisfactory council member before the official's term expires. Again a petition is required.

Proponents of direct democracy contend that these devices are essential to keep legislative bodies in check and to provide the opportunity for citizens to act directly on local policy issues. Skeptics feel that most voters are not well enough informed to vote intelligently on the kinds of matters often placed on these ballots. Indeed, some referendum items are complex and esoteric, and many people simply are not interested in them. The result frequently is to turn the initiative and referendum into tools for special interests that have the time and money to take advantage of the processes. Because of this, some authorities insist not only that referendum outcomes are influenced by well-financed interest groups, but also that overall the process has a deleterious effect on the normal legislative process.[18] Defenders counter that these voting procedures should not be condemned because of occasional misuse; in fact, they represent an effective means to enhance citizen control of local government.[19]

HOME RULE AND THE LEGAL STATUS OF THE CITY

Despite the restricted view of municipal power reflected in Dillon's rule, courts permit cities to exercise a greater degree of control over strictly local affairs in areas where home rule charters have been granted. Municipal home rule provided by state law or constitution allows cities to "frame, adopt, and amend a charter for their governments and to exercise all powers of local self-government, subject to the constitution and general laws of the state."[20] It may be granted to all cities or just a few, generally on the basis of population. In Oklahoma, for example, any incorporated place with a population of 2,000 or more can adopt a home rule charter by following certain procedures spelled out in the state constitution. Among other things, a home rule charter allows the city to determine its own form of government, type of ballot (partisan or nonpartisan), and method of electing council members (ward or at-large). In effect, the charter becomes the basic law, or constitution, of the city. Most states now provide for home rule, but less than half of cities of 5,000 or more operate under a home rule charter.[21]

Does home rule really give cities greater independence? Apparently so, at least in some areas of governance. Clearly, home rule cities are free to choose the form of government they want to use, but in other areas, such as finance, charter cities may have little more authority than other cities. For example, in Pennsylvania home rule cities can set property tax rates, but the general assembly retains the power over taxation and over rates of taxation on nonresidents.[22] States always can preempt local powers or determine that some powers may be exercised concurrently by the state and local governments. In effect, then, home rule powers are largely subject to restraints imposed by state legislatures.[23] But administrative flexibility is only one aspect of home rule; its greatest importance may be psychological. Home rule encourages state legislators to stay out of local affairs for fear of interfering with the rights of local self-government, of violating "the principle of home rule."[24]

Traditionally, home rule supporters have feared state encroachment. Lately, though, more concern has been expressed over federal preemption of local law. In 1982, for example, in *Community Communications Co. v. City of Boulder,* the U.S. Supreme

Court held that cities, in regulating private business, were not exempt from federal antitrust laws unless they were acting directly as an agent of the state or carrying out clearly expressed state policy. That decision was later modified by a ruling in *Town of Hallie v. City of Eau Claire* (1985) and the Local Government Antitrust Act (1984), so that local governments may now regulate private activity under the general authority of state law. Of greater worry to home rule supporters is the 5-to-4 decision in *Garcia v. San Antonio Mass Transit Authority* (1985), in which the Supreme Court ruled that federal wage and hour standards apply to states and their local governments. The Court reasoned that the political process followed by Congress in passing laws provides sufficient protection to ensure that states and localities will not be unduly burdened. Although legislation lessened the impact of the *Garcia* ruling, some point to this case and other recent action at the national level (for example, federal laws preempting state and local regulations prohibiting tandem trucks and imposing national standards for cable franchise issuance and renewal) as evidence that home rule continues to shrink as the federal government expands its role under the commerce clause of the Constitution.

SUMMARY

The council-manager plan is now the most popular in the country for cities with a population of 25,000 or over. Mayor-council government remains more common, however, in the very smallest and the very largest municipalities. Debates persist over the alleged advantages and disadvantages of various electoral arrangements. Nonpartisanship is pervasive regardless of city size, but the at-large electoral form has not been as overwhelmingly adopted. An interest in city government structure is more than academic. Although structure alone does not determine who gets what, certain arrangements may benefit some groups while working to the disadvantage of others.

Cities remain creatures of the state, although evidence suggests home rule provisions have given municipalities greater freedom to frame a charter and choose their own form of government. But some worry about growing federal preemption and encroachment under provision of the commerce clause of the U.S. Constitution.

Notes

1. Charles Adrian and Charles Press, *Governing Urban America,* 5th ed. (New York: McGraw-Hill, 1977), p. 153.
2. Ibid., p. 154.
3. Boynton, "City Councils," p. 71.
4. Sanders, "Government of American Cities," p. 181.
5. Adrian and Press, *Governing Urban America,* p. 167.
6. Marvin G. Weinbaum, "Partisan or Nonpartisan?" *National Civic Review* 59 (November 1970): 532-37 and 566.
7. Albert Karnig and Susan Welch, *Black Representation and Urban Public Policy* (Chicago: University of Chicago Press, 1981).
8. Willis D. Hawley, *Nonpartisan Elections and the Case for Party Politics* (New York: Wiley-Interscience, 1973), p. 33.
9. Susan Welch and Timothy Bledsoe, "The Partisan Consequences of Nonpartisan Elections and the Changing Nature of Urban Politics," *American Journal of Political Science* 30 (February 1986): 137.
10. Eugene C. Lee, *The Politics of Nonpartisanship* (Berkeley: University of California Press, 1960), p. 50. For similar findings from the Bay Area, see Kenneth Prewitt, *The Recruitment of Political Leaders: A Study of Citizen-Politicians* (Indianapolis: Bobbs-Merrill, 1970), p. 142.
11. Eugene C. Lee, "City Elections: A Statistical Profile," *Municipal Year Book 1963* (Chicago: ICMA, 1963), p. 78.
12. Hawley, *Nonpartisan Elections,* p. 122.
13. Murray S. Stedman, Jr., "Why Urban Parties Can't Govern," *National Civic Review* 61 (November 1972): 501-4.
14. William J. D. Boyd, "Local Electoral Systems: Is There a Best Way?" *National Civic Review* 65 (March 1976): 136-40 and 157.
15. Ibid., p. 139.
16. Timothy Bledsoe and Susan Welch, "The Effect of Political Structures on the Socioeconomic Characteristics of Urban City Council Members," *American Politics Quarterly* 13 (October 1985): 467-83.
17. Sanders, "Government of American Cities," pp. 185-86.
18. Stanley Scott and Harriet Nathan, "Public Referenda: A Critical Appraisal," *Urban Affairs Quarterly* 5 (March 1970): 313-28.
19. George S. Blair, *Government at the Grass-Roots,* 2d ed. (Pacific Palisades, Calif.: Palisades, 1977), pp. 85-86.
20. Adrian and Press, *Governing Urban America,* p. 138.
21. Alan Klevit, "City Councils and Their Functions in Local Government," *Municipal Year Book 1972* (Washington, D.C.: ICMA, 1972), p. 17.
22. See Charles Hoffman, "Pennsylvania Legislation Implements Home Rule," *National Civic Review* 61 (September 1972): 390-93.
23. See, for example, the discussion in Samual Gove and Stephanie Cole, "Illinois Home Rule: Panacea, Status Quo, or Hindrance?" in *Partnership Within the States: Local Self-Government in the Federal System,* ed. Stephanie Cole (Urbana, Ill.: Institute of Government and Public Affairs,

University of Illinois; Philadelphia: Center for the Study of Federalism, Temple University, 1976), pp. 158-61. The authors conclude that home rule has made some difference, but after five years the changes have not been dramatic (p. 167).

24. Adrian and Press, *Governing Urban America,* p. 142.

Suggested for Further Reading

Clavel, Pierre. *The Progressive City.* New Brunswick, N.J.: Rutgers University Press, 1986.

Gluck, Peter, and Meister, Richard. *Cities in Transition.* New York: New Viewpoints, 1979.

Hawley, Willis D. *Nonpartisan Elections and the Case for Party Politics.* New York: Wiley-Interscience, 1973.

Prewitt, Kenneth. *The Recruitment of Political Leaders: A Study of Citizen-Politicians.* Indianapolis: Bobbs-Merrill, 1970.

Riordan, William L. *Plunkitt of Tammany Hall.* New York: Knopf, 1948 (originally published 1905).

States and Their Local Governments

How have all of the state reform activities affected local government, traditionally strongly interdependent with the states? Have improvements at the state level translated to advances for substate jurisdictions? Do the states treat their local units much as they always did, sometimes placing them in an intergovernmental straitjacket? Or, have more urban-oriented legislatures loosened a few strings and allowed them more freedom to deal with their problems and aided them in areas where local efforts are insufficient? In short, what effect has state government reform had on state relations with their local governments? In order to deal with these questions, it is necessary, first, to examine what the role of state government is in regard to local units.

STATE RESPONSIBILITIES FOR LOCAL JURISDICTIONS

For almost all local jurisdictions—the notable exceptions being Indian reservations and the District of Columbia—state governments hold the key to many matters determining their well-being and success. The states are, in fact, major decisionmakers in local government affairs. In addition, they coordinate and supervise local administration of state programs; assist substate governments in improving their capability to carry on their own activities as well as those mandated for the administration of state law on the local level; bear a significant portion of the costs of local operations; intervene in local emergencies; and, to some degree, ensure "good government" at the local level.

Moreover, in recent years states increasingly have become intergovernmental managers of federal programs administered at the local level. While this role is not new, it has expanded dramatically with the growth of federal assistance programs and the vesting of administrative responsibility for the new block grants in the states. Often the decision as to which local units will receive federal funds is made by the states. In addition, it may be necessary for them to plan, supervise, monitor, provide technical assistance and perform other oversight activities in connection with the federal-aid programs.

STATES AS DECISIONMAKERS FOR LOCAL GOVERNMENTS

As decisionmakers for local governments, states determine, either through the state constitution, or by statute or charter, what local governments there will be; the proper allocation of powers to and among them; their functional assignments; their internal structure, organizations and procedures for local operations; their fiscal options in regard to revenue, expenditures and debt; the extent of the interlocal cooperation; how their boundaries can be expanded

---

Advisory Commission on Intergovernmental Relations, *The Question of State Government Capability,* Report A-98 (Washington, D.C., 1985), 186-291, 304. Reprinted from *Capitol, Courthouse, and City Hall: Readings in American State and Local Politics and Government,* 7th ed., edited by David L. Martin (White Plains, N.Y.: Longman, Inc., 1988), 34-42. (Notes have been renumbered.)

or contracted and to some degree their land use patterns. When one government exercises this kind of influence over others, its decisions affect those subordinate governments critically.

Because there is no federal Constitutional provision for local governments, they owe their existence to the states. In the absence of a state constitutional restriction, the state legislature may create or abolish local governments at will. While public opinion and countervailing local political forces may prevent any precipitant moves to disestablish a local unit, the legal authority to do so is there. In the words of Judge John F. Dillon, local governments are "mere tenants at the will of the legislature."[1]

Likewise, the state constitution or, more usually, the legislature, determines which units of local government can exercise which powers and functions. Often these allocations are made on the basis of traditions, and, usually, once a unit has authority to perform a function it rarely loses it. Nevertheless, the state decides whether cities, counties, towns, townships, or special districts, or all or none can or must engage in land use planning and zoning, operate the public school system, construct an airport or engage in other functions. In most states, without a specific grant of authority from the state, local units are unable to act. They have only the powers granted to them; and the courts, following Dillon's Rule, are inclined to interpret authorizations strictly. The rule states:

> It is a general and undisputed proposition of a law that a municipal corporation (read: local government) possesses and can exercise the following powers and no others: First, those granted in *express words;* second, those *necessarily or fairly implied* in or *incident* to the powers expressly granted; third, those essential to the declared objects and purposes of the corporation—not simply convenient but indispensable. Any fair reasonable doubt concerning the existence of power is resolved by the courts against the corporation and the power is denied.[2]

Other states are more liberal with the powers of their local units.

While it might seem that the determination of local government structure, organization, and procedures should be the preserve of the citizens of the locality concerned, such is not entirely the case. Both state constitutions and state legislatures prescribe forms of governments, duties of officials and operating procedures for local jurisdictions. For example, in 1975 New York had 11 statutes running to 19 volumes containing 6,000 pages dealing directly with powers and structures of its local governments.[3]

In another example, a recent amendment to the Tennessee Constitution providing for an elective executive form of government included the following statement concerning the county legislative body:

> The legislative body shall be composed of representatives from districts in the county as drawn by the county legislative body pursuant to statutes enacted by the general assembly. Districts shall be reapportioned at least every ten years based upon the most recent federal census. The legislative body shall not exceed 25 members, and no more than three representatives shall be elected from a district.[4]

The Tennessee legislature then provided in detail for the establishment of the county executive form of government.

States determine the fiscal options of their local governments in a number of ways. In the first place, they decide what revenue sources local governments can use, a decision predicated on protecting the state's own income. Property taxes and license and service fees have been the traditional sources, but in recent years revenues from income or payroll taxes, sales taxes and other sources have been authorized in some states. Limits on the rates of taxes imposed are frequently attached. States also stipulate the purposes for which local funds may be spent, impose spending limits, set salaries and fees, require certain budgetary procedures and sometimes approve local budgets. In addition, their requirements that local governments engage in specific activities often necessitate local outlays for these purposes. Such state mandated activities limit local expenditure options by absorbing local revenues.

Nowhere is local discretion more hindered than in the incurrence of debt. State constitutions and statutes impose limits on the amount of debt, the purposes for which it may be incurred, procedures for repayment and the investment of funds set aside for repayment. Although instituted to preserve the credit of both the state and other local governments by preventing default on debt obligations, such arrangements frequently stimulate local ingenuity in circumventing the state constraints. One example is the issuance of revenue bonds, repaid from the earnings of the enterprise for which money was borrowed, that are not considered "debt" since the general credit of the local government is not pledged to their repayment.

State decisionmaking also extends to determining the extent of and procedures for interlocal cooperation and external structural changes. State law will prescribe what agreements are allowable and sometimes the procedures for entering into them. Frequently, the creation of substate districts for handling local matters is specified by state statute. State legislatures also set out the terms of, and procedures for annexation, extraterritorial jurisdiction and consolidation. In one instance, Indianapolis and Marion County, Indiana, the state legislature merged the two governments without a referendum.[5] In another, the Kentucky State Board of Education consolidated the Louisville and Jefferson County school districts.

Land use control is an area in which state involvement has grown in recent years. From 1922 until recently, local governments largely exercised authority over the use of land except where states determined the location of state facilities and took land by eminent domain for such purposes as highways, parks, prisons, educational institutions, hospitals and other public uses. Following the publication of a model zoning enabling act by the Department of Commerce in 1922, most states adopted legislation authorizing municipal governments to classify land within their boundaries and to regulate its uses. When the department published model legislation for local planning control in 1928, the states adopted this code as well.[6]

Because local control of land use did not work well in many instances, frequently permitting urban sprawl, traffic congestion, air and water pollution, and loss of prime agricultural land, states undertook to regulate land use at the state level, revoking powers previously allowed local governments. A variety of techniques were used. States resorted to the requirement of permits for certain types of development, established mechanisms to coordinate state land use-related problems, and required local governments to establish mechanisms for land use planning and zoning. More recently, they moved to participate in the coastal zone management program of the federal government, took on the management of wetlands, determined the siting of power plants and related facilities, acted to regulate surface mining and established rules for identifying and designating areas of critical state concern (e.g., environmentally fragile or historic areas).[7] Moreover, they began to settle land use disputes among local jurisdictions, to forbid exclusionary zoning and to handle large developments. All of these activities enabled states to engage in decisionmaking concerning land use to a greater degree than once was the case. As a consequence, local governments find that although state decisions often relieve them of some of the pressures relating to development, they also limit their options in this as well as in other areas.

STATES AS ADMINISTRATIVE SUPERVISORS OF LOCAL IMPLEMENTATION

All states coordinate and supervise to some degree local administration of state functions. These activities encompass a wide range of state actions extending from informal conferences through advice and technical assistance, requirement of reports, inspection, imposition of grant-in-aid requirements, review of local actions, prior approval of local action, orders, rulemaking, investigations, removal of local officials and appointment of local officials, to state takeover of local administration. The employment of these devices to influence local administration varies widely, not only from state to state but from function to function within a state. In general, the less coercive appear to be the most effective and most frequently employed. The most stringent—substitute administration—rarely occurs and, when it does, it is in crisis situations such as financial, health or disaster emergencies....

STATES AS ENHANCERS OF LOCAL CAPABILITY

States frequently engage in efforts to improve the capability of local governments to carry on their own activities. They also try to upgrade local abilities to administer state law on the local level. Toward this end, they offer a wide range of technical assistance in such matters as purchasing, accounting procedures, drafting of charters, and design of personnel systems, not to mention a host of other subjects.

Local governments do not rely on such technical assistance extensively. A General Accounting Office survey indicates that approximately 50 percent of local officials responding never asked the state for technical assistance. Nonetheless, state officials are contacted more often than any other type of outside organization—including the federal government—to meet local technical assistance needs. Apparently local officials perceived fewer programs and less paperwork in dealing with state officials than with federal agencies.[8]

All states now have state agencies specifically designated to assist local governments.[9] Although Pennsylvania set up the Bureau of Municipal Affairs in 1919,[10] widespread adoption of special agencies for local affairs did not occur until the 1960s. Following a recommendation of the Council of State Governments, endorsed by public interest groups representing local governments, and a 1964 recommendation from ACIR, states began to create or designate such agencies. Currently, 35 of the agencies are separate cabinet departments, 9 are within other departments, and 6 are located in the governor's offices.[11]

The agencies offer a wide range of programs and services to local governments and try to promote intergovernmental cooperation, upgrade local management and planning capabilities, and facilitate the administration of programs in such areas as economic development and housing.[12] Some provide assistance for small jurisdictions in such matters as applications for federal grants. Few exercise control functions, emphasizing their assistance capabilities.

Other state aid may take the form of efforts to improve local government structure in order to enhance decisionmaking capacity and administration. This could involve the requirement for county executive (or manager) government as occurred recently in Arkansas, Kentucky, and Tennessee. It could include the extension of home rule or discretionary powers to local units broadening their authority to cope with local problems. Local boundaries might be altered by the state, as in Indianapolis, to make political jurisdiction correspond more closely to the geographic area of the problems. State statutes might impose merit systems, stipulate auditing practices, or require training for local officials. All of these are done by one or more states, although they are only examples of the many types of state assistance.

STATES AS BANKERS OF LOCAL GOVERNMENTS

A major facet of state involvement in local affairs is the part they play in financing local government. They are the principal external providers of funds to local governments. They transfer large sums of state money to the local units and, in addition, they serve as conduits of much of the federal money that local governments spend. Most of this is in the form of grants-in-aid, although states also share taxes as well as receipts from state businesses, such as liquor stores, and some other funds. They also provide payments to local governments in lieu of taxes on state property, share facilities, and sometimes give state real or personal property to local jurisdictions. State aid currently comprises approximately one-third of the funds local governments spend.[13] In addition, states pass through to local units about 27 percent of the federal funds they receive.[14]

STATES AS ENSURERS OF EQUITY, EFFECTIVENESS, EFFICIENCY AND ACCOUNTABILITY

To a substantial degree, states are the ensurers of "good" government at both the state and local levels. Through their constitutions, statutes and court decisions, they can mandate equity in representation, distribution of resources, and governmental operations. While they operate within the limits of human constraints, their legal controls over local units allow them to improve responsiveness of local institutions and to ensure accountability and openness of and access to governmental processes. They exercise significant control over such matters as apportionment for representation. They can establish formulas for the distribution of resources and require fair governmental practices. State "sunshine" statutes, aimed at ensuring open decisionmaking in public matters, can apply to state and local levels alike.

The steps states can take to ensure effective government cover a wide range of possibilities. On one hand, they can grant charters that allow local officials the leeway to deal with their problems. On the other end of the scale, they can oversee locally administered state programs to ensure that they accomplish the intended results, authorize sufficient revenues to carry out government programs and remove barriers to effective management. Often they can play a positive role through standard setting, technical assistance and advice. The same thing applies to encouraging efficiency. Although those who actually deliver government service are the largest factor in the efficiency of the operations, states can exert influence by promoting cooperation among localities, sharing expertise and promoting local competency. They can refrain from imposing procedures and requirements that impair economical government operations. State restrictions on local debt, accounting, purchasing and auditing requirements, while often necessary to prevent financial crises, must be imposed with care. Otherwise, requirements intended to encourage efficiency in some instances may produce the opposite effect.

Each state performs differently in these matters, a fact that makes nationwide assessment of their actions difficult. They have, as well, unique political cultures, economic and social systems, and other characteristics that make for different patterns of response to problems.

CRITICISMS OF STATE ACTIONS AFFECTING LOCAL GOVERNMENTS

The heavy reliance of local governments on the state affords the latter substantial options in regard to improvement of local governmental operations. The choices made, nonetheless, have not always provided the maximum opportunity for local excellence. They have, in the past, often retarded local efforts at effective and efficient decisionmaking and administration. In the words of a 1969 ACIR report:

> The deadly combination of restricted annexation and unrestricted incorporation; the chaotic and uncontrolled mushrooming of special districts; and limitations upon municipal taxing and borrowing powers; the deliverance of all important police powers of zoning, land use and building regulations into the hands of thousands of separate and competing local governments—these are but a few of the byproducts of decades of state governments; nonfeasance and malfeasance concerning urban affairs.[15]

Many critics would agree that states often have been unmindful of local problems, particularly those of big cities. In discussing the "reluctant states" in this connection, Roscoe C. Martin blamed part of the problem on the "state mind." He wrote, in 1965:

> Rural orientation, provincial outlook, commitment to a strict moral code, a philosophy of individualism—these are the components of the state mind. If they evoke memories of the oil lamp and the covered bridge, why this very spirit of nostalgia is also characteristic of the state mind. One of the most unhappy features of the state (and its leaders and institutions) is its intermittent and imperfect contact with the realities of the modern world.[16]

In Martin's view, this state of mind gave birth to certain myths that have had important influences on state policies toward local problems. Chief among the myths is the conviction that little government, both in the sense of local governments and a minimum of state government, is "both virtuous and democratic." Conversely, big government, be it state or federal, tends to be corrupt and undemocratic. Moreover, urban problems "spring from unhealthy soil" and lack the legitimacy of established claimants to state attention. States claim a lack of resources to deal with all these matters. Finally, the federal government, large and distant, is an object of distrust.

The "state mind" has had the consequence of engendering a dedicated intransigence and "negativism" on the part of the states, according to Martin. Their addiction to the status quo produces an unfavorable reaction to almost anything new. In summing up the effects of the state of mind and mythologies that he attributes to the states, Martin wrote:

> In summary, three overriding deficiencies flow from the state of mind and the mythology which grip the states. The first is in orientation—most states are governed in accordance with the rural traditions of an earlier day. The second is timeliness—the governments of most states are anachronistic; they lack relevance to the urgencies of the modern world. The third is in leadership—state leaders are by confession cautious and tradition-bound, which ill-equips them for the tasks of modern government.[17]

If Martin's analysis is correct, such a negative outlook on the part of the state does not augur well for local governments. Are the criticisms set out above valid at the present time? Have the states been willing to change in this important aspect of their responsibilities? What recent actions have they taken to improve their relations with their local governments? How do these balance others that increasingly circumscribe local options and initiatives?

CHANGING STATE STRATEGIES TOWARD LOCAL GOVERNMENTS

If, as the Walkers pointed out, "the acid test of the States' real strength lies in their relationship with their own localities,"[18] that relationship needs to be examined to determine if it permits localities enough freedom to manage their own affairs effectively and efficiently at the same time that it preserves state authority to deal with statewide problems. The dichotomy presented by building both strong state and strong local governments need not force a choice between the two. Strong, viable governments at both levels do not preclude effective sharing of responsibility and, in fact, may enhance it. The growing interdependence of states and their local governments, as reflected in the growth of shared functions and fiscal aids, underscores the necessity of increased cooperation and coordination between them....

In the past quarter century, states have broadened local powers through increased grants of home rule and optional charters, through devolution of powers and through permission to make interlocal agreements. Counties have been the principal beneficiaries of the greater autonomy, although other types of local jurisdictions also have profited. States have coupled this strengthening of local legal authority, however, with a dramatic increase in mandates on local governments to undertake new functions and activities. These requirements have proved costly to the localities. Despite the attachment of cost estimates in the form of fiscal notes to state legislation mandating local action, the expense has fallen largely on the smaller jurisdictions, thus limiting their options because of fiscal constraints. The trade-offs between more discretionary authority on the one hand and increased state mandating on the other have varied from state to state. Consequently, it is difficult to assess the overall impact of these two opposite developments.

Notes

1. City of Clinton v. Cedar Rapids and Missouri Railroad Company, 24 Iowa 455, 462, 463 (1868).
2. John F. Dillon, *Commentaries on the Law of Municipal Corporations*, 5th ed. (Boston, Mass.: Little, Brown and Co., 1911), vol. 1, sec. 237. Emphases in the original excerpt "read: local government."
3. Joan Aron and Charles Brecher, "Recent Developments in State-Local Relations: A Case Study of New York," a paper prepared for the Conference on the Partnership within the States: Local Self-Government in the Federal System, November 18-20, 1975, 1-2.
4. Article VII, Sections 1 and 2, adopted March 7, 1978.
5. Daniel R. Grant, "Urban Needs and State Response: Local Government Reorganization," in The American Assembly, *The States and the Urban Crisis,* edited by Alan K. Campbell (Englewood Cliffs, N.J.: Prentice-Hall, Inc., 1970). For recent activity on city-county consolidation, see Parris N. Glendening and Patricia S. Atkins, "City-County Consolidation: New Views for the Eighties," *1980 Municipal Year Book* (Washington, D.C.: International City Management Association, 1980), 68-72.
6. Land Use Planning Reports, *A Summary of State Land Use Controls*, Report 2 (Washington, D.C.: Plus Publications, Inc., January 1975), 1. For a discussion of the spread of innovations in land use legislation among the states, see Nelson Rosenbaum, *Land Use and the Legislatures* (Washington, D.C.: The Urban Institute, 1976).
7. Council of State Governments, *State Growth Management* (Lexington, Ky.: May 1976), 24-25. The Council has published a series of studies on state land use programs and policies developed by the Task Force on Natural Resource and Land Use Information and Technology. The Council sponsored the Task Force in cooperation with the U.S. Department of the Interior. The studies are *State Alternatives for Planning and Management* (Final Report of the Task Force); *Land Use Management: Proceedings of The National Symposium on Resource and Land Information; A Legislator's Guide to Land Management; Land Use Policy and Program Analysis Number 1: Intergovernmental Relations in State Land Use Planning; Land Use Policy and Program Analysis Number 2: Data Needs and Resources for State Land Use Planning; Land Use Policy and Program Analysis Number 3: Organization, Management and Financing of State Land Use Programs; Land Use Policy and Program Analysis Number 4: State of the Art for Designation of Areas of Critical Environmental Concern; Land Use Policy and Program Analysis Number 5: Issues and Recommendation—State Critical Areas Programs;* and *Land Use Policy and Program Analysis Number 6: Manpower Needs for State Land Use Planning and Public Involvement in State Land Use Planning.*
8. U.S. General Accounting Office, *State and Local Government's Views on Technical Assistance* (GGK-78-58) (Washington, D.C.: July 12, 1978), ii, 38, 45.
9. ACIR, *State-Local Relations Bodies: State ACIRs and Other Approaches*, M-124 (Washington, D.C.: U.S. Government Printing Office, March 1981), 37.
10. Joseph F. Zimmerman, "State Agencies for Local Affairs: The Institutionalization of State Assistance to Local Governments," mimeographed (Albany, N.Y.: State University of New York at Albany, Graduate School of Public Affairs, Local Government Center, 1968).
11. ACIR, M-124, *op. cit.*, 38-39.
12. Ibid.
13. ACIR, *The States and Intergovernmental Aids* (A-59) (Washington, D.C.: U.S. Government Printing Office, February 1977), 9.

14. See Table 5, ACIR, *Recent Trends in Federal and State Aid to Local Governments,* M-118 (Washington, D.C.: U.S. Government Printing Office, 1980), 8.
15. Advisory Commission on Intergovernmental Relations, *Urban America and the Federal System,* M-47 (Washington, D.C.: U.S. Government Printing Office, 1969), 2.
16. Roscoe C. Martin, *The Cities and the Federal System* (New York: Atherton Press, 1965), 77. See also The American Assembly, *The States and the Urban Crisis*, edited by Alan K. Campbell (Englewood Cliffs, N.J.: Prentice-Hall, Inc., 1970); Lee S. Green, Malcolm E. Jewell, and Daniel R. Grant, *The States and the Metropolis* (University: University of Alabama Press, 1968); A. James Reichley, "The States Hold the Keys to the Cities," *Fortune Magazine* (June 1969); and Paul N. Ylvisaker, "The Growing Role of State Government in Local Affairs," *State Government* (Summer 1968).
17. Ibid., 79.
18. Jeanne and David Walker, "Rationalizing Local Governments' Powers, Functions and Structure," in *States' Responsibilities to Local Governments: An Action Agenda*, prepared by the Center for Policy Research of the National Governors' Association, Washington, D.C., 1975, 39.

Principles of Fiscal Federalism

A serious assessment of Federal-State-local fiscal relations must address a wide variety of issues. They range from the appropriate assignment of service responsibilities among levels of government to the obligation of the Federal government, if any, to moderate disparities in the fiscal capacities of the States and local governments.

The size, diversity, and dynamic character of the American federal system make these issues particularly complex. After India, the United States is the world's second-largest federal democracy, with far and away the most complicated governmental structure. The core of that structure consists of 50 States, the District of Columbia, a number of territories, and several hundred native American governments.[1] In contrast, West Germany has 11 länder and citystates, Australia 6 States, Canada 10 provinces and 2 territories, India 22 States and 9 union territories, and Switzerland 25 cantons.

Additionally, localities represent a distinct and quasi-autonomous level of government. While legally creations of and subordinate to the States, about 80,000 units of local government have a high degree of *de facto* autonomy, and make independent claims upon both the Federal and State governments as well as the private sector. Moreover, the structure, responsibilities, and revenue-raising powers of local governments vary enormously among the States, as does the division of authority between the State government and localities. Some of these arrangements are prescribed by State constitutions, many are deeply rooted in tradition and accommodations of long standing. Change does not come easily, but it has occurred at an historically unprecedented pace in recent decades. Underlying the formal structure of American federalism is a highly pluralistic society characterized by dynamic social and economic change and mobility.

Given these realities, the notion of a definitive, unambiguous theory or set of principles for the structuring of government finance and intergovernmental fiscal relationships is illusory. Rather, federalism demands continuing adjustments and reallocations of responsibilities and resources in response to changing circumstances and improving understanding of inherently complex situations. Nonetheless, such adjustments and reallocations are more likely to be constructive in the long run if their consideration is informed by a consistent and clearly articulated set of theoretical principles and the policy guidelines that flow from them.

Federalism can be addressed from numerous theoretical perspectives ranging from legalistic discussions of Constitutional provisions relating to the authority of the national government and the States to elegant mathematical representations of intergovernmental fiscal relationships. The question addressed in this discussion is what perspective provides principles that offer the most promising guidance in addressing the contemporary issues of American federalism.

Reprinted from *Federal-State-Local Fiscal Relations*, Report to the President and the Congress (Washington, D.C.: Office of State and Local Finance, Department of the Treasury, September 1985), 9-29.

The central issues of federalism in the United States of the 1980s are financial. They involve decisions relating to the 43 percent of the nation's income that is produced or redistributed by the public sector.[2] With a view to the primary objectives of efficiency, equity, and accountability, this chapter outlines a set of basic economic principles that provide a conceptual framework for this report. The discussion is organized into three major sections:

- *Basic Concepts:* The role of democratic governments in a market economy, the rationale for a general bias in favor of governmental decentralization, and the general conditions that must be satisfied if a decentralized system is to be economically efficient, equitable, and accountable to the electorate.
- *Structure of Responsibilities:* Specification of the roles and responsibilities of each level of government based on the geographical incidence of the benefits and costs of specific public services and fiscal disparities.
- *Implementation of Responsibilities:* Basic guidelines to ensure efficiency, equity, and accountability in a structured system of federal relationships.

The chapter concludes with a discussion of the limitations of this conceptual framework and a summary of its major implications in the form of a set of specific criteria for federalism reform.

THE ECONOMIC THEORY OF FEDERALISM: BASIC CONCEPTS

The world's great federal democracies emerged as responses to two essential political concerns—the protection of individual liberty from abuse by government power and the preservation of national unity in highly pluralistic societies. These concerns of our Founding Fathers were shared by those who shaped federal democracies in nations as diverse as Canada, India, and Switzerland. The concerns shaped principles of federalism cast in terms of constitutional rules and legal precepts buttressed by political philosophy.

National unity and personal liberty are secure today in large measure because of the enduring wisdom of the principles of federalism incorporated in the Constitution by its authors. Today, the central issues of federalism relate to the more mundane pursuit of equity, efficiency, and accountability in the very large proportion of the nation's resources that flows through the public sector.

These issues of the 1980s were undreamed of two centuries ago, when the public sector commanded an insignificant fraction of the nation's income. While the traditional principles of federalism offer general guidance, relatively little of practical value in rationalizing the public sector can be gleaned from the language of the Constitution or the Federalist Papers.[3]

Fortunately, a body of well-understood economic theory offers considerable practical guidance in addressing the issues of the 1980s. It must be stressed that economics does not offer a definitive resolution of every matter on the agenda, such as whether a single level of government should have exclusive responsibility for a particular service, and which level that should be. Many key questions of fact identified as relevant by economic theory are not susceptible to precise measurement.[4]

Even when there is agreement about facts, value judgments by policymakers are often required on matters that are beyond the purview of economic analysis. On many issues, conflicts between the objectives of efficiency and equity are real, and trade-offs must be resolved through the political process. Nonetheless, economic theory provides a useful basic framework for considering the key questions involved in structuring government and intergovernmental fiscal relations to the ends of efficiency, equity, and accountability. The elements of that theory are outlined in this section.[5]

Why Government?

Practical experience as well as economic theory demonstrate that, in general, the productivity of the economy and the welfare of individuals are most likely to be maximized when decisions about the production and consumption of goods and services are made in the marketplace. The intervention of government in such an economy can only be justified to the extent that the market can be shown to be incapable of dealing effectively with a situation.

While specific limitations or failures of markets constitute necessary conditions for government action, they are not, in themselves, also sufficient conditions. Before government action is appropriate, there must be a reasonable prospect that it will improve on the performance of the market at reasonable cost.

In this context, economists argue that, beyond defining and ensuring conformance with the rules of the game for the market, governmental action can be justified only (1) to ensure the overall performance of the economy at high levels of employment with reasonable price stability; (2) to provide or to subsidize the provision of goods and services that people are willing to pay for but that are not provided in sufficient amounts by the private sector; and (3) to ensure an equitable distribution of income and wealth among individuals and households, and its corollary, an equitable distribution of fiscal capacity among subnational governmental jurisdictions.[6]

Economic Stabilization

At a very minimum, government must regulate the supply of money. Market economies are subject to cycles in the level of business activity that, if left totally unchecked, can result in deteriorating overall economic performance and excessive social costs. Recent history suggests that modern market economies are also characterized by institutions that give rise to inherent tendencies toward inflation. In light of these considerations, there is general agreement that some level of government action is required to maintain economic performance at a steady pace.

There is, however, considerable controversy about the appropriate scope and nature of such intervention. In general, there is growing agreement among economists of all persuasions that such action should be confined to measures designed to promote economic growth and maintain a stable monetary system, and should not involve the sorts of efforts to "fine tune" the economy with tax and expenditure (fiscal) policies that were popular in decades past.

Allocation of Resources

Certain goods and services that people would be willing to pay for simply cannot be provided adequately by the private sector. Obvious examples of such public goods are national defense and the control of communicable diseases. The essential attribute of goods and services whose supply can be left to the private sector is that they are marketable. That is, an individual can consume or benefit from them only if he or she pays the market price. Candy bars and movies benefit only those who consume them, and an individual unwilling to pay the market price can easily be excluded from their consumption.

However, all Americans benefit from outlays for national defense, and none could be denied those benefits for failure to pay. The involvement of the government in the provision of services characterized by the inapplicability of this principle of exclusion is, therefore, clearly a necessary function of the public sector.[7]

The production and consumption of certain types of goods and services that can be privately produced and sold in the marketplace generate benefits or costs that are important to people who are not directly involved in their production or consumption. For example, the primary beneficiary of education is the student, and those benefits can be denied to an individual who is unwilling to pay. However, more is at stake in education than the benefits received directly by students. It is widely believed that society as a whole benefits from educational attainment. Without some collective action through government to support educational services, less would be provided than most people believe would be desirable and would be willing to pay for.

Such circumstances justify a role for government in the provision or financing of services with significant "external" benefits. The objective of government action in such cases is to ensure that the total amount produced reflects the demand of the indirect (external) as well as the direct beneficiaries of the services.

Similarly, the production of some goods and services may give rise to costs to society that the market does not require to be paid by the private producers. In the absence of intervention by the government to ensure that such external costs are included in private production costs, the market prices of such goods and services will be artificially low, and excessive quantities will be produced and consumed.[8]

A standard example of external costs is the toxic wastes created by the production of such goods as gasoline. The manufacturer may be able to avoid the costs of neutralization or safe disposal of the wastes by dumping them in a nearby river. Should he do so, the costs of the environmental degradation will be borne by those downstream, rather than by the producer and consumers of the product. Government action may be justified to ensure that all of the costs of such goods are paid by the manufacturer and the consumer.[9]

Distribution of Income and Wealth

A market economy is a demonstrably superior mechanism for the generation of income and wealth. There is no guarantee, however, that it will produce a distribution of income and wealth that Americans would deem acceptable.

Distributional issues arise in a number of contexts. Some are unable because of poor health, mental incapacity, age, or family circumstances to compete effectively in the labor market. The effective operation of the market requires that some individuals accumulate resources beyond those required for current consumption to devote to productive investments. Economic growth, which generates rising living standards for most Americans, has inevitable costs in the short run as labor and capital can rarely shift instantaneously and costlessly from declining to growing industries. The role of government in facilitating such reallocations of resources and in ameliorating the burdens on specific individuals adversely affected is a perennially contentious matter. As a result, distributional issues are an enduring feature of the political debates of nations with market economies.

There are, of course, serious disagreements about the appropriate extent and nature of redistribution by government. At a minimum, however, there is near-universal agreement that government should provide a basic "social safety net." This is designed to ensure that no Americans need go without minimum levels of food, shelter, clothing, and medical services when they are unable to provide for themselves. Decisions on these issues are inherently value judgments. Beyond pointing out the possible desirability of government action, and calling attention to the potential consequences of redistributive policies for economic incentives, economic theory has little guidance to offer.

A Note on Opportunity Costs

Economic theory delineates roles for government in ensuring the stability of the economy, in allocating resources, and in distributing income and wealth. It also demands that decisions about such activities take into account their potential costs. Such costs are measured in terms of resources withdrawn from the private sector and distortions of market incentives. Before a government activity is initiated (and, once initiated, before it is perpetuated indefinitely), two pertinent questions must be asked. The first is whether it is an appropriate function of government. The second is whether the activity's benefits exceed its costs.

These are not simple issues. For example, numerous public policies are designed to direct higher levels of investment to housing than would otherwise occur. Their justification rests on the external benefits widely believed to be associated with home ownership, including social stability and attachment to community. Such activities are also, in some cases, strands of the social safety net—elements of the government's distribution policy.

However, the diversion of resources into housing has costs in terms of the reduced availability of capital for investment in plant and equipment. Decades of debate have not resolved the relative costs and benefits of housing policies. What is unfortunate is not that precise dollar values have not been assigned to such external benefits as community cohesion and social stability. Rather, it is that—in these and other policy debates—the opportunity costs of governmental activities are often ignored. One of the most significant contributions of economics to policy discussions is its central maxim that "there is no such thing as a free lunch."

Many economists believe that certain structures and processes of contemporary American federalism tend systematically to downplay or obscure the opportunity costs associated with government activities. When consideration of policy choices focuses more intently on the benefits than on the costs of governmental action, there is a built-in bias toward an overexpansion of the public sector. These considerations are addressed here in a discussion of procedures for the expression of consumer preferences in public sector institutions.

Predisposition toward Decentralization

Economic theory provides a powerful rationale for structuring decision making on and the financing and delivery of public services, to the maximum extent possible, on a decentralized basis. This predisposition toward decentralization is rooted in considerations of efficiency, accountability, manageability, and equity. These considerations lead to a general principle of autonomy that calls for restraint on the part of the Federal government and, to a lesser degree, State governments in their intrusions into the affairs of lower-level units of government.

Efficiency

Given any distribution of income, the welfare of consumers in a market economy is maximized because each is free to allocate his or her income in whatever manner produces the most satisfaction. In the case of the types of services that must be provided by government, however, a high degree of uniformity is inescapable. Yet people's preferences for public goods are hardly more uniform than their preferences for private goods. Some assign high priority to security, for example, and are willing to pay high taxes to put a police officer on every corner. Others place a high value on education, and are willing to foot the bill for low pupil-teacher ratios and high-tech instructional equipment.

A centralized or unitary system of government has a limited capacity to respond to such differences in preferences. A decentralized system, on the other hand, can accommodate these differences by offering a range of choices in the level and mix of public services.

In a decentralized system, individuals and firms are free to locate in the governmental unit that provides the level and mix of public services that most closely accord with their preferences. Once located, of course, a democratic system offers them the opportunity to influence the decisions in their community and State. This potential for "voting with one's feet" promotes a closer match between public goods and private preferences. It also stimulates competitive pressures for governments to develop innovative, more efficient modes of service provision. Decentralization also lessens the likelihood that a government will get too far out of line with its neighbors; individuals and firms are free to pack up and leave when their preferences are no longer satisfied. Decentralization can thus be viewed as the governmental analog of the marketplace.[10]

Accountability

Economic efficiency requires effective mechanisms to discipline the producers of goods and services. In the marketplace, producers are disciplined by the choices made by consumers. Accountability in the public sector is maintained through the political process.

Decentralization significantly enhances the effectiveness of this process. In a decentralized system of government, choices about expenditures are most directly linked to costs. If the people who benefit from a public service have to bear the full costs of that service, they are likely to be sensitive to whether output levels are appropriate and whether the services are produced efficiently. Decentralization also allows for more accurate identification of the public official responsible for the provision of a particular service and therefore makes possible more effective electoral discipline.

Manageability

The imperatives of effective management demand a high degree of decentralization. The experience of corporate institutions suggests that centralized bureaucratic structures responsible for large-scale activities are simply unmanageable due to an inability of central decision-making authorities to process information. Corporate structures are almost universally characterized by high levels of functional and/or geographic decentralization in order to make effective management possible. If decentralization is a necessity for the effective management of major corporations, it is an absolute imperative for the conduct of governmental activities for a nation as large and complex as the United States.

Equity

Equity considerations cut two ways in the context of a decentralized system. On the one hand, differences in fiscal capacities among State and local governments result in differences in the "tax prices" of public services among jurisdictions. This issue is discussed further later in this chapter, but here it need only be noted that, to some, this is an inequitable situation.

At the same time, if a major equity consideration is that the costs of government services be borne to the maximum possible extent by those enjoying the benefits (this "benefit principle" is also considered later in this discussion), decentralization can improve the prospects of this result. The smaller the governmental unit, the easier it tends to be to tailor a revenue system to satisfy the benefit principle, for reasons closely related to those considered earlier in connection with efficiency.

Principle of Autonomy

The structure of government in a federal system is not entirely decentralized, but—for reasons explored in detail later here—is made up of a national government and one or more lower levels. In the United States, of course, there are three basic levels: Federal, State, and local. If the full advantages of decentralization are to be realized, what may be called the principle of autonomy must receive strong recognition and support. In essence, this principle is that the autonomy of lower levels of government should only be impaired by higher levels of government when their activities have significantly adverse consequences for other units. In practical terms, this means that the Federal government should exercise restraint in its involvement in the affairs of any State, unless that State's activities generate significant costs for other States.

Given that local governments are, legally, creatures of the States, the principle of autonomy cannot appropriately be applied as rigorously to State-local relations as it can to relations between the Federal government and the States. Nonetheless, the full benefits of decentralization are only likely to be realized if State governments grant substantial autonomy to their localities, and exercise genuine restraint in their involvement in the decisions of those local governments.

The principle of autonomy is a central, though often implicit, theme of the discussion in the remainder of this chapter. The next section considers the issue of the assignment of responsibilities among levels of government. The final section outlines a set of specific guidelines for the implementation of these responsibilities and for fiscal relations among levels of government in a federal system that flow from the economic theory of fiscal federalism.

THE STRUCTURE OF RESPONSIBILITIES: SPILLOVERS, DISPARITIES, AND INCOME MAINTENANCE

While an overwhelming case can be made for a high degree of governmental decentralization, it is also clear that certain activities are most appropriately undertaken by the national government. The most obvious examples are providing for the nation's defense and stabilization of the economy through monetary and fiscal policies. The benefits of such activities clearly extend throughout the nation.[11] At the other extreme, the benefits of fire services are geographically limited, and are most appropriately the responsibility of local governments.

For most government activities, however, the appropriate roles for the national and subnational levels of government are not so obvious. The sorting out of responsibilities among levels of government requires careful attention to vertical and horizontal fiscal relationships.[12] Vertical relationships refer to the assignment of expenditure and revenue-raising responsibilities among the levels of government. Horizontal relationships refer to the relative fiscal capacities of States and localities to meet their service responsibilities.

Spillovers and Vertical Fiscal Relations

In a federal system, subnational jurisdictions independently decide their own levels of public services. Some types of services, such as fire protection, provide benefits only to the residents of a community (incidentally to visitors). However, other services benefit residents of neighboring jurisdictions, perhaps even entire regions. An example is wastewater treatment. The benefits of a particular jurisdiction's devotion of resources to waste treatment extend beyond its borders, though they tend to decrease with distance. Some services whose primary benefits are local may benefit the entire nation.

A jurisdiction's allocation of resources to a service can only be expected to reflect the benefits realized by its residents. They will, therefore, limit the amount of the service provided to the level at which their benefits equal their costs.[13] If a portion of the benefits (say, in the form of services provided to commuters) spill out to neighboring jurisdictions, it is rarely possible for that jurisdiction to negotiate with all outside beneficiary jurisdictions for remuneration. Without compensation for the external benefits, however, the service level will be too low from the standpoint of all potential beneficiaries.

In such situations, economic theory calls for a higher level of government to finance a portion of the costs incurred by the subordinate units if the allocation of resources to the service is to be optimal. The appropriate proportion is given by the ratio of the external benefits to nonresidents to the total benefits of the service. A suitable vehicle for the higher government's action is a matching grant based on the share of the benefits that spills out of the jurisdiction.

For example, if 20 percent of the benefits of local police services provided by a city is realized by commuters and visitors to the city from throughout the State, a State matching grant paying 20 percent of the city's total outlays for those services would ensure an appropriate level of provision.[14] The effect of the matching grant is to reduce the net cost of the services to the city to 80 percent of their nominal cost. As this is the proportion of the benefits realized by city residents, the decision of their government on the allocation of resources to the services could, therefore, be presumed to be optimal.

Some services generate external benefits that extend beyond the boundaries of local jurisdictions or States but are clearly less than national in scope. Economic theory suggests that these circumstances should be addressed by State action or action through some multi-State structure. Federal action, beyond possible third-party mediation of multi-State agreements, is only warranted if the spillovers are widely distributed throughout the country, as in the case of interstate highways.

While the concepts of benefit incidence and spillovers have powerful analytic implications for the assignment of governmental responsibilities, misapplication of the concepts is common. Arguments that Federal actions are justified because spillovers are involved that threaten economic efficiency must be carefully assessed with regard to the magnitude of the potential problem and the effectiveness of the presumed remedy. Even when some higher-level action is justified, Federal involvement is rarely necessary or appropriate.

For example, the benefits of public transportation often spill over the boundaries of individual localities. However, such benefits are normally encompassed by clearly bounded regions made up of a readily identifiable group of localities or, in some cases, States. Such circumstances provide scant justification for Federal action that would, in effect, force taxpayers in Maine to subsidize a public service whose benefits are only enjoyed by the residents of California, or of the San Francisco Bay area.

It should also be pointed out that there is considerable confusion between problems that are nationwide and spillovers that are national in scope. For example, every community must fill potholes and provide police patrols. These are nationwide problems, but they can hardly be viewed as problems requiring the attention of the national government. Since the benefits of such services essentially accrue exclusively to the residents of each community, there is little justification in economic theory for State, let alone Federal, involvement in their financing or provision. Federal intervention is appropriate only when a service involves benefits or costs that are widely dispersed throughout the country, such as nuclear waste disposal or basic scientific research.[15]

Disparities and Horizontal Fiscal Relations

In addition to spillovers, the existence of substantial fiscal disparities also provides a potential basis for action by higher levels of government. The conclusion that the market allocates resources efficiently to maximize consumer welfare rests on the acceptability of the underlying distribution of income and wealth. Correspondingly, the argument that local and State governments can be counted upon to allocate resources efficiently in the public sector if externalities are appropriately accounted for assumes that the underlying distribution of fiscal capacity is reasonably acceptable.

As there are large differences in the incomes and wealth of individuals, so too are there large differences in the fiscal capacities of State and local governments.[16] The central policy issue is whether disparities in fiscal capacities are serious enough to justify mitigating measures by the States and the Federal government to ensure equity and an efficient allocation of resources in the public sector.

There are significant differences in the abilities of States and localities to raise revenues from their own sources. These differences are traceable predominately to variations in the income and wealth of the residents of jurisdictions. However, they are also attributable, in some cases, to the differential abilities of State and local jurisdictions to shift the burdens of their taxes to nonresidents, that is, to export them.

There are also differences among jurisdictions in the underlying social and economic factors that give rise to service needs, such as the size of the school-age population or concentrations of low-income residents. In addition, there are differences in the costs of providing basic services. For example, road building is far more costly in mountainous areas than where the land is flat.

Concern with fiscal disparities flows from both equity and efficiency considerations. Equity considerations are implicit in such propositions as that all Americans should have access to minimum levels of public services or that they should bear comparable tax burdens for comparable levels of services.[17] There are major differences of opinion about what services should be included in any minimum standards and what constitute comparable tax burdens. Nonetheless, such equity concerns have played a significant role at the State level, where virtually every State has a program to offset fiscal disparities among local school districts. These programs generally employ complex allocation formulas that respond to local differences in revenue-raising abilities, educational needs, and costs of services.

Beyond equity considerations, there are important reasons to be concerned about fiscal disparities on efficiency grounds.[18] These flow from the proposition that government action should be neutral with respect to private economic decisions except where non-neutrality is an explicit objective of policy. For example, discussions of tax reform focus on how Federal taxes benefit some economic activities and sectors and penalize others.[19] In such circumstances, private economic choices respond to the Federal tax structure rather than to rates of return shaped by market forces. As a result, aggregate economic performance is impaired.

Fiscal disparities among States and localities tend to create analogous distortions of private economic choices. Disparities in the abilities of States and localities to finance their service responsibilities foster differences in tax rates and service levels. When such considerations, rather than market factors, induce households and firms to relocate (or discourage relocation, when market considerations call for it), the economy as a whole suffers.

The economic literature makes a strong case for some Federal action to reduce disparities in State-local fiscal capacities in the interest of economic efficiency, but several ambiguities are inherent in such actions. While there is widespread agreement that every American should have access to some basic set of essential public services, disagreements about the scope of the essential services are significant. Economic theory offers little help in resolving such differences, which are rooted in value judgments.

Even if there were no disagreement about equity standards, the design of disparity-reducing Federal policies would have to cope with several difficult issues. Clearly, disparity reduction should not so enhance the attractiveness of particular regions and communities that the locational choices of households and firms substantially detract from the nation's overall economic performance. In operational terms, economic theory suggests that policies to shore up the fiscal capacities of economically disadvantaged areas should be designed with a view to the fiscal consequences of economic decline, but should not provide so much assistance that low tax rates and/or high public service levels offset the underlying economic characteristics of the areas.

Particularly problematic is the question of the Federal role in reducing disparities among local governments, which range far more widely than disparities among the States. To a significant degree, intrastate disparities are shaped by the decisions of State governments regarding the geographical boundaries of localities, the assignment of service responsibilities, and restrictions on local revenue-raising options.

It is also true, however, that some intrastate disparities are in part shaped by Federal actions. Most obvious are jurisdictions that must provide education services to the children of military personnel and other Federal employees who live on Federal installations that are exempt from local taxation, or border jurisdictions whose economies are significantly influenced by international economic developments.

Another difficult issue is presented by the existence of communities with very low incomes whose local governments do not have the capacities to provide essential services, combined with the failure of the State government to respond. When such situations offend widely held national equity norms, strong pressures on the Federal government to take remedial action are predictable. However, inappropriately designed responses to such pressure may compromise the fundamental responsibility of State governments for the fiscal capacities of their local governments.

Historically, appeals directly to the Federal government by officials whose State governments have not been responsive to their needs were major factors in the proliferation of programs in the 1960s and 1970s providing Federal funds directly to local governments, including Revenue Sharing and Community Development Block Grants. Until such time as all States demonstrate a willingness to assume these responsibilities, these pressures are likely to continue, and some Federal response may be unavoidable. In such circumstances, Federal efforts to address serious fiscal disparities at the local level should be as limited as possible, should involve an efficient vehicle and explicit targeting, and should be designed to stimulate ameliorative action by State governments.

The Special Case of Income Maintenance

It has long been conventional wisdom among economists that the distribution and stabilization functions of public finance should be the responsibility of the Federal government, and that State-local governments should confine their attention to the allocation function.

This view rests on equity and efficiency considerations. The equity argument is that only a nationally uniform system of income-maintenance programs financed by a progressive income tax can be fair to all Americans. A system administered and financed by State and local governments would inevitably produce disparate benefit levels that would tend in the aggregate, because of competition among States and localities, to be lower than that for which a national consensus might exist.

The efficiency argument is that the differences in benefit levels and the tax rates that would be necessary to finance them (because of differences in State-local fiscal capacities) would result in significant, nonmarket-based incentives for migration, which would tend to reduce the overall productivity of the economy.

In recent years, there has been considerable rethinking of these arguments.[20] Support has been growing for the view that the only practicable option is an intergovernmental approach to income maintenance, though the predominant share of the responsibility for financing the "social safety net" should remain with the Federal government. This rethinking reflects a number of important considerations.

First, it is by now abundantly clear—after decades of experience with an *ad hoc* system of income-maintenance programs involving all three levels of government—that views about the appropriate level of benefits vary substantially among the States (and local governments). A wide range of benefit levels has persisted stubbornly in the face of fairly strong Federal incentives promoting greater uniformity. This suggests that support for a uniform national system is much weaker than has been supposed in the past.

Second, nearly two decades of efforts to design a national system of cash payments that simultaneously provides reasonable levels of benefits and preserves work incentives without being exorbitantly costly appear to suggest that such a system is beyond the reach of a policy based predominantly on cash assistance.

Third, it has become increasingly apparent that the American public does not view cash assistance with as much favor as economists do. In fact, the public appears much to prefer in-kind benefits—such as food stamps, housing vouchers, medical care, legal services, and school lunches.

Finally, recent experience suggests that a coherent, long-range strategy for dealing with the problems of poverty must go beyond mere income maintenance. Such a strategy would include services designed to improve employment prospects—remedial education; training; medical assistance; counseling; relocation assistance; provision for reduced minimum wages, wage subsidies, and other types of incentives for private-sector efforts; and even requirements for acceptance of work assignments in return for certain types of benefits.

A number of general policy implications seem to flow from these considerations. First, diversity is to be expected, indeed, is essential. Many of the problems are different in rural and urban areas, and in different regions of the country. Second, many of these approaches require high levels of administrative discretion. This is essential so that States and localities can tailor responses to the highest-priority problems of specific areas and devise innovative ways of helping dependent individuals and families achieve self-sufficiency.

Third, some significant level of continuing Federal financial involvement appears essential to ensure that minimal standards of benefit adequacy prevail throughout the nation.[21] At the same time, the States must be free to provide whatever supplementary levels of assistance they may be prepared to pay for. Beyond this, the need for decentralized administration requires that the States and local governments have a substantial stake of their own resources in the system if they are to have appropriate incentives to develop innovative approaches and to insist upon managerial efficiency.

Mixing Policy Objectives

In all federal democracies, national governments undertake policies to address spillovers and disparities. In Australia, Canada, and West Germany, the major thrust of national grant policy is directed toward the reduction of fiscal disparities. In contrast, most Federal grants in the U.S. came into being as responses to specific, perceived problems. Such programs should be evaluated on the basis of the appropriateness of their design as responses to the existence of benefit spillovers.

With the possible exception of revenue sharing, no major Federal grant program is designed specifically to reduce fiscal disparities among the States and local governments. Indeed, disparity reduction is not generally viewed as a major objective of revenue sharing. Paradoxically, many categorical grant programs are justified by some of their supporters on the ground that they respond to underlying fiscal disparities.

The disparity-reduction grant strategies employed in Australia, Canada, and West Germany appear to have allowed national policymakers to resist pressures to overreact to specific problems. The basic posture is that the national government has assured subnational units adequate fiscal resources to respond to most problems that may arise.[22]

IMPLEMENTATION OF RESPONSIBILITIES

The concepts of the incidence of benefits and costs and fiscal disparities provide useful guidance in sorting out responsibilities among the governments of a federal system. In addition, economics provides important general advice on how these responsibilities should be implemented in order to ensure high levels of efficiency, equity, and accountability.

Most pertinent to an overall assessment of Federal-State-local fiscal relations are guidelines that address (1) mechanisms for the expression of consumer preferences in the public sector, (2) standards for the design of efficient grants-in-aid, and (3) compensation of subordinate units for the burdens imposed by the pursuit of policy objectives by higher levels of government. This survey of implementation guidelines is far from complete and touches only major propositions.

Expression of Consumer Preferences in the Public Sector

In the private sector, the market choices of individuals and households provide clear signals regarding what and how much should be produced, and effectively discipline unresponsive producers. Thus, the expression of consumer preferences is simple, direct, and effective. However, the institutional settings and collective decision-making processes inherent in the public sector provide ample opportunity for distortions of consumer preferences. Consequently, economists have devoted considerable attention to the expression of preferences with an eye to enhancing the accountability of governmental institutions. This interest is focused on adapting market mechanisms to public sector choices and the organization of political processes for collective choice.

Market Mechanisms

The first line of defense for the expression of consumer preferences is maximum reliance on market and quasi-market mechanisms in public-sector activities. This is feasible when a significant portion of the benefits of a public service accrues to an identifiable individual or firm that can be excluded from consumption of the service. In such circumstances, revenue-raising procedures should be designed so that those who benefit from the service finance it to the extent of their benefits.

This proposition argues for the imposition of charges, fees, and payments for licenses whenever the exclusion principle applies and the costs of administration are reasonable. There are, however, curious patterns in the acceptance of such practices. For example, hunters and fishermen tend to be quite willing to accept the notion that they should pay for licenses, the proceeds of which are earmarked for wildlife management. In contrast, recreational boaters and library users have demonstrated far less enthusiasm about accepting an obligation to pay the costs of public services from which they directly benefit. One of the salutary consequences of the tax-limitation measures imposed in recent years on State and local governments has been moderation of the resistance to the imposition of service fees and charges.[23]

When the levying of fees and charges is not feasible, efficiency in the allocation of resources argues for so-called benefit taxation.[24] Although some controversy surrounds the incidence of the real property tax, the evidence suggests that its yield in residential areas is reasonably related to the distribution of the benefits from most local public goods. Benefit taxation may also involve the use of such devices as special districts, assessment areas, targeted sales taxes, and other procedures that allow a close linkage between the benefits of public services and their financing. These considerations also suggest that Federal policymakers should refrain from actions that unnecessarily influence how States and localities raise revenues, such as grant formulas that tend to discourage the use of fees and charges.[25]

Market or marketlike mechanisms are also useful tools for limiting inappropriate and inefficient intrusions into the private choices of firms and households. This is illustrated by approaches to the problems of service congestion and income maintenance.

The value of some public services is affected by how many people consume them at the same time—mass transportation is an especially good example. Large investments are required to meet peak-load service demands. The imposition of tolls or other access charges during peak-load periods makes possible a fairer allocation of the costs of such facilities and tends to reduce the required investment. Such practices are clearly applicable to parks, airports, museums, and other public facilities that suffer from peak-load congestion. The alternatives are cumbersome and intrusive procedures to ration access and a reduction of the benefits to all.

A general bias in favor of marketlike approaches is also reflected in the approach of most economists to income-maintenance programs. The improvement in the welfare of recipients attained from the existing budgetary cost of such programs would be significantly enhanced if in-kind grants were replaced by cash payments, which recipients could use freely in the marketplace. Short of cashing-out welfare programs, economists favor vouchers rather than direct provision of goods and services in areas as diverse as housing, medical care, legal services, and education. This reflects the judgment that low-income households can better judge what mix of goods and services suits their needs than legislators and bureaucrats, and that policies that constrain these choices in the marketplace introduce inefficiencies.

Political Mechanisms

In many circumstances, marketlike mechanisms are not feasible, and as a result economists have focused on the operation of mechanisms for collective political choices. The central proposition that flows from these considerations is that, to the greatest possible extent, units of government responsible for the provision of services also should be responsible for raising the revenues to finance them. This forces direct comparison of the costs and benefits of public services as well as private consumption possibilities and promotes informed judgments about the level and mix of services most consistent with public preferences.

Several notions flow from these propositions. Policies that tend to obscure either the costs or the benefits of services may result in misallocations of resources. For example, taxes or grants that obscure perceptions of costs tend to focus policy discussion on the benefits of a service. As a result, there is a tendency for governments to overinvest in that service. At the same time, policies that obscure service benefits promote underinvestment.

Additionally, effective political mechanisms for the expression of consumer preferences should not raise the cost of information so that it becomes difficult for citizens to identify the elected officials responsible for policy outcomes. This clearly requires that, to the greatest extent possible, responsibilities for raising revenues and expenditure be assigned to the smallest jurisdiction in which the benefits of a public service are concentrated, that intergovernmental grant procedures not bypass the elected officials of recipient jurisdictions, and that the structural complexity and compliance requirements of the grant system be minimized.

Grants-in-Aid

The preceding discussion suggests that intergovernmental grants are required to accommodate benefit spillovers and to reduce fiscal disparities.[26] While design criteria for grants-in-aid flow readily from economic theory, practical considerations often demand attention to other issues.

Spillovers and Categorical Grants

In general, economic theory suggests that all categorical grants should be matching grants, with the required match by the recipient government set equal to the proportion of the benefits that is realized by the residents of the jurisdiction. From this perspective, there are four essential characteristics of Federal or State grants intended to ensure that external benefits are appropriately reflected in the decisions of recipient governments.

First, they should be available to any subordinate unit providing the service. Second, the matching ratio should reflect the benefits of the aided service realized by the State or the nation as a whole. Third, funds should be available only to finance the aided service, but should not otherwise be restricted (e.g., to capital outlays or any particular technology). Finally, the funding for the matching grants should be open-ended.[27]

An open-ended categorical grant with a matching provision effectively reduces the price to the grantee jurisdiction of the designated service. The principle is that the costs of a service are shared according to the distribution of benefits. If 10 percent of the benefits of a service flow to nonresidents of a jurisdiction, that government would tend to underinvest in the service. An appropriate allocation of resources requires a grant reflecting the willingness of the nonresident beneficiaries to contribute 10 percent of the financing. If 10 percent of the benefits are realized by nonresidents regardless of the size of the program, the grant should be open-ended.

In practice, it is likely to be very difficult to specify the correct matching rates, which could well be different for every jurisdiction. Even if the rate were identical for all jurisdictions, its exact magnitude could be subject to dispute. What is required for a matching grant program of the State of Indiana, for instance, is an estimate of the benefits to the State as a whole of Gary producing an educated high school graduate, over and above the benefits to the graduate and the City. This is a difficult issue requiring policy judgment as well as solid technical analysis. It does not seem unreasonable to suppose, however, that careful analysis could come up with relatively accurate estimates of the relevant externalities.

Few, if any, existing Federal or State grant programs satisfy these basic criteria. A number of economists have observed that the matching rates of current Federal programs exceed by considerable margins any reasonable estimates of the relative external benefits of the assisted services.[28]

Given the excessive Federal matching rates, recipient governments have a powerful incentive to overspend. To avoid this, the Federal government responds by limiting the funding for the grants, in the aggregate and for individual governments. For any government whose own spending on the assisted service exceeds the match required to qualify for the maximum Federal grant for which it is eligible, the statutory matching rate is irrelevant. By all indications, this is the case for virtually every State-local government.

For example, if a jurisdiction planned to spend $1 million on a particular service, and a Federal program requiring a 20 percent local match but with a funding limitation of $300,000 were instituted, the matching rate could not be expected to influence the jurisdiction's spending on the service. In essence, the grant would have no effect at the margin, and the program would not have the intended effect of increasing the allocation of resources to the aided service.[29]

In effect, assuming the jurisdiction has a modicum of financial acumen, the funds would be virtually equivalent to general-purpose fiscal assistance. That is, the government would be able to finance $300,000 of its planned outlay of $1 million with the grant funds, freeing-up an identical amount to be spent for any other purpose, including reducing taxes.[30]

It is widely believed that open-ended matching programs would be more costly than the present system. At existing matching ratios, this would certainly be true. However, if matching rates were lowered to more appropriate levels, that is, if the Federal subsidy per dollar of grantee spending were decreased significantly, the funds would increase spending on the aided services with benefit spillovers rather than on services with no spillovers (the effect of current policy) at potentially lower cost to the Federal government.[31]

It has also been argued that the cost of an open-ended program would be unpredictable, and hence inconsistent with sound budgeting practice. This need not be the case. Reasonably reliable estimates of the relevant price elasticities of demand are available, and even better estimates could be developed. Moreover, prudence argues for setting the Federal match at the low end of any range of estimates of the spillovers associated with the service for which a grant is to be made available, in order to minimize the magnitude of the budgetary exposure. Experience would then produce evidence of the price elasticity of State or local demand for the aided service, and the Federal matching rate could subsequently be raised to a point closer to the middle of the range of estimates of the relative importance of the spillovers.[32]

In addition to not satisfying the basic criteria for what George F. Break has called "pure-price-subsidy" grants,[33] the existing system of Federal categorical grants-in-aid is not confined to a small number of services for which strong cases can be made that substantial underallocations of resources will result in the absence of the Federal assistance. Rather, the system has evolved over the past several decades to include hundreds of closed-ended programs, most of them requiring some degree of recipient matching, for an extensive array of narrowly defined services. In an attempt to ensure that the Federal funds are actually spent for the aided services, the programs have been encumbered by highly detailed compliance requirements. The resulting system is so complex, and its administrative costs so high, that efficiency and accountability have been substantially eroded from the perspective of the Federal government as well as recipient State and local governments.

For many years a standard response to these problems has been the aggregation of related categorical programs into block grants. These feature fewer restrictions on use of funds and negligible, if any, matching requirements. One problem with this strategy is that Federal funds are forthcoming in the first place because specific services produce external benefits. Even if the flypaper effect is relatively small, the fiscal impacts of the programs do end up being at least a modest increase in total spending for the aided service. When less specificity is introduced, the flypaper effect is likely to be further diluted, perhaps even to the point that there is no actual increase in spending for the targeted function.

This occurs because the grant recipient can be expected to consider only benefits to its residents, and—in the absence of a price effect from the grant—to ignore external benefits. These considerations, coupled with the closed-ended nature of block grants, makes them hardly distinguishable from general-purpose fiscal assistance, except for the associated administrative costs to the grantor and grantee.

In sum, block grants are preferable to much of the existing system of closed-ended categorical grants because of their lower administrative costs, reduced potential for distortion of local preferences, and potentially more defensible distribution. However, they do not address the misallocations of resources resulting from the existence of spillovers. Moreover, their administrative costs make them an expensive form of general-purpose fiscal assistance. Thus block grants have considerable value as an interim solution to the problems of closed-ended categoricals. In the long run, however, they would not appear to have a place in the system of intergovernmental payments contemplated by the theory discussed here.

The implications of the discussion so far of grants-in-aid can be summarized as follows: First, categorical programs should be restricted to a limited set of carefully defined services with significant benefit spillovers. Federal matching rates should be substantially reduced, and funding limitations removed. Second, since block grants are, in essence, a costly form of general-purpose fiscal assistance, their reform should be addressed from that perspective, which is discussed in the next section.

Disparities and General-Purpose Fiscal Assistance

The design of grants to respond to fiscal disparities is a relatively straightforward exercise. Problems emerge because of confusion regarding the objectives of the grant.

In the simplest case, the objective of a disparity-reduction grant can be formulated as providing payments that allow all eligible jurisdictions to raise some target level of revenues if they exert a standard tax effort. Central to this formulation are the measurement of potential recipients' revenue-raising capacities, the specification of a level of resources deemed adequate to finance a minimally acceptable level of services, and a judgment about what constitute tolerable tax burdens.

Implicit in this formulation for a capacity-equalizing grant is that all potential recipient jurisdictions have essentially the same service responsibilities. When these responsibilities vary among otherwise comparable jurisdictions, additional modifications may be required. In such cases, the objective of the grant would be reformulated to achieve a target ratio of tax burden to service responsibility when the recipients exert some standard tax effort.

It is important to stress that the legitimate objective of a disparity-reduction grant program undertaken by a national government is to equalize the potential to raise revenues relative to some specification of responsibilities among subordinate units. National governments should be indifferent to the actual level of revenue raised. Canada's system of fiscal-equalization payments to Provincial governments best illustrates this approach.

In the United States, much of the best thinking about equalization grants has been done in connection with State school-aid programs. Most State governments have instituted capacity-equalization grants to local school districts. However, the objective of these grants is the equalization of service levels rather than ensuring the potential to raise a minimum amount of revenues.

State governments are legally responsible for education, and school districts are the administrative vehicles for States to discharge this responsibility. With districts dependent on property taxes, disparities in the revenue-raising abilities of the districts are often large enough to result in substantial inequities in the provision of education services. However, State governments—being legally responsible for education—cannot be indifferent to these inequities. The response of the States has been either to assume the costs of local education or to provide equalization grants. Since the State government is ultimately concerned with the equity of service provision, such grants often provide incentives to raise revenues by rewarding the tax effort of school districts.

At the Federal level, the logic of State school finance has been inappropriately applied in discussion of the interstate allocation of revenue sharing funds. The powerful influence of tax effort in the program's allocation formula has been justified by the stipulation that the Federal government should help States on the basis of their willingness to help themselves. However, this is another way of saying that the Federal objective relates to the general levels of services that are actually provided by State and local governments. Such an objective is clearly inappropriate in a federal system in which actual service levels are the independent province of the States and local governments.

Fair Compensation

Actions of larger and geographically more encompassing governments affect lower levels of governments. When such activities inappropriately reduce the revenue-raising abilities or increase the costs of lower levels of government, economic theory suggests that fair compensation should be required. In the absence of compensation, the true costs of the decisions of the Federal or State governments are not likely to receive proper consideration, and economically efficient decisions are not likely to result. Such cost shifting might result from the ongoing activities of the States or the Federal government or from the imposition of mandates.

Ongoing Activities

The pursuit of national or State objectives can adversely affect lower levels of government in a variety of ways. For example, the presence of Federal or State office buildings increases the service costs of the localities where they are located to degrees indistinguishable from privately owned office buildings. Some school districts are burdened by the responsibility for educating children who reside on Federal properties, such as military bases.

Clearly, such circumstances demand that reasonable compensation be paid to the affected jurisdictions. Economic theory suggests that a reasonable general principle might be that the Federal and State governments should be subject to local taxes, fees, and charges on the same terms as private firms and individuals.

If local governments in fact financed their operations in full accordance with the benefit principles discussed earlier, this would be an appropriate principle. In reality, however, though considerable progress has been made in recent years, local finance in few areas can reasonably be judged to be conducted in thorough-going conformity with the principles of benefit-based finance.

For example, as noted earlier, the real-estate tax on residential property in most areas probably conforms fairly well to the benefit principle, but it is doubtful whether any such case could be made for commercial and industrial property. One need look no further than the intensity with which localities throughout the country strive to attract such property to suppose that the objective is to augment the local tax base in a manner that does not bring with it commensurate service costs. This observation is borne out by the fiscal-impact analyses commonly relied upon to make the case for such efforts. Such analyses typically show that commercial and industrial properties generate revenues that substantially exceed the additional costs of the public services that must be provided to them.

The implication is clear. For commercial and industrial property, the real estate tax is more accurately characterized as being based on the ability-to-pay than on the benefit principle. This being the case, it would clearly be inappropriate to expect the Federal and State governments to subject themselves to real property taxes, or to make in-lieu payments equivalent to their potential liabilities for such taxes. However, unless it can be demonstrated that local fees and charges do not bear a reasonable relationship to the costs of services actually rendered to properties owned by the Federal and State governments, considerations of efficiency and equity argue for those governments to be required to make such payments.

Regulations

Through direct regulations or conditions for the acceptance of grants, the Federal and State governments direct lower-level units of government to undertake activities without specific compensation for the costs.[34] In some cases, States or localities are directed to remedy violations of Constitutionally protected rights. In such circumstances, it is difficult to suppose that the Federal government has any obligation to defray the costs of the mandated remedy, although it may wish to do so in order to facilitate compliance. If, however, the regulation involves issues outside the scope of Constitutionally protected rights—such as environmental matters or historical preservation—two questions are in order. Is the regulation legitimate and, if so, what compensation for the costs of responding to it is appropriate?

Typically, regulations not involving Constitutionally protected rights originate in situations involving spillovers of costs of private- or public-sector activities. In such circumstances, a regulation is potentially legitimate. However, it is difficult to see why the Federal government should be under any more obligation to compensate the jurisdiction for the costs associated with such a regulation than it is to compensate the firm that is required to arrange for safe disposal of toxic wastes.

On occasion, the Federal government directs State and local governments to take actions directed at benefit rather than cost spillovers. In this relatively infrequent circumstance, the appropriate strategy is a matching grant designed as discussed earlier, rather than a regulation.

Moreover, if the costs or benefits are confined within the boundaries of a jurisdiction, a mandate to eliminate the costs or increase the benefits would not be a proper object of Federal concern. For example, if a watershed is totally within the boundaries of a particular State, it would be inappropriate for the Federal government to direct State action to control flooding or pollution in that watershed.

CAVEATS AND RECAPITULATION

Previous sections of this chapter allude to problems and limitations in the application of the theory of public finance in a federal system to practical problems. Most obvious are the significant uncertainties associated with many important issues. A current policy debate, for example, is focused on the sources and costs of acid rain, a classic spillover problem. Beyond the technological uncertainties, application of the principles of public finance theory must cope with economic tradeoffs, conflicts with noneconomic values, and necessary adjustments to a world of second-best options.

Actual policies very often involve difficult tradeoffs of values encompassed by economic theory. For example, single-minded pursuit of economic efficiency would call for the establishment of a separate local government for virtually every service, with its boundaries coincident with the geographical area over which benefits from the service range.[35] If this logic were fully implemented, citizens and public officials would be faced with a system of local governments of such structural complexity that information costs and the problems of coordination would be insuperable. Consequently, the structure of local governments reflects necessary tradeoffs between efficiency and accountability.

Further, public finance theory obviously does not comprehend all of the values expressed in American politics, nor is there any likelihood of public acceptance of an unqualified adherence to economic standards. Clearly, economic considerations recede in importance when there are serious threats to personal liberties or national unity. More generally, economic theory simply provides a framework to examine the consequences of policy options in terms of standards of economic efficiency, equity, and accountability.

Finally, public finance theory must cope with a world that all too often offers only second-best options. For example, economists are in substantial agreement that the most efficient method of income maintenance would involve a national program of cash grants to individuals and households. However, nearly two decades of welfare-reform efforts have demonstrated that the American people want income maintenance to be addressed by an array of in-kind and cash benefits. Consequently, for income maintenance and other policy areas, policy choices are frequently limited to second-best options in terms of economic efficiency.

Despite such limitations, public finance theory offers a powerful framework for structuring the analysis of Federal-State-local fiscal relations. The central propositions of this framework can be summarized in terms of criteria for the reform of federalism.

The criteria address two sets of issues—what responsibilities should be assumed by each level of government and what general guidelines should govern the implementation of those responsibilities. The general framework for viewing the role of democratic government in a market economy is consistent with established public-finance theory, which holds that governments have basic responsibilities relating to the overall stability of the economy, the allocation of resources, and the distribution of income and wealth.

Assignment of Responsibilities

The criteria for the assignment of responsibilities are rooted in two principal factors: (1) the existence of spillovers of substantial costs or benefits beyond the boundaries of subnational units of governments, and (2) the existence of disparities in the capacities of subnational units to finance their service responsibilities. In general, the responsibility for delivery of a public service should be assigned to the government with jurisdiction over the smallest geographical area within which a plurality of the benefits from the service are realized.[36]

Local Responsibilities

Public Services: In general, the role of government in the allocation of resources consists in serving as the agent of individuals (consumer/voters) in ensuring an optimal allocation of resources in situations in which consumer demand, expressed in the market, results in levels of production of goods and services that do not accurately reflect the true preferences of the residents of the jurisdiction.

Local governments should be responsible for providing "public goods"—that is, services whose benefits by their very nature accrue to every resident of a jurisdiction, none of whom can practically be excluded from benefiting by his or her failure to pay.[37] Local governments also have an obligation to subsidize the consumption of certain forms of private goods when significant external benefits are associated with their purchase by individual consumers. Police patrols are an example of a relatively pure public good; elementary education is an example of a service with significant external benefits.

Intrastate Spillovers: Local governments are responsible for dealing with situations involving costs and benefits that spill over their boundaries, but only significantly affect neighboring jurisdictions. They may discharge such responsibilities by negotiating joint-funding arrangements with the nearby jurisdictions or by appealing to the State government to mediate and perhaps enforce an agreement on arrangements acceptable to all of the affected localities.

State Responsibilities

Public Services: When a plurality of the benefits from a public service accrues to all or most of the residents of a State, the responsibility for delivering that service should be assumed by the State government—State parks and highway patrols are examples.

Intrastate Spillovers: A State government has an obligation to respond to spillovers of costs or benefits associated with public and private activities when they are substantial, to the extent that they are incident within the boundaries of the State. In general, if these spillovers are statewide, the financial involvement of the State government is appropriate. However, if the spillovers are confined to relatively small, discrete areas of a State, the responsibility for dealing with them should rest with local governments. If confined to an identifiable substate region, and the affected localities are unable to negotiate joint local solutions, there might be a State role in mediating and possibly enforcing (but not financing) a solution among the affected localities.

Interstate Spillovers: State governments are responsible for dealing with situations involving costs and benefits that spill over State boundaries, but that do not spill to the nation as a whole, by negotiating appropriate agreements with other States for joint action. The States may appeal to the Federal government for assistance in arriving at (and perhaps enforcing) such agreements, but Federal financial involvement is inappropriate.

Intrastate Fiscal Capacities: If the distribution of the capacities of localities to finance their service responsibilities offends State-level equity standards and/or affects intrastate locational choices, the State government has an interest in ensuring that an acceptable distribution of local fiscal capacities prevails and that intrastate locational choices respond only to market forces.

Federal Responsibilities

National Public Goods: The Federal government's primary responsibility is the provision of national public goods, that is, goods and services the benefits of which accrue to all Americans, none of whom can be excluded from benefiting by a failure to pay—national defense, economic stabilization, and communicable-disease control are examples of such services.

National Spillovers: The Federal government has an obligation to control external costs and provide matching grants to State-local governments reflecting benefit spillovers when the magnitudes of these costs or benefits are substantial and are widely dispersed throughout the nation—interstate highways and some environmental issues are examples.

Regional Spillovers: Some spillovers of costs and benefits are substantial but limited to discrete, multi-State regions. If the affected States cannot work out a mutually acceptable accommodation on their own, there is a legitimate Federal role in mediating the issues and perhaps in enforcing an agreement, but not in financing a remedy—flood control programs in a multi-State watershed, for example.

Distribution of Income and Wealth: To the extent that the distribution of wealth and income offends widely shared standards of equity, Federal action is appropriate—in conjunction with State and local governments—to ensure an acceptable distribution—progressive income tax, income maintenance.

Interstate Distribution of Fiscal Capacities: To the extent that the capacities of certain States are inadequate to finance minimum levels of services from the perspective of widely shared equity norms and/or seriously distort private locational choices, Federal action is appropriate to ensure that an acceptable distribution of fiscal capacities prevails and that locational choices respond only to market forces.

Intrastate Distribution of Fiscal Capacities: To the extent that the pursuit of Federal policies reduces the fiscal capacities of local governments, Federal action is appropriate to compensate the affected localities for the adverse impacts of Federal actions on their service responsibilities or their revenue-raising capacities.

In a perfectly operating federal system, the distribution of fiscal capacities among local governments would be the exclusive responsibility of State governments. In the American federal system of 1985, many States effectively address the problem of local fiscal capacities, but some have only begun to do so. The pressures on the Federal government to deal with the fiscal problems of localities are intense. Where such pressures must be responded to, the Federal response should (1) be as limited as possible, (2) provide assistance by an efficient vehicle with explicit targeting, and (3) be designed to stimulate State action.

Implementation of Responsibilities

General criteria for the implementation of responsibilities relate to four issues: (1) market and political mechanisms to optimize the expressions of consumer preferences on the producers of public goods and services, (2) standards for the design of grant programs whose objectives are to ensure that optimal levels of public services are provided, (3) compensation for the costs imposed in the pursuit of the policy objectives of higher levels of government, and (4) the implications of economies and diseconomies of scale in the production and delivery of public services.

Expression of Consumer Preferences

Market Mechanisms: Implement policies that take the fullest possible advantage of market and marketlike mechanisms for the expression of consumer preferences. This means that user fees should be charged whenever the exclusion principle applies and the costs of implementation are reasonable, although the costs of individual services should be subsidized from other revenue sources to the extent that external benefits are associated with their consumption.

This also means that, when it is not economical to finance a service by user charges, the incidence of the tax used should correspond as closely as possible to the incidence of the benefits from the service. Additionally, to limit political or bureaucratic intrusions in private choices, market mechanisms should be relied upon in program design wherever feasible.

Political Mechanisms: Implement policies in ways that enhance political mechanisms for the expression of consumer preferences. This requires that, to the greatest possible extent, units of government responsible for the provision of services also be responsible for raising the revenues to finance them, that the elected officials of governments receiving intergovernmental grants be responsible for their expenditure, that policies facilitate identification of the elected officials responsible for policy outcomes, and that grant requirements be limited to an absolute minimum.

Intergovernmental Grants

Categorical Grants: Federal or State matching grants intended to ensure that the external benefits to the nation or State as a whole of certain services are given appropriate consideration in State-local decisions should have four essential characteristics:

- They should be available to any governmental unit providing the service.
- The Federal or State match should equal the proportion of the benefits of the aided service that is realized by the nation or the State as a whole over the range of the service provided.
- Funds should be available only to finance the aided service, but should not otherwise be restricted (e.g., to capital outlays or any particular technology).
- Funding should generally be open-ended.

General Fiscal Assistance: The objective of general fiscal assistance is the reduction of disparities in the fiscal capacities of State and local governments. Such grants should have four essential characteristics:

- They should only be available to jurisdictions whose fiscal capacities are inadequate to permit the financing of levels of services deemed minimally acceptable without self-destructive tax burdens. Per capita payments should vary inversely with the fiscal capacities of recipient jurisdictions.
- Payments should be entitlements with no constraints but State-local law on the use to which they may be put.
- Recipients should be subject only to reasonable financial-accountability and civil-rights requirements.
- Annual payments should be predictable, but should be adjusted year-to-year by an open and explicit allocation process relying on the most recent available data.

Fair Compensation

Fiscal Capacities: If the pursuit of national or State policy objectives significantly increases the service costs or impairs the revenue-raising abilities of lower-level units of government, the affected governments should be compensated for these burdens. In general, this calls for the Federal and State governments to be subject to local fees, charges, and taxes that clearly reflect benefit-finance principles. It does not justify payments by the Federal and State governments for fees, charges, and taxes that are not benefit-based.

Regulations: The Federal and State governments should not direct lower-level units of government to take actions without compensation being paid to the affected governments through appropriately defined matching grants that reflect shares of the benefits from the mandated action that are realized by those who are not residents of the affected units of government. Compensation is not appropriate for three types of "mandates": (1) those relating to the Constitutionally protected rights of individuals; (2) those that are conditions of Federal grant programs; and (3) those reflecting Federal or State social and economic policy, such as wage and hour laws and social-insurance legislation, that is generally applicable to all entities and employers throughout the nation or the State.

Scale Effects

Economies of Scale: When the cost of producing a service can be significantly reduced by economies of scale, lower levels of government should arrange to buy that service from a higher level of government or an appropriate private firm. The contract-cities arrangement in Los Angeles County is an example of such an approach. The existence of major scale economies may dictate the assumption of responsibility for the performance of a function by a higher level of government that other considerations may suggest should be left to the market or to a lower level of government—an example is Social Security.

Another aspect of economies of scale may have significant consequences for the role of government, especially at the local level. This is the fact that major economies of scale are involved in the production of certain types of services to which the exclusion principle can practically be applied and whose consumption generates negligible external benefits. Hence these services are not candidates for government provision as public goods. However, the economies of scale in their production are so substantial that, left entirely to the market, a single producer is likely quickly to secure a monopoly—hence the common characterization of such services as "natural monopolies." Some obvious examples are water supply and sewerage (where individual systems are not practicable), electricity, telephone, and cable television.

In most areas of the country, water-supply and sewerage services are provided by public authorities. In some areas, electricity is provided by public authorities, though private firms are the most common providers. Telephone services are virtually exclusively provided by private firms, as are cable television services. When these services are privately provided, some form of local (or State) public regulation of the monopoly providers is universal. The diversity of approaches to services that are identical in their essential attributes is an indication of the diversity of the nation. The principles of public finance in a federal system offer little guidance to the appropriate handling of such services.

Diseconomies of Scale: When the cost of producing a service is characterized by diseconomies of scale, higher levels of government may appropriately arrange to contract for the provision of that service with private firms or lower levels of government—State employment agencies and environmental monitoring.

Notes

1. While not widely appreciated, many Indian nations possess sovereign authority that in some ways exceeds that of States.
2. This ratio is total Federal, State, and local expenditures in the national income and product accounts (adjusted to count Federal grants only once) as a proportion of national income. As a percentage of the gross national product, a more common but less appropriate referrent, the ratio is 34 percent. [*Economic Report of the President, 1985* (1985), 254 and 320.]
3. The evolution of interpretation of the Constitution as it relates to these issues is reviewed in chap. 3 of this report.
4. For example, a key concept in the economic theory of the public sector is the benefits generated by an activity. In market transactions, benefits are automatically measured by the terms of exchanges entered into voluntarily by sellers and buyers, that is, by market prices. In the absence of such transactions and in cases where market transactions give rise to benefits to third parties—essential attributes of the appropriate concerns of government—benefits must be evaluated by the political process.
5. For a constructive discussion of the limits of the economic theory of fiscal federalism from the perspective of a political scientist, see Samuel H. Beer, "A Political Scientist's View of Fiscal Federalism," in Wallace E. Oates (ed.), *The Political Economy of Fiscal Federalism* (Lexington Books, D.C. Heath and Company, 1977), 21-46. A number of reports by the Advisory Commission on Intergovernmental Relations include critical discussions of the economic theory. See, for example, *The Condition of Contemporary Federalism: Conflicting Theories and Collapsing Constraints,* Report No. A-78, Vol. II of *The Federal Role in the Federal System: The Dynamics of Growth* (1981).
6. This framework for analyzing the functions of government finance was originally articulated a quarter century ago by Richard A. Musgrave in his treatise, *The Theory of Public Finance* (McGraw-Hill, 1959), 3-27. Although the concept of three general functions—stabilization, allocation, and distribution—sometimes becomes cumbersome (for example, most government programs have both allocative and distributional aspects), it has stood the test of time and is used extensively in this report.
7. The phrase "involvement of the government in the provision of" is used advisedly. Government, by virtue of its exclusive power to tax, has an unavoidable role in financing services for which the exclusion principle does not practicably apply. This need not necessarily mean, however, that such services must be produced or delivered by public employees.

   For example, most public facilities have always been constructed by private firms under contract to the government, essentially because experience has demonstrated this to be the most efficient (least costly) approach. The same logic is today being applied to the production and delivery of many types of public services. That is, when private firms can be shown to have the capacity to produce or deliver a service at lower cost than public employees, efficiency dictates that such potential be exploited.

   A more general definition of the distinctive characteristic of public goods is that they involve high costs of restricting the benefits to those willing to pay. See Roland N. McKean, *Public Spending* (McGraw-Hill, 1968), 67-72.

8. External costs may also be associated with governmental activity—discharges of untreated effluent by municipal sewerage systems is an example.
9. The issues involved in policies for shifting external costs to producers and consumers are discussed further in chap. 3 (this report) in connection with Federal regulatory policies.
10. The classic statement of this view appears in Charles M. Tiebout, "A Pure Theory of Local Expenditures," *Journal of Political Economy* 64 (October 1956): 416-24.
11. It is a tribute to the wisdom and foresight of the authors of the Constitution that, well before economic theoreticians had articulated the concepts discussed in this chapter, they managed to identify as responsibilities of the national government a range of functions all of which satisfy the criteria of economic theory as appropriate functions of that level of government.
12. The issues relate to the responsibility for policy choices. The actual delivery of particular services may be undertaken by another level of government in response to economies or diseconomies of scale, discussed further below.
13. Strictly speaking, the decisions will be based on the equation of benefits and costs at the margin. To simplify the discussion, this technicality is abstracted from in this section.
14. In the particular case of services whose benefits are realized in substantial measure by visitors, a locality may be able to cover an appropriate share of the costs by adopting taxes that are paid by visitors. For example, resort communities typically rely heavily on occupancy and sales taxes that, effectively, shift a significant share of the costs of their services from which visitors benefit to those visitors. When this is possible, the external benefits essentially are "internalized," the allocation of resources may well be optimal, and involvement of higher levels of government may not be necessary.
15. As discussed in more detail later, Federal action may be required to ensure that Constitutional rights are not impaired by State and local programs or officials.
16. As discussed in detail in chap. 8 (this report), the fiscal capacity of a government is its ability to raise revenues from its own sources, relative to its fiscal responsibilities.
17. See James M. Buchanan, "The Pure Theory of Government Finance: A Suggested Approach," *Journal of Political Economy* 57 (December 1949): 496-505.
18. See James M. Buchanan and Richard E. Wagner, "An Efficiency Basis for Federal Fiscal Equalization," in Julius Margolis (ed.), *The Analysis of Public Output* (Columbia University Press for the National Bureau of Economic Research, 1970), 139-58.
19. See U. S. Department of the Treasury, *Tax Reform for Fairness, Simplicity and Economic Growth: The Treasury Department Report to the President,* Vol. 1, *Overview* (November 1984), 13.
20. See, for example, Henry J. Aaron, "Six Welfare Questions Still Searching for Answers," *The Brookings Review* (Fall 1984): 12-17.
21. See the recent article by Robert P. Inman, which concludes that Federal withdrawal from direct involvement in such programs as Food Stamps and AFDC would result in a drastic decline in outlays on these key programs. Inman argues that this would occur even if the Federal government were to provide general fiscal assistance sufficient to compensate the States for the direct Federal outlays on the programs. ["Fiscal Allocations in a Federalist Economy: Understanding the 'New' Federalism," in John M. Quigley and Daniel L. Rubinfeld (eds.), *American Domestic Priorities: An Economic Appraisal* (University of California Press, 1985), 1-33.]
22. It should be stressed that care must be taken in drawing direct policy implications for the United States from the experience of other federal systems. Nonetheless, the experience of other countries does provide useful insights into some of the key issues of American federalism.
23. Historically, the use of fees and charges for government services has been objected to on two types of grounds. The first is the somewhat mystical reasoning that seems to assume that government services are somehow different from those provided by the market, and that they should be paid for by everyone through taxes rather than predominantly by those who directly benefit. This belief remains widely held with respect to elementary and secondary education. However, its appeal appears to be waning for many other services traditionally provided by governments as it is increasingly appreciated that the only thing different about government services is the practical difficulties that preclude or impair market provision. The second argument against fees and charges is that they are unfair to the poor. This is, of course, a value judgment—if public sentiment favors exempting those with low incomes from certain fees and charges, that is a matter for each government to decide. It is hardly an argument against charges for most users.
24. The alternative is reliance on the ability-to-pay principle of taxation, which underlies the progressive Federal income tax. The problem with an attempt to apply this principle at the State and local level is the risk of inducing out-migration of well-off individuals and profitable firms. If individuals and firms are not called upon to pay taxes that are seriously disproportionate to the benefits they realize from public services, however, the problem of "tax competition" is likely to be minimized. This suggests that, as Edward M. Gramlich observes in a recent paper, "subnational jurisdictions ultimately have only one feasible taxing arrangement, the benefit principle." ["Reforming U.S. Fiscal Federalism Arrangements," in Quigley and Rubinfeld, *op. cit.*, 47 and 48.]
25. Certain forms of tax exporting—shifting of tax burdens to nonresidents—are serious violations of the benefit principle of taxation, and result in major distortions of public-sector choices. With the linkage between benefits and burdens severed, the residents of many tax-exporting jurisdictions face reduced tax prices for public services, and are likely to overinvest in those services. In some circumstances, however, tax exporting can be a useful and legitimate means of implementing the benefit principle, as in the case of resort communities mentioned earlier.
26. Two other rationales for intergovernmental grants deserve mention. The first is that grants are a vehicle for enlisting the involvement of the States and local governments in the delivery of services under a national program (or local governments under a State program). The clearest example is the Federal grants to the States for the administration of the Food Stamp Program. In FY 1985, these grants are estimated to total $840 million for the payment of benefits of $10.5 billion. [Office of Management and Budget, *Budget of the United States Government, 1986—Appendix* (1985), I-E89]. One recent study estimates that the Federal grants pay approximately half of the administrative costs of the program.

[Richard P. Nathan, Fred C. Doolittle, and Associates; *The Consequences of Cuts: The Effects of the Reagan Domestic Program on State and Local Governments* (Princeton Urban and Regional Research Center, 1983), 14.]

A more controversial example is the Medicaid Program, which involves open-ended matching grants to the States for benefit payments as well as administration. It is more controversial because there is disagreement whether Medicaid is a Federal program the States administer or a State program for which Federal grant assistance is provided. [See the discussion of this issue by Helen F. Ladd, "Federal Aid to State and Local Governments," in Gregory B. Mills and John L. Palmer, *Federal Budget Policy in the 1980s* (The Urban Institute Press, 1984), 177-81.]

A second rationale is that Federal grants are intended to induce the States and local governments to deliver minimum, national levels of services. The certain way to ensure that such minimum service levels are achieved would be for the Federal government to make lump-sum, non-matching grants sufficient to finance all the costs of the targeted service levels. This is, effectively, the approach used in the Food Stamp Program. However, assuming the States and localities have some level of demand for the service, the Federal budgetary cost of achieving the desired service levels can be minimized by providing grants with matching requirements for recipients calibrated to reduce the price of the service by just enough to induce the States and localities to provide the desired minimum. For such a program, variable matching rates would be necessary to minimize the Federal budgetary cost, since the demand for any service is likely to vary among States and localities.

For example, jurisdictions with low fiscal capacities can be expected to have lower demand for a service, other things equal, than jurisdictions with high fiscal capacities. The need for reliable measures of fiscal capacity for use in formulas involving variable matching rates for grants perceived as being designed to achieve minimum national service levels provided much of the impetus to the early research by the Advisory Commission on Intergovernmental Relations in the 1960s on the measurement of fiscal capacity. [For a discussion of minimum-service-level grants, see Wallace E. Oates, *Fiscal Federalism* (Harcourt Brace Jovanovich, 1972), 87-94.]

27. Issues involved in the design of efficient and equitable grant programs are discussed in chap. 7 of this report.
28. Gramlich, for example, estimates that the Federal share of the $29 billion of categorical matching grants in FY 1983 averaged 80 percent. He goes on to observe that "at the margin the ratio of internal to total benefits for these programs seems to be much higher than 20 percent." [*Ibid*, p. 57.]
29. Theoretically, a closed-ended matching grant with a "maintenance-of-effort" requirement would have a price effect at the margin. In the example in this paragraph, suppose that the maintenance-of-effort requirement were that a government must spend at least as much of its own funds on the aided service as it did in the year before the grant program was instituted. If that level of outlays for the jurisdiction were $900,000 (implying plans for an 11.1-percent increase in outlays absent the Federal grant), the availability of the new grant would reduce the cost to the locality of $375,000 of additional outlays on the service to $75,000, a deal the locality would probably find highly tempting. The result would very likely be a larger increase in outlays for the service than the locality had been planning—perhaps even to the level that would exhaust the available Federal funds: $1,275,000.

Although many existing categorical programs have maintenance-of-effort provisions, they are rarely as stringent as that hypothesized here, often referring to own-financed spending levels several years before. In such cases, they may have negligible effects at the margin. Moreover, if rigorously enforced (as they appear rarely to be), such requirements can involve high administrative costs to grantor as well as grantee, and they can be highly intrusive into the affairs of the recipient jurisdiction.

30. Econometric analyses have suggested that the fungibility of such grant funds may not be viewed by State-local governments quite as straightforwardly as this illustration suggests. That is, they have identified what has come to be called a "flypaper effect." This is the apparent tendency for some of the funds made available for a specific service by a grant program to stick where they land, rather than being treated as though they were perfectly fungible. In the illustration, the government might increase its outlays on the aided service by, say, $25,000. The empirical literature is discussed in chap. 7 of this report.
31. In the earlier example of a service involving a planned local outlay of $1 million, the Federal grant requiring a 20 percent local match with a $300,000 cap on the grant to the government would have no price effect. Local spending on the service might rise slightly because of the increase in the total resources available (the income effect) or because of the flypaper effect, but most of the Federal funds would be spent on other services, or even tax reductions. However, if the Federal grant required an 80 percent local match with no limit on the Federal funding, the effect would be quite different. The grant would reduce the price of the aided service by 20 percent. If the price elasticity of demand were 0.5, the locality would increase outlays for the service by 10 percent—to $1.1 million. The cost to the Federal government would be 20 percent of the total outlays, or $220,000, significantly less than in the earlier example.
32. During the 1960s and 1970s there was a tendency for Federal matching rates to be raised for existing categorical programs. Such "match creep" could occur without budgetary consequences because the programs retained their closed-ended nature. Similar match creep would be unlikely to occur in the case of the open-ended grants under consideration here, for any increase in the Federal matching ratio could be expected to have immediate budgetary consequences.
33. *Financing Government in a Federal System* (Brookings, 1980), 102-5.
34. This issue is discussed in chap. 3.D.4 (this report).
35. This concept of "perfect mapping" of jurisdictions is explored by Albert Breton in "A Theory of Government Grants," *The Canadian Journal of Economics and Political Science*, Vol. 31 (May 1965): 175-87. A more modest statement of this view appears in Albert Breton and Anthony Scott, *The Economic Constitution of Federal States* (University of Toronto Press, 1978).
36. This proposition is a variant of what Oates calls the "decentralization theorem." See *op. cit.*, 31-63.
37. The responsibility for "providing" comprehends decisions on what level of resources should be devoted to the service as well as how the service should be produced and delivered.

Local Public Economies: Provision, Production, and Governance

Ronald J. Oakerson

The last two decades have seen a major shift in thinking about patterns of public organization affecting local government. New ideas and concepts have generated new research with important, often counterintuitive, conclusions. Patterns once despised are seen to have virtues; those once welcomed are viewed with skepticism. Yet the traditional American commitment to local self-government appears to be as strong as ever. A new consensus may be emerging around a simple but powerful idea—that multiple local governments together constitute a "local public economy," consisting of a *provision side* and a *production side* that can be organized in quite different ways.

Distinguishing provision (taxing and spending) from production and delivery of local goods and services has far-reaching implications for the organization and governance of a local public economy, including a greater reliance on private and intergovernmental contracting to produce services, and a greater number and variety of local government jurisdictions to make provision for local services. Both of these implications raise issues of interlocal governance to a high order of priority.

CONCEPTUAL FOUNDATIONS

The structure of a local public economy rests on a distinction between provision and production of local public goods and services. *Provision* refers to collective choices that determine the following:

- What goods and services to provide (and what are to remain private)
- What private activities to regulate, and the type and degree of regulation
- The amount of revenue to raise, and how to raise it (whether by taxing or user pricing)
- The quantities and quality standards of goods and services
- How to arrange for production (whether by a department of local government, contracting or some other interlocal arrangement)

Production, on the other hand, refers to the more technical processes of transforming inputs into outputs—making a product or rendering a service. Although production is often viewed as entirely the work of agents, it is frequently better viewed as "coproduction," a process in which a specialized producer interacts with a citizen-consumer to produce a service.

The distinction between provision and production lays the conceptual foundation for a new understanding of the organization of local public economies. Different considerations apply in the choice of an organizational unit to *provide* a service from those involved in the choice of an organizational unit to *produce*. The work of local government is increasingly viewed primarily in terms of provisioning rather than producing. Although the organization of production can be and often is governmental,

Reprinted from *Intergovernmental Perspective* 13, no. 3/4 (1987): 20-25.

frequently it becomes a private responsibility. Patterns of organization on the provision side of a local public economy thus can differ from those on the production side, and a variety of different arrangements can be designed to link provision with production.

ORGANIZING THE PROVISION SIDE

The organization of the provision side of a local public economy involves a set of problems that fall into three main classes: (1) preference revelation, (2) fiscal equivalence and (3) accountability.

Preference Revelation

The problem of individual preference revelation derives from the incentives of individuals to conceal their true preferences for public goods and services if provision is organized strictly on a voluntary basis. The institutional requirement is for some process of collective choice from which an individual cannot simply opt out. (Individuals can of course move out of a local jurisdiction, but this is different from opting out of provision while continuing to live there.) Given some form of collective choice, *boundary issues* become critical. An optimal set of boundaries will include those directly affected by provision choices, but not extend so far as to include communities with widely different preferences. In sum, any provision unit should, as closely as possible, define a *community of interest* among a group of people who share a piece of local geography.

Fiscal Equivalence

Efficiency on the provision side of a local public economy depends on the degree of "fiscal equivalence" that is attained. This criterion means simply that individuals (households or firms) and groups (neighborhoods or communities) "get what they pay for and pay for what they get." A lack of fiscal equivalence undermines the local community of interest.

Accountability

Provision units also must deal with the potential for distortion in "principal-agent" relationships between citizens and officials. All communities stand in need of agents, including both elected officials and civil servants, who can represent the interests of members. Provision units need to be organized in such a way that ordinary citizens are able to exercise a significant measure of "voice" so that agents can be held accountable in the conduct of community affairs.

ORGANIZING THE PRODUCTION SIDE

Organization on the production side is based on considerations having to do with the technical transformation of resource inputs into product or service outputs. Unfortunately, no one has a recipe for producing good policing or education, for example, though somewhat more is known about producing good streets. Almost all local public goods and services, however, depend on the availability of specific time-and-place information, such as neighborhood conditions, to support effective production choices. Emphasis has to be placed on the scale and organization of a production process that allows individual producers to make locally informed judgments. This is a much different problem than involved, for example, in a typical assembly line.

Economies of Scale

An important distinction exists between local public goods that tend to be capital intensive and services that tend to be labor intensive. Capital intensive goods are more likely to be characterized by economies of scale, a decrease in the average unit cost of production as the scale of production increases. Labor intensive services are more likely to exhaust potential economies of scale quickly, in part because of greater dependence on specific time-and-place information.

Coproduction

Traditionally, production side considerations have placed a heavy emphasis on the importance of management. Some public services also depend on the participation of citizen-consumers in production—a process called "coproduction." While it is well known that the productivity of local public agencies such as schools and fire departments depends in part on the cooperation of citizens, it is not well understood how to incorporate citizens into production processes. Yet citizen-consumers are often a crucial source of the time-and-place information producers need to be effective.

LINKING PROVISION WITH PRODUCTION

Distinguishing provision from production in a local public economy opens up a range of possibilities for linking one to the other. The main options are as follows:

Self-production. A provision unit organizes its own production unit. This is the traditional model of local organization with departments for police, fire, public works and so forth.

Coordinated production. Two or more production units coordinate their activities in whole or in part.

Joint production. Two or more provision units jointly organize a single production unit.

Intergovernmental contracting. A provision unit contracts for production with another provision unit which then assumes responsibility for organizing production.

Private contracting. A provision unit contracts with a private vendor, who is responsible for organizing a production unit.

Franchising. A provision unit sets production standards and selects a private producer, but allows citizen-consumers to choose whether to purchase the service.

Vouchering. A provision unit sets production standards and decides on the level of provision (through its taxing and spending powers), but allows individuals (or groups) to engage different producers, public or private, at their discretion.

The potential variety in organizing and relating provision to production is much greater than a traditional view of local government would suggest.

GOVERNANCE

The governance of a local public economy is not concerned directly with either provision or production, but instead has to do with a choice of rules within which patterns of provision and production emerge, and with the resolution of conflict among participants, including maintaining agreeable and equitable arrangements. Viewed in this way, governance is separable from both provision and production.

When conflict occurs (for example, over municipal boundaries or the incidence of taxes), governance arrangements must exist to apply general rules to specific cases and constrain participants to reach settlements. Fiscal disparities among provision units are a potential source of conflict in most highly differentiated local public economies. Adjustments in the fiscal rules governing revenue capabilities—in particular the availability and possible sharing of various tax bases—are often responses to fiscal conflict.

DISTINGUISHING PROVISION AND PRODUCTION: IMPLICATIONS

Distinguishing provision and production implies a greater use of both private and intergovernmental contracting to produce local public goods and services.

Current Practice

Private and intergovernmental contracting is widely practiced. A recent ACIR study found that 90.8 percent of the municipalities in a national sample reported at least one service contract among 34 service activities. Most municipalities that contract out, however, use this method of production in only a small proportion of their service responsibilities.

Significant change in the nature of municipal contracting has taken place since the 1970s. Contracting in the period prior to 1970 was heavily skewed toward the public sector. ACIR found in a 1972 study of municipal governments that intergovernmental contracting was the preferred alternative to self-production. Because of a lack of private vendors and/or a lingering concern with corrupt practices in awarding contracts, municipal governments avoided private producers in favor of governmental jurisdictions when shedding service production. This reluctance to use private vendors has diminished significantly. The proportion of communities reporting at least one private service contract exceeds the percentage reporting at least one intergovernmental contract by 18 percent. This reflects the growing number of private service contracts, not an absolute decline in intergovernmental contracting.

Although contracting is employed to some extent by almost every community, such arrangements still are utilized to produce only a fraction of the total services provided by local government. The mean percentage of services contracted in our sample is only 27 percent. Almost half (45 percent) of cities contract for less than 16 percent of their service responsibilities.

Efficiency Gains from Contracting

Empirical studies of garbage collection, electrical power, fire protection, police protection, and an assortment of custodial and general services have found that contracted service production nets significant—but variable—savings over government self-production.

An economies-of-scale argument suggests that the advantages of contracting would tend to diminish, other things being equal, as provision units increase in population size. The ACIR study finds, however, that this relationship holds only over a range of small municipalities. Over the middle to upper size range, reliance on contracting tends to increase with size. This is not what one would expect if economies of scale lead municipalities to contract out.

The ACIR study confirms that competition among potential producers is important to a decision on the part of a municipality to contract out. Municipalities that are located in more competitive economic environments, such as densely populated metropolitan areas, tend to do more contracting. Competition does not always require, however, having alternative vendors in place. A municipality generally retains some capability for self-production (if only legal authority), thus ensuring at least that much choice between production arrangements.

Various political factors also are associated with a decision to contract out. Relatively liberal annexation or consolidation authority tends to diminish reliance on contracting. The incidence of contracting also tends to increase with the presence of fiscal rules that restrict local taxing and/or spending.

The Relevance of Provision Arrangements

In order for citizen-consumers to benefit from contracting, there must also be a provision unit able to acquire information about alternative producers, choose a production method, select a producer, negotiate a contract and monitor performance. Provision arrangements are crucial to the utility of contracting.

Provision arrangements also determine how efficiency gains will be distributed. Who benefits? Is it citizen-consumers, either through tax savings, increased levels of service, or both? Or do local politicians, managers and bureaucrats grab the lion's share of benefit by in effect distributing efficiency gains to the advantage of their particular interests?

The ACIR study contains some interesting results relative to these questions. First, contracting tends to reduce expenditures when municipalities contract out less than 25 percent of their service responsibilities, but tends *not* to reduce expenditures when contracting moves beyond 25 percent. This makes economic sense. If there are efficiency gains from contracting, it follows that the more a municipality is able to contract out (presumably within some limit), the lower the tax-price of services provided. As the tax-price decreases, services demanded by citizens can be expected to increase.

The fundamental importance of contracting is the ability of provision units to choose whether or not to contract out. The availability of a marketplace on the production side does not necessarily mean that provision units should always choose to enter the market as collective consumers, rather than produce for themselves. A basic function of provision units is to decide how to arrange for production. That ability to choose, not the inherent superiority of one mode over another, becomes the key factor in determining relative efficiency.

Organizing the production side of a local economy is likely to involve a mixture of production arrangements.

The differentiation of the production side of a local public economy is the result of choices on the provision side. *Distinguishing* provision and production conceptually does not always—even usually—lead to their actual *separation*. Most provision units, except small neighborhoods, choose to organize the production of some services for themselves. *Differentiated production*—dividing a set of closely related production tasks among different production units—rests on the fact that most public services actually consist of a number of different service components. Production criteria vary among components of the same service.

For example, consider police services. Police patrol, including response to emergencies, can be distinguished from criminal investigation. In addition, patrol can be distinguished from dispatching, and investigative work in the field from the work of a crime lab. As a classification scheme, patrol and investigation can be considered "direct services," those activities that deliver services directly to citizen-consumers, while dispatch and crime lab can be considered "indirect services" that support the production of direct services. With respect to each component of a service, different production arrangements are possible. Economies of scale may differ sharply. If one component of a service is labor intensive, while another is capital intensive, the economies of scale are almost sure to be different. Depending on specific circumstances, different production components may be produced internally, contracted out, or produced jointly with another jurisdiction.

A traditional concern about multiple production units is possible duplication of effort. A recent ACIR study of police, education, fire and street services in St. Louis County, Missouri, found little duplication in spite of a multiplicity of production units. Specialization, not duplication, is characteristic of production systems that rely on multiple units. A mutual interest in avoiding duplication may be sufficient to minimize its occurrence.

In addition to coordination, production units specialize by "alternation"—dividing responsibility on the basis of time, space or clientele—to avoid duplicating one another. This tendency of multiple and/or overlapping units to avoid duplication may account for the failure of consolidation efforts to result in demonstrable cost savings, as often predicted by metropolitan reformers.

Distinguishing provision and production draws attention to the potential economic viability of very small local governments as "pure provision" units.

In the past, analysts frequently evaluated local government units on their ability to *perform* a range of functions. This language—functional performance—does not distinguish provision and production. Inability to *produce* was equated with inability to *perform*. But, as is now widely accepted, inability to produce does not entail inability to *provide*. The acceptability of contracting raises the possibility of "pure provision" units—local governments that produce very little for themselves, but remain very active as providers—raising revenue, holding elections, deliberating on the needs of the community, choosing desired goods and services and determining supply levels, shopping for vendors, negotiating contracts and monitoring service flow.

Small units of local government—those under 1,000 population—have been characterized as toy governments, postage-stamp governments and "lilliputs." Somehow, the term "government" is identified with greater concerns than maintaining the livability of a few thousand—or several hundred—households living within a dozen or so blocks. The legal nomenclature is often no help. Fourth-class cities in Missouri, for example, have a maximum size of 3,000 people. If a city of 3,000 attempted to function as a city of 30,000, it would not be economically viable. But such units are not, in any functional sense, cities. Nor are their governments city governments, except in name, despite the presence of mayor and council. This fact does not make small local governments insignificant. It makes them, functionally, neighborhood governments, providing a limited set of services. With few exceptions, they tend to be pure provision units, with most services contracted out either to public or private vendors.

The provision side of a local public economy will tend to be highly differentiated among a variety of units, small and large, with some "nested" inside others.

Types of Provision Units

The variety of potentially useful provision units is quite large, but the basic types are as follows:

Municipalities. State laws generally enable local citizens to create a variety of municipal units—cities, towns and villages—varying along the dimensions of population size and governing authority. The limiting factor is the rule that one municipality cannot overlap another—municipal governments are, by definition, mutually exclusive jurisdictions.

Counties and townships have the virtue, in this context, of being able to overlap municipalities. Usually, counties are larger than municipalities; townships are more likely to be smaller and, in some cases, contain only parts of municipalities in addition to unincorporated territory. Counties and municipalities (and to some extent townships and municipalities) have the potential to function as complementary provision units. Small municipalities can function effectively as neighborhood governments when county government (among possible jurisdictions) is able to provide for larger scale public concerns. The limitation is that county and township boundaries are predetermined and relatively fixed.

Special districts are governmental units, usually created at local discretion with citizen initiative and consent, that can overlap municipalities and have flexible boundaries. The variety of special districts is greater than any other type of provision unit. Their purpose, in general, is supplementary. Some special districts are nested inside existing units; some overlap existing units, often including both incorporated and unincorporated territory; still others are coterminous with existing units but are created to add specific, specialized provision arrangements. This variety and flexibility can allow the organization of communities of interest that do not happen to coincide with existing local government boundaries. To be sure, not all special districts are equally worthy, but each should be evaluated on the basis of its performance, especially its ability to represent citizen-consumer interests. A blanket bias against special districts does not appear to be warranted, given the limitations inherent in the design of general-purpose governments.

Performance Differences

No single type of provision unit is equally well suited to providing for all local public goods and services. One dimension on which provision units vary widely is size. Another key issue is the extent to which a variety of units can efficiently coexist within a metropolitan area. Traditionally, there has been concern about fragmentation of metropolitan areas, and also a parallel concern about possible inefficiencies from overlapping jurisdictions. If provision is not sorted out from production, these traditional concerns make a great deal of sense. Local public economies function in part by finding ways to avoid the inefficient consequences that are potentially associated with both fragmentation and overlap.

Elinor Ostrom and her colleagues at the Workshop in Political Theory and Policy Analysis, Indiana University, Bloomington, have carried out an extensive research program to determine the effect of jurisdictional size on citizen evaluations of police, among other measures of police performance. Their work consistently demonstrates that smaller units tend to be more responsive providers of police services. Similarly, William A. Niskanen and Mickey Levy at the Graduate School of Public Policy, University of California, Berkeley, found in a study of California school districts that larger district size has a consistent negative effect on various measures of school performance.

Recent empirical research has found *lower* levels of local government expenditure to be associated with *higher* levels of fragmentation and overlap, even when controlling for the level of community service demand. Although it would be incorrect to claim that more fragmentation is always better than less, it has been shown that a variety of provision units can efficiently coexist and frequently do.

A highly differentiated local public economy need not "fragment" a metropolitan community.

The term used to describe a differentiated local public economy is "fragmentation." Unfortunately, this term mixes description with evaluation. It is one thing to say that a metropolitan area contains a large number of provision units; it is another to say that the multiplicity of those units fragments the area. Degree of fragmentation is usually measured, by opponents and proponents, as the number of jurisdictions per 10,000 population. Such a measurement, however, tells us nothing about the "fragmenting" effect of multiple jurisdictions.

The important questions are whether, and the degree to which, a more highly differentiated local public economy subtracts from the coherence of a metropolitan community. A coherent political community is one that is able to act in relation to communitywide concerns; a metropolitan political community is one that is able to act on metropolitan-wide concerns.

Daniel J. Elazar of the Center for the Study of Federalism at Temple University has argued that a complex of local governments can be understood as a "civil community" constituted on the basis of intergovernmental relationships. One mark of a civil community would be an ability to tend simultaneously to common and diverse interests. The recent ACIR study of St. Louis County found a civil community of nearly a million people and of immense vitality. The community finds diverse expression in 90 municipalities, a vigorous county government, 23 school districts and 25 fire protection districts, plus countless organized subdivisions. It also finds common expression, not only in the county government but also in organizations of municipalities, fire chiefs and police chiefs, the Cooperating School Districts of St. Louis County, a special district for special education, and, most especially, in the county delegation to the state legislature and occasional countywide referenda. The county delegation—31 representatives and seven senators, all elected from districts—become, in effect, "constitutional" decision makers for the civil community. Special state legislation for the county, together with the traditional legislative deference on local bills, gives the civil community a significant "constitutional" capability.

The civil community thus is able to maintain a form of metropolitan governance without having to create a metropolitan government. The ideal of metropolitan government would consist of a *single provision unit* for an entire metropolitan community. A local public economy on the other hand generally consists of a variety of provision units. A single unit would, almost certainly, be nonoptimal. Instead of thinking of metropolitan governance only in terms of large general-purpose governments, it is possible to think in terms of a civil community that maintains a set of rules. These rules, usually embodied in state law, become a kind of "local government constitution," a framework within which local citizens are able to constitute the provision units that become the building blocks of a local public economy.

To maintain an efficient local public economy requires structural flexibility and continued availability of alternative arrangements for provision and production.

A local public economy is not static. The sources of change include shifting citizen-consumer preferences, population growth (or loss) and developing technology. Adaptation depends on the availability of alternatives and the development of new ones. On the production side, the availability of alternatives is simply another way of saying "competition." In a public economy, however, the competition is not simply among private vendors but also between public and private vendors and among public suppliers. If competition among private suppliers is not well developed, it may be important to maintain the option of public production. Maintaining the public option may mean, in turn, not contracting out everything that could be. Maintaining a competitive environment could also mean, for a large provision unit, choosing to divide up the production of some service among different contractors rather than contracting with a single vendor. Where there are a large number of small provision units, however, competition on the production side tends to be self-generating.

The development of new production alternatives is a key both to adaptation and to productivity improvement—it is also a source of change. This sort of development depends on *entrepreneurship,* which can be both public and private. In both cases, initiative is a necessary condition. Initiative increases with the number of possible entrepreneurs. Counting the number of police chiefs, fire chiefs, directors of public works, city administrators or managers, and school superintendents yields a crude measure, in each of these services, of the potential for public entrepreneurship in a metropolitan area. Such activity in St. Louis County, for example, is ongoing, and results in many successful joint production efforts from the formation of educational consortia for computer technology to drug enforcement programs.

The continued availability of alternatives must extend also to the provision side. Provision alternatives are sustained in several ways. One way consists of creating nested provision units with somewhat overlapping authority, e.g., municipalities within a county. A form of political competition exists between officials in overlapping jurisdictions, allowing "voter sovereignty" (analogous to consumer sovereignty) to exercise a choice. Provision alternatives can also be maintained by means of special districts. In general, the greater the number of available provision units, either in place or to be created at citizen option, the more likely it is that citizens will be able to obtain satisfaction of their preferences.

Distinguishing provision and production suggests the possibility that redistribution on equity grounds may be more effective when recipient communities are organized as separate provision units, able to make their own production choices.

A difficulty posed by a large number and variety of provision units is the emergence of fiscal disparities. Provision-side efficiency implies a degree of disparity in spending from own-source revenues. At the same time, principles of equity suggest limits to the permissible range of disparity—although no objective definition of those limits is possible.

The problem of equity in local service provision is complex. If it were possible to achieve equity simply by reducing disparities in revenue potential, then any pattern of organization that tended to increase those disparities would earn a negative rating on equity in its overall scorecard. Matters are not, however, so simple. The expenditure side of local government is at least as relevant to equity as the tax side. What is more, the efficiency with which money is spent, and the responsiveness of service provision to community preferences, intervene between expenditures and equity. Equity is an attribute of service, tax and expenditure outcomes.

Several unanswered empirical questions are at issue. How do differences among jurisdictions in a highly differentiated local public economy compare to the differences among communities or neighborhoods within local jurisdictions, especially large cities? How do fiscal disparities *among* jurisdictions compare to service disparities *within* jurisdictions? Moreover, how is this comparison affected by intergovernmental fiscal transfers? Which pattern of organization provides for better trusteeship of intergovernmental revenues?

Future research should also study both the instruments of fiscal transfer used by overlapping jurisdictions, including state and federal grant-in-aid formulas, and the performance of provision units that receive funds. At issue is the ability of both granting and receiving jurisdictions to focus assistance on those communities in greatest need. Historically, ACIR has closely monitored metropolitan fiscal disparities. The challenge now is to expand the scope of inquiry to include neighborhood disparities within urban jurisdictions in order to render a comparative assessment and formulate an effective intergovernmental strategy for addressing both urban and suburban equity problems.

Conclusion

No one can determine the "correct" or "best" pattern of organization for a local public economy a priori. Instead of trying to determine what an ideal structure of metropolitan organization ought to look like, our efforts should go into studying the "rules of the game" to help individuals and communities better order their relationships.

References

Elazar, Daniel J. *Cities of the Prairie: The Metropolitan Frontier and American Politics.* New York: Basic Books, 1970.

Kolderie, Ted. "Rethinking Public Service Delivery." In Barbara H. Moore, ed., *The Entrepreneur in Local Government.* Washington, D.C.: International City Management Association, 1983.

Niskanen, William A., and Mickey Levy. "Cities and Schools: A Case for Community Government in California." Working Paper No. 14. Berkeley: Graduate School of Public Policy, University of California, 1974.

Ostrom, Elinor. "Size and Performance in a Federal System." *Publius* 6, no. 2 (Spring 1976): 33-73.

Ostrom, Vincent, and Elinor Ostrom. "Public Goods and Public Choices." In E. S. Savas, ed., *Alternatives for Delivering Public Services: Toward Improved Performance.* Boulder: Westview Press, 1978, 7-49.

Schneider, Mark. "Fragmentation and the Growth of Government." *Public Choice* 48 (1986): 255-63.

Stein, Robert, and Dolores Martin. "Contracting for Municipal Public Services." ACIR Working Paper, 1987.

Stevens, Barbara. *Delivery of Municipal Services Efficiently.* Washington, D.C.: U.S. Department of Housing and Urban Development, 1982.

Whitaker, Gordon P. "Coproduction: Citizen Participation in Service Delivery." *Public Administration Review* 40, no. 3 (May-June 1980): 240-46.

Government as Competitor: Alternatives to Privatization

Marc Holzer and Arie Halachmi

INTRODUCTION

Advocates of privatization argue that the private sector is the appropriate structure for the delivery of many services that are now public. Despite the momentum for privatization, governments as service providers should not be "written off" so quickly. As an alternative to privatization, governments can and should compete with the private sector for services which are appropriate for private or public sector delivery. Taking this even further, agencies which are now monopolies might redefine themselves, competing widely for government contracts against other government agencies and/or private firms.

The debate over privatization is premised on the same assumption by both sides: everyone wants *productivity*. Advocates of privatization, such as E.S. Savas (1974), have emphasized relatively tangible concerns of productivity, narrowly defined as efficiency and/or effectiveness. Under the banner of "privatization," government has been attacked through the twin assumptions that monopolistic government is inherently inefficient and the competitive private sector is inherently efficient. The privatization movement, loosely defined, is also identified as "contracting out," "downsizing," and "rightsizing."

According to Katz (1991), proponents of privatization "have lived by the mantra that anything government can do, business can do better." Privatization is marketed as a solution which will typically

- lower costs, while improving quality;
- allow economies of scale;
- allow public vs. private comparisons of cost and performance;
- avoid large start-up costs;
- provide access to specialized skills and training;
- promote flexibility in the size and mix of services;
- make it possible to hire and fire as necessary;
- allow for experimentation in different modes of service provision;
- reduce dependence on a single supplier;
- bypass inert bureaucracies; and
- allow quicker response to new service areas (Savas 1987).

The term "privatization," as it is commonly used, is actually a bifurcated concept. One meaning of the term is the shift of government services to the private sector, establishing a direct relationship between the private provider and the private consumer. This includes steps such as divestment or sale of government enterprises and assets, load shedding, and demonopolization of government services to allow private alternatives to emerge (Bailey 1987; Brudney 1987; Savas

---

Marc Holzer is executive director, The National Center for Public Productivity, and professor of public administration, Rutgers-The State University of New Jersey, at Newark; Arie Halachmi is professor of public administration, Institute of Government, Tennessee State University.

1992). In these public-to-private shifts, privatization signifies moving services from government-as-provider to the firm-as-provider. A direct relationship between the service provider (a firm) and the consumer or client is a defining characteristic. The financial relationship is between the two as private parties, without a payment through government. No contract with the government entity is involved, although government may have a regulatory, policing, or indirect financing role.

In its alternative usage, privatization is "contracting out," or moving services from direct supply by government to an indirect relationship between the service provider (a firm acting on behalf of government as a formal contractor) and the consumer/client. The financial relationship is then between three parties: government as the conduit and monitor, the firm as the service provider, and the customer/client as the service recipient.

In contrast to the proponents of private business as the provider (whether directly or indirectly funded) of public services, there are those who offer a less enthusiastic perspective on privatization. Advocates of public provision of such services (Barnekov and Raffel 1992; Stahl 1988; Ogilvy 1986-87) offer a range of questions for the public manager to answer when considering whether to privatize in order to enhance productivity. Namely, to what extent will privatization likely

- reduce services?
- lower employee morale?
- result in incomplete contracts?
- produce cost overruns?
- lower quality at the expense of quantity?
- place short-term profits over long-term planning?
- negate the service ideal inherent in public service?
- provide opportunities for graft and corruption?
- duplicate services?

Although the debate on privatization has been polarized, each set of advocates needs to address the concerns of the other and of the public: privatized services must be responsive to public policy, and services delivered by government must be efficient and effective. That dialogue is important because privatization is very much in the forefront of the political debate. It must, however, move beyond superficial rhetoric. Competition is frequently presented as the primary means to achieving efficiency, but only *one* form of competition—privatization—has been assumed. Savas (1992) proposes a thesis: "Competition, achieved by prudent privatization, is the key to improving the productivity of public agencies and, more broadly, of public programs and public services.... Competition must be introduced and institutionalized, and privatization is the technique of choice for accomplishing this."

Competition can certainly improve organizational performance, but, in linking competition to privatization, the former concept has been defined too narrowly. An alternative—government as competitor—expands the discussion. This permits defining government as competitor as an intragovernmental (i.e., internal) approach to public service delivery. Such approaches open up alternatives or substitutes to private sector delivery of what are now public sector services.

This discussion reviews three approaches to competitive government: public vs. private competition; public vs. public competition; and competitive federalism.

PUBLIC VS. PRIVATE COMPETITION

Governments put particular services up for bid, with reason. The average U.S. city contracts for 20 percent of its services. According to Savas (1974, 1992), surveys show that public officials are very satisfied with contracting, with documented savings on the order of 25 to 35 percent and virtually no loss of quality or reduction in service levels.

When bids are allowed from the public department faced with losing its monopoly status, the winning bidder, surprisingly, may turn out to be the public agency. This is called "contracted in." Phoenix, Arizona, presents a good case study of this approach (Holzer 1991). Faced with growing budget problems, the city started awarding municipal contracts to private organizations. Responding to the situation, the Department of Public Works developed a nontraditional approach—competition with privatization—competing against prospective private sector providers to offer the highest level of municipal service to the taxpayer at the lowest possible cost. The competition resulted in the Department of Public Works winning back contracted services by lowering the real cost per unit of output.

Phoenix enhanced the competitive atmosphere in which it operates through increased technology, labor-management cooperation, innovative practices, and community involvement and support. Since these substantial results were achieved in solid waste collection services, a service affecting every household, citizens were able to evaluate municipal services on a firsthand basis. The primary objective of entering the competition had certainly been to win back city sanitation contracts, but the ultimate result was a savings of city revenues. In one year alone, savings and cost-avoidance totaled approximately $1.5 million. The program also improved employee morale and labor-management relations which, in turn, resulted in productivity enhancements, innovations (e.g., a retread tire program), and participation in the competitive bidding process by department employees.

A competition with privatization concept allows government services to compete with private industry on an equal footing since no decision to contract out is made prior to the call for private bids. Therefore, municipal agencies are encouraged to compete with private firms, rather than adopt a "do nothing" approach to providing services to the public.

Although this public vs. private model can work, it is not widespread enough to slow the rush toward privatization. The momentum is unimpeded despite Savas' caution that not all services lend themselves to contracting and careful procedures must be followed in order to realize the full benefits. Although Savas (1992) acknowledges that government "should be given an opportunity to compete with the private firms in an even-handed bidding process," he is rather pessimistic about contracting in. He does, however, acknowledge that competitive bidding by government agencies has been effective in the United Kingdom. (See also Hetzner 1987.) In particular, Savas points to problems of determining full pricing for agency bids so as to provide fair competitive comparisons with the private sector.

PUBLIC VS. PUBLIC COMPETITION: AN EXPANDED MODEL OF GOVERNMENTAL COMPETITION

Although competition with the private sector may be feasible and beneficial, not all public services are good candidates for private bids. An alternative model—in which agencies or units of government compete with one another to provide services—is particularly appropriate for government's largest functions: law enforcement and education.

The model of public vs. public competition is built upon certain principles. It accepts the concept of pure privatization as it applies to limited services which government can no longer easily or appropriately provide. Further, it adopts the premise of government's critics that monopolies are inherently inefficient. As Savas (1992) argues:

> A government agency that enjoys a monopoly or is otherwise shielded from competition can be expected to behave no differently than a private monopoly: without the spur of competition, managers and workers alike generally lack the motivation to innovate, to seek better ways, to make changes, to work smarter or harder, or to increase productivity.

However, this public vs. public competition model rejects the premise that the private sector is inherently more efficient or effective. First, the use of private providers does not assure the existence of meaningful competition. Second, where productivity improvement rates are measurable, the annual rate of improvement of public services is similar to that of the private sector (Mark 1983). Third, there are cases where private sector contractors failed to deliver public sector services as promised. Fourth, there are successful state and local improvement projects which exhibit efficiency and effectiveness (Holzer 1991).

Public agencies can, and do, innovate in service delivery. This suggests other forms of competition for the provision of government services.

1. Open Competition: Although many services are appropriate for possible contracting out to the private or not-for-profit sectors, in the competitive spirit of increasing the number of bidders virtually all public agencies should be encouraged to bid on a project. If competition implies greater choices, then elected officials and the public are likely to have more alternatives by cultivating public sector options.

To maximize competition, bids from a variety of public agencies would be acceptable, regardless of their locus within the government or in another jurisdiction and regardless of their mission. As examples, a school district might provide vehicle maintenance services to a police department, or a state highway agency might bid on project management services for a local park department. These bidding agencies would likely have the ability to capitalize on existing investments through economies of scale or enjoy excess capacities that cannot be reduced due to technical, financial, or legal reasons.

Acceptance of public bids would not preclude service delivery bids from the private or not-for-profit sectors. The best providers could come from any number of settings. The competition by government-owned and private airlines for government contracts in some European countries is a case in point, in which either public or private organizations may triumph. Another case is successful competitive bidding by the vehicle maintenance division of the New York City Department of Sanitation, in which it won contracts to service emergency medical service and police vehicles (Holzer 1988).

2. Open Competition Only within Government: In contrast to routinely privatized functions such as sanitation, training, printing, or maintenance, some public sector functions are relatively intangible or complex. Their delivery may be appropriate only to public organizations for purposes of public accountability and policy making under the control of democratic institutions. Privatization could conflict with such values as democratic control and retention of management and emergency capacities. Services where privatization might not be appropriate include public safety, public schools, public higher education, social services, public health, and environmental regulation. Policy-sensitive functions such as the drafting of legislation and writing of speeches have also been proposed as inappropriate candidates for contracting out.

Bidders might include units of the contracting organization, other units or subunits of the same jurisdiction or of similar jurisdictions, and units of other levels of government, including federal, state, and local agencies, and public authorities or special districts. In many cases, legislation would be necessary to allow agencies the flexibility to bid on projects which go well beyond their stated missions.

Although examples of internal competition of government-funded programs exist, they occur infrequently. Shared services, as between local governments or school districts, represent an informal application of this model. The school voucher concept is a movement toward the marketplace, but one which is generally limited to the public schools.

COMPETITIVE FEDERALISM

Introducing the market to relationships between governments has value. Dye (1990) posits such competition between units of government as an opportunity for customers to "vote with their feet." Thus, for example, an injured party can seek help from a state's civil rights agency or from its federal counterpart, the Equal Employment Opportunity Commission (EEOC). One can work through a city, county, or state agency, or several federal agencies to facilitate starting a small business. By the same token, one may ask any one of three agencies for help on matters involving banks and security trading.

While the model is valid, it appears to present two problems. First, Dye (1990) like others (Kanyon and Kincad 1991), describes the competition among government entities at the three levels of government in the United States. However, the competition for "clients," and thus for resources, exists not only *between* levels of government but *within* levels of government (Halachmi and Holzer 1993; Halachmi 1995). Recent initiatives by federal agencies to establish a "Franchising Fund," i.e., to offer on a competitive basis various logistical services such as fleet maintenance, telecommunication, and data processing or payroll administration to other federal agencies for a fee, suggests that the competition is intensifying. These initiatives indicate that there is a public market for certain services. The prospect of contracting out some of a sheriff department's services to other government entities such as other sheriff departments, the U.S. Marshal, or vice versa (Halachmi and Boydston 1994) is an illustration of the possible competition within and among levels of government.

The other difficulty with the Dye (1990) model is that it lacks a normative prescriptive quality. It was not Dye's intention in his discussion to reform or to optimize the performance of government entities. Yet, it is shortsighted to leave out an explicit reference to the existing competition among government entities within and among levels of government, and to the normative value of such competition. As noted by Holzer (1995), the logic of critics of government as competitor to deliver services is that turning over services to the private sector results in savings without loss of quality. However, if competition exists and is encouraged within government, what does the private sector have that government doesn't have? After all, the only reason Savas (1974, 1992) prefers private providers to public ones is that the competition keeps the former on their toes.

QUESTIONS RAISED BY INTRAGOVERNMENTAL COMPETITION

The approaches to competitive government discussed above stimulate a range of questions, and partial answers:

1. *What if an agency is too successful, becoming a monopoly or part of an oligopoly?* Possible success should not be a deterrent to innovation and experimentation. If an agency or unit designed to increase competition becomes dominant instead, then policy makers should limit its size, splitting it into one or more smaller agencies. Following Darwin's survival model of reproduction one of its "offspring" might then become the "fittest," displacing unsuccessful government bidding units or groups in those units.

2. *What will agencies do with "profits" generated by contracts?* As opposed to the now typical situation in which government agencies do not retain income as "profits," all or a significant portion of profits can be retained or reinvested by the public contractor.

3. *Can government make decisions as rapidly or flexibly as its private sector counterparts?* Very possibly. This might, however, require extensive rewriting of regulations or legislation.

4. *Are public agencies now equipped to compete with the private sector?* Competition by government might require new investments in technology, although in other cases the investment already exists in terms of excess capacity. One advantage of privatization is that firms might have access to investment capital that is not as available to their public agency counterparts.

5. *Will internal competition have dysfunctional consequences?* Of course, but they can be minimized if they are anticipated and monitored. Following are some possible dysfunctions:

    a. Information pirating: managers could attempt to ferret out confidential information to gain unfair advantage.

    b. Corruption/bribes: government managers might attempt to influence each other inappropriately.

    c. Undue political influence: politicians could attempt to direct contracts to agencies in which they have more influence.

6. *Will agencies be able to tolerate "slack" in order to invest in writing bids?* Will public agencies be able to take a long view that successes will eventually emerge? Possibly, especially considering the popular argument that there is now substantial slack, or underutilized capacity, in government.

7. *Are public agencies unwilling to transfer functions to other agencies, but more willing to contract out?* Contracting out does not imply giving up territory, while letting another agency provide a service may be perceived as surrendering turf. The paradox of internal competition may be a bias against other public entities, even to the point of paying a private provider more.

CONCLUSION

Enhanced competitive capacities may help convince skeptics that government is, or can be, productive. Under a model of "government as competitor" the change in public opinion is not likely to be dramatic, but the direction is likely to be positive as government reasserts its legitimate missions and reestablishes its competency.

References

Bailey, R.W. 1987. Uses and misuses of privatization. In *Prospects for privatization*, 138-52. S.H. Hanke, ed. New York: Academy of Political Science.

Barnekov, Timothy K., and Jeffrey A. Raffel. 1992. Public management of privatization. In *Public productivity handbook*, 99-116. Marc Holzer, ed. New York: Marcel Dekker, Inc.

Brudney, Jeffrey L. 1987. Coproduction and privatization: Exploring the relationship and its implications. *Journal of Voluntary Action Research* 16, no. 3 (July-Sept.): 11-21.

Dye, Thomas R. 1990. *American federalism: Competition among governments*. Lexington, Mass.: Lexington Books.

Halachmi, Arie. 1995. The challenge of a competitive public sector. In *The enduring challenges in public management*, 220-46. Arie Halachmi and Geert Baccarat, eds. San Francisco: Jossey Bass.

Halachmi, Arie, and Robert Boydston. 1994. The political economy of outsourcing. In *Case studies in public budgeting and financial management*, 3-17. Aman Khan and W. Bartley Hildreth, eds. Dubuque, Iowa: Kendall/Hunt Publishing Company.

Halachmi, Arie, and Marc Holzer. 1993. Toward a competitive public administration. *International Review of Administrative Sciences* 59, no. 1: 29-46.

Hetzner, Candace. 1987. Lessons for America one hundred years after Pendleton. *Public Productivity Review*, no. 43: 15-30.

Holzer, Marc. 1988. Productivity in, garbage out: Sanitation gain in New York. *Public Productivity Review* 11, no. 3: 37-50.

——————. 1991. Exemplary state and local (EXSL) awards program. Newark, N.J.: National Center for Public Productivity, Rutgers University.

——————. 1995. The public productivity challenge. In *The enduring challenges in public management*, 413-18. Arie Halachmi and Geert Bouckaert, eds. San Francisco: Jossey Bass.

Kanyon, D.A., and John Kincaid, eds. 1991. *Competition among states and local governments*. Washington, D.C.: The Urban Institute.

Katz, Jeffrey I. 1991. Privatizing without tears. *Governing* 4, no. 9 (June): 38-42.

Mark, Jerome A. 1983. Productivity measurement of government services: Federal, state and local. White House Conference Background Paper. Washington, D.C.: Bureau of Labor Statistics, June.

Ogilvy, James A. 1986-87. Scenarios for the future of governance." *The Bureaucrat* 15, no. 4 (Winter): 13-16.

Savas, E.S. 1974. Municipal monopolies versus competition in delivering urban services. In *Improving the quality of urban management*, 473-500. Willis D. Hawley and David Rogers, eds. Beverly Hills, Calif.: Sage Publications, Inc.

——————. 1987. *Privatization: The key to better government*. Chatham, N.J.: Chatham House Publishers.

——————. 1992. Privatization and productivity. In *Public productivity handbook*, 79-98. Marc Holzer, ed. New York: Marcel Dekker, Inc.

Stahl, O. Glenn. 1988. What's missing in privatization. *The Bureaucrat* 17, no. 2 (Summer): 41-44.

The Three Policy Arenas
Paul E. Peterson

Since cities have an interest in policies that enhance their economic well-being, local public policies are treated differentially, depending upon their impact on the economic vitality of the community. Three types of public policies can be logically deduced from this fact.[1] *Developmental* policies enhance the economic position of the city. *Redistributive* policies benefit low-income residents but at the same time negatively affect the local economy. *Allocational* policies are more or less neutral in their economic effects. These definitions are very general and require further elaboration and specification. In doing so, we shall discover that just as policies have varying economic consequences, so they are produced by different economic and political conditions. For one thing, for each policy type different factors affect the level of fiscal support state and local governments can and will provide. Also, the level of government responsible for financing a policy varies with the policy arena. Finally, the kinds of politics associated with each type of policy are highly variable. To say more would anticipate much of the remainder of my argument. In this discussion we shall be content with laying out the three policy arenas and showing how the factors that produce variation in their level of fiscal support vary from one policy arena to the next.

Developmental policies are those local programs which enhance the economic position of a community in its competition with others. They strengthen the local economy, enhance the local tax base, and generate additional resources that can be used for the community's welfare. They are praised by many and opposed only by those few whose partial interests stand in conflict with community interests.

Developmental policies enhance the local economy because their positive economic effects are greater than their cost to community residents. The most obvious cost is any increase in taxes the program requires. Other costs may include the opportunity costs of allocating land for the designated purpose. The creation of an industrial park or a shopping center may come at the expense of parkland or residential neighborhoods. Any air, water, or noise pollution associated with the policy is also a cost the local community must bear. But in return for these costs, the community may gain new employment opportunities, increased demand for locally provided services, increased land values, and higher local government revenues.

Developmental policies need not always entail the attraction of business and industry to a community. It may be that the creation of a wildlife preserve will so enhance the attractiveness of surrounding residential property that any opportunity costs involved in allocating land for such a purpose will be more than offset by the increased market value of the adjacent areas. Under some circumstances, improvements in local schools will make an area such an attractive place for families that the increased cost of supplying the service will be more than offset by the increased value residents will place on living in a locale with excellent schools. The same can be said for other local government services.

Reprinted from *City Limits* (Chicago: The University of Chicago Press, 1981), 41-65, 232-33. By permission of the publisher.

A convenient way of roughly calculating whether or not a policy is in the interest of a city is to consider whether its benefit/tax ratio is more or less than 1.0, that is, whether the marginal benefits exceed the marginal cost to the average taxpayer. If the average or above average taxpayers (the persons who receive no more than the mean level of marginal benefits from their marginal taxes) find their benefit/tax ratio enhanced by the policy, then they will place a higher value on remaining in the community. Those policies which can be financed out of user charges paid by community residents or taxes levied on users of the service can usually be treated as developmental policies. In these cases, the people receiving the service indicate by their behavior that they value the service more than what they must pay to supply it. The fact that toll roads can be financed solely out of costs imposed on drivers indicates that road building of this sort is a developmental policy.

But although a self-financing program is usually a developmental policy, not all developmental policies must be self-financing in a narrow, cost accountant sense of the word. Tax concessions to businesses locating in a community are not literally self-financing, but the economic benefits to the area of their choosing the community as their center for economic activity may be so great that in the long run the program pays for itself. And it is the judgment by local officials that a program will cost the community little or nothing in the long run that is the best indication that a program is a developmental policy.

At the opposite end of the scale are those public policies that are not only unproductive but actually damage the city's economic position. Many kinds of economically harmful policies can be imagined, but most are not sufficiently viable to be serious contenders for the public purse. No serious participant in local politics suggests that every city employee be given a black Cadillac with a full-time chauffeur. Apart from any other consequence, these sorts of policies would bankrupt City Hall. On a smaller scale, of course, regressive policies are tolerated. Through long-established political connections, a fire commissioner may be able to retire handsomely in the Caribbean on an extraordinary pension, even though such a concession is a cost to taxpayers, with no apparent compensating benefits. But except for those interested in political corruption, most economically regressive policies have little theoretical relevance.

One kind of unproductive local policy can make a plausible claim for public support, however. Because *redistributive* policies help the needy and unfortunate and because they provide reasonably equal citizen access to public services, such policies are sometimes incorporated into local government practice, even when their economic consequences are pernicious.

I wish to limit my use of the term "redistribution" in two ways. First, I speak only of redistribution from the better off to the less well off segments of the community. Although technically redistribution can refer to any transfer of money, in recent years it has been given the more specific meaning of income transfers from higher to lower income segments of the population. Second, I speak only of those redistributive policies that have negative effects on local economies. In some cases redistribution may be economically beneficial. Whenever a local community needs additional low-income residents to help staff its service industries or more unskilled workers to operate its manufacturing industries, then the city may have an interest in supplying these workers some redistributive services, such as low-cost housing or free medical care. But in the contemporary United States such shortages of unskilled workers are rare, and it must be recognized that in most cases redistributive programs have negative economic effects. While they supply benefits to those least needed by the local economy, they require taxation on those who are most needed. Such a strong claim can be made on behalf of the poor and the needy that, although local governments often shy away from these painfully regressive redistributive policies, they are the one kind of regressive policy cities sometimes undertake.

One can roughly calculate whether a policy is redistributive by estimating whether those who pay for the service in local taxes are recipients of the service. Where there is no overlap at all, a pure case of redistribution is indicated. Welfare assistance to the nontaxpayer is the purest case. More generally, any service which increases the marginal benefit/tax ratio of those above the mean ratio for all taxpayers is a redistributive service. Without the service they already are privileged recipients of local services; with the service their relatively high level of benefits (as compared with taxes paid) is enhanced still more. Because low-income residents usually pay the lowest absolute amounts in taxes (however high their tax rate as a proportion of their income), it is these low-income residents who have relatively high benefit/tax ratios and who are the most likely beneficiaries of redistributive services.

Once again, this is only a rough way of determining whether a policy is regressively redistributive. Under some circumstances the nontaxpayer may be making such significant contributions to the local economy that he indirectly supports a local government's revenue base. A private university excused from paying property taxes but which generates in its environs numerous secondary and service industries that do pay local taxes is a case in point. Yet in most cases redistributive programs which help those whose benefit/tax ratio is already relatively high only make the community a more costly locale for the more productive community members. As desirable as many redistributive programs may be in other ways, they harm the local economy.

Allocational policies are neither developmental nor redistributive. Marginal expenditures for such services have neither much of a positive nor much of a negative effect on the local economy. In a sense, the category only gives a formal classification to the midpoint of the range between the policies that help develop the local economy and those that do the most to redistribute valued things to nontaxpayers. But inasmuch as many local government services fall into this middle ground and local conflicts often focus on allocational policies, the midpoint on the continuum deserves as much consideration as the two extremes.

The housekeeping services of local government are the best example. On the whole, they are neither redistributive nor developmental in character. Instead, all members of the community benefit from the most valued aspects of police and fire protection, and from systematic, community-wide collection of garbage and refuse. These services reduce the likelihood of catastrophic conflagrations, wholesale violations of persons and property, community epidemics, and the use of public spaces as dumps and junkyards. The value each individual places on these services may vary, but all receive important benefits. Moreover, it is likely that marginal allocations for these services are appreciated more by richer taxpayers, who have more resources in need of protection.

These housekeeping services are usually performed with greater effectiveness in areas of a community where tax payments are greater. In the parts of the city where property is more valuable and owners pay more in taxes, one also characteristically finds lower crime rates, less fire damage, and cleaner streets.[2] One cannot claim that these outcomes are simply a function of the overt efforts of city departments. Indeed, police, fire, and sanitation efforts are more concentrated in lower income neighborhoods.[3] The relative peace and quiet of the more wealthy areas is a function of environmental variables influenced more by local government zoning laws than the overt efforts of specific city departments. Nonetheless, a combination of urban government policies produces city services that operate with higher levels of effectiveness in areas of the city where more valuable property is located.

Housekeeping services are thus widely and proportionately allocated. On the one hand, they do not particularly benefit a needy segment of the community at the expense of the average taxpayer. On the other hand, these programs do not pay for themselves in the same way that developmental policies do. Housekeeping policies, administered by local monopolists, operate with less than perfect efficiency, and user charges are seldom levied in ways that rationalize use. As a result, the distribution of benefits is different from the distribution of costs and, above a bare minimum of service, there is little likelihood that the marginal benefits to the average taxpayer are greater than 1.0.

Many of the employment policies of local government are another type of allocational politics. Apart from the levels of wages and benefits, which must be kept competitive with other cities, local governments can pursue a range of policies in the recruitment of personnel without endangering the local economy. One city may prefer to hire in accord with specified professional qualifications, such as length of schooling, scores on civil service examinations, and the like. Other cities prefer to hire political cronies of elected leaders. Some cities prefer strict adherence to merit criteria, while others balance their employment opportunities among the city's racial and ethnic groups. Since these approaches probably have equal chances of finding willing and able recruits, any of them can be followed without having much effect on local efficiency.

Formally, allocational policies are those which provide the average taxpayer with an average ratio of benefits to taxes. Increased expenditures on allocational policies neither increase nor decrease the attractiveness of the city to this average taxpayer (who, of course, is probably well above the average citizen in wealth). This means that the marginal benefit from allocational policies is less than the marginal cost in local taxes. For example, even though the average taxpayer wants police services, he would prefer that the marginal dollar spent on such services be saved. At the same time, there is some other allocational policy for which the average taxpayer would be willing to pay an increased tax in order to receive it. But were he provided that service, his benefit/tax ratio would increase and some other individual who did not want that increment would become the average taxpayer, still suffering from a modest benefit/tax ratio. Thus, to the average taxpayer allocational policies always provide too little service at too great a cost.

VARIATION IN THE LEVEL OF PUBLIC SERVICES PROVIDED

The level of developmental, redistributive, and allocational policies provided by local governments varies from one community to the next. The factors producing this variation differ among policy arenas. To give a formal explanation for these differences, I shall rely on the language of benefit/tax ratios to which the reader has already been introduced. This is necessary to give precision to the presentation of the argument. But the reader should always recognize that local governments are not run by narrow-minded, pettifogging cost accountants who calculate the balance between direct taxes paid and direct services received. It is the more general impact on the local economy which in the end is their greatest concern.

Three factors affect the supply of developmental, redistributive, and allocational policies: fiscal capacity, the cost of supplying the service, and the demand for the service. First, other things being equal, the fiscal capacity of a community affects its level of expenditure. *This is due to the relatively small amount of variation among localities in the rate of taxation of their economic resources.* Because the benefit/tax ratio to the average taxpayer for most government expenditures is less than 1.0, relatively higher local tax rates make a community relatively less attractive. To protect a community's economic resources from net outward flow, tax rates must not be significantly greater in any one community than they are in competing areas. At the same time, communities will spend up to the tax rate levied by communities in competing areas, because the demand for services by the average taxpayer will always be less than the supply. Where greater fiscal capacity exists, a higher percentage of these demands can be supplied without imposing a relatively high tax rate. The local community has every incentive to meet service demands until the benefit/tax ratio drops below that of its competitors.

Although numerous exceptions can be found, rates of taxation of economic resources thus tend to become similar among jurisdictions competing in similar markets. For example, if one looks at the total per capita general expenditures by state and local governments, one finds considerable differences among the 50 states. In 1973, the state-by-state standard deviation in expenditures varied by $229 around a mean of $637, producing a coefficient of variation of 0.36. As can be seen in Table 1, grants from the federal government reduced these interstate differences only marginally. However, the amount of revenue raised by state and local governments per $1,000 of personal income varied within one standard deviation by only $19 around a mean of $162, yielding a coefficient of variation of only 0.12. In other words, states differed considerably in their expenditures for public services while the rate at which they taxed personal income for these services was fairly similar. Moreover, similarities in rates of taxation cannot be attributed to differential revenue support from the federal government.

As these data show, similarity in rates of taxation produces substantial variation in the level of local government expenditures. At the same tax rate, communities with greater per capita economic resources have greater revenues per capita available for public expenditure. It can thus be hypothesized that differentials in local government expenditure are positively correlated with indicators of a community's fiscal resources, whether these be median family income, per capita income, median property value, sales and gross receipts, or some combination thereof.

Second, the cost of supplying public services affects levels of expenditures among state and local governments. If the labor and materials governments must purchase to supply a good are in relatively short supply, their costs increase and so do levels of public expenditure. At least, this is true for those govern-

Table 1: *State and Local Finances, 1973*

	Mean	Standard Deviation	Coefficient of Variation
General expenditure per capita excluding federal aid	$637	$229	.36
General expenditure per capita including federal aid	$860	$276	.32
General revenue from own resources per $1000 personal income	$162	$ 19	.12

Source: Maxwell and Aronson 1977, tables A-7 and A-9.
Note: Data are for the 50 states.

Table 2: *Hypothesized Determinants of Local Government Expenditure*

	Determinants of Expenditure			
Type of Policy	Fiscal Capacity	Demand	Supply	Need
Redistributive	High	…	Low	Low or negative
Allocational	Moderate	Moderate	Moderate	…
Developmental	Low	High	Moderate	…

ment services for which the price elasticity of demand is less than 1.0. Although the number of units that will be purchased declines as costs increase, the total expenditure for the service increases.

Third, government expenditures are a function of the economic demand for public services. As demand increases, governments purchase more services and expenditures increase. These relationships seem obvious and straightforward, but it is to be remembered that the concept of demand is used in the sense employed in a market analysis. Unlike most studies of public policy, demand here is not equated with the preferences of the median voter. It is the demands of the potentially migratory taxpayer which are critical. Preferences become demands only to the extent that the individual is willing and able to pay for the service desired. Resident preferences are considered demands only in proportion to the level of taxes they pay (or, more generally, the amount they contribute to the economic vitality of the community). One does not therefore expect to find local government responsiveness to each and every resident or voter in the community. It is the concerns of the above-average taxpayer that are given the greatest weight.

How these three factors—fiscal capacity, supply, and demand—vary with the level of expenditures depends on the type of public policy in question (see Table 2). In the case of redistributive policies, the relationship between fiscal capacity and expenditure levels is strong. Because the beneficiaries of the policy are different from the taxpayers, any increase in the tax rate for redistributive services is likely to have particularly harmful economic consequences. Consequently, tax rates financing redistributive policies must be much the same from one community to another, and variations in fiscal capacity will determine much of the variation in expenditure. Measures of the "need" for redistributive policies, on the other hand, will be weakly correlated with expenditures. Because the need for redistributive policies is unlikely to be felt by taxpaying residents of the community, there is no way for the need to become translated into effective demand. Similarly, one does not hypothesize a strong relationship between the cost of supplying a service and expenditure levels. Because the benefit/tax ratio is low, redistributive policies are the one type of local government service for which demand elasticity is probably equal to 1.0. As costs of the service increase, the supply of the service will decrease by a comparable amount so that overall expenditures will remain the same.

Exactly opposite patterns of correlation are expected in the case of developmental policies. Because the marginal benefit/tax ratio for these services is high and the perceived benefits may even exceed costs, fiscal capacity is not likely to have a significant effect on expenditure levels. Even those communities with relatively low fiscal capacities will find it in their interest to spend money on programs that help develop that fiscal base. Measures of demand, on the other hand, will be strongly correlated with expenditures. A community that benefits from the tourist trade will spend more on parks and recreational programs because there is a demand for the service. The costs incurred by the local government are offset by the increase in the tourist trade. Supply variables can also be expected to affect expenditures, as the demand elasticity for such policies is likely to be less than 1.0. To take the tourist trade example once again, communities will probably provide fewer recreational services as their costs increase, but the service decline will probably be less than the cost increase, thereby producing higher overall expenditure levels.

Allocational policies fall somewhere in between these polar extremes. Because the benefit/tax ratio is less than 1.0, fiscal capacity will affect the level at which services are provided. Communities with weak fiscal capacities cannot afford to levy much heavier taxes simply to provide higher levels of allocational services. On the other hand, economic demand and the cost of supplying the service will also affect expenditure levels. Not only will service provision be greater where taxpayers perceive greater needs, but since demand is less price elastic than in the redistributive arena, increases in the cost of supplying the service are not fully offset by decreases in the amount of service provided. As policemen cost more, fewer policemen are hired; nevertheless, overall expenditure levels still increase.

In sum, different policies have different effects on a city's economic interests, and therefore the level at which they are provided is determined by different economic factors. The amount of financial support for developmental policies, which promote a city's economic growth, is determined by the economic demand for such policies. Cities that need more industry will give tax concessions to in-migrating businesses. Cities that need more tourists will spend more on recreational services. Cities that are more geographically dispersed will spend more on streets and highways. These needs are satisfied because they are the equivalent of economic demands in the private market. Satisfaction of the needs by local government enhances the economic welfare of the community and the revenue base of City Hall.

Redistributive policies that weaken the local economy are only provided at a level which the city can afford. A community with a weak fiscal base does not provide a high level of redistributive services, even if many are poor and needy. To do so would require a higher rate of taxation, which would make the community less attractive to commerce, industry, and productive labor, all of which are needed to sustain the local economy. Note that these relationships are exactly the opposite from what one would expect were local policies determined by the politics internal to the city. Where poor people are present in abundance, one would expect to find higher levels of redistribution. But insofar as the presence of the poor weakens a local fiscal base, one must expect to find instead an inverse relationship between poverty and redistributive expenditures.

Allocational policies are neither fish nor fowl. They have little effect on a city's economic growth. The level at which they are provided is a function not just of fiscal capacity but also of economic demand and the cost of supplying the service.

EMPIRICAL DIFFERENTIATION OF THE POLICY ARENAS

The connection between the three types of policies and the environmental conditions in which a city finds itself is simple and straightforward. Yet, it is not easy to find a way of showing these connections with readily available information about city governments. There are two major types of problems. The most troublesome is finding comparable units of analysis. The word "city" does not mean the same thing in every place. Some "cities" operate a host of public services; other "cities" direct little more than the police and fire departments. Some "cities" raise most of their own revenues; other "cities" get large grants from their state governments.

I have concluded that one cannot examine "city" expenditures by themselves. Because state-local relationships are so intertwined, it is necessary to examine the combined expenditures of state and local governments. The comparable units of analysis thus become the 50 state-local government systems in the United States. I treat the combined activities of each state-local system as theoretically comparable to the combined activities of each of the others.[4] Any differences in their expenditure patterns can thus be meaningfully related to the varying economic environments in which they find themselves. Not only does this procedure solve the unit-of-analysis problem, but it has the added advantage of providing a "hard" case against which to test the propositions that have been developed. What has been said about local governments applies with somewhat less force to state governments, which are responsible for a larger land area and therefore somewhat less sensitive to external economic forces than are cities. If the propositions are supported by data collected on the combined expenditures of state and local governments, they almost surely hold for the activities of cities and other local government jurisdictions.

The second problem is that state and local governments do not nicely classify their policies as developmental, redistributive, and allocational. Any attempt to apply this system of classification to those used by governments will necessarily be less precise than one would like. However, the categories by which governmental expenditures are classified in the United States census provide a breakdown which permits some reasonable approximations of the pure distinctions I have outlined. State and local expenditures for welfare and for health and hospitals seem fairly obvious examples of relatively redistributive policies. In general, there is at best only a loose correspondence between the individuals who pay for these services and the individuals who receive them. There may be some question as to the degree to which these policies redistribute benefits across class lines, whether these services really benefit the people they are supposed to help, and whether the primary beneficiaries are the recipients or the employees providing the services. But, at the very least, few claim that in these policy areas there is a close correspondence between taxes paid and services received. Additional measures of welfare policy are provided by the average payments made by state and local governments in old age assistance, aid to dependent children, and unemployment benefits. These amounts, which are subject to state and local discretion, give particularly good evidence of a state-local system's commitment to redistributive objectives.

In the United States, developmental policies on which high levels of expenditure are made are more difficult to discern. Most types of services whose beneficiaries can be readily identified and charged accordingly are handled by the private market. But, for some government policies there is at least a rough correspondence between taxpayer and beneficiary. The most obvious examples are governmental efforts to improve the transportation and communication systems of the society. In many of these cases, the direct consumers of these services pay charges covering their costs. Gasoline taxes and automobile and truck licenses cover the costs of highway building. More generally, states and localities benefit economically from being better connected with the transportation of the larger society. Thus, in the analysis that follows, expenditures for highways constitute the one example of a developmental policy for which data were readily available.

The best examples of allocational policies are expenditures for police and fire services. As stated earlier, these are designed to benefit the community as a whole and have little redistributive impact, and yet their marginal benefit to the average taxpayer is probably substantially less than their marginal cost.

I have classified education separately in the following tables, because the classification of this governmental function is particularly difficult. Another discussion has documented the significantly greater redistributive impact of education in central cities than in suburban areas. In general, one must conclude that educational services are slightly redistributive—more so than police and fire services, but less so than expenditures on welfare and health. However, educational services are heavily financed at the local level, and they are the single most costly item to the local taxpayer. Since it is the most expensive of the redistributive programs local governments finance, expenditure levels for even this modestly redistributive program may still be sensitive to a community's fiscal capacity.

Eight independent variables were selected to identify the relative importance of fiscal capacity, demand-supply factors, and noneconomic "need." The two indicators of the fiscal capacity of state and local governments were median family income and per capita property value. Three measures of urbanization—the percent living in metropolitan areas, population density, and the percent employed in nonagricultural occupations—provided indicators of variation in the economic demand for and the cost of supplying several of the dependent variables. Because urbanization is correlated with wage rates and the price of many materials, it may be accepted as a proxy for variations in the cost of supplying government services. At the same time, urbanization provides an indicator of increased demand for allocative policies, such as police and fire protection. Urbanization is also negatively associated with the economic demand for roads and highways. Besides these three measures of urbanization, a more direct indicator of the cost of supplying government services was included—the average wage paid in the manufacturing sector. Finally, two indicators of need for redistribution unable to reflect themselves in economic demand were included—the percent with low incomes and the percent of blacks. A full description of all the independent and dependent variables is given elsewhere.[5]

In the tables that follow, I analyze the ways in which these eight factors affect redistributive, allocational, and developmental expenditures. To show that the relationships are robust, I analyze the data in a variety of different ways, introducing different combinations of variables in each table. Some readers may find the presentation, which demands some familiarity with statistical techniques, too technical to warrant detailed scrutiny. The reader who is willing to accept my claim that the information presented generally supports the hypotheses I have offered may move to the conclusions of this discussion. The reader who wishes to peruse the tables that follow should keep in mind the distinction between low and negative correlations. If a coefficient of correlation is low, that means that the two variables are apparently unrelated. In Table 3, for example, the low .06 coefficient of correlation between property values and highway expenditures means that highway expenditures were no higher in states with high property values than those with low ones. A negative coefficient, if strong, shows that two variables are inversely related. For example, in the same table, the –.58 between metropolitan population and highway expenditures indicates that per capita expenditures on highways are less in those states where a higher percentage of people live in metropolitan areas. From this inverse, negative correlation, one may infer that more expenditures per capita are provided in rural areas to accommodate the needs of a low-density population.

The simple correlations between these eight independent variables and each of the nine public policies are presented in Table 3. In general, the pattern of correlation is consistent with the hypotheses. The two indicators of fiscal capacity, median family income and property value, were the variables most strongly associated with expenditures for redistributive and educational purposes. Factors associated with variations in the cost of living for low-income people, including population density and urbanness, were positively but less strongly related to the level of redistribution. Significantly, percent black and percent low income, presumably measures of need and of the political power of needy groups, were negatively related to expenditures for redistribution.

The determinants of expenditure levels for developmental policies differed significantly from those in the redistributive arena. Highway expenditures were not significantly affected by the fiscal capacity of the state-local government system. Instead, they were most strongly affected by indicators of the demand for the service and the cost of supplying it. The density of the population, the percent living in metropolitan areas, and the percent employed in non-

Table 3: *Simple Correlations between Public Policy and Fiscal Capacity, Demand-Supply, and Need*

	Determinants of Expenditure							
	Fiscal Capacity		Demand-Supply				Need but No Demand	
Type of Policy	Income	Property Values	Density	Metropolitan Population	Nonagricultural Employment	Average Wage	Percent Poor	Percent Black
Redistributive								
Old-age assistance	.50	.44	.12	.20	.32	.26	–.41	–.25
Aid to dependent children	.71	.59	.45	.26	.45	.37	–.76	–.57
Unemployment benefits	.81	.74	.46	.53	.58	.47	–.70	–.33
Welfare expenditures	.59	.58	.53	.47	.56	.22	–.50	–.28
Health and hospitals	.33	.47	.16	.33	.42	.17	–.14	.19
Educational	.74	.54	.11	.22	.35	.70	–.66	–.46
Allocational								
Police	.70	.73	.37	.60	.65	.39	–.50	–.11
Fire	.69	.73	.55	.64	.71	.28	–.56	–.20
Developmental								
Highways	.12	.06	–.35	–.58	–.25	.38	–.15	–.44

Source: Peterson 1979a.

agricultural employment were negatively related to highway expenditures, because the economic demand for highways is greater in less densely populated rural parts of the country. Expenditures were also greater where wage levels were higher. Determinants of allocational policies took still a different form. For these policies, the fiscal capacity variables and the demand-supply variables were about equally important for explaining expenditure levels.

The simple correlations presented in Table 3 can be misleading. Apparently strong relationships may turn out to be spurious when controls are introduced; apparently weak relationships may become stronger once variables that impede identification of the relationships are removed. At the same time, the problem of multicollinearity when several highly correlated independent variables are included together in a regression analysis creates other problems of interpretation. After numerous analyses, in which we sought to minimize these contrasting but uniformly exasperating problems, it was discovered that almost as much of the variance in the public policies could be explained by just three variables—income, metropolitan population, and percent black—as by regressions including twice that number. Since the three variables provided one indicator of each of the three theoretically significant concepts that had been elaborated, the simple regression presented in Table 4 proved to be the best test of the hypotheses.

In this table, it becomes even more apparent how important fiscal capacity is for determining redistributive policies. The level of old-age assistance, the amount of aid to dependent children, and the level of unemployment benefits are all heavily dependent on the fiscal resources of state and local governments. To a lesser extent, overall expenditures on welfare and on health and hospitals are also dependent on the fiscal resources of the jurisdiction. Educational policies, too, are a function of the state's income level. Even though education is a less redistributive policy than the others, it is heavily financed by local governments and therefore seems especially sensitive to fiscal factors.

It is equally important to note the variable with which redistributive policies are unrelated. Although blacks are one of the most needy groups in the American population, for most redistributive policies there is but a weak relationship between their percentage of a state's population and the level of benefits received. Indeed, the negative sign in the table

Table 4: *Income, Metropolitan Population, and Percent Black as Determinants of Public Policy*

	Determinants of Expenditure			
Type of Policy	Fiscal Capacity: Income	Demand-Supply: Metropolitan Population	Need but No Demand: Percent Black	Multiple R
Redistributive				
Old-age assistance	.58**	–.14	–.01	.51
Aid to dependent children	.63**	–.07	–.32**	.78
Unemployment benefits	.71**	.12	–.07	.81
Welfare expenditures	.35*	.29*	–.18	.63
Health and hospitals	.48**	.00	.38**	.48
Educational	.88**	–.29*	–.09	.79
Allocational				
Police	.59**	.24*	.08	.74
Fire	.42**	.40**	–.10	.75
Developmental				
Highways	.67**	–.97**	–.06	.81

Source: Peterson 1979a.
Note: Table gives standardized beta coefficients. Single asterisk (*) indicates *T* statistic significant at .05 level. Double asterisk (**) indicates *T* statistic significant at .01 level.

indicates that the larger the percentage of blacks, the less the redistributive expenditure. Nor does the result change when the percent of low-income people living in the state is substituted for the percent black. As can be seen in Table 3, both the presence of blacks and the presence of poor people have only negative effects on redistributive expenditures. The only exception to the pattern is the case of health care and hospitals, where the percent black is positively related to redistributive expenditures. In this single case, there is a hint that black need for health care actually increases expenditures for the service. The peculiar mechanisms by which this need becomes an effective determinant of locally financed public health care seem worthy of special attention. But if the presence of blacks increases state and local expenditures for health care, it has the opposite effect on welfare policy. Even when controls are introduced for a state's fiscal resources (as in Table 4), the presence of blacks dampens the amount of support for dependent children.

Allocative policies were, as predicted, responsive to both fiscal capacity and demand-supply factors. In the case of fire expenditures, the two seemed roughly equal in importance. On the other hand, police expenditures seemed somewhat more responsive to fiscal capacity than to demand-supply factors. Perhaps by 1970, the year for which these data were compiled, local authorities were beginning to believe that marginal increments in police expenditures yield relatively small marginal benefits to average taxpayers, and therefore more is paid for these services only if fiscal capacity is ample.

Developmental policies proved to be very strongly related to demand-supply factors in just the way that had been anticipated: the more rural the state, the more it spends on highways. Given the greater importance of highways for the economy of the rural state, such policies are certainly sensible. Yet, the strong responsiveness of this developmental policy to the demands of the rural economy contrasts sharply with the impotence of the needs of blacks and low-income groups as determinants of redistributive policy. On the other hand, my hypotheses had not anticipated the smaller but nonetheless strong relationship between fiscal capacity and highway expenditure. Apparently, capital must be available before even economically prudent investments can be made.

Skeptics may raise three objections to these findings: (1) the effects of economic demand for services and the cost of supplying them have not been separated; (2) the relationships among the variables may change once the impact of federal assistance is taken into account; and (3) the findings may be heavily influenced by the presence of the southern states in the sample of 50 states. All three possible criticisms gain little support from additional data analysis.

First, consider Table 5, which makes an attempt at separating out the effects of the economic demand for services and the cost of supplying them. Income remains the indicator of fiscal capacity, and in this table metropolitan population is treated as an indicator of positive demand for allocational services and of negative (because rural areas have greater per capita needs) demand for highway expenditures. I also include the average hourly earnings in manufacturing as a plausible indicator of the cost of supplying public services. The findings confirm the initial propositions in almost all details. Redistributive policies are strictly a function of fiscal capacity; the other variables have little effect. As might be expected, educational policies are influenced both by fiscal capacity and by the cost of supplying this labor-intensive service. Relationships for allocational policies are also much as hypothesized. They are influenced by both fiscal capacity and demand, though the cost of supplying the service is not positively related to expenditure levels. Finally, highway expenditures, the one example of a developmental policy, are most heavily influenced by the higher demand for the services in rural areas, but it is quite consistent with our expectations that they are also influenced by cost factors. The one unanticipated finding is that highway expenditures are also a function of fiscal capacity.

Next, consider the impact of federal aid on locally financed expenditures. In doing so, remember that the dependent variable includes only those expenditures not directly financed by federal grants-in-aid. Table 6 nonetheless shows that federal aid is strongly associated with welfare and highway expenditures locally. The causal direction of this relationship is not easily discerned. On the one hand, the availability of federal assistance may encourage local spending on these programs. On the other hand, matching formulae produce increased federal commitments whenever local contributions increase. In any case, these correlations are not my primary consideration;

Table 5: *Income, Metropolitan Population, and Average Wages as Determinants of Public Policy*

Type of Policy	Determinants of Expenditure[a]			
	Fiscal Capacity: Income	Demand: Metropolitan Population	Cost of Supply: Average Wages	Multiple R
Redistributive				
Old-age assistance	.71**	−.18	−.16	.52
Aid to dependent children	1.04**	−.30**	−.24*	.76
Unemployment benefits	.82	.06	−.08	.81
Welfare expenditures	.69**	.13	−.27*	.64
Health and hospitals	.25	.20	−.04	.37
Educational	.71**	−.28**	.30**	.82
Allocational				
Police	.57**	.28*	−.05	.74
Fire	.67**	.30**	−.23*	.77
Developmental				
Highways	.47**	−.93**	.31**	.84

Source: Peterson 1979a.
[a]See note to Table 4.

what is relevant to the argument presented in this discussion is whether federal aid changes the relationships between expenditures and the fiscal capacity, demand, and supply factors. Table 6 reveals that the federal impact on these relationships is minimal. Fiscal capacity remains the primary determinant of redistributive expenditures; demand-supply variables remain the most important determinant of developmental expenditures; and allocational policies remain affected by both fiscal capacity and demand-supply factors. Except for health policy, the needs of minorities have no significant effect on expenditure levels.

Finally, the pattern of relationships changes only slightly when the southern (Confederate) states are deleted from the analysis. We do not know any particularly good reason for deleting the South from the analysis; it is part of the market economy of the United States and is subject to the same external pressures as any other region. Cultural differences are not so great that entirely different patterns of interaction among variables are to be expected. But for those who insist that interstate comparisons take into account the distinctiveness of the South, Table 7 reports the findings for the 39 nonsouthern states only. When the table is compared with Table 5, it will be noticed that the beta coefficients in the two tables are very similar. Redistributive policies continue to be mostly a function of a state's fiscal capacity, the developmental policy (highways) remains more a function of the nonmetropolitan character of the state than of any other factor, and allocational policies are still influenced by both fiscal capacity and demand-supply factors.

REVIEW OF RELATED STUDIES

Although this typology has not previously been used to analyze state and local finance, my findings are consistent with a good deal of previous, largely atheoretical research. Although different statistical techniques are applied and different samples are used for testing the data, and even though methodological problems abound, the results are surprisingly consistent with mine.[6] Consider first Fisher's study of state and local government expenditures in 1960, which reports beta coefficients for seven independent variables that account for expenditures in a number of policy areas.[7] In Table 8, I present the specific findings from his analysis which best test the hypotheses we have presented. First, note the moderate correlations between indicators of fiscal capacity and expenditures for redistributive government functions,

Table 6: *Federal Aid and Local Expenditure*

	Determinants of Expenditure[a]				
Type of Policy	Federal Aid	Fiscal Capacity: Income	Demand-Supply: Metropolitan Population	Need but No Demand: Percent Black	Multiple R
Redistributive					
Welfare expenditures	.67**	.62**	.02	−.08	.89
Health and hospitals	−.06	.47**	.03	.38**	.49
Educational	.19*	.88**	−.37**	−.14	.81
Allocational					
Police	.15	.54**	.33*	.08	.76
Fire	.12	.38**	.47**	−.10	.76
Developmental					
Highways	.65**	.34**	−.47**	.02	.94

Source: Peterson 1979a.
[a]See note to Table 4.

and then note the weak relationships between expenditures and population density, a measure of the cost of supplying these goods. From an egalitarian perspective, it might be said that education and health care are most badly needed in those states where adult educational attainments are low. Yet, since this need is unlikely to be translated into an effective demand for the product, these services are least provided where they are most needed. Second, expenditures for two types of allocational policies—police and fire—are moderately correlated with measures both of fiscal capacity and of demand and supply. Only sanitation expenditures are considerably more a function of fiscal capacity than of demand-supply variables. With this exception, the pattern of allocational expenditures is quite consistent with what I found in my own analysis. Finally, the relationship between economic demand and level of expenditure is particularly strong for the one example of a developmental policy included in the Fisher study. For the most relevant measure of economic demand—density—the correlation coefficient attains a high negative value of .62. Although some relationship between fiscal capacity and expenditure also exists, it is comparatively modest.

Consider next the relevant findings from Dye's massive study of state and local expenditures given in Table 9.[8] Dye presents data for only redistributive and developmental policies, and only simple correlation coefficients were reported, making it difficult to identify the separate effects of fiscal capacity and demand-supply variables. But, within these limitations the contrasts between redistributive and developmental policies are dramatic. Whereas his indicator of fiscal capacity is always strongly associated with redistributive expenditures, it is not at all correlated with expenditures for highways. Also, it is quite apparent that education, welfare, and health expenditures are not concentrated in states where, from an egalitarian perspective, there might seem to be the greatest need. In fact, the opposite pattern obtains. On the other hand, for the developmental policy arena, there is a strong relationship between need for a policy and the level of expenditures. The less densely populated, less urban areas spend more monies per capita on roads and highways. In this case, need becomes translated into effective demand. Dye himself noticed these differences between the redistributive and developmental policy arenas. "The states which spend more on highways," he says, "do so by digging deeper into state treasuries and into personal incomes. This is in contrast to the states which spend more on education and welfare; we have found that these states are wealthier and able to spend more on these functions without using a larger share of personal income to do so."[9]

Dye's research has spawned a considerable body of statistically more sophisticated studies on the determinants of state and local expenditures. For the most part, these studies have concentrated on the relative

Table 7: *Determinants of Public Policy in Nonsouthern States*

	Determinants of Expenditure[a]				
		Demand-Supply			
Type of Policy	Fiscal Capacity: Income	Metropolitan Population	Nonagricultural Employment	Need but No Demand: Percent Black	Multiple R
Redistributive					
Old–age assistance	.54**	–.17	.09	–.14	.52
Aid to dependent children	.58**	–.01	.01	–.25	.59
Unemployment benefits	.61**	.29	–.07	–.08	.76
Welfare expenditures	.13	.28	.32	–.21	.62
Health and hospitals	.27	–.18	.39*	.18	.55
Educational	.98**	–.28	–.32*	.04	.70
Allocational					
Police	.39*	.13	.24	.09	.72
Fire	.17	.31*	.42**	–.17	.76
Developmental					
Highways	.72**	–1.04**	–.10	–.01	.84

Source: Peterson 1979a.
[a] See note to Table 4.

importance of environmental as opposed to political variables. But the studies do document, if only in passing, the differential characteristics of redistributive and developmental policies. The most extensive documentation exists on redistributive policies, which tend to attract the interest of political scientists. Here the studies convincingly demonstrate (by a variety of statistical techniques) the continuing significance of a state's fiscal base for its commitments to redistribution. Cnudde and McCrone, for example, demonstrate that with but one exception the inclusion of income in a regression analysis significantly reduces the causal power of apparently important political variables.[10] On the other hand, they show that the two demand and supply indicators—urbanization and percentage not employed in agricultural occupations—do not have the same effect on these redistributive policies.[11]

More recently, Tompkins has included both economic and political variables in a complex analysis that attempts to show the political path by which economic variables explain welfare policy.[12] Once again, the one economic variable whose explanatory power persisted throughout his analysis of this redistributive program was the best indicator of the fiscal capacity of the state—its per capita income.

It is a factor analysis by Sharkansky and Hoffbert that produces the most suggestive set of findings.[13] In an attempt to differentiate among different kinds of public policies, they empirically distinguished two factors: "welfare and education" and "highways and natural resources." Without much distortion, the two factors could be just as easily relabeled "redistributive" and "developmental," for the first was heavily loaded with indicators of a state's commitment to high welfare payments to its poor, and the second with indicators of a state's commitment to build roads and develop its natural resources. Of greatest interest in this context are the simple correlations between two environmental factors that the analysts labeled "affluence" and "industrialization."[14] The first is an excellent measure of a state's fiscal capacity, and the second a good inverse measure of the demand for roads and other assets disproportionately utilized in rural areas. The simple correlations among the four items are given in Table 10. Here we can see that both affluence and industrialization are correlated with both redistributive and developmental policies. However, fiscal capacity is by far the more important correlate of redistributive policies, and the demand factor the more crucial determinant of expenditures for highways and natural resources.

Table 8: *Determinants of State and Local Expenditure—the Fisher Study*

	Determinants of Expenditure				
	Fiscal Capacity		**Demand-Supply**		**Need but No Demand:**
Type of Policy	Income	Tax Yield[a]	Density	Urbanization	**Education**
Redistributive					
Health and hospitals	.38	.41	.22	...	...
Educational					
Schools	.56	.29	...	...	...
Allocational					
Police	.40	...	.36	.25	.35
Fire	.47	...	.34	.36	...
Sanitation	.98	...	...	...	.50
Developmental					
Highways	.30	.31	−.62	−.22	...

Source: Fisher 1964, Table 2.
Note: Table gives beta coefficients generated by a seven-variable regression analysis. Correlation coefficient not given, if statistically insignificant.
[a] The expected tax yield from a standard pattern of taxation applied to all states.

Table 9: *Determinants of State and Local Expenditure—the Dye Study*

	Determinants of Expenditure			
	Fiscal Capacity: Income	**Demand-Supply**		**Need but No Demand: Education**
Type of Policy		Industrialization	Urbanization	
Redistributive				
Unemployment compensation	.80	.30	.55	.67
Aid to dependent children	.74	.26	.51	.55
General assistance	.76	.39	.58	.43
Health expenditure	.56	.39	.45	.42
Educational	.83	.36	.51	.59
Developmental				
Highways	.02	−.51	−.37	.04

Source: Dye 1966, tables IV-2, V-5, and VI-2.
Note: Table gives simple coefficients of correlation.

Table 10: *Determinants of State and Local Expenditure—the Sharkansky-Hofferbert Study*

	Determinants of Expenditure	
Type of Policy	**Fiscal Capacity (affluence)**	**Demand (industrialization)**
Redistributive		
Welfare, education	.69	.37
Productive		
Highways, natural resources	.43	−.69

Source: Sharkansky and Hofferbert 1969, Table 8.
Note: Table gives simple coefficients of correlation (Pearson's R).

Besides these statewide analyses, examinations of local government finance contain numerous findings that bear upon the distinctions among the three policy arenas that I have drawn. In general the findings are quite consistent with those that have been reported in the text.

CONCLUSIONS

Redistributive policies differ from developmental policies, while allocational policies share some of the characteristics of each. Redistributive policies are not easily implemented by local governments. To the extent that they are promulgated, they are located in areas where there appears to be the least need for them. Only where the fiscal base of a community is relatively substantial can policies of benefit to minorities and the poor be implemented. Because the greater tax base in the prosperous communities allows greater fiscal resources to local governments at no greater a rate of taxation, these communities can provide for some degree of redistribution. But in less advantaged communities, where low-income people are probably found in greater abundance, the level of redistributive programs must be held to a bare minimum. The great irony of redistribution at the local level is that it occurs most where the poor are relatively scarce, and vice versa.

Developmental policies are relatively free from these fiscal constraints. Where there is a need for the policy, that need can be met by the less as well as the more prosperous communities. In fulfilling the need, the community enhances its own economic prosperity, thereby strengthening its capacity to provide other services. To some extent the same can be said of allocational policies, and it is in these two arenas that local governments are particularly active.

For all three policy arenas the level of fiscal support is strongly influenced by factors which in the short run are quite beyond the realm of local politics. The strong relationships between expenditures, fiscal capacity, economic demand, and the cost of supplying services are fully apparent even when no attention is paid to the internal political processes of the city. A great deal can be said about local public policy without considering any variations in the recruitment of elected officials, the strength of political parties, the degree of organized group activity, or the level of turnout in local elections. Powerful forces external to the city carry great weight in local policy-making.

I thus find myself in some agreement with Thomas Dye, whose work on public policy has emphasized the environmental rather than the political determinants of public policy.[15] Yet the debate which Dye's work has spawned is artificial, drawing a false dichotomy between the economic and the political, as if events in the complex political economies of our cities and states can be neatly inserted into the arbitrary pigeonholes that divide the social sciences. The decisions taken by local governments in the developmental, redistributive, and allocational arenas are political decisions taken by local government officials. Yet these men and women operate within certain constraints. Uppermost in their minds must be the long-term economic welfare of their community. Although exceptions can be found, in the aggregate they are sane, reasonable, prudent individuals with a sense of the limits on what is possible. To say that environments constrain what these officials do hardly means that politics is absent.

Notes

1. Cf. Lowi 1964.
2. Levy et al. 1974, chapter 4.
3. Ostrom et al. 1973.
4. This is possible because I have a "unitary" model of state-local policymaking processes. This is made explicit in Peterson 1979.
5. Peterson 1979.
6. One of several difficulties with which the expenditure literature has wrestled is the problem of multicollinearity. When independent variables are correlated with one another, it is difficult to distinguish their separate influences. In the research reported in the text, I have given as much attention to simple correlation analysis as to multiple correlation analysis, I have preferred findings from regression analyses where fewer rather than more independent variables have been introduced, and I have given special weight to research where analysts have taken special pains to reduce problems of multicollinearity. Such selectivity is especially important in an area of research where so little attention has been given to developing a theoretically defensible rationale for the selection of independent variables and where scholars, taking advantage of high-speed computers, run "barefoot" through the data.
7. Fisher 1964.
8. Dye 1966.
9. Ibid., 169.
10. Cnudde and McCrone 1969.
11. Ibid., 864.
12. Tompkins 1975.
13. Sharkansky and Hofferbert 1969.

14. We are using the simple, not the partial, correlations that Sharkansky and Hofferbert provide on p. 877 because the partial correlations control for political variables. Sharkansky himself has elsewhere pointed out that these are theoretically inappropriate variables to use in an analysis of the combined expenditures of state and local governments.
15. Dye 1966.

References

Cnudde, C.F., and D.J. McCrone. 1969. Party competition and welfare policies in the American states. *American Political Science Review* 63: 858-66.

Dye, T.R. 1966. *Politics, economics, and the public: Policy outcomes in the American states*. Chicago: Rand McNally.

Fisher, G. W. 1964. Interstate variation in state and local government expenditure. *National Tax Journal* 17: 57-74.

Levy, F.; A.J. Meltsner; and A. Wildavsky. 1974. *Urban outcomes: Schools, streets, and libraries*. Berkeley and Los Angeles: University of California Press.

Lowi, T. 1964. American business, public policy, case studies, and political theory. *World Politics* 16: 677-715.

Ostrom, E.; W. Baugh; R. Guarasci; R. Parks; and G. Whitaker. 1973. *Community organization and the provision of public services*. Beverly Hills, Calif.: Sage.

Peterson, P.E. 1979. A unitary model of local taxation and expenditure policies in the United States. *British Journal of Political Science* 9: 281-314.

Sharkansky, I., and R.I. Hofferbert. 1969. Dimensions of state politics, economics, and public policy. *American Political Science Review* 63: 867-79.

Tompkins, G.L. 1975. A causal model of state welfare expenditures. *Journal of Politics* 37: 392-416.

Economic Base: What Our Jobs Are Tied To

Eva C. Galambos and Arthur F. Schreiber

The most important characteristic distinguishing the local economy from the national economy is the degree of openness of the local economy. A local economy is less self-sufficient than the national economy is; in other words, a local economy is more specialized in terms of what its industries produce. Thus, the local economy will sell a larger portion of its total production to buyers outside of its boundaries (exports); likewise, the local economy will buy a greater portion of its goods and services from outside its boundaries (imports). The greater the proportion of exports and imports, the more open the economy; the smaller the geographic area of the local economy, the more open it is likely to be.

Economic base analysis concentrates on the importance of exports to the local economy. A local area has little influence on the demand for the goods and services it exports; such export demand is determined outside the local area by economic conditions in the region and the entire nation. Sales to buyers outside of the local economy generate labor and business income. Some of this income from export activity is spent in the local area on additional purchases of locally produced goods and services, thereby generating still more income or employment within the local area. In other words, if income from export sales increases, the total income of the local economy will increase by an even greater amount—it will be multiplied.

In this article, the local economy is divided into two parts: (1) export activity (called the economic base) and (2) all other local economic activity. Methods are presented for determining the size and composition of the economic base; the application of these results for local economic development and planning is also discussed.

WHAT IS THE ECONOMIC BASE?

The underlying theory of economic base is that exports are the moving force that determines the total level of local economic activity. As indicated in the introduction, income from export activity is determined mainly outside of the local economy; this export income will be spent principally on additional purchases of locally produced goods and services, generating a multiplier effect. For example, a local area has a factory that produces military vehicles; if an increase in orders is received, export activity increases. Producing military vehicles is obviously an export activity; these vehicles will be purchased by the U.S. government and not by local business firms or citizens. As a result of the increased export orders, retail merchants and other local business firms will enjoy higher sales generated by added employees engaged in producing military vehicles. The expanded payrolls will be spent on basic living items such as food, clothing, and housing. Thus, $10 million of additional export sales may result in a $30 million expansion of total local sales, the export sales having a threefold multiplier effect.

Reprinted from *Making Sense Out of Dollars: Economic Analysis for Local Government* (Washington, D.C.: National League of Cities, 1978), 13-25. Research and publication funded by Office of Policy Development and Research, U.S. Department of Housing and Urban Development.

The export activities of the local economy are called the economic base. The remainder of local economic activity, nonexport activities, includes all locally produced goods and services that are consumed or purchased within the local area; these are called nonbasic. Thus, the total economic activity in the local area is classified as either basic or nonbasic. The basic activity determines the level of nonbasic and, therefore, the level of total economic activity.

How are we to measure the basic and nonbasic activities of the local economy? There are three possible approaches. One would be the dollar value of all goods and services produced. Another would be the quantities of various goods and services produced. The third method is to measure economic activity in terms of employment. Because employment data are more readily available for local areas than are dollar or production statistics, employment is used to measure economic activity in the discussion that follows. Thus, the size of the economic base and of the total local economy is measured by employment.

HOW IS THE ECONOMIC BASE USED?

Unstable growth in the local economy is undesirable, subjecting the community to the problems associated with major booms and busts in employment and income. Rapid but temporary economic growth may result in overcrowded schools and other public facilities, necessitating large capital expenditures for new roads, water and sewer line expansions, more schools, and other capital projects. A sharp decline in the local economy can result in declining tax revenues at the same time that demands for welfare-related services are increasing. Thus, rapid growth or decline presents problems for local government. A local economy that grows at a moderate rate is usually preferred to one that fluctuates seriously.

Local decision makers have no control over a general economic decline or recession in the national economy. They may, however, lessen the local impact of national economic conditions if they are able to diversify the local economic base. If the economic base is narrow by being heavily tied to one or two industries, the level of local economic activity will be largely determined by swings in these industries; however, if the sources of export employment are diversified, the local economy does not have "all of its eggs in one basket." In such a case, the fortunes of one or two industries will not dictate the fortunes of the local economy to such a great extent. Determining the economic base, and then the extent to which total export employment is spread among various industries, helps in evaluating the degree of instability the local area may encounter. A narrow economic base signals local planners to seek additional export employment in industries not included in the present economic base.

Economic base analysis is also useful for projecting the effects of a new industry on the total local economy. Total employment divided by export employment gives the export employment multiplier referred to above. This multiplier provides local planners with a rough idea of the increase in total local employment that would result from an increase in export employment.

Most communities are already aware of the obvious parts of their economic base, such as the local steel mill or coal mine. But there are many small industries which, when closely examined through the techniques presented here, will also be identified as part of the economic base. An economic development strategy might be designed around these less obvious industries comprising the local economic base.

HOW DO YOU DETERMINE THE ECONOMIC BASE?

When the economic base is determined by using employment as the measure of economic activity, total employment of the local economy must be divided into basic (export) and nonbasic (nonexport) categories. Local employment data are not normally listed separately for each business firm, but rather by industry or in groupings of individual firms producing similar products. This section discusses the most frequently used industrial classification scheme and the methods of dividing employment by industries into two categories: basic and nonbasic employment.

Industry Classifications

Published employment statistics for local areas usually follow the classification scheme of the *Standard Industrial Classification (SIC) Manual*.[1] The SIC Manual divides industries into groups designated by SIC codes. Each establishment is assigned a four-digit industry code on the basis of its major activity in terms of products handled or services rendered. SIC codes provide four levels of detail. The first digit represents the following broad industry groups:

- Agriculture, forestry, and fisheries
- Mining
- Construction
- Manufacturing
- Transportation, communication, electric, gas, and sanitary services
- Wholesale trade
- Retail trade
- Finance, insurance, and real estate
- Services
- Government

Each industry group is then divided into so-called two-digit categories, and these are further subdivided into three- and four-digit categories. An example of each of these four levels of detail is shown in Table 1. For each level of industry detail, 19X3 employment is shown for the United States as a whole and for an actual Midwestern SMSA local area with a 19X0 population of approximately 130,000. This local area will be referred to as "Midwestern SMSA" throughout the example in this article to illustrate the technique of economic base analysis.

Determining Export Employment

Once available data on local employment by industry are obtained, employment in each industry is classified as employment for the production of exports or of nonexports. What methods are available to make these classifications? If local staff conducting the economic base study had intimate knowledge of how much each local industry sells within or outside the local area, they could split employment in each industry into export and nonexport categories. In a very small local area, there might be a group of persons having the personal knowledge to arrive at a relatively accurate classification of export and nonexport employment. In most cases, however, there are too many employers in a local area for any small group of persons to possess the required knowledge.

The most direct method for determining export employment would be to conduct market surveys of all employers, or of a carefully selected sample, through personal interviews with employers or mail questionnaires. Surveys to determine employers' export and nonexport production or sales (and resulting employment) are time consuming and costly. In addition, firms do not usually maintain records that will quickly reveal the amount of their exports from a local area. Thus, indirect methods are usually employed.

As a first step in using indirect methods, the employment of all local employers or industries that are obviously engaged solely in export production are classified as export employment. For example, the Midwestern SMSA contains a manufacturer of large electrical transformers (SIC Code 3612). It is highly unlikely that any of these transformers are for local use. Accordingly, all such employment would be classified as export employment of the local economy. Similarly, there may be some employment that is obviously totally nonexport, such as most city or county government employment.

Table 1: *The Four Levels of Detail Provided by the Standard Industrial Classification (SIC) Manual*

		19X3 Employment	
SIC Code	Description	United States	Midwestern SMSA
(Industry Group)	Manufacturing	19,768,681	17,179
20	Food and Kindred Products	1,526,231	1,575
201	Meat Products	304,944	D[a]
2011	Meat Packing Plants	165,975	D
2013	Sausage and Other Prepared Meats	50,373	
2015	Poultry Dressing Plants	88,195	
202	Dairy Products	181,530	183
2021	Creamery Butter	5,732	
2022	Cheese, Natural and Processed	21,965	
2023	Condensed and Evaporated Milk	9,588	
2024	Ice Cream and Frozen Desserts	19,742	
2026	Fluid Milk	124,319	D

Source of Employment Data: U.S. Bureau of the Census, *County Business Patterns, 1973* (Washington, D.C.: Government Printing Office, 1974) United States Volume (CBP-73-1), 15 and appropriate state volume.

[a] In accordance with federal disclosure laws, data that disclose the operations of an individual employer are not published As a result, data are not shown separately for any industry that does not have at least 100 employees or 10 establishments in the reporting area (county, in this case).

The remaining employment in the local area cannot be readily identified as production of goods and services that are sold completely in local markets or completely exported. For example, in Table 1, regarding the 183 employees engaged in producing dairy products in the Midwestern SMSA, some of their milk and other dairy products will be sold in grocery stores within the Midwestern SMSA and some will be exported to grocery stores outside of the county. For the majority of industries that are not completely export or nonexport, location quotients (discussed below) are frequently used as the indirect method for classifying export and nonexport employment.

Using Location Quotients to Estimate the Economic Base

Location quotients are used in Table 2 to obtain an estimate of export employment for the Midwestern SMSA in 19X3. For the sake of brevity in this example, employment is shown only at the two-digit SIC level. In practice, however, the most detailed data should be used; in many cases these are available at the three- and four-digit SIC levels as discussed in the next section.

If the Midwestern SMSA were self-sufficient in producing goods and services in each two-digit industry, neither exporting nor importing them, how much local employment would you expect in each industry? One reasonable answer is the same percentage in each industry locally relative to total local employment as that industry comprises of national employment. In other words, if local employment in a specific industry were 5 percent, and nationally this industry also accounted for 5 percent of total employment, we could assume the local economy is neither importing nor exporting.

When a local industry has a greater percentage of total local employment than is true for the nation, the industry is exporting. When the local industry has a lower percentage than is true for the nation, it is importing. The location quotient is the ratio of the local industry's actual percentage of total local employment to the percentage of that industry nationally. A location quotient greater than one indicates export employment. These concepts are discussed below with reference to the 19X3 employment data in Table 2, which are obtained from *County Business Patterns*.

U.S. employment by two-digit SIC industries is shown in column 1, Table 2, and totals 61,275,000. In column 2, employment in each industry nationally is shown as a percentage of the total 61,275,000. For the Midwestern SMSA, employment in each industry is shown in column 3, and totals 39,353; the percentage of local employment by industry relative to the 39,353 total employment is shown in column 4.

For the United States, SIC 20 (food and kindred products manufacturing) represents 2.49 percent of U.S. total employment. For the Midwestern SMSA, this industry comprises 4 percent of local employment. The location quotient for SIC 20 in the Midwestern SMSA is:

$$\frac{4\%}{2.49\%} = 1.61$$

Because the location quotient is greater than one, SIC 20 in the Midwestern SMSA is an export industry.

How much of the Midwestern SMSA's SIC 20 employment is for export? The excess of 4 percent over 2.49 percent represents export employment. In column 5, local requirements are shown; these equal what local employment would be if the national percentage applied locally. If 2.49 percent of the Midwestern SMSA's total employment of 39,353 were employed in SIC 20, the industry would have 980 workers. In reality it has 1,575, as shown in column 3. The excess of 1,575 over 980 (or 595) is the export employment shown in column 6 for the food and kindred products manufacturing industry in this local area.

The same procedure as discussed for SIC 20 is used to compute export employment for the Midwestern SMSA in 19X3 for all other industries in Table 2. The resulting export employment is shown in column 6. When local employment is less than the employment estimated to meet local requirements, the number in column 6 is negative; this indicates that the local area is a net importer for that industry. In summary, the steps for estimating export employment are:

a. Calculate the percentage that employment in each industry for the nation is of total employment in the United States (as shown in column 2, Table 2).

Table 2: *Export Employment Computed from Location Quotients: Midwestern SMSA, 19X3*

Employment Category		U. S. Employment		Midwestern SMSA Employment		(5) Midwest, SMSA Employment for Local Requirements (col. 2 × 39,353)	(6) Excess Employment= Export or (deficit) (col. 3 − col. 5)
SIC Code	Description	(1) Amount (thousands)	(2) Percentage of Total	(3) Amount	(4) Percentage of Total		
	CONTRACT CONSTRUCTION						
15	General Building Contractors	1,099	1.79	956	2.43	704	252
17	Special Trade Contractors	1,973	3.22	773	1.96	1,267	(494)
	All Other	660	1.08	1,051	2.67	425	626
	MANUFACTURING						
20	Food and Kindred Products	1,526	2.49	1,575	4.00	980	595
25	Furniture and Fixtures	510	.83	615	1.56	327	288
26	Paper and Allied Products	650	1.06	423	1.07	417	6
27	Printing and Publishing	1,091	1.78	450	1.14	700	(250)
33	Primary Metal Industries	1,231	2.01	2,260	5.74	791	1,469
34	Fabricated Metal Products	1,414	2.31	1,394	3.54	909	485
35	Machinery, Except Electrical	1,949	3.18	845	2.15	1,251	(406)
	All Other	11,397	18.60	9,617	24.44	7,320	2,297
	TRANSPORTATION AND UTILITIES						
42	Trucking and Warehousing	1,135	1.85	742	1.89	728	14
49	Electric, Gas, and Sanitary	663	1.08	562	1.43	425	137
	All Other	2,220	3.62	617	1.57	1,425	(808)
	WHOLESALE TRADE						
	RETAIL TRADE	4,224	6.89	1,496	3.80	2,711	(1,215)
52	Building Materials and Farm Equipment	523	.85	461	1.17	335	126
53	General Merchandise	2,320	3.79	1,352	3.44	1,491	(139)
54	Food Stores	1,773	2.89	1,018	2.59	1,137	(119)
55	Auto Dealers and Service Stations	1,829	2.98	1,180	3.00	1,173	7
56	Apparel and Accessory Stores	803	1.32	522	1.33	519	3
58	Eating and Drinking Places	2,894	4.72	2,262	5.75	1,857	405
	All Other	2,236	3.65	1,796	4.56	1,436	360
	FINANCE, INSURANCE, AND REAL ESTATE SERVICES	4,138	6.75	1,535	3.90	2,656	(1,121)
80	Medical and Other Health Services	3,425	5.59	2,315	5.88	2,200	115
	All Other	8,406	13.72	3,191	8.11	5,399	(2,208)
	ALL OTHER EMPLOYMENT	1,186	1.94	345	.88	763	(418)
	Total Employment	61,275	100.00%	39,353	100.00%		

b. Multiply the percentages obtained in (a) by total employment in the local area to obtain what local employment would be in each industry if it followed the national patterns (as shown in column 5, Table 2).

c. Subtract the estimated employment for local requirements obtained in (b) from the actual employment in each local industry (column 3, Table 2). If the result (shown in column 6, Table 2) is positive, the remainder equals export employment; if the result is negative, the local area is a net importer for that industry.

d. To obtain the total export employment (economic base) for the local area, sum up all positive export employment as obtained in (c).

Table 2 shows the computations of export employment for 19X3 for the Midwestern SMSA for two-digit SIC industries. Table 3 shows total local employment and export employment for 19X3 as taken from Table 2. Table 3 also shows total local employment and export employment for 19Y6, computed by the same methods as shown in Table 2, using 19Y6 employment data.

WHERE DO YOU OBTAIN THE EMPLOYMENT DATA?

The employment data for the Midwestern SMSA shown in Tables 1, 2, and 3 are from the U.S. Bureau of Census publication, *County Business Patterns,* which is published annually.[2] One volume gives total U.S. employment data and a separate volume for each state shows employment by counties and SMSAs. The employment data pertain to mid-March of each year.

There are two basic problems with *County Business Patterns* data: (1) not all employment is included and (2) local employment data for the most detailed SIC code industrial category may not be given. These two problems, and methods of dealing with them, are discussed below.

Employment Data Not Included

County Business Patterns includes only data for employment covered by social security, derived from employers' quarterly payroll tax returns. Thus, the following types of employees are excluded: government employees, self-employed persons, farm workers, and domestic service workers. In 19X3, *County Business Patterns* employment data accounted for about 75 percent of total U.S. employment. For urban counties and SMSAs, the major exclusion is government employment. Government agencies should be able to provide employment data for local, state, and federal government employment to supplement the employment data contained in Tables 2 and 3.

Undisclosed Employment Data

Tables 2 and 3 compute the Midwestern SMSA economic base using two-digit SIC code employment data. This was done to keep the tables short. *County Business Patterns* contains three- and four-digit employment data, and in practice the economic base should be computed on the basis of the most detailed information available. Although three- and four-digit employment detail is available for many industries in the Midwestern SMSA in 19X3, the data become more incomplete as industry detail becomes finer, as indicated in Table 1 for SIC 20. For SIC 20, food and kindred products, three-digit employment is available for code 202 (dairy products). However, employment in the Midwestern SMSA is not shown for code 201 (meat products), nor for any of the four-digit codes shown in Table 1. The symbol "D" in Table 1, used with a detailed three- or four-digit code, means that disclosure rules prevent publication of data that would reveal individual employer statistics.

Employment for SIC codes with a "D" designation may still be estimated, however, by using the number of reporting establishments in the industry and the distribution of these establishments by employment-size class. Even when total employment is not given for an SIC marked by "D," the number of reporting establishments and their employment-size class are published. Although Table 1 does not disclose Midwestern SMSA employment for SIC 201 and 2011, *County Business Patterns* does show that the 201 (meat products) industry in the Midwestern SMSA is comprised of two establishments, one with 8 to 19 employees, and the other with 500 or more employees. *County Business Patterns* also reveals that there is only one establishment under code 2011 (meat packing plants) and that this establishment has 500 or more employees. From this information, we can infer that SIC 201 employment in the Midwestern SMSA is comprised of one meat packing plant

Table 3: *Economic Base Computed from Location Quotients: Midwestern SMSA, 19Y6 and 19X3*

Employment Category		Total Employment		Export Employment	
SIC Code	Description	19Y6	19X3	19Y6	19X3
	CONTRACT CONSTRUCTION				
15	General Building Contractors	747	956	95	252
17	Special Trade Contractors	830	773		
	All Other	516	1,051	114	626
	MANUFACTURING				
20	Food and Kindred Products	1,803	1,575	711	595
25	Furniture and Fixtures	495	615	192	288
26	Paper and Allied Products	303	423		6
27	Printing and Publishing	427	450		
33	Primary Metal Industries	1,822	2,260	941	1,469
34	Fabricated Metal Products	1,345	1,394	496	485
35	Machinery, Except Electrical	1,111	845		
	All Other	10,281	9,617	2,750	2,297
	TRANSPORTATION AND UTILITIES				
42	Trucking and Warehousing	465	742		14
49	Electric, Gas, and Sanitary	487	562	71	137
	All Other	826	617		
	WHOLESALE TRADE / RETAIL TRADE	1,255	1,496		
52	Building Materials and Farm Equipment	392	461	89	126
53	General Merchandise	1,097	1,352		
54	Food Stores	904	1,018		
55	Auto Dealers and Service Stations	1,050	1,180	46	7
56	Apparel and Accessory Stores	375	522		3
58	Eating and Drinking Places	1,435	2,262	65	405
	All Other	1,508	1,796	317	360
	FINANCE, INSURANCE, AND REAL ESTATE SERVICES	1,364	1,535		
80	Medical and Other Health Services	1,397	2,315	115	
	All Other	2,682	3,191		
	ALL OTHER EMPLOYMENT	309	345		
	Total Employment	35,226	39,353	5,887	7,185

with at least 500 employees, and one other firm with 8 to 19 workers. More accurate information on employment in the local meat products industry might be obtained through the voluntary cooperation of the business firm, or from a local Chamber of Commerce directory.

The number of Midwestern SMSA industries, by SIC levels, for which employment is *not* shown in the 19X3 *County Business Patterns* because of disclosure rules is shown in the last column of Exhibit 1.

Because of the missing data, the economic base information in Tables 2 and 3 for the Midwestern SMSA is incomplete. When detail is not available by two-digit SIC code, Tables 2 and 3 show an "all other" employment category under each industry group. Employment in the "all other" categories is

Exhibit 1

	Number of Industries		
SIC Level	Total	Employment Data Given	Employment Data Not Given Because of Disclosure Rules
Industry groups	9	9	0
Two-digit SIC codes	41	35	6
Three-digit SIC codes	84	65	19
Four-digit SIC codes	38	16	22

obtained by subtracting employment in the two-digit SIC codes that are known from total employment in the relevant industry group. For example, employment in 19X3 for the contract construction industry group is 2,780. Subtracting employment in SIC codes 15 and 17 (956 + 773) leaves a remainder of 1,051 as "all other" employment in this industry group.

Note that the amount of employment assigned to the "all other" category under manufacturing is quite large. The Midwestern SMSA has four large firms (with more than 500 employees each) under SIC codes 36 (electrical equipment and supplies) and 37 (transportation equipment) for which disclosure rules prevented publication of employment statistics. Therefore, employment in SIC codes 36 and 37 is thrown into the "all other" category. This could be avoided, of course, by direct contacts with these employers. With data from these companies, export employment could be computed for SIC codes 36 and 37.

In summary, the economic base of the local economy can be determined for any year for which adequate data are available. If the health of the local community is to be continuously monitored, however, the economic base of the local economy should be analyzed on a periodic basis, perhaps, every one or two years. In order to make meaningful comparisons of changes in the economic base between years, a consistent source of data and consistent methods of computing the economic base are required. *County Business Patterns* is the most practical source of basic information for computing the economic base on a regular cycle because it is published annually and is readily obtainable. Employment information that is not covered or disclosed by *County Business Patterns* must be obtained locally.

WHAT DO THE RESULTS MEAN?

The results of computing the economic base of the Midwestern SMSA shown in Table 3 can be used to determine the extent to which total export employment is spread among various industries and whether the economic base is becoming more diversified over time or more widely spread among industries. As indicated in the second section, a broad economic base is usually preferred to a narrow one, so that the level of local economic activity is not largely dependent on the fortunes of only one or two industries. Table 3 also provides information on the approximate size of the employment multiplier, giving a rough idea of the impact on the local economy of the change in total employment that would result from a change in export employment. A discussion of these uses of the results follows.

Diversification of the Economic Base

Calculation of the location quotients for 19Y6 and 19X3 shown in Table 3 indicates that the economic base for the Midwestern SMSA has changed over this seven-year period, becoming more diversified in 19X3 than it was in 19Y6. Several measures can be obtained from Table 3 to evaluate whether diversification in the Midwestern SMSA has increased:

a. Compare the amount of export activity in the major local industries over time. For example, as shown in Exhibit 2, the three largest sources of export employment in the SMSA in 19Y6 accounted for approximately 75 percent of export employment in all local industries. This was reduced to about 61 percent by 19X3.

b. Compare over time the number of distinct local industries that produce exports. There were 12 separate industries in 19Y6 in Table 3 for which export employment is shown. By 19X3 diversification increased, with 16 industries showing exports. (The same industry classifications are used in both years.)

c. Compare for each industry group the change in the total percentage of export employment over time. The percentages shown in Exhibit 3 are obtained by adding the export employment percentage for each two-digit industry within the relevant industry group in Table 3.

As the above comparison indicates, manufacturing export employment became less important, while the other four sources of export employment increased, meaning that the economic base has become more diversified.

Each of these three measures, as well as others that could be devised, indicates that the economic base of the Midwestern SMSA became more diversified over this seven-year period. These conclusions are based on the limited data contained in Tables 2 and 3, however. As pointed out before, the actual computation of the economic base would use all of the two-, three-, and four-digit data contained in *County Business Patterns,* as well as in government agency and other local data sources. Accordingly, a much more detailed breakdown of the Midwestern SMSA's economic base and its changes over time would be obtained. For continuous monitoring of the health of the local economy, these data can be obtained regularly for annual revisions of the economic base computations.

The Export Employment Multiplier

The total local employment and total export employment numbers shown in Table 3 are frequently used to form an export employment multiplier, as shown in Exhibit 4.

The multipliers for these two years indicate that total employment is five to six times as large as estimated export employment in Table 3. The export employment multiplier provides local planners with a rough idea of the impact on the local economy of total employment changes that would result from a change in export employment. In other words, an export multiplier of five indicates that if export employment increases by 100, total local employment is likely to increase by about 500. Similarly, a decrease in export employment of 100 jobs would likely result in a reduction in total local employment of about 500 jobs.

The multiplier derived from one year's employment data should be used with caution. A multiplier based on employment data and computed from location quotients may differ significantly from one year to another. Some changes may reflect spurious dif-

Exhibit 2

Employment Category	Percentage of Total Export Employment	
	19Y6	19X3
All other manufacturing	46.71%	31.97%
Food and kindred products	12.08	8.28
Primary metal industries	15.98	20.45
Total	74.77%	60.70%

Exhibit 3

Industry Group	Percentage of Total Export Employment	
	19Y6	19X3
Contract construction	3.55%	12.22%
Manufacturing	86.46	71.54
Transportation and utilities	1.21	2.10
Retail trade	8.78	12.54
Services		1.60
Total	100.00%	100.00%

Exhibit 4

Year	(A) Total Employment	(B) Employment Export	Multiplier: A ÷ B
19Y6	35,226	5,887	5.98
19X3	39,353	7,185	5.48

ferences because of the limitations discussed in the next section rather than actual changes in the export base. A more accurate estimation of the local multiplier may be obtained by comparing the annual relationship of export employment with total employment over a longer period, such as 10 years.

Identifying the local economic base and measuring its changes over time are an integral part of understanding the local economy.

QUALIFICATIONS

The preceding discussion focused on the local economic base, measured in terms of employment by applying location quotients to compute export employment. Employment is not a perfect measure of local economic activity, and the use of location quotients has its limitations. Also, changes in export employment are not the only causes of change in the level of local economic activity. These three qualifications to economic base analysis are discussed below.

Employment Data

Employment statistics are not always a precise measure of the level of local economic activity as depicted in terms of income or production. The employment data in *County Business Patterns* count a part-time job the same as a full-time job as one employee. Obviously, the two jobs do not produce the same amount of income or output. If employment were adjusted by some measure such as hours worked, a more accurate accounting of the level of economic activity would result.

Location Quotients

Location quotients are the most frequently used method for estimating local export employment because they involve less time and cost than surveys or other methods. Several assumptions that underlie the use of location quotients do not always apply, however. First, this approach assumes that consumer practices and production methods are uniform throughout the nation. In the case of consumer practices, for example, the number of swimming pools purchased in different communities varies by climatic differences. The assumption of a national average percentage of total employment in the construction of swimming pools will not hold in comparing southern Florida, where the number of swimming pools constructed is above the national average, and northern Minnesota, where it would be below the national average. In such a situation, location quotients based on national averages would overstate export employment in swimming pool construction for southern Florida and understate it in northern Minnesota. Except for a few products like swimming pools, however, there are probably no significant differences in consumption patterns among different regions of the United States.

With respect to production methods, location quotients based on employment data assume that it takes the same amount of labor input to produce a given amount of output anywhere in the nation. If industry is more automated in some parts of the country than in others, the amount of employment required to produce a given amount of export product will differ across areas.

The location quotient estimate of export employment assumes that no industry will have any exports until local requirements are met. For example, in SIC code 56 (apparel and accessory stores) in Table 2, total employment is 522, local requirements employment is 519, and export employment, as estimated by the location quotient method, is 3. However, not all sales represented by local requirements employment of 519 are likely to be local purchases. Some residents of the Midwestern SMSA will purchase clothing outside the SMSA (for example, on trips to larger cities); on the other hand, some nonresidents, using funds from nonlocal sources, such as students of the local university, will purchase clothing in the SMSA. Thus, in employment terms, exports might be equal to 103, but they are offset by imports equal to 100 for a net export of 3. In general, the location quotient method understates export employment (and overstates the multiplier).

The amount of export employment identified by location quotient computations will also depend on the SIC code digit level used. The more disaggregated the data are, the less likelihood there is that imports by some firms or sectors within an industry will offset exports by other firms or sectors of the industry. For example, two-digit SIC data may hide underlying exports for a certain sector of an industry that become apparent when greater detail at the three- or four-digit levels is used.

Thus, the key to minimizing the problems of understating export employment is to use the most detailed employment data available in computing location quotients and resulting export employment by industrial classification.

The Role of Imports

Economic base analysis focuses on the role of export production and its impact on total local economic activity. Imports should not be neglected, however, in assessing methods for stimulating local economic growth. Several two-digit SIC industries in column 6, Table 2, show employment less than the estimated local requirements. These negative numbers indicate industrial categories in which goods and services are imported on balance. In contrast to the effect of export employment, import means that local income is being expended outside the local area. Attempts to increase local employment in industrial categories that show imports (thereby reducing imports and the outflow of income) can be just as effective in stimulating local growth as increasing export employment.

In summary, economic base analysis has its limitations. Nevertheless, the computation of the annual economic base over a period of several years (using consistent data sources, level of detail, and technique) yields comparisons that are meaningful. The changes in the economic base revealed by such comparisons mirror the trends and underlying changes in the local economy even though the absolute numbers obtained for the export base might differ if other data sources, level of detail, and computational methods had been used.

TIME, COST, AND EXPERTISE

Obtaining published employment data from *County Business Patterns* and computing location quotients for those employment categories for which the most detailed SIC code data are available is a relatively easy task. For example, the time spent obtaining the data and computing the results in Tables 2 and 3 for the Midwestern SMSA for two years took only about four hours. The location quotient method need not be used to determine export employment when it is obvious that all employment in an industry is exclusively export or nonexport employment. Also, it is prefer-

Export Employment Worksheet Year: _____

Employment Category		U. S. Employment		(3) Local Employment	(4) Local Requirements Employment (col. 2 × total of col. 3)	(5) Export Employment (col. 3 − col. 4; do not enter if less than zero)
SIC Code	SIC Description	(1) Amount (thousands)	(2) Percentage of Total			
___	___	___	___	___	___	___
___	___	___	___	___	___	___
___	___	___	___	___	___	___
___	___	___	___	___	___	___
___	___	___	___	___	___	___
___	___	___	___	___	___	___
___	___	___	___	___	___	___
___	___	___	___	___	___	___
___	___	___	___	___	___	___
___	___	___	___	___	___	___
___	___	___	___	___	___	___
___	___	___	___	___	___	___
___	___	___	___	___	___	___
___	___	___	___	___	___	___

able to supplement published data with local information giving detail on employment categories that cannot be disclosed in published data because of federal disclosure laws. The time and effort involved in collecting and integrating these supplementary data should not be significant; a few phone calls or consulting locally published industrial directories may provide the information. Once these data sources are identified, an annual updating of the local economic base is relatively easy in terms of time and cost. No expertise is required to determine the economic base other than a familiarity with the sources of data and with the techniques contained in this article. The computational techniques are simple division and multiplication that can be done with a hand calculator.

A sample worksheet, similar to Table 2, is provided here for use in computing the local economic base. This form can be reproduced in sufficient quantity to compute the economic base for several years at the greatest level of employment detail available from *County Business Patterns* and supplementary sources of local employment data.

Notes

1. Executive Office of the President, Bureau of the Budget, *Standard Industrial Classification Manual* (Washington, D.C.: Government Printing Office, 1972). This manual is revised every five years.
2. U.S. Bureau of the Census, *County Business Patterns* (Washington, D.C.: Government Printing Office)—United States and appropriate state volumes. *County Business Patterns* is found in the reference room of most local public or college libraries. It can also be obtained at a reasonable cost (different volumes are different prices) directly from the Government Printing Office in Washington, D.C. Separate volumes give employment totals for the United States and for each state; thus, purchase of the U.S. volume and the state volume would provide all data required to compute the economic base for a given year as in Table 2 or 3. *County Business Patterns* was first published in 1946 and has been published annually since 1964.

Budget Setting

Productivity and the Budget Process
Gerald J. Miller

I. INTRODUCTION

Is productivity achieved through public budgets? As part of management systems, budgets are designed to achieve an amalgam of values, including productivity. To understand the relationship between productivity and budgets, this discussion outlines purposes attached to budget systems, and draws their implications for achieving greater productivity in government organizations.

While we describe large-scale budget structures in terms of their relationship to productivity, we argue that the form of budget process may not be as important to productivity as the symbol that budget process strongly projects. In the first section of the article, we review budget forms and later examine and report research results on the symbolic content of budget processes. In a later section, we report the basis for the argument that productivity efforts can employ budgets as symbols by providing research in one instance.

II. TYPES OF BUDGET AND THEIR CONTRIBUTIONS TO PRODUCTIVITY

In summarizing the financial problems facing public officials, one noted observer has outlined two problems: increasing the amounts of revenue and using present amounts to their best advantage. The second, he says, is the more difficult to solve: "Without open market or profit tests, there are no clear widespread indications of what...government services are wanted, in what quantity, at what quality, and what prices" (Hatry, 1972, p. 263). Lacking the marketplace on which to base decisions, elected officials are expected to choose courses of action "which contribute most to governmental objectives ...[and, rationally, to]...insure maximum use of scarce resources" (Grossbard, undated, p. 4). Those who design budget methods and procedures, then, must bear the responsibility of making the choice process contribute to productivity.

A. Productivity Is More Than Decision Rationality

Other considerations for making more rational choice processes relate to the "pressures on cities, counties and states [and, presumably, the federal government] to reach out and find ways of improving their understanding of problems and of the consequences of alternative courses of action to meet them" (Mushkin, 1969a, p. 4). To improve understanding of problems, officials must realize that problems in governments are compound, "highly interrelated with complex behavioral relationships" (Mushkin, 1969a, p. 4). That is, government action may relieve only one part of a larger problem or instead create another.

In addition, the effect of multiagency action has been "merely fragmented attacks on multiple disabilities of single individuals and families" (Mushkin, 1969a, p. 5). Governmental efforts, especially

---

Reprinted from *Public Productivity Handbook,* edited by Marc Holzer (New York: Marcel Dekker, Inc., 1992), 227-51. By permission of the publisher.

realizing the number of considerations that must be taken into account, seem to lack any system of application and evaluation. Jernberg (1971, p. 10) asks more generally, "Can decisions concerning public services and facilities, which affect the quality of urban life and create a better environment for social interaction, be made in a systematic manner which assures rationality, dependability, and predictability?" He offers the budget process as the means to achieve these productivity goals.

B. Budget Principles and Practices

Freeman (1972, p.10) offers several definitions of a budget. A budget is "a plan of financial operation embodying an estimate of proposed expenditures for a given period and the proposed means of financing them, or a process for systematically relating the expenditure of funds to the accomplishment of planned objectives." He offers another more comprehensive, complementary definition (1972, p. 10):

> (1) a financial expression of a [jurisdiction's] plans for a specified period of time, (2) a control device during the operating period, and (3) a vehicle by which actual results may be compared with planned results and the variances analyzed so that we may improve both our operations and budgeting in the future.

If we consider, like Sundelson (1935, p. 243), what the ideal budget might be,* we would find a set of generally agreed upon ideas** relating the requirements of informed voters and responsible decision makers. These ideas include comprehensiveness, exclusiveness, unity, annuality, accuracy, clarity, and publicity. Comprehensiveness requires that the budget hold all authority for expenditure and revenue which the government provides. Exclusiveness reflects the importance attached to separating fiscal matters from substantive ones; the budget should include financial matters, not other matters of substance. Unity suggests the need to relate all of the parts of the budget to each other—what revenues support what expenditures if earmarked. Annuality forces regular review of expenditures and revenues by commanding the length of the period between them. Accuracy means that estimates of needs and resources be near the mark rather than the product of wishful thinking or suggested by political strategy. Clarity demands that who pays what and how much as well as what is spent be unmistakable rather than obfuscatory or simplistic. Finally, budget making must seek publicity, essentially the airing of needs, grievances, and policy positions of representative and represented.

Yet, Sundelson's (1935) eight principles might be compressed to one, according to Burkhead (1956, p. 107):

> There is probably only one principle which is likely to be useful—that of operational adequacy. The budget cycle and the budgetary process must be capable of coping with the governmental problems at hand. This means that there must be an emphasis on flexibility and adaptability, not an emphasis on an ideal that is intended to be unchanging.

Among the budget processes widely used in governments, we find much evidence that Burkhead (1956) is right.

Within these principles are the basic tenets for defining a management device, above all. The actual practices of governments today are more times at the one extreme of meeting the very basic definition Freeman (1972) offered (expenditures and financial means) than at the other extreme, combining planning, control of expenditures, evaluation of actual results with planned results, and evaluation of alternative methods to achieve a desired result. We shall consider both definitions in succeeding portions of this discussion: first, the line-item budget as a rudimentary way of assessing expenditures and means; performance budgeting as a method of going one step beyond the line-item budgeting by classifying items by function; program budgeting, as a means of combining planning; and budgeting for the more effective use of resources and relatively newer combi-

---

*Others who have devoted their lives to principles include Rene Stourm, *The Budget,* translated by Thaddeus Plazinski (New York: Appleton & Company, 1917), pp. 144-68; and G. Findlay Shirras, *The Science of Public Finance* (London: Macmillan & Co., Ltd., 1936), Vol. 1, pp. 82-83; Vol. 2, pp. 968-74.

**We attempted to determine whether current budget theorists and practitioners still mention these principles presently. Both theorists, such as Aaron Wildavsky, *Budgeting,* rev. ed. (Piscataway, New Jersey: Transaction Books, 1987), and practitioners such as those reached through the near legendary "Green Books"—see Lewis Friedman, "Budgeting," in *Management Policies in Local Government Finance,* ed. J. Richard Aronson and Eli Schwartz (Washington, D.C.: International City Management Association, 1981), pp. 99-111.

nations of these methods, zero-base budgeting and balanced-base budgeting.

i. Line-Item Budgeting: The Control Orientation

An early approach to budgeting—a line-item, or object of expenditure, budget—is still the most popular approach in local government owing to its simplicity and the strict accountability or control it allows. This budget, however, has limited utility as a management tool.

The line-item budget allocates funds to specific items or objects. Salaries, office supplies, and printing costs are forecast for the next year, limiting the administrator to a certain increment per objective over the amount budgeted for that object the last fiscal year (Table 1).

The Jeffersonian line-item approach was implemented again around the turn of the twentieth century as means to reform uncontrollable spending. It was devised to hold governmental units accountable for expenditure by setting an item-by-item spending schedule.

The greatest advantage of line-item budgeting is the control it exerts on financial administration. The intentions of governmental decision makers are defined as to what will be spent on what. This, in turn, provides some control over work by casting expenditures along departmental lines and characters of expense.

Grossbard (undated, p. 6) argues the insufficiency of the line-item budget. He views line-item budgeting as the result of "short run thinking and a tendency to put off both expenditure increases and revenue measures until a later period." The problem with the traditional line-item budget format, Grossbard further argues, is that "it does not do enough." Specifically, the budget is difficult to relate to objectives. There is no relation of expenditures to accomplishment, no concept of alternatives to policy, and no integration of planning, budgeting, and control. Line-item budgeting promotes inertia in that changes are produced only as marginal changes from the previous year. Levels of service, organization structure, and methods of operation become permanent, although they may be unsatisfactory.

Anton (1964), in his study of budget practice in three Illinois cities, illustrates the marginal or incremental practices of line-item budgeting. Because the only information available to a city was the past year's budget and the marginal increases asked by each department, the budget hearing was found to provide the only clues as to what to cut and what to leave as it was. Anton (1964, p. 16) observes:

> Precisely because the "stakes" are inherently so political in meaning, the criteria used to decide [budget] questions are seldom relevant to departmental goals. Instead, the deciding criteria become such political factors as power and influence of the department head, the ability of the department to mobilize support for its demands, or the ability of the council to gain prestige by granting or refusing the demand.

The increases in the budget were not based on any demonstration that services from any particular department would improve or suffer as a result of increases or cuts. In fact, all departments could have made a persuasive case for increases to improve their operations.

The departments, however, were not equal in their ability to marshal influence. Anton (1964, p. 17) continues, "what is most significant here is the demonstration that in the absence of detailed information on the part of the council and in the absence of strong central control over various departments, each department is relatively free to seek improvement in its financial position by putting pressure on the council. Clearly, the advantage lies with the strong."

Table 1: *Line-Item Budget Illustration*

Park and Recreation Fund Budget

Account Number	Account Title	199X Actual ($)	This Year Estimated ($)	Next Year Proposed ($)
#10-1	Recreation Section			
A-1	Salaries	10,000	11,000	12,000
A-2	Social security	1,000	1,100	1,200
A-3	Insurance	500	600	700
B-5	Telephone	100	150	200
B-6	Office rent	1,000	1,000	1,000
B1-	Utilities	300	500	700
C-12	Equipment	4,000	5,000	6,000
C-15	Expendable supplies			
C-15a	Baseball supplies	500	550	600
C-15b	Basketball supplies	400	425	450
C-15c	Tennis supplies	300	310	320
	Total	18,100	20,635	23,170

ii. Performance Budgeting: The Management Approach

Owing to limitations in line-item budgeting and increasing levels of expenditures, the federal government began turning to a new approach—a management approach—in the early 1930s. This change grew out of several circumstances. First, the increase in activities and expenditures under New Deal programs made some type of aggregate of activities performed more important for informational purposes than itemized objects. Second, Keynesian economics stressed more public spending to reduce economic disadvantages during the depression; therefore, the number of expenditures increased and their performance as a group had to be measured. Third, the President's Committee on Administrative Management in 1937 advocated management of spending by the president and subsequently called for expanding the Bureau of the Budget and consolidating it in the Executive Office of the President (Schick, 1966; pp. 257-58). Fourth, the Hoover Commission in 1949 recommended "that the whole budgetary concept of the Federal Government should be refashioned by the adoption of a budget based upon functions, activities and projects" (Schick, 1966, p. 258). In fact, from the Hoover Commission came the new name performance budgeting.

The management approach or the idea of performance budgeting referred to by the Hoover Commission was also promoted by the Municipal Finance Officers Association (MFOA, 1954), and both included several new concepts. This budget related expenditures to performance. Appropriations were made to activities—jobs to be performed—rather than objects. The new concept introduced operational analysis, a method of measuring inputs—personnel services, contractual services—against outputs and how many units of activity occurred as a result. Generally, the budget calls for more information on what the activity was, what the procedures used were, and what level of service could be provided for what amount (Table 2).

Necessitated by increased economic activity, the new approach was tailored to provide distinct advantages over the line-item concept. By its orientation to management, performance budgeting's principal thrust went toward helping administrators assess the work efficiency of operating units by casting budget categories in functional terms, and providing work-cost measurements to facilitate the efficient performance of prescribed activities. At the height of performance budgeting's acceptance, Ridley and Simon (1943) identified four types of measurement needs: results, costs, efforts, and performance, the last three of which were their measures of "admin-

Table 2: *Performance Budget for a Public Works Department Street Lighting Section*

Operation	Unit Man-Hours	Rate per Man-Hour ($)	Unit Labor Cost ($)	Unit Material ($)	Unit Equipment ($)	Total Unit Cost ($)
Washing luminaires	0.23	1.29	0.30	0.01	0.02	0.33
Lamping	0.39	2.11	0.82	0.96	0.12	1.90
Painting standards	0.77	2.23	1.72	1.04	0.08	2.84

What is the best level of service?
  Washing luminaires Twice per year
  Lamping Twice per year
  Painting standards Once every other year

Number of lights in service   5,010
  Washing luminaires 5,010 multiplied by 2 and by $0.33 = 3,306
  Lamping 5,010 multiplied by 2 and by $1.90 = 19,038
  Painting standards 5,010 divided by 2 multiplied by $2.84 = 7,114
Routine maintenance budget   29,458

Source: Sherwood and Best (1975, p. 395).

istrative efficiency" and, commonly today, productivity. For the first time, standards were set based on the measurements made, worker hours, cost accounting, and ratio of personnel to activity.

Many found disadvantages in performance budgeting's application in the federal government. Budget estimates were no more meaningful than those in line-item budgets. The reason for making one particular expenditure rather than another was not clear. No alternatives were presented on which to base a "best" choice. The same limitations were true in the states and cities where performance budgeting was being employed.

Work measurement presented the second difficulty for budget officers. There were inherent difficulties in measuring government output with precision. It was easy to measure government purchases, generally easy to measure government activities, but "it is perennially difficult to measure government output except for repetitive discrete products such as postal service" (Burkhead, 1972, p.73).

Last, performance budgeting lacked the tools to deal with long-range problems. With planned expenditures set within a one-year perspective, "almost all options [for future action] have been foreclosed by previous commitments" (Schick, 1966, p. 258).

Robert Luther, budget officer of Fairfax County, Virginia, explained the application and implementation of some performance budget concepts in a suburban county. Problems arose in several areas. Quantifying or categorizing units of work within a department met with difficulty. Collection of data on work units was not done accurately; therefore, it was unreliable. Department heads questioned the concept of data collection and the need for it; there was little departmental cooperation (Luther, 1972, p. 347). The difficulty was symptomatic of little or no commitment by elected officials or department heads to concepts of work measurement.

The development of a management approach to budgeting is, in retrospect, an evolutionary step toward use of the budget as a tool in both quantifying the results of a particular expenditure and in evaluating the entire budget program. The performance budget was a middle step between the traditional line-item method of control as productivity and the planning approach to productivity—how do we solve this policy problem—adopted by performance budgeting's successors, program budgeting and planning, programming, budgeting system (PPBS).

iii. Program Budgeting

Program budgeting suffers a severe identification crisis in the budgetary literature. It is used synonymously with performance budgeting as well as with the planning, programming, budgeting system. Even when the Hoover Commission introduced the term *performance budget,* its task force report utilized the term program budget interchangeably with performance budget. Schick observed "no uniformity in usage, some preferring the *program budgeting* label, others *performance budgeting* to describe the same things. The level of confusion has been increased by the association of the term with the PPB movement" (Schick, 1966, p. 250).

Burkhead (1956, p. 139) attempted to distinguish between performance budgeting and program budgeting. A program may be defined in relation to a higher level of organization than performance. Since a program may encompass several performing organizational units, the program budget is broader and more integrative than a performance budget. Program costs are broad summary costs which may be developed through aggregation of performing units' costs. Performance details need not be incorporated into a program budget, since it is not necessarily based on performance units (see Table 3).

Also, a department or agency may be involved in several programs simultaneously, but operating units within a department are directly responsible for performance. Therefore, in terms of organizational structure, the program budget may respond to higher-level organizational needs, whereas the performance budget may serve lower-level operating needs better. In other words, the program budget is more centralized.

The program budget has a longer range and is forward looking. Performance budgets are based on records of past performance and accomplishments, whereas program budgets are built around estimates of what performance is reasonable to expect in the future. Program budgets are thus better prepared to project the social and economic policies of government.

According to these distinctions, different purposes are served by these two types of budgets. A program budget is more suited to the requirements of overall budgetary planning, including review by the central budget office, the chief executive, and the legislature. It is most useful for decision making at

Table 3: *Program Budget Illustration*

Crime Prevention Program Budget—Central Business District		
Subprogram	City ($)	Private Sector ($)
Street lighting improvements in CBD		
Public Works Department	25,000	
business		25,000
Police street patrols		
Police Department	10,000	
business security departments		5,000
Alarms from businesses		
Police Department hookups	50,000	
business store hookups		125,000
Intensive garbage pickup		
Sanitation Department	50,000	
business stockroom efforts		10,000
Intensive street cleaning		
Sanitation Department	12,000	
business effort on curbs and gutters		20,000
Employment and training program		
juvenile	100,000	
adult	25,000	
Business job potential		100,000
Totals	272,000	285,000

Goals:
1. Increase ability to police area through patrols and better notification.
2. Increase attractiveness and pedestrian population of area.
3. Increase number of jobs and decrease number of jobless.

or above the departmental level. Performance budgets must likewise provide information for review purposes, but must also be detailed enough to serve management purposes at or below the departmental level.

Program budgeting involves an attempt to arrange budget expenditures around program or functional needs in order to meet broad objectives. By relating inputs to outputs, cost-benefit analysis is facilitated with the aim of allocating resources to the most efficient and effective means for achieving ends. The key elements of the process include long-range planning, goals setting, program identification, quantitative analysis, including cost-benefit measurement, and performance analysis.

There are four essential steps in the construction of a program budget:

1. Definition of the ends to be achieved
2. Definitions of the method and timetables by which they are achieved
3. Determination of the costs for each action required
4. Determination of measurements of success, whether goals are actually being achieved, through the budgeted programs

The Second Hoover Commission task force recommended that the term *program budgeting* be used to emphasize the review of proposed new programs over the review of the performance of previously authorized programs.

a. Advantages

Program budgeting focuses on goals and outcomes, and helps provide perspective for budget expenditures. The budget requires consideration of future implications of programs and effects of current actions. It also emphasizes the role of planning in budget decision making.

b. Disadvantages

However, program budgeting may require modification of activities which have an impact on many related activities. Economic, social, and political events may not follow the anticipated pattern which may undermine the intentions of program budgeting's long-range planning efforts. Analysis of relationships between inputs and outputs does not necessarily consider unintended consequences or side effects of actions taken or proposed. Quantitative measurement of outputs may not be possible; even where quantitative analysis is feasible, the criteria of economy and efficiency may preclude the consideration of quality and productivity. Finally, the budget requires central coordination, since programs may cross agency lines.

iv. PPBS: The Planning Orientation

The planning, programming, budgeting system (PPBS) has been characterized by Schick (1966) as the product of an evolutionary process from management to planning of federal governmental expenditure allocation.* Schick outlines this development (1966, p. 250):

---

*But see my argument that it is not evolution so much as a titanic struggle that created PPBS (Miller, 1991).

1. Economic analysis at both micro- and macro-levels has had an increasing part in determining fiscal and budgeting policy.
2. The development of new informational and decisional technologies has enlarged the applicability of objective analysis to policy making.
3. Planning and budgeting have gradually converged.

Wider acceptance of Keynesian economic principles set the stage for PPBS in its call for governmental action in planning economic growth for the nation. Moreover, utilization of planned spending as both an impetus and a constraint on growth had been used during the underemployment-plagued economic depression years. Finally, a planned taxing policy has forced the implementation of a governmental economic plan.

Coupled with these developments, new means or technologies have increased government's ability to analyze objectively the alternate policies available to it. The introduction of operations analysis during World War II and cost-benefit analysis during the 1950s both allowed the federal government more depth in optimizing the coordination of resources to reach objectives. The introduction of systems analysis along with wider application of operations research and cost-benefit analysis by the RAND Corporation in 1961 in the U.S. Department of Defense consolidated approaches in one package. All these techniques spurred the development of PPBS.

Based on Defense Department's success with PPBS, President Lyndon B. Johnson introduced the same package in the other departments and agencies in 1965 as a means of budgeting to meet objectives. Planning and budgeting converged.

Following the example of the national government, local governments also experimented with the new system. Mushkin (1969b, pp. 16-21) outlined the development: New York City in 1966, Philadelphia shortly afterwards, and, through the 5-5-5 Intergovernmental Demonstration, five cities, counties, and states before the end of the year.

Most characterize PPBS as a rational means of fusing planning processes, programming efforts, and the budget system. Many found little new among the components but a revolutionary concept in the combination. Thus, planning is the determination of the basic goals of the organization and the selection of the programs best calculated to achieve these goals. Programming entails the scheduling and execution, as efficiently as possible, of the specific projects required to implement these programs. Budgeting is the process of converting the goals, programs, and projects into money estimates for review within the administrative branch and final action by the legislative branch. The basic advantage of PPBS is the emphasis on rational decision making. To improve rationality, PPBS allows policy makers to

1. establish goals and objectives after observation,
2. assign alternative means toward accomplishing objectives,
3. predict the consequences of each alternative,
4. select the most beneficial alternative, and
5. program all work toward achieving objectives.

There are disadvantages, however, in the PPB system, both internal and external. For local governments, there are distinct adaptations to be made to the system to make it applicable and workable.

First, internal difficulties concern the dynamics of the structure itself, the goal-setting procedure, and cost-benefit analysis. Within the structure of procedure of PPBS budgeting, there is a tendency to centralize decision making. The responsibility for goal setting and policy choice is centrally determined, resulting in better coordination of activities, but at the cost of initiative in innovation and development of new alternatives at lower levels of policy making.

The stress of PPBS on the cross structural nature of goals and objectives diminishes the importance of existing organizational boundaries. This approach disrupts present channels of communication between administrative agencies. Because there will be different cross structural arrangements for each objective, the PPBS approach has not been found to establish a single channel to replace it.

Emphasizing the alternative results in uncertainty among all participants in the system. Uncertainty becomes the replacement for the last budget system's stability.

Goal setting itself is difficult because of both the complexity of problems and the different outlooks of each goal setter. Wildavsky (1969, 1966, pp. 292-

310) notes the ultimate problem with PPBS: "Budgeting, in PPBS, is intimately linked to policy; however, the basic problems in policy formulation and development stem from the fact that we do not know what it is that we are trying to accomplish."

Cost-benefit analysis itself is not sufficiently sophisticated yet to meet all the demands placed upon it. Hatry and Cotton (1967, p. 6) argue that there are "difficulties in considering a time stream of costs and benefits and not simply the evaluation of costs and benefits for a single point in time." In its present procedural form, the most apparent deficiency of cost-benefit analysis is that such variables as social systems and highly intangible services elude measurement. Moreover, Jernberg (1971, p. 370) finds two points of view on cost-benefit's application. One view holds that cost-benefit analysis should include all considerations, including political costs and benefits. The opposing view points out that this leads to sole reliance on political considerations and rejection of the economic or rational considerations. In conclusion, Jernberg states (1972, p. 372) that "cost benefit analysis [is presently viewed] as serving a more modest role of assisting and providing a more sound base for intuitive judgment." Hirsch (1966, p. 156) agrees, saying, "Policy makers want to know which groups benefit the most and where the losses are distributed as a result of their decisions."

There are other major political problems as well. In the very process of changing systems, existing programs have built up definite constituents convinced of the validity of the present approach; "members of an organization and their clients have a vested interest in the policies of the past" and fight change (Wildavsky, 1966, p. 294).

The first, and still basic, evaluation of PPBS in use comes from George Washington University's 5-5-5 Project mentioned earlier. In that project, PPBS was introduced to five cities, five counties, and five states. The project began in the spring of 1966 under the guidance of task forces from the university.

Mushkin (1969a, 1969b) summarized the approaches, the problems, and the successes encountered in the process of her review of the 5-5-5 Project. The approach, she concluded (1969a, p. 2), was basically incremental, "resulting in halfhearted endorsement with no real desire to implement more than one small step at a time. [The participants] were cautionary with a long timetable." Eleven of the 15 jurisdictions chose to continue the program formally. She concluded that the project yielded the following:

1. The beginning of a more questioning attitude toward budgeting and program planning
2. A new emphasis on the beneficiaries of public services; i.e., on the people for whom the government functions
3. A new emphasis on formulation of objectives and programs
4. A new enthusiasm about state and local government work among staff assigned to PPB work
5. A start in a few governments toward an interagency dialogue on common objectives and interrelated programs

The experiences of three of the cities bear close scrutiny. Meiszer (1969), the assistant city manager of Dayton, Ohio, explained the development of PPBS used in Dayton in terms of four subsystems: program structure, program analysis, program budget, and program evaluation. His evaluation of the implementation of the several subsystems indicated that sufficient progress had been made from the program structure to be completed. In addition, analysis had already exerted an influence on decision making. However, while program budgeting was producing good results, evaluation was lagging. Meiszer terms Dayton's implementation as still in the development stage but progressing sufficiently. Horton (1969), director of administrative analysis for Metropolitan Nashville-Davidson County, observed that "even with problems PPBS has increased awareness of administrators of the need to improve the decision making process." The city, however, did experience administrative problems, lack of trained personnel at the beginning of the program, inadequate staffing, and a lack of teaching materials. In sum, there was plenty of theory, but no methods of application.

Progress in PPBS implementation in Dade County, Florida, was characterized as being slow to develop. Grizzle (1969) stated that the system had yet to be infused into the process it would replace, and that planning had not been linked to budgeting. In fact, PPBS was initially "used primarily to comply with federal planning requirements in certain federal programs."

v. Zero-Base Budgeting

Theoretically, zero-based budgeting (ZBB) requires that each previously funded program or new program proposal be justified, without regard to previous funding levels. This procedure is designed to promote objective comparisons among diverse programs requesting resources, based on their merits alone and negating the effects of historical bias.

In practice, the definition of ZBB is much less comprehensive. Pyhrr (1973), an early proponent of ZBB and to many its inventor, recognizes the impracticality of a true zero-base budget and leans toward a more practical definition, one in which evaluation has a profound effect but not an exhaustive use.

Four basic steps are required to employ ZBB. First, the jurisdiction must identify decision units, or basically the units of analysis, be they programs or organization units. Second, the jurisdiction defines decision packages, or bundles, of decision units which in reality correspond to the organization at which the lowest-level choices will be made and priorities set. Those responsible for decision packages develop appropriations requests based on rankings of decision units within decision packages and, ultimately, across decision packages.

A decision unit identifies a discrete activity, function, or operation. A decision package identifies and sets priorities among decision units based on each decision unit's purpose, need (expressed usually as the consequences of not performing the activity, function, or operation any longer), performance measures or methods of detecting success and failure, alternative ways of performing the activity, function, or operation, and the costs and benefits of various levels of budgetary support as they affect performance and are observed in the measures defined in the package (see Figure 1).

The key to ZBB is the evaluation of alternatives among the decision units in the decision package.

Figure 1: *Zero-base Budgeting Decision Package Ranking Process*

STEP 1: Managers A, B, and C each rank packages for their units and send to Manager X.	**STEP 2**: Manager X receives packages and evaluates and ranks them within each unit.	**STEP 3**: Manager X (and Y) ranks packages for units A, B, and C against each other, and sends to Manager R.	**STEP 4**: Manager R evaluates packages from Managers X and Y, and then ranks them against each other.

Decision Unit A

Package	% Previous FY
A1	100
A2	125
A3	75
A4	0

Package	% Previous FY
A1	125
A2	100
A3	75
A4	0

Decision Unit B

Package	% Previous FY
B1	0
B2	75
B3	100
B4	125

Package	% Previous FY
B1	75
B2	100
B3	125
B4	0

Decision Unit C

Package	% Previous FY
C1	100
C2	0
C3	75
C4	125

Package	% Previous FY
C1	100
C2	75
C3	0
C4	125

(Other sections and departments follow the same process)

X1	A1
X2	A2
X3	C1
X4	B1
X5	C2
X6	B2
X7	B3
X8	C3
X9	C4
X10	A3
X11	A4
X12	B4

Y1	M1
Y2	N1
Y3	L1
Y4	L2
Y5	L3
Y6	L4
Y7	M2
Y8	N2
Y9	N3
Y10	M3
Y11	N4
Y12	M4

1	A1
2	N1
3	A2
4	C1
5	M1
6	L2
7	L1
8	B1
9	C2
10	L3
11	B2
12	L4
13	N3
14	N2
15	M2
16	B3
17	C3
18	M3
19	C4
20	A3
21	N4
22	M4
23	B4
24	A4

Given the information in the process, choices hinge on the different ways of performing the same function (the decision unit) and the outcomes based on the different levels of budgetary effort. Managers, having identified the consequences of no longer performing the activity, function, or operation, estimate the differences in performance due to lower than current budget support, continued but stable levels of support, and greater future support. Thus, ZBB's uniqueness lies in information formatting.

The literature on the conceptual evolution of ZBB is sparse. In essence, ZBB was developed at either Texas Instruments, Inc., in 1969 or in the U.S. Department of Agriculture in 1964 (Wildavsky, 1975). In the former, Pyhrr reports success; in the latter, Wildavsky reports failure. The greatest fame of ZBB came through its introduction into public agency administration by Jimmy Carter, then governor of Georgia and later president of the United States.

a. Advantages

The literature implies that ZBB has at least 10 advantages: (1) ZBB yields increased information from managers throughout the organization, particularly operating managers who are responsible for the actual performance of activity for which they budget. (2) It results in improved plans and budgets which themselves result from combining planning and goals setting, budgeting, and operational decision making into one process requiring detailed scrutiny of every activity. (3) ZBB encourages the use of continued evaluation of program efficiency and effectiveness throughout the budget-operating year. (4) Programs and managers who have committed themselves to certain levels of performance can be reviewed during the operating year to gauge progress. (5) ZBB's priority ranking system facilitates assigning cutbacks or reductions when necessary. (6) ZBB helps set priorities and sharpen overall objectives. (7) The ZBB approach shifts budget attention away from incremental approaches to last year's budget and focuses on minimum levels of operation. (8) ZBB promotes the search for alternatives to programs, performance, and funding levels and may be most useful in reallocating funds among programs within an agency. (9) The ZBB approach can readily identify low-yield or low-priority programs which may be eliminated. (10) ZBB reduces the opportunity for manipulation of budget presentation information, or "gamesmanship." If the information is present in ZBB formats, attempts at gaming become transparent.

b. Disadvantages

From a theoretical perspective, the disadvantages of ZBB may include problems of implementation: Users are threatened by the need to reevaluate pet projects. Also, the number of decision packages generated can overwhelm managers reviewing them; the paperwork produced can have more volume than meaning. Zero-based budgeting is limited to use with only those controllable elements in budgets. In the federal budget, controllables may amount to no more than 25 percent of the total. The ranking system remains susceptible to subjective decision and ZBB does not aid in judging priorities among dissimilar activities such as defense, education, and energy. It is difficult to apply ZBB to state and local programs whose genesis is not local but federal, and whose support does not lend itself to their control. In addition, there is difficulty in identifying appropriate decision units, in gathering accurate supporting data to produce effective analysis, and in determining minimum levels of effort. Zero-based budgeting requires vast improvements in agency evaluation systems necessary to make program comparisons and rankings and is expensive and time consuming to implement.

Practically, ZBB's disadvantages include its failure to fundamentally change the practice of federal budget making. Second, the Office of Management and Budget (OMB), in trying to simplify paperwork needs, drained the decision packages of their decisional utility. Third, managers decided priorities in a vacuum, without knowledge of how interrelated programs might be affected by rankings done partially by others. Thus, Program A may have been related to Program B, but A was included in a set of priorities distant from B; one's operation may have depended on the other but one's fate could not be revealed to the other.

vi. The Balanced-Base Budget

After ZBB, a rash of citizen-led initiatives redefined productivity, radically, as lower tax rates and smaller budgets. The first of a series of budget procedures aimed at controlling the rise of and even cutting expenditures came from Kansas in the form of the balanced-base budget (Muchmore and Duncan, 1982).

This form of budgeting reverses what has until recently been the normal process. That is, the process calls for estimating future revenues and then using this estimate as the budget limit.

The first step in the balanced-base budget process calls for the top manager to send issue papers to agency heads. Each issue paper outlines a specific problem that the agency is to solve. The issue paper process is a means to collect information about trends in service demand or other relevant factors that must be considered in order to arrive at prudent base allocations among agencies.

The second step in the process occurs when top managers allocate budgets for all agencies. The top manager allocates on the basis of the strength of the arguments presented in the issue papers and on the basis of his or her own comprehensive view of organization needs. These allocations exist at the agency level, not at the program level; therefore, agency heads distribute the money within their organizations according to agency priorities.

The third step in the budget process is the preparation of program planning documentation by the agencies. Each agency must decide how to divide its responsibilities into separate programs or clusters of activity that serve a common objective or set of objectives, and that are so closely related they must be managed jointly. Programs detail how problems are to be solved.

The fourth step in the process requires the top manager to give each agency three expenditure levels (A, B, and C) upon which detailed budget proposals are to be constructed. The B level is the most important because it reflects an allocation of all expected general revenues. The B level is the base for a balanced budget. The A level represents a reduction of funding below the base level by a specified amount. The C level budget represents additional funds beyond the balanced base in specified amount. The information contained in the three-level submissions together with agency explanations of the difference in services that would result from adopting alternative service levels is the basis for the final budget recommendations.

Since the allocations are established for agencies rather than for programs, chief administrators for agencies must distribute the allocations among the programs under their jurisdictions. This is done by assigning an A, B, or C level of spending to each program. These levels of funding relate to the alternative approaches to problems that were discussed in the issue papers.

The two final steps in the balanced-base budgeting process are the hearing and review sequences, and finally the governor's announcement of the final executive budget and its submission to the legislative branch.

The balanced-base budget format, like all other budgets, focuses attention in certain ways, controlling the premises behind leaders' decisions. The budget controls expenditures by publicly listing agency allocations that are not to be exceeded. It is also an executive budget because the chief executive is responsible for determining allocations and deciding what programs are to be introduced, continued, or discontinued by determining the levels of funding for those programs. In turn, the chief executive's actions, and the actions of the agencies, are controlled because once the budget is published, it cannot be altered without careful scrutiny by those in control.

The issue papers help determine the most urgent problems in the jurisdiction and provide the means to instruct agency heads to design programs to solve those problems. When designing programs, agency heads must outline what projects are necessary to achieve the objectives of the program. To structure projects, one determines the most efficient way to perform the individual tasks necessary for the completion of projects. This form of budgeting establishes management control because employees are told what client group they are to help, what activities they are to accomplish, and how long they have to produce the desired effect.

Balanced-base budgeting also focuses on the outcomes of activities. This budget form considers both the needs of the public and the cost of solving those needs. The central elements—goals and long-range planning—provide predictability and stability to agency activities and a means for controlling them. Every activity must contribute to the ultimate objective of the program.

The BBB approach, as radical change in budgeting, took away the normal premises underlying budgeting. We choose here to explore its ramifications in more depth, both in substance and process. In the next sections, we discuss the "radically different" approach substantively first, followed by the BBB process.

III. REALITY CONSTRUCTION IS THE IMPLICIT THEORY OF PRODUCTIVITY IN BUDGETING

Although the budget methods we have reviewed suggest otherwise, financial management has never laid serious claim to "finding the best means to a given end," as economic efficiency principles dictate, but has considered "isolating alternative behaviors and their consequences" instead (Simon, 1976). Storing (1962) views the latter as still forcing one to ignore criteria for "good" consequences: What are good and what are bad and what makes one better than another? Edelman (1964) argues, over a review of Mead's work (1934), that one seldom knows good from bad consequences, and, by that, appropriate behaviors, until one has experienced them. Said another way, having experienced a consequence, one can then rationalize or give meaning to what happened, calling it good or bad in terms of some other, socially derived or affect-based set of criteria.

That set of socially derived or affect-based criteria is usually thought of as "culture." Organization culture, or even a culture in which organizations interact, has prescriptive value. Culture implies "shared meanings, shared paradigms, and shared languages..." (Pfeffer, 1981, p. 11) as well as an ideology, rituals, myths, and knowledge that "prescribes what work is to be done and how it can be changed over time" (Walker, 1986, p. 7).

Two alternative approaches to the study of budgeting, the ritualistic, ceremonial approach and a random choice approach, relate to each other and explain how culture can transmit criteria of "good" consequences. We consider each in the sections which follow as concepts. Then we apply each empirically. Finally, we draw conclusions about their applicability by comparing them to the cognitive approach attributed to more traditional ways of thinking about financial management.

A. The Symbols and Rituals of Budgets

Consider for a moment the affective approach to understanding public life. We respond to symbols such as a balanced budget with concern. We believe in the rituals such as the competitive bid process in awarding the sale of general obligation bonds. We listen closely to understand the language of economic forecasts because they tell us in their arcane way to be optimistic or not.

In all, we ascribe much importance to the pomp and circumstance that we see. This affect we feel comes from at least three sources, which we want to consider here in an administrative context: symbols, rituals, and language.

i. Symbols

Symbols are quite simple representations of quite complex matters. They may be defined as a stimulus object, "the meaning or significance of which is socially generated and cannot be inferred from its physical form" (Elder and Cobb, 1983, p. 142). Symbols focus attention in such a way that they bind people together through the shared attention brought about. Symbols also bring with them associations for people which create a discipline for individual behavior in favor of larger goals. This latter use of symbols is what we want to describe here: the leader's use of symbols to bind and discipline followers.

ii. Rituals

In addition to a leader's use of symbols, we also explore the rituals and ceremonies that take place in government organizations. These practices are accepted and desired by organization members as dramatic manipulation of symbols by legitimate persons, usually making those inside the ritual feel differently from those outside, and in so doing "structure, validate, and stabilize collective action" (Trice et al., 1969, p. 42). Ceremonials provide cues, even explanations, for individuals confronted by novel or ambiguous information. Ceremonials also invest organization decisions with legitimacy.

Edelman (1964, pp. 16-17) defines a ritual as physical activity that gets people involved symbolically in a common effort; the ritual's efficiency is the way it compels attention to individuals' relatedness to each other and their joint interests. The result is conformity but also "satisfaction and joy in conformity" (p. 16). He goes on:

> Men instinctively try to find meaning and order when placed in a confusing or ambiguous situation. In dances and other motor activity in which primitive man celebrates season changes, the basic order of the universe underlying the "blooming buzzing confusion" of sensations is reaffirmed and the individual reminded of the need to conform to a basic order himself. In rain dances and victory dances men achieve symboli-

cally something they collectively need or want by reaffirming their common interest, denying their doubts, and acting out the result they seek. The motor activity, performed together with others, reassures everyone that there are no dissenters and brings pride and satisfaction in a collective enterprise. A simplified model or semblance of reality is created, and facts that do not fit are screened out of it. Conformity and satisfaction with the basic order are the keynotes; and the acting out of what is to be believed is a psychologically effective mode of instilling conviction and fixing patterns of future behavior.

Moreover, says Edelman (1964), the ritual serves at least three purposes: to quiet resentments and doubts about particular political acts, reaffirm belief in the fundamental rationality and democratic character of the system, and thus fix conforming habits of future behavior.

iii. Language

Language, finally, plays an important part in understanding as well. Edelman (1977, p. 16) argues that we "naturally define ambiguous situations by focusing on one part of them or by comparing them with familiar things." Language is useful in evoking those familiar ways of thinking about things. By using a particular language, in fact, we define what we see in not only understandable but often believable and legitimate ways as well.

We can see the basic financial management procedures pursued by governments as using language as a tool to gain compliance inside and acceptance outside the organization. Budgeteers' fiduciary role, according to research, has led to the creation of a language vital to conserving resources and averting risk (Wildavsky, 1975). This language often unintentionally implies that guarding resources has more value than productively employing them; however, the intent of the language is to show that managers "consult relevant people, consider alternatives, gather information, act decisively" (March and Olsen, 1986, p. 22). Decision-making processes, therefore, use language which assures society that human existence is built around intelligent choice.

The chief executive's attention to the ramifications of symbols, rituals, and language can spell the difference between successful and unsuccessful governing. In the research we report here, the attention to affect meant the difference between a consolidation of executive power after decades of slow reform in the executive branch and a slide to further fragmentation.

B. The Role of the Financial Manager in Interpreting Fiscal Reality

We contend that a budget manager's major function is that of manipulating symbols, producing rituals, and employing a unique language to get the budget and impose it. It is the financial manager's job, and that of all managers, to give reason and meaning to the process of work. The process of work has larger meaning in public administration, for lacking the widespread notion of making a profit as do private sector organizations, each public organization must look for a unique vision which gives meaning to the processes each follows. That particular process can be protecting the weak from the evil or defending the free world but all have in common the notion of doing everything possible with as little help from the taxpayer as possible, a short version of financial management's fiscal vision.

We argue that finance departments create the reality that organizations have by symbolically, ritualistically, and rhetorically coping with the most critical problem each organization has, i.e., resource restraints. Coping gives the finance department the clout to be able to enforce the use of a special language. In that language, the term *budget* becomes an overarching metaphor. Creating a reality in which resources are contingent and in which the finance department is the critical agency for commanding resources and wisely allocating them among uses, the financial manager provides much of the affective utility of financial management procedures.

C. The Research on Reality Construction in Budgeting

To build this case for financial management as largely symbolic in nature, we survey literature presently available. Most of the literature explains long-held notions of administrative reform that assume a relationship between process and outcome. One authority claims that "the form in which information is classified and used governs the actions of [decision] makers, and conversely, that alterations in form will produce desired changes in behavior" (Schick, 1966, p. 257).

Linked to the idea of an executive budget, this idea has power. Process-leads-to-outcome lends responsibility to the administrative organization and allows for steering of local, state, and national economies.

On the question, the evidence is mixed (Grizzle, 1986; Wanat, 1973; Jernberg, 1969). We look at existing studies and experience to illustrate both sides.

The affirmative side—process dictates outcome—clearly believes that budget format decides outcomes (Grizzle, 1986), owing primarily to the fact that decisions depend on information.

Those who disagree tend to point out that process and format often diverge. An outcome oriented toward distribution of values or benefits cannot be pushed by a process that points out an optimal, goal-oriented distribution. Rarely does an evaluation report intrude in political decision making, say the others (Lauth and Abney, 1986; Lauth, 1985).

But can they both be true? If so, is there a point of reconciliation at which we find the two approaches actually working in harmony? The purpose here is to argue for integration—that the symbols, language, and rituals create and maintain a reality no longer sustainable with hierarchical relationships alone.

D. One Case of Reform: The Balanced-Base Budget System

If we consider budget decision making as fragmented, we see vastly different sets of attention rules used by budget actors. Process more or less formalizes the application of some rules. Budget reforms come about, therefore, as methods of forcing budget actors to attend to budget decisions in particular ways with an agreed-upon timetable.

What these particular ways are, it turns out, are sources of competition. Budget actors evade those rules which bind them and abide by those that do not. In this section, we expand the discussion on balanced-base budgeting and describe in more depth this one instance of budget reform. It is a case study, and its generalizability is limited, as are all conclusions found using this method.* However, the conclusions do make a persuasive argument for the case of budget signaling from top to bottom of the hierarchy using symbol, ritual, and language.

---

*This section relies primarily on Muchmore and Duncan (1982), and the information is used with their permission.

i. Executive Reorganization in Kansas

Until 1972, governors of Kansas had limited power. Their ability to appoint heads of departments had been superseded by the appointment of boards and commissions, which then appointed the department heads. Moreover, the budgeting authority belonged essentially to the legislature and the agencies which together decided budgets without the 2-year-term governor having much say. The legislature met every other year for fiscal matters, leaving much of the oversight function in budget matters to a budget office jointly controlled by the governor and the legislature.

In 1972, the legislature passed and the voters approved a sweeping consolidation of management control in the governor's office. The governor gained responsibility for initiating and proposing an executive budget. In addition, boards and commissions were often abolished with appointment authority over department heads reverting to the governor, further strengthening gubernatorial power. The legislature, for its part, created greater fiscal oversight with beefed up staffing in its Legislative Research Division and its Ways and Means Committee.

The separation of executive and legislative control over budgeting that resulted from the 1972 effort forced the passage of information through the governor's office. In fact, the 1972 law provided that the governor's budget agency stipulate the form of budget requests, and that agency requests would be provided the legislative committees simultaneously with their submission to the governor. Such a form precluded some agency-legislative committee interaction because "no cabinet secretary relishes the prospect of appearing before a Ways and Means Committee to defend both his agency request and his governor's recommendation when the two do not coincide" (Rein and Brown, 1982, p. 33).

a. The balanced-base budget (BBB) process

From 1972 to 1982, the governor, legislature, and agencies worked through an annual budget accommodation. The legislature retained much control over budgeting. The governor, not quite having full power over the executive branch, let the budget director retain control over minutiae, and influenced state agencies through wide-ranging efforts to increase federal aid, reform the tax system, and appoint personally loyal cabinet secretaries. The budget office, nominally a part of the governor's staff, remained a joint legislative executive shop (Bibb, 1984).

By the beginning of the term of John Carlin, however, budgeting had become a routine, giving the new governor little strategic leeway. Legislative committees insisted on appropriating federal funds, such as revenue sharing, refused to reform the tax system by levying a minerals extraction tax, and used the budget to drive a wedge between the governor and his most loyal cabinet members (Muchmore and Duncan, 1982).

The BBB process was created to neutralize some of the legislative hegemony over the budget. The budget reform was meant to achieve two goals: provide strategic control and, in so doing, consolidate the governor's management control over the executive branch.

ii. Revisions to Kansas Budgeting to Bring BBB into Being

Muchmore and Duncan (1982), the inventors of the BBB reform, described it as an effort to gain the attention of executive branch officers. This attention shift came about through scarcity production. To illustrate, previous to the installation of a new budget system in Kansas, revenue estimates were made only after agency budgets had been prepared. They first came into play as the central budget staff began work with the governor to reconcile requests to available resources.

Since the BBB system introduced resource limitations as a first step, the revenue-estimating schedule was advanced by 6 months—from November to the preceding May. After the early projections had been reviewed, the governor allocated expected State General Fund revenues among agencies in order to create a "budget base" that would become the centerpiece for all ensuing budget construction.

Each agency was directed to prepare a budget in which total General Fund outlays equaled the assigned base level. Hence, the summation of all planned agency outlays exactly equaled expected revenues, and the base was a balanced budget.

To retain the characteristic of balance, gubernatorial recommendations for expenditures in any agency in excess of the allocated base amount had to be offset by a corresponding reduction elsewhere in the budget.

The governor's base allocations applied at the agency level and not at the program level. Agency managers were left free to propose a distribution of the base amount across programs within their jurisdiction.

A critical element of the revised process was the information base available to the governor for deciding base budget allocations to agencies. In April, agencies were directed to prepare "issue papers" on major policy questions they believed the governor should consider in dividing expected revenues among agencies. The issues and alternatives posed in the papers, accompanied by budget office analyses, constituted the data base for the governor's deliberations.

In the second year of implementation, the issue paper process was expanded to include input from private interest groups as well as state agencies. This broadened the array of issues and the variety of expertise available to the governor when allocations were made.

A form of zero-based budgeting also became part of the balanced-base budgeting system. It was felt that the governor would also need information on the changes in agency operations and public benefits that would occur if an agency received an amount of money that differed from the base allocation. Having assigned a base allocation and directed agencies to formulate budgets at that base level, the governor also assigned a second allocation at a higher level and a third allocation at a lower level. Agencies were then directed to prepare budget submissions at each of these supplementary levels to reflect potential agency adjustments to reduced funding and to express the priorities that might be executed if funding were raised above the base. Thus, the product with which the governor was presented, in anticipation of final budget decisions, was an array of alternatives that approximated the information required for optimal choices.

The array of alternatives focused not only on expenditures but also on variations in output. If the principles of constrained maximization were to be observed, it was thought, equal emphasis had to be placed on measurement of performance and service delivery. Therefore, the revised system obligated agencies to provide performance indicators and measures for each expenditure level.

These measures provided a means of assessing progress toward achieving stated program goals. Ideally, they also permitted a rough comparison of costs and benefits across a range of possible outlays, enabling the evaluation of adjustments either above or below the base allocation. In practice, the shift in emphasis from cost data to a combination of cost and benefit data was difficult to achieve in the short run.

The reasons were easily recited. First, benefit and performance information was hard to obtain for some programs, and its reliability could be subject to challenge unless it reflected an established data-gathering process. Second, even when performance data were available, they were vulnerable to conflicting interpretations. Costs, on the other hand, were easily obtained, thoroughly documented, backed by extensive historical information, and relatively unambiguous. Budgetary discussions, therefore, gravitated toward costs, particularly when the final fiscal plan adopted by the legislature was written in terms of cost control and not in terms of expected performance. The presumption in favor of cost data as the overriding element of decision making was not easily countered.

The revised system also imposed both a program structure and a program planning requirement on agencies. The operations of state agencies were reviewed to determine how activities could more logically be clustered so that a budget unit was defined by reference to one or more common objectives and coherent management. The results were a breakdown of state government into approximately 350 programs. In some instances, subprograms were defined as subsidiary but discrete activity clusters within programs. The fundamental unit for budget preparation purposes was the program.

The creation of programs logically preceded a second step; namely, the preparation of operations plans to spell out in detail the goals and objectives for every budget unit: to describe the operational characteristics of the program, to identify long-term factors affecting the need for the service, and to provide indicators that could be used to monitor performance. Such program plans were commonly used in the central management and budget systems of the states from which members of the Division of Budget were recruited.

iii. Questions for a Study of BBB

As with any new official taking office, the investiture may provide considerable amounts of information to nominal subordinates and actual competitors. Thus, we wanted to determine what the components of the Kansas governor's investiture included. Specifically, what symbols and what rituals took on importance through the BBB system? Did they add to a plausible interpretation? Did the ritual leave the governor open to plausible alternative interpretations?

iv. Methods Used in the BBB Study

The balanced-base budgeting system had constant scrutiny from both executive branch agencies who experienced it and legislators who contended with the governor for control of spending priorities. To ascertain the views of those who experienced the system, interviews and questionnaire surveys were conducted to create data sets.

Four sets of data on these budget actors and their reactions provide detail about what the budget system became useful for and how the system became implanted in the larger system of state government decision making. One of these data sets came from a survey of agency budget officers, the primary officers who responded for agencies to the Division of Budget (Miller and Olson, 1983). Two surveys looked at legislators and their views on the system (Solomons, 1983; Tinkum, 1982). A battery of face-to-face interviews with cabinet secretaries surfaced conclusions made by high-level managers.

The research design had one longitudinal feature. The questionnaires to agency budget officers and one of the legislator questionnaires (Tinkum, 1982) were administered within 6 months of the end of the first budget formulation cycle using BBB, as were the interviews with high-level managers. The second legislator survey (Solomons, 1983) was conducted after the second budget formulation cycle.

v. Findings and Discussion

The agency budget officials tended to see the new budget system as a sign of change. For small agencies, the writing was on the wall to begin responding to queries in programmatic terms rather than service delivery terms. Large agencies, accustomed to a program view of the world, nevertheless felt that they gave away a source of leverage by giving away problem analyses and policy initiatives before the budget season even got started.

In both cases, however, the governor, it appeared, had accomplished two objectives. First, he had consolidated executive power through the budget process laying full claim to the values and imperatives of responsible administration. He may not have begun the executive reorganization movement in Kansas, but, it was said by a cabinet secretary, he did finish it with the BBB system.

It was in the BBB system that agencies felt the allocation power an executive budget brings to responsible administration. In this case, the allocation nominally resulted from decisions premised on agency policy papers, problem studies, and strategic environmental scans.

The governor, in any case, was able to achieve his second objective through the allocation decision. He was able to produce the political spectacle of a decision, and a major one at that, by announcing in grand style a direction for the budget to take before the first line-item form was ever filled out.

The grand allocation gesture came without the normal hearings process presided over by budget office officials. Previously, "cat and mouse games" had taken place. According to a previous budget director (Bibb, 1984, p. 126),

> Kansas law provided that the director of the budget review the requests of the state agencies and recommend a tentative budget to the governor from which the agencies could appeal to the governor for restoration. We had established the practice of periodically excluding programs from my recommended list so that, in the appeal process, they would be evaluated and a decision made as to whether each program should be continued and, if so, at what level.

The budget director could force the agency to reveal data that would not ordinarily come out in the budget review process, and the director could hand the governor the hot political potatoes that the budget director found it unwise to handle himself. This stopped. With BBB, the governor could ask what the agency was doing to ensure his objectives. A game still, the budget hearing became a stage in which the governor could play by his own script, not by the agencies', in holding them accountable for his agenda.

Thus, on the administrative side, symbols, rituals, and language were brought into play in support of the consolidation of gubernatorial power. The allocation decision symbolized initiative and decisiveness on the part of the leader. In so doing, the allocation encouraged individual agency discipline in favor of larger goals—Elder and Cobb's (1983) arguable primary role for symbols.

The budget hearing, normally a ritual demonstrating budget office mastery over accounting detail, was replaced by a ritual of a different sort. The hearing ritual provided the governor an opportunity to use the dramaturgy of probing agency budget requests to play the roles of both provider to the faithful and punisher of the wicked. At once the governor could ask for information in broad sweeping terms, pointing out the value a program provided. At others, he could command the damnation of those who failed his sense of vision and who allowed events to take his initiatives in directions he did not want, all before an audience newly enamored with gestures, scenes, and spectacle.

The governor's use of BBB fulfilled Edelman's three purposes for rituals (1964). By personally presiding and "leading" in his visionary way, the governor could quiet the resentment his early allocation had stirred. Yet, the allocation itself, affirmed and defended by agencies in the hearings, became the grand gesture that reaffirmed the role of the executive in the democratic system. Finally, by both quieting resentment and reaffirming the governor's role, the hearing ritual in BBB gave the governor the ability to gain agency conformity.

Balanced-base budgeting led administrators to talk a different language. The system encouraged "cost control," program-level responsibility for "priority setting," and an "early spot" of problems. Most of all, the BBB system, temporarily perhaps, stilled the agencies' claims to a common "fair share" of additional budget authority each year, instead pushing large, new-money budget increments toward single objectives that the governor's strategy favored.

The legislative reaction was slow but stubborn. As both Tinkum (1982) and Solomons (1983) found, legislators refused at first to believe that the reform had any relevance for them. Only when legislators observed the way the system consolidated the governor's power did they begin to encourage agency dissent.

That dissent came first from the state universities, a traditionally independent group, especially experienced in the ways of legislative processes like budgeting. Disgruntled university officials ultimately gained an attorney general's opinion of the constitutionality of the BBB process; the opinion lent support to the maintenance of some close agency/institution-legislative committee relationships, especially when these unique institutions had not been swept under the governor's full control through previous executive reorganizations.

The effect of the balanced-base budgeting system for theory was to demonstrate the potential applicability of investiture rituals in signaling a change in emphasis to important subcultures. The governor, using the hearing ritual, forced the allocation to be a symbol of executive power, and through the allocation, signaled change to all executive agencies who could not escape his dominance through special legislative dispensation. These confrontations lent support to the budget process and its language under the new BBB regime, ritual consolidated power, and through spectacle, quieted resentment, reaffirmed the budget allocation role, and gained conformity. The upshot was the final consolidation of a 20-year centralization of management prerogatives in the office of governor.

IV. CONCLUSIONS

This discussion has explored the productivity ramifications of different budget procedures. We first looked at existing budget types, from the control-oriented line-item budget format to the more complex balanced-base budget format established in the state of Kansas. Each has its own unique contribution to make to productivity improvement, but each, we argued, has a common goal: to signal the intention of chief executives.

This goal, we now argue, may have a more sweeping impact on productivity improvement. To the extent that this budget role helps unite the organization members in a purpose, it both decentralizes decision making and integrates activities from lowest to highest levels. The budget signals intent by specifying activities that must take place, the deadlines by which time they are to be completed, the information which is to be reported, the avenues through which communication is to be achieved, and the appropriate arguments which may take place in making decisions. Each of these is specified by some budget form, question, date, or meeting agenda.

Whether the budget process functions to further the public interest in productivity is a matter which voter control over chief executives decides. To the extent that the goals of the chief executive are those of the voting population—as well as legislators and others who have critical decisions to make in budgeting—the budget system can equip the system to operate productively.

References

Anton, T. J. (1964). *Budgeting in Three Illinois Cities,* Institute of Government and Public Affairs, Urbana, Illinois.

Bibb, J. W. (1984). A retrospective look at state budgeting, *State and Local Government Review,* 16 (3): 123-29.

Burkhead, J. (1956). *Government Budgeting,* Wiley, New York.

Burkhead, J. (1972). The budget and democratic government. In Lyden, F. J., and Miller, E. G., (eds.), *Planning, Programming, Budgeting,* Markham, Chicago, p. 73.

Cohen, M. D., and March, J. G. (1986). *Leadership and Ambiguity: The American College President,* 2d ed., Harvard Business School Press, Cambridge, Massachusetts.

Edelman, M. (1964). *The Symbolic Uses of Politics,* University of Illinois Press, Urbana, Illinois.

Edelman, M. (1977). *Political Language: Words That Succeed and Policies That Fail,* Academic Press, New York.

Edelman, M. (1988), *Constructing the Political Spectacle,* University of Chicago Press, Chicago.

Elder, C. D., and Cobb, R. W. (1983). *The Political Uses of Symbols,* Longman, New York.

Freeman, R. J. (1972). Municipal budgeting, accounting, reporting and auditing 1972-1999, *Alabama Municipal Journal,* 29 (June): 10.

Grizzle, G. (1969). PPBS in Dade County: Status of development and implementation, A Report to the Joint Economic Committee, United States Congress, U.S. Government Printing Office, Washington, D.C.

Grizzle, G. (1986). Does budget format govern actions of budget-makers, *Public Budgeting and Finance,* 6 (Spring): 60-70.

Grossbard, S. I. (n.d.). *PPBS for State and Local Officials,* Bureau of Government Research, University of Rhode Island, Kingston.

Hatry, H. P. (1972). Reflecting the consumer viewpoint in state and local government fiscal and expenditure decisions, *National Tax Journal,* 25 (September): 363.

Hatry, H. P., and Cotton, J. (1967). What is PPB? In *Program Planning for State, City, and County Objectives,* PPB Note 10, George Washington University State and Local Finances Project, George Washington University, Washington, D.C., p. 6.

Hirsch, W. Z. (1966). State and local government program budgeting, *Regional Science Association Papers,* 18: 156.

Horton, R. A. (1969). PPBS in metropolitan Nashville-Davidson County, Tennessee. A Report to the Joint Economic Committee, United States Congress, U.S. Government Printing Office, Washington, D.C.

Jernberg, J. (1969). Information exchange and congressional behavior: Caveat for PPB reformers, *Journal of Politics*, 33 (August): 722-40.

Jernberg, J. E. (1971). Financial administration. In Banovitz, J. M. (ed.), *Managing the Modern City*, International City Management Association, Washington, D.C., p. 10.

Lauth, T. (1985). Performance evaluation in the Georgia budgetary process, *Public Budgeting and Finance*, 5 (Spring): 2.

Lauth, T., and Abney, G. (1986). *The Politics of Administration*, State University of New York Press, Albany.

Luther, R. A. (1972). PPBS in Fairfax County: A practical experience. In Lyden, F. J., and Miller, E. G. (eds.), *Planning Programming Budgeting*, Markham, Chicago, p. 347.

March, J. G., and Olsen, J. P. (1986). Garbage can models of decision making in organizations. In March, J. G., and Weissinger-Baylon, R., (eds.), *Ambiguity and Command: Organizational Perspectives on Military Decision Making*, Pitman, Marshfield, Massachusetts.

March, J. G., and Olsen, J. P. (1989). *Rediscovering Institutions: The Organizational Basis of Politics*, Basic Books, New York.

Mead, G. H. (1934). *Mind, Self and Society*, University of Chicago Press, Chicago.

Meiszer, N. M. (1969). Developing a planning, programing, budgeting system in Dayton, Ohio. A Report to the Joint Economic Committee, United States Congress, U.S. Government Printing Office, Washington, D.C.

Merewitz, L., and Sosnick, S. H. (1971). *The Budget's New Clothes*, Markham, Rand McNally, Chicago.

Miller, G. J. (1991). *Government Financial Management Theory*, Marcel Dekker, New York.

Miller, G. J., and Olson, K. (1983). *Preliminary Assessment of Specific Dimensions of Balanced Base Budgeting, State of Kansas*, State of Kansas, Division of the Budget, Topeka.

Moak, L. L., and Hillhouse, A. M. (1975). *Concepts and Practices in Local Government Finance*, Municipal Finance Officers Association, Chicago.

Morstein Marx, F. (1957). *The Administrative State*, University of Chicago Press, Chicago.

Muchmore, L., and Duncan, H. (1982). *The Kansas Budget Process: Concept and Practice*, Capitol Complex Center, University of Kansas, Topeka.

Municipal Finance Officers Association (1954). *Performance Budgeting and Unit Cost Accounting for Governmental Units*, Municipal Finance Officers Association, Chicago, p. 1.

Mushkin, S. J. (1969a). Innovations in planning, programming and budgeting in state and local governments. A Report to the Joint Economic Committee, United States Congress, U.S. Government Printing Office, Washington, D.C.

Mushkin, S. J. (1969b). PPB in Cities, *Public Administration Review*, 29 (March-April): 16-21.

Pfeffer, J. (1981). *Power in Organizations*, Pitman, Marshfield, Massachusetts.

Pyhrr, P. (1973). *Zero-Base Budgeting*, Wiley-Interscience, New York.

Rein, M., and Brown, S. (1982). *The Appropriations Process in the Kansas Legislature*, University of Kansas, Capitol Complex Center, Topeka.

Ridley, C. E., and Simon, H. A. (1943). *Measuring Municipal Activities*, International City Managers Association, Washington, D.C.

Schick, A. (1966). The Road to PPB: The stages of budget reform, *Public Administration Review*, 26: 243-58.

Sherwood, F. P., and Best, W. H. (1975). The local administrator as budgeter. In Golembiewski, R. T., and Rabin, J. (eds.), *Public Budgeting and Finance*, F. E. Peacock, Itasca, Illinois, pp. 386-96.

Simon, H. A. (1976). *Administrative Behavior*, 3d ed., Free Press, New York.

Solomons, A. (1983). *Legislators' Attitudes toward the Balanced Base Budgeting System after Two Fiscal Years*. Unpublished Masters of Public Administration Policy Paper. Department of Public Administration, University of Kansas, Lawrence.

Storing, Herbert J. (1962). The science of administration: Herbert A. Simon. In Storing, Herbert J. (ed.), *Essays on the Scientific Study of Politics*, Holt, Rinehart and Winston, New York.

Sundelson, J. W. (1935). Budgetary principles, *Political Science Quarterly*, 50 (June): 243.

Tinkum, M. W. (1982). *Legislators' Attitudes about the Balanced Base Budget System of the State of Kansas*. Unpublished Masters of Public Administration Policy Paper, University of Kansas, Lawrence.

Trice, H. M., Belasco, J., and Alutto, J. A. (1969). The role of ceremonials in organization behavior, *Industrial and Labor Relations Review*, 23: 40-51.

Waldo, D. (1948). *The Administrative State: A Study of the Political Theory of American Public Administration*, Ronald Press, New York.

Walker, W. E. (1986). *Changing Organizational Culture: Strategy, Structure, and Professionalism in the U.S. General Accounting Office*, University of Tennessee Press, Knoxville.

Wanat, J. (1973). Budget format and budget behavior, *Experimental Study of Politics*, 2 (October): 58-69.

Wildavsky, A. (1966). The political economy of efficiency, *Public Administration Review*, 26 (December): 292-310.

Wildavsky, A. (1969). Rescuing policy analysis from PPBS, *Public Administration Review*, 29 (March-April): 189-202.

Wildavsky, A. (1975). *Budgeting: A Comparative Theory of Budgetary Processes*, Little, Brown, Boston.

Mandates: Cases in State-Local Relations

States always have mandated functions, standards, tax limits, and other rules for their local governments. These mandates require local governments either to take certain specific actions (e.g., undertake obligations) or not to take certain specific actions (e.g., comply with prohibitions). In recent decades, the number and costs of state mandates have grown, sometimes substantially, in most states. Local officials, therefore, have voiced increasing concern about them—what New York City's former mayor, Edward I. Koch, referred to as the "mandate millstone."[1] This concern is particularly pronounced when considering unfunded state mandates.

The concern over state mandates centers around an array of issues, including the decline in federal aid relative to state and local own-source revenues, the shift of more programmatic responsibility from the federal government to state and local governments, questions of accountability, public opposition to rising taxes, the difficulties faced by many local governments in meeting the financial demands of mandates, and the implications of mandates for local self-government, including the willingness of citizens to hold office, especially in small jurisdictions that lack the administrative support to cope with mandates. These circumstances have produced a renewed focus on state-local relations in the 1980s and 1990s.

This information report on state mandates is an effort to shed more light on an increasingly controversial aspect of state-local relations. It continues a line of research begun by the Advisory Commission on Intergovernmental Relations (ACIR) in 1978.[2] The initial report and a 1982 update[3] were the first systematic attempts to survey states' activities concerning mandates to local governments. On the heels of ACIR's 1978 report, Catherine Lovell et al. published a study of issues and impacts of federal and state mandates on local governments.[4]

Now, with renewed and growing concern about mandates, other organizations also are pursuing the issue. The U.S. General Accounting Office (GAO), the National Conference of State Legislatures (NCSL), and The Urban Institute have studied state mandates recently.

GAO's study viewed state experiences as a source of ideas for the treatment of this issue by the Congress. GAO found that the critical factors in prompting states to limit or to reimburse mandates included legislators' concern about imposing costs on local governments, a healthy fiscal climate, and a constitutionally established or voter-initiated requirement that the state reimburse local governments for the cost of mandates.[5]

NCSL's examination of mandates found them to be a major source of concern in state-local relations. It recommended that states review mandates to local governments and consider relaxing or eliminating those requirements, and in some cases assuming the cost of complying with them. NCSL encouraged states to develop some method, such as requiring fiscal notes,

---

Reprinted from Advisory Commission on Intergovernmental Relations, *Mandates: Cases in State-Local Relations*, M-173 (Washington, D.C.: ACIR, September 1990), 1-9.

to assure that the costs of all prospective mandates are taken into account before they are enacted.[6]

The Urban Institute's book *Coping with Mandates: What Are the Alternatives?* addresses several aspects of federal and state mandates. The contributing authors and editors examine the history of mandates and the recent experience of federal and state governments in responding to complaints from governments receiving the mandates. They place the mandates issue in three larger contexts: the policy goals that intergovernmental regulations are meant to achieve, the tensions among governments in the federal system, and the assessment of regulation as an instrument of government policy.[7]

DEFINITIONS OF MANDATES

In general, mandates arise from statutes, constitutional provisions, court decisions, and administrative regulations or orders that demand action from "subordinate" governments under pain of civil or criminal sanctions. There are, however, many variations on this basic definition.

Those who subscribe to a strict legal definition construe mandates as direct orders with clear intent to demand positive action allowing no legal choice but to carry out that action. Others view mandates from a broad financial perspective—considering the aggregate financial impact induced by a "superior" government. By this definition, mandates are interpreted as covering a wide array of governmentally induced costs. These added costs may result, for example, from conditions of grants-in-aid accepted "voluntarily" by recipients. These conditions may add a new function for local governments to administer; require that local governments fund part of this new function themselves; set higher standards of service than local governments would set for themselves; and require specific, unnecessarily expensive, or inappropriate means of achieving the mandate locally. In addition, mandates sometimes are defined to include commands that local governments not raise certain revenues, thereby causing revenue losses or "negatively" induced costs.

State laws contain many variations in the definition of mandates. For instance, Connecticut, Florida, Massachusetts, and Rhode Island focus on provisions that require local governments to spend more. Massachusetts mandates take effect only if the state assumes the cost.[8] Florida includes state actions that impose "costs" through an erosion of the local tax base[9] and encompasses actions that place limitations or requirements on local governments without compensating them for the costs necessary for compliance.[10] Connecticut specifically excludes court orders and any legislation necessary to comply with a federal mandate.[11] In Rhode Island, only that portion of a state mandate that exceeds the federal requirement is defined legally as a state-mandated cost.[12]

In addition to the legal variations, different working definitions have been developed by state-local relations bodies assigned to catalog mandates or to prepare fiscal notes. For instance, the South Carolina ACIR's working definition includes "statutes, regulations or orders that require the locality to undertake an activity or comply with some standard, even when the locality would have undertaken the activity or complied with the standard voluntarily." By the same token, it includes actions that prevent the locality from undertaking the activity, "even when the locality would not consider undertaking it in the absence of statute, regulation, or order."[13] The definition crafted by the Ohio Local Government Advisory Commission includes any constitutional, statutory, or regulatory provision requiring local governments to establish or modify a specific activity or provide a service to meet minimum state standards.[14]

Much of the variation among definitions of mandates stems from the imposition of unfunded service mandates. For those who take a broad interpretation, what counts is the bottom line, namely, net costs. Those who subscribe to a narrow interpretation of mandates believe that money is secondary; if something is mandated, it must be done, regardless of the cost.

A central controversy, therefore, arises from the question of what is reimbursable. Some analysts think the term "mandate" is pejorative because it characterizes regulations as imposing excessive, and thus compensable, costs on state and local governments.[15] Others accept the term as a nonprejudicial descriptor of a common class of intergovernmental activities.

WHY THE MANDATE REVOLUTION?

The rise of mandating as a salient issue in the federal system still remains to be explained in an adequate fashion. No doubt, a number of factors have combined to spark the mandate revolution.

One likely factor is that the policy demands on the Congress and state legislatures often outrun the fiscal resources needed to meet the demands. In the absence of sufficient funds—whether by legislative choice or economic constraint—there is a strong temptation to satisfy policy demands by mandating that functions be performed by other governments. Furthermore, policy demands tend to grow continually. Many policy demands of the past are institutionalized in today's budgets, thus requiring policymakers to expand their budgets with new resources or to shift new demands onto other budgets.

Another possible factor has been the growing professionalization of state governments. Better staffing for governors and legislatures, four-year gubernatorial terms, annual legislative sessions, enhanced administrative capacities, and other reforms advocated during the post–World War II era were intended to increase the policymaking abilities of state governments. The situation is not unlike Parkinson's Law: work expands to fill the time available for its completion. Key assumptions underlying these reforms were that states are better able than local governments to raise revenue, and that states actually would raise sufficient revenues to exercise their new capabilities, especially in light of what was then a rising tide of federal aid. Furthermore, the reform of state courts, coupled with the models of activism forged by federal courts, has resulted in growing state judicial activism and, thus, more state judicial mandates.

In addition, the professionalization of state governments attracted more interest groups to state capitols, a trend that appears to have accelerated again as the federal government shifts more responsibilities to the states and as states assume more responsibilities on their own. Interest groups have incentives to focus on state government rather than on many different local governments, just as they have incentives to focus on the Congress rather than on 50 state legislatures.

Thus, state governments are much more powerful policy engines than they were in the past, but the fiscal fuel needed to operate those engines is often in short supply. To some extent, therefore, to make use of their policymaking abilities and also to comply with federal mandates, states must commandeer the engines of their local governments.

The reform of state government, moreover, often was accompanied by attempts to centralize policymaking so as to provide for better policy coordination, more efficient administration, and more uniform implementation of public policy. The logic of state centralization frequently benefited local governments when states could provide some support to fund new policies and assume the performance of certain local functions; consequently, there was a tendency to overlook the inevitability that centralization would produce unfunded mandates.

Another likely factor in the rise of mandating is that citizens expect governments to conform to much higher standards and to protect individual rights more extensively than was true in the past. Movements to improve individual rights protection, consumer protection, environmental protection, social welfare, public service provision, government efficiency, and public accountability, for example, all require governments to behave in new ways, some of which were virtually unheard of a few decades ago. Many of these issues, moreover, are not subject to local variability, at least below certain levels. If the environment is to be protected, for example, then all governments must conform to and enforce certain minimum standards. State and local governments might be permitted to set higher standards, but not lower ones. Hence, states are called on to set or enforce standards in a wide variety of fields—standards that must be applied uniformly to all local jurisdictions or to jurisdictions of a certain type, regardless of the variability of local jurisdictions' capacity to cope with the costs of compliance.

Ironically, it is quite possible that local innovations contribute to state mandating, too. That is, when a local government comes up with a good idea, the state legislature may think that it is a good idea for all local governments and, therefore, mandate it statewide, even though what works in one locality may not work well or at all in other localities.

Sometimes, local officials request state mandates, not usually for themselves but for other local officials. A mayor may desire a state mandate to counteract city council opposition to a policy, and vice versa. County officials may want the state to mandate certain municipal policies, and vice versa. Suburbs may want the state to mandate certain policies for central cities, and vice versa. Independently elected county treasurers or sheriffs may ask the state to mandate salary increases, jail conditions, service levels, and so on. As one observer has noted, "Counties can be their own worst enemies when it comes to mandates."[16]

Of course, mandates also stem from genuine deficiencies in local government performance. Where one or more local governments decline to remedy a problem, the state may be compelled to mandate a remedy. Local deficiencies may give rise to interest group activity and media coverage demanding state action.

SOURCES AND LEGITIMACY

State mandates come from many sources—constitutional provisions, citizen initiatives, legislative statutes, judicial decisions, and administrative regulations. It can be argued that those sources closer to the people have more democratic legitimacy, while those farther removed from the citizenry have less democratic legitimacy because their political accountability is less direct.

Constitutional mandates have the closest links to direct democracy because, in effect, the people are imposing these mandates on themselves by ratifying a new constitution or constitutional amendment. Citizen initiatives, whether they result in constitutional amendments or new statutes, also have direct linkages to the electorate and have a potentially high degree of accountability. Perhaps the principal problem with such mandates is that citizens are not always aware of the policy consequences or tax costs of the proposals they support at the ballot box.

Statutory mandates have less direct links to citizen consent because they come (with gubernatorial approval) from the legislature, which is elected to represent the people. Here, questions can be raised about whether a mandate is motivated merely by political pressures to shift costs from the state to local governments or by careful, disinterested consideration of the extent to which the mandate represents genuine statewide (or greater than local) interests and whether it really should be paid for by the state.

Mandates issued by state courts are linked to the people insofar as they are tied closely to specific provisions of state constitutions and statutes. Judges do interpret the law, however, and their interpretations adhere more or less to the intentions of the citizens or elected officials who made the law. Court mandates, especially those based on constitutional grounds, generally are perceived by voters as having a high degree of legitimacy, thus making the courts an attractive forum for interests seeking to promulgate mandates. If a mandate is perceived as being too onerous, however, citizens can respond by amending the constitution, initiating a new law where this is permitted, or, in most states, unseating judges in selection or retention elections.

Administrative mandates are more likely to be created by processes more insulated from the people than those that emerge from the legislative process. A classic problem with administrative mandates is that they can be more rigorous, detailed, and inflexible than originally envisioned by the governor or legislature. Once embedded in the bureaucracy, moreover, a mandate sometimes can be hard to dislodge. At times, however, the executive branch may weaken a mandate or decline to enforce it vigorously. Hence, the executive branch itself can become a battleground for mandate compliance and enforcement. Administrators, of course, can be held accountable by judicial challenge and by corrective action by the legislature and the governor.

GOVERNMENTS AFFECTED

State mandates also can be considered in terms of the governments they affect. The legitimacy of imposing requirements or induced costs perhaps can be said to differ for home rule municipalities and counties, cities and counties without home rule, school districts, and special districts. These differences depend on the relationship of a local government to the state.

It may be argued, therefore, that mandates undermine home rule and should be applied more sparingly to home rule municipalities and counties. By contrast, non–home rule municipalities are subject to many state restrictions in any event, and non–home rule counties usually are considered to be administrative arms of the state, at least in part, and naturally subject to a broad range of state mandates. School districts, once largely a local concern, now are viewed as so important to equal rights, equal opportunity, and economic development that states have come to play a stronger role in financing and setting standards for them. Some special districts, by contrast, perform such obviously local functions that they remain relatively removed from state regulation. Other districts, however, have responsibilities in such fields as environmental protection and transportation, in which district activities cross local boundaries and take on "state" purposes.

THE ISSUE OF FUNDING

Local governments face their public responsibilities with varying degrees of fiscal capacity to respond to federal and state mandates. Governmental theory aside, the major mandate issue for many local governments is whether they can meet the financial demands of state mandates within the financial limits imposed by the state, that is, limits on local taxing, borrowing, and/or spending authority, plus limits on state and federal funding. Decisionmakers in state governments are pressured strongly by policy advocates to consider only the substantive merits of individual programs when weighing whether to assign specific responsibilities and costs to local governments. Local governments, however, have to contend with the aggregate impact of all mandates, compared with their total taxing capacity and any federal and state aid that is available. State officials do not always consider local tax capacities before making decisions that require the expenditure of local revenues. In addition, states sometimes simultaneously place further limits on local taxing or borrowing authority as they expand mandates.

Much of the mandate controversy surrounds the mismatch between mandated responsibilities and local funding capacities. Several means can be used to close the gap. These include expansion of local revenue authority, increased state aid for specific and general purposes (with or without fiscal capacity equalization features), state reimbursement of specific mandates, and provisions making certain types of state mandates unenforceable if they are not funded by the state.

One potential side effect of state mandates when they place financial burdens on local governments is that they can induce privatization. Costs passed from the federal government to state governments, and from state governments to local governments, in turn, can be passed on to the private sector. One example is the rise of residential community associations (RCAs) that remove some demands for public services from the local budget.[17] Another example is the use of developer fees (and privately donated public facilities) in some states to cover a portion of the costs of new roads, schools, sewers, parks, and other facilities that must be built before development is allowed to proceed.[18] Such privatization can increase the influence of private developers in the development of communities and diminish the influence of public policies. Jurisdictions in need of economic development may be particularly prone to passing on mandated costs to the private sector.

Who Should Pay?

Obviously, someone has to pay for mandates, but answering the question of who should pay is not easy. This question is most complicated in the case of state-local relations because, unlike the relation of the states to the federal government, local governments do not have co-sovereign status with their state. In the absence of specific state constitutional provisions regarding mandates or local autonomy, a state has broad legal authority to promulgate mandates for local governments.

Responsible Parties?

One argument for reimbursement is that those who make policy should bear the responsibility of paying for it. By this reasoning, the state should either raise revenue or take revenue from other state sources to provide payment for local mandate compliance. A mandate reimbursement requirement would compel the state to confront the real costs of public policy and to weigh priorities. In the absence of a reimbursement requirement, state officials do not have a strong incentive to assess costs, short term or long term. Weighing priorities is also important because an unfunded mandate may displace not only a local priority but also another state priority embedded in another unfunded mandate with which local governments are expected to comply.

The Greater Good?

The counter argument is that the legislature and the governor represent all of the people of the state and therefore can be understood as representing the people's interests. As such, state officials may be said to have a broader perspective on policy issues and to be less tied, as a group, to particular parochial interests. Given that citizens must pay for a mandate in any event, the state is obligated to consider the wisdom of a mandate itself, but is free to decide whether the costs of compliance are to be paid through local revenues, state revenues, or some combination thereof. Furthermore, if a state is obligated to reimburse all mandates, then the state may at times be deterred from making policy where it should make policy. If local officials, who also represent citizens in their various local capacities, object to a mandate, then the appropriate arenas for settling this local-state difference can be said to be the legislative, judicial, and electoral arenas. If local officials cannot prevail in those arenas, then the state cannot be said to be obligated to reimburse local governments for the cost of complying with the mandate.

Equity

Meeting compliance costs with local revenues rather than state revenues is not necessarily inequitable if it means that citizens pay for their own jurisdiction's compliance and not for compliance by other jurisdictions. Reimbursement from state revenues could mean that citizens in some jurisdictions will bear the costs of compliance in other jurisdictions as well as their own. This arrangement could be inequitable if citizens in jurisdictions that already behave in ways that conform to the mandate must pay for compliance in those jurisdictions whose deficient behavior prompted the state mandate. Thus, under a reimbursement system, citizens of an environmentally progressive jurisdiction, for example, may end up paying for the environmental insensitivities of other jurisdictions. A reimbursement system, therefore, could encourage less enlightened jurisdictions to sit on their hands waiting for state money rather than acting on their own. Such behavior could produce a general climate of local reluctance to initiate change and innovation. At the same time, if the state is obligated to provide reimbursement for all or most mandates, the state, too, could become less open to change and innovation.

An argument for reimbursement, however, is the extent to which the state tax system imposes tax burdens more equitably than most local tax systems. If local tax systems are more regressive than the state tax system, or are too limited geographically to match costs with beneficiaries equitably, then unfunded mandates may exacerbate these conditions. Yet, a reimbursement system may aggravate other problems, such as fiscal disparities, if revenues are transferred to both poor and wealthy jurisdictions for mandate compliance.

When a state or the voters statewide impose limits on the taxing, borrowing, and spending authority of local governments, however, the state cannot then equitably impose unfunded mandates on those local jurisdictions. It also would appear inequitable for a state to set limits on its own taxing, borrowing, and spending authority, and then shift the costs of policy initiatives to local governments in the form of unfunded mandates.

Passing the Buck

Virtually everyone recognizes, however, that unfunded mandates sometimes represent little more than an unwillingness on the part of state officials to confront voters directly with the true costs of public policy. Unfunded mandates can give citizens the impression that they are getting something for nothing. If local officials later must raise taxes or fees to comply with mandates, they are not likely to be able to shield themselves from adverse voter reaction by pointing to a state mandate millstone. Consequently, a constitutional or statutory mandate reimbursement requirement can act as a check on the ability of state officials to pass the tax bill on to local officials.

Moral Objectives

Even if the principle of reimbursement is accepted, however, not all mandates carry a clear moral obligation for reimbursement. Is a state, for example, obligated to reimburse a jurisdiction for compliance with a mandate that is intended to remedy racially discriminatory policies or corrupt activities long practiced by the jurisdiction? In other words, some mandates fall into a category in which it can be said that the mandate is a state response to some abuse or dereliction of responsibility by a few or many local jurisdictions. In these cases, one might argue that local officials ought to be required to face up to their responsibilities.

State Policy Change

At the same time, however, a case for reimbursement can be made where a mandate requires local governments to do something previously prohibited by the state or to stop doing something previously permitted or required by the state. In other words, when a state changes its policy, it would seem to be under some obligation to bear some of the costs imposed on local governments by that change.

Cost Differentials

Reimbursement systems also can mask the true costs of living in particular kinds of communities. That is, certain kinds of costs to citizens arise from living in a big city, a suburban municipality, or a rural community, for example, and in different areas of a state. A particular mandate, therefore, may impose a heavier burden on one type of jurisdiction than another; yet, to the extent that citizens choose to live in one type of jurisdiction rather than another, a reimbursement system can mask the true cost of that choice and allow citizens to enjoy a residential choice at less than true cost to themselves and more cost to others.

Practical Problems

It is not always easy, of course, to estimate the fiscal impacts of mandates across time and across a multiplicity of jurisdictions. No matter how refined and nonpartisan the estimating techniques used in fiscal notes processes, those techniques are subject to error. Estimating equitable rates of reimbursement becomes all the more problematic when reimbursements are to be provided over a period of years or, theoretically, in perpetuity.

Another practical problem is that legislators are inclined to circumvent mandate reimbursement requirements. Debates arise over cost estimates, definitions of mandates, and whether a particular act is a mandate falling within a reimbursement requirement. Thus, the process can become politicized, with the state seeking to pay the least and local governments seeking to obtain the most.

Need for Mandates

The debate over reimbursement, however, obscures the more fundamental questions, namely, what and how should the state mandate? It is not self-evident that states need to enact a large number of mandates. The problem for local governments often lies in the proliferation of highly detailed mandates, and mandates that serve mainly to micromanage local governments and public services. Where such mandating occurs, an argument can be made for reimbursement because such detailed mandating converts local governments into mere administrative arms of the state, thus defeating one of the major purposes of having local governments in the first place.

THE ISSUE OF LOCAL AUTONOMY

State mandates are of considerable concern to local governments because they reduce local autonomy. Essentially, a mandate substitutes state priorities for local ones, although state and local priorities sometimes may coincide. Some local officials believe that by depriving local governments of control over a significant portion of their budgets, state mandates diminish local governments' ability to respond to their own citizens' needs and priorities. In some cases, however, localities may be happy to shift the political responsibility for a necessary but unpopular mandate to the state, and let state officials take the heat.

State mandates also may be inappropriate because the state is not close enough to the operating details of mandated programs to establish them in the most effective and efficient forms. On the other hand, being too close to the problem and all of its political controversies, as local officials often are, may paralyze needed public action. Although local government decisionmakers have to maintain their accountability to their own citizens, they also are accountable to the state and have a responsibility to help meet statewide needs that have effects beyond the borders of individual localities. This spillover effect, however, creates arguments for state financial responsibility.

MANDATES AS VIRTUE AND VICE

The issue of mandates is difficult to deal with, in part because mandates are both a virtue and a vice of a federal system. They are a virtue in the sense that citizens can turn from one government to another in order to obtain action on their concerns. If local government is not responsive to a particular concern, then citizens may turn to their state government or to the federal government. Such forum shopping, or "pragmatic federalism,"[19] expands citizen choice and opportunities to influence government. This is a major reason for not having centralized government.

At the same time, mandating is a vice in the sense that it encourages centralization and reduces accountability by removing decisionmaking from local arenas and, in the case of unfunded mandates, by allowing one government to satisfy a set of citizen concerns while requiring other governments to confront citizens with the tax bill. Mandating encourages citizens to do end runs around their local governments rather than engaging their fellow citizens in the debate and action that might be necessary to alter or introduce a local policy.

Mandates rarely are invented by legislators out of thin air; instead, they are generated by constituents seeking action for their own benefit or for the benefit of their neighbors. As more legislators become full-time legislators, moreover, they are likely to face more constituent pressures for mandates. Consequently, whether or not there are constitutional or statutory provisions for reimbursement or fiscal relief, local governments will have to be attentive to the political dynamics of mandating in today's highly interdependent and intergovernmentalized environment.

SUMMARY OF STATE MANDATING POLICIES

State mandating policies include a substantial number of different elements. Each of the following strategies has been drawn from the practices and recommendations of states represented in this report, as well as other states:

- A definition of mandates acceptable to all parties concerned.
- A comprehensive inventory of mandates, updated periodically.
- A mandate review program to modify or repeal mandates as appropriate.
- Use of mandating as a last resort, after other cooperative approaches fail, and after careful consideration of whether a state interest really needs to take priority over the right of local self-government.
- Involvement of local officials in the formulation of necessary mandates.
- Use of the state ACIR as a key point of interaction and mediation.
- Requirements that legislative intent and compliance criteria be clear, perhaps requiring the legislature to specify a policy objective in a statement attached to or combined with mandate legislation.
- Procedural requirements for committees and each house of the legislature for action on mandates (e.g., recommission to a substantive committee on a point of order, an extraordinary majority-vote rule).

- Emphasis on results rather than process in mandates.
- Provision for local flexibility in methods of compliance.
- An appeals process, especially for localities that may have particular compliance problems, and especially when process is detailed in a mandate.
- Inclusion of a sunset provision in mandates.
- A fiscal notes process—or at least establish that fiscal notes are important in principle—to determine the probable fiscal impact of mandates on local governments. (About 42 state legislatures have some type of fiscal notes process, as does the Congress.)
- A mechanism for measuring local government fiscal stress, with mandate costs included in the measure.

Approaches to Mandate Funding

Several options are available to fund state mandates to local governments:

- Mandate reimbursement. As of 1988, at least 14 states had either a constitutional or a statutory general mandate reimbursement requirement[20] (*Constitutional:* California, Hawaii, Michigan, Missouri, New Hampshire, New Mexico, and Tennessee. *Statutory:* Colorado, Florida, Illinois, Massachusetts, Montana, Rhode Island, and Washington).[21]
- Rules that allow local governments to ignore certain mandates that are not funded by the state. (This still requires a definition of mandates, however.)
- State assumption of responsibility for selected local functions, or swaps of functions between the state and local governments. (A state ACIR could examine such issues and make recommendations.)
- Specific functions or services treated as shared state-local responsibilities and, therefore, financed on a cost-sharing basis.
- Expansion of local government revenue authority to help localities meet mandate compliance costs.
- Provision of more general aid to local governments, especially through a program of fiscal

capacity and fiscal equalization revenue sharing. (So long as the state assumes responsibility for ensuring local capacity to perform functions, both mandated and nonmandated, state mandates are less likely to be burdensome, and the state itself can link policies with costs. This approach does not solve the problem of determining the costs of mandates, but it may simplify matters and be more equitable than mandate-by-mandate reimbursement.)

Notes

1. Edward I. Koch, "The Mandate Millstone," *The Public Interest*, no. 61 (Fall 1980): 42-57.
2. U.S. Advisory Commission on Intergovernmental Relations, *State Mandating of Local Expenditures* (Washington, D.C., 1978).
3. U.S. Advisory Commission on Intergovernmental Relations, *State Mandates: An Update* (Washington, D.C., November 1982).
4. Catherine H. Lovell, Robert Kneisel, Max Neiman, Adam Z. Rose, and Charles A. Tobin, "Federal and State Mandating on Local Governments: An Exploration of Issues and Impacts," (Riverside, Calif.: Graduate School of Administration, University of California, 1979).
5. General Accounting Office, *Legislative Mandates: State Experiences Offer Insights for Federal Action*, September 1988, GAO/HRD 88 75, 30.
6. Steven D. Gold, *Reforming State-Local Relations: A Practical Guide* (Denver: National Conference of State Legislatures, 1989), 105.
7. Michael Fix and Daphne A. Kenyon, eds., *Coping with Mandates: What Are the Alternatives?* (Washington, D.C.: Urban Institute Press, 1990), xiv.
8. Massachusetts General Laws c. 29, s. 27C.
9. U.S. Advisory Commission on Intergovernmental Relations, "Florida State Mandates on Local Governments," in *Mandates: Cases in State-Local Relations* (Washington, D.C., 1990), 29.
10. Florida Statutes, Section 11.076.
11. Public Act 83 12, (June Special Session), An Act Concerning State Mandates to Local Government.
12. General Laws of Rhode Island, 45 13 7, "State Mandated Costs Defined."
13. "South Carolina: State Mandated Local Government Expenditures and Revenue Limitations," in *Mandates*, 13.
14. Ohio: Devising a Workable Solution to the Mandate Dilemma," in *Mandates*, 11.
15. U.S. Department of the Treasury, *Federal-State-Local Fiscal Relations: Report to the President and the Congress* (Washington, D.C., 1985), 80.
16. Jane Massey, "Approaches to the Mandate Problem," in Tanis J. Salant, ed., *Rethinking State County Relations* (Tucson: Office of Community and Public Service, University of Arizona, May 1990), 79.
17. U.S. Advisory Commission on Intergovernmental Relations, *Residential Community Associations: Private Governments in the Intergovernmental System?* (Washington, D.C., 1989).
18. Arthur C. Nelson, ed., *Development Impact Fees: Policy Rationale, Practice, Theory, and Issues* (Chicago: American Planning Association, 1988).
19. Parris N. Glendening and Mavis Mann Reeves, *Pragmatic Federalism*, 2d edition (Pacific Palisades, Calif.: Palisades Publishers, 1984).
20. U.S. General Accounting Office, *Legislative Mandates: State Experiences Offer Insights for Federal Action* (Washington, D.C., September 1988).
21. Florida has a constitutional amendment for mandate reimbursement on the November 1990 ballot. Connecticut has a voluntary reimbursement program, but no reimbursements have been made yet. The state has increased general aid to local governments.

Financial Indicators for Local Government

Sanford M. Groves, W. Maureen Godsey, and Martha A. Shulman

During the 1970s, governments at all levels experienced an increasing number of financial problems. These problems were related to rising demand for services, unionization of public employees, structural changes in the economy, shifts in population, double digit inflation, and changes in intergovernmental relationships.

When cities such as New York and Cleveland developed serious financial problems, government officials across the nation began asking specific and penetrating questions regarding the financial condition of their own communities. Clear, straightforward answers, however, were unavailable because most governments relied on conventional budgetary, balance sheet, or operating statement analysis. For reasons which will be discussed, these conventional types of analysis did not always identify existing or emerging problems. In addition, they tended to focus on a single year and failed to provide either a broad perspective or the types of data which could easily be communicated to city councils or the community-at-large.

The purpose of this discussion is to introduce a technique called "indicator analysis." This technique has been used by the private sector for many years and is usually referred to as financial ratio analysis. The term indicator analysis for the public sector as used in this article is a process that consists of the following.

1. Developing quantifiable measures of financial condition usually in the form of financial, demographic, and economic ratios.
2. Gathering these indicators into an overall system of indicators that highlights the relationship between the indicators.
3. Drawing conclusions regarding the financial health of the governmental entity by identifying the changes taking place and analyzing the direction and speed of those changes, and the relationships among the indicators.

This article will discuss one system of indicators, the Financial Trend Monitoring System (FTMS), developed by the International City Management Association.[1] The system provides tools which a city could use to

- monitor changes in financial condition;
- identify emerging financial problems in time to take corrective action;
- identify existing problems of which the city may not be aware;
- develop remedial action to deal with these problems;
- project future financial needs;
- obtain a clear picture of the city's financial strengths and weaknesses for presentation to the city council, citizen groups, credit rating firms, and other groups with a need to know; and
- provide a long-range perspective for budget deliberations.

Reprinted from *Public Budgeting & Finance* 18 (Summer 1981): 5-19. By permission of Public Financial Publications, Inc.

This article: (1) discusses the meaning of "financial condition" and the problems associated with measuring it, (2) presents the Financial Trend Monitoring System and its 36 indicators, and (3) discusses the experiences which 24 cities have had in using the system.

WHAT IS FINANCIAL CONDITION?

The term "financial condition" has many meanings. In a narrow accounting sense, it refers to a government's capacity to generate enough cash or liquidity to pay its bills. This is referred to here as "cash solvency." Financial condition can also refer to "budgetary solvency"—a city's ability to generate sufficient revenues over its normal budgetary period to meet its expenditure obligations and not incur deficits.

In a broader sense, financial condition refers to the long-run ability of a government to pay all the costs of doing business, including expenditure obligations that normally appear in each annual budget, as well as those that show up only in the years in which they must be paid. Examples of these latter obligations are pension costs, payments for accrued employee leave, deferred maintenance, and replacement of capital assets such as streets, equipment, and buildings. Although these costs will eventually show up in a budget or will otherwise make themselves known, an analysis of the next one to five years may not reveal them. Therefore, this long-run balance between revenues and costs warrants separate attention and is referred to here as "long-run solvency."

Finally, financial condition refers to whether a government can provide the level and quality of services required for the general health and welfare of a community. This can be called "service level solvency." A lack of such solvency would be seen, for example, in the case of a government that happens to be in sound financial condition but is not able to support an adequate level of police and fire services.

Few local governments face such severe and immediate financial problems that they are likely to default on loans or fail to meet payrolls and other current obligations. Therefore, this article adopts a broad definition of financial condition to encompass the four types of solvency described above. By using this broad definition, we hope to deal with the concerns of the many local governments that find themselves in one or more of the following situations:

1. They are under the strain of a few identifiable problems and are seeking to put these problems in a broader perspective.
2. They sense the emergence of problems but are having difficulty pinpointing them.
3. They are in good financial condition but are searching for a systematic way to monitor changes and anticipate problems.

OBSTACLES TO EVALUATING FINANCIAL CONDITION

If we had chosen a definition of financial condition that considered only cash and budgetary solvency, we would have narrowed the range of measurement issues. By including long-run and service level solvency, however, we encounter three sets of problems.

The Social Purpose of a Public Entity

The primary objectives of government include "health and welfare," "political satisfaction," and other values that can be measured only subjectively. Therefore, by including the concept of service level solvency within our definition of financial condition we have to settle for something less than precise measurement.

The State of the Art

Until recently, practitioners and researchers in public finance concerned themselves primarily with cash and budgetary solvency and did not pay much attention to long-run and service level solvency. The main exception has been the investment community, but it has specifically concerned itself with debt-carrying capacity. During the last few years local governments have broadened their concern, but no one has yet developed a comprehensive and practical way to evaluate the financial condition of a particular government.[2]

This lack can be attributed to a number of factors. First, the growth-oriented environment of local government prior to the 1970s discouraged close attention to the broad range of issues that affect financial condition. Second, data on economic and demographic events are difficult and sometimes impossible to obtain. Third, available data cannot always be compared from one city to another, because each city is unique in size, function, geography, revenue structure, and other significant characteristics. Fourth, there is no accepted theory to explain the links between the economic base and city revenue—for example, the extent to which a decline in employment or a shift from manufacturing to retail affects the revenues of a city.[3]

Last, the state of the art does not provide normative standards for what the financial characteristics of a city should be. There is no agreement as to what is a healthy per capita expenditure rate, level of reserves, or amount of debt. The credit-rating industry has many benchmarks for evaluating cities, but these have to be considered in combination with other criteria, such as the diversity of the city's tax base and its proximity to regional markets.[4] Some attempts have been made to develop standards by averaging various cities or comparing one city to another, but, because of the uniqueness of each city and the lack of sufficient objective data, these intercity comparisons have not gained authoritative acceptance.

The State of Municipal Accounting Systems

During the early 1900s, local government accounting systems grew with an emphasis on auditability and on providing visibility to dollars passing through government accounts. The accounting systems stressed legal compliance by tracking the flow of money in and out of the local treasury. The concepts of fund accounting and flow of funds were developed with little attention to cost accounting and to measuring long-run financial health.

The result is that most cities produce budgets showing revenues and expenditures, and most states require cities to balance them in one fashion or another. In addition, most cities produce year-end financial statements including balance sheets and operating statements.

These reports show the flow of dollars during a particular year, but they do not provide the information needed to evaluate a city's long-run financial condition. They do not show in detail the costs of each service provided, or all the costs that are being postponed. They do not necessarily display the accumulation of unfunded pension liabilities or employee benefit liabilities. They do not disclose the loss of flexibility in the use of funds that results from state and federal mandates. In addition, they do not show the erosion of streets, buildings, and other fixed assets that are not being maintained, nor do they re-

late changes in the economic and demographic conditions to changes in revenue and expenditure rates. Finally, they cover a one-year period and do not provide a multi-year perspective on changing conditions.[5]

THE FINANCIAL TREND MONITORING SYSTEM

As can be seen from the foregoing discussion, evaluating a jurisdiction's financial condition can be difficult. It is a process of sorting through a large number of pieces. The pieces include the national economy, population trends, and the internal finances of the city itself. Not only are there a large number of factors to evaluate, but many of them are difficult to isolate and quantify.

No single piece tells the whole story. Some are more important than others, but one usually cannot be sure until the pieces have been assembled. For example, revenues may be higher than ever in absolute amounts and may be exceeding expenditure levels by a comfortable margin. However, if a city fails to consider the effects of sustained high inflation on its purchasing power, it might be lulled into thinking that its financial condition remains as healthy as ever.

In view of this complexity, the lack of complete accounting data, and the lack of accepted theories and normative standards, one might question whether it is possible to rationalize the process of evaluating financial condition.

The answer is yes. Regardless of the obstacles, a city can collect a great deal of useful information, even if this information is only part of what there is to know. Medical science has learned little about the human body compared with what remains to be learned. This lack of total knowledge, however, does not prevent doctors from using what they do know to diagnose and prevent diseases.

The Financial Trend Monitoring System (FTMS) identifies and organizes the factors that affect financial condition so that they can be analyzed and, to the extent possible, measured. It is a management tool that pulls together pertinent information from a city's budgetary and financial reports, mixes it with appropriate economic and demographic data, and creates a series of indicators that, when plotted over a period of time, can be used to monitor changes in financial condition. The indicators deal with 36 separate conditions such as cash liquidity, level of business activity, changes in fund balances, unfunded liabilities, and external revenue dependencies.

The system does not provide specific answers to why a problem is occurring, nor does it provide a single number or index to measure financial health. It does provide the following:

1. Flags for identifying problems
2. Clues to their causes
3. Time to take anticipatory action

It also provides a convenient tool for describing the city's financial strengths and weaknesses to a city council, a credit-rating firm, or others with a need to know. It can assist a council in setting long-run policy priorities, and it can provide a logical way of introducing long-run considerations into the annual budget process.

The Financial Trend Monitoring System (FTMS) is built on 12 "factors" representing the primary forces that influence financial condition. These financial condition factors are then associated with 36 "indicators" that measure different aspects of seven of these factors. Once developed, these can be used to monitor changes in the factors, or more generally, to monitor changes in financial condition. The 12 factors together with the 36 indicators make up FTMS. The factors will be discussed first, and then the indicators.

The Financial Condition Factors

The 12 financial condition factors are shown in Figure 1 in bold type within each box. They are more fully described by the items listed within the brackets.

Each factor is classified as an environmental, organizational, or a financial factor. The chart arranges the factors as if they were inputs to and outputs from each other. This type of relationship is not the only one that exists. For example, many factors at times feed back into themselves and to other factors. In addition, the arrangement of the factors suggests a clear cause-and-effect relationship between the environmental and the financial factors, although this is not always true. The relationships shown here, however, are the primary ones and are the focus for this system.

In short, the environmental factors representing the external influences on a city government are filtered through a set of organizational factors. The result is a series of financial factors which describe the internal financial structure of the government unit.

The *environmental factors* affect a city in two ways. First, they create demands. For example, a population increase may force the city to add police, and the acceptance of a grant may require new audit procedures. Second, the environmental factors provide resources. An increase in population may also increase community wealth and tax revenues, while the grant may provide funds to build a new city hall. One way or another, the environmental factors may create demands, provide resources, or establish limits. Underlying an analysis of the effects of environmental factors on financial condition is the question: Do they provide enough resources to pay for the demands they make?

The *organizational factors* are a government's responses to changes in the environmental factors. We assume that any government can remain in good financial condition if it makes the proper adjustments to adverse conditions by reducing services, increasing efficiency, raising taxes, or taking some other appropriate action. This assumes that public officials have sufficient notice of the problem, understand its nature and magnitude, know what to do, and are willing to do it.

These are optimistic assumptions, especially in light of political constraints, deficiencies in the state of the art, and limitations in municipal accounting. Underlying an analysis of the effects of organizational factors on financial condition is the question: Do your legislative policies and management practices provide opportunity for appropriate responses to changes in the environment?

The *financial factors* reflect the condition of the government's internal finances. In some respects they are a result of the influence of the environmental and organizational factors. If the environment makes greater demands than resources provided, and if the organization is not effective in making a balancing response, the financial factors would eventually show signs of cash, budgetary, or long-run insolvency. In analyzing the effects of financial factors on financial condition, the underlying question is: Is the government paying the full cost of operations without postponing costs when revenue might not be available to pay these costs?

Figure 1: *Financial Condition Factors*

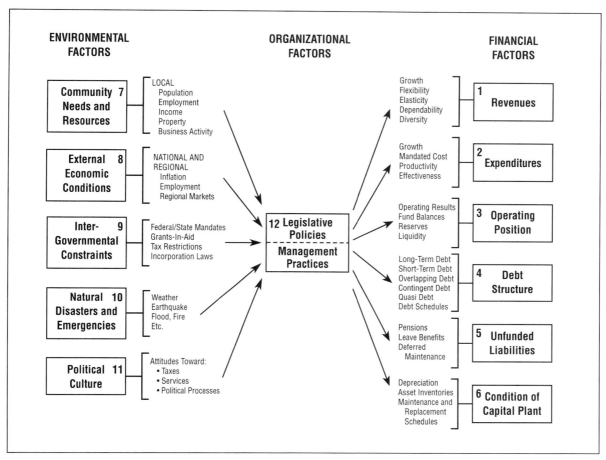

The Indicators

The indicators are the primary tools of the system. They represent a way to quantify changes in the factors discussed above. Figure 2 shows the 36 indicators along with the factors with which they are associated. Next to each indicator is an arrow pointing either up or down. These arrows should be read as "increasing" or "decreasing." If a city's indicator is moving in the direction shown, it should be considered a potential problem requiring further analysis. The mathematical formula for each indicator is shown in Figure 3.

Indicators are shown for only 7 of the 12 factors. Not all the factors are quantifiable in a meaningful management sense; some, such as Political Culture and Natural Disasters and Emergencies, have no indicators. Some indicators apply to more than one factor but are shown in only one place. For example, Percentage of Intergovernmental Revenues, shown under Factor 1 (Revenues), could also be considered an indicator under Factor 9 (Intergovernmental Constraints) insofar as it measures a city's dependence on grants. Likewise, Operating Deficits, shown under Factor 3 (Operating Position), could be considered an indicator under Factor 12 (Legislative Policies and Management Practices). The indicators have been grouped under the factors into which they most logically or conveniently fit.

Once a city quantifies the indicators for a period of years, it can combine them into a single chart or groups of charts which would represent a historical profile of the city. This profile would display many of the financial, economic, and demographic trends of the city.

124 / BUDGET FORMULATION: BUDGET SETTING

Figure 2: *Financial Trend Monitoring System*

```
                                                              FINANCIAL
                                                               FACTORS

  Revenues Per Capita ↑↓          Revenues
  % Restricted Revenues ↓          ├── Growth
  % Elastic Tax Revenues ↑         ├── Flexibility
  % Intergovernmental Revenues ↑   ├── Elasticity
  % One-Time Revenues ↑            ├── Dependability
  Property Tax Revenues ↓          └── Diversity
  % Uncollected Property Taxes ↑
  % User Charge Coverage ↓
  Revenue Shortfalls ↑

  Expenditures Per Capita ↑       Expenditures
  Employees per Capita ↑           ├── Growth
  % Fixed Costs ↑                  ├── Mandated Cost
  Fringe Benefits Per Employee ↑   ├── Productivity
                                   └── Effectiveness

  Operating Deficits ↑↓           Operating
  Enterprise Losses ↑              Position
  General Fund Balances ↓          ├── Operating Results
  Liquidity ↓                      ├── Fund Balances
                                   ├── Reserves
                                   └── Liquidity

  % Short-Term Liabilities to     Debt
    Operating Revenues ↑           Structure
  % Long-Term Debt to:             ├── Long-Term Debt
    • Assessed Valuation ↑         ├── Short-Term Debt
    • Population ↑                 ├── Overlapping Debt
    • Personal Income ↑            ├── Contingent Debt
  % Debt Service to Operating      ├── Quasi Debt
    Revenues ↑                     └── Debt Schedules
  % Overlapping Debt ↑

  % Unfunded Pension Liability ↑  Unfunded
    • Assessed Valuation ↑         Liabilities
    • Population ↑                 ├── Pensions
  % Pension Assets to Benefits     ├── Leave Benefits
    Paid ↓                         └── Deferred
  % Unused Vacation and Sick           Maintenance
    Leave ↑

  Maintenance Effort ↓            Condition of
  Level of Capital Outlay ↓        Capital Plant
  % Depreciation to Value of       ├── Depreciation
    Fixed Assets ↓                 ├── Asset Inventories
                                   ├── Maintenance and
                                   │   Replacement
                                   └── Schedules
```

- - - - EARLY WARNING TRENDS - - - -
- - - - FACTORS AFFECTING FINANCIAL CONDITION - - - -

ORGANIZATIONAL FACTORS

Legislative Policies / Management Practices

ENVIRONMENTAL FACTORS

LEGEND
↑ Increasing
↓ Decreasing

Population ↑↓
Median Age ↑

Personal Income ↓
Poverty Households ↑
Public Assistance Recipients ↑

Property Value ↓
Residential Development ↑
Vacancy Rates ↑

Employment Base:
• Unemployment Rate ↑
• No. of Community Jobs ↓

Business Activity:
• Retail Sales ↓
• Gross Business Receipts ↓
• No. of Businesses ↓
• Business Land Area in Use ↓
• Value of Business Development ↓

Community Needs and Resources
LOCAL
Population
Employment
Income
Property
Business Activity

NATIONAL AND REGIONAL
Inflation
Employment
Regional Markets

External Economic Conditions

Inter-Governmental Constraints
Federal/State Mandates
Grants-In-Aid
Tax Restrictions
Incorporation Laws

Natural Disasters and Emergencies
Weather
Earthquake
Flood, Fire
Etc.

Political Culture
Attitudes Toward:
• Taxes
• Services
• Political Processes

Evaluation Questions

- Does your external environment provide sufficient resources to pay for the demands it makes?
- Do your internal legislative policies and management practices provide the opportunity to make the appropriate response to changes in the environment?
- Is your governmental unit paying the total cost of operating without postponing costs to a future period when the revenues may not be available to pay the costs?

Figure 3: *Summary of Indicator Formulas*

Indicator No.	Title	Formula	Indicator No.	Title	Formula
1.	Revenues per Capita	Net Operating Revenues in Constant Dollars / Population	20.	Debt Service	Net Direct Debt Service / Net Operating Revenues
2.	Restricted Revenues	Restricted Operating Revenues / Net Operating Revenues	21.	Overlapping Debt	Overlapping Long-Term Debt / Assessed Valuation
3.	Intergovernmental Revenues	Intergovernmental Operating Revenues / Gross Operating Revenues	22.	Unfunded Pension Liability	Unfunded Pension Plan Vested Benefits / Assessed Valuation
4.	Elastic Tax Revenues	Elastic Operating Revenues / Net Operating Revenues	23.	Pension Assets	Pension Plan Assets / Pension Benefits Paid
5.	One-Time Revenues	One-Time Operating Revenues / Net Operating Revenues	24.	Accumulated Employee Leave Liability	Total Days of Unused Vacation and Sick Leave / Number of Municipal Employees
6.	Property Tax Revenues	Property Tax Revenues in Constant Dollars	25.	Maintenance Effort	Expenditures for Repair and Maintenance of General Fixed Assets / Amount of Assets
7.	Uncollected Property Taxes	Uncollected Property Taxes / Net Property Tax Levy	26.	Level of Capital Outlay	Capital Outlays from Operating Funds / Net Operating Expenditures
8.	User Charge Coverage	Revenues from Fees and User Charges / Expenditures for Related Services	27.	Depreciation	Depreciation Expense / Cost of Depreciable Fixed Assets
9.	Revenue Shortfalls	Revenue Shortfalls[1] / Net Operating Revenues	28.	Population	Population
10.	Expenditures per Capita	Net Operating Expenditures in Constant Dollars / Population	29.	Median Age	Median Age of Population
			30.	Personal Income	Personal Income in Constant Dollars / Population
11.	Employees per Capita	Number of Municipal Employees / Population	31.	Poverty Households or Public Assistance Recipients	Poverty or Public Assistance Households / Households in Thousands
12.	Fixed Costs	Fixed Costs / Net Operating Expenditures			
13.	Fringe Benefits	Fringe Benefit Expenditures / Salaries and Wages	32.	Property Value	Constant Dollar Change in Property Value / Constant Dollar Property Value Prior Year
14.	Operating Deficits	General Fund Operating Deficit / Net Operating Revenues			
15.	Enterprise Losses	Enterprise Profits or Losses in Constant Dollars	33.	Residential Development	Market Value of Residential Property / Market Value of Total Property
16.	General Fund Balances	Unrestricted Fund Balance of General Fund / Net Operating Revenues	34.	Vacancy Rates	Vacancy Rates
			35.	Employment Base	• Rate of Unemployment • Number of Community Jobs
17.	Liquidity	Cash and Short-Term Investments / Current Liabilities	36.	Business Activity	• Retail Sales • Number of Community Businesses • Gross Business Receipts • Valuation of Business Property • Business Acres Developed
18.	Current Liabilities	Current Liabilities / Net Operating Revenues			
19.	Long-Term Debt	Net Direct Long-Term Debt / Assessed Valuation			

Note: This figure is intended as a summary of the indicators, the data each requires, and their formulas. For a more detailed look at how each piece of data is to be derived, see Sanford M Groves *Financial Trend Monitoring System: A Practitioner's Handbook* (Washington, D.C.: International City Management Association, 1980); and Handbook 1, *Evaluating Financial Condition* (1980).

[1] Net Operating Revenues Budgeted Less Net Operating Revenues (Actual).

Figure 4 illustrates what a trend profile might look like. It is a hypothetical case of a city which might be developing serious problems. The potential for serious problems can be seen by examining the direction and interrelationships between such trends as increasing operating deficits (indicator # 14), decreasing general fund balances (# 16), and decreasing liquidity (# 17). Emerging problems can be seen by looking at increases in the city's unfunded liabilities (#22 and #24), decreases in its business activity (#36) and in its property tax collection rates (#7), and by examining the expenditure trends for capital facility maintenance (#25). In sum, a chart of this sort can be used to help make an assessment of the city's current strengths and weaknesses, and to assist the city in determining what it should do in the future. While these indicators will not necessarily provide answers as to why a problem is occurring or what the appropriate solution is, they will enhance the opportunity for an informed management response.

TESTING THE FINANCIAL TREND MONITORING SYSTEM

The Financial Trend Monitoring System was developed with the assistance of over 50 city managers and finance directors across the country. After the system was developed, draft handbooks were written with detailed worksheets for collecting data and calculating the indicators. The final version of these handbooks is referenced in the first footnote to this article. The system was then tested in 24 cities of varying size, geographical location, financial condition, and urban-rural characteristics.[6] The cities were selected to provide a cross section of these characteristics.

The work was performed by the cities' staff with minimum assistance from ICMA. Each city was asked to develop trends for a 10-year period, to analyze the data, and then provide ICMA with the data and an appraisal of the usefulness of the information as a management tool. The cities were asked the following: (1) Did FTMS give you information you did not already have; (2) was it useful and worth gathering; and (3) how did you use it?

Successes

The results of this test have been positive. First, the test cities have found FTMS to be a useful management tool. The managers and finance directors stated that for the first time, it gave them "hard numbers" to substantiate what they knew intuitively, but which they had difficulty demonstrating. In addition, they felt it provided a broad perspective on their city's financial condition which is readily explainable to individuals such as council persons who do not have a background in municipal finance and economics.

Test cities used FTMS to identify the extent to which user charges no longer covered the cost of specific services; the potential effect which unfunded liabilities such as accumulated employee leave might have on future budgets; and the extent to which the city was deferring maintenance on capital equipment and facilities. Two of the user cities, Rockville, Maryland, and Spokane, Washington, successfully used the results of the study in presentations to the bond rating firms of Standard & Poors and Moody's.

Some cities found that FTMS made them aware of weaknesses in their financial condition. For example, one city, prior to using the system, believed that it was financing its recent growth from revenues derived from rising property values. The city was using growth in assessed valuation as a gauge of how much expansion it could afford. However, when the city adjusted the property value and other related indicators for inflation and then compared them to other revenue indicators, it found that revenue growth from taxes related to property value was a smaller percentage of total revenue growth than had been previously believed. As a result, the city stopped using increases in assessed valuation as a measure of the amount of service expansion they could afford.

A second city, prior to using the system, believed it was in good financial condition although not without problems. However, after analyzing a number of indicators, such as increasing operating deficits, decreasing fund balances, decreasing liquidity, and negative real dollar growth in property tax revenues, the city found that its problems were much more serious than previously believed. In addition, the test cities found creative ways to use the system which were not conceived of when it was developed. For example, some used it as a report card that demonstrated to the council how effectively the city was meeting community objectives. Others used it as an orientation tool to educate new council members. The staff of one city used it to convince its council that the city both needed and could afford to issue bonds; another used it to demonstrate to the council that the city needed to raise its property tax rate.

Figure 4: *Financial Trend Profile*

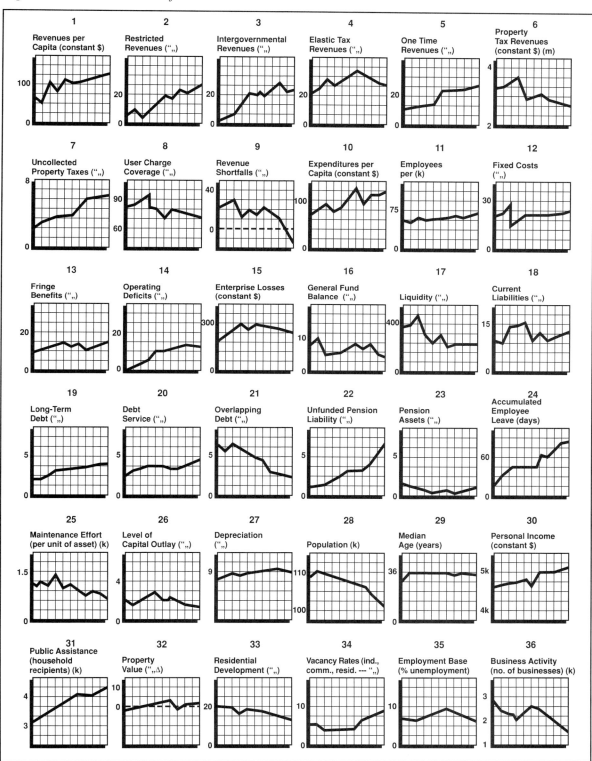

Note: These trendlines represent 10 years of data.

PROBLEMS

Although the results of the test were positive, many of the cities encountered problems developing the indicators. Generally, these problems were technical or managerial.

Technical Problems

The most common technical problem related to the availability of data, especially data going back more than five years. Although all of the participating cities adhered to Generally Accepted Accounting Principles (GAAP) and had independent annual audits, many found that much of the financial data for prior years did not exist in the form which was needed, and that they had to do a considerable amount of disaggregation of accounting data. This was especially true when cities tried to break down the indicators for departments that had been reorganized several times over the past 10 years. It also occurred if a city tried to separate the costs of a particular activity such as street maintenance from the expenditure history of its entire public works department.

Many of the smaller communities discovered that economic and demographic data were difficult to locate. Much of the needed economic and demographic data could be taken directly from the U.S. Census Reports. However, the census reports do not provide timely information for communities under 25,000 in population. Thus, many of the smaller cities had to find alternatives to gather this information. Some went to county or state sources and approximated the data by calculating their percentage share using population, land area, or other appropriate criteria. Others relied on local resources such as utility billing records to estimate the number of households, or occupation tax records to estimate the number of jobs within the city.

Managerial Problems

The managerial problems related primarily to the commitment which top management was able to make. Cities found that a high level of commitment from top decision makers was vital to get the project under way and to make effective use of the results. Twenty-eight cities started the testing process while only 24 completed it. Two of the "dropouts" had a change in city manager during the test period. A third city withdrew because the assistant manager who was directing the project changed jobs. In the fourth city, the council voted not to commit staff time to the project shortly after it was begun.

Some test cities faced initial resistance from their finance staffs. Several finance directors interpreted the manager's decision to begin indicator analysis as an intrusion in their domain or as a lack of faith in the finance staff. However, after they became involved in developing the indicators, the finance directors supported the system and felt it made their job of communicating financial information easier.

CONCLUSION

When FTMS was first developed, it was intended as a management tool for systematically organizing the multitude of factors which affect financial condition. As such, it represents an *analytical approach* which can be used in the various ways discussed above. However, it stops short of providing concrete answers as to whether a particular trend indicates a problem. While the handbooks indicate that certain trends could be a problem and provide suggestions of what to look at if a particular trend is occurring, they leave the determination of whether a trend portends a problem to the judgment of the individuals performing the analysis. The emphasis is put on the analyst's professional experience, knowledge of the city, and judgment. With the exception of credit industry benchmarks for six of the indicators, the handbooks offer no standards by which a city could measure the existence or magnitude of a problem.

The deliberate omission of normative standards was due to imperfect understanding of the factors affecting financial condition, the lack of adequate research data, and the uniqueness of individual cities. Surprisingly, the staffs of the test cities did not find the lack of standards a major drawback. Rather, they felt that the system provided sufficient data and flexibility to draw their own conclusions, and appreciated not being locked into arbitrary standards.

Although the creation of standards for individual indicators is fraught with serious problems, FTMS does take one step in this direction by establishing operating definitions for some of the variables. With sufficient time and research, standards are possible. Meanwhile, additional cities are using FTMS or similar indicator systems to provide useful graphic and explainable information.

Notes

1. This article is based on a five-part handbook, "Evaluating Financial Condition," written by Sanford M. Groves and W. Maureen Godsey and published by the International City Management Association in 1980. The research and testing for these handbooks were made possible through grants from the National Science Foundation and the Department of Housing and Urban Development.

2. For a comprehensive review of work on evaluating financial condition, see Richard J. Aronson, "Municipal Fiscal Indicators," *An Information Bulletin of Management, Finance and Personnel Task Force of the Urban Consortium* (Washington, D.C.: U.S. Department of Housing and Urban Development, 1979); and Robert Berne and Richard Schramm, "The Financial Solvency of Local Governments: A Conceptual Approach," A Report Prepared for the International City Management Association, March 1978.

   Individual works of particular interest include: Municipal Finance Officers Association, *Is Your City Heading for Financial Difficulty: A Guidebook for Small Cities and Other Governmental Units* (Chicago: Municipal Finance Officers Association, 1979); Philip M. Dearborn, *Elements of Municipal Financial Analysis,* Special Report, Parts I/IV (Boston: The First Boston Corporation, 1977); George Peterson et al., *Urban Fiscal Monitoring* (Washington, D.C.: The Urban Institute, 1978); Terry N. Clark et al., *How Many New Yorks?* (Chicago: The University of Chicago, 1976); and Richard J. Aronson and Eli Schwartz, "Determining Debt's Danger Signals," *Management Information Service,* vol. 8, no. 12 (Washington, D.C.: The International City Management Association, December 1976).

3. See, for example, Roy W. Bahl, Alan K. Campbell, and David Greytak, *Taxes, Expenditures, and the Economic Base: Case Study of New York City* (New York: Praeger Publishers, Inc., 1974).

4. For a discussion on how credit rating firms rate local government bonds, see Wade S. Smith, *The Appraisal of Municipal Credit Risks* (New York: Moody's Investors Service, Inc., 1979); Hugh Sherwood, *How Corporate and Municipal Debt Is Rated: An Inside Look at Standard and Poor's Rating System* (New York: John Wiley and Sons, 1976); Moody's Investors Service, Inc., *Pitfalls in Issuing Municipal Bonds* (New York: Moody's Investors Service, Inc., April 1977); and John E. Peterson, *The Rating Game* (New York: The Twentieth Century Fund, 1974).

5. For an in-depth discussion of some of the problems associated with current municipal accounting systems, see Roger Mansfield, "The Financial Reporting Practices of Government: A Time for Reflection," *Public Administration Review,* March/April 1979; and Coopers and Lybrand, *Financial Disclosure Practices of the American Cities: Closing the Communication Gap* (Boston and New York: Coopers and Lybrand, 1978).

6. The test cities and their populations are listed below: Abington, Pennsylvania (60,000); Allentown, Pennsylvania (107,000); Anniston, Alabama (34,000); Auburn, Maine (23,000); Chapel Hill, North Carolina (31,000); Columbia, Missouri (68,000); Eau Claire, Wisconsin (49,000); Ellensburg, Wisconsin (13,000); Englewood, Colorado (35,000); Newport, Rhode Island (33,000); Overland Park, Kansas (81,000); Richfield, Minnesota (42,000); Richton Park, Illinois (10,000); Rock County, Wisconsin (140,000); Rockville, Maryland (44,000); St. Augustine, Florida (12,600); Scottsbluff, Nebraska (14,500); Selah, Washington (4,200); Sparks, Nevada (32,000); Spokane, Washington (174,000); Tallahassee, Florida (90,000); Tipton, Iowa (2,800); Walden, New York (5,800); and Yakima, Washington (53,000).

Cutback Management in an Era of Scarcity: Hard Questions for Hard Times

Charles H. Levine

We are entering a new era of public budgeting, personnel and program management. It is an era dominated by resource scarcity. It will be a period of hard times for government managers that will require them to manage cutbacks, tradeoffs, reallocations, organizational contractions, program terminations, sacrifice, and the unfreezing and freeing up of grants and privileges that have come to be regarded as unnegotiable rights, entitlements, and contracts. It will be a period desperately in need of the development of a methodology for what I call "cutback management."[1]

The challenge of *scarcity* and public sector *contraction* to the viability of our political and administrative systems should be obvious: growth slowdowns, zero growth, and absolute declines—at least in some sectors, communities, regions, and organizations—will increase the probability of rancorous conflict, decrease the prospects for innovation by consensus, and complicate the processes for building and maintaining support for administrative systems and democratic processes. In this potentially turbulent environment, the dominant management imperatives will likely involve a search for new ways of maintaining *credibility, civility,* and *consensus;* that is, in an era of scarcity, we will need new solutions to problems of how to manage public organizations and maintain the viability of democratic processes.

WHY CUTBACKS?

The most familiar cause of cuts is *problem depletion;* cuts occur when a problem is solved, alleviated, brought under control, or when the demand that it be solved diminishes. Perhaps the best example of problem depletion has been the effect of demographic changes on the education system. Because our population has aged, schools have been forced to close or curtail activities considerably.

Recent experiments with sunset legislation (where programs are brought under review usually three to five years after their initiation) are aimed at attuning public funding to problem depletion rather than to an agency's survival needs.

A second familiar cause of cuts in public budgets stems from the *erosion of the economic base* of some of our cities and states. The litany of problems in our older cities and in the northeast in general over the past twenty years underlines the agony of managing decline: the growth of dependent populations, the suburbanization of business and industry, and the shifts in economic activity to the sunbelt from the frostbelt have put some areas in the impossible position of needing to do more but being forced by declining tax bases to do less. The well-publicized fiscal problems of New York City and Cleveland and the retrenchment of their bureaucracies represent just the most advanced cases of a widespread national problem.

Reprinted from *Intergovernmental Personnel Notes* (January/February 1979), published by the U.S. Office of Personnel Management. An earlier version of the article was presented as an address to the American Association for Budget and Program Analysis, Washington, D.C., November, 1978.

The third type of cause for cutbacks is *inflation*. The cost of government has risen rapidly over the past ten years—at least doubling in most cases—and has really taken off over the last five years. Because of its service nature, most government costs are incurred by personnel. In an environment of leveling or declining economic growth, something has to give. This means that in order to make any appreciable savings, cuts must be made in personnel and subsequently in the services government agencies offer.

Taxpayer revolt, a fourth cause of cutbacks, has surfaced recently along with much speculation —mostly tied to Proposition 13—about its cause. These explanations usually include reference to the difficulty of tracing the well-being of individual taxpayers to specific government services, the desire of voters to alleviate the impact of inflation on their personal disposable incomes, the backlash of taxpayers against the salary increases of unionized public workers and the services offered to the poor and minorities, and the cumbersomeness of financing local services through the mechanism of the property tax.

A fifth cause of cutback—*limits to growth*—directly or indirectly overarches the others. Our dependence on depletable resources and foreign energy sources has created a severe imbalance between exports and imports, and it is not clear whether we will be able to find substitutes or additional sources of energy by the end of this century. We can also anticipate a further slowing down in the rate of economic growth, at least for the next decade or two.

WHAT IS CUTBACK MANAGEMENT? WHY IS IT DIFFERENT?

Cutback management means managing organizational change toward lower levels of resource consumption and organizational activity. Cutting back an organization involves making hard decisions about who will be let go, what programs will be scaled down or terminated, and what clients will be asked to make sacrifices.

These are tough problems that are compounded by four aspects of resource scarcity. First, behavioral scientists have demonstrated that change is most easily accomplished when the people affected have something to gain, but under conditions of austerity the acceptance of change will be unlikely because the rewards required to gain cooperation and build consensus will be unavailable.

Second, public organizations are confronted with norms, civil service procedures, veterans' preferences, affirmative action commitments, and collective bargaining agreements which constrain the ability of management to target cuts.

Third, organizational contraction produces some serious morale and job satisfaction problems which makes it difficult to increase productivity to make up for the cuts.

Fourth, cutbacks reduce the enjoyment of working and managing in an organization because nearly everyone is forced into a position of having to do with less.

A declining organization confronts its management with several unique problems. The first problem I call *"The Paradox of Irreducible Wholes."* This problem refers to the fact that an organization cannot be reduced piece-by-piece by simply reversing the sequence of activities and resources by which it was built. The "lumpiness" of public organizations stems from the growth process in which critical masses of expertise, political support, facilities and equipment, and resources are assembled. Taking a living thing like an organization apart is no easy matter; a cut may reverberate throughout a whole organization in a way no one could predict by just analyzing its growth and pattern of development.

The second problem is *"The Management Science Paradox."* This problem is caused by the way public organizations invest in and use their data systems and analytic capacity. When organizations have slack resources, they often develop elaborate management information systems, policy analysis capabilities, and hardware and software systems. But, when resources abound, this capacity is rarely used because public agencies usually prefer to spend slack resources building and maintaining political constituencies. In a decline situation, on the other hand, maintaining and using this analytic capacity often becomes impossible for a number of reasons including political pressures. Therefore, in brief, the Management Science Paradox means that when you have analytic capacity you do not need it; when you need it, you do not have it and *cannot* use it anyway.

The third problem is *"The Tooth Fairy Syndrome."*[2] In the initial stages of contractions, few people are willing to believe that the talk of cuts is for real or that the cuts will be permanent. The initial prevailing attitude in the organization will usually be optimistic; i.e., that the decline is temporary and the cuts will be restored soon by someone—in some cases as remote as the tooth fairy. Under these conditions, management's credibility suffers and resistance, cynicism, and sarcasm tend to dominate responses to calls for voluntary budget cutting. The preferred tactical response for nearly everyone is to delay taking action while waiting for someone else to volunteer cuts or for a bailout from a third party.

The fourth problem is *"The Participation Paradox."* The field of organization development teaches that the best way to manage change is to encourage the maximum amount of participation by all affected parties. But a rational cutback process will require that some people and programs be asked to take greater cuts than others. By encouraging participation, management also encourages protective behavior by those most likely to hurt the most. The Participation Paradox confronts management with a nearly insoluble problem: How does one single out units for large sacrifices which have people participating in the cut process? The usual answer is to avoid deadlocks or rancorous conflict and allocate cuts across the board.

"The Forgotten Deal Paradox" is the fifth problem. Ideally an organization or unit should be able to plan cuts and attrition on a multi-year basis. Such an optimum arrangement would allow an organization to plan its cuts so that six months, two years, or further on it will be allowed to fill *some* vacancies, replace some equipment, or restore some services when needed. In the private sector it is possible to make bargains for restoring some cuts later on knowing that they will likely be honored by the management team in the future. This kind of arrangement is much less likely in the public sector because the top management team usually lacks the continuity required to make and keep bargains with a long time frame.

The sixth problem is *"The Productivity Paradox."* Briefly stated, when dealing with productivity, it takes money to save money. Productivity requires up front costs incurred by training and equipment expenses. Under conditions of austerity, it is very difficult to find and justify funds to invest in productivity improvement, especially if these funds can only be made available by laying off employees or failing to fill vacancies.

These six problems are illustrative of the difficulty involved in managing cutbacks. They tend to force management to rethink the process of organizational development and growth; and they force managers to make new kinds of strategic choices in the face of perplexing uncertainty.

WHAT STRATEGIES?

At the present stage of our knowledge about cutback management, strategies are easier to describe than prescribe. So at this point, we need to be satisfied to raise appropriate questions and hope that later their answers can help managers cope with austerity. A proper start, therefore, is to investigate the major steps in the cutback process. That is, the strategic choices that an organization must make about confronting, planning, targeting, and distributing cuts.

Resist or Smooth Cuts?

When confronting possible cuts, managers and political leaders will have to choose between resisting these cuts or smoothing them out by limiting their impact on the organization's most important functions, procedures, and long-term capacity. Since no organization accedes to cuts with enthusiasm, some initial resistance is likely. But resistance is risky because "stonewalling" financial stress may ultimately force the need to make cataclysmic cuts like massive layoffs; missed paydays; defaults on loans, bonds, and notes; and the selling off of physical facilities and equipment. Therefore, sometimes, usually quite early in the planning process, an organization's or government's leadership will have to make the choice between struggling to resist cuts or struggling to minimize the negative effects.

Deep Gouge or Small Decrements?

This choice is affected by The Forgotten Deal Paradox; that is, the utility of taking deep cuts initially in order to rebuild the organization later is limited by the risk that the resources needed to build back capacity later will not be available. The alternative strategy is to take the cuts year-by-year in small decrements to minimize their impact in the hope that public support for the agency will increase and the cuts will stop.

The deep gouge strategy tends to make the most rational *management* strategy, but the small decrement strategy *may* make the only rational *political* strategy.

Share the Pain or Target the Cuts?

Sharing the pain of cuts by allocating them across-the-board to all units may minimize pain, help to maintain morale, and build a good team spirit in the organization; but it is not responsible management. Not every unit in an organization or every agency in a government contributes equally to the goals, purposes, and basic functions of that organization or government.

If an austerity situation gets bad enough, some leadership will emerge to identify and rank priorities and allocate cuts to units based on them. These hard choices will be accompanied by intense debates over such matters as the importance of different services, the method of ranking priorities, and the difficulty of maintaining excellence in an organization when it is declining.

Efficiency or Equity?

Perhaps the most difficult strategic choice to make in the cutback process involves the tradeoff between efficiency and equity. This dilemma stems from both the cost of delivering services to different populations and the composition of the public work force.

The most dependent parts of our population—minorities, the poor, the handicapped, and the aged—are often the most costly to serve. Blind cost cutting calculated on narrow productivity criteria could do grave harm to them. The dilemma is also compounded by the recent rise in minority public employment and the salience of seniority criteria in laying off public employees; last-in, first-out criteria for layoffs usually means that minorities and women will be differentially hurt—*irrespective of their productivity*.

Since there will always be a tendency to allocate cuts disproportionately to the politically weak, and productivity criteria *could* be used to disguise such an intent, we can expect cutbacks to spark much litigation as they become more widespread. The outcome of this litigation will, of course, greatly constrain, but never completely eclipse, managerial and political discretion over the locus and extent of cuts.

DIRECTIONS FOR FUTURE RESEARCH

To begin to answer these hard questions, a commitment must be made to develop a research program on the management of fiscally stressed public organizations. We know almost nothing about what works best under different kinds of cutback conditions. So, the first thing we need to develop is a baseline inventory of tools and techniques for managing cutbacks along with case studies of their application. With this information we can begin to sort out methods for scaling down public organizations and make some judgments about their appropriations to solve cutback problems of different types of severity.

Second, we need to find methods for solving the credibility, civility, and consensus problems that plague organizations and governments during periods of large-scale cutbacks. We need to invent and perfect democratic processes for allocating cuts which will make cuts effective yet equitable.

Third, we need to devote a great deal of thought to the ethical dimensions of cutbacks. We need to ask, for example, what the ethical responsibility of an organization is to its terminated employees and de-coupled clients.

Finally, we need to understand how cuts affect public expectations and support for government, i.e., whether expectations about government performance will be lowered and tolerance for poor services will be increased. If the post–World War II era has been until recently characterized by rising expectations and optimism about an active public sector's ability to solve public problems, will this new era produce a downward spiral of expectations and a pessimism about the efficacy of government to help create a better society? On a similar, but more narrow note, how long and to what depths will Americans tolerate the effects of reduced public services on their lives? In other words, if support for government services swings back and forth like a pendulum, how poor will services have to become before support for their improvement begins to build?

These are some hard questions we need to worry about. These, I predict, will be some of the dominant issues of public management in the decade ahead.

Notes

1. For another explication of this theme, see Charles H. Levine, "Organization Decline and Cutback Management," *Public Administration Review* (July/August, 1978): 316-25.
2. I credit Robert W. Wilson of Montgomery County (Maryland) Government for first labeling this phenomenon for me.

Six Steps for Communities in Crisis

Allen J. Proctor

The current economic recession has created difficult budget problems for localities throughout the United States. The prospects for a slow economic recovery with low inflation, while favorable for long-term economic growth, are very unfavorable for tax revenue growth. If this is the most likely economic scenario, then localities will face enormous budget pressures for at least the next several years. Except for those fortunate, and few, localities which still have large fund balances, the prospect of depressed revenue growth for the next several years means that governments must find ways to do business differently if they are to keep their budgets in balance.

The most important factor that will single out the localities that will successfully weather the next several years is the capacity to adopt and adhere to a program of actively anticipating budget problems and responding in the early stages. For a finance officer, this policy would support comprehensive risk analysis (what are the problems one might expect to emerge?) and contingency planning (how will one respond should the problems materialize?). Such a program would make it possible to routinely set aside appropriate reserves for delinquent taxes, adverse judgments and disallowances, extraordinary spending needs, etc. It would also establish a routine timetable for revising revenue and expenditure estimates and responding to those revisions with new tax and spending plans. Without such a program, budget problems are unlikely to be recognized until they come to a head, and responses are unlikely to be formulated and approved until cash is literally running out and a crisis is at hand.

Unfortunately, the point in time when a finance officer is given his or her strongest mandate is too often after a crisis has begun. Once that occurs, a finance officer needs to implement simultaneously six steps that are designed to enhance the ability to maintain budget balance and to begin a process of restoring stability to government policymaking and service delivery. The six steps are as follows:

- Disrupt purchasing and hiring
- Establish and maintain close monitoring of revenues and spending
- Determine whether stopgap financing is needed until budget actions reach full savings potential
- Utilize the media to build public awareness of the crisis
- Initiate analysis of why the problem became a crisis and how this can be avoided in the future
- Consider requesting state oversight or intervention

These steps are designed to achieve three goals. First, establish control of current developments. Above all, don't be a passive victim of economic developments. Second, expect to encounter problems and try to anticipate where they will occur and how

---

Reprinted from *GFOA Budget Bulletin* (Chicago: Government Finance Officers Association, September 1992). By permission of GFOA.

to respond promptly. Third, make sure the fix includes rehabilitation so that your budget planning and control mechanisms will be stronger when the next set of problems emerges.

1. Disrupt Purchasing and Hiring

In a crisis, the foremost priority must be to stop, or at least slow, the momentum of spending. Even when budget problems are well known, the bureaucracy exhibits the human tendency to maintain the status quo, continuing to handle purchasing, hiring, and contracting in routine ways. This routine must be interrupted. While the obvious objective is to make permanent changes in appropriations and spending policy, the first step must be to prevent the fiscal problem from needlessly worsening.

Spending is most effectively disrupted through immediate freezes on hiring and purchasing. The purpose of such freezes is to buy time until analysis and decisionmaking is completed so that permanent spending changes can be implemented. At that time, freezes should be lifted.

Any freeze must have exceptions, and the determination of exceptions is the most important decision to be made. Personnel turnover always occurs; the finance officer should know in what departments and titles to expect turnover and what the dollar value of leaving those positions vacant will be. In addition, a hiring freeze must have a procedure for granting exemptions for critical positions which, if left vacant, would lead to undesirable breakdowns in basic service delivery. Ideally, attrition analysis and exemption planning will have already been completed as part of routine contingency planning. If not, valuable time will be lost while the analysis and planning is performed. On the other hand, if the freeze is imposed without analysis and planning, the effectiveness of the freeze will be compromised because department heads will hesitate in hopes that decisions aren't final and that they will ultimately be granted exemptions.

Effective ways to rapidly slow purchasing are necessarily less specific. First, if the current budget includes funds to offset inflation, that inflation funding should be cancelled immediately. In addition, all encumbrances should be cancelled, to be restored on a case-by-case basis only after review by budget officials as to the government's contractual obligations and the relative importance of the purchase to basic service priorities.

2. Establish and Maintain Close Monitoring of Spending and Revenues

One cannot contain the budget crisis without knowing if the disruption to spending is succeeding. That knowledge can come only through a vigilant monitoring process. The process should ensure that departmental spending adheres to annual *and monthly* targets. It should ensure that your solutions are working: spending reduction initiatives are meeting targeted monthly savings; tax and fee increases are meeting targeted monthly collections.

It is essential that accountability for implementing the response to crisis go beyond central budget and finance staff and reach deeply into departments. Major initiatives should have detailed implementation schedules with progressive deadlines. Specific individuals in the departments should be held accountable for achieving targeted savings by pre-specified dates. The budget or finance office should establish prespecified dates to review progress of each initiative and to decide whether and how to redirect budget-balancing efforts when slippage is identified. The process can be successful only if departmental managers know that their efforts are being monitored and that any effort to postpone or avoid the spending cuts will be identified and foiled.

3. Determine Whether Stopgap Financing Is Needed until Budget Actions Reach Full Savings Potential

Having disrupted spending and established effective controls to ensure budget actions are taking place, there may be a temporary period of cash shortfall before all the new actions achieve enough savings to close the budget gap entirely. This situation is more likely the more severe the budget crisis because substantial changes in tax policy or service delivery typically take six months to a year to develop the proposals, attain any necessary legislative approvals, and implement the changes. (At the simplest level, for example, the annualized savings called for in the budget will take 12 months to reach full value.) Thus, while the budget fixes are coming up to speed, some sort of stopgap financing may be necessary, ranging from cashflow assistance within a fiscal year to deficit financing across fiscal years.

While the precise possibilities will differ across jurisdictions based on varying legal authority and financing arrangements, temporary financing has three basic sources: publically issued notes, the state government, and the public pension system. The most common and straightforward method of temporary cashflow financing is the public issuance of tax anticipation notes or revenue anticipation notes. In difficult circumstances, the issue may be feasible only if it can be privately placed. If the fiscal crisis is sufficiently severe and public confidence is weak, one may need to look to the state government or public pension system.

Since state aid is a significant part of most localities' budgets, the schedule of receipt of state aid can be a significant source of temporary cashflow help. In particular, arrangements can be made with the state to distribute aid on an accelerated basis in order to build cash balances while cash needs are gradually slowed by the locality's budget actions. If the need is more prolonged, direct short-term loans (or guarantees of private loans) can be sought from the state.

The public pension system can be a safe and responsible source of temporary funding when other alternatives are not available and solvency is at risk. Obviously, the pension system must not be abused and the fiduciary obligations of government require that even a hint of abuse be avoided. In that strict context, there are responsible ways to seek assistance from the pension system as a sympathetic creditor while providing safeguards to the system that are identical to those demanded by private lenders. Temporary help can take the form of delays in scheduled payments to the pension system, with interest paid to the system at the same average rate of other system investments. Payment at a lower rate would be a clear abuse of the pension system. Alternatively, this can be done more formally through direct loans or through private placement of tax or revenue anticipation notes which have pledges and escrow procedures identical to publically placed notes. Provision of weaker pledges and procedures would be an abuse of the pension system. Fiduciary considerations may warrant supplementing these pledges with state guarantees of repayment of these funds to the pension system if there is any question that, without those guarantees, the fiduciary obligations of the pension system would not be met.

4. Utilize the Media to Build Public Awareness of the Crisis

A major tool in catalyzing a response to the budget crisis is the media. In particular, the media must be utilized to ensure that there is a widespread perception that a budget problem truly exists and continues to exist. An effective media effort can also develop the essential awareness that the solutions available are limited, the services one receives and the taxes one pays are in immediate jeopardy, and therefore the establishment of priorities and the elimination of low-priority programs must be confronted.

The primary objective of outreach to the media is to challenge complacency, inertia, routine, and "business as usual" among bureaucrats and elected officials. The reason for this is that, once implementation of a budget reduction program begins, the abstraction of budget cuts becomes concrete reality, and support for the budget balancing effort can quickly erode both among the bureaucracy (who hope the crisis will go away) and among the elected officials (who will bear the brunt of citizen complaints about the spending cuts and the tax or fee increases). This tendency toward erosion of support must be actively countered through extensive discussions and interviews with all available media.

Ideally, you will have developed your credibility with good, responsible reporters well before the need for media attention arises. Remember that the effort to sustain commitment to fiscal repair is easily undermined by speculation, "crying wolf," and idle threats of worst-case spending cuts. Therefore, you must avoid them at all times. Instead, your contact with reporters must be dominated by facts: what deficits already exist, what service effects are known versus what effects are speculative, what options are available and what options are not available, what decisions have been made and what decisions have not been made, what was the cashflow deficiency for the month and what is its significance, and so forth.

5. Initiate Analysis of Why the Problem Became a Crisis and How This Can Be Avoided in the Future

Once you have set up a way to slow spending, kept it from getting worse, arranged short-term financing to buy time for your actions to take effect, and established a media effort to sustain the effort, it is time for some reflection and reform. Given the weak outlook for the federal budget and the national economy, getting out and staying out of today's budget problems will require a multi-year effort, which means multi-year financial planning.

One should first view the crisis as an opportunity to establish a better mechanism for anticipating problems, since this crisis developed because one didn't get ahead of the emerging problems. This new mechanism should include procedures for risk analysis and contingency planning as well as establishment of adequately funded reserve funds, as discussed earlier.

Second, one must try to identify long-term solutions. This is difficult and involves confronting very hard choices; however, the media effort that is helping sustain support for current budget actions can also help to build support for discussing long-term solutions including the basic options of permanently eliminating services, raising taxes, introducing new or higher fees, and reducing the cost of existing services. The sense of immediacy of long-term changes is subjective but essential. Early identification of critical near-term deadlines for implementation of multi-year solutions will allow distant goals to make immediate demands on policymakers, the bureaucracy, and the citizenry. However ambitious or naive this objective may seem, one must not let the present opportunity for change and reform slip away as the memory of the budget crisis fades with time.

Exploitation of that opportunity requires thoughtful analysis of the fundamental problems that led to the budget crisis. One must determine if there were persistent errors in budget estimates or procedures that were not corrected and thereby led to crisis. One must determine if the problems were transitory or structural. Transitory problems allow one to have a solution that primarily buys time until the problem disappears on its own. In these circumstances, one should focus reform on developing better monitoring and more effective ways to anticipate problems. On the other hand, structural problems require major policy changes. Examples of structural problems are a sustained decline in the local economy and tax revenues; service demand growth that chronically exceeds the growth capacity of the local tax base; legal mandates or contractual rules that limit the controllable share of expenses so much that the normal volatility of revenues becomes a major budget balancing problem; and, of course, permanent changes in the level or type of federal or state budget support.

6. State Oversight or Intervention

If anticipating, responding, and getting ahead of problems is beyond the scope of local financial and political resources, it may be appropriate to seek state oversight or intervention to attain these three objectives. The possible roles of the state can include establishment of formal oversight agencies, statutory prohibition of practices that chronically lead to local budget problems, and various forms of credit enhancement such as statutory dedication of revenues, statutory bond covenant pledges, statutory escrow procedures, or other statutory means of forcing behaviors on the locality that have otherwise proved elusive.

FILLING POSITIONS DURING A HIRING FREEZE

Hiring freezes are common strategy for reducing expenditures over the short term. The Department of Management and Budget of Volusia County, Florida, designed a scoring system to evaluate requests to fill positions during a hiring freeze. The table in the next column lists the evaluation criteria, weighting, and points that make up that system.

An agency requesting approval to fill a position must rate the position on its relative importance within the agency and its impact on operations if it remains vacant. The criteria for scoring the request are grouped accordingly under "position impact" and "vacancy impact." Each criterion, in turn, is weighted (e.g., funding availability for the position is given a weight of 6 percent of the total 100 percent).

There are two or more possible responses for each criterion. Each response is assigned a point value (e.g., 5 points for external support). Responses under three criteria are assigned a point range. The score for each criterion is determined by multiplying the points for the chosen response by the percentage weight for that criterion (e.g., 5 points × 7.5%). The scores for all of the criteria are then tallied to calculate the total score. In theory, the higher the tally, the greater justification there is for filling the position.

Criteria for Evaluating Position Requests

% Weight		Points
	POSITION IMPACT (30% of Total Score)	
7.5	Position Support	
	• External (public)	5
	• Internal support	2
4.5	Type of Position by Category	
	• Administrative support/clerical	2
	• Professional/technical	2
	• Manual/skilled worker	4
	• Public health/safety	5
4.5	Position Revenue Link/Funding Source	
	• Property tax supported/internal service	1
	• Partially tax supported	2
	• Enterprise	4
	• Fully grant funded	5
	• Partially grant funded	3
	• Direct revenue link	1-5
4.5	Positions—Division	
	• Number of similar positions by category	
	(0-1) 5 pts. (2-4) 3 pts. (5+) 1 pt.	
	• Percent of similar positions by category	
	(75-100) 5 pts. (50-74) 3pts. (25-49) 2 pts. (<25) 1 pt.	
3.0	Positions—Department	
	• Number of similar positions by category	
	(0-1) 5 pts. (2-4) 3 pts. (5+) 1 pt.	
	• Percent of similar positions by category	
	(75-100) 5 pts. (50-74) 3 pts. (25-49) 2 pts. (<25) 1 pt.	
6.0	Funding Availability	
	• Available	5
	• Marginal	2
	• None	0
	VACANCY IMPACT (70% of Total Score)	
28.0	Service Delivery—Vacancy will result in:	
	• Elimination of the service	5
	• Significant delay in providing service	3-4
	• Slight delay in providing service	1
	• None	0
21.0	Financial	
	• Overtime	
	– Cost exceeds position	5
	– Cost between 75 and 100%	4
	– Cost between 25–74%	3
	– Cost less than 25%	1
	• Additional cost of filling position (subtract):	
	> $10,000	3
	> $5,000	1
	$0	0
21.0	Reasons for Vacancy	
	• Management decision	5
	• Attrition	1
	• Transfer	2
	• New positions authorized in current fiscal year	5

Managers must make some tough choices as they fill positions during a hiring freeze. This scoring system does not make those decisions any easier but does help to measure the results.

BUDGET BALANCING STRATEGIES

Listed below are some common strategies used by local governments to avoid budget deficits. The strategies are not presented in any particular order and the list is by no means exhaustive. No one strategy is recommended or discouraged. Each government must decide which techniques best serve its unique situations and adapt those techniques as needed.

- Reduce hours of operation for public facilities (e.g., libraries, recreation centers, swimming pools)
- Close facilities that are receiving low use or are in need of extensive repair
- Reduce service frequency (e.g., reduce garbage collection service from twice a week to once a week) or scale back existing programs
- Investigate the possibility of regional service consolidation
- Use fund reserves or contingencies
- Postpone hiring of selected positions or freeze all vacant and new positions during a specified period
- Refinance debt
- Examine the duties and hours of part-time and temporary staff to determine if the positions are truly needed
- Use volunteers wherever possible to reduce salary and benefit costs
- Replace full-time staff with less costly part-time personnel
- Spread out capital equipment costs over several year period through lease-purchase agreements
- Limit or reduce overtime and callback pay
- Increase user fees, licenses, and permits
- Create new service charges for user-specific services currently funded by other means
- Update asset inventory list to assure purchases are for essential items
- Institute safety programs for employees to reduce claims and employee absenteeism
- Extend the useful life of equipment
- Examine departmental organizations and employee responsibilities for possible position consolidation, transfer to needier department, or position downgrading
- Postpone the implementation of new programs or services or provide a scaled-back version
- Use inexpensive employee recognition practices to generate cost-saving ideas
- Provide early retirement incentives to produce salary and benefit savings by keeping the position vacant or filling it at a lower salary
- Institute a mandated or voluntary employee furlough (unpaid leave of absence)
- Delay or cancel capital projects
- Require employees to pay part of health insurance or increase the amount that employees pay
- Freeze spending in controllable areas of the budget (i.e., office supplies, travel, subscriptions, and capital)
- Sell assets no longer needed or in use
- Transfer services or programs to enterprise funds, if appropriate, in order to free up general fund dollars
- Lease or rent property that the government owns but currently has no plans to use
- Maximize net collections through timely billings and aggressive pursuit of delinquent tax payments
- Establish a joint purchasing agreement with other government agencies to take advantage of reduced prices for larger purchases
- Use attrition to incur savings over time
- Implement across-the-board cuts

How to Read a Budget

James D. Carney and Stanley Schoenfeld

An operating budget is a reflection of a government's financial plans—in its basic form, a listing of anticipated revenues and planned expenditures in the coming year. Although in a more complex form, a budget may contain a great volume of supporting information, readers of budgets should remember that no amount of this information changes the basic form, which should make any budget easy to read and understand. The degree to which it clearly presents its basic message is a measure of the value of the budget document.

Although supporting information is intended to add a more thorough understanding of the government's plan and purpose, it can and often does confuse the reader. However, the absence of supporting information leaves the reader uninformed and dubious about the budget's content and may spur inquiry. We will explore in this article the elements of a representative budget document,* the type of information it presents and omits, and the deductions a reader can draw from it, together with examples of analysis that the reader could conduct.

This discussion is not intended to pass judgment on budget types or present alternate forms. It is intended only to help you, as the reader, better understand the budget example.

ELEMENTS OF A BUDGET DOCUMENT

Budget documents come in all sizes and formats, ranging from concise pamphlets to tomes several inches thick. Fortunately for the reader, they almost all contain four basic sections.

Budget Message

The budget message is generally a narrative preface to the document highlighting the economic climate, community service priorities, special circumstances, general constraints on budget building, and key changes in the budget, both financial and programmatic. It is normally prepared and signed by the government's chief executive, elected or appointed, and is often the only narrative analysis of the planned change included in the budget. The other sections of a budget are most typically in tabular form.

Summary Schedules

This section usually immediately follows the budget message and contains several schedules summarizing the budget. The exact number and type of sched-

---

Reprinted by permission of Peat, Marwick, Mitchell & Company. This article appeared in *Casebook in Public Budgeting and Financial Management,* edited by Carol W. Lewis and A. Grayson Walker III (N.J.: Prentice-Hall, Inc., 1984), 18-35.

*A modified program budget, prepared for a city of 200,000 people, has been used in the various exhibits presented here. Despite its programmatic structure, this budget can also be viewed organizationally, because at the lowest level, the program elements are identical with organizational elements. The example also lists line item data by object of expenditure. Although other types of exhibits could have illustrated a traditional line item approach or a classic program budget, the selected budget contains elements of both and is representative of most budget documents in current use.

ules included will vary with legal requirements, which classification structure in use (i.e., program, organization, line item), and with the preferences of the government.

The following summary schedules are the most commonly used:

- property tax calculation (Exhibit 1)
- total revenues and expenditures (Exhibit 2)
- total expenditures by classification structure (Exhibits 3, 4)
- total revenues by source (Exhibit 7)
- expenditures by fund—used in governments with multiple fund structures (Exhibit 9)

In addition to these five general summaries, individual budgets may often contain other summary schedules of data related to items such as budgeted positions and prior-year fund balances.

For comparison, the document will often show both appropriated and actual prior-year budgets and expenditures, if available.

Detailed Schedules

This section presents the most detailed data. The government normally organizes detailed schedules according to the classification structures it uses. These structures will generally be one or more of the following:

- program—type of service delivered (e.g., fire protection, snow removal)
- organization—unit of organization delivering services (e.g., public works department, crime prevention unit)
- object of expenditure (line item)—type of goods and services to be purchased (e.g., personnel services, office supplies)

In addition to planned expenditures by major classification (Exhibit 8), these schedules may furnish successively lower levels of detail within classifications (Exhibits 5, 6). They may also display expanded information on intended results (service objectives), the current year's achievements, and the planned method of reaching the service objectives (the service plan). Sometimes they show revenues generated by the program or department or expenditure budgeted elsewhere but attributable to the program (e.g., fringe benefits). Comparative data on prior budgets and requested budgets are also generally supplied.

The following detailed schedules are among the more commonly used:

Exhibit 8—Detailed budget by classification (program and object): summary of a program by sub-programs.

Exhibit 5—Detailed budget by classification (program and object): summary and sub-program by program element.

Exhibit 6—Detailed budget by classification (program, organization, and object): lowest level of detail—program element, department, object detail.

Supplemental Data

This last section contains any additional information the government chooses. Placed here because it does not fit appropriately into other sections, it will vary widely from government to government. The most common supplemental schedules are as follows:

Unappropriated funds—a schedule of revenues and expenditures for a self-supporting activity not formally budgeted, such as an airport.

Ordinances—the enabling legislation for adopting the budget, authorizing expenditures, and levying taxes.

Capital outlays—a schedule of planned capital outlays, which may also include the funding source (i.e., bonds, notes, or current revenue).

Debt service—a schedule of debts, planned interest, and principal payments.

Trust and agency funds—a schedule of assets held for others under specific instructions. These assets may include funds for retirement systems or funds donated to a local government to purchase something as a commemoration.

Grants—a schedule of revenues received from outside sources (usually a higher level of government) to undertake specific programs or activities for a fixed period of time. These may also not be formally budgeted.

HOW TO UNDERSTAND A BUDGET

The title *How to Read a Budget* implies more than just a cursory review of the document. It really means *How to Read and Understand a Budget*. To understand a budget, the reader needs to analyze its contents, but such analysis need not imply sophisticated techniques. Indeed, the reader can readily understand a great deal without much effort. The observation notes included with each exhibit are examples of very basic but important analysis a reader can use to understand a budget. By synthesizing various items of information, identifying gaps in data, and noting unexplained changes, the reader can draw even further deductions.

When analyzing a budget, keep the following general rules in mind:

- Focus your examination on the largest dollar amounts. Small items, unless of specific interest, are not material to understanding.
- Look at absolute as well as relative percentage changes. Although an item may increase by only 7 percent, if the amount is in the millions the change can be very significant.
- If you cannot find information on an area, ask about it; don't assume you lack the skills to locate it. The data may not be supplied when perhaps it should be. Indeed, it may be intentionally omitted to make understanding more difficult.
- Look for trends over several years. Year-to-year changes, both large and small, may be misleading since they can be caused by one-time circumstances.
- Review revenues as well as expenditures. They are equally important.
- Try to understand something about the background of each item. Certain revenues, such as sales tax receipts, grow with inflation and the economy. Others, such as license fees, will tend to be flat in the absence of specific changes. Expenditures in certain areas, such as education, may be largely for personnel, but in others, such as road maintenance, the distribution should be balanced with material and equipment purchases. Any deviation from the expected should be questioned.

QUESTIONS

The general questions that the budget reader should attempt to answer to better understand it are examined below. They are as follows:

1. How is the property tax rate changing?
2. Is the budget in balance, and has it been balanced in prior years?
3. How is the program expenditure plan changing?
4. Which department expenditure plan is changing the most?
5. Which program element is changing the most?
6. What is happening in the program element expenditure plan?
7. How is the revenue plan changing?
8. How are the individual revenue sources changing?

Each of these questions is answered for the sample budget. The analysis should be read in conjunction with the cited exhibit. An analytical reading of a budget will usually raise questions that cannot be fully answered by reading the budget alone; sometimes the budget message may supply the answer, but sometimes it does not. In order to facilitate scanning, the material is formatted as follows:

question
exhibit where data may be found
comments regarding analysis
unanswered questions (if any)

The exhibits include notes defining elements of the schedule and observations derived from a careful reading.

1. How Is the Property Tax Rate Changing? (See Exhibit 1)

Comments

The Property Tax Calculation schedule shows that the overall combined tax rate is increasing by $2.94 per thousand dollars of assessment, or a 4.3 percent increase. It shows that the city has two separate tax rates, one for general city purposes and the other for education. Although the general city rate is declining by $1.86 per thousand (9.2%), note that the actual tax levied ($13,035,648) declines by only 7.4 percent. This difference is because total assessments are increasing by 1.9 percent, enlarging the base for the rate calculation. Indeed, as happened in 1979-80, the rate can decline while the total tax levy increases.

How to Read a Budget / 143

Exhibit 1: *Property Tax Calculation*

Schedule shows the calculation of the tax rates for the general city and education. The latter is broken out by law.

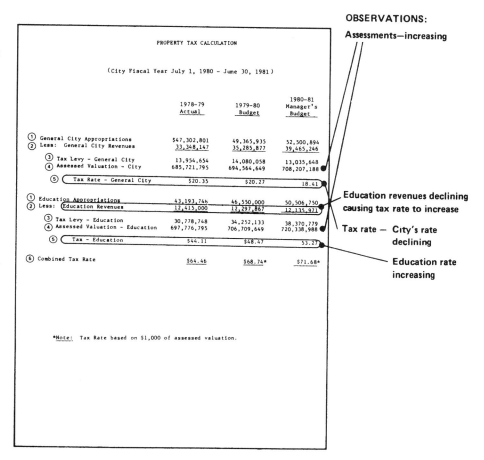

DESCRIPTION:

To estimate the tax rate the schedule takes the total expenditures ① less the total revenues excluding the property tax level ② to compute the amount of tax to be raised ③ This is divided into the total assessment ④ for the tax to establish the tax rate per $1000 of assessment ⑤

Note that Education's assessments are higher than the general city due to fewer exemptions

The two rates are summed to show an approximate rate per $1000 ⑥

OBSERVATIONS:

Assessments—increasing

Education revenues declining causing tax rate to increase

Tax rate — City's rate declining

Education rate increasing

In addition, the combined tax rate is increasing because the education property tax rate is increasing by $4.80 per thousand (9.9%).

By looking at other data on the schedule, another fact becomes apparent. While both the general city and school *expenditures* are increasing, only general city *revenues* are increasing; school revenues are not. Therefore, all education expenditure increases must be funded through a local property tax rate increase.

Unanswered Questions

What is the dollar impact of the tax rate on an average property owner in the community?

How does the tax rate compare to other neighboring communities?

Why are school revenues declining?

Can education expenditures be further reduced to minimize the tax rate increase?

How does the tax rate increase compare to other measures of change, such as, (a) added or reduced service? (b) increases in school population? (c) inflation rate fluctuations?

2. Is the Budget in Balance and Has It Been Balanced in Prior Years? (See Exhibit 2)

Comments

A budget is balanced when planned expenditures equal anticipated revenues; most governments are required by law to submit a balanced budget. The

Exhibit 2: *Summary of Revenues and Expenditures*

Schedule summarizes total revenues and expenditures as well as the change in the tax rate.

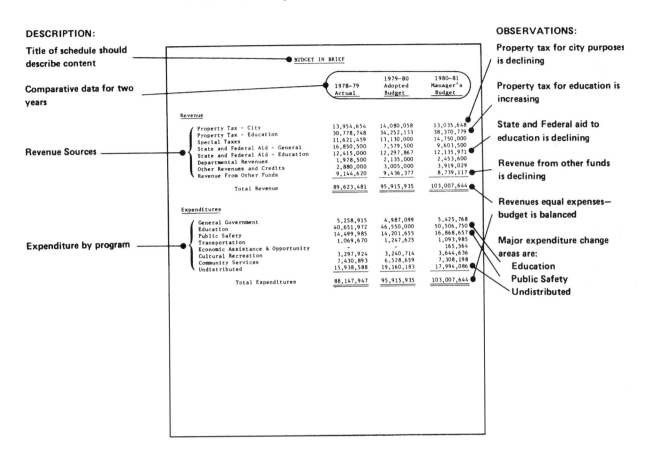

manager's budget column shows that total revenues and total expenditures are equal, and hence the sample budget is balanced, as was also the prior year's budget (1979-80).

The actual operating results for 1978-79, however, show that revenues exceeded expenditures by $1.47 million. This differential does not mean the budget for that year was out of balance; it means rather that the actual result of the year's operations was a surplus of revenues over expenditures, generally a positive indication of performance.

Similar information could also have been estimated for 1979-80, but it was not. Such an estimate of actual operating results for the preceding year would be useful in assessing how realistic the new budget is.

Unanswered Questions

What items legally must be budgeted?
Are any expenditures and revenues not budgeted?
How was the prior-year surplus achieved?

3. How Is the Program Expenditure Plan Changing? (See Exhibit 3)

Comments

The schedule entitled *Summary of Budget by Program and Sub-program* is the most useful of the summary schedules available to answer this question. It displays areas of expenditure by service with a reasonable amount of detail. Total expenditures increased by $7,091,709 (7.4%) compared to 1979-80.

Exhibit 3: *Expenditure by Program*

Schedule shows expenditure by program only. It does not distinguish fund or organization.

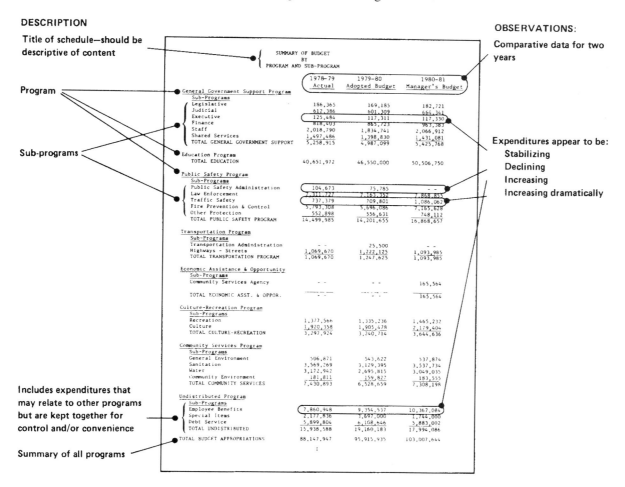

By examining the change in each program and within programs and sub-programs the reader can begin to isolate those areas where significant changes are occurring. For example, when comparing program areas to those in 1979-80, five are increasing, two are declining and one is new. Of those, public safety has increased the greatest percentage (18.8%). When examining the sub-programs within public safety, two areas emerge with major increases—fire prevention and control (25.8%) and traffic safety (53.2%). Note, however, that in absolute dollars, fire protection's increase is much larger—$1.5 million compared to $300,000 for traffic safety. In addition, both programs had lower budgets in 1979-80 when compared to actual expenditures of 1978-79. This discrepancy may suggest that these areas were under-budgeted in 1979-80 and that the current increase is a two-year catch-up attempt. By examining each program, the reader may isolate areas for more careful review of their detailed budgets.

Unanswered Questions

Is the new program area being added to the budget or is that item a separate identification of a program previously grouped elsewhere? If so, why?

Why are the transportation and public safety administration sub-programs eliminated, and where are these expenditures now reflected?

4. Which Department Expenditure Plan Is Changing the Most? (See Exhibit 4)

Comments (See also Exhibit 8)

The schedule of departmental expenditures ignores programs and sub-programs. It is worth noting that "finance" is both the title of a department and a sub-program (see Exhibit 3). This is unnecessarily confusing.

The Community Development Department has grown 20.5 percent over 1979-80, although much less than the departmental request, which was an increase of 46.6 percent over 1979-80. This change suggests that functions and services are being added.

Two departments, Legislative and Law, show higher manager's budgets than the departments requested, although by small amounts. Managers are usually faced with limiting spending plans or at least making choices between competing needs, so it is unusual to see increases in departmental requests unless the government is moving an activity from one department to another. The occurrence is sufficiently unusual to warrant further inquiry.

The Parks, Recreation and Conservation Department has had its budget reduced for two consecutive years, although it requested a substantial increase. The planned reduction may imply a reduction of service and/or a deferral of maintenance.

Unanswered Question

What services will the new Community Services Department provide?

Exhibit 4: *Expenditure by Department (Organization Unit)*

Schedule shows departmental expenditures for the general fund only. Expenditures from other funds are shown in Exhibit 9, "Expenditures by Fund"; but not by department, an inconsistency in preparation.

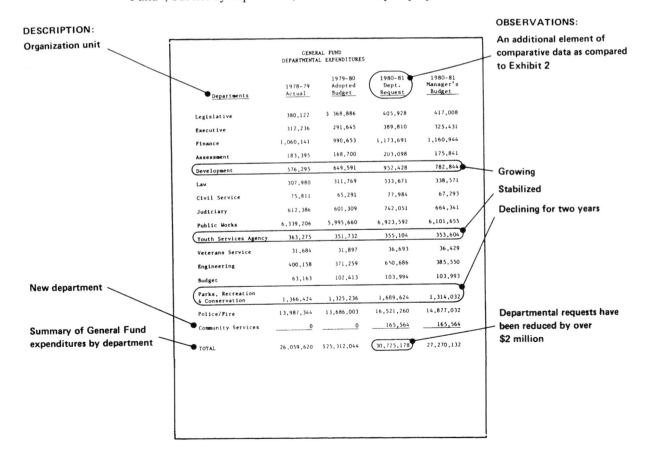

5. Which Program Element (Lowest Organizational Unit in Budget) Is Changing the Most? (See Exhibit 5)

Comments

There are four program elements within the Finance Department: Purchasing, which is increasing at a 19.1 percent rate, the Comptroller's Office which is increasing at a 14 percent rate, and Budget and Assessment, which are increasing at very modest rates. While the manager's increase in the budget sub-element is only 1.5 percent, the increase in 1979-80 is 62.1 percent over 1978-79. A change of that magnitude usually implies either an increase in staff or a transfer of staff and function from one organization to another.

The forecasted expenses for 1979-80 are 4.7 percent less than the adopted budget. Most of that reduction is in personal services—indeed, the forecasted expenses for personal services for 1979-80 are less than the actual expenses in 1978-79.* The manager's budget shows a decrease on each line from the department request.

Unanswered Questions

What did the manager eliminate from the department request?

---

* The manager's budget is 12.5 percent higher than the 1979-80 budget but 18.4 percent higher than the forecasted expenses.

Exhibit 5: *Detail Budget by Classification (Program and Object)*

Schedule shows expenditures for sub-program by line item and program element.

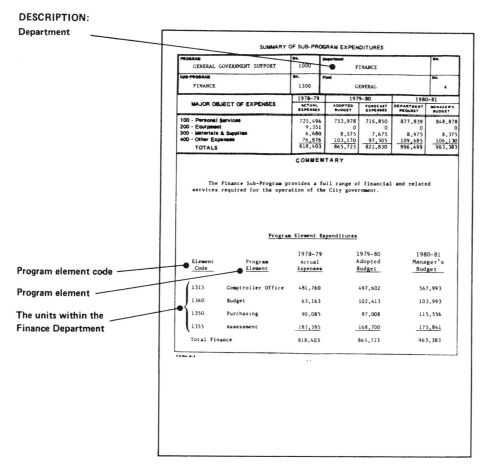

DESCRIPTION:
Department

Program element code

Program element

The units within the Finance Department

OBSERVATIONS:
The Finance program is comprised of four organization units

Budget had a major increase in prior year

148 / BUDGET FORMULATION: BUDGET SETTING

What staffing or organizational change resulted in the personal service budget fluctuation?

6. What Is Happening in the Program Element Expenditure Plan? (See Exhibit 6)

Comments

The information for program elements is the lowest level of detail in the budget, and is also for the organization unit. Exhibit 6 shows the purchasing unit's budget. The commentary indicates that the print shop has been added to this program element, which may account for the almost 34 percent increase. However, no definite statement is made.

The largest increases are in wages, indicating that people are being added to the unit.

Interestingly, the final budget is higher than that requested, suggesting that the decision to add the print shop was made by the city manager and not the department. Note also that the miscellaneous categories are being dropped.

Finally, the fact that the forecast expenses are significantly lower than budgeted in 1979-80 suggests that positions were budgeted but not filled.

7. How Is the Revenue Plan Changing? (See Exhibit 2)

Comments

In addition to the changes in property taxes discussed in Question 1, other revenue sources are changing, and, in fact, the change in the property tax in part depends on what happens to all other revenues, since property tax is used to balance revenues with expenditures.

Generally the other revenue sources fall into four categories:

Special taxes—These are taxes from which the government receives all or a portion of the receipts. The government may or may not control the tax rate and base. Most tax receipts are subject to economic conditions.

Exhibit 6: *Detailed Schedule by Classification (Program, Organization, and Object)*

Lowest level of detail in budget; program element, department, object detail

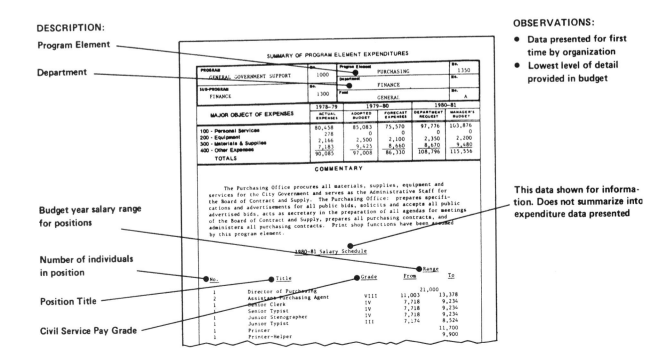

State and federal aid—These are revenues received for both general and special purposes. Most often they will be controlled by the government providing the funds.

Department revenues—These revenues, usually controllable, result from department operations, including fees, charges, fines, etc.

Other revenues and credits—These revenues and credits do not fall into any of the above categories.

Of the six other revenue categories shown in Exhibit 2, four are increasing while two are declining. The decline in *state and federal aid—education* is interesting because overall, *state and federal aid—general* is increasing sharply. This discrepancy may indicate that aid to education is being capped or limited for some reason. The second declining revenue source is *revenue from other funds*.

Unanswered Questions

Why is aid to education declining, especially in view of the increases in other aid? Are revenues declining in all other funds, or only in specific funds?

8. How Are the Individual Revenue Sources Changing? (See Exhibit 7)

Comments

To answer the above question, each category of revenue should be reviewed. In Exhibit 7, all categories of general fund revenue are increasing, with state and

Exhibit 6: *Detailed Objects of Expense (continued)*

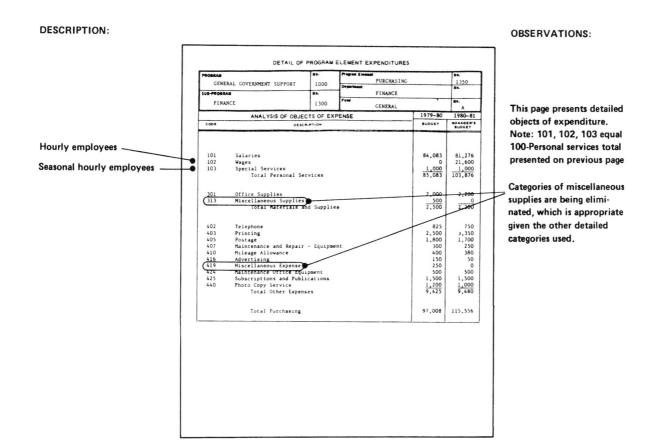

federal aid increasing the most, proportionately. However, within this category, most sources are stable, and only state revenue sharing is increasing dramatically. It is also the largest source of state and federal aid.

Under special taxes, a new real estate transfer tax is planned. The sales and use tax, the largest of all general fund revenues, is increasing at 10.4 percent.

Departmental revenues, the smallest category, is relatively stable, with several new types of revenues shown.

The other revenues and credits category has perhaps the largest number of changes. We can note two new revenue sources, one of which, maintenance of state and county roads, should perhaps be shown under state aid or departmental revenues. Most significantly, sale of real estate is large and increasing. Revenues from the sale of any assets are one-time revenues and because of this, are not wise to budget as a revenue source, especially if significant. The following year either an asset of similar worth must be sold or another source must be found to replace the revenues. The city may have a problem next year. Finally, the reserve for uncollected taxes, which is used to offset delinquency, is increasing more than the total tax levy, indicating that greater tax delinquency is expected.

Unanswered Questions

What is the exact source of the new revenues shown?

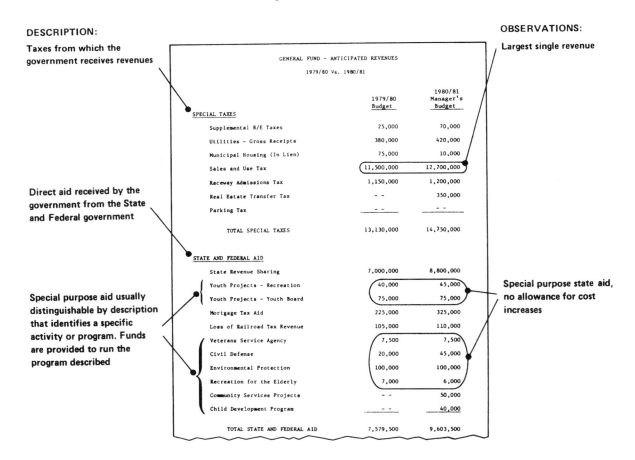

Exhibit 7: *Revenues by Source*

This schedule shows general fund revenues by type (tax, aid, direct user charge) and source (kind of tax or aid).

What is the real estate to be sold and how will this revenue be replaced or offset next year?

Why is state revenue sharing increasing when other aid is stable?

Once these questions have been answered, the budget reader can feel certain in identifying

- how many dollars the government is spending for what services;
- what has changed significantly from year to year;
- what factors most affect revenues and expenditures; and
- what additional questions still may need answering.

Two additional exhibits (Exhibits 8 and 9) have been included.

Exhibit 7: *Revenues by Source (continued)*

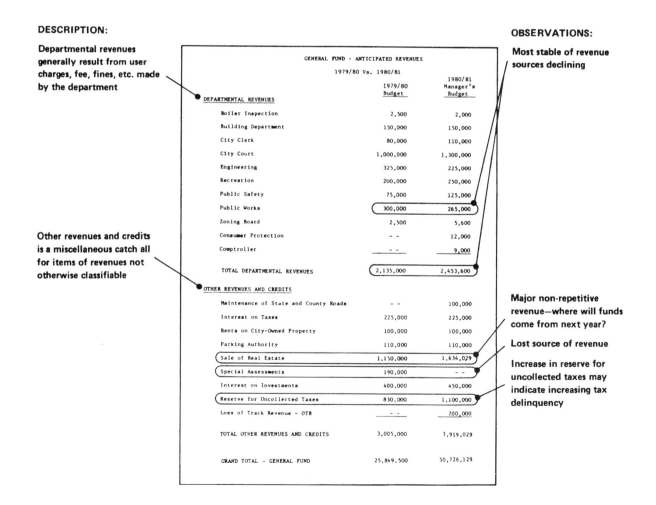

DESCRIPTION:

Departmental revenues generally result from user charges, fee, fines, etc. made by the department

Other revenues and credits is a miscellaneous catch all for items of revenues not otherwise classifiable

OBSERVATIONS:

Most stable of revenue sources declining

Major non-repetitive revenue—where will funds come from next year?

Lost source of revenue

Increase in reserve for uncollected taxes may indicate increasing tax delinquency

152 / BUDGET FORMULATION: BUDGET SETTING

Exhibit 8: *Detail Budget by Classification (Program and Object) Summary of a Program by Sub-Programs*

Schedule shows expenditures for a program and its sub-programs, also for line items.

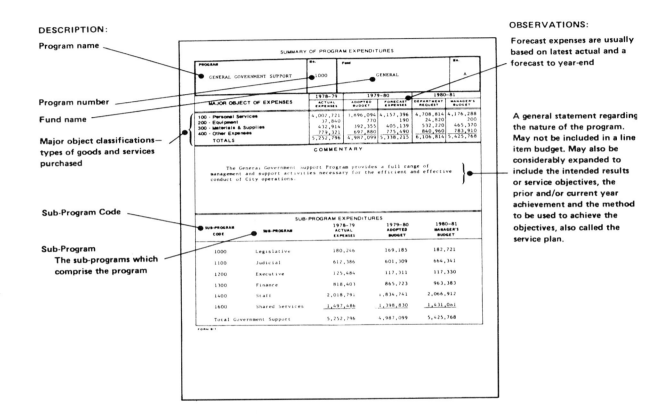

DESCRIPTION:

- Program name
- Program number
- Fund name
- Major object classifications—types of goods and services purchased
- Sub-Program Code
- Sub-Program
  The sub-programs which comprise the program

OBSERVATIONS:

Forecast expenses are usually based on latest actual and a forecast to year-end

A general statement regarding the nature of the program. May not be included in a line item budget. May also be considerably expanded to include the intended results or service objectives, the prior and/or current year achievement and the method to be used to achieve the objectives, also called the service plan.

How to Read a Budget / 153

Exhibit 9: *Expenditures by Department*

Schedule shows expenditures for each fund and equals the total appropriation shown in Exhibit 1. Funds are generally self-explanatory.

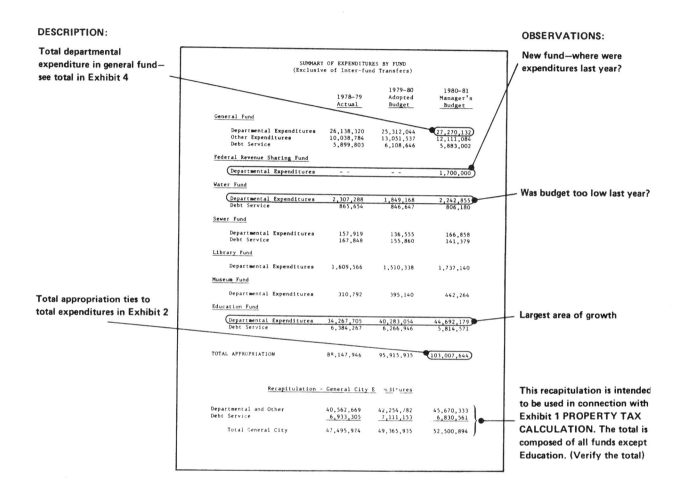

Revenues

Criteria for Evaluating a Tax (Revenue) System

Debate on fiscal policy seldom makes clear the basis for selecting one revenue source over another. Several factors may be at work to discourage explicit statements; e.g., lack of data as to the economic effects of a tax, uncertainty as to who will bear the tax burden, and the complexity and multiplicity of tax effects. Nevertheless, when a subnational (state/local) government makes the political decision to use one tax form rather than another (or use some more intensively than others) there is a need to have a set of criteria by which to make policy choices. The following are those generally accepted criteria by which a given tax or tax system should be evaluated.

REVENUE PRODUCTIVITY

The primary job of a tax system is to produce revenues. Thus, the system as well as each particular tax, must be judged on the basis of its revenue generating potential. For those who want the jurisdiction's revenue to expand at least as rapidly as its population and economic activity, there is an advantage in selecting taxes whose revenues are automatically responsive to changes in employment, volume of business, price level, or, as a general proxy, the dollar value of personal income received in the jurisdiction. Such taxes (e.g., personal income taxes) are said to be income *elastic*. That is, for every 1 percent increase in the economy's personal income, tax revenues automatically rise by more than 1 percent. Such elasticity helps avoid the need for frequent tax rate and/or base changes, thereby minimizing political strains. However, one danger of income elastic taxes is that during recessions revenues may decline faster (in percentage terms) than the jurisdiction's income. Such a drop in revenues may force cutbacks in existing public services and also prevent adequate monies for tax relief.[1]

In contrast, income inelastic taxes (e.g., liquor and tobacco excises) provide revenues which are stable whether the level of business activity rises or falls. The intensive use of such taxes requires more frequent legislation to raise taxes, since revenues do not increase rapidly even during periods of economic growth.

As a result, then, there is a policy tradeoff between elastic and inelastic revenue sources. Heavy reliance on elastic taxes provides the government with revenues which tend to automatically change more than is proportionate to general economic growth. But, by its nature, this growth responsiveness fails to provide an element of revenue stability, particularly during recessions.

Although there is no explicit coefficient which represents an optimal tax system, past state/local experience indicates that a tax structure should contain both types of revenue sources, with a somewhat greater reliance on the elastic taxes. This helps a government achieve a fairly constant level of public services and still avoid oversusceptibility to recession.

Excerpted from "The Policy Framework," in *Financing an Urban Government* (Washington, D.C.: The District of Columbia Tax Revision Commission, 1978, Robert D. Ebel, executive director), 11-15. (Notes have been renumbered.)

NEUTRALITY

Neutrality in taxation requires that taxes accomplish certain *intended* objectives, but beyond this they should minimize interference with private economic decisions. Special emphasis here must be placed on the word "intended." Sometimes a government deliberately chooses to raise some prices through taxation and thus discourage consumption—as in levying specific excises on gasoline or in enacting various antipollution fees or taxes.

Similarly, the structure of a broad-based tax can be designed in order to accomplish certain other social goals. For example, some economists argue that land in the District [of Columbia] could be more efficiently used if we were to reduce or eliminate that part of the real property tax levied on land improvements (i.e., buildings). However, others argue for higher taxes on certain types of improvements. Whether these proposals lead to desirable policy must be largely determined by empirical analysis. What is important to note now, though, is that in any tax policy there may result an unintended handicapping of some industries or firms by taxing them more heavily and arbitrarily than their competitors, thus imposing a social loss on the community.

A tax-distortion of private economic decisions may, indeed, be justified in the public interest. But awareness of the neutrality criterion requires that any such distortion be deliberate and not merely inadvertent. It is of great importance to be aware that even though a given tax may have an intended and "desirable social purpose" (and, in fact, may even accomplish that purpose), it can also have unintended effects which, on net, may make its use a poor policy tool.[2]

EQUITY

Few questions of public finance are more obviously judgmental—and therefore political—than the question of who should pay. Nevertheless, tax equity is a proper concern in economic analysis and must be addressed as objectively as possible. For our purposes here, there are two types of equity concepts which can be distinguished: horizontal and vertical.

Horizontal equity requires the equal tax treatment of persons in equal circumstances (equal treatment of equals). For example, if the criterion for determining a resident individual's tax liability is income, expenditure, or wealth, then horizontal equity requires that all persons having equal amounts of these measures regardless of the source derived, pay the same sum in taxes.[3]

Vertical equity deals with the fairness of the distribution of tax liabilities among persons not in similar circumstances. Here, the most commonly used index is income, and discussions of vertical equity usually focus on the distribution of the burden of a tax structure. Tax structures (or individual taxes) may be progressive (tax burden varies directly with income), regressive (tax burden and incomes are inversely related), or proportional (no change in tax burden as income changes). Accordingly, for a given set of public expenditures a policy of income distribution in favor of the poor would require the heavier use of progressive net income taxes and taxes on inheritances and estates. Taxes on consumption, such as the retail sales, liquor, tobacco, and gasoline taxes are generally regressive and thus redistribute income in favor of the wealthy.

What is the appropriate or "fair" distribution of the tax burden? There are two general approaches. The first is based on the *benefit* principle and defines equity in terms of the incidence of government expenditures. Thus, if *on net,* expenditures on District government goods and services tend to be directed largely toward low (high) income persons, the benefits criterion would require that an equitable tax system be regressive (progressive). In short, distribution of the tax burden depends upon the expenditure structure.

Despite its theoretical soundness, however, the application of the benefits principle is operationally difficult to apply as an equity guideline on a general basis. The principle is easily applied to a select subset of publicly provided goods—specifically those taxes or charges which have a direct price or cost-of-service relationship to the user of a government service (e.g., motor fuel taxes, user charges) and to general business taxation.

The principle is not applicable to the bulk of public services comprised of

1. pure public goods where persons cannot be excluded from the benefits of a service (e.g., public health programs, provision for human rights);

2. services which have "third party" or "external effects" of an economic action which are not taken into account by the actor (e.g., the general welfare loss to society of pollution or the gain of public education); and
3. programs specifically designed to redistribute income.

A second approach to equity is provided by the *ability to pay* principle—that persons should contribute to the cost of government on the basis of one's ability as usually measured by income or wealth. Unlike the benefit principle, the ability principle is unrelated to the expenditure side of the government budget and lacks a scientific foundation. Nevertheless, in the United States, the ability principle more closely conforms to the conventional social and political bases for distributing the tax burden.

Although the vertical equity issue is an important one for tax policy, concern over tax regressivity (or progressivity) should be kept in a total fiscal perspective. Two points are particularly relevant. First, what is important in regressivity discussions is the distribution of the entire tax system. Because all types of taxes have certain inherent structural inequities, a jurisdiction must rely on a mix of taxes so that it is not forced to employ a few levies so intensively that those inequities will become intolerable. It follows, then, that government will have both progressive and regressive taxes in its system. Accordingly, it is the distribution of the entire tax system, not that of any single levy, which should be of policy interest in discussions of vertical equity.

Second, this focus on the distribution of the tax burden ignores half of the total budget. Expenditures have their own distributive effect. Indeed, it is quite possible that a government could have a regressive tax system and a progressive expenditure structure—with the net budget effect being neither regressive nor progressive.

TAX EXPORTING

Most state/local governments rely—sometimes quite heavily—on taxes which are designated to be paid by nonresidents. This design to *export* taxes should not be based on a political preference to "beggar our neighbors," but from the realization that nonresidents may generate substantial costs to a jurisdiction in traffic policing, health problems, congestion, and environmental degradation.

Similarly, the concentration of large federal installations in the District creates both costs (e.g., tax base erosion) and benefits (as a source of jobs and personal incomes). Thus, it is appropriate to consider whether the operations of these U.S. agencies are contributing a fair share to D.C.'s tax revenues. Judged by the criterion of enhancing tax exporting, a nonresident income tax, business taxes, and taxes levied specifically at tourists receive high marks. The federal government's presence also provides some opportunity for tax exporting. However, because of constitutional restrictions, federal agencies can be taxed only indirectly, primarily by taxing the income and consumption of their employees. Of course, one major opportunity to export taxes to the federal government is the deductibility of most state/local taxes (e.g., District taxes against federal income taxes).

INVESTMENT AND ECONOMIC GROWTH

It is frequently alleged that state or local taxes will frighten away prospective investors and producers, but there is much literature which testifies that neither tax increases nor tax exemptions have had significant effects on the location of industry within the United States. At some point, of course, extremely high, discriminatory or uncertain taxes could have adverse effects on the jurisdiction's economic growth. Accordingly, D.C. policymakers must be alert to the possibility that particular segments of the District's economy might be jeopardized by sudden increases and/or unusually high levels in the effective tax rates they are required to pay.

ADMINISTRATIVE FEASIBILITY

Another basis commonly advanced for choosing among tax alternatives is the ease or difficulty, costliness, or cheapness of collecting any levy in a reasonably uniform way. Surely, other things being equal, it is preferable to choose taxes which are easy to collect.

The trouble is that the "other aspects" are rarely equal. A poll tax is extremely easy to administer, but also completely contrary to most people's idea of fairness. Sales taxes are simpler to collect than income taxes, but this difference is rarely the grounds for choosing the one over the other.

Indeed, there are few taxes proposed to city councils or state legislatures which, assuming that they are constitutional and otherwise lawful, cannot be administered if the government has the will, the facilities, and staff to do so.

There are, of course, differences in the costs of collecting various taxes, measured by the ratio of administrative outlays to revenues from each levy. Thus, a dollar of revenue from a gasoline tax or liquor tax, collected from only a few wholesalers, requires smaller administrative costs than a dollar of general excise tax, which is paid by many thousand taxpayers. The general excise, in turn, is less costly to administer than a net income tax, which is more complex and therefore more difficult to audit. However, the range of differences among major taxes is seldom so wide as to make this efficiency criterion critical for making the choice, since the collection ratio is usually somewhere between a half percent and a few percentage points of the revenue collected.

TAXPAYER COMPLIANCE COSTS

There is a wide range of compliance costs—the costs borne by the individual or business taxpayer in keeping records, computing and filing tax returns, undergoing audits, etc. Little data on compliance costs is gathered, however, and so policy groups do not have much to go on in considering this aspect of choosing taxes. Nevertheless, failure to consider the taxpayers' views in the mechanics of tax preparation can result in both widespread tax evasion and contempt for the government legislative body.

POLICY TRADEOFFS

It is important to recognize that in choosing to enact a new tax or modify an existing one, there will inevitably be tradeoffs among these criteria. For example, a heavy reliance on consumer taxes produces large and stable revenues, but it tends to distort vertical equity. Or, a higher property tax on local business may be an efficient way to reduce overall tax burdens on residents, but it may also come at the cost of reduced economic growth in parts of the city.

Notes

1. The overall coefficient of revenue elasticity is defined as the ratio of the percentage change in revenues to the percentage change in income or some other measure of economic growth. If the ratio is greater than one, the revenue source is said to be *elastic*; if less than one, *inelastic*. If the ratio equals one, there is *unitary elasticity*.

    The magnitude of the revenue elasticity is a function of the jurisdiction's tax rate and base as well as of the economy's structure. Thus, one can break down the overall coefficient of elasticity into elasticities with respect to population, growth in output per capita or per worker as a result of productivity increases, or increases in the general price level. These component elasticities are likely to differ. For example, consider the D.C. personal income tax.

    In the absence of any dramatic demographic changes, the elasticity with respect to population is likely to be unity. However, due to the progressive rate structure, elasticity with respect to real income growth is expected to be greater than one. This elasticity (with respect to nominal income growth) would be expected to further increase in inflation due to the inflation erosion of the real value of the personal exemptions and credits, standard deductions, and tax rate brackets.

    Finally, it should be noted that it doesn't follow that the more progressive an income tax is, the more elastic it will be. The progressivity/elasticity relationship is a function of the income distribution of a jurisdiction's taxpayers. For example, as more taxpayers move into the top bracket, (for subnational government this is often a relatively low income level compared to the federal tax structure) the automatic growth responsiveness of tax revenues to further income changes necessarily levels off.

2. Some economists view *neutrality* in a much narrower sense. They define a *non-neutrality* as any interference with the private market decisions of consumers and producers, e.g., decisions regarding such issues as the optimal input mix in a production process, locational choices, and the satisfaction behavior of consumers. This view has merit in that it emphasizes that any government interference (e.g., taxation) in the market distorts private choices from what they would be in the absence of government and, as a result, can involve some costs. Thus, this narrow view of neutrality is based on the assumption that the initial, pretax allocation of resources and distribution of income in the private market is optimal in an economic sense. Clearly, if such is the case, any alteration of private sector behavior would, by definition, introduce allocative *in*efficiency.

    In contrast, the broader view of neutrality rejects the notion that the unobstructed private market is optimal in the sense of reaching the "best" of all solutions. Rather, it not only implicitly recognizes that by its very nature the private market system fails to allocate all resources efficiently (e.g., as in the case of the inability to exclude users from a given service), but also recognizes that government interference may not be harmful if the previously existing (e.g., pretax) state of resource allocation, income distribution, or economic stabilization is not necessarily optimal.

    Thus, although each of these views of neutrality expresses concern to minimize distortions in the private sector (an important goal!) the emphasis differs. However, in order to have an adequate policy criterion, the emphasis of the broad view approaches the issue in a more realistic framework. For further discussion, see Bernard P. Herber, *Modern Public Finance,*

3d ed. (Homewood, Ill.: Richard D. Irwin, Inc., 1975), chap. 6; and Richard A. Musgrave, *The Theory of Public Finance* (New York, McGraw-Hill, 1959), chap. 7. 17.

3. Martin Feldstein, "Compensation in Tax Reform," *National Tax Journal* (June 1976), argues that all horizontal inequities arise from changes in tax laws rather than from the structure of the laws themselves. This argument is based on the premise that individuals make commitments (e.g., education, occupation, location) based on existing tax laws and the market factors (e.g., wages) will be adjusted until net after tax rewards are equalized. It follows, therefore, that ending certain tax subsidies or special tax treatments for persons creates its own set of horizontal inequities, since commitments may be irreversible or reversible only slowly.

Evaluating Alternative Revenue Sources
Ian J. Allan

Local governments continue to operate in a difficult fiscal environment made worse by the effects of an economic recession. Of increasing concern to many finance officers is the drop in revenues from economically sensitive sources that has led to budget shortfalls and deficits. The financial difficulties encountered by state governments has led to cutbacks in state aid to localities and compounded the problems faced by local governments.

While reductions in spending can be a part of the solution to the fiscal problems of local governments, many have found that expenditure demands have increased during the current recession. As a result of this situation, many local governments are considering the adoption of alternative sources of revenue to bolster sagging collections. This task has been made more difficult by tax revolts in some areas that have made it increasingly problematical for local governments to raise needed revenues through the use of the real property tax.

The purpose of this article is to provide guidance to those finance officers contemplating the adoption of alternative revenue sources and to encourage local governments to develop formal statements of revenue policy. It includes discussion of local government revenue policy and appropriate policy goals, a procedure for identifying tax and other revenue alternatives, a method for evaluating specific tax and user charge alternatives, and the implications of revenue structure reforms for a local government's credit standing. This information can assist finance officers in conducting evaluations of their revenue structure and in providing policy advice to the elected officials who are ultimately responsible for adopting changes.[1]

EVALUATING LOCAL GOVERNMENT REVENUE POLICY

Revenue policy, in its simplest form, represents the set of decisions made regarding the raising of revenues to fund the operations of government, and is reflected in the taxes, fees, and user charges imposed within a particular jurisdiction. Many local governments lack a formal, comprehensive statement of revenue policy; their tax and revenue actions are made, instead, on an ad hoc, fragmentary basis.

Ideally, revenue policy will reflect a community's fundamental values, such as the desire to ensure that the living standards of elderly and/or low-income homeowners are not adversely affected by rising residential property values and property tax bills. In reality, state restrictions on local revenue-raising authority prevent revenue policy from fully reflecting these fundamental values. In many states it is not possible to reduce local dependence on the real property tax and, thus, blunt the impact of rising property tax bills, because state governments have restricted the ability of local governments to diversify their revenue structures through the imposition of income or sales taxes.

Reprinted from *Research Bulletin* (Washington, D.C.: Government Finance Research Center, Government Finance Officers Association, January 1992), 1-8. By permission of GFOA.

Why reform the current revenue structure? Reforms are often proposed as a means of defusing a fiscal or political crisis. For example, at the present time an economic slowdown is forcing many local governments to review and revise their existing revenue structures in order to generate sufficient funds to meet growing expenditure demands. Another typical example of reform is where a local government responds to growing complaints about rising property tax bills by attempting to diversify the jurisdiction's revenue base and reduce its dependence on the real property tax. Revenue policies are also reformed because one feature of the tax and revenue system has fallen out of line. For example, the need for and pursuit of revenue adequacy may create inequities in the tax burden that must be addressed at some point in time.

Policy Goals

While opportunities for comprehensive reform of a local government's revenue policy and revenue structure are rare, evaluation of individual revenue sources is quite common. Prior to conducting an evaluation of the local revenue structure, it is important to review what are generally considered to be the appropriate goals of revenue policy. The goals discussed below are not listed in order of importance nor are they mutually exclusive: conflicts and trade-offs between them will be inevitable.

Political Acceptability. Taxpayers expect fairness in the distribution of the tax burden and an understanding of how the burden is allocated. To increase taxpayer understanding of the tax and revenue system, complexity should be kept to a minimum and the assumptions underlying the revenue policy made explicit.

Politically acceptable revenue policies will to a certain extent reflect local tradition and political attitudes. Prior to altering existing revenue policy, a review of the political environment must be conducted. An important component of this review is an examination of existing revenue capacity and revenue effort, including comparisons with other jurisdictions if such data are available. Revenue capacity gauges the ability of a government to raise revenues and is measured in terms of per capita personal income. Revenue effort is a measure of the actual amount of revenue raised by a government, and is often measured in terms of revenue per capita. Evaluating local revenue capacity and effort can reveal citizens' attitudes and preferences towards taxation and the level of taxation that they are willing to bear.

Revenue Adequacy and Stability. The revenue structure should provide the government with sufficient revenues to finance desired public services. Creating an equilibrium between the growth of revenues and the activities that governments finance will be difficult to achieve, but is a worthwhile objective. Ideally, revenue yields, while responsive to income and population shifts, will be dependable and predictable. Economic recessions and changes in state and federal aid distributions can have a negative impact on revenue growth. At the present time, due to the effects of economic recession, revenue adequacy is a major concern of governments at all levels.

Revenue Diversification. An optimal revenue structure includes a balance among the major taxes of property, sales and income; minimizes the use of nuisance taxes; and relies on user charges where feasible. Taxes should be as broadly based as possible to allow for lower tax rates and improve economic efficiency. Diversity in the revenue structure is desirable for political and social reasons.

A diversified property tax base with a balance between the different classes of property is desirable because it will be less vulnerable to economic shifts. To achieve this aim, linkages between tax policy and planning/zoning policy should be forged. In the short term, a balance between the various classes of property will be hard to achieve; in the long term, particularly in growing communities, such balance is a good possibility.

Equity. The distribution of the tax burden and the benefits of public services should be equitable. Horizontal equity requires that the treatment of persons in similar economic circumstances be equal. Vertical equity requires fairness in the distribution of liabilities among persons in different circumstances.

Economic Neutrality. The tax and revenue system should maintain economic neutrality, promoting growth and the efficient allocation of the economy's resources. The goal here is to minimize unintentional interference with private economic decisions in the process of raising needed revenues.

Administrative Feasibility. The complexity and cost of collection of revenues must be considered prior to adoption of a particular tax or revenue source. Compliance should be made simple, certain and inexpensive for the taxpayer, and administration easy and economical for the tax collector.

Self-Sufficiency. To the extent possible it is important not to be overly reliant on federal and state aid so that aid reductions or cutoffs do not interfere with the provision of vital services or distort budget decisions.

Political Feasibility. The use of particular taxes or revenues by state governments may preclude their use at the local level because states may wish to reserve the tax or revenue base for their use alone. Local governments should consider this when evaluating revenue alternatives, and pursue those alternatives which are politically feasible. Legislative advocacy may be required in some cases.

Political Accountability. Increases in local taxes or other revenues should be the product of deliberate legislative action and not inherent structural features of the tax and revenue system that result in automatic rate hikes. A good example is the real property tax and property assessments that have increased from the previous year, resulting in higher property tax bills unless the tax rate is lowered. Some local governments deal with this phenomenon by adopting a truth-in-taxation law that sets a constant property tax yield rate and prohibits increases in property tax levies unless public hearings are held.

Accounting for Tax Exemptions, Abatements, and Relief Programs. By tracking and accounting for the value of taxes and other revenues foregone by a local government for the purposes of providing incentives to businesses or for tax relief for low-income property owners, a government can more easily compare its costs with the benefits obtained.[2] A word of caution: it can be difficult to measure the benefits associated with tax abatements and other relief programs, and local governments should be careful not to exaggerate their size.

Exporting the Tax Burden. Tax exportability can be defined as the ability to levy taxes or other revenues in such a way that the burden is borne by taxpayers outside of the jurisdiction of the local government. Exporting the tax burden is a desirable goal because it lessens the burden on a local government's residents. Retail sales and hotel/motel accommodations taxes are generally the most exportable.

Taxes can also be exported to the federal government when local governments take advantage of the deductibility of local property and income taxes from the federal income tax. When searching for revenue alternatives, deductibility (or the lack of it) should be a consideration.

Ordinance Consolidation. To ensure greater control over a government's revenue policy, local laws regarding taxes, fees and user charges should be consolidated. This will enable the local legislative body to review them on a regular basis—easily and comprehensively—and reduces the chance that "old" rates will remain in effect due to administrative neglect.

Other Valid Goals. A local government revenue policy may reflect other goals of the community, such as the preservation of historic properties or provision of property tax relief to homeowners. These goals may conflict with other policy goals, such as the need for revenue adequacy and stability or the desire to maintain economic neutrality.

In the process of examining alternative revenue options, the goals outlined in this section can be used as a means of assessing the feasibility and desirability of the various options as they might be applied in a local jurisdiction. Failure to fully consider these goals could lead to future fiscal and/or economic difficulty, particularly if decisions are made regarding revenue sources that account for a large proportion of the jurisdiction's revenue base. The application of these goals to specific revenue alternatives is more fully discussed in the section on evaluating alternative revenue sources.

Linkage with Fiscal Policy

Revenue policy is inextricably linked with fiscal policy. An evaluation of revenue policy should not be undertaken without an evaluation of expenditure policy. Of particular importance is the identification of the level and mix of services that taxpayers wish to support. Essentially a political decision, this is one of the more difficult challenges facing any government. Nonetheless, only by identifying this "target level of taxation" can reform of the revenue structure be completed successfully. An additional concern is that the revenue structure continue to generate sufficient revenues to meet future spending requirements, while meeting other revenue policy goals.

Linkage with Economic Development Strategy

The revenue policy in place in a local jurisdiction directly affects the business climate and economic development efforts. Policy makers need to understand how the current revenue structure affects the economy and how proposed changes may improve or hinder future economic activity and take into account the interaction between taxation and economic activity when adjusting local tax rates.

Local government policy makers, aware that they are in competition with other jurisdictions for economic development projects, attempt to maintain a healthy business climate in order to discourage businesses from relocating to another jurisdiction and to encourage businesses located elsewhere to relocate in the local jurisdiction. Fear of developing a less competitive tax climate than neighboring jurisdictions has caused many local governments to raise revenues through the imposition of additional user charges and fees rather than by raising major tax rates. This can result in a more balanced tax and revenue system and may ultimately be of greater benefit to a local government's residents and enhance economic development efforts.

Important questions to ask are: Would a tax or other revenue change force a business to leave? Have any businesses complained of heavy tax burdens and financial difficulties? Would tax incentives offered to businesses undermine revenue stability? Would a tax or other revenue change contradict past policies, including the granting of tax abatements to businesses?

STEPS IN THE IDENTIFICATION OF ALTERNATIVE REVENUE SOURCES

Local governments considering the reform of their revenue policies will want to identify alternative revenue sources. The identification of such alternatives can be accomplished systematically through an examination of existing local revenue-raising authority, a review of the experience of other jurisdictions, and an evaluation of the local economy.

Examine Local Revenue-Raising Authority

Local revenue-raising authority varies from state to state depending on a number of factors, including whether the state in which the local government is located allows "home rule" or is governed by what is known as "Dillon's Rule." Local governments granted home rule status are often allowed wide latitude in the selection of taxes and other revenue sources, and only those taxes and revenues specifically prohibited by the state constitution or statutes are unavailable for their use. Dillon's Rule states that only those tax and revenue sources specifically approved by the state for local government use are available to those governments. Currently, forty-one states have granted home rule to their cities, while twenty-eight states have provided home rule to their counties.

Taxes and other revenues that are not currently legal under state constitutional or statutory law would require changes in those laws or the passage of enabling legislation prior to their adoption at the local level. This does not preclude local governments from pursuing such changes, but may make it difficult to adopt certain types of taxes and revenues.

Once the review of the state constitution and statutes has been conducted, the next step is an examination of local law. Two things are important: what revenue-raising authority currently exists, and what enabling legislation would need to be passed in order to adopt new taxes or other revenues. In most jurisdictions, local ordinances will be necessary in order to adopt new taxes, fees or user charges.

Examine the Experience of Other Jurisdictions

Along with the review of local revenue-raising authority it is usually worthwhile to examine the experience of similar jurisdictions, both within the state and in other states. The revenue-raising experience of other local governments located within the state is particularly helpful because the residents of those jurisdictions may have similar attitudes and traditions regarding taxation. This information will be helpful in gauging the feasibility of imposing new taxes or other revenues in a jurisdiction.

The experience of jurisdictions in other states is often the best source of information about potential tax and revenue options. Such a review will not only provide information on tax and other revenue options that are not permitted in your state, but can also provide a sampling of innovative revenue-raising practices in use around the nation.

In evaluating the experience of other jurisdictions, the tax and user charge evaluation criteria discussed in the next section can be utilized. By reviewing the experience of other jurisdictions it will be possible to get a better idea as to what has worked in the past and is likely to work in the future.

Evaluate the Local Economy

Finally, it is important to consider the state of the local economy when evaluating revenue policy. Of particular importance is an examination of relevant economic and demographic trends, including: population, per capita personal income, proportion of AFDC recipients, job trend and workforce, fair market value of real property, and taxable retail sales. Such trend analysis will help to provide the framework for any redesign of revenue policy, can lead to a greater understanding of the environment in which budgetary policy operates, and enable a more practical evaluation of revenue alternatives, including a better understanding of the revenue potential of different options.

While all revenue alternatives may impact or be affected by the local economy, certain alternatives should be evaluated in greater detail. In some instances, the state of the local economy will preclude a local government from imposing certain taxes, fees, or user charges. For example, imposing a tax on energy consumption, such as electricity usage, could have a substantial negative impact on an energy-dependent industrial firm that may be experiencing financial difficulty due to the effects of an economic downturn. The loss of jobs and tax revenues due to the closing of such a business could have a devastating effect on a community.

EVALUATING ALTERNATIVE REVENUE SOURCES

A local government's evaluation of alternative revenue sources should involve taxes, fees, and user charges. The evaluation of taxes and user charges is slightly different and documented in the following paragraphs. The evaluation of fees can be conducted along these same lines.

Tax Evaluation Criteria

The following criteria can be used in evaluating specific tax options. The criteria provide a means by which each can be measured against the goals of revenue policy; they can also force local government policy makers into explicit choices when selecting one alternative over another. Exhibit 1 shows how these criteria were applied in an actual analysis of alternative revenue sources conducted by the Government Finance Research Center for Baltimore County, Maryland, in 1989.

Economic Efficiency. This criterion is concerned with the possibility that the imposition of a tax or a change in the tax rate or base will result in a change in the relative price of a good or service sold in a jurisdiction and have an effect on private economic choice. A change in relative prices could cause consumers to shop elsewhere for goods and services (the so-called "border city" effect), or cause businesses and individuals to alter their locational choices. If businesses and/or individuals alter their decisions, the tax is said to create efficiency costs.

The price elasticity of demand for a good measures the sensitivity of demand to changes in price. The higher the price elasticity of demand for a good, the more sensitive demand will be to changes in price. The price elasticity of demand for a good is determined by the availability of substitutes. The more substitutes for a good available, the higher will be the price elasticity of demand for that good, thus, that good will be a less likely candidate for taxation. If demand for a good is price inelastic, demand will be unaffected by price, and there will be little need to be concerned about the effect of the imposition of a tax on private economic choice, as there will be little effect.

It is possible to calculate the price elasticity of demand for a wide range of goods, but local governments in the process of evaluating their revenue structures rarely do so. Instead, many governments rely on assumptions regarding price elasticities when making revenue policy decisions. For example, when considering the imposition of a local retail sales tax, local governments often assume that the price elasticity of demand for retail goods is high when there are a number of shopping centers located in adjacent communities that do not impose a local retail sales tax and are viable substitutes for local retailers.

In order to minimize efficiency costs, taxes can be imposed on goods with price-inelastic demand. Efficiency costs are also minimized when broad-based or flat-rate taxes are imposed.

Exhibit 1: *Alternative Revenue Options for Baltimore County, Maryland*

Option	Proposed Revenue Change	Economic Efficiency	Equity Issues	Administrative Effort	Political/Legal Issues	Projected Yield (FY91)
Ambulance Service Charge	Charge of $50/run	Demand is price inelastic	Benefits-based	Low (third-party collection)	Narrowly-based	$700,000
Increase in Hotel/Motel Occupancy Tax	Increase rate to 10%	Demand price inelastic—exportation possible	Benefits-based/high income elasticity	Low	Narrowly-based	Additional $1,095,000
Expansion of Energy Taxation	Natural gas: $.01/therm	Demand is price inelastic	Regressive	Low	Broadly-based	$2,360,000
	Electricity (res): 7.5% of value	Demand is price inelastic	Regressive	Low	Broadly-based	$13,407,000
	Fuel oil: $.02/gallon	Demand is price inelastic	Regressive	Low-moderate	Narrowly-based	$1,471,000
	Coal: $1/ton	Demand is price inelastic	Regressive	Low-moderate	Narrowly-based	1,688,000
Transaction Tax on Automotive Rentals	$2/transaction	Demand is price inelastic	High income elasticity	Moderate-high	Narrowly-based	$370,000+
Boat Mooring Tax	$10/foot of length	Demand probably price inelastic	High income elasticity	Moderate	Narrowly-based	$566,000
Commercial Parking Tax	$10/space	Price inelastic demand	Benefits-based	Low	Narrowly-based; potential legal problem	$428,000
Commercial Rent Tax	2.5% of gross rents	Price elastic—could affect locational decisions		High	Probably legal; businesses opposed	$6.5 million
Motor Vehicle Tax	$25/vehicle	Little effect on number of registrations	Benefits-based	Moderate-high	May be legal; broadly-based	$13.9 million
Bulk Collections Charge	$10/pickup	Price inelastic demand	Benefits-based	Low-moderate	Narrowly-based	$580,000
Title Transfer Tax	Expansion of title transfer tax base	Negligible impact on volume of transactions		Low-moderate	Narrowly-based	$5,700,000
Classification of Recordation Tax Rate Structure	Increase of $.50/$500 for commercial transactions	Negligible impact on volume of transactions		Low	Narrowly-based	Additional $444,000
911 Fees	Increase of $.20/month	Price inelastic demand	Negligible effect on disposable income	Low	Broadly-based—requires state action	Additional $737,000
Motor Fuel Tax	2% of value or $.02/gallon	Negligible effect on consumption	Benefits-based	Moderate	May be legal; less opposition than other major taxes	$5.1–7.6 million; $8.5 million
Liquor License Fees	50% increase in fees	Price inelastic demand		Low	Narrowly-based—requires BLC and state approval	$292 000
Classification of Property Tax Rate Structure	Increase of $.25/$100 for commercial/industrial properties	Could have adverse effect on business location decisions		Low	Affects business broadly—requires state action	Additional $6.4 million

Exhibit 1: *Alternative Revenue Options for Baltimore County, Maryland (continued)*

Option	Proposed Revenue Change	Economic Efficiency	Equity Issues	Administrative Effort	Political/ Legal Issues	Projected Yield (FY91)
Local Individual Income Tax	Increase local share to 60% of net state income tax	Could affect locational choices	Would compound regressivity of income tax	Low	Broadly-based—would have opposition—requires state action	$50 million
Local Sales and Use Tax	Imposition of .5% tax	Would alter consumption slightly	Would compound regressivity of sales tax	Low-high	Broadly-based—requires state action	$30.3 million
Local Corporate Income	Imposition of 3.5% tax	Would affect locational decisions		High	Broadly-based on businesses—requires state action	$24 million
Sales Tax on Automotive Rentals	Imposition of 2% tax	Price inelastic demand		Moderate-high	Narrowly-based—requires state action	$927,000
Capital Gains Tax on Real Property	Imposition of 1% tax on incremental increase in property values			Moderate-high	Broadly-based—requires state action	Will increase over time

Equity. This criterion is concerned with the effect that a tax change will have on equity between individual taxpayers. The important question to answer is: Who bears the burden of the tax?

One of the basic goals of revenue policy is to design an equitable tax and revenue system. While there has been basic agreement that each taxpayer should contribute his or her "fair share" to the cost of public services, there has been disagreement over what that "fair share" represents. Two approaches have been developed that attempt to deal with this issue. The first approach involves the application of the so-called "benefit principle," while the second approach rests on the "ability to pay" principle.

Applying the benefit principle, an equitable revenue system is considered to be one in which each taxpayer contributes in accordance with the benefits he or she receives from public services. The ability-to-pay principle, on the other hand, requires that taxpayers contribute to the cost of public services in line with their ability to pay. Although the benefit principle is utilized as a justification for the imposition of fees or charges for certain types of public services, such as for the use of recreational facilities, the ability-to-pay principle is widely accepted by economists as the appropriate guide to the determination of equity for revenue policy purposes.

The ability-to-pay approach utilizes two rules in the determination of equity among taxpayers that are important to this analysis. The horizontal equity rule requires that people with equal incomes pay the same amount of taxes, while the vertical equity rule requires that people with greater incomes pay a higher proportion of their incomes as taxes. Generally speaking, the use of a graduated (progressive) rate structure improves vertical equity, while the use of a flat-rate tax structure is better for horizontal equity.

Progressivity, proportionality, and regressivity are important equity concepts used in describing the burden of a tax or group of taxes across income levels. Progressivity refers to a situation in which taxes as a proportion of income increase as income increases. Proportionality occurs when taxes as a proportion of income are the same for all individuals. Regressivity refers to the case where taxes as a proportion of income decline as incomes increase.

In evaluating tax equity, it is important to determine the effect of a tax on disposable income; i.e., what amount of purchasing power was taken away by the tax? Equity may not be as important an issue if a tax amounts to an insignificant proportion of a low-income taxpayer's total income. Equity will be an issue if a great deal of purchasing power is taken away.

The income elasticity of demand is another important concept that indicates what percentage of marginal income is spent on a good. If the percentage of marginal income spent on a good increases as incomes increase, this is a potential candidate for taxation. Although it is possible to calculate the income elasticity of demand for a wide range of goods, local governments rarely attempt to do so when evaluating revenue alternatives. Rather, many governments rely on assumptions regarding income elasticities when making revenue policy decisions. For example, the federal government taxes luxury items, such as yachts and expensive jewelry, in an effort to exact additional revenues from the wealthiest taxpayers and because these types of goods have a high income elasticity of demand.

Administration. This criterion is concerned with the administrative burden of a tax. Several questions should be answered, including: 1) is the tax easy to evade? 2) what does the tax cost to administer? 3) who pays the cost of administering the tax? and 4) what is the cost of administration of alternative taxes? The point of this exercise is to ensure the efficient collection of taxes and other revenues. Failure to accurately estimate the burden of administering new taxes or other revenues could lead to situations in which the cost of administering a tax exceeds the cost of alternative taxes or exceeds the revenue collected from the tax.

Determining the cost of administering new taxes may be difficult without detailed study. Information on such costs, particularly for small revenue generators, is almost nonexistent. Generally speaking, broad-based and flat-rate taxes are easier to administer, while taxes with graduated rate structures (such as a progressive income tax) offer incentives for taxpayers to avoid paying.

Political/Legal Considerations. In evaluating the political feasibility of imposing a new tax or increasing a tax rate, it is worth reviewing the findings of the U.S. Advisory Commission on Intergovernmental Relations, which has consistently found that the public's attitudes are generally positive towards the taxation of sales, but negative towards the taxation of income and property.[3] It is also generally accepted that taxes with broad bases and/or graduated rate structures are harder to "sell" to the taxpayer, while taxes with narrow bases and/or flat rates are easier to sell.

As noted earlier, part of the review process involves a determination of the extent to which a local government has state constitutional or statutory authority to impose particular taxes, fees, or user charges or increase their rates. In evaluating a specific tax option, it is important to determine the legal steps necessary for its imposition.

Once a new tax has been adopted, the possibility exists that legal difficulties related to this option will arise involving such things as conflicting interpretations of statutes or challenges on the grounds of discriminatory taxation. The experience of other jurisdictions in these matters may assist a local government in gauging the likelihood of such a situation occurring.

Yield and Elasticity. This criterion examines the potential revenue yield and elasticity of each tax option. The yield depends on the size of the base and the rate applied. It is important to note that higher yields are often possible at lower rates if a broader base is used.

The elasticity of a tax measures the responsiveness of tax revenue to changes in the underlying base of the tax. For example, the elasticity of an income tax is often measured as the percentage change in income tax revenue divided by the percentage change in personal income. A key question to answer is: will revenues generated by the tax match the growth in expenditures? In order to answer this question, it is important to examine the elasticity of the tax and of the expenditure structure. Elastic taxes feature revenue growth greater than growth in the underlying base of the tax, such as local personal income or the local economy. On the other hand, revenue growth for income-inelastic taxes increases at the same or a lower rate than that of the underlying tax base. Graduated (progressive) tax rates can increase the elasticity of a tax, while flat rates often result in limited revenue growth.

What is a good tax? Although there are many who would argue that there are no good taxes, public finance economists generally believe that a good tax has some of the following characteristics:

- it is imposed on a good with price-inelastic demand

- it is imposed on a good with a high income-elasticity of demand
- it is simple and inexpensive to administer
- it is acceptable to the vast majority of taxpayers and is beyond legal challenge
- its revenue yield grows at a rate that matches or exceeds growth in expenditures

Evaluating User Charges

When public sector goods or services are similar to those offered by the private sector, the possibility exists that local governments will be able to charge individuals for the use of those goods and services. The ability of local governments to impose user charges for the goods or services that they provide depends on the technical and economic feasibility of the user charge in question. A proposed user charge is technically feasible when the benefits of a good or service accrue to particular individuals and when it is possible to exclude nonpayers from receiving the benefits of that public good or service. User charges are economically feasible when it can be determined that the costs of administering the proposed charges are less than the benefits expected from the substitution of user charges for taxes.

User charges should be set at levels that will allow a local government to recover the costs of providing a service, including: direct labor costs, supervisory and administrative costs, supplies and materials costs, and appropriate indirect costs. By setting user charge rates in such a way, the unintentional subsidization of services with tax revenues can be avoided. In some instances, such as with municipal electric utility charges in several states, charges may be set above cost in order to earn additional revenues for a government. In both cases, state statutes often provide guidance as to appropriate user charge rates.

Local governments considering the imposition of user charges should also note that they are not deductible from federal income taxes, as real property and income taxes are.

IMPLICATIONS OF REVENUE STRUCTURE REFORMS FOR CREDIT STANDING

Reform of a local government's revenue structure could have important implications for its credit standing. Today, the most common reasons why a local government chooses to undertake these reforms is to bolster sagging revenue collections and/or reduce reliance on the real property tax. The most common method used to achieve this is revenue diversification.

Credit analysts generally consider revenue diversification a good thing, up to a certain point. The introduction of income and sales taxes, which can reduce a government's dependence on a single revenue source, such as the real property tax, and add elasticity to the revenue structure, is generally regarded as a positive step. Ideally, a balance between these major revenue sources will be established. Overreliance on a local retail sales tax is not looked upon favorably by credit analysts, however, because its revenues are susceptible to swings in the business cycle.

The real property tax is considered to be the foundation of the local government revenue structure due to its reliability and predictability. Credit analysts view this as a good thing because it indicates that the government has a steady source of revenue to meet its debt service obligations and fund government operations. Reliance on other revenue sources may not provide the stability necessary to conduct the affairs of government in an orderly manner.

Overdiversification could have an adverse impact on a local government's credit standing. Replacing a reliable revenue source, such as the real property tax, with a number of smaller, more volatile revenue sources could be interpreted as an indicator of a weaker fiscal position which could have adverse credit impacts. A well thought out program of implementation that is not viewed as a scrapping of the real property tax probably would not have such impacts.

Notes

1. For those interested in additional information on the evaluation of revenue sources, see Robert L. Bland, *A Revenue Guide for Local Government,* Washington, D.C.: International City/County Management Association, 1989; and Robert Berne and Richard Schramm, *The Financial Analysis of Governments,* Englewood Cliffs, N.J.: Prentice-Hall, 1986. For additional information on fees and charges, see the forthcoming publication, *Catalog of Fees and Charges,* Chicago, Ill.: GFOA.
2. For more information on accounting for tax abatements, see Edward V. Regan, *Government, Inc.: Creating Accountability for Economic Development Programs,* Chicago, Ill.: GFOA, 1988.
3. See U.S. Advisory Commission on Intergovernmental Relations, *Changing Public Attitudes on Governments and Taxes: 1991,* Report S-20, Washington, D.C.: U.S. ACIR, 1991.

Property Tax and Assessment

THE PROPERTY TAX

Money for schools, parks, police and fire protection, and other government services comes from taxes. According to recent census data, in the United States, one tax, the *property tax,* provides over 40 percent of local government revenue raised from local sources. Elected officials, for example, city councillors, county commissioners, state legislators, and members of school boards, levy taxes. That is, they decide how much money should be raised by the property tax and other taxes.

Assessors have a very different role. They *administer* the property tax, and their chief task is to estimate the value of all taxable property in their jurisdictions.

Property is usually taxed according to value (ad valorem), which means that the tax levy is divided among taxpayers according to the value of each taxpayer's property. Each owner's share of the total property tax is the same as his or her share of the total value of taxable property. Taxes are imposed on *real property* (land and buildings) and, in some areas, on *personal property* (machinery, equipment, livestock, furniture, automobiles, and so on).

The Importance of the Property Tax in Government Finance

In Canada, the United Kingdom, the United States, and some other nations, the property tax is an important source of local government revenue for several reasons. The property tax is a more stable revenue source than sales and income taxes because property values reflect long-term economic considerations, not short-term economic fluctuations. For example, because property values rarely decrease suddenly, the property tax continues to provide stable income during a recession when sales and income taxes may decline sharply. Property tax rates can be easily adjusted to meet changing revenue needs as long as rate ceilings have not been reached. Real property is immobile, so property taxes are difficult to avoid. The property may be viewed as a security for the tax imposed. If taxes are not paid, ownership of the property will be transferred to the taxing jurisdiction. Finally, when property values rise because of public expenditures for community services, the property tax captures some of the increase for the community.

The Property Tax Base

For the most part, property taxes are levied against the value of real property, although in some areas, personal property is also taxed. Property may be taxed on the basis of full estimated market value or on some fraction of that value specified in legislation or officially stated by the local government. The value that is the basis of taxation is known as the assessed value. The ratio of assessed value to market value is the assessment ratio.

Accuracy, Equity, and Fairness

Assessors are expected to achieve accuracy, equity, and fairness in their estimates of value. Accuracy is

---

International Association of Assessing Officers, *An Introduction to the Assessment Profession* (Chicago: IAAO, 1987), 1-7. Reprinted by permission of IAAO.

achieved if the value of property is neither under- nor overestimated. Equity is achieved if all like properties are assessed alike. Fairness is achieved if each taxpayer pays a share of taxes proportional to the value of his or her property. The International Association of Assessing Officers (IAAO) develops and publishes assessment standards to help assessors achieve fair, accurate, and equitable assessments.

The Calculation of Property Tax Rates and Bills

The calculation of individual property tax bills is the last in a series of actions taken by local government revenue officers (see Exhibit 1). Usually, a budget is established by elected officials who determine the spending requirements of the government. Total expenditures include those for debt service of the government and those needed for the operation of schools and other government agencies. Financial aid from other governments, income from local taxes other than the property tax, and income from fees and the like are subtracted from the total budget, leaving a net amount to be raised by the property tax.

The assessor, working outside the process of budget development, estimates the assessed value of all taxable property within the jurisdiction. The budgeted revenue to be raised from the property tax is then divided by the total assessed value established by the assessor. The result is the nominal tax rate (Exhibit 1).

For example, suppose a town had budgeted $120,000 in revenue to come from property taxes, and the assessor had determined the total assessed value to be $3,000,000. The nominal tax rate is .04, or 4 percent ($120,000 ÷ $3,000,000). Individual property tax bills are then calculated by multiplying the nominal property tax rate by the assessed value of the individual property. Thus, the property tax bill for a home with an assessed value of $37,500 would be $1,500 (.04 × $37,500). Many jurisdictions will have several rates, one for the school district, one for the fire district, and so on.

Tax rates may be expressed in dollars per $100 of assessed value, in dollars per $1000 of assessed value, or in mills per dollar. A mill is one tenth of a cent or one thousandth of a dollar (see Exhibit 2).

The effective tax rate provides a useful way of thinking about the property tax when different classes of property are assessed at different ratios. The effective tax rate is the property tax bill expressed as a percentage of the market value of the

Exhibit 1: *Determining Tax Rates and Bills*

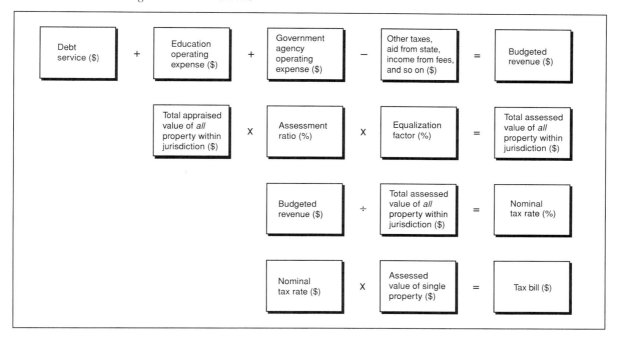

Exhibit 2: *Calculation of Taxes and Tax Rates*

> Amount to be raised by property tax divided by jurisdiction's total assessed value equals nominal tax rate.
> $120,000 ÷ $3,000,000 = .04 = 4 percent
>
> Tax on a home with a market value of $100,000 and an assessed value of $30,000:
>
> Assessed value × nominal tax rate = tax
> $30,000 × .04 = $1,200
>
> *Tax rate* of 4 percent expressed in mills per dollar = 40 mills/dollar.
>
> Taxes = 40 mills/$1 × $30,000 = 1,200,000 mills = $1,200 dollars
>
> Effective tax rate:
> Tax ÷ market value
> $1,200 ÷ 100,000 = 0.012 = 1.2 percent

property. The nominal tax rate will not be the effective tax rate when the assessed value differs from market value. For example, assume that the property in the example above has a market value of $125,000. The effective tax rate is .012, or 1.2 percent ($1,500 ÷ $125,000). It can also be seen that the property is assessed at 30 percent of market value ($37,500 ÷ $125,000 = 0.30, or 30 percent). This percentage, the assessment ratio, or assessment-sale price ratio, should be close to the legal assessment ratio.

Another method of developing the effective tax rate is to multiply the assessment ratio by the nominal tax rate. In the example the effective rate is .012 – .30 × .04.

THE ASSESSMENT FUNCTION

Authority of the Assessor— The Legal Framework

Property tax laws establish the legal framework for the assessor's work. The laws establish which property is taxable and which is exempt, whether property is to be appraised on the basis of current market value or some other standard, how frequently property is to be reappraised and reassessed, and when each part of the assessment process is to be completed. The laws also define the duties of assessment officials, their authority, and the limits of their authority. Assessors should be familiar with the legislation governing assessment in their jurisdictions.

Responsibilities

In simple terms, an assessor is responsible for discovering and describing property, valuing property, identifying property owners or taxpayers, and making assessments. An assessor also has related responsibilities: providing information about assessment and property tax matters to property owners, government officials, and others, and responding to complaints and appeals of assessments. Because assessors usually require assistance in carrying out their functions, they are responsible for administering the personnel and material resources of their offices.

The primary responsibility of assessors is the preparation of an annual assessment roll, which forms the basis for taxation in the jurisdiction (state, province, county, city, town, village, township, or school district) for which it is prepared. The assessment roll lists all properties in the assessment jurisdiction, identifies property owners or taxpayers, and states an assessed value related to the assessor's estimate of the market value (or use value) of the property.

The primary tasks performed by the assessor in completing the assessment roll are as follows:

1. Locating and identifying all taxable property in the jurisdiction. An accurate set of maps that plot every parcel of land is the assessor's major tool for identifying and locating taxable real property. If personal property must be assessed, the laws usually prescribe administrative procedures to locate and identify it. For example, the taxpayer may be required to file a return listing taxable personal property with the assessor, who then audits the return.

2. Making an inventory of the quantity, quality, and important characteristics of all taxable property. An inventory is essential to the proper assessment of properties and to the assurance of equity in the taxation of similar properties. An on-site inspection is almost always necessary to complete an inventory. Legislation often *requires* the assessor to view a property before appraising it. Some appeal courts have ruled that the failure of the assessor to view a property will invalidate the assessment placed on it.

3. Estimating the value of each taxable property. Assessors use all appropriate appraisal techniques to estimate value. The quality of their estimations is critical to the equitable distribution of the tax burden. Assessors use three basic approaches to estimating value: the cost approach, the sales comparison approach, and the income approach. Historically, properties have been appraised one at a time. Increasingly, properties are appraised in groups (mass appraisal).

4. Determining the extent of taxability of each property. To determine the extent of taxability of each property, the assessor must review legislation affecting the taxable status of properties in the jurisdiction. A thorough review must include not only the general taxable and exempt provisions of state or provincial legislation, but also provisions of local legislation affecting individual property or property owners. Some legislation will provide that properties exempt from taxation must, nonetheless, be assessed; other legislation will provide exemption from assessment as well as taxation. The assessor must also research case law that may have interpreted the legal meaning of a specific legislative provision relating to the taxability of a particular type of property—a difficult task unless the assessor keeps up with legal interpretations as they occur. Recognized case reporting systems, such as IAAO's *Assessment and Valuation Legal Reporter,* are essential tools.

5. Calculating the assessed value of each property. The property tax rate of each tax district in which a property lies is applied to its assessed value, the value appearing on the assessment roll, to determine the amount of the property tax. Ideally, assessed value will be the same as market value.

An increasing number of states and provinces have established by law a percentage of market value at which the assessed value is to be set. Several have defined classes of property and assigned percentage factors to each. For example, single-family residential properties might be assessed at 12 percent of market value and industrial properties at 16 percent. The percentage factor is then applied to the market value of all properties within each class to generate assessed value. Other states have weakened this already tenuous link between assessed value and estimated market value by imposing limits on assessment increases (Proposition 13 in California, for example)—a practice that IAAO opposes.

6. Preparing and certifying the assessment roll of the entire jurisdiction. The assessor lists all properties in the assessment jurisdiction, usually on a printed form satisfying legislative requirements for preparation of the assessment roll. Then the assessor prepares a certificate (usually in a form regulated by statute) attesting to the sufficiency of the roll and to compliance with the statutory provisions for its preparation. Preparation may be done by computer, Addressograph, typewriter, or hand. The assessment roll is then presented to the appropriate agency by the statutory date set for its return. The roll is reviewed, taxes computed, and tax bills sent out. Monies are usually collected by another agency.

7. Notifying owners of the assessed value of their properties. The laws of most states and provinces require that owners of properties be notified of the assessed values of their properties at the same time as, or immediately prior to, the date set for the return of the assessment roll. In some jurisdictions, tenants must also be notified. In several jurisdictions, notification is required only when a change has been made from the previous assessment. The formal notification is called an assessment notice.

8. Defending value estimates and methods used to assess value during appeals by taxpayers. All assessment legislation provides taxpayers with the right to appeal the assessed value of their property. Assessors should be thoroughly familiar with the pertinent legislation and with the operating procedures of the appeal body. They should be prepared to justify all valuations and methods to the satisfaction of the appeal body and, ideally, to the satisfaction of the taxpayer.

Pricing Public Services

Kevin Neels and Michael Caggiano

BENEFIT-BASED FINANCE

For many years, city government operations throughout the country expanded rapidly as tax receipts increased and state and federal governments became more generous in providing aid. From 1960 to 1978, real per capita general expenditures for local government nationwide grew from $302 (in 1978 dollars) to $520. In 1978, however, the trend was reversed. That year was marked by the passage of Proposition 13 in California, one of a series of measures intended to limit taxes and curb the growth of local government. Federal and then state aid to localities also began to decline as other levels of government experienced their own financial difficulties. By 1980, real per capita local government expenditures had fallen to $484 (in 1978 dollars), and since then, the downward trend has continued.

Nationwide, the revenue source that has grown most rapidly and has done the most to offset declining intergovernmental revenues is benefit-based finance. Unlike many other sources of funding, benefit-based finance is controlled by the city itself. Hence, it can increase self-reliance and reduce dependence on decisions made at other levels of government.

Beneficiary charges share some important characteristics that distinguish them from property taxes and other sources of general revenue. First, they represent payments for specific city services. Unlike property taxes, which support a wide range of activities, beneficiary charges are frequently earmarked. For example, the fee that a golfer pays to use a city golf course covers the course's operation and maintenance. The golfer knows what he is buying when he pays his fee. Second, beneficiary charges are paid by the consumers of the service—the people, businesses, or institutions that benefit. A general sales tax earmarked to support a regional transit system would not constitute a beneficiary charge, but transit fares would.

Beneficiary charges that a citizen can avoid paying by not consuming the service are generally called user charges. A special assessment for street maintenance, which might be regarded as a form of benefit-based finance, would not be a user charge, since there is no way that property owners can avoid paying the assessment. Recreation fees, on the other hand, can be avoided by not using the city facilities. These are user charges.

Advantages

Beneficiary charges offer four primary advantages over other forms of finance. First, they can raise substantial sums of money at times when legal, political, or economic limitations restrict other potential revenue sources. Second, beneficiary charges encourage a change in management outlook. They can be administered so that the city unit providing a service in effect raises its own money through sales of the service, thus focusing attention of city managers on the concerns and demands of the people they serve, rather than on budgetary politics. As citizens become

---

Reprinted from *The Entrepreneurial City: Innovations in Finance and Management for Saint Paul*, R-3123-SP/FF (Santa Monica, Calif.: RAND, 1984), 8-26. By permission of RAND.

customers rather than clients, managers must become more directly responsive to their needs. Third, beneficiary charges can improve horizontal equity. Polls indicate that the public perceives beneficiary charges as a fair and appropriate way of paying for city services, because they guarantee that services are paid for by the people who use them. Reliance on beneficiary charges prevents limited public resources from being diverted to benefit special interests. Finally, benefit-based finance, especially user charges, rations the demand for public services and encourages people to be more careful in their use of public resources. A recent report to municipal leaders in Massachusetts emphasizes this point:

> Setting a fee can also be used to lessen inefficient or wasted use of community resources. If a police or fire department has offered assistance to those locked out of homes or cars free of charge in the past, instituting a fee for this discretionary service may discourage individuals from relying on the service, and prompt citizens to give more thoughtful attention to protecting their homes and their cars. In this particular instance, the fee is instituted recognizing that it is not a big "money maker," but an attempt to limit the discretionary assistance previously provided by public safety personnel. Because many services are seen as "free," citizens may overuse the service. If there is a fee or charge, unnecessary use will be better regulated.[1]

Disadvantages

Beneficiary charges have two major disadvantages: The revenue stream they generate can be unpredictable, and they can have an adverse impact on the poor and the disadvantaged.

Income from beneficiary charges tends to be less stable than traditional sources of city revenue such as property taxes or state aid. This is especially true of user charges, where consumption of the service and payment of the fee are voluntary. A spell of bad weather can significantly decrease the fee income generated by a city's recreational facilities. A slowdown in construction can wipe out most of the revenue from development fees. A city department that is heavily dependent on user-charge income therefore must maintain much larger working capital reserves and must be able to respond much more quickly to changing circumstances. The job of departmental management becomes more demanding.

Beneficiary charges can in effect deny some services to citizens with limited incomes. Many services have traditionally been provided at no charge (that is, financed from general revenues) to make certain that they are equally available to all members of the community. Imposition of a user charge may limit access to services, i.e., poorer households may forgo use of the service rather than strain their already limited budgets.

However, a move toward user charges need not necessarily place undue burdens on the poor. This situation can be avoided by making careful decisions about when to charge for city services, and paying close attention to the design of the charges that are imposed.

CANDIDATES FOR USER CHARGES

To assess the feasibility and desirability of beneficiary-charge financing, city services can be grouped into three categories: public goods, private goods, and merit goods.

Public goods are the services that supply general benefits to the public at large. The best examples of public goods are police and fire protection. It is impossible to identify the extent to which each individual benefits from such services. One individual's use of the service redounds to everyone's benefit, since everyone has an interest in preventing crime and inhibiting the spread of fires. As another example, enforcement of planning and zoning regulations results in a more livable city for everyone. Traffic signs and signals ensure orderly traffic flow and thereby provide a general benefit to all travelers.

True public services should be funded out of general revenues. Indeed, the city has very little choice, since these services lack identifiable consumers.

Private goods are the polar opposite of public goods. It *is* possible to identify individual consumers of private goods. The benefits of private services accrue solely to those consumers, and the public at large has no stake in any individual's consumption of the service. Although responsibility for provision of private goods and services is generally left to the private market, the city may be active in this area for a number of reasons.

One of the most common reasons for public provision of private services is that the service represents a natural monopoly. For example, it is overwhelmingly cost effective for all the water service in a built-up area to be provided by a single organization. When a service such as water is provided on a monopoly basis, there are no market forces to constrain the behavior of the producer. The monopoly must be publicly regulated to assure that it does not exploit its powerful position. Under these circumstances, there is no advantage to private provision of the service, so services that involve natural monopolies are often provided by public entities. The major monopoly services that Saint Paul provides are water service, sewer service, and provision of streets.

A city may offer private services because they are naturally complementary to other services the city provides. Although use of a copier is clearly private, the library provides copiers because people who come to the library often need them—making copiers available is a natural extension of the library's basic mission. The city maintains concession stands in the Como Park Zoo for similar reasons.

In other instances, the city may provide private services for no other reason than historical accident.

The city should try to recover the full cost of providing private services from the people who consume them. Failure to do so means that in effect the city is using general revenues to subsidize particular individuals and special interests. In a city with continuing financial problems, such subsidies are hard to justify.

The final category of city services is merit goods, which occupy an intermediate position between public goods and private goods and share some of the characteristics of both. They are like private goods in that they are generally consumed by identifiable individuals; they are like public goods because the benefits of the service spill over into the community at large. One of the best examples of this type of service is the treatment of communicable diseases. Clearly, the person who is sick and being treated is the prime beneficiary of the service; however, the community as a whole also benefits from the reduction of the risk of contagion that his treatment brings about.

IDENTIFYING THE PUBLIC GOOD COMPONENT IN CITY SERVICES

A major portion of the Saint Paul budget is allocated to merit goods, which in many ways are the hardest of the three categories to deal with. Because there is a private benefit, consumers of the service should pay some charge. The charge should reflect the size of the private benefit, but it is not always easy to determine the relative public and private shares, and in many cases the dividing line reflects value judgments that are expressed through political decisions.

The public component of a service can take a number of different forms. Allowing people with contagious diseases to go untreated increases the health risk to the population at large. Thus, the reasons for the public interest in their treatment are clear and direct. In other cases, the public component can reflect a collective value judgment. For example, the citizens of Saint Paul have decided that they want to live in a community of well-read, well-educated people, so they have chosen to use public resources to support an extensive system of public libraries. The public component can reflect a general concern for the welfare of disadvantaged community members. The city provides extensive recreational services partly because it does not want the poor to be denied access to recreation.

Because they embody a mix of public and private goods, services in the merit good category should rely on a mixture of funding. A portion of their cost should come from contributions by consumers of the service, and the remainder should be supplied from general city revenues.

The city's leaders must identify the fraction of the cost that reflects general public benefits and that should come from general revenues. In Saint Paul, decisions have already been made about what fractions of the cost of citywide support services the various Special Fund activities will have to bear.[2] A number of services, including the Oxford Swimming Pool and the Municipal Athletic Facility, have relied on a mixture of general funding and user fees. In September 1983, the city council decided to cover 25 percent of the cost of summer street maintenance from general revenues.

Decisions about the funding mixture for different services tell the city's middle-level managers how much additional income they are expected to raise. With a target to shoot for, a manager can concentrate on developing the user fees, beneficiary charges, and enterprise operations that best fit the needs of his clientele and the characteristics of his operation.

We recognize that Saint Paul must make its own judgments about the services it has a vital stake in providing. However, we have devised some broad guidelines that can be used in making decisions about the financing of merit good services. These guidelines are based largely on the work of the Saint Paul Responsive Services Task Force, as reported in the minutes of their May 4, 1983, meeting. Task Force members were asked to delineate the issues the city should consider before changing the way a service is provided. The group developed 26 issues and rated them in importance. We organized these 26 issues into seven basic categories, which we converted into a checklist (see Exhibit 1). We then assigned a weight to each item on the checklist. The weights are the sum of the ratings assigned to each question by the Task Force, normalized to 100 and rounded to the nearest 5 for simplicity.

For any service, a "yes" or "no" answer should be recorded for each question. The percentage of the full cost to be paid by a beneficiary charge is then the sum of the weights for those questions to which a "yes" answer is recorded. In cases where Task Force issues pertain to more than one of the categories we developed, the total rating is divided equally among the categories into which the issues fall.

Examples of how two services, computer-based library searches and sewer-system capital improvements, might be scored are shown in Table 1. These examples are hypothetical and do not necessarily reflect the values of the citizens of Saint Paul.

This scoring exercise suggests that the library should try to recover 90 percent of the cost of literature searches it runs for its clients, while the sewer division should charge users a little more than half the costs of infrastructure improvements.

We must emphasize that before dividing the charges for a service between the consumers and the community, the city's overall financial condition must be considered. Saint Paul can afford to provide only a limited array of services free of charge to everyone. In times of fiscal stress, the margin of generosity has to be smaller. For this reason, decisions about financing the production of merit goods must always be consistent with the volume of general revenues that are available.

PROTECTING DISADVANTAGED RESIDENTS

As local government officials around the country have turned toward beneficiary charges as a source of revenue, they have worried about the effects of such charges on lower-income groups. In Saint Paul, city officials, workers, and citizens have all emphasized the importance of maintaining access to city

Exhibit 1: *Checklist for Evaluating Merit Good Services*

Question	Weight
A. Does consumption of the service generate minimal spillover effects on other members of the community?	25
B. Is it possible to identify a specific beneficiary for the service?	20
C. Is the imposition of beneficiary charges for this service statutorily and administratively feasible?	15
D. Would the imposition of beneficiary charges for this service evoke negligible political opposition?	15
E. Would the imposition of beneficiary charges for the service lead to substantial revenues for the city?	10
F. Would benefit-based funding of this service through Revenue Centers result in enhanced efficiency?	10
G. Would beneficiary charges for this service have negligible effects on the city's competitive position?	5

Table 1: *Hypothetical Checklist Scores of Two City Services*

Service Question	Computer-Based Literature Searches by Library	Sewer System Capital Improvements
A	25	0
B	20	20
C	15	15
D	15	0
E	0	15
F	10	0
G	5	5
Total	90	55

services by all members of the community. Consequently, in developing the Revenue Center design, we sought to build in assurances that disadvantaged groups will be treated equitably.

The equity safeguards for disadvantaged groups would take three forms: (1) the continuing provision of basic public services, (2) the manipulation of the charge structure for private and merit good services to ease the burdens it places on the poor and the elderly, and (3) the Safeguard system, a program of vouchers that the poor can use to pay beneficiary charges and obtain services.

Provision of Essential Services

The point of establishing Revenue Centers is to guarantee that essential city services will be provided to all members of the community. Collecting revenue from consumers of private goods will relieve pressure on property taxes and other General Fund revenue sources. That means the General Fund can be used to provide public or essential services freely and openly to everyone. These services constitute the first line of defense for the poor, the elderly, and the disadvantaged.

Designing Charge Structures

Even where fees and charges are imposed, it is often possible to structure them in such a way as to minimize their inequitable impacts. Such built-in protections constitute the second line of defense for disadvantaged groups in Saint Paul.

An example of this form of protection is lifeline electricity rates, which provide some minimum level of consumption at a low cost. Beyond that level, the price per unit rises. Thus, poor families in small houses with few appliances pay low rates, while wealthier families in large, well-equipped houses pay more. This example has direct relevance for Saint Paul in the water utility and in sewer services.

Another example of equitable charge structures is the system of group fare discounts used on most public transit systems. School children, the elderly, and the handicapped are charged lower fares than other passengers.

There are many possibilities for building equity protection into charge structures. Recreational programs and other city services for which people pay a fee at the point of sale can offer group discounts. Services that might be financed through special assessments, such as street maintenance, street lighting, and neighborhood parks, could allow elderly homeowners with limited cash incomes to defer payment until their houses are sold. It might also be possible to establish fees whose level varies with the income of the neighborhood. Discounts could be offered in low-income neighborhoods for libraries, recreation centers, and health clinics, or even in special assessments. In general, each charge mechanism that the city might use will suggest its own set of possibilities.

The Safeguard System

The Safeguard system is the most comprehensive way of maintaining access to city services. This system would provide vouchers to members of disadvantaged groups for access to a wide range of responsive city services. These vouchers, financed from the city's general revenues, would reimburse Revenue Centers for services provided to the poor, the elderly, and the handicapped. The administrative feasibility of such a system has not yet been determined. Clearly, its costs would be substantial, and it is not clear whether its potential benefits would offset those costs.

The main issues in the design of the Safeguard system are eligibility, form of payment, and accountability. Defining eligibility requires a value judgment on the "appropriate" income level, age, or degree of disability that triggers admittance to protected status. Certifying eligibility requires a way of rating individual applicants. One way would be to administer specially designed means tests to applicants. However, such tests can be difficult and expensive to administer, and they are often a degrading experience for the people involved. Alternately, eligibility could be based on the tests and certifications already conducted in Saint Paul for welfare, food stamps, unemployment compensation, health care, and other programs.

A simple form of payment would be scrip that people could exchange for responsive city services. This is the approach now used in the food stamp program. Reimbursement of the Revenue Center would be based upon the amount of scrip collected.

Accountability problems are relatively easy to resolve in a system based upon the issuance of scrip. As long as the scrip could not be easily duplicated, the system could be policed. Clients could spend only as much scrip as they possessed, and the Revenue Centers would be reimbursed for only as much scrip as they turned in. Controlling the use of the scrip by ineligibles would present more difficult, but not insurmountable, problems. Identity cards could be issued along with the scrip, to be checked when the scrip was used. A political judgment would have to be made on the acceptability of permitting development of a "white market" in scrip. Selling of scrip by eligibles would provide extra resources for those to whom it was issued, but not necessarily in the form of city services.

ESTABLISHING CHARGES FOR CITY SERVICES

Once the decision to charge for a service has been made, a number of practical questions arise. Every charge has three components: a unit of measure, a rate per unit, and a collection mechanism. The unit of measure defines the quantity of service consumed. The charge per unit of measure sets the revenue yield for the charge. The collection mechanism is the administrative procedure for passing the payment from consumers to the producer of the service. Each of these three components must be defined and in place before the charge can be implemented. In addition, it is important to prepare the public for the charge through advance notification. These issues are discussed below.

Units of Measure

The unit of measure for a charge determines its magnitude for a particular individual. Gasoline is sold by the gallon, for example, and potatoes are sold by the pound. In general, charges for public services should be based upon similarly specific measures of the quantity of service consumed.[3] However, it is often difficult to define a unit of measure for public services, so cruder measures must be used. The possible units of measure for assessing beneficiary charges fall into three categories: general levies, proxy measures, and quantity measures.

General levies rely on diffuse estimates of the benefit an individual receives from a service; they establish the weakest link between service consumption and charge level. In many instances, they differ little from a general tax earmarked for a specific use. Examples include a flat per-household fee for police protection, a property tax millage for fire protection, or a front-footage charge for street maintenance. In all these cases, there is a rough relationship between the basis and the benefit received, but it is only a rough relationship. Many general levies are compulsory and hence fail to qualify as true user charges. They do, however, help to focus public attention on the cost and quality of specific services. General levies are used most often for services that have a large public good component (i.e., spillover benefits) and for which output measures are hard to define.

Proxy measures rely not on direct measurements of usage, but on approximations. For example, most states finance highway construction and maintenance through a tax on gasoline sales. An ideal user charge would be based upon the number of miles driven by each vehicle operator, but since that information is not available, gasoline sales provide a very serviceable approximation. Someone who drives a lot will contribute more to the support of the highway system than one who drives very little. Saint Paul now uses a proxy measure in charging for sewers. The city does not meter volume of effluent—the ideal basis for a user charge—but since what goes in must go out, except for lawn watering, winter water usage provides a good approximation, and it is used to assess sewer charges.

In cases where the service is not standardized, such as the review of building and site plans, the cost of providing the service is used as a way to estimate consumption. Saint Paul also uses this approach in charging for police protection at some special events.

When good output measures are available, charges can be based directly on consumption. In Saint Paul, water service and golf course charges are based on usage. The use of output measures as a basis for assessing beneficiary charges provides the strongest incentives to producers and consumers and in one sense, at least, the fairest apportionment of costs.[4] Unfortunately, quantity-based user charges often require a more elaborate billing system than flat fees, and the costs of operating the system may outweigh the potential benefits. Practicality sometimes requires that compromises be made.

Setting the Rate per Unit

One of the most difficult problems in establishing charges for services is deciding how much people should pay. In practice, these decisions are often made on an ad hoc basis. In an effort to provide a more systematic basis for setting charges, we shall consider the various procedures that have been suggested and present a set of guidelines for choosing among these procedures in specific cases.

Procedures for setting fee and charge levels are either cost-based, revenue-based, or income-based. Cost-based procedures yield charge levels that reflect the costs of providing the service. They differ in the particular measure of costs that each considers. Most municipalities that have an explicit policy for setting charge levels follow some form of cost-based pricing. In some cases, cost-based pricing is legally mandated. California cities, for example, are prohibited from setting fee and charge levels any higher than the costs of providing the corresponding services. Similar restrictions apply to the fees collected by the water utility of Saint Paul. Even when they are not prohibited from doing otherwise, municipalities will often set charges equal to costs out of a sense that this is an appropriate rule for a nonprofit entity to follow. In effect, officials have applied nonprofit status not only to the city as a whole, but also to the individual activities it engages in.

One common form of cost-based pricing sets charges equal to the direct costs of providing the service. Direct costs include all the expenses immediately associated with the particular service. The costs of all materials and fuels used for a city asphalt plant, for example, the salaries of all personnel working at the plant, and the amount spent on its maintenance and upkeep would be summed. Dividing this sum by the number of tons of asphalt produced would give the average direct cost, and hence the charge per ton.

A second form of cost-based pricing sets charges equal to average full costs. Full costs are higher than direct costs and lead to a correspondingly greater charge. They include, in addition to direct costs, appropriate shares of administration, overhead, and other indirect costs that are common to many activities.[5] These costs are apportioned on the basis of the activities' share of the allocation "base." The simplest base is direct cost. Thus, if the direct cost of the asphalt plant is $1 million and the direct costs of all the other activities within the department to which it belongs add up to $19 million, the full cost of asphalt would include 5 percent of departmental administrative costs. Similar apportionments would be made for administrative costs at the citywide level. In particular instances, it may be appropriate to use a different allocation base for some overhead cost items. For example, Saint Paul now allocates Personnel Department costs to the Special Fund activities on the basis of their numbers of employees.

In its 1983 budget, Saint Paul instituted full recovery of central support service costs for Special Fund activities. These activities now have to pay the General Fund back for the administrative and citywide support services they receive, an important step toward adoption of full cost as a basis for setting beneficiary charges.

Costs vary with the quantity of service provided. Obviously, if the level of output increases, total costs will generally also increase. However, the average cost per unit may increase or decrease. Consider once again the case of the asphalt plant. Some costs of operation will remain the same regardless of the level of output. If the volume of asphalt produced is very small, these fixed costs will be spread over a small base. As the volume of output increases, the share of fixed costs that each ton of asphalt must bear will shrink, and thus average costs will decline. As the volume of output increases, the decline in average costs may continue for some time until production begins to approach capacity. After that occurs, average costs will rise. It may become harder to schedule the delivery of materials efficiently. At higher rates of output, machinery is likely to break down more often, requiring greater expenditures for repair and upkeep. As the facility becomes busier and more crowded, individual worker productivity may decline because of the difficulty of managing a larger workforce. The overall result will be increasing difficulty in coaxing each successive ton of asphalt out of the plant. When this occurs, average costs will tend to rise.

Although the above example referred exclusively to direct costs, similar volume-related effects can be found for indirect costs. In most situations, these can be regarded as fixed, so that as the level of service (and hence also the allocation base, however defined) grows, average indirect costs will decline. However, the workload in accounting, personnel, and the other overhead divisions may eventually grow to the point that it becomes necessary for them to expand. At that point, average indirect costs would rise.

In situations where average costs depend significantly on the level of output, economists advocate setting charges on the basis of marginal cost. The marginal cost of a service is the cost of the last unit of service provided. Conceptually, marginal cost is measured by the change in total cost (both direct and indirect) that would occur if output were increased by one unit. Setting prices to cover marginal costs leaves the city no worse off than it would be if it cut the service, and at the same time it guarantees that the public gets maximum use of the service.

Because indirect costs and many direct costs do not change with the quantity of service provided, marginal costs are usually below full costs and often even below direct costs. For this reason, the use of marginal-cost pricing often leads to a situation where beneficiary-charge revenues must be supplemented by funds from other sources.

The marginal cost of providing a service may also include a congestion component when provision of the service involves the use of a facility with a fixed capacity, such as a swimming pool. As swimmers fill up the pool, a point may be reached at which the addition of an extra one starts to detract from the enjoyment of those already there. In this instance, the cost of serving an additional swimmer includes not only the maintenance and operating costs associated with his use of the facility, but also the cost of the degradation in the quality of the service that his use causes for everyone else. In such cases, a simple way to institute marginal-cost pricing is to set fees high enough to cover operating costs and avoid overcrowding, but low enough to keep the facility fully used.

The second major class of procedures for setting charges looks at the revenue rather than the cost side of the picture. These revenue-based procedures reflect not what it costs to provide the service, but rather what people are willing to pay for it. There are two major variants here: market pricing and exemplary pricing.

Some of the services the city provides are also available on the open market from private producers. The going market price then provides a strong signal about how much the city should charge. The city cannot charge more than market price, since citizens could then be expected to obtain the service from cheaper private producers. But unless the city wants to subsidize a service to make it more readily available to disadvantaged members of the community, there is no good reason to charge less than the market price.

It should be noted here that the service available on the open market need not be precisely identical to that provided by the city. The basis for market pricing is the way demand for the service reacts to changes in the charge. City libraries, for example, have to compete with paperback book stores, which offer different but closely related services. If services available on the open market can substitute for what the city provides, there will be some charge level above which the city has almost no customers, and below which it has almost the whole market. That is the charge level that would be defined by market pricing.

For services that are not available in any form from private suppliers, the city may obtain some guidance in setting charge levels by examining fee structures in neighboring jurisdictions. With exemplary pricing, the city follows the example set by its neighbors. Their experience provides important, though limited, information. In most cases, charge levels in neighboring jurisdictions mark the bottom of the range the city should consider in its own pricing decisions. The fact that these charges have been successfully established proves their feasibility, both administratively and politically. There is less reason to believe that they have been set at an appropriately high level. Stronger finances, for example, may let neighboring jurisdictions be more generous in subsidizing services out of general revenues than Saint Paul can afford to be.

The final set of principles for setting charge levels is based on the amount of income generated. These principles consider both the cost and revenue sides of the equation. The three main alternatives here are full cost plus markup, income maximization, and discriminatory pricing.

Under full cost plus markup, charges are set at a fixed percentage above full cost. With every unit of service provided, the city collects enough revenue to cover both direct cost and overhead plus some amount of net income. This principle primarily applies to basic utility services that the city provides on a monopoly basis and finances through a well-established user charge. In these cases, setting prices on the basis of full cost plus markup can turn the service into a source of income. Where the service is widely used, this form of pricing allows tax-exempt institutions to contribute something toward the operation of the city government. It may also simply be a convenient way for the city to expand its revenue base if demand for the service is such that modest increases in its price will have little effect on the amount consumed, if the city is legally empowered to raise the fee, if the billing and collection mechanisms are already in place, and if the distributional effects of the increase are not unacceptable.[6] In many situations, there are legal restrictions against setting charges above costs, so careful legal work is needed before this principle can be used.

Under income maximization, charges are set at the level that generates the greatest net income for the city. If the service is available from private suppliers, income maximization probably dictates that the charge be set at the going market price. If the city alone provides the service, the income maximizing charge depends on both the nature of the demand for the service and its cost structure. In the case of a necessity like water or sewer service, the income-maximizing charge is likely to be well above full cost. For services that have fairly close private market substitutes, like some recreational services, the income-maximizing charge might not even be sufficient to allow recovery of marginal costs. In such cases, it might be more appropriate to speak of minimizing losses.

When all consumers pay the same fee for a service, determination of the income-maximizing fee level requires some experimentation and a consideration of both costs and revenues. If a fee is raised, the total number of consumers of the service will decline, but each of the remaining consumers will be paying more. Total revenue can thus either increase or decrease, depending upon the relative strengths of the two effects. Because less of the service is now being provided, costs of providing it should decline. If raising the fee increases net income, the income-maximizing charge is higher than the present charge. If raising the fee decreases total revenues, evaluation is more complex. If the decline in costs exceeds the decline in revenues, the income-maximizing charge may be higher than the present charge, since raising fees has still increased net income. If the revenue decline exceeds the cost decline, the fee may be too high, and income would be maximized at a lower fee level.

The idea behind discriminatory pricing is to avoid the tradeoff described above by setting high charges for those who are willing to pay a lot and lower charges for those who are not. This is hard to do, both because of the difficulty of determining what any individual is willing to pay and because of legal and ethical pressures to treat everyone equally. In practice, discriminatory pricing is accomplished by packaging the service in different ways that are aimed at different groups of people. For example, rates for parking in city garages close to the downtown area could be set higher than those for garages located farther out. Alternately, the city could charge higher fees for the use of swimming pools located in higher-income neighborhoods. Fees for the use of city golf courses could be lowered during off-peak periods to encourage more people to use them then. Successful applications of discriminatory pricing involve either offering the "high" end of the market a little extra convenience in exchange for a higher price, or offering discounts for times and places high-end consumers are unlikely to use. The service being offered must lend itself to alternate forms of packaging, and those setting the rates must have a sophisticated knowledge of their clients.

Because of the widespread impacts and policy implications of decisions about charge levels, it is impossible to spell out simple rules for using the procedures described above. Circumstances vary from one case to another, and inevitably political judgments have to be made. Nonetheless, it is possible to derive some general guidelines.

The simplest case to deal with is that of public goods. Here, charges are neither feasible nor appropriate. Thus, the rule to follow is not to charge for these services.

For merit goods, the range of choices is bounded by zero and the full cost of providing the service. If the public component in the service is very large, the charge should be set very close to zero. If the public component is very small, the charge should be set very close to average full costs. Where the actual charge should fall along this spectrum depends upon the relative importance of the public and private components.

In the case of private goods, there are more options, and the choice is more complex. In general, full-cost pricing is the appropriate way to set charges. But following this rule too slavishly may result in inefficiencies and missed opportunities. To assure responsiveness to citizen demands and financial health, a more sophisticated and flexible approach must be taken to the pricing of private goods.

Three factors should be considered in setting the rate per unit for private goods: the revenue potential of the service, the cost of providing it, and the distributional implications of the charge.

It is necessary first to determine how much consumers of the service would be willing to pay. Consumers would be willing to pay a great deal for water service, since water is a necessity. They would be willing to pay much less for public library service, because there are many alternatives to public library service, and in a pinch people can do without it.

Market pricing and exemplary pricing both base charges exclusively on measures of what people are willing to pay. Even if a different charge principle is finally adopted, these two should be considered in evaluating the revenue potential of the service.

If revenue potential exceeds the full cost of providing the service, a decision must be made about how much net income the city should make from the service. It is here that the distributional implications of the charge become important. If a service is widely used by all segments of the community and all income classes, the effects of turning it into a source of net income may well be regressive. Under these circumstances, full-cost pricing would be most appropriate. If a service is directed primarily at large businesses or wealthier members of the community, it may be appropriate to price it so as to maximize the amount of net income it generates for the city. Full cost plus markup provides an intermediate procedure between these two extremes.

If the income potential of a service is below the full cost of providing it, a decision must be made about whether to continue providing the service. If consumers are not willing to cover the marginal cost of providing a service that is truly private, then it probably ought to be abandoned.

If consumers are willing to pay something between the full cost and the marginal cost of a service, its provision can still be financially beneficial to the city. Deciding these borderline cases requires considerable sophistication. The danger is that they will occupy personnel and resources that could be put to better use. But on the other hand, they increase the responsiveness of city government and can generate a certain amount of income that otherwise might not be available. It may also eventually be possible to develop them into profitable lines of business for the city. Charge levels for borderline services should be set so as to maximize net income to the city. Although such charges may not fully cover fixed costs, those costs would have to be paid regardless of how much or how little of the service is provided.

Collection Mechanisms

The third big issue in establishing a charge for a service is the method of collection. There are many possibilities, but one in particular is important enough to warrant some discussion: payment by mail.

Services that are widely and regularly consumed often lend themselves to a mail-based billing system. Saint Paul sends out regular water bills and Northern States Power sends out electric bills.

In many cases, a city can collect charges through a billing system established for some other purpose. In Saint Paul, for example, sewer charges are placed on the water bill, and special assessments are put on the property tax bill. The practice could be extended to applications such as collecting fees for fire inspections through the property-tax billing system.

The city could also make use of billing systems maintained by other organizations. If vehicle ownership were used as a basis for street assessments, the fee might be collected by the state along with registration fees and remitted to the city. This approach has been used by some states to collect local parking fines. In areas where telephone companies will collect fees for incoming calls, a modest fee could be collected for calls to the library's reference desk, for example. There are probably many possibilities of this nature, although each would have to be negotiated carefully with the outside party.

The advantage of using an outside billing system is that it saves the city the cost of establishing its own system. The disadvantage, in all cases, is that these systems are likely to be imperfectly suited to the requirements of the charge the city would like to collect. The alternatives are to add new capabilities to the existing billing system (generating costs that the city will probably have to bear), or to accept the use of a crude proxy measure.

The question of when to establish a new mail billing system depends upon the relationship between the magnitude of the charge, the cost of running the billing system, and the cost of alternative methods of collecting the charge. If the cost of collecting a bill exceeds the amount of the bill, there is clearly no point in going to the trouble. And, of course, there is no reason to establish an independent billing system if a cheaper alternative exists.

The costs of mailing out a bill and processing the reply tend to decline as the number of transactions increases. Higher volumes allow more automation and spread fixed costs further. Thus, charges that everyone pays (such as water bills or property taxes) tend to have their own billing systems.

Costs per transaction increase with the complexity of the bill; therefore, pulling together a lot of information in order to compute a complex bill is justified only if the sum of money involved is substantial. Conversely, for very simple bills (e.g., a flat fee for a season pass to the city golf course), it may be cost-effective to collect charges through the mail.

Notification of the Public

Any move toward user charges is likely to be met with grumbling and even some outright opposition on the part of citizens. People always resist having to pay for things they previously received free of charge. This is especially likely to be the case if the new fees are not accompanied by reductions in taxes, a situation that Saint Paul's financial difficulties make very likely.

To deal with this problem, Revenue Center management may have to engage in some marketing. Citizens should be notified in advance of proposals for new fees and charges so that they will not be taken by surprise. Notification is especially important in a city like Saint Paul that has a strong tradition of citizen involvement in city affairs. At the time of notification, Revenue Center management should be prepared to make a case for the charge. They should be able to show how much the service costs and who is using it, and they should be prepared to explain why making consumers bear the cost of the service is fairer than funding it from general revenues. Management should also be prepared to meet expectations for higher quality that the imposition of fees will create among users.

In spite of the fact that no one likes user charges, the recent financial difficulties of many cities have made people more receptive to the idea of having to pay for city services. In many cases, the alternative to paying a fee was to give up the service. Against this backdrop, fees and charges do not look quite so bad. Although the easing of fiscal pressures during the preparation of Saint Paul's 1984 budget removed some of the impetus toward fees and charges, it may ultimately result in a smoother period of transition. Citizens are less likely to be hit from all sides at once with proposals for new fees. The city as a whole will be able to reexamine its product line and make more considered decisions about which services should be charged to consumers and which services provide general benefits and hence should be financed from general revenues.

Notes

1. Massachusetts Executive Office of Communities and Development, *Costing and Pricing Municipal Services,* Commonwealth of Massachusetts, August 1982, p. 14.
2. Saint Paul's Special Funds apply to most of the services whose costs are covered by beneficiary charge revenues.
3. A close relationship between consumption and charge level will encourage citizens to be careful about their use of the service and will encourage Revenue Center management to optimize the volume of output.
4. There are two commonly used standards for judging the fairness of a charge: (1) whether it is paid by the person receiving the benefit, and (2) whether it is paid by the person who can afford to pay. Beneficiary charges are fair in the former sense, but not necessarily in the latter.
5. These indirect costs also include allowances for retirement of outstanding debt and the upkeep and replacement of all capital equipment. For a complete discussion of the concept of full cost, see Massachusetts Office of Communities and Development, op. cit.
6. In many cases, a city moves from direct to full-cost pricing simply to increase the yield of well-established user charges and to funnel some of the revenue into the General Fund.

Projecting Local Government Revenue

Charles D. Liner

We cannot foresee changes in the many economic, political, and administrative factors that affect local government revenue. Nor can we expect statistical methods, techniques, or computers to do the impossible. Still, certain methods, techniques, and approaches can aid local governments in estimating future revenue. By analyzing current trends and the forces that underlie them, we can make a projection of future revenue.

> Projection: An estimate of future possibilities based on current trends.
> — Webster's Dictionary

The key to good projections is good analysis. Good analysis requires understanding the revenue system and the forces or events that have affected past revenues, having adequate and timely information, and exercising good judgment. This article presents an introduction to one approach—time-series analysis. Although this approach incorporates certain statistical methods that may be helpful, the value of the approach lies in its emphasis on analyzing current trends by dividing the past record of collections (the time series) into its component parts and using this analysis as the basis for making projections.

For a revenue projection method to be useful to local governments, it must meet certain criteria:

- It must be straightforward and uncomplicated so that local officials untrained in mathematics, statistics, or economics can use it during the budgeting process.
- It must require only information or data that are easily obtainable on a timely basis from local government administrative records or from the state government.
- Finally, it must be possible for the required calculations to be performed manually rather than by computer, since many local governments do not have computers.

Some methods proposed for local government revenue projections—for example, multi-variate-regression analysis—do not meet these criteria. Time-series analysis, on the other hand, is a method that can be understood easily and requires only simple computations that can be performed on a hand-held calculator. It does not require projections or current data on population, per capita income, retail sales, gross national product, or other variables. Instead, it involves analysis of data readily available from internal records or recent state government reports. Even when a computer is available, manual computations and graphing techniques are preferable to use because they give the analyst a better "feel" for factors that affect revenues. Finally, the projections can be understood by members of governing boards, who are responsible for the budget and for making long-range plans.

The first step in making a time-series analysis is to separate total revenue into its major components—funds, local revenues, state-shared and state-collected revenues, and individual revenue sources. This

Reprinted from *Popular Government* 43 (Spring 1978): 32-45.

breakdown is necessary because different sources are affected by different variables and because budgeting requires some separation of revenue sources. Once total revenue is separated into its components, the analyst must decide whether to analyze *actual* revenues or the *base* of the revenue source. For example, property tax revenue is the result of several factors—the total assessed value of taxable property (the base), the tax rate, and the collection rate; therefore, the base should be projected separately from the tax rate and the collection rate. It may be necessary to divide the property tax base into its components—real versus personal property or residential versus commercial property. For other revenue sources it may be infeasible or unnecessary to analyze the base. For example, it is usually sufficient to analyze retail sales tax collections rather than retail sales, which is the base, because the tax rate is not expected to change and because the composition of the base is not likely to change in a way that will affect revenues significantly.

Once the analyst has broken down the revenues into components, he must decide how to allocate his time. Usually it does not pay to spend much time on minor revenue sources. These sources can be projected by using the previous year's collections or by using the department heads' judgment. The analyst should devote most of his attention to important revenue sources.

The next step is to collect the historical record of actual collections or the tax base for each year. This chronological series of data is a "time series." A time-series component is a factor that causes the time series to change over time. The object of time-series analysis is to break the time series down into its components in order to analyze the components separately. Four types of components will concern us—trend, cyclical, seasonal, and irregular. These are discussed below.

TIME-SERIES COMPONENTS

Trend

A trend is a continuing direction of movement in the time series. The trend is the most important type of time-series component for use in projecting local government revenue because many revenue sources are affected by long-term trends in underlying economic and demographic variables. Communities with growing population and increased economic activity are likely to have an upward trend in their property tax base and in retail sales tax collections. A dramatic example of a downward trend appears in Figure 1, which shows a time series of parking fee revenue. The downward trend in revenue is due to the long-term downward trend in shopping and commercial activity in the city's central business district.

Underlying trends in population and economic activity that are stable over time can be used to project revenue if we can assume that the same trends will continue or if we can forecast future changes that may occur in the trends. Population trends are not entirely stable over time because they depend on changes in birth, death, and migration rates. But these rates do not change dramatically or unexpectedly over short periods of time, and we are generally aware of changes that are occurring. In fact, past changes in birth rates, such as the "baby boom" after World War II and recent declines in birth rates, provide good clues to future changes in family formations, school enrollments, age distribution, and other factors that will affect local governments.

Similarly, although economic activity is very susceptible to business cycle influences, economic growth or decline in local areas is usually based on fundamental trends that can be expected to continue for several years. For example, [some] states have had economic growth rates higher than those in other regions of the country, and the basic economic and

Figure 1: *Parking Meter Receipts*

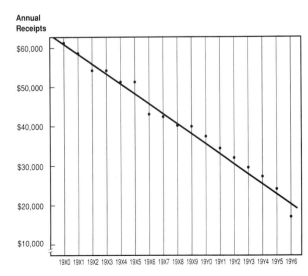

social factors that contributed to these growth rates should continue in the near future. One of the most pervasive causes of population and economic change in recent decades has been the long-term downward trend in the rural farm population and the large increase in urban and nonfarm rural population. Another basic trend that has had important implications for local governments is the decentralization of economic activity within communities. Growth has tended to occur outside or at the edge of municipal boundaries, and as a result many central business districts have declined and changed in character.

Thus a key to analyzing local government revenue is to analyze basic trends that affect the local revenue base. Current trends are the best indication of future trends, providing the basis for making assumptions about the future and alerting us to those factors that may change in the future and thus affect future revenue.

Cyclical Factors

Revenues may be affected by cyclical, or wave-like, movements that occur irregularly over a period of several years. Three types of cycles may affect revenues: business cycles, interest-rate cycles, and stock-market cycles. Although related, they must be analyzed separately.

The most important cyclical influence on local revenues is the business cycle, wavelike fluctuations in the general level of economic activity. Business cycles tend to affect almost all economic activities and are characteristic of modern industrial economies in which economic decisions are largely decentralized. Production, employment, income, retail sales, property values, and prices affect local revenues either directly or indirectly and are affected by the phases of the business cycle—expansion, downturn, contraction, and recovery. Business cycles do not occur regularly, and it is difficult to foresee their occurrence or their size.

In projecting revenues, it is important to have some appreciation of the current state of the economy and the current phase of the business cycle. Although the analyst cannot be expected to make sophisticated economic forecasts, he should be aware of current analyses and forecasts of economic conditions, which are reported frequently in newspapers, news magazines, financial publications, and government publications.

If revenue projections are to be based on past trends in revenue collections, it is essential to analyze the effects of previous business cycles. The historical pattern of business cycles can be seen in time series of gross national product, industrial production indexes, employment, or unemployment rates.

The effect of business cycles on tax revenues is usually not as dramatic as the effects on such economic variables as production, income, and employment. Tax revenues may not fall precipitously during recessions, and they may not increase proportionately during expansions. People who become unemployed during recessions must still buy food, utilities, and housing. Unemployment compensation and personal savings permit many families to maintain their standard of living. Since property is usually assessed only every eight years in North Carolina, for example, normally the tax base would not fall, even if property values fall, but growth in the property tax base may lessen and some collections may be delayed. Sales tax collections, franchise tax revenues, and privilege license tax collections should not reflect the full extent of economic recessions.

Cyclical fluctuations in interest rates have two effects on local government revenue: they affect the cost—and therefore the desirability or feasibility—of government borrowing, and they affect the property tax by influencing the amount of new construction, which is sensitive to changes in mortgage rates.

A final but less important cyclical effect comes from stock-market cycles. Since the value of stocks owned by residents in some states is part of the base of the intangible property tax, revenue from this tax may respond somewhat to fluctuations in stock prices.

Seasonal Components

Revenue collections during the course of a year may vary according to seasonal influences. For example, parking fee revenues and retail sales tax collections will vary with seasonal patterns of shopping. Utility franchise tax collections, which depend on consumption of electricity and gas, will also vary with the season. Recreational fee revenues will usually be much higher in summer than in winter. In these cases, revenue collections vary seasonally because the base varies seasonally. Legal and administrative provisions of revenue sources are another important cause of seasonal variations. For example: most property tax collections occur in the late fall, local governments receive their share of state-shared and state-collected taxes quarterly.

In analyzing and projecting revenues it is usually necessary to examine both annual and monthly time series. Normally, one analyzes annual data to study long-term trends and cyclical influences, but in making projections for the coming fiscal year it is often necessary to examine monthly data for the most recent years. Annual data will not reflect seasonal variations—the only components will be the trend, cyclical, and irregular components; but in a monthly time series, the seasonal component may have the strongest influence on variations.

Figure 2 demonstrates seasonal variation in retail sales tax collections. Sales tax collections increase dramatically in December because of Christmas shopping. Since we are interested in the long-term trend underlying the monthly data, we must smooth out the seasonal variation to establish the trend. This can be done by calculating a twelve-month moving average and plotting the average in the seventh month. (The box on page 188 shows how to calculate a moving average.) The twelve-month moving average eliminates the seasonal variation and also smooths variations due to irregular and cyclical influences; the plotted average indicates the underlying trend, although cyclical influence may also be revealed. For example, in Figure 2 retail sales tax collections exhibit a strong upward trend, but the dip in the moving average during 19X4 and 19X5 reflects the cyclical effect of the recession that occurred in those years.

Figure 2: *Monthly Collections, 3 Percent Retail Sales and Use Tax*

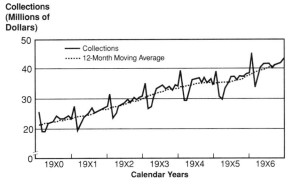

During the course of a year it may be useful to analyze monthly collections from some local or state sources to see whether collections are in line with previous estimates and to detect cyclical or other changes that may be affecting collections. But it is often very difficult to analyze weekly or monthly collection data because of seasonal or irregular influences. For example, unusually large collections may occur in one period or differences in the number of business days in each month may affect collections. A good example is provided by the record of monthly gasoline tax collections shown in Figure 3. It shows a seemingly erratic pattern of collections. Calculating and plotting a seven-month moving average, as shown in Figure 3, reveals a regularly occurring seasonal pattern. Monthly collections of gasoline taxes fall in the winter months and then increase during the spring and summer as the number of miles driven increases. The seven-month moving average also smooths out unusual variations in collections. For example, collections were unusually low in April 19X3 and unusually high in the following month, presumably because some collections that normally would have occurred in April were collected in May. The seven-month moving average smooths these large variations and shows them to be in line with the normal pattern of collections.

A moving average of less than twelve months also gives an indication of trend and cyclical effects without completely eliminating the seasonal component. The seven-month moving average plotted in Figure 3 permits the trend of collections from year to year to be evaluated. For years before 19X3, the seven-month moving average would reveal a continuing increase in the level of seasonal collections. The moving average for 19X3 is similar to that of 19X2 but at a higher level. However, the sharp increase in gasoline prices late in 19X3 and early 19X4 had an important effect on gasoline consumption and therefore on revenue collections, which are based on the number of gallons sold. This effect is not immediately apparent from actual collections but is readily apparent from the moving averages. The moving average for 19X4 shows the same seasonal pattern but at a lower level, while the moving average for 19X5 appears to be roughly at the same level. This pattern is confirmed by total collections for calendar years—collections increased 6 percent in 19X3, declined 2.6 percent in 19X4, and increased only 1.4 percent in 19X5.

Figure 3: *Gasoline Tax Monthly Collections*

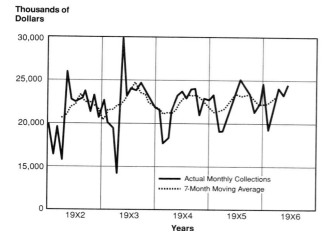

Irregular Components

Irregular components of time series include a multitude of possible events, legal and administrative changes, or other factors unrelated to trend, cyclical, or seasonal components. Irregular components show up as deviations from the trend or from cyclical patterns. We should devote our time and efforts to analyzing the trend and cyclical components and those irregular components that can be explained easily or have had significant effects on revenues. Since so many factors or variables can affect revenues, and since these factors or variables change constantly, almost every number in a time series will be affected by irregular or erratic components. We have neither enough information nor enough time to investigate each variation from the trend or cyclical pattern.

For some revenue sources, the irregular components may have such an important effect on revenues that no trend or cyclical components are apparent. This may be true, for example, of a time series of water tap charges. These charges are assessed when a home or building is connected to a public water system, not necessarily when the structure is built. The amount of water tap charges may depend on such irregular events as the extension of sewer line to an existing neighborhood, annexation, the construction of a new industrial plant, additions to water system capacity, or construction of new homes near existing water lines. Revenue from parking fines may vary with administrative policies regarding enforcement. Other revenue sources that are likely to have strong irregular components are the municipal property tax (due to annexations or revaluations), sewer assessments, sewer charges, street cut revenues, and interest on investments of idle cash.

For some of these sources, analysis of trend and cyclical components may not be very helpful in projecting revenues; for others, such as the property tax, the analysis must account explicitly for irregular components such as annexations and revaluations as well as trend and cyclical components. It may be possible to discover some pattern or causative factor associated with variations and to use this information in estimating future revenue. Sometimes it may be appropriate merely to use some rough average or an informed guess to estimate future revenues, especially if the amount is not large relative to total revenue. In any event, the time-series analysis methods discussed below will be of little value when the irregular component overwhelms trend, cyclical, or other components.

For revenue sources that are not overwhelmingly affected by irregular components and have important trend or cyclical components, two types of irregular components are very important in analyzing local revenues: tax-rate and tax-law changes (including enactment of new taxes), and specific occasional factors that significantly affect revenue.

Revenue projections must, of course, take into account expected changes in tax rates and in the tax laws, but past changes must also be taken into account in order to analyze past trends in revenues. For example, analysis of property tax revenue requires distinguishing between tax-rate changes and tax-base changes.

Revenue projections and analysis of past trends must also take into account specific events and developments that have had or are expected to have an effect on revenues. One example, previously mentioned, is the sharp rise in gasoline prices in 19X4, which caused a decrease in gallons of gasoline purchased and, therefore, of funds available for municipal street improvements. Revaluations of property is another important example. The opening of a new shopping center may affect sales tax revenue if it draws customers from outside the county. A new industrial firm or the closing of an existing firm may have a significant effect on revenue.

> *Calculating a Moving Average*
>
> For a three-month moving average, add the amounts for the first, second, and third time periods and divide by three to obtain the moving average, which should be centered in the second time period. Then add the amounts for the second, third, and fourth time periods and divide by three. And so on. Thus:
>
> | Month | Collections | Moving Average (rounded) |
> |-------|-------------|--------------------------|
> | 1 | $21 | |
> | 2 | 16 | (21+16+20) ÷ 3 = 19 |
> | 3 | 20 | (16+20+15) ÷ 3 = 17 |
> | 4 | 15 | (20+15+16) ÷ 3 = 17 |
> | 5 | 16 | (15+16+22) ÷ 3 = 18 |
> | 6 | 22 | (16+22+22) ÷ 3 = 20 |
> | 7 | 22 | (22+22+23) ÷ 3 = 22 |
> | 8 | 23 | (22+23+21) ÷ 3 = 22 |
> | 9 | 21 | (23+21+23) ÷ 3 = 22 |
> | 10 | 23 | (21+23+20) ÷ 3 = 21 |
> | 11 | 20 | (23+20+22) ÷ 3 = 22 |
> | 12 | 22 | |
>
> For a seven-month moving average, add the amounts for the first seven time periods, divide by seven, and center in the fourth time period. Then add the amounts for the second seven time periods, divide by seven, and so on. A moving average for an even number of time periods must be placed off-center (e.g., the seventh month for a twelve-month moving average). Reference: F.E. Croxton and D.J. Cowden, *Applied General Statistics*, 2d ed. (New York: Prentice-Hall, Inc. 1955).

ANALYSIS OF TREND

For many local revenue sources, the trend component will have a strong influence; therefore, analysis of the trend component will be the basis for making projections. Once the trend is estimated, the influence of cyclical and irregular components can be analyzed, since they will show up as deviations from the trend. The trend in time series can be estimated by "fitting" a straight line to the time series so that the line approximates the trend.

Graphing the Time Series and the Trend Line

Although it is preferable to calculate trend lines from the actual data in the time series rather than to fit a trend line visually, it is important to plot the time series on graph paper. In fact, graphing each time series may be the single most important part of the analysis. A graph gives a picture of the basic pattern of each revenue source. It immediately calls to attention major variations in the time series, and it forces the analyst to explain the revealed patterns. The graph can also be used to plot the calculated trend line so that variations from the trend line can be analyzed and so that the trend line can be projected to future periods. Figure 1 is an interesting example of such a graph, which shows the pattern of parking meter collections. As stated previously, the graph reveals a consistent downward trend in parking meter receipts in a city that has experienced a decentralization of shopping and other economic activity from the central business district. Variations from the calculated trend line are relatively small, suggesting that the underlying trend is very important in determining collections and that cyclical and irregular components have had relatively little influence on collections. The calculated trend line can therefore be expected to serve well as the basis for projecting future collections. (Rate changes, of course, will have to be taken into account.)

Calculating the Trend Line

The trend line can be calculated quickly and simply from the time series by using a short-cut "least-squares" method. The least-squares method produces a straight line that minimizes the sum of deviations from the line and the actual data. It provides an estimate of the slope and level of the trend and allows us to calculate and plot future trend values. But this method must be used with judgment and discretion since the calculated line does not necessarily produce a good fit with the data and does not necessarily reflect a true trend. The actual trend in the time series may be a curve rather than a straight line, or irregular influences may produce such large variations from the calculated trend that the calculated trend is meaningless.

A trend line is defined by its level and slope. The level is represented by the calculated value of the trend line in a given year. The slope represents the change in the time series for each period of time. The slope may be negative or positive, depending on whether the trend is down or up. The slope is the change in the calculated value of the trend line for each period. The change will be the same for each period. In the short-cut least-squares method the trend values for each year of the time series are calculated according to the following formula:

Calculated trend value = level in central year + (slope × number of years from central year)

To calculate the trend line, we must (1) calculate the "level in central year," and (2) calculate the slope of the trend line (as explained in the box in the next column). Calculation of the trend values is simplest when the time series has an odd number of years. The middle year then is the "central" year. For an even number of years, the "central" year is between the two central years, and the calculations must be adjusted accordingly. The slope will be a positive (+) number for upward trends and a negative (−) number for downward trends. After the level in the central year and the slope are calculated, one can calculate the values of the trend line for each year in the time series and project the trend line to future years.

Adjusting for Trend

The least-squares trend line can be used to project revenues into the near future as long as there is no reason to believe that the trend will change. Before using the trend line for this purpose, however, we will need to know how much confidence we can place in the trend as a predictor of future revenues. We also will need to analyze the contribution of cyclical and irregular components to the behavior of the time series in order to adjust the projections according to our assumptions about future cyclical and irregular influences. One method that can be used for both purposes is to "adjust the data for trend."

To adjust the data for trend, the actual data for each year are divided by the calculated trend value for that year and multiplied by 100 to produce the "percentage of trend." The formula is as follows:

$$\frac{\text{Actual collections}}{\text{Calculated trend value}} \times 100 = \text{Percentage of trend}$$

The calculation is illustrated in the box on this page.

The percentage of trend is a useful measure of the relative variation of the actual data from the trend line. If the percentage-of-trend values are all close to 100 percent, this suggests that most of the variation in actual collections is due to the underlying trend, and we can have more confidence in projections based on the trend. On the other hand, if the percentage-of-trend values vary significantly above or below 100 percent, the actual data are clearly being influenced importantly by cyclical or irregular components in addition to, or instead of, a trend, and the trend line will not give us a means for making trend-line projections with confidence.

Calculation of Percentage of Trend

Fiscal Year	Actual Collections (thousands)		Calculated Trend Value				Percentage of Trend
19X1–X2	($142.8	÷	$118.6)	×	100	=	120.4%
19X2–X3	(105.8	÷	139.6)	×	100	=	75.8
19X3–X4	(166.5	÷	160.4)	×	100	=	103.8
19X4–X5	(173.0	÷	181.3)	×	100	=	95.4
19X5–X6	(213.9	÷	202.2)	×	100	=	105.8

Adjusting for trend may be helpful in analyzing cyclical and irregular components. Besides analyzing the percentage-of-trend values for each year, it may be helpful to graph them. Cyclical components will show up as high or low percentage-of-trend values during years of expansion and contraction, respectively. Major irregular components may show up as one-time deviations.

PROJECTING REVENUES

Time-series analysis provides an approach to understanding the trend, cyclical, seasonal, and irregular influences on local government revenues. The knowledge that we gain from time-series analysis can serve as the basis for projecting revenues into the future. But a word of caution is in order. Time-series analysis is a method for analyzing revenues, and the analysis can serve *as the basis* for making revenue projections. But simply calculating a trend line and projecting the trend line into the future does not necessarily produce reliable estimates of future revenue. Time-series analysis must be used with good judgment and discretion.

Analysis of trend is the starting point for projecting revenues when trend is found to be an important influence. If it is apparent that the trend is an important component of the time series, a study should be made of the factors that account for the trend. For example, the property tax base should be analyzed by looking at the record of changes in components of the base in past years. Trends in commercial, residential, and apartment construction should be under-

Calculating and Plotting a Least-Squares Trend Line

The object is to calculate a trend line for the time series for fiscal years 19X2-X3 to 19X6-X7 (in actual practice a longer period would normally be used), plot the trend line along with the actual data, and project the trend line for fiscal years 19X7-X8 and 19X8-X9. The first step is to calculate the slope and level in the central year.

Column (a) Fiscal Year	Column (b) Collections (thousands)	Column (c) Years from Central Year	Column (d) Cross-products (b) × (c)	Column (e) Years-squared (c) × (c)
19X2-X3	$142.8	−2	−285.6	4
19X3-X4	105.8	−1	−105.8	1
19X4-X5	166.5	0	0	0
19X5-X6	173.0	+1	+173.0	1
19X6-X7	213.9	+2	+427.8	4
Total	802.0		+209.4	10

Calculate the slope:

$$\text{Slope} = \frac{\text{cross-products total}}{\text{years-squared total}} = \frac{209.4}{10}$$

Calculate the level in the central year:

$$\text{Level in central year} = \frac{\text{total collections}}{\text{number of years}} = \frac{802.0}{5} = 160.4$$

Calculate the trend line and project the trend line to fiscal years 19X7-X8 and 19X8-X9:

Fiscal Year	Level in Central Year		Number of Years from Central Year		Slope		Trend Line Value
19X2-X3	160.4	+	(−2	×	20.9)	=	118.6
19X3-X4	160.4	+	(−1	×	20.9)	=	139.5
19X4-X5	160.4	+	(0	×	20.9)	=	160.4
19X5-X6	160.4	+	(+1	×	20.9)	=	181.3
19X6-X7	160.4	+	(+2	×	20.9)	=	202.2
19X7-X8	160.4	+	(+3	×	20.9)	=	223.1
19X8-X9	160.4	+	(+4	×	20.9)	=	244.0

Graph the time series and the trend line:

1. Plot actual revenues.
2. Plot the trend-line values for 19X2–X3 and 19X8–X9 and connect with a straight line.

    Calculating a trend line for an even number of years is similar except that the "central year" is between the two central years. For these two central years, the trend-line values are calculated by adding or subtracting half the value of the calculated slope to or from the calculated "level in the central year."

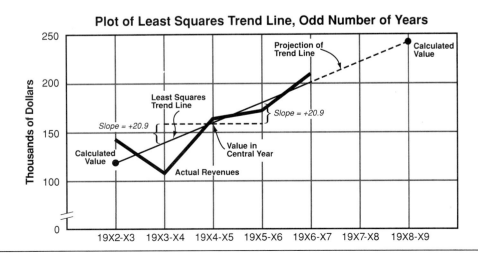

Plot of Least Squares Trend Line, Odd Number of Years

stood. Local population and economic trends should be analyzed. After the basic trend is analyzed, deviations from the trend should be analyzed. Are the deviations due to cyclical influences, to changes in tax law, or to special events? How sensitive are local revenue sources to the business cycle? Do current collections suggest any changes from the trend?

After the time-series components have been analyzed, assumptions must be made about the future. Projecting a trend line into the future involves the implicit assumption that the underlying trend will not change and that cyclical or irregular factors will not cause future revenue to depart significantly from the trend. The assumptions should be explicit. For example, explicit assumptions should be made about population growth, the level of economic activity, the business cycle (e.g., "the national economy will continue to recover from the recession," or "there will be no recession during the next two years"), interest rates, new major industrial firms, annexations, and so forth. It may be advisable to have alternative assumptions—pessimistic and optimistic, high and low, for example—and to make different projections according to the alternative assumptions. Analysis of each major revenue source enables us to know what assumptions are necessary or important. The projections then follow according to the assumptions.

SUMMARY

The reader may be disappointed to find that no mathematical, statistical, or mechanical methods have been presented that would enable him to produce precise projections for each revenue source. Unfortunately, such techniques do not exist. We cannot produce adequate projections by feeding data into a computer. Rather, good projections must rest on thorough analysis, good judgment, realistic assumptions, and a sound approach.

The reader who wishes to know more about time-series analysis and other methods of forecasting and projecting should see Frederick E. Croxton and Dudley J. Cowden, *Applied General Statistics,* 2d ed. (New York: Prentice-Hall Inc., 1955), and Steven C. Wheelwright and Spyros Makridakis, *Forecasting Methods for Management,* 2d ed. (New York: John Wiley and Sons, 1977).

Adjusting for Inflation When Comparing Revenues or Expenditures

David N. Ammons

Comparing the amount of revenues received by a local government one year to the amount received in another year can be misleading. Although the more recent number may be larger, it might represent resources with less "buying power" than the smaller figure from an earlier year. Similarly, steadily increasing expenditures may be more attributable to inflation than to service expansion or loss of efficiency. Meaningful comparisons across years are possible only if the figures are adjusted to reflect "constant dollars."

◆ Keystone, Nevada

The city manager of Keystone, Nevada, was already worried about next year's budget, even though the budget hearings were still three months away. Years ago in college, a professor had described what he called "rational-comprehensive decision making" and its application to the budget process, but very little seemed rational about the decision making taking place in Keystone these days.

Never mind population growth. Never mind citizen demands for improved services. With city council elections coming next spring, incumbents were already bracing for the onslaught of challengers grumbling about runaway expenditures. This morning, a coalition of councilmembers sent word through the mayor that it expects the city manager to hold the line on expenditures and would, under no circumstances, consider a property tax increase for next year.

"Mayor, how can you and the others preempt me like this?" asked the city manager. "We're addressing important community needs, and we're managing our resources wisely. I had hoped to get a fair audience for what I am sure will be a solid budget proposal. Why the panic? Our increases haven't been extravagant."

"How can you say that?" responded the mayor. "Municipal expenditures are up 19 percent in two years' time. Don't think for a minute our opponents haven't pointed that out to potential supporters."

The mayor and the councilmembers now banding together were clearly worried about their public image and the upcoming election. The mayor had been elected on a campaign that emphasized his business experience and his fiscally conservative philosophy. No wonder he was stung by the 19 percent increase!

Soon after the mayor left, the city manager called the budget officer to his office. After describing the substance and tone of the mayor's message, the city manager said, "It won't be business as usual this year. There's no way that we'll be allowed to tap our resources as in the past few years. The best we can hope for is a modest increase in expenditures funded by tax base expansion rather than a tax rate increase. But we won't even get that if we aren't prepared."

The city manager laid out a strategy for meeting the "runaway expenditures" charge head-on. He directed the budget officer to prepare a comparison of expenditures for this year and the previous two years using "constant dollars" rather than "current dollars."

Reprinted from David N. Ammons, *Administrative Analysis for Local Government: Practical Application of Selected Techniques* (Athens: Carl Vinson Institute of Government, University of Georgia, 1991), 68-73.

"Start with our highest priority items—like police patrol. Let's see if we can get some information out that will help us—and the mayor and council—defend what we've been doing."

IMPLICIT PRICE DEFLATOR

When a shopper mutters, "A dollar doesn't go as far as it used to," he's right. An item that costs $1.25 today may have cost, say, $1.00 only a few years ago. Inflation diminishes the value of money. Five quarters in that shopper's hand may *look like* $1.25 (and it *is* $1.25 in "current dollars"), but it is only $1.00 in "constant dollars" if they can buy no more than what $1.00 could buy in the base year.

Converting current dollars to constant dollars is a simple matter. Various price indexes are available for that purpose, the most popular one being the Consumer Price Index (CPI), compiled by the Bureau of Labor Statistics. The CPI measures changes in a variety of consumer products and is used frequently in labor negotiations and as a guide to various cost-of-living adjustments.

A second index—one more tailored to the needs of local government—is the Implicit Price Deflator (IPD), compiled by the U.S. Department of Commerce's Bureau of Economic Analysis. The IPD is a better choice for most local government purposes because it reports an index based specifically on state and local government purchases of goods and services. Even so, the IPD, like all other indexes, is an imperfect gauge of inflation and users should be aware of that.

Implicit price deflators are published throughout the year in *Survey of Current Business*, by the U.S. Department of Commerce. A table from the publication, which shows the IPD for state and local government purchases of goods and services, is provided in Exhibit 1. Annual IPDs for that category are shown in Table 1.

Exhibit 1: *Implicit Price Deflators for Gross National Product*
[Index numbers, 1982=100]

	1986	1987	Seasonally Adjusted					
			1987			1988		
			II	III	IV	I	II	III
Gross national product	113.9	117.7	117.3	118.2	118.9	119.4	121.0	122.4
Personal consumption expenditures	114.3	119.5	118.9	120.2	121.5	122.2	123.9	125.2
Durable goods	105.6	107.9	107.5	108.6	108.9	109.1	109.6	110.3
Nondurable goods	107.8	112.1	111.9	112.9	113.7	113.8	116.0	117.3
Services	122.4	128.5	127.6	129.1	131.0	132.2	134.0	135.5
Gross private domestic investment								
Fixed investment	103.5	105.2	105.3	105.1	105.4	105.3	105.1	105.2
Nonresidential	100.2	100.4	100.8	99.9	99.8	99.6	99.5	99.7
Structures	107.1	111.1	111.2	111.7	111.8	113.0	113.8	114.2
Producers' durable equipment	97.2	96.2	96.8	95.3	95.1	94.8	94.6	94.8
Residential	111.1	116.2	115.2	117.7	118.7	119.5	119.5	119.5
Change in business inventories								
Net exports of goods and services								
Exports	100.0	100.0	100.1	99.9	100.1	100.3	102.1	104.1
Imports	93.6	99.0	99.4	98.9	100.0	100.8	101.4	101.3
Government purchases of goods and services	114.6	118.5	118.6	119.1	119.5	121.7	122.7	123.3
Federal	109.8	112.7	113.7	112.9	112.6	115.2	115.3	114.6
National defense	110.4	111.5	111.3	111.3	111.6	112.8	113.4	114.7
Nondefense	108.2	117.0	122.9	119.0	116.0	125.5	122.7	114.1
▶ State and local	118.2	123.0	122.3	123.9	124.9	126.5	128.1	129.4

Source: U.S. Department of Commerce, Bureau of Economic Analysis, *Survey of Current Business* 68, no. 11 (November 1988): 14.

Table 1: *Implicit Price Deflators (1982 = 100.0)*

State and Local Government Purchases of Goods and Services	
Year	Implicit Price Deflator
1980	86.2
1981	93.4
1982	100.0
1983	104.7
1984	109.9
1985	114.9
1986	118.3
1987	123.2
1988	128.8
1989	135.0

Source: Data drawn from Table 7.4 in various issues of U.S. Department of Commerce, Bureau of Economic Analysis, *Survey of Current Business*.
Note: IPDs for 1986 and 1987 differ slightly from those reported in Exhibit 9.1 due to revisions made by the Bureau of Economic Analysis subsequent to 1988. In July of each year the bureau revises the national income and product account estimates for the three prior years.

Figure 1: *Using the Implicit Price Deflator (IPD)*

Formula for converting "current dollars" to "constant dollars" for a selected base year:

$$\text{current dollar revenue or expenditure} \times \frac{\text{base year IPD}}{\text{current IPD}} = \text{current revenues or expenditures in base year dollars}$$

Converting current dollars to constant dollars involves simple mathematics. The formula for doing so is provided in Figure 1. First, a base year of the analyst's choosing is selected. Then, current dollars are multiplied by the ratio of the base-year IPD to the current IPD. The resulting figure will be the buying power of current dollars in base-year dollars. The term "current" is used for convenience; it may refer to this year or to any year other than the selected base year.

CONVERTING POLICE PATROL EXPENDITURES TO "CONSTANT DOLLARS"

The budget officer compiled a brief summary of police patrol positions and expenditures for the three most recent fiscal years (Table 2). The increase in expenditures was slightly greater than the municipal average—20 percent, rather than 19 percent. The increase was in part attributable to adding two patrol officers and three public service officers during the last two years. Those increases, of course, had nothing to do with inflation. But what would the increase have been had it not been for inflation?

The budget officer converted each of the expenditure figures in Table 2 to constant dollars. Fiscal years in Keystone begin in July of one calendar year and end with June of the following year, so the budget officer could have used the IPD for the year in which the fiscal year began, the year in which it ended, or perhaps the first quarter IPD or the mid-point between two annual IPDs. For the sake of simplicity, he decided to use the IPD for the year in which a given fiscal year ended. The 1985 IPD of 114.9 was used as the base year, and the unadjusted 1984-85 expenditures were regarded as 1985 dollars. The calculations for converting total expenditures for 1985-86 and 1986-87 to 1985 constant dollars for the patrol activity of the Keystone cops are shown in Figure 2. The full set of expenditures converted to 1985 dollars is shown in Table 3.

BUDGET STRATEGY

"This will help, but we still have a lot of work to do," remarked the city manager when the budget officer showed him the constant dollar figures. "We're still up 12 percent in constant dollars in just two years' time, but that's a lot better than having to explain a 20 percent jump."

Table 2: *Police Patrol: Positions and Expenditures, City of Keystone*

Position allocation	1984-85 Actual	1985-86 Actual	1986-87 Budget
Sergeants	4	4	4
Patrol officers	26	27	28
Public service officers	2	4	5

Expenditures	1984-85 Actual	1985-86 Actual	1986-87 Budget
Salaries and benefits	$1,047,621	$1,132,262	$1,241,173
Supplies	13,500	19,442	18,926
Other services	4,980	6,620	8,295
Maintenance	135	400	400
Capital	59,791	64,985	83,285
Total	$1,126,027	$1,223,709	$1,352,079

Figure 2: *Converting Keystone Police Patrol Expenditures for 1985-86 and 1986-87 to 1985 "Constant Dollars"*

$$\text{current dollar expenditure} \times \frac{\text{base year IPD}}{\text{current IPD}} = \text{current expenditures in base year dollars}$$

Total Expenditures for 1985-86

$$\$1,223,709 \times \frac{114.9}{118.3} = \$1,188,539$$

Total Expenditures for 1986-87

$$\$1,352,079 \times \frac{114.9}{123.2} = \$1,260,989$$

Table 3: *"Constant Dollar" (1985) Comparison of Police Patrol Expenditures, City of Keystone*

Expenditures	1984-85 Actual	1985-86 Actual[a]	1986-87 Budget[a]
Salaries and benefits	$1,047,621	$1,099,720	$1,157,555
Supplies	13,500	18,883	17,651
Other services	4,980	6,430	7,736
Maintenance	135	389	373
Capital	59,791	63,117	77,674
Total	$1,126,027	$1,188,539	$1,260,989

[a] All figures for 1985-86 and 1986-87 have been converted to 1985 "constant dollars" using Implicit Price Deflators for state and local government purchases of goods and services.

"We've increased the number of positions in that division by 16 percent to try to improve services and meet the demands of a growing population," commented the budget officer.

"That's true," responded the city manager, "Let's try to attack this thing on two fronts. See if you can come up with some performance indicators that would show improved service quality to help us defend expenditures in excess of inflation. Also, let's adjust our expenditure figures to account for a growing population as well as inflation. Get the best population figures you can from the planning department and convert those constant dollar numbers to expenditures per capita reported in constant dollars. With the growth we've experienced in the last two years, I think the per capita figures will show a very modest increase. When we make those adjustments and compile our improved performance indicators, I'm confident we will present a very defendable record."

UTILITY OF INFLATION ADJUSTMENTS

Opportunities for the application of inflation indexes in local government are numerous. Such indexes are often used to peg cost-of-living increases in employee wages, annual adjustments in multiyear service contracts, and multiyear revenue and expenditure comparisons. Adjusting figures to constant dollars in such comparisons permits a more reasonable evaluation of fiscal trends.

Suggested for Further Information

Leazes, Francis J., Jr., and Carol W. Lewis. "Now You See It, Now You Don't." In *Casebook in Public Budgeting and Financial Management*, edited by Carol W. Lewis and A. Grayson Walker III, 189-94. Englewood Cliffs, N.J.: Prentice-Hall, 1984.

Expenditures

Evaluating Public Expenditures: A Guide for Local Officials

Therese A. Freeman, Ernest G. Niemi, and Peter M. Wilson

FUNDAMENTAL CONCEPTS: COMMUNITY RESOURCES, COSTS, AND BENEFITS

Public expenditures almost always have impacts that extend beyond the budget. When local officials consider only the budgetary effects of a public program, they may be ignoring some other important effects that influence the program's desirability to the community. The full range of public and private impacts should be evaluated to determine if, on balance, a program is worthwhile.

Consider a hypothetical public program. Before the program begins, the community (individuals, businesses, and the government) possesses a set of "resources." These resources include all the community's goods and services: money, real property, labor, governmental services, clean air, civic pride, etc.—everything of value. Carrying out the program uses some of these resources—public as well as private, monetary as well as non-monetary. In return, the program creates a new set of resources which would not have been available without it. The resources that a program uses are the program's *costs*. The new resources that exist as a result of the program are its *benefits*. In addition to the program's effect on the total amount of resources available to the community, it may redistribute resources among individuals. Both aspects are important in evaluating the program.

THE BEGINNING STEPS: CLEARLY DEFINING THE SITUATION

Because public programs can affect a community and its resources in complex ways, completely evaluating a program's costs and benefits may be difficult. The magnitude and value of a program's costs and benefits often cannot be predicted with certainty. The resources devoted to evaluation will depend on the nature of the program. Some programs, due to their size and expense, will warrant a full-scale look at costs and benefits. For many other programs, much simpler evaluations will suffice.

Evaluating a program in terms of its effects on community resources will indicate the extent to which the program contributes to the community, even in cases where the costs and benefits cannot be assigned monetary values. The critical tasks are to decide which costs and benefits are relevant to the expenditure decision and identify the resources the community would possess with and without the program. Therefore, an evaluation should begin with the following two steps:

Step 1: Define the community whose resources are relevant to the program evaluation.

Step 2: Identify all the changes in the community's resources (public and private) that will occur if the program is undertaken.

Reprinted from a document prepared by the Department of City and Regional Planning, Harvard University, under contract to the Massachusetts Executive Office of Communities and Development, Division of Community Services, June 1978. By permission of the Massachusetts Executive Office of Communities and Development.

Many government programs will affect people who live outside the boundaries of the governmental entity. Step 1 involves deciding whether or not to include these effects in the analysis. Usually this decision is based on the community's political situation and each program's individual characteristics.

EXAMPLE 1-1: Building an Athletic Field
The city of Newport is considering a proposal to build a multiple-use athletic field. Opponents of the program argue that many of the field's potential users will not be residents of Newport, and that the city should not build facilities for non-residents. Proponents argue that for recreational facilities, the concept of community should include not only the city's residents but also their close neighbors.

Which view of the community is correct? There is no "correct" answer to this question. The city's political process will have to provide the answer.

Step 2 sets the stage for determining the program's costs and benefits. As the following sections explain in detail, the new resources available to the community as a result of the program are the program's benefits and the decreases in available community resources are program costs. Figure 1 summarizes the logical sequence of steps for thoroughly evaluating a program's impacts on a community.

COSTS

This section (1) defines in more detail the concept of a program's costs to the community; (2) discusses why it is valuable for local officials to consider this concept of costs when making spending decisions; (3) explains how to distinguish between real costs to the community and "transfers" between individuals; (4) describes how to measure costs; and (5) illustrates how to use the cost concept in making decisions.

Defining Costs

The costs of a local government program are the resources used in carrying it out. From an overall community perspective, costs are relevant whether they are incurred by government or directly by households and businesses. They also are relevant whether they entail dollar outlays or the use or consumption of non-monetary resources. The following four categories cover the complete range of resources that should be considered as costs if used by public programs.

Group 1: Resources purchased by the government for the program.
Outlays of public funds for construction, equipment, or salaries are examples of this type of cost. Standard financial budgetary analysis usually deals with only this type of cost.

Figure 1: *Steps for Analyzing Public Programs*

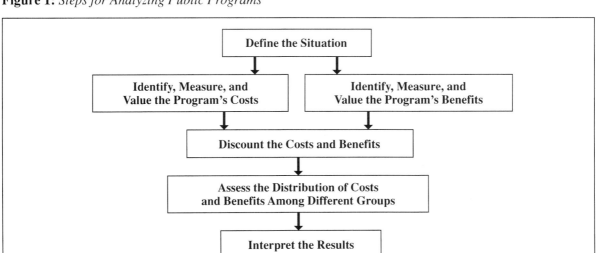

Group 2: Resources already owned by the government.

When a program uses a previously acquired government asset such as land or office space, a real cost is incurred even though there may be no dollar outlay related directly to the program.

Group 3: Resources owned or purchased by local residents.

Some government programs use or consume privately owned resources, thereby imposing costs on the community. For example, if a program requires households to use larger septic tanks, the extra costs to the households should be counted as part of the program's costs.

Group 4: Intangible resources.

Programs often require some sacrifice of community resources such as clean air or uncongested streets. While such losses can be important costs, their monetary value usually cannot be estimated. However, these sacrifices can sometimes be quantified in physical terms; for example, congestion could be measured by a change in traffic flow.

When important choices between programs must be made, a full accounting of each of these four types of costs is worthwhile even if some estimates must be very rough.

Distinguishing between Real Costs and Transfers

When resources are neither used up nor created but just shifted from one set of individuals to another, the shift is called a *transfer.* A transfer differs from a cost in that it does not decrease a community's total amount of resources. Instead, it changes the shares of those resources enjoyed by different individuals.

EXAMPLE 2-1: Abating Local Property Taxes
Riverside is considering a program that would abate the property tax payments of elderly persons. If the program is implemented, the taxes of other taxpayers would increase to compensate for the abatements. Some opponents of the program claim that these tax increases would be an excessive cost for the community.

The abatement program does *not* have a cost from the perspective of the community as a whole. The program would make elderly persons better off and nonelderly persons worse off than they would be without it, but it would not decrease the community's total amount of resources. The program would, in effect, only transfer resources (tax money) from nonelderly taxpayers to elderly persons.

Of course transfers are important attributes of government programs and have considerable bearing on local officials' decisions. However, when evaluating programs it is important to distinguish between transfers and real program costs. Later sections further discuss transfers.

Measuring Costs

Determining Monetary Values

Whenever possible, costs should be valued in monetary terms so that different types of costs are measured in the same units. In principle, a program's costs should be valued according to individuals' general willingness to pay for the resources the program will use. For goods and services in Group 1, willingness to pay is indicated by the price the government must pay to buy them. When a program uses publicly owned assets in Group 2 it is necessary to estimate what the value of those assets would be on the open market. For example, if a program uses office space in a government building, the program's costs should include the estimated rental value of that space. Costs in Group 3 should be valued in the same manner as those in Groups 1 and 2.

It is much more difficult, however, to assign a monetary value to a program's effects on intangible resources such as clean air or quiet streets. A community's willingness to pay for intangible resources must be determined through the judgment of local officials.

EXAMPLE 2-2: Removing Snow
Youngsville must decide between continuing municipal snow removal and contracting with a private company. To determine the annual cost of the current snow removal program the finance committee examines the budget. They find that only direct salaries are reported separately for snow removal. Outlays for pension benefits, administrative expenses and vehicle maintenance are reported in the municipal accounts as single "line items" encompassing many programs. How

can the actual costs of the current snow removal program be determined?

The problem of determining a program's true total costs comes up repeatedly when decisions must be made about continuing existing programs. Budget costs are an example of the costs in Group 1, resources purchased by the government for a particular program. Although they are reflected in the budget, they are not always apparent. To make a choice, the finance committee needs to know the total cost of the service. The committee should therefore estimate the portion of the line-item costs attributable to the snow removal service, and add these to the salaries.

The committee also should look beyond the budget and estimate the value of the trucks, equipment, storage area, and other previously acquired resources that are part of the current program. These resources are important elements of the program's costs, and if the committee excludes them from its calculations, it will underestimate the program's full costs.

EXAMPLE 2-3: Constructing a Parking Garage
Louisburg is considering two ways of developing a downtown block which is owned by the city. One option is for the city to build and operate a parking garage. The other is to sell the site to a private firm which would construct a parking garage.

Proponents of a municipally built garage argue that it would be less expensive for the city to build the facility than for a private operator. They claim that, since the city already owns the land, the only costs under this option would be for construction and operations. Since a private firm would have to buy the land, it would need to charge higher fees in order to recover its costs.

From a community-wide perspective, the proponents' argument is *not* correct. There is no saving in land costs if the city builds the garage. The costs of using scarce publicly owned land, buildings, and equipment are sometimes overlooked because they do not entail a dollar outlay. Yet these resources have many alternative uses, so committing them to one program has a cost, namely the lost opportunity to use them for other purposes. Therefore, using the site has the same real costs whether the site is privately or publicly owned. The same scarce resource is used in either case. The cost calculations for each option should contain the land's estimated market value.

Determining Values in "Constant Dollars"

When programs involve costs occurring at different times, the values of the costs should be expressed in terms of "constant dollars," that is, in terms of the present purchasing power of dollars without building in inflation. For example, if a program presently uses an office that rents for $4,000 per year and will continue to use the same office in future years, the program's cost calculations should show this amount as the value of the office for each future year. Using constant dollars insures that all costs are measured in dollars with the same purchasing power.

BENEFITS

Benefits are the resources which the community will gain as a result of a public program. This section (1) defines benefits in detail; (2) explains the differences between real benefits to the community and transfers of resources among individuals; (3) demonstrates how to measure benefits; and (4) shows how to use the benefit concept to make spending decisions.

Defining Benefits

Benefits are the resources the community will possess if a program is undertaken but will not possess if it is rejected. Thus, a program can produce benefits by making resources available to the community. Resources created, freed from other uses, or conserved by a program are all considered benefits.

EXAMPLE 3-1: Renovating an Office (Part 1)
The city of Rimpton wants to renovate a usable but deteriorated office. The benefits of this project will not be the value of the entire renovated office. Instead, the benefits will be just the value of the improvements made to the office. Since some aspects of the office (walls, windows, etc.) are not new resources made available by the project, they should not be viewed as benefits.

Distinguishing between Real Benefits and Transfers

When a program redistributes resources between groups of individuals, these actions often are mistakenly counted as a benefit instead of a transfer. From the recipient group's perspective, the program appears to produce benefits; however, the gain to the recipient group is a loss to some other group in the community. From a community-wide perspective, the program has not made any new resources available.

EXAMPLE 3-2: Constructing New Bleachers
A citizens' group in Scranton has urged the School Committee to construct bleachers at the high school's football field and to charge admission to the school's games. The group claims that within 10 years, the admissions fees will have covered the construction costs. The group also claims that, "This project will benefit the entire community not only by giving us a set of bleachers, but also by creating added revenues for the school from the eleventh year onward."

In this example, the bleachers clearly would be a benefit. However, it is incorrect to consider the admissions fees as benefits—even during the first 10 years. No new resources will be created when spectators pay money to sit in the bleachers. Because the admission fees can be used to support school expenditures, they represent a transfer from spectators to taxpayers. Counting the fees as benefits would be double-counting, i.e., counting the benefits from the bleachers twice.

The following impacts are frequently cited as benefits, but they usually are transfers among individuals: increased revenues, increased taxes, increased sales, and increased property values. These impacts are benefits only if they make new resources available to the community.

EXAMPLE 3-3: Developing a New Playground
Riverton is considering developing a new playground. In a feasibility study, a consultant stated that the project would "benefit Riverton in two ways: (1) provide 10,000 user-days of recreational opportunities annually and (2) increase the value of surrounding residences by a total of $95,000."

It is not correct to count as benefits both the additional recreational opportunities *and* the increased property values. The additional recreational opportunities are the only new resources and thus the only benefits. The property value increases do not represent new resources, they only indicate that the surrounding property owners will have access to the playground, and, in a rough sense, will be the recipients of the project's benefits.

(Note that if the value of the additional recreational opportunities cannot be measured directly, the property value increases can be used as an *indirect* measure. Either the direct or the indirect measure—not both—must be chosen to represent the project's benefits.)

Measuring Benefits

Whenever possible, a program's benefits should be measured by estimating how much the community values them. Placing a value on benefits is important because a program's desirability primarily depends on whether the value of its benefits exceeds the value of its costs.

As earlier noted, the fundamental measure of a resource's value is the community's willingness to pay for it. However, public programs often produce benefits for which it is difficult to determine this measure. Consequently, for measurement purposes, benefits can be divided into three groups:

Group 1: Resources measurable in monetary terms.
Group 2: Resources measurable in physical units, but not in monetary terms.
Group 3: Resources valued by the community, but not measurable by any means.

Benefits in Group 1 typically are (or are similar to) goods and services that are sold in the marketplace. In such cases, the value of the benefits is the market price of the good or service. As earlier explained, these resources should be valued in constant dollar terms if they occur at different times in the life of the program.

EXAMPLE 3-4: Renovating an Office (Part 2)
This example in the previous section demonstrated that the benefits from a renovation would be the improvements to the office. To find the

value of these benefits, it is necessary to first estimate what the price would be for a comparable, renovated office in the private real estate market. From this value should be subtracted the price that people would have paid in the private market for an office comparable to the deteriorated office before it was renovated. The difference between the two prices represents the value of the renovation's benefits.

Although the monetary value of the benefits in Groups 2 and 3 cannot be determined, these benefits are no less important than those in Group 1. Personal judgment must be relied upon for estimating the value of these benefits to the community.

The important difference between the benefits in Group 2 and Group 3 is the amount of information available to help local officials make their judgments about value. By definition, officials have a nebulous idea of the value of the benefits in Group 3. The benefits in Group 2, on the other hand, can be estimated in discrete physical units. Clearly, in most instances, this additional information can be useful.

The playground in Example 3-3 illustrates the difference between the last two groups of benefits. Assume that, besides the 10,000 user-days of recreational opportunities, the program will produce another important benefit, increased neighborhood pride. Neither of these benefits can be measured in monetary terms. However, the increased recreational opportunities can be measured in physical terms (10,000 user-days); this benefit belongs in Group 2. The increase in neighborhood pride, which cannot be measured at all, belongs in Group 3.

DISCOUNTING

The costs and benefits of public programs can occur in complex patterns over time. To compare and evaluate programs, each program's stream of future costs and benefits—in constant dollars—must be converted to a single value by discounting. This section introduces the discounting concept. It discusses (1) what the discount rate means; (2) the mechanics of discounting; and (3) the ways discounting can aid individuals making public spending decisions.

Defining Discounting

A familiar notion is that a dollar tomorrow is worth less than a dollar today. This notion is partly based on inflation, but it is also true with the constant dollar concept used for evaluating a program's costs and benefits. One way to look at the impact of time on the value of money is to consider that, through investments, money can "grow." For example, suppose someone asks to borrow $100 from you today and gives you a guaranteed promise to repay $100 (in constant dollars) in one year. You probably would not accept the offer because having $100 now is more valuable to you than having $100 next year. One reason for this is that if you keep the money you can invest it and by next year have more than $100. If your best investment opportunity pays 10 percent annual interest you would have:

$$(\$100) \times (1 + \text{interest rate}) = (\$100) \times (1.1) = \$110$$
This Year   Next Year

As a result, you would consider $100 today to be equal in value to $110 next year. Unless the person promised to repay this amount, you would not make the loan.

What if the person wanted to borrow the money for two years? In this case, if you make the loan you will forgo a second year of interest. You would consider $100 to be equal in value to:

$$(\$100) \times (1.1) \times (1.1) = \$121.00$$
This Year   In Two Years

When evaluating public programs, the role of time is the same but the perspective is reversed. One knows the program's stream of estimated future costs and benefits for which monetary values can be determined. The objective is to find out how much a specific dollar amount that will be realized in a future year is worth today. For example, how much money today would be equivalent to having $100 a year from now? To find the *present value* of $100 a year from now you *discount* using a *discount rate,* which is another term for the interest rate. With a 10 percent discount rate, the present value is:

$$(\$100) \times \left(\frac{1}{1 + \text{discount rate}} \right) = \$100 \times \left(\frac{1}{1.1} \right) = \$90.91$$
Next Year   This Year

This reasoning also applies to longer periods. A $100 payment two years from now has a present value of:

$$(\$100) \times \left(\frac{1}{1.1}\right) \times \left(\frac{1}{1.1}\right) = \$82.60$$

In Two Years · This Year

In practice, a table of *discount factors* is used rather than the preceding calculations. Discount factors show how much $1 in a future year is worth today. A table of discount factors appears on page 205. The following equation uses the discount factor to recalculate the present value of a $100 payment two years from now:

($100) × (Discount factor: 10% per year for two years) = ($100) × (0.826) = $82.60

Discounting can be used to convert any flow of dollar values in future time periods to an equivalent single present value. The dollar amounts in each year are multiplied by the appropriate discount factor, then added together to produce a single present value. The examples and cases that follow illustrate the uses of discount factors.

How Discounting Can Aid Local Spending Decisions

Discounting is useful whenever dollar *flows* are compared over time. If dollar values can be estimated both for a program's costs and its benefits, discounting can be used to calculate the program's *net present value*. For each year of the program, costs and benefits are added together to give a net cost or benefit. Then, the net cost or benefit for each year is multiplied by the appropriate discount factor. These yearly values are summed to give a net present value. If the net present value is positive, the program's benefits exceed its costs; if the net present value is negative the costs are greater than the benefits.

Discounting also can be used to compare alternative programs that differ in the timing of their costs and/or benefits. If a net present value can be determined for each alternative, the program with the greatest net present value has the greatest surplus of benefits over costs. If it is necessary to compare just the costs or just the benefits of the alternatives, discounting can indicate which alternative is least costly or most beneficial.

EXAMPLE 4-1: Upgrading a Rural Road
Pine County wants to upgrade a dirt road to accommodate more traffic. Either graveling or paving would be adequate to carry the road's traffic. The county wants to choose the option with the lowest costs over an 11-year period. Paving would have a high initial cost of $35,000 but low maintenance costs of $1,000 per year. Graveling would have a lower initial cost of $28,000 but higher maintenance costs of $2,000 per year. Which alternative is less costly for the county?

Discounting can yield the answer by converting the stream of costs for each alternative to a single equivalent present value. Pine County has a 10 percent discount rate. The costs are shown on the following page in thousands of dollars.

If annual costs were simply added together with the initial expense, graveling would have a total cost of $48,000 and paving would have a total cost of $45,000, but this would neglect the time value of money. Future costs are less of a sacrifice than current costs, since until they are used for this project, resources can yield a return in other uses. By applying discounting to each flow of costs, each alternative can be expressed as a single present value. Using a discount rate of 10 percent (see "Choosing a Discount Rate," p. 204), the cost of the gravel alternative has a present value of $40,260; the paving alternative cost has a present value of $41,140. Discounting indicates that graveling is the least expensive alternative.

Choosing a Time Period for the Analysis

To calculate a program's present value, it is necessary to choose a time period for the analysis. In other words, it is necessary to decide how far into the future to count the program's costs and benefits. Sometimes the time period can be determined by the lifetime of a program or the local government's official planning period. In other cases, a program may have a very long or indefinite lifetime, and it is necessary to choose a somewhat arbitrary period of analysis. As a general rule, a time period of less than 15 years is adequate for most present value calculations. Using a period longer than 15 years rarely yields results much different than using a 15-year period, because discounting greatly reduces the present value of costs and benefits that will occur in the distant future.

Incorporating Capital Costs in Present Value Calculations

Recognizing Capital Costs

Because capital investments last for many years, they require special consideration in present value calculations. The first consideration is that if land, buildings, and equipment are purchased for use in a program, their full value should be recorded as costs in the year in which they are purchased. This is the case regardless of the pattern of cash outlays such as bond payments for the assets. When resources are committed to a program, they are unavailable for other uses for the rest of the time period of analysis. Their full cost should be recognized in the year they are committed to a program.

A second consideration is that land, buildings, and equipment that are already part of the community's total resources when a program is being evaluated must be included in present value calculations. In the present value analysis, the use of capital stock that is already owned should be treated just like an initial purchase. When it is committed to the program, its full estimated current market value should be recorded as a cost.

A third consideration is that neither depreciation nor finance charges are counted as part of a program's costs. This follows directly from the concept of costs as resources used by the program. Depreciation is an accounting technique that is not applicable in present value calculations. Since costs should be recognized when the resources to be used by the program are committed to it, the full values of capital investments are counted at the time of their purchase. Subsequently including depreciation as costs would therefore be double-counting. Similarly, including financing charges—interest and principal repayments—as costs would also be double-counting. The discounting procedure automatically accounts for interest. Principal repayments have already been charged to the program by counting capital investments at the time of purchase.

Accounting for Salvage Value

If capital investments are not completely consumed during the time period of analysis, their remaining value should not be counted as a program cost. For example, a new vehicle that is purchased and used for two years has a resale value at the end of the two-year period. In this instance, the resale value of the vehicle should be deducted from program costs in the year of its sale. Similarly, capital investments used in ongoing programs may have some value at the end of the time period used for analysis. This remaining value should be discounted and deducted from the program costs in the final year of analysis.

Salvage value is the term used for the resale value of capital items and the remaining value of capital investments at the end of the period. Salvage value is deducted from program costs to show that

Table 4-1: *Summary of Costs for Example 4-1*

Year:	This Year	+1	+2	+3	+4	+5	+6	+7	+8	+9	+10
Annual Costs in Constant Dollars (in thousands):											
1. Graveling	28	2	2	2	2	2	2	2	2	2	2
2. Paving	35	1	1	1	1	1	1	1	1	1	1
3. Discount Factor at 10 Percent	1	.91	.83	.75	.68	.62	.56	.51	.47	.42	.39
Present Values at 10 Percent (costs × discount factor):											
4. Graveling (line 1 × line 3)	28	1.8	1.7	1.5	1.4	1.2	1.1	1.0	.94	.84	.78
5. Paving (line 2 × line 3)	35	.91	.83	.75	.68	.62	.56	.51	.47	.42	.39
Total Present Values at 10 Percent (sum of costs × discount factor):											
Graveling (sum of line 4):	$40,260										
Paving (sum of line 5):	$41,140										

the program has not consumed the capital asset entirely; some of the resource still remains available for additional uses. An equivalent procedure is to add the salvage value to program benefits. The important point is to account for the resource's remaining value.

EXAMPLE 4-2: Estimating the Capital Costs of an Existing Building
Glenville is assessing the costs of its recreation program over the next 10 years for comparison with other programs. The recreation program uses a building which has an estimated market value of $100,000. Because of aging, wear and tear, the building will be worth less (in constant dollars) 10 years from now than it is worth now. The assessors' office judges that 10 years' aging will reduce the building's value to $80,000. In calculating the present value, the planning department accounts for the capital cost of the building in the following way:

1. The building's existing market value is recognized as a cost in the initial year of the time period.
2. Its salvage value at the end of 10 years (in constant dollars) is discounted and deducted from costs in the final year.

The following entries are made in the present value worksheet:

	Capital Costs for Building (This Year)	Salvage Value (+9)
	−$100,000	+$80,000
10% Discount Factor	1.000	0.424
Present Value	−$100,000	+$33,920
Net Present Value	−$ 66,080	

The discounting calculations show that using the building for 10 years costs the community $66,080.

EXAMPLE 4-3: Leasing versus Buying a Typewriter
The Holfield Senior Citizen's Council needs another typewriter. The typewriter can be leased for $280/year or purchased for $815. The typewriter company requires a 15 percent downpayment with the balance repayable over two years at $12\frac{1}{2}$ percent interest. The council routinely replaces the typewriters it owns every two years. Past experience has shown the resale value of a two-year-old machine to be about 50 percent of its original price. Should the council lease or buy the additional typewriter?

Year:	This Year	+1
LEASE OPTION		
1. Costs	−$280	−$280
2. Resale Value	0	0
3. Net Value	−$280	−$280
4. 10% Discount Factor	1.000	0.909
5. Present Value (line 3 × line 4)	−$280	−$255
6. Net Present Value (sum of line 5)	−$535	
PURCHASE OPTION		
7. Costs	−$815	0
8. Resale Value	0	+$408
9. Net Value	−$815	+$408
10. 10% Discount Factor	1.000	0.826
11. Present Value (line 9 × line 10)	−$815	+$337
12. Net Present Value (sum of line 11)	−$478	

The above table illustrates the net present value (NPV) calculations for each option. A two-year time horizon is used in the analysis because of the council's typewriter replacement policy. The leasing costs for a two-year period when discounted at 10 percent yield a NPV of −$535. The NPV of the buy option is −$478. Note that interest and principal repayments are not counted as costs in this calculation. Interest is accounted for by the discounting procedure; the price of the typewriter is counted as an initial investment so that including the payments would be double-counting. The typewriter can be resold after its two years of use, hence the positive entry in year +1. A two-year discount factor is used here because the typewriter is held for two years and sold at the beginning of year +2. The NPV calculations show that the council would save $57 in present value terms by purchasing rather than leasing the typewriter.

Choosing a Discount Rate

The example at the beginning of this article explained that a person generally does not lend money to someone else unless the borrower agrees to repay at least as much as the lender would have by investing the money and earning interest. The same principle applies for the resources used in public programs. A public program should not be undertaken unless its benefits are worth at least as much as the resources the community would have without it (except where equity impacts override this conclusion as explained in the next section). The discount rate represents the average rate of interest that public funds would earn if, instead of being used on a public program, they were returned to private households and firms. Thus, the discount rate is the cost of drawing resources from the private sector for use in the public sector.

Local governments using discounting need to choose a single discount rate and apply it to each program that is evaluated. Discount rates of between 5 and 15 percent are commonly used. The local government's bond rate is sometimes used as the discount rate, on the principle that it measures the cost of public funds. This is not correct, because the bond rate represents only one source of public funds. The discount rate should reflect the average cost of all public funds, whether acquired through borrowing or taxes.

The Federal Office of Management and Budget has estimated the cost of public funds to be 10 percent. This rate is widely used by federal agencies for program evaluation. Because it is quite difficult to determine a community's exact discount rate, it is recommended that local governments also use the 10 percent rate.

The choice of a discount rate can sometimes affect the ranking of alternative programs. High discount rates give a relatively heavy weight to dollar flows in the first year of a program, while low discount rates give relatively more weight to dollar flows further in the future. In Example 4-1: Upgrading a Rural Road, discounting at 10 percent indicated that the costs of the gravel alternative had the lower present value of the two options. If Pine County considered 10 percent too high a time value of money, and instead used 5 percent, then the ranking of the alternatives would be reversed. Paving would have the lower cost in present value terms ($42,720 for paving versus $43,440 for graveling). Because graveling has a lower initial cost but higher future costs, it becomes relatively less attractive with a lower discount rate.

For some programs it is useful to see if the present values change considerably when different discount rates are used. A reasonable range of alternative rates is 8 to 12 percent. However, for most cases, the 10 percent rate will be appropriate.

Discount Factors

The following table presents discount factors that show how much $1 in a future year is worth today. The table includes discount factors for discount rates of 8, 10, and 12 percent. The discount factor for a given discount rate and a time in years into the future is determined using this formula:

$$\text{Discount factor} = \left(\frac{1}{1 + \text{discount rate}}\right)^n$$

The discount factor for the present year (n=0) is 1.000.

Discount factors are used to discount (convert) dollar amounts occurring in future years to their equivalent present value. The formula for discounting is:

$$\text{Present value} = \begin{array}{c}\text{(Dollar amount)}\\\text{at year n}\end{array} \times \begin{array}{c}\text{(Discount factor)}\\\text{for year n}\end{array}$$

Discount Factors: How Much $1 in a Future Year Is Worth Today

Year	Discount Rate		
	8%	10%	12%
This Year	1.000	1.000	1.000
+1	0.926	0.909	0.893
+2	0.857	0.826	0.797
+3	0.794	0.751	0.712
+4	0.735	0.683	0.636
+5	0.681	0.621	0.567
+6	0.630	0.564	0.507
+7	0.583	0.513	0.452
+8	0.540	0.467	0.404
+9	0.500	0.424	0.361
+10	0.463	0.386	0.322
+11	0.429	0.350	0.287
+12	0.397	0.319	0.257
+13	0.368	0.290	0.229
+14	0.340	0.263	0.205
+15	0.315	0.239	0.183
+16	0.292	0.218	0.163
+17	0.270	0.198	0.146
+18	0.250	0.180	0.130
+19	0.232	0.164	0.116
+20	0.215	0.149	0.104

EQUITY IMPACTS

Very few programs will affect every member of the community equally. If a program involves transfers, one group within the community acquires resources from another group. For some programs one group may receive most of the benefits without incurring many of the costs.

Since the distribution of costs and benefits can have important consequences for the community's overall well-being, identifying and considering this distribution is as important as looking at a program's total levels of costs and benefits. For example, because of its distributional consequences, a program may be judged to be undesirable even though its benefits outweigh its costs. This section (1) introduces the concept of a public program's equity impacts; and (2) presents a method for evaluating these impacts.

Defining Equity Impacts

A program's equity impacts are its effects on the distribution of resources among different groups within a community. Note that EVERY PUBLIC PROGRAM HAS SOME IMPLICATIONS FOR EQUITY, either because it changes the present distribution or because it keeps this distribution the same.

Assessing Equity Impacts

Although methods exist for extensively evaluating programs' equity impacts, the focus here is limited in the most fundamental and important steps—identifying and roughly measuring the impacts. These objectives can be accomplished by following three steps:

> *Step 1:* Identify which group receives each benefit and which group incurs each cost.
>
> *Step 2:* Quantify, as far as possible, the program's impact on each group.
>
> *Step 3:* Determine whether the pattern of distribution of costs and benefits affects the program's desirability.

Successfully completing Step 3 is the crux of our concern with equity impacts. Note, however, that a local official can complete Step 3, deciding on the importance of the equity impacts, only by using his/her judgment. A concern for equity involves feelings about justice—feelings that are personal and subjective.

Steps 1 and 2 can systematically explain what a program's equity impacts will be and provide useful information for making decisions. Merely identifying each group's costs and benefits (Step 1) may sometimes be sufficient. The equity impacts may be so obviously overwhelming or inconsequential that further consideration is unnecessary. If more information is needed, then the costs and benefits each group will experience should be quantified (Step 2).

Following these steps requires classifying members of the community into groups. The following list presents several commonly used distinguishing characteristics:

— Income and Wealth
— Homeownership
— Geographic Location
— Age
— Race or Ethnic Group
— Family Size

EXAMPLE 5-1: Locating a Day-Care Center
The director of the city of Banfield's subsidized day-care program is considering expanding the program. Residents in the Fairmount neighborhood have asked that a new day-care center be located in their neighborhood. Fairmount is a low-income area and residents have complained that it is very costly for them to take their children to the existing, downtown center. However, the director's staff recommends that the existing center be expanded since, although both alternatives would yield the same benefits, the expansion alternative would have lower costs. Although most costs would be the same for both alternatives, a new center in Fairmount would require additional new equipment and an extra supervisor. The total annual additional costs for the new center would be $20,000. However, the director's staff estimates that if the new center were located in Fairmount, residents in the area would save a total of $4,470 each year in transportation costs. Thus, the net additional costs for the new center would be $15,530 a year (the additional costs to the city minus the savings to the Fairmount residents).

Which alternative should the director choose? There is no obvious answer. The community, as a whole, would be better off with the expansion, but the residents of Fairmount would be better off with the new center. Although the director still must base the decision on judgment, the analysis of equity impacts and costs and benefits gives him/her a clear understanding of the implications of each alternative.

INTERPRETING THE RESULTS OF A PROGRAM ANALYSIS

This section (1) suggests how to summarize the findings of a program analysis to highlight the critical choices which must be made; (2) discusses how to assess the effect on the analytical results of alternative assumptions about future conditions; and (3) provides a checklist of questions which should be asked when reviewing an analysis to ensure that it has been conducted appropriately.

Summarizing the Findings of a Program Analysis

An analysis of spending alternatives provides officials with predictions about the outcomes of different proposals. These predictions provide a good basis for choosing an alternative. However, in almost any decision, officials must add their own judgment of community needs and priorities to the findings of a program analysis in order to make a choice. Cost and benefit estimates need to be closely scrutinized. Costs and benefits expressed in monetary terms should be compared with those that are measured in units other than dollars. Concerns for equity should be weighed against other objectives.

Consideration of all the impacts of alternative programs is made easier if impacts are placed in a summary format. A program analysis should include a table summarizing the costs, benefits, and equity impacts of each spending alternative. Costs and benefits in a summary table can be divided into those which have been estimated in monetary terms and those which are measured in non-monetary units. Costs with monetary values should be given as a total, with a listing of the cost elements included in the total. Benefits with monetary values should be summarized in the same way. When alternatives differ in the time-flow of costs or benefits, discounted present values should be given in the table. Costs or benefits which are not measured in dollar terms should be represented by other measures such as "number of persons served," or "increase in daily traffic," or "change in water quality."

Often, statements of program impacts can include a measure of "cost effectiveness," which is the cost per unit of output or capacity. Cost effectiveness measures are most useful for programs which have benefits that cannot be valued in monetary terms. For example, the cost per sewer connection for alternative sewer plans or cost per student for special education programs are measures which can aid decisions in the absence of quantified benefits.

EXAMPLE 6-1: Choosing a Landfill Site
Bayport is seeking a site for a new sanitary landfill. Alternative sites are being evaluated on several criteria, including acquisition cost, capacity, potential pollution hazards, and recreational value. Officials wish to minimize any hardships on nearby residences from odors or traffic, and they would prefer to purchase a site from an owner willing to sell rather than using eminent domain. The following costs and benefits have been discussed and measured in either quantitative or qualitative terms:

Monetary Costs:
– Site acquisition costs (present value)
– Site development costs (present value)
– Operating costs (present value)

Other Costs:
– Potential for groundwater pollution (none; slight; moderate; serious)
– Suitability of site for recreational use (no potential; some potential; great potential)
– Proximity to residential areas (number of homes within $1/4$ mile of site)

Benefits:
– Site capacity (tons of solid waste)
– Market value of site after it is filled and landscaped (present value)
– Potential for public reuse as recreational land (no potential; some potential; great potential)

The costs, benefits, and equity impacts for each alternative site are summarized in a table similar to the table on the next page.

Using Site #1 will concentrate collection truck traffic on Fuller Street and create congestion at the intersections with Oregon Avenue and California Avenue.

With the analytical findings summarized in this form, Bayport officials have some useful information to make complex tradeoffs between good and bad features of each site. Officials must decide which site would yield the greatest net benefits, and they must assess whether use of that site would be equitable for the site owner and for nearby residents.

Changing the Assumptions of the Analysis

In estimating a program's costs and benefits, many assumptions must be made about future conditions in order to estimate the most likely values of the program's expected impacts. However, there may be a great deal of uncertainty about the true magnitude of some cost or benefit elements. It is important to know how a program's desirability would change if the assumptions prove to be incorrect. Sometimes large uncertainty about a particular cost or benefit estimate will be inconsequential because the item is only a small part of total costs or benefits. In other cases, changing one assumption may greatly affect a program's attractiveness. In the latter instance, further research may reduce the uncertainty of the original assumption, but frequently local officials will have to rely on their judgment about the likelihood of future events.

The importance of an uncertain assumption to a program's desirability can be tested in the following manner:

Step 1: Determine a range of plausible values for the uncertain cost or benefit.

Step 2: Re-estimate the program's impacts using the lowest and highest values of the range.

Step 3: Summarize the results and compare them with the original results using the most likely assumption.

Step 4: Where possible, indicate the likelihood that the cost or benefit will be higher or lower than the most likely value.

EXAMPLE 6-2: Increasing the Frequency of Bus Service
Parking congestion is a problem in Pelman's business district. One proposal to reduce congestion is to increase the frequency of downtown bus service. It is projected that 500 drivers per weekday could be attracted to the transit system

Summary of Estimated Impacts for Site #1

Costs
Monetary Costs* (present value)	$600,000
Other Costs	
Potential for Groundwater Pollution	Slight
Lost Recreational Value	None
Number of Affected Residences	22

Benefits
Market Value After Rehabilitation (present value)	$100,000
Capacity	40,000
Recreational Reuse Potential	None
Cost Effectiveness: Dollar Cost per Ton of Capacity	$15.00

Equity Impacts
Site #1 is occupied and farmed by an elderly man who has lived there all his life. He has stated that he would not be willing to sell the farm and move to another residence.

*Includes costs for site acquisition, development operations, and rehabilitation. Discounted at 10 percent over the expected life of the landfill.

with a particular expansion in bus service. The service expansion would be costly, however, because new buses and additional drivers would be required. It is estimated that the cost of expanding service would be about five times as great as the additional revenues which could be expected. Officials rejected the proposal because the city has a policy of implementing service expansions only if additional revenues will cover at least one-half of additional costs.

There could be objections to the decision not to extend service based on the possibility that the projected ridership increases are too low. However, ridership must increase by more than 1,000 riders per weekday for revenues to cover one-half of the additional costs. An increase in ridership of this magnitude is considered extremely unlikely. Therefore officials have a strong basis for rejecting the proposal, even though ridership estimates are somewhat uncertain.

A Checklist for Reviewing an Analysis

The following questions are presented for local officials to use as a checklist for determining if a program has been analyzed thoroughly and correctly.

1. Have the program's objectives been clearly and completely stated?
2. Has the population affected by the program and relevant to the analysis been identified?
3. Have the program's costs been estimated correctly?
   a. Are the estimates of future budget outlays complete, or have some important expenditures been overlooked?
   b. Have the costs of land, building space, or equipment already owned by the government and used by a program been included as a program cost?
   c. Have other non-budget costs been overlooked?
   d. Have any costs been counted more than once?
4. Have the program's benefits been estimated correctly?
   a. Have all of the benefits been identified?
   b. Have any benefits been overstated or counted twice?
5. Has the time value of money been accounted for by discounting those future costs and benefits for which dollar values can be determined?
   a. Have present values been computed?
   b. Was an appropriate discount rate used in the present value calculations?
6. Have the program's distributional impacts been considered?
7. Have the findings of the analysis been tested for their sensitivity to changes in assumptions about the magnitude of important costs or benefits?

IMPLEMENTING THE USE OF PROGRAM ANALYSIS

This section (1) suggests criteria for choosing the issues which should be analyzed; (2) discusses the resources needed to undertake program analysis; and (3) suggests how program analysis can be incorporated into local government operations.

Selecting Programs to Analyze

The issues and methods discussed in this guide can be applied to virtually all local government expenditure decisions. However, for many programs a simple "back of the envelope" analysis of costs, benefits, and equity impacts can provide local officials with sufficient information. In addition, because thorough investigations of program costs and benefits do take time and money, officials will have to set priorities on which decisions will be aided by extensive analysis, and which will be subject only to cursory analysis.

Several criteria can be used to choose whether a spending decision should be analyzed in detail:

1. *The magnitude of the program.* The greater the cost of proposed programs or projects, the greater the potential savings from a systematic comparison of alternatives.
2. *The length of the program.* Which decisions will have impacts over a long time period? If a project will have a long life, then a projection of future conditions, costs, and effects is worthwhile.
3. *The political nature of the program.* Which decisions are likely to be controversial? If a consensus exists that a particular spending proposal should be approved, then an elaborate comparison with "straw man" alternatives will be of little use. However, if a lively debate about a program is expected, then the factual base provided by a systematic evaluation can help focus the arguments on the important issues.

Resources Needed to Analyze Programs

The major resource required for analytical studies is the time of skilled personnel. Program analysts need not have a great deal of specialized training, but they should be familiar with basic analytical techniques and the use of quantitative data. They also need an ability to clearly define the problems being analyzed and to identify the alternative ways of solving those problems. Persons with backgrounds in engineering, economics, public administration, planning, or business usually have the skills necessary for program analysis. A single individual with administrative experience, analytical skills, and familiarity with the needs of local officials can effectively direct analytical efforts of other personnel who may lack extensive experience or training in program analysis.

The cost of a program analysis will depend on the complexity of the issues, the availability of data, the experience of the analysts, and the thoroughness of the study.

Incorporating Program Analysis into Local Government Operations

Having the in-house capability to do program analysis has strong advantages over the use of consultants. Local government personnel have an ongoing familiarity with the policy issues faced by officials. Consultants hired for a single study must first familiarize themselves with the unique circumstances of the locality. At the conclusion of a consultant's study, the expertise gained by the consultant is usually not available to local officials in the future. Studies which are performed in-house can be considered investments in the knowledge and skills of government personnel as well as aids for specific decisions. In addition, in-house analyses are likely to be less costly than analyses performed by consultants. For major studies requiring highly specialized knowledge, use of consultants is advantageous. However, for regular reports of modest scale, government staff members are usually preferable to consultants.

States and large cities which are using program analysis often place responsibility for program analyses within a special department which may also undertake evaluations of the performance of existing programs. These departments usually are closely associated with the budget office. Small cities or towns may find that analysis can be introduced most effectively by individuals within an operating department, with the encouragement of the executive officer.

Cost-Benefit Analysis
Gerald J. Miller

I. INTRODUCTION

Government allocation decisions have a significant influence on the nation's productivity—its economic efficiency—and, particularly, on government productivity. Specific allocation decisions, those in budget and regulatory policies, have a profound effect on societal and economic affairs as well. Therefore, understanding allocation decision making can provide insight about just how and with what consequences allocation decisions are made to enhance productivity as well as mollify contending social forces.

One allocation tool, cost-benefit analysis, has grown in popularity, at least among policy analysts, in the three most recent presidential administrations, as *the* tool of choice in determining allocations. Therefore, this tool takes on greater significance, and we should wonder how much we understand its foreseen and unforeseen consequences.

Allocation refers to government action to define the country's needs and set priorities for fulfilling them. It is through allocation policy, substantially, that public expenditure policy and regulatory policy are made. Both spending and regulation decisions determine in concrete terms what it is that government agencies and staff members do and how they do it.

Allocation technology is not value-free. In allocation, ideological positions compete for the critical premise or assumption. Allocation policy is quite often framed in terms of equity versus efficiency, with policies and programs that give to each according to his needs and take from each according to her abilities set against policies and programs that result in at least one person being better off and no one worse off.

As a result, determining what technology to employ in making allocation choices has great allure and great controversy. One controversial method of organizing information is cost-benefit analysis. In this article, we look at the rationale and method of cost-benefit analysis. Then, we critique the use of cost-benefit analysis in achieving productivity. We define productivity as economic efficiency and seek to determine whether productivity can be achieved with the methods provided by cost-benefit analysis.

II. RATIONALE AND METHOD OF COST-BENEFIT ANALYSIS

One of the reasons a government exists is to act as agency of last resort. Government usually gets asked to do those things everyone else is either unwilling or unable to do. Formally, therefore, one of the major concerns of government policymakers has to do with compensating for what markets fail to provide or which markets leave as a consequence of what they do provide. For the purpose of description here, we call government action to remedy market failures, the provision of public goods. This article describes the way governments make choices in coping with market failure. First, we reintroduce the fiscal allo-

---

Reprinted from *Public Productivity Handbook*, edited by Marc Holzer (New York: Marcel Dekker, Inc., 1993), 253-79. By permission of the publisher.

cation role of government and briefly explain how governments fulfill it. Second, we explain how market failure occurs. Third, we discuss the decision-making process that is used to determine the proper amounts of public goods that should be produced by governments. Finally, we discuss the relatively new concept of "nonmarket failures" and the contributions of economic reasoning to the financial management of government agencies.

A. Fiscal Functions of Government

Regardless of the forces government fiscal policies are meant to loosen or harness in the name of doing those things no one else will do, there are certain goods which few will produce—often leaving it to government to provide some things everyone needs. For instance, national defense, the classic case, is a commodity which is too expensive, too complicated, and, in general, too hazardous to society to leave for each citizen to provide for himself or herself.

The last reason—hazardous—may be the most important reason for not having an every-man-for-himself situation. That is, if everyone had the responsibility to look out for himself or herself, we would have lost the very reason for having a nation in the first place, the acknowledgment that we are one and want to act together to protect and further our collective interest.

In any case, we find government as provider of last resort when "market failure" occurs. Market failure strikes when the normal processes of the giant auction we call the economy do not work efficiently, specifically when rationing is either not feasible or not desirable (Stiglitz, 1988; Musgrave and Musgrave, 1980).

Rationing is not feasible when no one can be excluded from use of a product or service. Fire services to a complex of abutting apartments may not be feasible, since containing a fire in one gives benefits to all. Since no one is excluded, all except the one who pays become free riders. No price system for rationing makes sense.

Rationing may also be undesirable even though feasible. For instance, an uncrowded bridge could be paid for with a toll device forcing drivers to pay as they entered. Because the bridge is uncrowded, the toll may actually decrease traffic and provide an incentive to seek alternative routes to avoid the tariff.

In both cases, rationing through normal market mechanisms does not work as it would otherwise.

Other methods must be used to decide allocation: how much each apartment dweller should pay for fire protection and how big a bridge to build.

Government's allocation functions relate to the provision of public goods. Generally, the problem is to decide how much and what type of public goods to provide. Decision makers need some sort of mechanism for deciding these questions, and, luckily, they have not just one but three mechanisms: the Pareto criterion, the Kaldor criterion, and the mechanism in place which allows us to invoke these criteria.

i. Pareto Criterion

Named after the nineteenth century economist, the Pareto criterion guides selection of a policy by favoring those in which at least one person is better off and no person is worse off as a result of the policy.

What policies have such an unambiguous goodness attached to them? Education might, but some suffer lost earnings from going to school that they will never recoup. What about water and air quality? There are sunk costs in pollution that we could say one would suffer loss in remedying.

ii. Kaldor Criterion

A second method of dealing with welfare, the Kaldor criterion, is slightly less demanding: Should we not accept a policy if those in the community benefiting from the policy compensate those who lose by the policy, especially if the winners or beneficiaries still have some gain left over?

Consider this example. If the strict private goods only requirement were not relaxed (libertarianism), we would never get such goods as pristine ocean beaches. One finds it extremely difficult to slice up pieces of the ocean in order to allocate maintenance responsibilities to protect the beach. Moreover, nature's ways in forcing erosion and so on would make such coercion folly. Will one person maintain the beaches? Not by the table of benefits, especially when those benefits are held down by the inability to divide the resource or exclude others from its use.

But should the beaches be maintained? If costs equal the expense of maintaining the beaches and benefits equal the sum of everyone's perception of betterment, common sense would tell us yes. For example, in the following illustration, what would the Pareto criterion tell us if the cost were shared equally by all individuals?

Individual	Benefit ($)	Cost ($)	Condition
A	3,000	2,000	Better off
B	3,500	2,000	Better off
C	2,000	2,000	No worse off
D	3,000	2,000	Better off
E	2,500	2,000	Better off
Total	14,000	10,000	

The Pareto criterion—at least one is better off and no one is worse off as a result of a public program—supports a program, in which costs are shared equally, of $10,000. As the illustration above shows, that program would make no one worse off—even C—and at least one person, and in this case A, B, D, and E, would be better off. A $10,000 program passes muster.

The $10,000 program, however, provides greater benefits to some than to others. As shown in the table above, the surpluses range from $1,500 for B to $500 for E.

We might say that the $10,000 version of beach cleanup is less equitable than it is efficient. Defining productivity as a balance between equity and efficiency, we want to find the program that would achieve both. The Kaldor criterion is meant to suggest a way to find that program.

Recall the Kaldor criterion provides for winners compensating losers in a given situation. Without assuming any losers, however, we can still create a Kaldor-like result, as the situation below suggests.

Individual	Benefit ($)	Cost ($)	Surplus ($)
A	3,000	2,999	1
B	3,500	3,500	0
C	2,000	2,000	0
D	3,000	3,000	0
E	2,500	2,500	0
Total	14,000	13,999	1

To ensure that the winners bore their fair share of the costs and still stood to reap some gain, the maximum project would have to be $13,999. We can compute this amount by distributing the costs in the same way as the original surpluses so that one person gains $1 of surplus, whereas all others have benefits that equal their costs.

This distribution of costs and benefits underlies the progressive tax structure and redistribution of income programs which guided the construction and maintenance of the American version of the welfare state for some 50 or more years. More to the point of this discussion, however, the Kaldor criterion underlies the measurement of productivity and, especially, cost-benefit analysis. Cost-benefit analysis, like the Kaldor criterion, argues that as long as the benefits exceed the costs of a project, the project should go forward.

iii. Voting

The problem with cost-benefit analysis and with the Kaldor criterion is the determination of benefit. In a country that values individualism and decentralized decision making, we assume that each person can value a policy alone. The sum of those values becomes the public welfare. However, this makes it difficult to calculate individual benefits. Instead, the political system and, specifically, the voting system, take care of that.

But what vote should be required? Unanimity, majority rule, three-fourths, two-thirds, plurality? The answer lies in the analysis of voting by legislative bodies. Following Buchanan and Tullock (1962), the analysis falls on the interaction of two variables: (1) the loss of value that occurs when we do not include in any decision each individual's own calculation of benefit from a given project, and (2) the cost of making an effort to ascertain each individual's preference.

As an alternative to the price system as a method of determining what and how much of a public good to produce, voting applies in finding the expected cost to the individual and to the group or public, which the individual alone can calculate, of implementing a public project. How much effort to exert in finding these individual preferences, or, specifically, in determining when we can feel sure we have solicited the opinions of enough people and when enough people desire a project to warrant its implementation constitutes the basis of voting analysis.

Voting analysis demands that we know individuals' preferences toward a project. Obviously, 100% voting participation resulting in a consensus decision on the project would guide decision makers in making a valid decision. The first variable in voting analysis, therefore, is the probability of violating the

Pareto criterion as we depart from unanimous consent. Such a problem occurs in sampling as well as in choosing majority rule over consensus.

Nevertheless, gaining unanimity has drawbacks, not the least of which is the cost entailed in cajoling participation and informing voting. The counterbalance to total participation and consensus is the cost that both would entail. The more closely we near total participation and consensus in voting, the higher the cost of the voting process. The lower the cost of the voting process, the less likely we will have valid facsimiles of the voters' preferences; that is, majority votes of whatever number of voters may not be valid expressions of the total population's preferences even though such an election may cost less than any method we could use to secure unanimity.

Obviously, the appropriate system of voting involves trading off the cost of exclusion against the cost of the election, a calculation easier than it looks. We seldom have single issues in which individuals have two choices and perfect information about them both. Rather, we have a continuous stream of issues about which individuals have varying levels of intensity of preferences.

It can be shown through studies of public opinion that our knowledge of and attention paid to issues faced by members of Congress is relatively low—over the 10,000 or so measures members see in every session, we, as voters, probably know something—anything at all—about less than 1% (100) and have intense preferences about even fewer, say 0.1% (10). We probably have full and complete knowledge of even less, say 0.01% (1).

Also the intensity of preferences among voters tends to form a regular pattern. Very few voters feel intensely about an issue either way. The vast majority, the middle, have no feeling about an issue at all and probably do not find the issue itself salient.

Such arrays of preferences yield themselves to vote trading or logrolling* as well as coalition building. In cases where we have public provision of private goods, we have all the conditions for bargaining: costly participation, isolated issue salience, and unclear estimates of who benefits through policies and by how much.

---

*That is, some defer to others on issues about which others feel intensely and vice versa.

iv. Overspending

In cases in which we have public provision of public goods, we have conditions for overspending, say Buchanan and Tullock (1962), or underspending, says Downs (1960).

Consider an example Buchanan and Tullock offer as support for the idea that logrolling tends to create more expenditure than would ordinarily be the case if economic efficiency controlled. Consider the case of 100 farmers in a locality, each of which is served by a separate access road which requires maintenance. Maintenance of a specific road must have the consent of a majority of voters and, if so, is financed out of general tax revenues levied on all farmers equally. If each road's maintenance is voted on separately and no logrolling takes place, no road improvements would pass under general tax financing. Each road improvement benefits only one person but the cost is borne by several.

Suppose vote-trading agreements can take place. In order to have his or her road repaired, each farmer must agree to support the road repairs of 50 other farmers in order to get the 51 votes required for his or her own road repair. The benefit to this farmer is the benefit of having his or her own road repaired; the cost to him or her of the agreement is his or her share of the repairs to be done on the 50 other roads he or she agrees to support. In the general case, each of the farmers will attempt to secure an agreement with 50 other farmers and the agreements will probably be overlapping, since all 100 farmers want to get their own roads repaired. In the end, each farmer will have secured agreement to have his or her road repaired. In determining the level of road repairs on each road, the benefit to the farmer whose road is being repaired is weighed against the costs of 50 farmers of repairing it. The costs incurred by the other 49 farmers not included in that particular agreement are neglected. Overall, the cost to all farmers will exceed the benefits from the chosen level of repairs in each road. The logrolling process will have resulted in overexpenditure.

v. Underspending

Downs (1960) demonstrates the opposite case, the case for spending less than would be necessary. If we consider the same example above but substitute higher education for road repair, we might find that the calculation of benefits each farmer made would result in undervaluing the public expenditure. Arguments, except for the agricultural experiment station, the cooperative extension service, and the college of agriculture at the state land grant university, would probably tend toward belittling most benefits and accentuating higher education's costs. In the end, higher education might be underfunded, given some notion of adequate or efficient funding, and the entire government budget made smaller than economic efficiency might otherwise dictate.

vi. Summary

Allocation may be approached through logrolling or through cost-benefit analysis. Cost-benefit analysis is that allocation principle in which a project is selected if the costs and benefits are weighed and the result makes the society better off. The problem with cost-benefit lies in implementing shared benefits in such a way that those who bear most of the costs get enough of the benefits to offset their losses.

Logrolling—using the political process to allocate—examines a project in the context of all projects on the agenda for study at one time. The supporters of a project ultimately get their way only because they trade favors with supporters of other projects. The result is a sharing of costs and benefits so that both sets of supporters, as a whole, are better off. The problems with logrolling tend to be those related to overspending, a condition supporters of logrolling think is a function of viewing of the needs of the individual as greater than the needs of society. That is, those who favor cost-benefit analysis, and who believe logrolling results in overspending, tend to be those who favor the right of the individual to reach his or her goals in competition with others without government's help. Those who favor logrolling rather than cost-benefit analysis see the needs of society as paramount, at least those needs which, in the end, make society's benefits greater than society's costs.

III. ALLOCATION, ORGANIZATION, ANALYSIS—MICRO AND MACRO: AN INTRODUCTION

Cost-benefit structures* drive project-by-project or budget-by-budget decisions. At the micro-, or project, level, an analyst delves into the preferences for that project versus its cost. At the macro-, or budget, level, decision makers must cope with combining, into some meaningful whole, projects that have overcome microlevel constraints. The systematic aggregation of microdecisions is not truly a macrodecision. In reality, budgets are constructed from both microviews and from some systematic macroview—often called ideology or a political platform—that details how the entire basket of public goods should be chosen. This section describes both levels of analysis and describes practical ways the two levels may complement each other.

A. Micro-Cost-Benefit Analysis

To begin a cost-benefit analysis, one has at least one project which can be studied. In this case, the concept is straightforward: determine benefits and costs; then find the ratio of dollar-quantified benefits, at their current value, to dollar-quantified costs, at their current value (B/C). If that ratio is greater than 1, the analysis suggests that the project should be considered for inclusion in the jurisdiction's budget.

The concept, as just outlined, includes two major ideas which influence the analysis: the notion of measuring benefits and costs and the idea of measuring them at their current value. Measuring benefits and costs involves estimating, forecasting, and costing them, all difficult to do in the public good sector. The second, calculating benefits and costs at their current value, requires knowledge of preferences about the time value of money.

i. Uncertainty and the Measurement of Costs and Benefits

Measuring costs and benefits involves carefully considering both the obvious and not so obvious elements that a project will entail, forecasting changes that will occur and affect these elements over time, and including—costing—the elements properly, that is, in both accounting and economic terms. This section describes the hazards of estimating, forecasting, and costing.

a. Estimating

The first element of measurement is estimation. Estimation deals with the type of cost or benefit to be counted and costs and benefits that are real or pecuniary types, tangible or intangible, as well as direct

---

*We follow Schmid's organization (1990) here, and the distinction is made for simplicity's sake only.

or indirect benefits. First, real costs and benefits are those which have a real or absolute consequence for society as a whole. That is, on balance the cost or benefit to society was not one in which the cost to one group of individuals was offset by the benefit to another group of individuals. The cost or benefit was not merely redistributed—as a pecuniary cost or benefit would describe—but an absolute change in the well-being of society as a whole.

Second, tangible and intangible costs and benefits describe the difference between those which can be priced or which society can agree relatively easily on a price and those which cannot. A tangible cost-benefit to many is a project such as a dam, with its measurable construction costs and irrigation, flood control, and recreation benefits. An intangible cost might be the endangered species which is destroyed as a result of the dam's displacement and destruction of the species' habitat.

The last type of cost and benefit which must be confronted in estimating the numbers that feed the cost-benefit analysis is the direct-indirect contrast. Direct costs are those immediately apparent from the project. The dam example, both tangible costs and tangible benefits, illustrates this idea. The indirect or secondary costs from the dam's construction might include poorer or better drainage in streams and marshes that fed the undammed stream, greater air and noise pollution as a result of recreational equipment used on reservoirs created by the dam, and even climate changes that result from large bodies of water replacing water flows.

In each case, the analysis would not be complete without considering the pecuniary, intangible, and indirect costs and benefits of a project. Most analyses suggest this to be difficult and controversial.

b. Forecasting

The policy problems and consequences of forecasting are often not based on political differences. Since no forecaster can know the future and, instead, must monitor various data sets, judgments must be made about what to consider important enough to follow closely, what is novel, and what is a trend. One's assumptions, built not only through political views, but also through organizational and professional effort, guide one to search for answers to all three questions (Pierce, 1971, p. 53). Thus, forecasting has great interpretive potential. Likewise one can influence the course of events. If one's view is substantially influential, the guidance this forecast provides can influence the course of events (Pierce, 1971, p. 41). As Klay (1985) has pointed out, moreover, what one wants to see can happen; views do become self-fulfilling prophecies.

Many different classification schemes help us to understand forecasting as a rational exercise. Quantitative methods are those depending on empirical data and in which theories play a central role. Qualitative methods also may come into play; forecasters may have only a fuzzy understanding of their theories' production under various conditions. Finally, forecasters may combine both forms, implicitly reflecting organization biases; forecasters may even reason backward from a desirable conjectured state of affairs to data and assumptions necessary to support the conjecture (see Dunn, 1981, p. 195).

Quantitative methods. Quantitative methods are those forecasting methods involving data and mathematical analysis. These quantitative methods fall into two basic categories: time series analytical methods and causal models.

1. Time series analysis. A time series is a sequence of observations of phenomena of interest. Usually these observations are spaced at specific and constant intervals. For example, the expenditures of a state government would form a time series when these expenditures, or a specific class of expenditures (the variable), were measured over a period of years. Analysis of a time series involves describing the source of the sequence of realizations, the factor generating the time series. The simplest method of forecasting time series assumes that present trends may be extrapolated. The basic methods used for extrapolation are least squares and other forms of regression analysis.

   Least squares and simple regression require that a relationship between two variables exist and that enough history describing this relationship be accessible to determine quantitatively the degree to which movement in one variable may be predicted by movement in the other. Yet, decision makers often express doubt that what lies ahead will have repeated the past. Many discredit regression techniques which assume linearity where none exists.

2. Causal models. A model consists of explicitly stated relationships among variables which portray an abstraction of some phenomenon such as taxes and economic growth. Most models build on history but, in addition, on elaborate theoretical relationships, such as that involving the curvilinear relationship among productivity, tax rates, and revenue yields (Wanniski, 1978).

Forecasting models range from relatively simple judgmental models to highly complex econometric models. All may be used in any context but especially economic ones.

> (a) Judgmental models. A judgmental model is a method of economic analysis which is relatively unstructured and informal. The forecaster generally does not use mathematical equations to represent the economy, but relies instead on any information that seems useful—information about future investment intentions and upcoming political events, judgments and hunches of people familiar with economic events, and other considerations not explicitly a part of the national income accounts framework.
>
> (b) Econometric and mathematical models. An econometric model, at the other extreme, is a system of analysis in which the economic system of a country is represented by a complex system of statistically estimated mathematical equations. The number of equations that are needed to adequately represent the economy depends on the number of actors that are to be considered. The larger the number of equations, the greater the number of subtle economic variations that can be accounted for by the model.
>
> (c) Policy analysis with models. The same model can be used for policy analysis as well as for forecasting. To investigate any specific set of possible government actions, the policymakers simply insert the change into the model and solve to find out what the impact of the action is likely to be. In periods of inflation, the figure for taxes might be raised and expenditures lowered. In periods of depression, the opposite actions might be taken.

An econometric model allows the government to predict the effects of a policy action before enacting it. The quality of the model depends on the accuracy with which it can predict these values. The distinguishing feature of econometric models is, in summary, an attempt to depict the economy by a set of statistically estimated mathematical equations. Particular emphasis is placed on having as many variables as possible explained within the system of equations, on the use of hard economic data, and on the simultaneous solutions of the model without the introduction of other considerations.

Qualitative approaches. Qualitative forecasting methods are those in which subjective estimation predominates. Such methods have greatest utility in murky or confusing areas of activity, those areas where our knowledge of the relevant variables and the patterns of interaction among these variables may not be well developed. Often qualitative methods' loudest partisans are those who reject a priori reasoning or positive theory.

The most basic qualitative forecasting technique is the judgmental forecast. Using judgment, individuals create a relatively unstructured and informal process. Those people with information relevant to the phenomena being considered essentially pool that knowledge and make educated guesses about the future. Hunches and intuition play a large role in the outcome of a judgmental forecasting process.

The delphi technique is a well-known form of judgmental forecasting (Brown and Helmer, 1962). To employ this method, one empanels a group of experts. These experts respond to a sequence of interrogations in which their responses are communicated to each other. Specifically, their responses to one questionnaire are used to produce a subsequent questionnaire. Any set of information available to some experts and not others is passed on to the others through this sharing process. This information, the method envisions, sharpens judgment among experts and focuses attention and forecasts.

Brainstorming is another information-gathering technology, one useful in aiding judgment and forecasting future events (Osborn, 1953). This method follows a very disciplined format. Criticism of any source of information or of the information provided is banned. In fact, farfetched ideas are encouraged as an aid to eliciting a large number of practical ideas. The quantity of data is emphasized. The first step in the process—the generating phase—rests primarily on creativity. The second phase is a winnowing out phase in which individuals evaluate ideas generated earlier. The third phase builds on the best ideas surviving the second phase by focusing attention on synthesizing these best ideas. Finally, the evaluation phase forces the elimination of all but the best idea or forecast.

Finally, many organizations employ the nominal group technique (Delbecq et al., 1975) to forecast future events. A nominal group is a group composed of the pooled outputs of randomly chosen individuals who have worked alone.

Problems in Forecasting. Forecasting in government is hardly ever the prerogative of only one group. Intergroup effort, in fact, describes what takes place when both legislative and executive bodies cooperate, of course (Kamlet et al., 1987), but such effort is also required among different offices within the executive branch (Pierce, 1971).

Common to all whose task is forecasting is ambiguity. Seldom is there a clear definition of cause-effect relationships. Seldom less is there agreement about what one wants to happen. Thus, forecasting is often a judgmental process, one especially influenced by forecasters' social construction of reality.

To understand the judgmental process, and thus revenue forecasting, it is necessary to understand the elements that interact to construct cause-effect relationships and desired outcomes. The interaction among actors in forecasting, as in all other organizational and judgmental exercises, assumes that all want stability; all participants interact and confine behavior in ways to trade stable expectations about behavior.

Explaining reality construction solely as an economy of social interactions is incomplete. March and Olsen (1989, p. 62) suggest that the market centers on bias:

> Although there seems to be ample evidence that when performance fails to meet aspirations, institutions search for new solutions, changes often seem to be driven less by problems than by solutions.... When causality and technology are ambiguous, the motivation to have particular solutions adopted is likely to be as powerful as the motivation to have particular problems solved, and changes can be more easily induced by a focus on solutions than by a focus on problems. Solutions and opportunities stimulate awareness of previously unsalient or unnoticed problems or preferences.

All parties to making judgments have a solution in mind. Judgment in a collective choice situation is a matter of convincing other parties of the connection between a preferred solution and the problem at hand.

The argument about one's preferred solution may be easier to make when the party realizes the importance of sequential attention. Parties to the making of a judgment have limited time and limited willingness to devote more than a fair share of that time to a given judgment call. Any party realizing the limited time problem can choose to focus attention, or not, on a given solution.

One's ploy may well be to focus on the aspect of the problem which a given solution seems most capable of resolving. Or one's time may best be spent in characterizing a problem as one for which a favorite solution has always been chosen by the group to use. In fact, Brunsson (1989) has argued that it is possible to sustain a coalition among members who have what appear to be strictly inconsistent objectives because of sequential attention. Pierce agrees (1971, p. 50):

> By adroitly applying technology and expertise, [executives] can manage the assumptions and judgments which must be made to combine... forecasts in some reasonable way and predict... change.

The recognition of biases, and the understanding that differences may be useful, underscores much research in judgment making (Wright and Ayton, 1987). That is, differences create a healthy skepticism about others' views and assumptions, bringing them out in the open (Golembiewski and Miller, 1981). Research by Klay (1985, 1983) and Ascher (1978) suggests that airing such differences may reduce overreliance on outdated core assumptions, or "assumption drag," in forecasts, improving their accuracy.

c. Costing

Finally, cost-benefit analysts must cope with the assignment of some quantitative value to the stream of costs and benefits. This has special difficulty in the public goods sector, since markets have not "priced" these goods, owing to market failures in either rivalry or divisibility. Three specific costing problems bedevil analysts: estimating shadow prices, final prices, and opportunity costs.

Shadow Prices. First, the cost of a project or the benefit of it may often be estimated by analogy. Some equivalent market may exist for a project, somewhere; that equivalent is employed as the basis for costing out the elements of the project for analysis. The problems of finding such a shadow or of using the most nearly correct one still create problems. Would a roller coaster ticket price mirror a subway fare?

Final Prices. Second, the lack of a shadow price leads to additional problems. That is, most public goods tend to be oriented toward outcomes rather than mere outputs. Outcomes are extremely hard to envision, much less estimate in dollar-denominated consequences. For example, street sweeping and cleaning are often touted as popular programs, even though they have no meaningful outputs (pounds of garbage collected, raves from residents) but definite outcomes. "Clean streets" has a meaning all its own and is an end in itself. Such an end in itself is hard to measure for cost-benefit analysis.

Opportunity Costs. Third, a project without a shadow price always carries an opportunity cost that might be measurable and meaningful for analysis. The opportunity cost of any project is the cost and benefit of another project foregone to proceed with the present one. The true worth of any project, therefore, is the cost (and benefit) of the most obvious substitute. Clean streets may carry the cost of an opportunity, such as a rat amelioration program, foregone. The illustration also suggests the problem of lack of adequate quantifiability in opportunities foregone, the biggest problem in calculating costs.

d. Summary

Problems abound in estimating, forecasting, or costing project elements for analysis. Estimating costs and benefits accurately requires knowledge that far exceeds that available to an analyst. Forecasting demands an objectivity and a knowledge of theoretical relationships far beyond that normally expected of economists and social observers. Costing public programs has special difficulties in that few analogous, meaningful, or quantifiable projects exist on which to base estimates.

ii. Valuation Over Time
and by Different Selection Criteria

The selection of projects through cost-benefit (CB) analysis is commonly derived from an investment theory utilizing comparisons between a stream of costs and a stream of benefits *measured at their current value*. Generally, these comparisons are made on the basis of one or the other of two calculations, net present value (NPV) or internal rate of return (IRR).

The NPV measures future streams of costs and benefits by "netting" or subtracting current value costs from current value benefits. A variation of this measure is the more popularly known ratio of current value benefits over current costs. The differences are nil. The criterion for selection in the former is a positive number; the criterion for the ratio is a number greater than unity (1).

A second method of selecting a project is to determine its rate of return (IRR). This calculation suggests that projects whose current value benefits exceed their current value costs by a given rate or percentage are better than those that do not.

The difference between NPV/CB ratio and IRR is in the former's discrimination in favor of large numbers. That is, IRR corrects for extremely large differences in scope among projects. It is more appropriately applied at the macrolevel where projects compete against other projects than at the microlevel where a project's benefits compete against its odds.

a. Discounting

Nevertheless, the calculation of NPV and the CB ratio depend on establishment of current value costs and benefits. Current value costs and benefits are also known as discounted elements.

Discounting is based on a preference for the time value of money. For example, if given the choice between $100 now and $100 a year from now, most people would prefer to have the $100 now.* If forced to wait, we would want the year-from-now choice to be equal in value to the $100 today alternative. The amount that would make the $100 a year from now equivalent in value to the $100 today alternative is our preference for the time value of money. Some of

---

*To those like Henny Youngman, this is "nem di gelt," or take the money: "Don't believe all the baloney people tell you about what they'll do for you tomorrow. Take the money" (Youngman, 1990).

us prefer more under some circumstances than others. To illustrate: The delay in getting the $100, such as when we lend money to a college student daughter or son to buy an automobile in return for the promise to repay it—we would want to have compensation for the delay. What would the time preference be?

The calculation of time value may shed light on finding preferences. Consider that if you put $100 in a bank at 5% interest, you would have $105 in a year, if interest is compounded annually. The future value of that $100 (the amount it would be worth in one year) is $105, or:

Future value of $100 = $100 × (1 + 0.05) = $105

A sum of $100 at the present time is equivalent to $105 next year at a 5% interest rate. A person's choosing not to put money in the bank tells us that the $100 sum we have today is equivalent to an amount next year of at least $105 and maybe much more. If the person feels that having $100 today or $105 one year from now are equivalent, then the 5% interest rate represents the time value of money—of waiting one year for the money. The 5% interest rate measures the willingness to trade $100 today (present value) for $105 one year from now (future value).

If we know the interest rate that reflects the tradeoff to the citizens of a community between $100 in benefits today versus some greater level of benefits in later years, we can convert the value of the future benefits into their present-day worth. Two examples illustrate the need to know the present value of future benefits. In the first case, many governments often buy fleets of automobiles for their police forces and for many other departments. The government's decision makers face the quandary, Should we buy or should we lease the automobiles? Present valuing the terms of the lease is the only true way to compare, on financial terms, the buy-versus-lease alternatives.

In a second case, governments often sell bonds in the marketplace to finance capital improvements such as roads and bridges. These bonds will be redeemed with principal payments the government will make annually over a period of years. The bond financings are, more often than not, competitively bid. Ordinarily, investment banks bid on bonds by offering an interest rate for each annual principal payment. If a bond financing covered a redemption period of 10 years, an investment bank would often bid on each of 10 annual payments or maturities. The government decision maker who evaluates the competing bids must calculate the present value of each principal payment on which the bank submitted a bid because, presumably, the interest rates the banks bid were different, leading to different total amounts of interest the government would pay.

Essentially, we calculate the present value in the opposite way we calculate interest earnings of future value. That is, if the formula for the future value of a sum of money is

Future value =
Present value × (one + interest rate)

The formula for finding present value is solved by algebra (dividing both sides of the equals sign by the term "one + interest rate") to get the formula:

Present value =
Future value / (one + interest rate)

In other words, if we know any two terms—future value, interest rate, or present value—we can find the third. And if we know the future benefits of a project with any certainty at all, as well as the interest rate, we can find the present value of the project.

We should note one fact about terminology related to the time value of money. The rate used to calculate future value is best thought of as an interest rate; most of us are familiar enough with that process through savings accounts and like investments. However, the rate used in present value calculations is known as the *discount rate* because the value of a benefit we receive at some future time is smaller today by comparison because we deduct an amount to compensate us for the delay. In other terms, we deduct from the future value by a factor that relates time and the discount rate.

Projects often begin to have benefits much later than 1 year after they have been built. The construction of a project, for example, may take 3 years. The benefits, while forecast to be a certain amount, may have to be adjusted because of the delay. The adjustment would be done in the same way as three separate 1-year present value calculations. That is, if the present value of a forecasted benefit of $1,000 (at 5%) for one year were

Present value = $1,000 / (1 + 0.05) = $952.38

then the present value for the second year would be

$952.38 / (1 + 0.05) = $907.03

and the present value for the third year would be

$907.03 / (1 = 0.05) = $863.84

The formula may be simplified by

Present value (of $x over 3 years at 5%) = $\frac{\text{Future value}}{(1 + 0.05)^3}$

Thus, by cubing the discount factor (1 + 0.05), we calculate precisely as we did by the long method formerly.

b. Annual costs and benefits

Many projects have costs and benefits continually over a period of years. In other words, these projects have a benefit (or cost) stream. To find the total value of the stream from this succession of periods, we add terms to the basic formula for present value that we looked at earlier. If a project had annual benefits for n years, we would use the following formula:

$$\text{Present value} = \text{Annual value} \times \frac{[(1 + \text{discount rate})^n - 1]}{\text{discount rate} (1 + \text{discount rate})^n}$$

Consider the following example. If a city were offered $1,800 for a piece of property today that it was leasing to a business for 5 more years at $300 a year with the option to purchase at the end of the 5-year period for $500, which would you advise the city leaders to choose? Using an interest rate of 5%, let's consider the two alternatives.

1. The lease
   Annual benefit = $300
   One time benefit = $500
   PV annual benefit = $300 × $\left(\frac{(1.05)^5 - 1}{0.05 \, (1.05)^5}\right)$
   = $1,299
   PV one time benefit = $500 / (1.05)^5
   = $392
   Total benefits = $1,299 + $392
   = $1,691

2. The sale
   The sale, theoretically, at least, would take place today; therefore, its present value is $1,500

3. Comparing the two alternatives
   Lease/purchase = $1,691
   Sale = $1,800

We would probably advise the city to sell the property. Of course, the difference is small because, above all, we are dealing with rather small sums. Yet, if the differences were small even with bigger numbers, other considerations would be called into play to decide the question, such as the disposition of the property—given other city policies—if sold; the reliability of payments by the present lessor; other plans the city might have for adjoining property; and so on.

The city's main advantage in knowing the present value of the lease is the ability to compare directly the value of a sale and the value of the lease. These types of calculations make comparisons meaningful, since the cash flow from the lease— [(5 × $300) + $500] = $2,000—might have led decision makers to believe that the lease's value was more than it actually was.

B. Macro-Cost-Benefit Analysis or Portfolio Construction

On a project level evaluation of benefits and costs, the net present value idea has some merit. Certainly, one hesitates to spend taxpayers' money on projects whose worth cannot be shown readily. However, selection problems occur when the comparison is between projects of unequal size or projects of unequal economic or useful lives, as well as when an entire budget of projects is being selected. We find two strategies normally used to overcome these selection problems: a scheduling strategy and a strategy to construct portfolios.

i. Cost-Benefit Analysis without Constraint

First, capital projects are also often submitted with no expenditure ceiling specified. Consequently, more projects are submitted than can be funded. Prioritization is necessary to achieve the required cutbacks.

Prioritization is frequently achieved by scheduling. Scheduling helps alleviate waste by ensuring construction of facilities required initially; that is, before primary construction. For example, sewers will be scheduled for construction prior to building a street so that it will not be necessary to cut new pavement during sewer construction.

A danger of prioritization by scheduling is that rarely are projects completely eliminated. More often, they are postponed and placed further down the schedule. As projects stay on the schedule for several years, there can be a maturation effect; they may become bona fide projects with funding even though they logically do not have a high priority.

Prioritization requires review to ensure the project relates to the overall goals and policies of jurisdiction. Projects must be scrutinized to find the value they add to programs which, in themselves, are not of equal rank. Using program or zero-base budgeting rather than the department or functional approach, managers can force these comparisons.

ii. Marginal Rate of Return Analysis

A second approach to cost-benefit analysis, one that overcomes the scheduling problem, employs marginal analysis in selecting productive projects. This method has greatest utility when projects are quite different in scale or useful life.

Marginal analysis requires three steps. First, a range of discount rates is evaluated to determine the likely field of opportunity costs for projects such as those being evaluated. Second, the analyst determines the internal rate of return for the entire set of projects and discards those which fall below the opportunity costs of capital. Third, the preferred choice is selected by finding that project which has the highest internal rate of return for the employment of capital.

a. Finding the range of discount rates and opportunity costs

Determining opportunity costs of projects provides the information one needs to discount future costs properly. That is, to be systematic in judging the value of public projects, the projects must be compared not only to the population of candidate *public* projects, but also to all investment opportunities, public and private. In this way, the economic efficiency of all institutions is preserved.

An opportunity's cost is the cost of a project foregone. That is, if one chooses one project over another, the true value of the choice is the value foregone to gain it. Consider the example of desserts. If we forego one that contains 1,000 calories for one that has 100 calories, we value the one we chose at its 10:1 savings rate. The one we chose is 10 times the value of the one we did not choose.

In this same sense, public projects compete with private sector projects. If we decide to spend money on public capital projects, we forego the economic benefits of leaving the money in the private sector, where, presumably, it generates economic growth.

Since we cannot grasp the long-term costs and benefits of collective goods very well, the opportunity cost gets fixed as a discount rate by which we judge what costs and benefits we do know. We measure costs and benefits and discount this stream by the opportunity cost of capital.

Many consider the market to have done this costing for us, at least in constructing a range of opportunity costs for portfolio purposes. The difference between the tax-free yield on municipal bonds and the taxable yield on these bonds or on corporate bonds of equal risk of default might serve as the floor in our range. The yield on federal long-term bonds might be our range's ceiling.

Why these? If the opportunity cost of capital is value foregone, the small difference in the former represents such a comparison. The tax exemption represents the subsidy or cost of pushing investment dollars from the private to public sector. These bonds would not be sold, or the projects they finance built, we assume, if they had to be offered at market rates.

The top of the range is that market rate that attracts capital. The federal government's long-term taxable bond rate is such a rate.

b. Determining the internal rate of return of the projects

Instead of determining a cost-benefit ratio, many analysts follow the private sector practice of solving for the rate of return on investment, or the *internal rate of return* (IRR). Having discovered this internal rate, analysts discard those projects whose rates are less than the opportunity cost of capital—the floor of rates.

Consider the example of a project with an initial outlay of $20,000, annual costs of $10,000, and annual benefits of $13,000, all of which are paid or received at the end of the fiscal year. The projected life of the project is 10 years, and there is no residual benefit at the end of the project. This project's costs and benefits are represented with the following cash flows:

Year	Costs	Benefits
1	−30,000	+13,000
2	−10,000	+13,000
3	−10,000	+13,000
4	−10,000	+13,000
5	−10,000	+13,000
6	−10,000	+13,000
7	−10,000	+13,000
8	−10,000	+13,000
9	−10,000	+13,000
10	−10,000	+13,000

To find the IRR, we determine that discount rate at which the net present value (NPE or discounted costs and benefits) are zero. In the table below, we show four possible discount rates and the net current value for the cash flows above.

	Discount Rate (%)			
	5	10	15	20
Project A	4,118	253	−2,334	−4,088

Given the numbers that appear in the table, the discount rate of 10.41% brings the discounted benefits and costs into equality. That is, the net costs and benefits are almost zero.

The internal rate of return of a given set of cash flows (outflow in payments for construction and such, inflow in benefits received) is that discount rate at which the current value of the inflow equals the current value of the outflow. Finding the IRR is a matter of eliminating all those discount rates at which the two flows are not equal.

Take, for illustration, three projects with unique cash flows, each over 10 years.

Project	Capital Costs	Annual Costs	Annual Benefits
A	20,000	10,000	14,000
B	30,000	10,000	15,000
C	50,000	17,000	25,000

With computers, it is possible to program to find the rate, since hunting for it is time consuming and tedious.

	Discount Rate (%)			
Project	5	10	15	20
A	11,839	6,396	2,684	103
B	10,037	3,450	(993)	(4,038)
C	14,155	3,702	(3,328)	(8,127)

Just as large numbers may make projects less practical, even though benefit-cost (BC) ratios make them look better, projects which have large internal rates of return also may not be practical. This may be so in limited budget situations particularly. For example, a budget with a limit of $15,000 simply cannot afford any of the projects, no matter what their IRR. Not only does the internal rate of return calculation limit the population of possible projects to those which exceed the minimum rate or the opportunity cost of capital, but, obviously, it also limits projects to those that a government can afford.

c. Selecting projects by their marginal rates of return

The actual method of choosing a portfolio of projects which have internal rates higher than the minimum is by determining marginal rates of return among those which have not been weeded out already. This method operates on the principle that each additional dollar invested in a project should have at least the same, if not a higher, rate of return than the last. We would first employ the minimum acceptable rate criterion to projects to weed out those projects that alone could not produce a rate of return great enough to justify taxation to finance them. Then, we would ask which combination of projects yields the highest marginal rate of return.

Taking the projects just described, and establishing a 7% minimum acceptable rate,* arriving at net current values and benefit-cost ratios comes first. The net current values and ratios are displayed in the following table:

---

*This is a fairly low rate. As of this writing, municipal bond rates are in this range.

	Capital Required	Net Present Value @7%	BC Ratio	IRR
A	20,000	9,403	1.11	20.2%
B	30,000	7,081	1.07	13.7%
C	50,000	9,460	1.06	12.4%

Then, the process requires finding the differences between any and all projects. The marginal analysis method requires comparison between successively larger projects—between one project and another with larger capital requirements—and not the other way around (Gohagan, 1980, pp. 209-11).

In our example, our process requires moving from Project A to Project B (and on to Project C) or from Project A to Project C. We ask whether it is justifiable to spend additional capital to mount a larger project. The marginal additions are portrayed below.

Marginal Increase	In Capital	Annual Costs	Annual Benefits	MIRR (%)
From A to B	10,000	0	1,000	0%
From A to C	30,000	7,000	11,000	7.06%

The analysis suggests two facts. The first is that there is no additional benefit to be gained by investing in Project B rather than Project A. However, because we set the rate of return floor at 7%, the move from A to C would be justifiable, since the $30,000 extra dollars, invested in what we presume to be a popular project, would return at least that minimum. As a result of our analysis, the marginal internal rate of return calculation would suggest Project C to be the most productive use of the public's money.

iii. Portfolio Construction

A third approach to cost-benefit analysis deals with the most productive combination of projects by using investment portfolio approaches of choice. Finding this combination is the subject of capital budget deliberations. How does one build a portfolio?

Constructing a portfolio requires three steps. First, we set the minimum rate of return for capital. Second, we determine the marginal internal rate of return for each project or combination of projects over each other project or combination. Finally, we choose that combination which exceeds our minimum rate by the greatest margin.

a. Setting the minimum rate

In our last example, we set the minimum rate at 7%. We will be using the same data; however, let's make the hurdle a higher one (10%), since we will be dealing with large net current values as the following table reveals:

	Capital ($)	Annual Benefits ($)	Annual Costs ($)	NPE 10%	BC 10%
A	20,000	14,000	10,000	6,396	1.08
B	30,000	15,000	10,000	3,450	1.04
C	50,000	25,000	17,000	3,702	1.02
A + B	50,000	29,000	20,000	9,847	1.06
A + C	70,000	39,000	27,000	10,098	1.04
B + C	80,000	50,000	27,000	7,152	1.03

b. Determining marginal rates for all combinations

As with the last group of projects, we will determine marginal rates, but with the portfolio approach, we will also combine projects and calculate IRR and MIRR for these combinations as well. For an illustration of this with our project data, see the table below. In it we report only the largest capital projects. The marginal rate of return is the rate of return on the extra capital invested in projects with higher capital requirements. In the A + C versus A + B example, the A + C required $20,000 more capital than A + B; therefore, the marginal rate is the return on that extra $20,000.

	Marginal BC	Marginal IRR
A + C over A + B	1.00	10.41%
A + C over C	1.08	20.24%
B + C over A + C	0.68	0.00%

c. Choosing the best combination

The criterion for choice is based first on total present value, then marginal benefit-cost ratios, and finally the marginal internal rate of return. In setting up the last comparison, we took only the portfolio with the highest total present value, A + C with $10,098. Then we compared it to those projects just smaller in capital requirements to determine whether the expenditure of the extra money was justified. The extra $20,000 resulted in at least equal costs and benefits when compared to the combination of A + B and a positive benefit-cost ratio when compared to Project C. Each of the MIRR measures—that compared to A + B and that compared to C—were greater than the 10% hurdle we set up. We conclude that the extra $20,000 was a justifiable expenditure on these measures.

If A + C is a justifiable project, what about the next one, B + C, which requires larger amounts of capital? Is the extra $10,000 expenditure justifiable when we select B + C over A + C? According to the chart, it is not. The extra $10,000 represents substantially greater costs than benefits (a marginal benefit-cost ratio of 0.68). Also, the extra capital brings no return at all.

We conclude with the choice of a simple portfolio of Projects A and C. The total current value of benefits and costs was a positive $10,098. The marginal gain over the next lower capital cost alternatives was above the minimum rate of return we established as well.

IV. THE RESEARCH

To test the assumption that the marginal internal rate of return method will provide the best guide to projects to select, we conducted a research project involving seasoned state government executives. We asked them to compute the rates of return, but then asked them to select the best portfolio, using their experience as a guide. The research can suggest some of the important steps actually used in considering which projects are apparently in the best interest of a public authority to fund.

A. Methods

Thirty state government analysts, acting as research subjects, were given a cost-benefit analysis to conduct as they saw fit. They were divided into five groups for analysis and discussion, in order to ensure that whatever special expertise in urban problems that existed was spread evenly across the groups. The choice concerned the best use of $250,000 in state funds for an economically and socially destitute but politically sensitive (hometown of the governor) area of the state. The groups were given one month to decide their portfolios. The five project choices are briefly described below:

1. A transportation project. A wooden trestle bridge, having an estimated economic life of 25 years, would cost $80,000 for initial construction and would need annual maintenance costing $4,000. The wooden bridge would have to be rebuilt after 25 years, which would require a 1-month closure to traffic. The wooden bridge would be built in an area subject to flooding, one in which the "100-year flood" probabilities indicate some likelihood of a flood that would destroy the bridge up to three times during a 50-year period. There would be intangible, tourism-related benefits to such a structure.

2. A transportation project. A steel replacement bridge, constructed on the same site as, but instead of, the wooden bridge, would have a 50-year economic life. The initial cost would be $160,000 with annual maintenance of $2,000. The bridge would be invulnerable to the 100-year flood.

3. A jobs training program. The journeyman training program would recruit 100 trainees per year for 6 years, 50% from the hard-core unemployed and 50% from nonunion construction workers (who now make $8,000 per year). The trainees would enter a 4-year training program. Once in, students would be paid $7,000 and upon successful completion, would be hired at $14,000. A trainee dropout rate of 10% per year could reasonably be anticipated; graduated journeymen would face an average 10% unemployment rate. Administrative costs for the program would be $100,000 per year.

4. A jobs training program. The clerical training program would also recruit 100 trainees per year over a 6-year period. The trainees would enter a 1-year program and be placed in jobs that paid $7,000 upon successful completion but receive nothing while training. Ninety percent of the trainees would come from the hard-core unemployed. Administrative costs for the program would be $100,000 per year.

5. An urban renewal project. The redevelopment project covers a 100-block area of an urban area and involves land purchases, resident relocation, redevelopment and improvements, public facilities, and administrative costs. The total of tangible costs equals $4.6 million. The total of tangible benefits equals $3.7 million. However, planners and proponents suggest large intangible benefits.

The respondents were asked to use the internal rate of return method to establish relative worthiness and the marginal rate of return method to help identify components of the best mix. They were also asked specifically to include the managerial implications of the portfolio and change recommendations in that light, especially considering fraud and abuse and difficulty in evaluating project success substantively.

B. Findings

Four major sets of findings emerged from the research. First, the cost-benefit analysis could be swayed by both the assumptions built into the projects as well as assumptions projected, by the analyst, onto the study. For example, many questioned the low dropout rate in the training programs, and this assumption was crucial to the benefit stream. Also, the subjects divided equally over the forecast unemployment rate, with those otherwise favoring the project forecasting a lower unemployment rate than graduate trainees would face in future job markets.

Second, intangibles tended to play a large part in the analysis of social infrastructure programs such as the urban renewal project. Arguments made to include tangibles pointed toward all manner of benefits from redevelopment—from better health of residents to pride in community. Hard-headed numbers analysts deprecated these measures and discarded this project from their portfolios.

Third, all subjects pointed out the fraud potential of the projects and added this factor into their analysis. Urban renewal was the consensus choice of the project most prone to abuse. Training programs were thought to be abused but able to be quarantined from such a problem by good management, an intangible cost.

Fourth, subjects suggested that a short-term bias pervaded analysis. This short-term bias affected judgments about training programs particularly, since their benefits and social consequences may not be apparent for a generation. The short-term bias was also manifested in the consumption-orientedness of the analytical approach. Conservation or patrimony benefits often are difficult to envision much less measure, owing to their intergenerational quality.

Finally, undergirding all of the findings was the ever presence of political considerations. In other words, what would "sell" politically, subjects always wondered. Despite its advantage in IRR terms, "Would a wooden bridge be politically as well as physically vulnerable?" one subject asked. "Could the bridge be explained in the face of conventional opposition, much less justified in the battle for funding by interest groups representing other proposals?"

Some pointed out that the cost-benefit analysis imputed values and demands to individuals without actually verifying them. The value of a bridge, for instance, was the individual's opportunity of traveling the next best route. However, no one ever asked an individual whether that was the route he or she would take or whether he or she would take that trip at all if there were no bridge. Some mentioned that the analysis would skirt politics when the political process was the only true gauge of what real individuals wanted or were willing to tax themselves to finance.

Politics, in the form of equity, also became an issue. One subject argued, "Cost benefit analysis is not particularly sensitive to the way in which income is distributed in society." The subject noticed that cost-benefit analysis tended to infer the same amount of value to rich and poor individuals. Also apparent to this subject was the method's conservatism.

When used with the five alternatives here, the method tended to minimize the need for government intervention on behalf of the poor.

C. Conclusions

Despite the large number of caveats made to an otherwise quantitative analysis, subjects generally agreed that there are "serious public policy implications in undertaking a project that is not rational with respect to tangible costs that exceed benefits, particularly in times of fiscal austerity." The number of biases that emerge in analyzing the costs and benefits of a range of projects—fraud potential, short-term returns, consumption instead of conservation, tangible items to measure—suggested the extreme conservatism of the method to the subjects. Yet, the last comment on fiscal austerity is revealing. It suggests that the political environment for tax policy, the willingness of individuals to pay taxes, and the civic mindedness of taxpayers serve to condition analysts to the need to be conservative or otherwise in the assumptions and use of bias in analysis. Presumably, times other than fiscal austerity might prompt different analytical procedures.

D. Summary

This research has tested the idea that the internal rate of return method of cost-benefit analysis would guide seasoned state executives in their choice of an optimal, even if hypothetical, portfolio. The findings suggest that a large number of other considerations, both managerial and political, guide judgment in addition to quantitative techniques. However, the surprising finding was the large role that the IRR calculation actually played—that it is not sound, "not rational," to select a project in which tangible costs exceed benefits. Moreover, surprisingly, subjects were loath to project their own political leanings or their social philosophies on the analysis, content instead to act conservatively, in hopes, we would infer, that the political process would take over where they left off in creating an equitable as well as efficient portfolio.

V. ECONOMIC REASONING IN GOVERNMENT FINANCIAL MANAGEMENT

We now place cost-benefit analysis within the even larger body of literature characterizing economic reasoning in government. This review forms a critique and is meant both to support the research findings of the previous section, and also to suggest the larger sources and consequences of the approach for choice.

Economics, or more specifically, rational choice theory, exerts a strong influence on thinking about government financial management through cost-benefit analysis. Thus, government productivity is often closely associated with the idea of economic efficiency, which cost-benefit analysis was introduced to maximize.

A. The Maximizing Behavior of Government Actors and Agencies

The fundamental principle of economic reasoning states that "bureaucratic officials, like all other agents in society, are motivated by their own self interests at least part of the time" (Downs, 1957, p. 2).

In parallel fashion, political actors seek advantage for both themselves and their constituents and tend to maximize gain and minimize loss. Both bureaucratic and political actors reach their targets through a maze of rules: communication and coordination rules for bureaucratic officials and voting rules for political actors. The world within which behavior bends around rules is an unpredictable one, and gaining greater certainty about the acquisition of advantage may offset in part the size of the advantage itself. The actors, therefore, constantly calculate what is literally a risk-return relationship, given their preferences for different kinds of advantages to begin with.

B. Economic Decision Making

Economic decision making tends to be deductive and because of that has an elegance given to mathematics-like precision in detailing "proof" as well as an otherworldliness in which few argue its practicality.

The idea of looking at the world in terms of "decision" instead of some other concept, say sovereignty (another abstraction but one loaded with ideology) or resource problems (topical, practical ways of dealing with phenomena) is tribute to economists following a "scientific" approach to studying the world.

Decisions cut across all of mankind's activities; they occur every minute of every day and cover everything from the mundane to the spiritual, and especially the sensible. Dimensions of decisions seem to cover all bases: psychological, political, remunerative, making the decision a truly fundamental element of life.

Having based microeconomics, or the theory of the firm, on the idea that firm owners maximized their firms' welfare, economics could assert something called optimal decisions. These decisions were based on the thinking of a group of philosophers called logical positivists.

Logical positivism started in early twentieth century Vienna and became known through the work of Ayer (1936). Positivists hold that only two kinds of statements have meaning:

1. Those which are true merely because of the definitions employed (all bachelors are unmarried).
2. Those that could be shown to be true or shown to be false by some possible sense-experience, such as a scientific experiment (water changes from a liquid to a gaseous state as greater heat is applied). If it cannot be verified by scientific means (empirically verifiable), the statement loses meaning. Thus, the statement "there is a God" or "Jane loves Dick" has no meaning.

Logical positivists, not to take it too far, argue that there can be no meaning attributable to that "known" independently of experience. In fact, Ayer himself said (1936, p. 721),

> [T]he admission that there were some facts about the world that could be known independently of experience would be incompatible with one fundamental contention that a sentence says nothing unless it is empirically verifiable.

Ayer and his fellows ran into mathematics—not verifiable independently but the truths which are certain and necessary.

Others had tried to square the two. John Stuart Mill, for instance, had argued that mathematics cannot be proved universally true until we have seen all of the cases. Natural sciences and mathematics, he said, were very similar; their truths are probably so, but we have no guarantee—there may be an exception.

So what happens when there is found an exception to a mathematical statement? Suppose, for instance, that we accept as probably true the statement that 2 times 5 equals 10, and when we count 5 pairs of objects we find 10 objects. Then, once we count and do not find 10 objects. In such a case, we would say

1. We were wrong to suppose there were 5 pairs to begin with.
2. An object was taken away when we were not looking.
3. The counting was wrong.

We would explain the phenomenon so that it fit the facts, but 2×5 would still $= 10$.

In effect, there is logic and mathematics on the one hand and there is observation and experience on the other. Or as Kant would have it, a synthetic proposition depends on what we see: Its validity is determined by the facts of experience; and an analytic proposition is valid solely because of the definitions of the symbols it contains.

Consider a brief example (Ayer, 1936). A statement such as "There are ants which have established a system of slavery" awaits experience for confirmation or falsification. However, a statement such as "Either some ants are parasitic or none are" depends solely on "either," "or," and "none" and acquires truth independently of experience. The truth of the matter is we know nothing about parasitic ants after reading the last statement, but we could through observation know something about slavery among ants from the first statement. Analytical statements have no factual content. No experience will ever refute them.

There is no lack of use here, in any case. Because, as Lincoln reasoned through the problem of what to do with rebellious Southerners after the War between the States, (1) all Southerners are rebels, (2) all Southerners are Americans, therefore (3) all rebels are Americans.

These statements are tautologies, obvious truths, internally so. The tautological form holds through all analytical propositions: If P implies Q, and P is true, Q is also true.

Still analytical propositions do not increase knowledge, they are a priori knowledge. In even more direct terms, as Simon (1976) would say, they are values. Simon based his thinking on roughly the same analytic-synthetic distinction. Decision making in administrative contexts stems from a set of premises—value premises and factual premises. Roughly, people having defined the situation in a certain way (provided for themselves the value premise) readily choose the one best way to act (ascertain the facts and choose the optimal way). But Simon went on to show that the latter may not be so.

Thus, individuals in administrative contexts have less than full knowledge of or capacity (time, resources) to gather the facts. Rather than optimize, people satisfy or choose the first satisfactory alternative, given their value premise.

Economics steps in via cost-benefit analysis, using logical positivism, in two ways. First, economists argue that given the value premise, and ignoring the individual who is about to make a choice, one can judge, from the external situation, behavior optimally adapted to the situation. Cost-benefit analysis can provide a standard of optimality against which competing alternatives may be judged.

Second, economists also argue the need for aids to calculation which will help individuals suffering with bounded rationality to cope with complex situations. Thus, cost-benefit analysis can uncover masked or hidden facts or even suggest ways to limit one's boundaries to insight.

Cost-benefit analysis is a class of analytical methods that evaluate the economic or the choice—aspects of given decisions. Others are *utility theory*, which examines the relative worth of various alternatives measured subjectively and generally incorporating probability and the decision makers' attitudes toward risk; *cost-effectiveness analysis,* a measure of the relative efficiency of various technologies in achieving an already-decided maximum result; and *cost-benefit analysis,* a measure of the relative efficiency of projects economically—Are the intended effects worth the cost.

The cost-benefit analysis approach has its limits in government decision making, as the research reported here has suggested. That is, cost-benefit analysis is often used to justify ex post facto a position already taken; the most significant factor in cost-benefit analysis is often its sponsor. Cost-benefit analysis tends to neglect the distributional consequences of a choice. The method systematically undervalues projects that improve the distribution of wealth and systematically overvalues projects that exacerbate economic inequality. In the Kaldor-Hicks terminology, cost-benefit analysis would recommend a course of action that could potentially allow the winners to compensate the losers so that no one is worse off, but the method does not guarantee that the winners *will* compensate the losers.

Over and above the operational problems with cost-benefit analysis, and by extension economic reasoning in government, there are intangibles of fundamental importance that cost-benefit analysis cannot conceive. There is, for example, a moral significance in the duties and rights of individuals and of government in relation to the individual that is not comprehended in the measurement of consequences alone. Related to this idea, certain rights, such as due process of the law, cannot be conceived simply because they are processes valued for themselves rather than outcomes.

Cost-benefit analysis has been blamed for damaging the political system. Some argue that politics is superior to analysis because of the wider scope of ideas and concepts the people practicing politics can fathom. Others argue that analysis enfranchises unelected policy analysts and disenfranchises those who do not understand, do not believe, or cannot use analysis to make their arguments to government. Such a situation creates a loss of confidence in government institutions.

To return to cost-benefit analysis's basis in economics, others argue that the basis insofar as it describes or prescribes government action is flawed. That is, cost-benefit analysis assumes that there can be no market failure. There are always opportunity costs and shadow prices with which public sector goods can be valued. Research on markets suggests that markets are not perfectly competitive, that that lack of competition leads inevitably to failure, and that the public goods are produced to remedy that failure. Without a way to value public goods, therefore, cost-benefit analysis fails to inform the decision-making process.

Another economic idea—that any alternative must be judged in terms of other alternatives—lends support to analysis. These proponents of cost-benefit analysis argue that there is no alternative to cost-benefit analysis; none as explicit or systematic. In fact, cost-benefit analysis's formalized, explicit nature allows the public to hold its public officials accountable to a larger extent than under normal politics and management. Systematic analysis is less likely to overlook an important fact or consideration which when placed in an adversarial process such as politics, may lead to the determination of the public interest far sooner than mere impressionistic surmise.

The controversy over the use, misuse, or lack of use of analysis often pits those who believe in government against those who see the market as the predominantly positive force in society. Typically, what cost-benefit analysis overlooks is what most progovernment action proponents find government most useful in providing, equity. Promarket proponents argue that government intervenes for spurious reasons and, in doing so, creates more problems than it solves, certainly leading to less rather than more economic efficiency.

VI. CONCLUSIONS

We have defined productivity in terms of both equity and efficiency in this discussion. We have also shown that the Kaldor criterion for allocating government services fulfills that criterion in theory. In demonstrating the Kaldor criterion, we have demonstrated cost-benefit analysis and have elaborated most of its important technical facets. In doing so, we demonstrated that cost-benefit analysis—and productivity—rely on comparisons made among programs at the suborganization, then organization, then interorganization levels, and that the real outcome of these comparisons is the construction of portfolios of investments. The technology which might be used to improve these comparisons, and thus improve productivity, we argued, could be borrowed from portfolio construction models in business investment practice, since they too are based on cost-benefit analytic principles.

We further argued the heuristic, if not the absolute determinative value of this technology. Moreover, we demonstrated through a small piece of research that cost-benefit analysis is a crucial learning tool in understanding policy problems. Nevertheless, the research revealed the limited nature of this technology in that real decision makers in a simulated decision-making situation used other, different criteria in making final choices. These other, different criteria, often more heavily weighted than cost-benefit analysis, included managerial feasibility and a project's tendency toward encouraging fraud and abuse.

In the end, we classed cost-benefit analysis with other methods of thinking which are basically deductive in nature. These methods ignore intuition, feeling, and other means of informing decisions. While practical in a limited way, the analytical methods underlying cost-benefit analysis are often self-defeating. Especially inappropriate to government productivity, the methods defy reality, an administrative reality which must reconcile plural views, each of which describes more than monetized utility, in allocation policy choices.

References

Ascher, W. (1978). *Forecasting: An Appraisal for Policy-Makers and Planners,* Johns Hopkins University Press, Baltimore, Maryland.

Ayer, A. J. (1936). *Language, Truth and Logic,* Knopf, New York.

Brown, B., and Helmer, O. (1962). *Improving the Reliability of Estimates Obtained from a Consensus of Experts,* Rand Corporation, Santa Monica, California.

Brunsson, N. (1989). *The Organization of Hypocrisy,* Wiley, Chichester, England.

Buchanan, J. M., and Tullock, G. (1962). *The Calculus of Consent,* University of Michigan Press, Ann Arbor.

Delbecq, A. L., Van de Ven, A. H., and Gustafson, D. H. (1975). *Group Techniques for Program Planning: A Guide for Nominal Group and Delphi Processes,* Scott, Foresman, Glenview, Illinois.

Downs, A. (1957). *An Economic Theory of Democracy,* Harper & Row, New York.

Downs, A. (1960). Why the government budget is too small in a democracy, *World Politics,* 12 (4): 541-563.

Dunn, W. N. (1981). *Public Policy Analysis,* Prentice-Hall, Englewood Cliffs, New Jersey.

Gohagan, J. K. (1980). *Quantitative Analysis for Public Policy,* McGraw-Hill, New York.

Golembiewski, R. T., and Miller, G. J. (1981). Small groups in political science. In Long, S. (ed.), *Handbook of Political Behavior,* Vol. 2, Plenum Press, New York, pp. 1-71.

Kamlet, M. S., Mowery, D. C., and Su, T.-T. (1987). Whom do you trust? An analysis of executive and congressional economic forecasts, *Journal of Policy Analysis and Management,* 6 (3): 365-384.

Klay, W. E. (1983). Revenue forecasting: An administrative perspective. In Rabin, J., and Lynch, T. D. (eds.), *Handbook of Public Budgeting and Financial Management,* Marcel Dekker, New York.

Klay, W. E. (1985). The organizational dimension of budgetary forecasting: Suggestions from revenue forecasting in the states, *International Journal of Public Administration,* 7 (3): 241-65.

March, J. G., and Olsen, J.P.(1989). *Rediscovering Institutions: The Organizational Bias of Politics,* Basic Books, New York.

Musgrave, R. A., and Musgrave, P. B. (1980). *Public Finance in Theory and Practice,* 3d ed., McGraw-Hill, New York.

Osborn, A. (1953). *Applied Imagination: Principle and Procedures of Creative Thinking,* Scribners, New York.

Pierce, L. D. (1971). *The Politics of Fiscal Policy Formation,* Goodyear, Pacific Palisades, California.

Schmid, A. A. (1990). *Benefit-Cost Analysis: A Political Economy Approach,* Westview, Boulder, Colorado.

Simon, H. A. (1976). *Administrative Behavior,* 3d ed., Free Press, New York.

Stiglitz, J. E. (1988). *Economics of the Public Sector,* 2d ed., Norton, New York.

Wanniski, J. (1978). "Taxes, Revenue and the 'Laffer Curve,'" *The Public Interest,* Winter: 3-16.

Wright, G., and Ayton, P. (1987). *Judgmental Forecasting,* Wiley, Chichester, England.

Youngman, H. (1990). "Nem di Gelt" (Take the Money), *New York Times,* July 31: A19.

23 Local Government Financial and Budgetary Analysis

Kenneth D. Sanders and Charlie Tyer

A strong relationship exists between a government's financial condition and the new fiscal year budget. A *financial condition analysis* examines the financing of public services and the jurisdiction's ability to meet its current and future obligations. *Budget analysis* focuses on the recommended services and revenues for a particular fiscal year. These two types of analysis are important sources of information for public officials.

A financial condition analysis should precede any budget analysis since the results may affect budget decisions. If a jurisdiction's financial condition was rated "poor," officials should be alerted to the need for appropriate actions to deal with the situation. Conversely, if the financial condition was rated "good," officials may be inclined to recommend different types and levels of expenditures. The main point is that the budget is only one facet of the overall financial framework of a jurisdiction and should be analyzed in relation to the financial condition of the community. Accordingly, public officials should analyze their jurisdiction's overall financial condition, as well as their annual budgets.

The first section describes a method of determining the financial condition of a jurisdiction, an analysis which encompasses two separate studies. The first concerns the government's financial resources, its ability to finance and deliver services, and its general financial practices. The second study focuses on selected local economic trends to determine the community's economic health. These two facets of the financial condition analysis make up the micro and macro view of the community and should provide officials with a reasonable understanding of their jurisdiction's overall financial condition.

The second section describes how a public official can evaluate the budget document in relation to the previously determined financial condition of the jurisdiction. This particular budget analysis method is based on the utilization of detailed budgetary information to effectively analyze the expenditures and operations of various departmental services. Officials can modify the detail presented throughout this discussion to meet the circumstances and needs of their own jurisdiction.

FINANCIAL CONDITION ANALYSIS

Review of Financial Resources

An effective way to begin a financial condition analysis is with a review of the way in which government services have been financed over the past several years. This will provide information on the jurisdiction's financial resources as well as its ability to provide future services. The primary analysis centers on revenue and expenditure patterns. Although similar to the analysis used for evaluating the budget, the primary difference is the level of detail used. In this particular analysis, more general revenue and expenditure categories are reviewed compared to the specific detail needed in a budget analysis. An example

---

Adapted from *Local Government Financial and Budgetary Analysis*, Financial Management Series, no. 7 (Columbia, S.C.: Bureau of Governmental Research and Service, University of South Carolina, 1982), 31-78. By permission of the Bureau.

of the more general summary is shown in Table 1. The fiscal years are labeled X9, Y0, Y1, Y2, Y3, and Y4 to convey six successive years. Here, Y3 is the year being budgeted, while X9 is the oldest period shown.

Determining Historical Financial Occurrences

The analysis of the information in Table 1 can reveal much about the financial condition and practices in a jurisdiction. As an example, several observations of FY X9 to FY Y3 activities are listed here:

(1) Of the total increase in revenues of $499,000, more than 40 percent came from property taxes ($210,000).

(2) All other revenue sources increased only 23.3 percent. This is an average increase of only 7.5 percent each year. The largest increases in this revenue group were attributed to sanitation rate increases in FY Y1 and the proposed increase in FY Y3, and from transfers from other funds.

(3) Revenues received from outside sources (Beer and Wine Tax, Liquor Tax, Federal Assistance and the Bank Tax) increased only $55,000, or less than 4 percent annually.

(4) The increase in the total operating budget of $597,000 was greater than the growth in total revenues of $499,000.

Table 1: *Historical Revenue and Expenditure Summary, Six Years*

	General Fund (dollars in thousands)						
Revenues	Actual FY X9	Actual FY Y0	Actual FY Y1	Estimated FY Y2	Proposed FY Y3	Projected FY Y4	Percent Change FY X9-Y3
Property Tax	611	680	712	745	821	840	+ 34
Beer and Wine Tax	59	60	72	74	76	77	+ 29
Liquor Tax	54	56	67	70	72	74	+ 34
Licenses and Permits	190	196	209	204	218	220	+ 15
Federal Assistance	206	206	206	215	215	215	+ 4
Fines and Forfeitures	64	65	60	64	67	68	+ 4
Sanitation Fees	86	89	102[a]	106	129[b]	130	+ 49
Bank Tax	16	18	18	20	23	24	+ 43
Interest	30	34	38	43	54	45	+ 80
Recreation and Park Fees	3	3	3	4	5	5	+ 67
Sale of Property	8	2	0	4	53	0	+562
Miscellaneous	0	0	0	0	3	0	—
Transfer from Other Funds	0	0	0	105	87	50	—
Fund Balance	19	31	20	30	22	15	+ 16
TOTAL	1,346	1,440	1,507	1,684	1,845	1,763	+ 37
Expenditures (in thousands)							
Personnel Services	733	769	804	998	1,128	1,157	+ 54
Supplies and Materials	88	96	109	120	132	135	+ 50
Utilities	96	106	119	134	153	158	+ 59
Debt Service	62	65	69	75	98	107	+ 58
Other Operating Expenses	154	163	187	198	219	225	+ 42
TOTAL OPERATING BUDGET	1,133	1,199	1,288	1,525	1,730	1,782	+ 53
Capital Projects	150	169	133	90	75	75	− 50
Capital Equipment	48	54	51	46	40	40	− 17
TOTAL BUDGET	1,331	1,422	1,472	1,661	1,845	1,897[c]	+ 39

Note: The fiscal years are labeled X9, Y0, Y1, Y2, Y3, and Y4 to convey six successive years. Y3 is the year being budgeted; X9 is the oldest period included in this analysis.

[a] Includes rate increase of 10 percent. [b] Includes rate increase of 20 percent. [c] FY Y4 shows a projected deficit of $122,000.

(5) The dollar level of Capital Improvement Projects and Capital Equipment purchases declined each year, except in FY Y0.

(6) Personnel Services costs increased 54 percent or $395,000. This represents 66 percent of the total increase in the operating budget ($597,000) for this period.

Table 2 presents a sample summary that can be used to further understand the increase in personnel service costs. Observations concerning the information in the table are presented as follows:

(1) While the number of full-time regular city positions increased by 15 from FY X9 to FY Y3, the most significant growth in these positions (19) occurred between FY Y1 and FY Y3.

(2) The number of part-time positions increased by 2 from FY X9 to FY Y3.

(3) Overall, a total of 20 additional positions were funded by city revenue sources during this period.

(4) In FY Y2, the city funded 6 previously supported federal aid positions when that funding was eliminated.

(5) In FY Y2, 4 full-time positions were added to staff a new recreational facility.

(6) A total of 5 additional police officer positions were funded in FY Y2 and FY Y3. Other position changes are listed at the bottom of Table 2.

(7) Salary increases for all employees occurred in FY Y0 (6%) and in FY Y2 (5%).

(8) Insurance premiums increased in FY Y1 and FY Y2 by 12 percent and 8 percent respectively.

(9) Retirement contributions made by the city increased in FY Y2 by 8 percent.

Analyzing Historical Financial Occurrences

A public official may wonder how this information can be used to determine the financial condition of the jurisdiction. The following section discusses many of these observations in relation to several financial premises considered to be both practical and sound. The most important aspect of the analysis includes the understanding of how the government functioned during the period reviewed and then to relate these activities to sound financial practices. It should be

Table 2: *Historical Personnel Summary*

Authorized Positions	General Fund					
	FY X9	FY Y0	FY Y1	FY Y2	Proposed FY Y3	Estimated FY Y4
Full-Time Regular City	78	76	74	86[a]	93[b]	93
Part-Time	4	4	4	3	6	4
Seasonal and Temporary	8	8	8	9	11	11
TOTAL CITY POSITIONS	90	88	86	98	110	108
Federally Funded	11	9	15	6	4	4
Personnel Costs—City Funded Only (dollars in thousands)						
Salaries	571	611	641	799	909	934
Insurances	63	61	68	86	95	97
Retirement Contributions	84	81	80	102	112	114
Other Personnel Costs	15	14	15	11	12	12
TOTAL	733	767	804	998	1,128	1,157

[a] Six federally funded positions picked up with city funds, new personnel added to fund a new recreation facility (4), plus 2 police officers added.

[b] Increase in Police (3), Fire Dispatch (1), Administration (2), and Maintenance (1).

Salary increases: FY Y0 by 6 percent and in FY Y2 by 5 percent. Insurance increases: FY Y1 by 12 percent and in FY Y2 by 8 percent. Retirement increases: FY Y2 by 8 percent.

noted that the occurrences listed on the prior pages do not include all possible observations that could be drawn from a financial condition analysis.

1. *Recurring and Nonrecurring Revenues.* One indication of how well services have been financed is revealed by the government's use of recurring and nonrecurring revenue. Sound financial policy recommends the use of recurring revenue sources for recurring expenditures. Recurring expenditures are considered to be those expenditures fundamental to the services performed from year to year. Of course, reductions in basic services would also reduce the amount of recurring expenditures. Recurring revenues are funds collected annually from what are considered to be stable and reliable sources of income. These revenue sources are derived from a legal basis, such as a local ordinance, state policy, or federal aid.

The appropriation of nonrecurring revenue to pay recurring operating expenses can have significant financial ramifications for a government. By funding normal recurring operating costs, such as personnel, utilities, and supplies with nonrecurring revenue sources, a jurisdiction may find itself in the difficult position of having to replace these funds by increasing other revenue collections or reducing expenditures if nonrecurring funds become unavailable. The use of nonrecurring revenues to fund recurring expenditures can therefore jeopardize sound financial management practices. Very often, a difficult political decision to reduce expenditures and services is avoided by using nonrecurring funds. Unfortunately, this is often an expedient remedy for a difficult financial situation. The limited use of nonrecurring funds will not necessarily cause financial problems in any given year, but dependence on such revenue sources to fund increases in recurring expenditures is normally not recommended.

As indicated in Table 1, the main sources of nonrecurring revenues for FY Y3 are transfers from other funds ($87,000), sale of property ($53,000), and fund balance ($22,000). A portion of interest earnings should also be considered as nonrecurring revenue, especially during periods of fluctuating interest rates. Obviously, if the recurring interest figure is based on interest rates of 10 percent or 9 percent, there would be less interest earned if the rates were to fall to 6 percent or 7 percent. In this example, approximately $11,000 of interest revenue is estimated to be nonrecurring in FY Y3. Therefore the total amount of nonrecurring revenue in FY Y3 is estimated at $176,000. This represents nearly 10 percent of the total budget.

Table 3 details the amount of recurring and nonrecurring revenue from FY X9 to FY Y4. Since the $176,000 is budgeted to pay for operations and necessary levels of capital expenditures in FY Y3, a decline in this amount could cause serious problems in the future. In this example, the amount of nonrecurring revenue projected in FY Y4 is only $65,000, or $111,000 less than in FY Y3. As the table indicates, this is the primary reason for the projected shortfall of $122,000 in FY Y4. To eliminate this shortfall, it may be necessary to reduce services or increase other revenue rates.

To reduce the risk of encouraging this type of situation, it is usually recommended that nonrecurring revenues be budgeted for one-time services or purchases. Such services might include a contract to paint a facility, remodel an office, or purchase equipment or furniture with a relatively long-term expected life. By following this policy, the government becomes less vulnerable to revenues that may not be available in the future. While there are few strict guidelines regarding the percentage of nonrecurring funds that may be used to fund recurring expenditures, the $176,000 total in FY Y3 represents a potentially significant problem. Prior to budgeting these funds, each jurisdiction should determine the difficulty and consequences of replacing nonrecurring funds if they suddenly became unavailable. Simple tables, such as provided in Table 3, can be most helpful in monitoring the dependence of an entity upon various sources of funds.

2. *Review of Additional Revenue Sources.* As noted in Table 1, over 42 percent of the increase in total revenue from FY X9 to FY Y3 ($499,000) was derived from a single source, property taxes ($210,000). The other major sources of additional revenue came from sanitation rate increases and from a nonrecurring transfer from other funds. Of the total increase of $350,000 in recurring revenue from FY X9 to FY Y3, property tax collections accounted for $210,000 or 62 percent, while sanitation fees accounted for $43,000 or 12 percent. Together these two sources contributed 74 percent of the overall increase in recurring revenue during this period. Exhibit 1 summarizes the major revenue increases for each fiscal year.

Table 3: *Recurring and Nonrecurring Revenue, Six Successive Years*

Revenue	FY X9	FY Y0	FY Y1	FY Y2	Proposed FY Y3	Projected* FY Y4
			(dollars in thousands)			
Recurring	$1,319	$1,407	$1,487	$1,545	$1,669	$1,699
Nonrecurring	$ 27	$ 33	$ 20	$ 139	$ 176	$ 65

*A deficit is projected in FY Y4 of $122,100.

The dependence on a few revenue sources for generating additional funds has been prevalent in many jurisdictions. Over the years, governments have depended primarily on property tax growth to balance their budgets. However, a disproportionate dependence upon property tax increases may lead to financial problems, particularly if a community has a relatively stable level of property development and limited growth in property values. In addition, since public pressure to reduce or limit property tax growth continues, dependence upon this revenue to generate further increases can present an even more difficult financial dilemma. The same situation applies to continuous rate increases for sanitation services, business licenses, and other fees. Eventually, increases in these fees cannot be relied upon to raise additional revenue. In some cases, adding a new revenue source may be an acceptable alternative to service reductions in the face of increasing service demands. In some communities, the trend of generating more revenue rather than limiting expenditures and service growth continues to occur. As Table 1 indicates, this situation can result in an unstable and vulnerable financial position if expenditure growth is permitted to increase faster than available revenues.

3. *Personnel Services History.* At this point in the analysis of a jurisdiction's resources, the reader may be aware that some basic financial problems exist in this community. In particular, nonrecurring revenues are being used to pay for recurring expenditures, and a dependency upon specific revenue sources has developed. Since the cost of personnel accounts for the largest percentage of most government budgets, an analysis of personnel staffing patterns is particularly important in understanding overall expenditure patterns. As Table 2 indicates, a total increase of 19 regular full-time positions, 2 part-time, and 3 temporary positions occurred between FY Y1 and FY Y3. Four of these positions were authorized to staff a new recreation facility, 6 were funded to replace federally funded positions, and 9 were authorized to increase various services to the public. Without providing the specific detail for each personnel change at this time, the apparent trend in personnel growth and its associated cost were substantially greater than the revenue growth to pay for these positions. In fact, at an average cost of $11,000 for each of the 19 full-time positions, the total cost of $209,000 was greater than the total amount of recurring revenue ($182,000) generated from FY Y1 to FY Y3. This type of situation should provide a clue that an imbalance exists and that further evaluation and action should be undertaken to bring operating costs more in line with available revenue. A more detailed discussion on the effect of this personnel

Exhibit 1: *Where Did Sources of the Revenue Increases Come From?**

FY X9 to FY Y0	($ 88,000)
Property Tax	$ 69,000
Licenses	$ 6,000
FY Y0 to FY Y1	($ 80,000)
Property Tax	$ 32,000
State Taxes	$ 23,000
Sanitation	$ 13,000
FY Y1 to FY Y2	($ 58,000)
Property Tax	$ 33,000
Federal Revenue Sharing	$ 9,000
FY Y2 to FY Y3	($124,000)
Property Tax	$ 76,000
Sanitation	$ 23,000
Licenses	$ 14,000

* There has been a property tax increase and sanitation rate increase between FY X9 and FY Y3. Most of the other revenues have grown at a considerably slower rate.

growth is contained in the discussion of budget analysis.

Another significant point related to personnel service costs concerns the use of federally funded employees. The use of federally funded positions has created financial problems for many jurisdictions over the past several years. For example, many local governments that hired grant-supported employees for important operating positions were forced to either terminate or fund these employees from regular local funding sources to retain these positions when federal funding was reduced. Instead of reducing or eliminating services, many jurisdictions decided to maintain these positions with own-source funds. Public officials should be particularly aware of how each federally funded position is utilized since these funds may be a nonrecurring source of revenue. Exhibit 2 is an example of a personnel summary that can be used to denote specific positions funded by federal sources.

4. *Shifting Resources to Personnel and Other Operating Expenses.* According to another prior observation, the growth of personnel and other operating expenditures between 19X9 and 19Y3 ($597,000) was greater than the growth in *all* revenue sources ($499,000) for the same period. The increase is even larger when compared to recurring revenue sources alone ($597,000 to $350,000).

Since revenues increased at a slower rate than the operating budget, the money to fund this growth had to come from other sources. Instead of increasing revenues at the same rate or reducing the growth in personnel and other operating expenditures, additional funds were made available from nonrecurring sources and by shifting the jurisdiction's expenditure patterns. The shift in expenditures occurred by reducing the funding for capital improvement projects (CIPs) to pay for part of the increases in personnel and other operating expenditures. In effect, this jurisdiction decided to neglect the funding of long-term capital assets in favor of increasing short-term operating needs.

The most obvious problem with this decision is the significantly low level to which the support for capital improvement projects (e.g., tennis courts, buildings, and roads) and necessary capital equipment was allowed to reach. Since capital assets reflect growth and economic viability, the question of what happens to a community unable to build a tennis court, maintain a playground, or purchase new

Exhibit 2: *Summary of Positions Using FY Y3 Federal Funds*

Total Personnel Budget	$44,385
Finance—	
Administer Grant Funds	
1 – Administrative Analyst	$12,477
Fire Department—	
Grant for Prevention of Arson	
1 – Research Analyst II	$13,869
2 – Accounting Clerks	$18,039
	$31,908

vehicles for its police or fire departments becomes extremely important. The need for reasonable levels of capital expenditures is considered necessary for a government to function effectively.

5. *Transferring Funds to the General Fund.* Another financial practice that some governments utilize to generate more revenue is the transfer of money from other funds to the General Fund. This is accomplished by setting high rates for such services as water and sewer to obtain a positive fund balance that is then transferred to the General Fund.

Some experts contend that this method of generating additional revenue is a poor financial practice because each fund should be self-balancing, based upon its ability to charge specific fees in order to meet its own expenditure needs. The intentional generation of surplus funds may indicate that user charges are unnecessarily high. Instead of raising the necessary revenue in the General Fund or reducing General Fund expenditures, revenue has been generated from outside the General Fund to pay for General Fund operations. This financial practice tends to ignore the real problems in the General Fund. An additional problem with this type of situation may occur if these surplus funds are not always available. If they suddenly become unavailable, the jurisdiction is confronted with the problem of using nonrecurring revenue for recurring expenditures.

The transfer of funds from the Insurance Reserve Fund into other funds has become prevalent in some cities. These funds are usually accumulated intentionally over a period of years to pay for current and future claims against the jurisdiction. Most insurance reserve funds operate on the principle of increasing their surplus account to adequately insure the jurisdiction against large unexpected future claims. This is particularly true for cities that are partially or fully self-insured against certain losses. Due to the financial problems many of these cities are facing, officials have "tapped" these resources to meet higher expenditure demands. The use of these funds is not considered sound policy. It reduces the current burden only by transferring the burden to the future and producing what are known as unfunded liabilities.

In addition to the financial practices already discussed, officials should also be aware of several other possible financial problems. Although the following conditions were not indicated in Tables 1 and 2, it is important to determine if they exist in individual jurisdictions.

6. *Increasing Debt.* Most local governments are limited in the amount of debt they can assume. The debt limit in one state is 8 percent of assessed property values for general obligation bonds, although there are exceptions to the limit. An increase in debt payment, however, may indicate a higher percentage of funds earmarked for debt repayment. A problem can develop as increasingly high debt repayment levels affect the availability of funds to pay for other services. In this situation, the jurisdiction may be spending an increasing percentage of its funds for future services. Increasing debt payments can become a fixed or mandatory expenditure and can reduce a jurisdiction's financial flexibility and independence. A general guideline which may be employed to determine whether a jurisdiction has a potential debt problem is represented by the formula presented below. If debt repayment appropriated in the General Fund divided by total General Fund revenues is

10 to 12 percent, the maximum desirable limit may have been reached;

6 to 8 percent, acceptable limits exist;

4 to 6 percent, good; and

under 4 percent, possible underutilization of debt exists.

In the earlier example provided in Tables 1 and 3, FY Y3 recurring revenue in our mythical entity equals $1,669,000 and debt repayment is $98,000. Using the above formula,

$$\frac{98,000}{1,669,000} = .059 = 5.9\%.$$

This is considered good.

The recent abuses of debt by many cities conjure up a negative image of debt. However, the proper use of debt can provide a community with long-term positive benefits. Debt financing is necessary to construct schools, buildings, and other facilities since the total amount of funds necessary for such important projects is rarely ever available. Debt is an important financial tool that should be incorporated into the overall financial structure as long as it does not become a solution to difficult short-term financial problems. Borrowing funds to repay previously borrowed funds or extending debt for a longer period than an asset's estimated life are situations in which the use of debt is not recommended. The latter occurs, for example, particularly when debt is used to purchase vehicles with a repayment schedule of 10 years, considerably longer than the useful life of most vehicles.

7. *Growth in Mandatory Expenditures.* Although related to an increasing debt, officials should be aware of increases in the growth of mandatory, contracted, and legislative mandated expenditures. These types of expenditures may include funds for outside organizations (health organizations, the arts council, etc.), matching funds for grants or other projects, leases and long-term commitments for services, and expenditures mandated by the state or federal government. An increase in these types of expenditures can also reduce the total amount of funds available for other services, thereby limiting the flexibility and independence of the jurisdiction.

8. *Increasing Use of Intergovernmental Revenues.* Intergovernmental revenues are funds received from other governments. An overdependence on these revenues, especially if they are used for recurring type expenditures, can cause financial problems for a jurisdiction. A noteworthy example of this type of situation was indicated in Tables 1 and 2, in which federal funds were used to pay for personnel in important service positions. When this funding was eliminated, the jurisdiction was compelled to fund these positions because of their importance in continuing current service levels. A similar situation could occur if a jurisdiction were to become overdependent on other intergovernmental aid.

9. *Deferring Pension Liabilities.* Each local government that establishes a pension fund for its employees creates a legal commitment to pay pension benefits some time in the future.

The two primary methods of paying for pension liabilities are (1) establishing a special pension fund that funds benefits as they are accrued and (2) paying benefits as they occur. Some local governments prefer to pay out benefits as they occur from their current budgets. By deferring the funding of these benefits until they occur, larger fixed payments are needed as the amount of money deferred increases. The problem becomes even more acute when revenue growth is limited while the amount of benefit payments increases dramatically. Government officials should review the adequacy of any pension fund annually, including a special analysis of the total amount of unfunded liability.

The examples used thus far in a jurisdiction's financial condition analysis consist of a historical review of how funds have been spent, how services were financed, and the ability of the jurisdiction to provide services in the future. At this point, each official should have a reasonable understanding of his or her government's financial resources and practices. The next section discusses the second part of the financial condition analysis, the review of the underlying economic conditions within the community. The results of both studies should be able to provide a clear notion of the jurisdiction's overall financial health.

Review of Economic Conditions and Indicators

The second part of the financial condition analysis consists of reviewing several of the most important economic indicators that pertain to the individual community. These general economic trends provide an indication of the local economy's current health while also establishing a basis for projecting future economic conditions. Since a community's economic condition directly affects its ability to generate current and future revenue, it is important to relate the economy of a jurisdiction with its financial outlook. For example, a declining economy usually indicates the presence of fewer dollars, less development, and lower tax revenues. On the other hand, a growing and viable economy is more likely to generate increased dollars, higher levels of development and, ultimately, additional revenue for the government. Although the economic indicators presented in this section comprise only a partial listing, their review should provide officials with a reasonable representation of the jurisdiction's economic situation. The indicators discussed here include: population, property value, building permits, new commercial units, new residential units, retail sales, and personal income. The information needed to analyze each indicator can be obtained from local government records, planning commissions, councils of governments (COG's), local chambers of commerce, and state agencies.

Population estimates provide an indication of whether the economic base is growing. An increasing population usually signifies a growing and expanding economy, while a declining population trend may signal a reduction in available economic opportunities. The importance of this indicator is based on the assumption that a growing economic base signifies higher levels of employment and, concurrently, the generation of additional taxes and other revenue.

Total property valuation, if analyzed independently, may not reflect a real increase in property development or an increase in economic activity. Rather, increases in property valuations may be due in part to annual reassessment efforts by the community. A more accurate gauge would be obtained from specific valuation figures for new or additional construction. This information is usually available from the property assessment office.

The *number of building permits* is associated with the construction of residential housing, commercial development, and modifications to existing structures. An increase in building permits usually reflects new development, higher property valuations, and additional property tax revenue.

New commercial units are defined as additional retail storefronts, manufacturing plants or wholesale firms that increase the total number of existing units in the economic base. Included in these figures are new establishments that have either renovated or constructed a new business on previously vacant property. (A new business that merely replaces an existing business through a change in ownership may not necessarily add to the community's overall commercial activity since it does not increase the total number of commercial establishments in the community. This is especially true if the size of the establishment remains the same.) The importance of this indicator is based on the assumption that additional businesses are established in response to new demands of a growing community, and that their existence will generate more funds throughout the economic base.

The *construction of residential homes and apartments* indicates a demand for new housing. An upward trend is a positive sign that the local economy is active and viable. New residential construction should also be correlated with the number of building permits issued. This important economic indicator is also based on the assumption that housing construction expands the economic base of the community and is positively correlated with the tax base.

Retail sales reflect the volume of basic economic activity in a community. As increases occur in the number of commercial businesses, housing units, and population, the community's overall retail sales should also increase. The trend of retail sales reflects the vitality of the local economy and, therefore, the government's ability to generate revenue.

Personal income figures are correlated with many of the preceding economic indicators. As personal income rises, growth in retail sales and housing purchases will usually also increase. Conversely, a decline in personal income can be a sign that government revenue collections may decrease, affecting construction sales and other economic activity.

In order to develop a more useful economic scenario for a community, it is recommended that each jurisdiction prepare economic projections for several future years. By expanding the projection of these indicators and combining this information with other economic factors, a clearer pattern of potential economic activity may be available for more effective long-term financial planning.

Evaluating the Community

To determine the overall financial condition of a community, the results from the government's financial resource study and the economic indicator study should be related. In this way, public officials can obtain a comprehensive perspective on the financial aspects of their community.

The community presented for analysis in this discussion has had a steady but slowly growing economy. Officials can assume that revenues will continue to grow slowly and that economic development will remain generally constant. The economic outlook for FY Y3 is assumed to improve, but the amount of improvement projected is only minimal. The jurisdiction's financial problems will not be solved by large increases in additional revenue generated by the community's fundamental economic activity but by better planning and the proper utilization of its resources. This community has allowed its operating budget to increase at a faster rate than its revenue growth. Consequently, over the next several years, expenditures will have to be reduced to meet the expected slower growth of revenues. If the economic analysis reflected a declining trend, the overall financial condition of this community would be even more problematic. In such a case, more drastic reductions of expenditure services would be necessary to offset the anticipated slower revenue collections. If the economic growth of the jurisdiction were projected to increase significantly because of an influx of new businesses, the jurisdiction's financial condition might be considerably different. For example, if property tax revenues were expected to increase $200,000 from new businesses, many of the current financial problems could be solved in FY Y4 without drastic reductions. To maintain financial viability after that time, the community would have to adhere to the sound financial policies recommended.

The results of a community's financial condition analysis provide the framework for subsequent budgetary decisions. In this example, officials should concentrate their budget analysis on ways of reducing operating expenditures, as well as on methods of reversing the poor financial practices that have occurred over the past fiscal years. Several possible recommendations that can be used as a basis for evaluating the budget in relation to the results of the financial condition analysis are summarized here:

1. Limit the use of nonrecurring revenues for recurring expenditures.
2. Reduce recurring expenditures, particularly personnel and other operating items by effectively analyzing the services planned in the budget document.
3. Explore the possibilities of creating additional or new sources of revenue. This may include a review of the existing fee structures or the implementation of user fees for services currently provided free.
4. Reestablish a commitment to fund Capital Improvement Projects and capital equipment.
5. Establish specific policies and guidelines regarding the type and level of service desired.

6. Ensure that adequate control of federally funded personnel exists.
7. Review current and proposed commitments that fund long-term contracts or services. A reduction would increase the jurisdiction's financial flexibility.

BUDGET ANALYSIS

The ability to evaluate a budget document and then to make sound budgetary decisions is an essential part of a public official's responsibility. Budgetary decisions should reflect the financial condition of the government, the economic health of the community, and the service needs of the citizens. This section describes a comprehensive method which can be employed in evaluating the budget for effective decision making.

The initial phase of evaluating the budget involves a review of each revenue estimate. Although the examples used here pertain to the General Fund, the analysis for other funds is similar. Each official, regardless of his or her budgetary experience, should be capable of understanding revenue projections. In most cases, common sense is the most important prerequisite.

The amount of revenue projected is extremely important since it will affect the total expenditure level that can be budgeted. Revenues that are overestimated because of optimistic assumptions can cause expenditure reductions during the fiscal year to cover anticipated shortfalls. Conversely, if revenues are underestimated, important expenditure items may be excluded at the time the budget is adopted. This can cause unnecessary reductions in personnel, operating expenses, and capital purchases. It is precisely for these reasons that each revenue estimate should be reviewed according to the underlying assumptions used in its forecast.

Beware of the Automatic Revenue Increase

The amount of revenue budgeted is often based on an automatic increase each fiscal year. These increases are usually correlated with the rate of inflation. However, this projection technique can create overly optimistic estimates since all revenue is not related to inflation. The example in Table 4 illustrates this point.

Table 4: *Automatic Revenue Increase Summary*

Revenue Source	Actual FY Y1	Estimated FY Y2	Proposed Budget FY Y3
Building Permit Fees	$ 48,420	$ 41,690	$ 54,500
License Fees	$130,335	$136,850	$137,000
Plumbing Permit Fees	$ 10,260	$ 9,450	$ 9,500

Table 4 represents the collection pattern of three revenue sources: building permit fees, license fees, and plumbing permit fees for three fiscal years. Notice that these revenues have not increased at the same rate. Building permit fees and plumbing fees actually decreased in FY Y2. Many government revenues are strongly affected by a variety of economic and financial considerations other than inflation. As a result, each revenue source should be projected according to the individual factors that affect its growth, decline, or status quo. The method used to estimate each revenue amount should be reviewed in terms of its validity and reasonableness. Public officials do not have to understand sophisticated forecasting techniques, such as regression analysis or statistical modeling, to determine whether revenue projections are based upon plausible assumptions and information. Table 5 is an example of a typical revenue summary included in the budget document for a General Fund. Several of these revenues are described below.

Analyzing Revenue Sources

Property Tax

Property tax, also known as ad valorem tax, is usually the largest revenue source for a local government. The amount of property tax anticipated is determined by the jurisdiction's tax rate (millage rate) and the total assessed value of its property. In most local governments, a small percentage of the expected total collection is subtracted in anticipation of taxes that will be delinquent. While this percentage may vary for each jurisdiction, it is usually between 1 and 5 percent.

To illustrate how property tax is computed, assume that a jurisdiction's assessed valuation is $6,512,345, and it allows for 3 percent noncollectible tax payments. The total amount of property tax anticipated with a 123 millage rate is $776,988. This is computed as follows:

Assessed value × millage* = tax revenue

$6,512,345 × .123 = $801,018

$ 801,018 × .03 = $24,030

$ 801,018 − $24,030 = $776,988

---

* one mill = $ .001

Since property taxes are usually the largest source of revenue, and the most politically sensitive, each public official should be familiar with the property assessment process and the determination of the millage rate. In many cases, a budget is balanced by estimating all other revenues prior to determining the amount of property taxes needed. Then the millage rate is adjusted to produce the needed amount of revenue to match total expenditures.

Table 5: *Typical Revenue Summary of a Budget Document*

	General Fund (dollars)			
Taxes	Actual FY Y0	Actual FY Y1	Estimated FY Y2	Proposed FY Y3
Property Tax	638,150	671,446	711,000	776,988
Delinquent Property Tax	41,627	40,831	33,688	44,500
	679,777	712,277	744,688	821,488
Licenses and Permits				
Business Licenses	127,404	130,335	136,850	137,000
Building Permits	43,205	48,420	41,690	54,500
Electric Permits	10,065	13,404	9,180	9,700
Plumbing Permits	8,954	10,260	9,450	9,500
Misc. Permits	6,130	7,061	7,144	7,500
	195,758	209,480	204,314	218,200
Other Governments				
Beer and Wine	60,133	72,244	74,400	76,000
Liquor Tax	56,005	67,988	70,122	72,000
Bank Tax	18,150	18,265	20,650	23,000
	134,288	158,497	165,172	171,000
Charges for Services				
Park Admissions	775	788	1,153	1,300
Tennis Fees	660	685	780	900
Adult Sport Leagues	1,598	1,627	2,080	2,758
Sanitation – Residential	72,340	80,606	82,404	99,500
Sanitation – Commercial	16,987	21,533	23,980	29,550
	92,360	105,239	110,397	134,008
Other				
Fines and Forfeitures	65,370	60,689	64,060	66,500
Transfer from State/Federal Aid	206,512	206,512	215,300	215,300
Transfer from Other Funds	0	0	105,000	87,000
Sale of City Property	2,000	0	3,958	52,850
Interest Earned	34,897	38,744	43,000	54,000
Miscellaneous	0	0	2,975	0
Fund Balance	31,220	20,400	30,000	22,000
	339,999	326,345	464,293	497,650
TOTAL	$1,442,182	$1,511,838	$1,688,864	$1,842,346

Although the millage rate may be reduced in any budget year, a tax increase may still occur if the same taxable property is reassessed at higher values. This situation is highlighted here:

FY Y3 proposed millage rate = 123 mills

FY Y3 taxable assessed property valuation = $6,512,345

Property tax budget: $6,512,345 × .123 = $801,018

The FY Y4 estimate for the same community is as follows:

FY Y4 estimated millage rate = 108 mills

FY Y4 estimated assessed property valuation = $7,590,683

Property tax budget: $7,590,683 × .108 = $819,794

Although the millage rate was actually reduced from 123 mills to 108 mills, the increase in assessed property valuation resulted in higher property tax revenue.

Licenses and Permits

Business license estimates can usually be accurately projected because a current listing of all business licenses is usually maintained by officials. The total license collections are estimated from the information retained on each business establishment. In some states, business license fees are based on a formula that includes gross sales. Since this revenue source is related to the economic conditions of the community, some judgment may be necessary in estimating the amount of new license fees that will be collected.

Building and construction permit revenues are affected by the economic condition of the housing and construction industry. High mortgage rates and lower demand for new homes can reduce the number of permits for new construction. The fee for a specific construction permit is based on one or more parameters, such as the number of square feet, the number of feet of piping or wiring, etc. These sources of revenue are considered to be reliable, but traditionally fluctuate according to local and national economic conditions.

Charges for Services or Fees

Each revenue in this category should be reviewed according to its individual characteristics. The most significant revenue included in this group is derived from residential sanitation fees. The FY Y3 estimate of $99,500 in Table 5 is based on a 10 percent rate increase for residential collection. Each official should be aware of any planned rate increases prior to the budget document being submitted for review. This will allow adequate time to analyze the proposed changes. Typically, most local governments require separate ordinances to implement revenue changes. In some cases, changes such as recreation charges, permits, fines, and licenses are established and changed by administrative decree.

Other Revenue

Fines and forfeitures are collected primarily from moving vehicle violations, and usually represent a consistent but slow-growing source of funds. Although there seems to be a fundamental relationship between the amount of miles driven per vehicle and the number of violations issued, a slight decline in recent years in the number of miles driven has had little effect on the amount of revenue collected.

Although state or federal grant funds are accounted for in a separate fund, they are usually transferred to the General Fund to pay for operating or capital items. The total budget estimate for this should be based upon firm information, but they will be vulnerable to changes in fiscal policy at those levels. This situation should be monitored carefully over time.

In many governments, the estimated year-end fund balance from the current fiscal year is budgeted in the new fiscal year. These amounts should be reviewed carefully since surplus funds are sometimes overlooked during the budget process.

Another source of money may be a transfer from other funds on a one-time basis. A fund that has a positive fund balance, for instance, may transfer some or all of its balance to another fund, i.e., a transfer from a sewer fund to the General Fund. These funds should be considered as a nonrecurring revenue since their continued availability is highly unlikely.

Analyzing Expenditures

Expenditures are the difficult part of the budget to analyze and evaluate. Expenditure information is far more voluminous and complex than the revenue estimates since there are a greater number of specific expenditure categories. The two types of expenditure analyses that will be discussed in this section are incremental budget analysis and service unit analysis. Prior to any detailed analysis, officials should make a preliminary review of the budget.

Preliminary Review of the Budget

Prior to performing any detailed analysis, officials should have a general understanding of the expenditure budget. A considerable amount of information should already have been gathered from the government resources study conducted previously. Additional information is contained in the budget message and other expenditure summaries. These summaries are often included in the budget document. Table 6 is an example of a departmental expenditure summary covering a three-year period. It indicates expenditure changes, particularly from the current fiscal year (FY Y2) to the proposed budget (FY Y3). Departments that have significant spending changes can be easily identified. This information provides a general view of the total budget size and indicates where funding is being planned.

In order to further understand the proposed personnel changes from year to year, it is recommended that a summary be developed that specifies how personnel costs have changed. This summary should include both financial changes and concise reasons for these changes.

By obtaining this type of general budgetary information, each official's understanding of personnel costs can be increased prior to the analysis of individual services. Similar to previous summaries, it provides a "feel" for the priorities of the budget.

Following are several other types of summaries that can provide additional general information:

- Summary by individual object code or object code grouping.
- Summary of significant operational changes, such as new services, reduced or eliminated services, rate changes or technological changes, and new methods of delivery services.
- Summary of federal programs.
- Summary of total debt service.
- Summary of payments to all outside agencies.

Incremental Budget Analysis

Incremental budget analysis is based on a historical review of expenditure patterns or trends. Since most

Table 6: *Expenditure Summary*

Department	General Fund (dollars in thousands)			
	Actual FY Y0	Actual FY Y1	Estimated FY Y2	Proposed FY Y3
Administrator's Office	43	45	48	51
Council's Office	27	30	33	36
Legal	20	22	24	27
Personnel	16	18	20	34
Finance	103	110	122	166
Police	397	418	460	508
Fire	360	378	424	440
Parks and Recreation	124	136	199	209
Public Works	203	196	180	206
Sanitation	129	139	151	168
TOTAL	$1,422	$1,472	$1,661	$1,845

budgets are presented in a line-item format, most officials ordinarily review the historical trend of each object code, object code grouping, or department total to determine whether the proposed budget is consistent with previous spending patterns. A simple incremental budget analysis for several line-items is shown in Table 7.

The incremental approach requires a review of each object code to determine whether the changes from year to year are consistent and reasonable. Since the increases proposed in FY Y3 for each line-item seem small and reasonable compared to both the original FY Y2 budget and the estimated FY Y2 actual expenditures, most public officials will be satisfied with these budget amounts. Additional information is usually requested only when a significant change in the proposed budget (FY Y3) is proposed.

The primary drawback of utilizing the incremental analysis technique is the underlying assumption that the type and level of a past expenditure has been acceptable and that future provision of the same level of service will incur only slightly higher costs. This type of analysis provides little information concerning planned expenditures, the need for certain services or the efficiency of the services planned. As a result, incremental analysis has some limitations and is not recommended for officials interested in a

Table 7: *Line-Item Summary*

Object Code	FY Y1 Actual	FY Y2 Budget	FY Y2 Estimated Expenditure	FY Y3 Proposed
Materials	$2,865	$2,944	$2,923	$3,018
Small tools	$ 142	$ 130	$ 120	$ 125
Utilities	$6,133	$6,388	$6,496	$6,847

more informative and comprehensive approach to budget analysis.

One of the benefits associated with the use of incremental analysis is its ability to provide a preliminary view of financial information. An incremental analysis can provide general information about spending patterns by focusing on unusual changes and trends in object codes or overall department totals. In this way, it often identifies expenditure areas which are likely to be analyzed in more detail. Most of the analyses conducted in the earlier financial condition section utilized this technique to determine important general information on the manner in which resources were employed and changes in expenditure patterns. Since the basic goal of the financial condition analysis is to determine a *general* overview of one's financial condition, the incremental technique of analysis is sufficient.

Service Unit Analysis

The service unit analysis requires detailed information concerning each specific service being provided, including the level of that service, how the service is delivered, and the specific expenditures necessary to provide the service. This analysis relies upon relevant operational and budgetary information for more effective decision making. It can be performed either during the budget preparation process (i.e., administrator's budget hearings) or when the budget is submitted for council approval. In the latter case, councilmembers may have to request any details or summaries of the budget document that are not included in the budget ordinance.

The fundamental philosophy of a service unit analysis is based on the belief that officials should determine the policies and guidelines that govern the utilization of public funds. Recently, the service unit analysis concept has become more prevalent due to the difficult financial problems faced by many jurisdictions. To confront growing fiscal pressures, many officials have begun to review the details of actual departmental operations and expenditures as a method of rationally reducing their budgets. The service unit analysis is considered to be a more systematic and objective approach to reducing expenditures compared with arbitrarily cutting department budgets across the board or using budget ceilings independent of analyzing expenditure needs.

Service Unit Format

As previously mentioned, a service unit analysis is significantly more comprehensive than an incremental analysis. Exhibit 3 is an example of one format used for a service unit analysis. A specific service unit format is prepared for each major service within each department and should provide a description of the service rendered, how the service is performed, and the related expenditure requests. Exhibit 4 provides the accompanying detail to Exhibit 3 and presents an example for several object codes. If possible, one should request this type of information for each object code.

There are several reasons for requiring a detailed list of proposed expenditures. Initially, each expenditure can be analyzed in relation to the service performed. This is accomplished by determining why the expenditure is necessary. Since a detailed list exposes each planned expenditure, those items that previously may have escaped detection and subsequently have been built into succeeding budget totals can now be identified and reduced. This method can also allow an official to identify possible expenditure abuses. For example, if telephone costs are separated into the categories shown in Exhibit 4, specifying the budgeted amount for long distance calls and basic telephone service, this information allows officials to question both the amount and the need for each telephone charge, rather than making a decision on the merits of the lump sum amount. Such a detailed analysis can be utilized for any object code being reviewed. Finally, requiring each department to analyze its own budget needs through an evaluation of its own operations can be very helpful.

The purpose of this approach to financial analysis is not to focus on each pencil, pad, or nail. Rather, it is designed to obtain a reasonable level of detail

Exhibit 3: *Service Unit Format*

SERVICE UNIT Police Patrol: Expended	DEPARTMENT Police

The city is currently divided into 2 police districts. Police patrol is provided 24 hours per day, 7 days per week.

Within each district, there are 2 squads. Each squad is made up of 4 patrol officers and 1 sergeant for a total of 10 uniformed officers per district or 20 uniformed officers for the entire patrol service.

The proposed budget includes an increase of 3 additional police to obtain the total of 20 officers mentioned above. These officers would be used primarily to increase patrol activities in the southern part of the city. There has been an increasing problem of assaults and robberies in this area over the past 6 months.

Each squad is assigned 3 vehicles and an additional 2 floaters to perform its patrol duties. The cars are used regularly throughout each day. Two new vehicles have been planned in the budget to replace older vehicles.

The sergeants receive their shift assignments from the captain each 90-day period.

Object Code	Object Name	Estimated Expenditure FY Y2	Proposed Expenditure FY Y3
10	Salaries	$238,200	$280,155
11	Overtime	1,200	500
12	Terminal Leave	1,970	2,000
14	Retirement Contributions	29,500	32,787
15	Life Insurance	3,015	3,380
16	Health Insurance	15,490	17,477
17	Worker's Compensation	4,305	4,560
18	Other Personnel Items	1,100	1,100
	TOTAL	$294,583	$341,959
30	Office Supplies	295	315
31	Other Supplies	2,297	2,365
32	Materials	560	600
33	Uniforms	2,015	2,100
34	Travel	0	1,095
35	Rentals	875	875
36	Postage	20	25
37	Printing and Binding	450	450
38	Dues, Subscriptions	110	120
39	Repairs, Maintenance	1,297	450
40	Contracts: Professional	1,500	0
41	Contracts: Maintenance	2,465	2,600
42	Contracts: Other	1,500	1,500
43	Telephone	2,720	3,000
44	Electric, Gas	6,016	6,335
45	Sewer Charges	1,101	1,100
46	Water Charges	790	950
47	Vehicle Operations	21,385	19,510
	TOTAL	$ 45,396	$ 43,400
50	Capital Equipment	1,887	1,705
51	Vehicles	14,980	16,500
52	Capital Improvements	0	0
	TOTAL	$ 16,867	$ 18,205
	SERVICE TOTALS	$356,846	$403,564

from which rational decisions can be made. It is not intended to force departments to go through an unnecessarily long and tedious budget process or to explain every individual expenditure dollar. Additionally, the detailed expenditures list presented should not be considered as the only expenditures a department will make during the fiscal year. Since government operations and priorities are continuously changing, it should be clear that these expenditure estimates are the department's best guess of future needs at the time the budget is being developed. Some expenditure needs will tend to change more often than others. However, there are many specific expenditures that can be accurately estimated both within these object codes and others. It is the identification of these expenditures, especially as they relate to the services performed, that are most important for the decision maker's success. The most important elements inherent in a service unit analysis is its avoidance of the extremes of the incremental method and the inundation of detail involved in a zero-base budget process. Good analysis is based on a philosophy of reasonableness in which fairly detailed expenditure information is related to actual services performed, thus permitting more logical expenditure decisions to be made. Utilization of this approach will enable officials to match the type and amount of expenditures with the particular service level desired, thereby reducing the likelihood of arbitrary reductions or increases.

Variations of service unit analyses can be developed. For example, productivity or output measures related to each service, such as the number of citizens benefiting from a service, can be used. This information can provide a better understanding of who receives the service and how it is delivered. The more information available for defining and describing the service, the easier it becomes for officials to understand the type and level of expenditures budgeted. Another variation of the service unit format consists of developing alternative levels of a service provision, such as 100 percent, 85 percent or 110 percent of the current or proposed service level. This analysis provides officials with a method of reducing or increasing funding by focusing upon the effects of alternative funding levels. This approach is similar to the alternative decision packages used in the zero-based budget process.

To aid the process of relating services to various levels of expenditure, the questions asked by public officials are very important. Examples of questions which may be used include the following:

1. Are there any legal requirements to provide this service?

Exhibit 4: *Service Unit Detail: Police Service*

Object Code	Object Name	Product or Service Name	Proposed FY Y3 Budget
30	Office Supplies	Paper, pads	$ 320
		Pens	40
		Ribbons, clips, and other supplies	140
			$ 500
31	Other Supplies	Ammunition	$ 2,750
		Electrical parts	1,100
		Cleaning supplies	610
		Medical supply kits	470
		Miscellaneous	150
			$ 5,080
33	Uniforms	Police uniforms replacement—full attire	$ 1,760
		Shields, nightsticks	270
		Bulletproof vests	4,400
			$ 6,430
34	Travel	Police Technology Conference	$ 475
		Productivity Seminar	620
			$ 1,095
41	Contracts: Maintenance	Pest control	$ 890
		Air conditioning —maintenance	480
		Machine service	280
		Janitorial services	2,500
			$ 4,150
43	Telephone	Basic service	$ 2,300
		Long distance	460
		Additional line	240
			$ 3,000
44	Vehicle Operations	Fuel – 15 vehicles	$11,650
		Maintenance	2,450
		Repairs	13,635
		Licenses	160
		Other	250
			$28,145

2. What citizens benefit from this service?
3. How many citizens benefit from the service either directly or indirectly?
4. How is the service performed by individual employees?
5. Are there any particular aspects of this service that can be reduced or eliminated without jeopardizing the entire service?
6. Can this service be provided another way?
7. What would be the effect of a specific reduction in personnel and operating costs?
8. What has been done to improve the service output and quality?
9. Have operations been reviewed in order to reduce expenditures?
10. Are there any other departments that provide a similar service?
11. How would the attrition of specific positions affect the service?
12. Are there any technological applications that can reduce costs or increase the level of productivity?

Capital Equipment Analysis

Since the purchase of capital equipment may not be considered as a part of normal operating expenditures, it is discussed separately here. Capital equipment consists of items that have a useful life of at least one year and have a minimum dollar value, usually established by the jurisdiction. Procedures similar to those outlined for operating expenses can also be used to analyze capital needs. Capital equipment purchases should also be reviewed in relation to the service provided. Officials should discuss the need for the equipment, how a service will be affected by the addition of the equipment, and whether current equipment is sufficient for another year or longer. A thorough analysis of capital equipment often results in the elimination of unnecessary expenditures.

Deciding the Budget Issues

As noted previously, a comprehensive service unit analysis allows officials to understand how each service operates so that appropriate budget amounts can be determined. This approach assumes that as more meaningful information is available, more logical budget amounts can be matched with services performed.

After each service unit analysis has been performed, government officials should decide upon the appropriate budget level for each object code. The particular service level should be established according to the demands and needs of the community. Overall, the budget decisions should reflect the results of the financial condition review.

UTILIZING THE ANALYSIS

Public officials have been entrusted with the responsibility of deciding what services are necessary and at what level they should be funded. They must decide whether cutbacks are necessary or if certain services should be expanded. They must also decide employee salary increases, the need for utility rate increases, and the construction of government facilities. Budgetary decisions based on a knowledge of governmental services and community needs are more likely to be good decisions. The service unit analysis offers an approach that increases an official's knowledge about each governmental service. In this manner, better budget decisions can be made in lieu of arbitrarily imposing reductions or modifying programs. With increasing financial stress confronting many governments, this type of budget analysis can provide officials with important and relevant information which can be utilized to control expenditure and revenue levels. It should be remembered that this process is a middle-of-the-road methodology that is based on using relevant information for decision making in a reasonable and logical manner.

Monitoring Performance

AN OVERVIEW

A popular interpretation of "productivity" among many government officials is that the best way to increase productivity is to work harder. This implies that low productivity is directly related to people. However, there are many other factors affecting productivity that are often overlooked by management. Some of these include equipment, working conditions, availability of supplies and materials, planning and scheduling problems, work force composition, physical layout of a community, and so forth. Working harder is rarely the best way to improve productivity. Often, more can be accomplished through improved planning and scheduling.

Officials and managers of smaller local governments who are trying to improve productivity should be aware that often no single factor determines any given level of productivity. Usually a mixture of variables should be looked at before action is taken. For a director or manager to begin to get a handle on productivity, a system is necessary to highlight both regular accomplishments and problems that arise.

In approaching productivity measurement and improvement, several steps can be taken. The following discussion provides a framework or approach—not a formal process—for the analysis of alternatives to improve productivity. Included in this framework is the use of productivity measures.

Any manager or department director is constantly engaged in the process of looking at needs, delivering services to answer those needs, and evaluating those services. While this process is almost self-evident, there are some opportunities for a manager to incorporate productivity and accountability more strongly into department operations. Breaking down this constant daily management process can illustrate the point. Managers in the public sector—

- Review the public service needs of the community and existing policies aimed at meeting those needs.
- Set objectives of service and determine how best to meet those objectives, i.e., what type and level of service.
- Evaluate whether any improvements in procedures or organization of resources are possible.
- Monitor the performance.
- Analyze the results and take management action to make needed improvements.

One of the key stages where productivity measurement becomes important is monitoring. That is the feedback link, giving managers the data with which to determine whether the particular service delivery system is on target.

ACCOUNTABILITY

Managers have always been accountable on a daily basis to the chief administrative officer and on an annual basis for their budget. However, the factual,

---

Reprinted from *Performance Measurement and Cost Accounting for Smaller Local Governments* (Providence: Rhode Island Department of Community Affairs, n.d.).

quantified record of performance on which to base good accountability has been less than adequate. Smaller communities simply do not have enough detailed records to really analyze their performance. The reason lies in daily pressures and lack of a system which could remove the daily burden from the department director. As a result, many department directors have relied on informal review of performance through supervisors or been reactive to whatever is the most pressing issue at the time, reviewing performance in that area in detail, and ignoring other activities temporarily. When issues arise or at annual budget hearings, expenditures are justified in terms of dollars, not output; and facts on what cutbacks would mean in terms of less service are lacking.

This [selection] is based on the premise that department directors in smaller communities can set up a manual system to be accountable for productivity in two ways:

1. To see that local services are truly meeting needs of the community (i.e., they are effective).
2. To see that local services are improved within available resources wherever possible (i.e., if they can be made more efficient, they will).

Accountability operates to insure the best use of the tax dollar. The purpose of this [selection] is to outline a system of performance measurement that, with a little initial effort, a manager in a small community can use to effectively quantify performance, monitor and report on all functions he or she is accountable for.

Right now the kind of performance measures which can really help highlight efficiency and effectiveness are not there, but they can be developed. They will be useful both internally and at budget hearings as factual data supporting each functional expenditure at the requested levels. Such detailed backup information is more and more being required by taxpayers.

WHAT TO MEASURE

A manager must be concerned with both efficiency and effectiveness which together constitute productivity. Both these aspects of service delivery should be measured. The types of measures that will indicate effectiveness are quite different from those which will help a manager to evaluate efficiency.

A. Effectiveness

The broadest level of decision about effectiveness involves the decision whether or not to provide a particular service at all, i.e., is there a true identified need or can a service that does not seem necessary be eliminated partially or in total. This type of decision will take place at a higher level of management. With services that are being provided, a department director needs to know if they are effective, if they do provide good quality service. Meeting the established public view of what constitutes an effective level of service is important.

The issue of effectiveness and effectiveness measures can be thought of as an evaluation of the service from the consumer's perspective to some extent. The quality of service is not always easy to quantify, but by using the "consumer" perspective certain general types of effectiveness measures can be identified:

> Percentage or volume of community use of a service.
>
> Percentage of community reached (i.e., by area, economic groups, by age group, "reached on schedule," etc.).
>
> Percentage of citizen satisfaction (survey of types of recreation programs wanted, for example).
>
> Response time (in public safety areas especially).
>
> Visual inspection using some type of rating system and trained observers to see that quality work is being done.
>
> Citizen complaints.

Other examples of the major types of effectiveness measures can be found in the publication of the Urban Institute and ICMA entitled *How Effective Are Your Community Services?*

For a smaller community, the key to selecting measures of effectiveness is the cost of data collection. Several of the types of measures just suggested are feasible because data can be collected through regular department record keeping. For example, citizen complaints, volume of use of facilities or percent of community reached are data easily collectible in standard message forms, schedules of use or by simply adding one or two pieces of data to collect on existing forms. Response time, likewise, can be monitored by most police and fire departments using radio equipment.

One of the most reliable measures of the quality of physical work performed, which includes most public work and maintenance type activities, is visual observation. While smaller communities will probably not use the highly developed system of ratings and trained observers suggested in the referenced publication, their size is, in fact, an advantage in being able to have someone out in the field periodically observing the quality of work. This particular individual may be required to be on site of the work anyway. Some regular follow-up discussion of observations may be all that is necessary.

While the type of rigorous measurement of effectiveness suggested in the literature is very often too costly to smaller communities and not worth the effort, a department director should definitely consider some of the effectiveness measures suggested as part of a system of measurement. The general objective is to use every possible method available to check on the overall quality and effectiveness of major services. If some quantifiable measure is not possible, the alternative is frequent firsthand observations of work quality.

B. Efficiency

After looking more broadly at measures of the general effectiveness of services, a director will want to look more closely at the details of how services are delivered. How have resources been allocated to each function, and what kinds of operating procedures, planning, etc., go into the actual accomplishment or performance of the activity? Is it being done efficiently?

At this point, the question of what level of work to monitor arises—a task, group of tasks, unit or an entire department? Selection of the appropriate level at which to measure efficient performance should be governed by the following rule:

> Ideally, performance measurement should begin at the lowest productive level—the level at which the work is actually done.

This means that where possible and practical, measures for each unique task should be identified.

Why measure each task? From the standpoint of the role of the accountable manager, the reason is that each task represents a specific cost to government involving a unique combination of men, equipment, materials and time; and also produces a specific result for which the manager is responsible. If it can be quantified, then it is a measurable activity and output obtained for dollars expended can be reported.

From the standpoint of the manager's own need to have information with which to manage, information resulting from the measures can be used to plan, execute and control future operations. As a practical matter, however, smaller local governments may not be able to afford the time required to gather information at the lowest productive level in every instance. Therefore, in some instances, productivity measures can and should be accumulated at some higher level, possibly at the lowest formal organizational level such as unit or section.

Before going into more detail on the process of selecting measures, it may be helpful to outline some circumstances which can help a department director determine the right balance between too much and too little measurement information.

A director should consider *detailed performance reporting* when—

> The activity is the subject of special attention by the Council or the public;
>
> The activity has not been looked at in detail in a long time, i.e., no updating of operating procedures, etc.;
>
> The activity is a labor intensive one which represents a large cost in the budget;
>
> A problem is known to exist which will require some sort of public policy decision in the near future involving expenditures;
>
> Existing data indicates a potential problem (e.g., once a community has set some targets, they are being missed by substantial amounts);
>
> A specific project is underway which involves a new method for delivering a service, especially designed to improve performance; there is a need to evaluate its effectiveness and efficiency compared to the previous method.

Less detailed performance reporting is satisfactory when—

> Good records are already kept at the work level and they are always available to look at for analysis if the more general measures being reported indicate a problem;

The activity is regularly observed firsthand by a supervisor who regularly reports to management, and has a good feel for whether problems exist without detailed reporting by employees;

The activity was recently reviewed in detail and is not of great concern because it is performed adequately or improvements were made and verified.

Each department director must carefully weigh the advantages and disadvantages involved in monitoring at a detailed task level. This decision can be made for each function and in no way has to be uniform among all work responsibilities in the department. Detail can vary.

What exactly is the best way to identify the lowest productive level? Street maintenance, for example, includes a wide variety of productive activities ranging from patching, resurfacing, and sweeping to snow removal and catch basin cleaning. As another example, a smaller community may have a buildings and grounds division or crew. Such a unit does many things including mowing, trimming, painting, etc.

There is a process which department directors can follow before deciding which "level" of activity to measure. Whether or not a department has a formal organization chart, for purposes of setting up a performance monitoring system, a department director can develop a work responsibility chart which simply lists all the various functions associated with the department, down to the level of detail of each task involved. Such a chart will help identify all tasks that could possibly be measured for results. In deciding the "level" to measure, a director can first consider each task. If this is impractical, then the chart helps group tasks together so that measuring productivity can be feasible at a "higher" level.

Exhibits 1 and 2 show two examples of detailed charts which list all tasks performed. Now, on the basis of reviewing the chart, a public works director may decide to measure a task, such as mowing, or a group of tasks, such as landscaping, which includes mowing, trimming, weeding, planting, etc. The same director may also choose simply to measure at an even "higher" or divisional (grounds and buildings) level which may include even more activities than

Exhibit 1

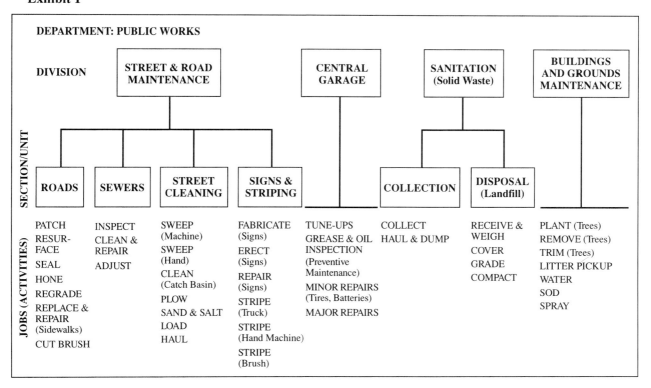

mowing, weeding and trimming, such as tree removal, pest control and so forth. On the other hand, for central garage operations, a very detailed accounting of time and resources used in each task may be required for decision making on vehicle replacement.

Creating a detailed work responsibility chart which lists every task permits the director to start by considering measures at this level, where the work is performed. To restate the point, there are advantages to measuring at the task level, not only for an accountability system but for internal use in planning, executing, and controlling operations. Not only can *street miles swept* indicate the level of service and measure performance, the records which provide this data also show whether scheduled work is too great, too little, whether machines are breaking down and unavailable, etc. In general, *more detailed* measures at the task level lead to—

Equal accountability for all, i.e., it is easier to pinpoint responsibility for performance on specific individuals or work units;

Data immediately available to more sharply define problems and help determine potential solutions;

Less likelihood of any activity being overlooked, i.e., no reporting required, therefore supervisors pay less attention.

In certain instances, a director may reject measuring a task because of unavoidable problems, such as—

Exhibit 2: *Program Structure, Community Protection*

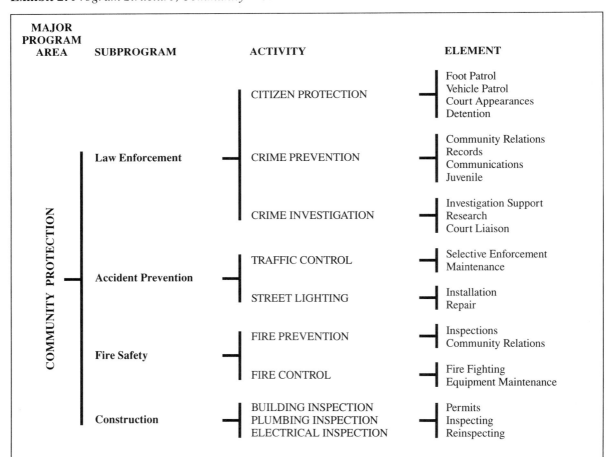

Time consuming;

Staff inadequate or retraining too difficult, placing accuracy of data in doubt;

Data too difficult to read and interpret, i.e. the sheer volume overwhelms a manager and/or the most useful data is hard to pick out.

The general rule for managers is accountability for efficient, effective management. A department director should have all the records and measurement data on performance which is needed for good accountability for all functions in the department. If there is no other apparent use for the information either immediately or in the future, excessive detail should not be required. Each decision should of course be reviewed at least annually, and preferably more frequently: each time the community's reporting system requires a performance report.

SELECTING MEASURES

Once those activities which will be measured are identified, several steps are involved in selecting the measures to be used to implement performance monitoring.

A. Identify the Work Unit

How can the activity be quantified? "Unit" in this sense means the physical unit of work accomplished which describes the activity for purposes of evaluation, such as miles, tons, number (made), calls answered. The unit plus the appropriate verb constitutes a workload measure. Workload measures are not too difficult to identify; miles traveled, tons collected, inspections conducted and calls received are a few examples. Exhibit 3 lists other examples of work units and the related workload measure.

Review the measures to make sure they actually define or reflect the activity. In areas such as public works, the measures are fairly straightforward. In crime prevention, there is obviously no way to measure "crimes prevented." In this instance, number of crimes reported and arrests made is the closest approximation, and the limitations of this data as a measure of crime prevention should be recognized.

Can the data be fairly easily identified and collected to provide the kind of information desired, i.e., useful for accountability, planning, scheduling, controlling? The "state of the art" in public sector productivity is not sufficiently defined that all measures suggested by the literature are applicable for the needs of smaller local governments. For example, some effectiveness measures require elaborate systems to collect data which may not be that necessary in a small community.

B. Identify All Appropriate Measures

Is a single measure adequate or are several necessary? In setting up a performance monitoring system, a director should consider a gradual implementation process. However, it should be pointed out that workload measures just discussed highlight output but do not really measure efficiency or effectiveness. Eventually, a manager must measure input, (i.e., costs) including manpower, materials used, etc., to evaluate efficiency. Other measures tell a manager whether the quality of work was satisfactory (effectiveness). A smaller community may "measure" workload at first but managers should look ahead to

Exhibit 3

Measuring workload can be a first step in establishing a PERFORMANCE MONITORING SYSTEM which will provide a department director with valuable information for planning, scheduling, and budgeting. Below is an example of some types of measures for monitoring performance at the function (activity) level where the work is performed.

FUNCTION	WORK UNIT	WORKLOAD (OUTPUT)
PUBLIC WORKS		
Streets and Highways Sweeping	Tons Miles Areas Tons	# Tons Collected # Miles Swept # Areas Cleared # Tons/Area
PUBLIC WORKS		
Central Garage Maintenance	Tune-ups Changes Repairs Inspection	# Tune-ups # Grease & Oil Changes # Repairs # Inspections
POLICE		
Uniform Service Patrol	Miles Beat Miles Arrests Responses Calls	# Miles Driven # Beat Miles Covered # Arrests # Responses # Calls for Service

eventually reaching the stage of measuring efficiency and effectiveness. Workload measures are a beginning. Measures of costs and quality are the ultimate goal.

C. Identify Forms on Which Data Can Be Collected

Can the data be collected accurately and reliably? This is critical. Accuracy demands a consensus on the data being collected, and the source of the data being collected. Is everyone defining terms the same way? Are there existing forms and procedures to gather and report the data, such as work order forms, logs, summary reports, etc.? If not, can they be easily designed? If individual employees have to report data, forms used should be preprinted, simple check-off or fill-in style that minimizes work and leaves less room for interpretation.

D. Identify Personnel Responsible for Data Collection

Are adequately trained personnel available to gather and report data? Will individual employees need to provide data or can supervisors maintain records? The more people involved in reporting source data, the more opportunity there is for inaccuracy. If a supervisor can handle the forms, there are likely to be fewer problems.

E. Identify All Data Needs

For what purposes are the productivity measures being collected? For immediate performance improvement? For the council? For departmental planning? This purpose relates to "level" of detail. Are major system changes required? The ability of existing budgeting and accounting systems to support the accumulation and analysis of output data with cost data must be considered.

In sum, selection of measures involves: Determining the work unit for the basis of measurement; reviewing forms and records to ensure that they support collection of good data. Ensuring that there is consensus on the data and source of data. (Is everyone defining terms the same way?) Assigning responsibility for collecting the data. One point to remember is that the more people involved in reporting source data, the more opportunity there is for inaccuracy.

USING MEASURES TO EVALUATE EFFICIENCY

After a local government has selected and implemented measures of workload for each task, it has the capacity to monitor the existing output of any given unit. The next step is to determine what inputs were necessary to produce the performance. Measuring inputs is a necessary step to measuring efficiency.

Manhours is the largest single input or cost. It is important for a city or town to monitor manhours *at the same work level at which measures of output are being used*. This is critical. The weekly time sheet indicates total hours worked by the individuals assigned to the street crew, but does not tell how much time was spent patching vs. cutting brush. That data has to be recorded daily on *actual* performance, not assigned time. The amount of labor time which it actually takes to accomplish the outputs being measured for each function is the major factor a department director needs to know, not only to report efficiency but also to plan and schedule future operations in order to control costs. Knowing the *manhours* involved in an activity is essential.

Monitoring manhours can be accomplished in a number of ways. The supervisor who assigns crews or the dispatcher who assigns patrol cars, etc., is probably the best source. A simple code can indicate the type of work assigned, number of men in the crew and even equipment or materials being used.

When measuring output at the task level, it is essential to record the number of hours each individual spends on each task. Three men working three hours on painting equals nine (9) manhours of painting.

It is possible to identify other inputs directly connected to particular activities by keeping some simple, but specific, records. These would relate to materials and supplies used, fuel consumed, equipment repair required and other objects directly associated with performing each function.

By associating these inputs of labor, materials, supplies and equipment which represent the *direct* cost involved with workload measures, a performance monitoring system can be developed for measuring efficiency. With data provided by line departments on all inputs, the finance department can calculate costs.

PUBLIC WORKS
Streets and Highways

ACTIVITY (FUNCTION): SWEEPING

INPUT (COSTS): MANHOURS, SUPPLIES, (GAS), EQUIPMENT, REPAIR.

Work Unit	Workload (Output)	÷ Input = Efficiency Measures
Tons	No. of Tons Collected	Cost per Ton
Miles	No. of Miles Swept	Cost per Mile
Areas	No. of Areas Cleared	Cost per Area
Tons	No. of Tons per Area	Cost per Ton per Acre

PUBLIC WORKS
Central Garage

ACTIVITY (FUNCTION): MAINTENANCE

INPUT (COSTS): MANHOURS, PARTS, SUPPLIES, ETC.

Work Unit	Workload (Output)	÷ Input = Efficiency Measures
Tune-Ups	No. of Tune-Ups	Cost per Tune-Up
Changes	No. of Grease and Oil Changes	Cost per Grease and Oil Changes
Repairs	No. of Repairs	Cost per Repairs
Inspection	No. of Inspections	Cost per Inspection

POLICE
Uniform Services

ACTIVITY (FUNCTION): PATROL

INPUT (COSTS): MANHOURS, EQUIPMENT, SUPPLIES.

Work Unit	Workload (Output)	÷ Input = Efficiency Measures
Miles	No. of Miles Driven	Cost per Mile
Beat Miles	No. of Beat Miles Covered	Cost per Beat Mile
Clearance	No. of Clearances	Cost per Clearance

USING TARGETS TO EVALUATE EFFICIENCY AND EFFECTIVENESS

Once a community has begun to use performance measures to get a clearer picture of existing levels of service delivery, several things may occur. A department director may spot areas where procedures have tended to get inefficient, and he may change some procedures to improve work. At the next level, once improvements are made a community may wish to have an ongoing way to compare performance from one year to the next. A very simple way to provide this point of comparison for analysis and decision-making is the use of targets. Targets are simply the planned level of service for a given time period. They may be informal, implied or specifically stated as part of an objective. For example, "to improve response time to breaking and entering incidents to three minutes." Three minutes is the target. Or, "to increase summertime streetsweeping operations and completely sweep the city once every month and the downtown area once a week." The target would be total miles of sweeping X number of sweepings for the time period involved, possibly 1,800 miles of sweeping that quarter.

Targets can be developed several ways:

1. Based on historical records—match or better last year's performance or meet the average of the last five (5) years.

2. Productivity improvement goal—based on careful analysis of existing performance and resulting work improvement efforts, a specific new level of performance is expected, e.g., a 10% increase in inspections.
3. Engineered standards—more and more communities have used industrial engineering techniques to carefully analyze the steps involved in a task. Based on the number of men and equipment involved, a standard of output is set. Several states are using standards for public works activities. This type of target works best with very repetitive, standardized operations where the same steps are used each and every time.

Whatever the source of the target, it is a highly effective means of analyzing productivity. It forms the basis of planned vs. actual reporting and is the type of accountability which can lead to productivity improvement when carefully analyzed and used for decision-making.

This [selection] recommends that smaller local governments measure activities over a period of time and then develop their own targets from this historical data. In some areas, targets are not so easily defined. To further complicate the problem, performance targets derived in one community are not usually directly transferable or comparable in another community. Targets should be constantly evaluated, not used as a black and white measure of success or failure.

SUMMARY

A community should aim to achieve a balance between efficiency and effectiveness. Measures of both should be used. Targets should be careful not to sacrifice quality for quantity. If concern for efficiency indicates that a more intense schedule would save dollars in terms of the inflationary cost of materials, concern for quality must be weighed and the results of any decision translated in terms of its effects on service.

This [selection] has discussed the process of setting up a productivity measurement system to aid in making these decisions based on the following:

Efficiency Measures—quantified indicators of *both* the direct outputs of each unique task (wherever possible) and the direct inputs required to produce that particular output (man-hours, materials, etc.).

Effectiveness Measures—quantified indicators of the quality or level of accomplishment of major services.

Targets—based on analysis of historical performance, efforts to improve existing performance where possible, and finally establishing *measurable* targets which are carefully and periodically reviewed by management.

The process of improving services relies heavily on effective evaluation of existing services—on being able to spot the difficulties and understand them, in order that they might be overcome. This vital step in the management process is monitoring performances....

Effective performance monitoring involves knowing what to measure and how to measure it. It is understanding how the relationship of cost to results can point to ways in which services might be made more efficient. And it is being able to determine whether the service effectively meets the needs of the community.

Service Efforts and Accomplishments: The Case of Road Maintenance

William A. Hyman and Joan A. Allen

INTRODUCTION AND SCOPE

All levels of government combined spend approximately $65 billion annually on highways, including $17 billion on maintenance and operations.[1] A large but not readily determinable amount of additional funds is spent on local street maintenance. Most transportation agencies' maintenance budgets are stretched thin, and they find it imperative to use their maintenance funds wisely.

It is generally agreed that roads should be maintained to a standard of reasonable quality over their useful lives rather than be allowed to wear out prematurely. A total lack of, or deferral of, maintenance usually results in significant increases in long-run total costs to both agencies and users. Maintenance (including repairs) retards or offsets the deteriorating effects of weather, aging, traffic, wheel loads, and vegetative growth. It also helps overcome damage, vandalism, failure of materials, and shortcomings in pavement design and construction.

Many agencies have implemented maintenance management systems or pavement management systems in order to assist them in allocating maintenance funds more efficiently and effectively. These systems, if well designed, offer significantly improved data on current road conditions and maintenance histories and result in more productive use of scarce funds, labor, material, and equipment. Enhanced financial accounting systems also provide information that can be used to assess the efficacy of road maintenance programs.

Most of the information collected and analyzed by road maintenance agencies is used for internal management and reporting purposes. Relatively little progress has been made in developing road maintenance service efforts and accomplishments (SEA) measures for presentation to the public, elected officials, and others outside road maintenance agencies. Even when suitable SEA measures are available internally, it is only the rare and exemplary organization that has also targeted such information toward external audiences.

The purpose of this discussion is to describe road maintenance SEA indicators that should be considered for communication to citizens and elected officials. Here we examine the ways local and state governments measure and report what they get for the dollars they spend on road maintenance: inputs to maintenance operations, the quantity and quality of work accomplished, the productivity of maintenance resources, and the efficiency with which road maintenance is carried out. The recommended SEA measures are illustrative of the type most suitable for external communication.

SEA measures aimed at external audiences can be helpful in obtaining increased funding by more objectively demonstrating the maintenance needs of the roadway system to budget officers and elected

---

GASB Research Report, Service Efforts and Accomplishments Reporting: Its Time Has Come, *An Overview*, is copyrighted (1990) by the Governmental Accounting Standards Board, 401 Merritt 7, P.O. Box 5116, Norwalk, Connecticut 06856-5116, U.S.A. Portions (pp. 247-62) are reprinted with permission. Copies of the complete document are available from the GASB.

officials, such as city council members or legislators. When an agency has surpassed its performance or productivity goals, such information can communicate maintenance successes to the public, including improved quality of roads. SEA measures may also help to determine whether it is more efficient to carry out various types of maintenance using agency personnel or by contracting with private firms. In addition, SEA measures tailored for external use improve the communication and interaction between in-house maintenance managers and appointed or public officials who must respond to the public concerns about road maintenance problems. Another valuable use of SEA measures is to provide information to the financial community to help, for example, bond raters assess the fiscal condition of various government jurisdictions.

Maintenance Defined

This article is generally confined to maintenance of the traveled way and the roadside and does not include cleaning, traffic signs, or traffic control. It does include some common maintenance activities in urban areas such as curb, gutter, and drainage repairs.

While definitions of maintenance are not clearly differentiated in practice and vary among jurisdictions, it is common to regard maintenance as actions that enable a road to achieve its intended useful life, rather than extend the road's life. Typical maintenance activities include pothole repair, crack filling, patching, applying seal coats, roadside vegetation control, roadway striping, guardrail maintenance, upkeep of roadside rest stops, blading of gravel roads and shoulders, and clearing drainage ditches and pipes of debris.

Some agencies also regard certain low-capital improvement options, such as bituminous resurfacing, as maintenance. The American Association of State Highway and Transportation Officials (AASHTO) defines physical maintenance of the traveled way as the resurfacing of hard surfaces with bituminous material less than three-quarters of an inch thick or replacement of the traveled way in kind for less than 500 continuous feet.[2]

Another way to characterize road maintenance is to distinguish among actions that are demand-responsive, routine, or periodic. Demand-responsive maintenance arises due to a sudden, urgent, or pressing need for maintenance. When pavements suddenly present hazards such as potholes or blowups, a "demand" is created for maintenance or repairs. In many agencies, certain maintenance activities are routine, such as crack sealing. Other maintenance may occur periodically, such as blading gravel shoulders.

Objectives of Road Maintenance

The principal objectives of road maintenance are as follows:

1. To provide a smooth, comfortable, expeditious, and safe ride for the public;
2. To reduce such user costs as fuel, repairs, accidents, and travel time;
3. To utilize labor, equipment, and material efficiently; and
4. To ensure that pavement lasts as long as it should, thereby reducing future costs, such as for rehabilitating or reconstructing it.

The widespread availability of powerful computers has resulted in the practical objective of providing the proper type and level of maintenance at the right time in the right location to bring overall maintenance costs to near the minimum.

Methodology

To determine what SEA indicators are used by local and state governments and how widely they are reported, we reviewed approximately 36 state budgets and 30 city and county budgets or performance documents. We also reviewed the literature pertaining to road maintenance practices, including information on maintenance and pavement management systems. From these materials, we identified jurisdictions that collected and reported service efforts, efficiency, and quality data.[3]

We identified several state and local governments that seemed to have made substantial progress in the identification and use of SEA indicators. We interviewed officials of 11 state and local governments in order to understand more fully the collection, use, and reporting of those indicators.

RECOMMENDED INDICATORS

The vast majority of states and large numbers of counties and cities collect data on the type and amount of work accomplished; funds expended for labor, equipment, and material; labor hours; equipment hours; material used by type and amount; and equipment types or classes used.

Most states have developed production standards (e.g., daily rates of accomplishment for different types of maintenance work) as part of performance standards that are intended to ensure uniform quality of each type of maintenance activity.[4]

In addition, many maintenance organizations have developed "level-of-service goals" against which accomplishments can be compared. Level-of-service goals sometimes serve as thresholds for determining when a certain type of maintenance work needs to be accomplished.[5] A particularly useful level-of-service goal is one that says, for example, that no more than 10 percent of the streets should be in "poor" condition, where poor is defined in some reasonably objective manner. As long as funding permits, when a street deteriorates into "poor" condition, this signals a maintenance need. Agencies can track the extent to which they are able to achieve level-of-service goals over time. If agencies are falling short of such goals, the shortfall can be used as a basis for requesting additional funding, or the level-of-service goal can be changed to reflect economic and political realities.

All states and a large number of cities and counties already have some type of pavement management system.[6] By early 1993, all states will be required to have a pavement management system acceptable to the Federal Highway Administration.[7] Therefore, current and historical data on pavement condition and distress should be routinely available at the state level and in many local jurisdictions.

Maintenance SEA has many dimensions, but the bottom line is productivity, efficiency, and cost-effectiveness. SEA measures are constructed from information concerning the inputs, outputs, and outcomes of maintenance programs.

The following paragraphs give examples of the types of information that should be used for regular external reporting of road maintenance SEA.

Inputs

The standard inputs to road maintenance should be reported: overall funding; funding by maintenance activity; person-hours; physical quantities of the most common material used, such as asphalt; and the number of different types of equipment that are representative of or account for the bulk of equipment used. Costs of each of the inputs should be reported in proper units and expressed in both current and inflation-adjusted dollars.

Outputs

A road maintenance agency should convey how much work has been performed. Following are typical measures of outputs:

- Miles of roads seal-coated
- Number of potholes repaired (or tons of pre-mix applied)
- Miles of curb/gutter/sidewalk replaced
- Number of street utility cuts repaired
- Miles of roadway striping

These measures could be strengthened significantly if information on accomplishments were compared to the total need or the goal for the year. Better measures of output would be as follows:

- Percentage of roads seal-coated out of total mileage requiring such work.
- Actual pothole repairs in comparison to planned pothole repairs.

Accomplishment should include preventive maintenance. Although what constitutes preventive maintenance is not generalizable from one agency to another, maintenance managers usually hold strong convictions concerning which type of maintenance can avoid or postpone more costly future actions.

The time period for which output measures apply should be clearly reported. Outputs reported in budget documents, budget requests, or reports aimed at the public are likely to be expressed in annual terms. Daily rates of accomplishment could be reported, but most agencies regard these as productivity figures rather than achievements of the maintenance organization.

Governments should overcome the great temptation to use only measures of output, to the exclusion of quality and efficiency indicators.

Measures of Quality/Outcomes

Road maintenance agencies should provide yearly reports on the condition of their roads to public officials and the public. Among the best indicators are the following:

- "Rideability" ratings, as determined by machines and/or trained observers.

- Measures of distress that have a direct bearing on maintenance SEA and needs, such as the miles of road that suffer from a specific type of cracking of a given severity and covering a certain percentage of the surface.
- Annual change in sufficiency scales, deficiency scores, or other composite indexes that reflect a variety of factors that contribute to road condition; these include roughness and pavement distress.
- Percentage of roads equaling or exceeding level-of-service goals such as "maintain in satisfactory condition" or "keep the present serviceability rating at 2.5 or above."
- Number of lane miles in poor, satisfactory, good, and excellent condition.

Quality assurance data are becoming more widespread, and more transportation organizations can be expected to administer surveys to assess public perceptions of road conditions and agency performance, although survey data is not without shortcomings. Examples of SEA indicators based on quality control efforts, evaluations of responses to citizen complaints, and well-designed citizen surveys are:

- Average and year-to-year change in response times to maintenance problems reported by the public.
- Miles of short bituminous resurfacing work whose "rideability" rating fell to an unacceptable level within three years compared to the total miles of such work done.
- Ratings from citizen surveys as to the quality of road maintenance practices and results.

Another good measure of outcomes is the average service life of different repairs and types of improvements. Many maintenance activities have service lives that can be well defined, for example, blading of gravel roads or shoulders.[8]

In addition, maintenance will affect the service life of pavement betterment and construction jobs, so that a measure of outcomes is the annual change in service life for such improvements as resurfacing, recycling, and reconstruction.

Another potential measure is the added cost to users of less-than-adequate road conditions. While agencies have attempted to estimate the effect of pavement condition on accidents and vehicle operating costs, this type of analysis is only now becoming widely practical as pavement management systems are being implemented throughout the country.

Measures of Efficiency

Most agencies do not make a distinction between productivity and efficiency indicators, though there is an important difference, and both should be reported. Productivity indicators reflect how well various inputs are used: money, labor, equipment, materials, and time. Unit costs, such as dollars per cubic yard of hand patching, are insufficient productivity measures. They need to be supplemented by separate productivity measures for each nonmonetary input, such as labor, equipment, materials, and time. An example is cubic yards of hand patching per person-hour of labor.

One way some agencies have portrayed productivity is to express the extent to which a certain maintenance activity is performed to production standards (daily production rates). For example, if the production standard is "x miles of chip seal per day," one could report the number of days per year when chip seals were being applied and the number of days the production standard was equaled or exceeded.

Efficiency measures portray the benefits the public receives in terms of better roads given *all* the maintenance resources used. It is recommended that efficiency measures be developed in addition to productivity measures. An example of a practical efficiency measure suitable for public reporting is the number of miles of road in a specific road category maintained in a satisfactory or better condition per dollar of expenditure on the road category. The categories should be defined so that roads are reasonably uniform in important characteristics such as surface type and expected service life.

A refinement of this measure would involve the use of a pavement-condition rating scale: "the number of miles of a category of road maintained with a pavement serviceability index (PSI) of 2.5 or better per dollar of expenditure."

Efficiency and productivity measures should be reported for two or more periods. To reflect accomplishments of the maintenance organization, it is not enough to present a figure that pertains to a single point in time; there must be a way to measure change in SEA.

Measures of productivity and efficiency should be developed not only for the entire maintenance program but also for key components of interest to the public, for example, pothole repairs, surface treatments such as seal coats, and maintenance resurfacing.

These measures are not without their problems. Changes in pavement condition can be attributed to many things besides the productivity of the maintenance organization, and it is important that public officials or others outside the agency understand when unusual weather, rapid increases in truck traffic, or other factors distort measures of efficiency or productivity.

Exhibit 1 provides a summary of recommended road maintenance SEA indicators with a rationale for each.

OTHER ISSUES

Disaggregation

SEA indicators should be tailored to the audiences for which they are intended. They should also be sufficiently detailed to be illuminating but not so detailed that the information cannot be quickly absorbed and interpreted. These precepts should affect the level of disaggregation of the data. If the audience consists of public officials, not only is overall information about the maintenance program appropriate, but the data should be broken down according to jurisdictions of concern to public appointees, legislators, and city council and county board members. When addressing the public, maintenance agencies will find that truckers will be most interested in information concerning truck routes while the average motorist is primarily interested in commuter routes and roads and gateways to recreational and vacation areas.

Maintenance accomplishments and efficiency are likely to be related to the type of road and traffic levels (especially truck traffic), and so breakdown by functional class within a jurisdiction is appropriate (e.g., interstate, other freeways and expressways, principal arterials, minor arterials, collectors, and local streets). Disaggregation by type of pavement also conveys useful information, for example, flexible versus rigid pavements. Additional breakdowns by climate and terrain are useful if road maintenance activities are spread over areas with different climate conditions and geography that significantly affect maintenance SEA and road conditions.

In some cases, the most reasonable level of disaggregation may be by maintenance district. This type of breakdown avoids presenting SEA measures subject to misinterpretation because of differences in staffing levels, experience, or time and distance to travel to maintenance sites.

Finding out what legislators and the public most want to know about road maintenance and giving them that type of data or level of disaggregation might produce the best results in terms of interest and support for the government's road maintenance program.

Comparison Information

SEA measures should be compared over time and geographically to national or other sources where appropriate. Comparisons should also be made with regard to level-of-service or other goals, or to standards or objectives set by maintenance managers, other top management, or public officials. In addition, where possible, maintenance performed in-house should be compared to maintenance contracted out.

Year-to-year comparisons are best suited for public presentations. Historical information that spans many years is more useful than short-run changes in road maintenance SEA measures.

Public officials frequently wish to compare the performance of their jurisdiction with others. To make these types of comparisons useful, they need to be performed with care. Comparisons should be made among jurisdictions with similar characteristics, that is, within "peer groups." States frequently compare the condition of their roads with others in the same region. Large cities should look to their populous counterparts in similar climatic regions to make comparisons. Smaller cities in similar circumstances make suitable mates.

Annual accomplishments should be compared against level-of-service goals. For example, if a jurisdiction decides that no more than 10 percent of the street mileage should be in "unsatisfactory condition" at the end of the year, one can compare the number of streets actually in unsatisfactory condition to this goal.

To improve efficiency, an agency's goal might be to achieve a 5 percent reduction in the cost per year to keep the same mileage of roads in "satisfactory condition." At the end of the year, it is possible to compare the change in cost from the previous year to the goal of the 5 percent cost reduction, assuming

Exhibit 1: *Recommended SEA Indicators for Road Maintenance**

	INDICATOR	RATIONALE FOR SELECTING INDICATOR

INPUTS	Expenditures (current and constant dollars)
	  Total
	  By activity
	Labor hours
	Quantity of material by type
	Equipment hours by type
		Data normally gathered; provides a breakdown by type of resources used

OUTPUTS	Pavement miles resurfaced Pavement miles seal coated Number of potholes repaired (or tons of premix applied) Miles of curb/gutter/sidewalk replaced Number of street utility cuts repaired Number of storm inlets repaired/cleaned Miles of preventive maintenance Miles of deferred maintenance (i.e., postponed work)	Measures accomplishments of maintenance program Important measures that require careful definition and typically must be based on engineering judgment
OUTCOMES / QUALITY	Number and percentage of lane miles of road whose condition was either improved or maintained at a satisfactory level (i.e., PSI > 2.5) Lane miles in poor, fair, satisfactory, and excellent condition Road rideability as measured by such devices as Mays Meter Pavement distress indicators measured by visual condition surveys that relate to maintenance performance (e.g., number of lane miles with severe alligator cracking) Percentage of lane miles at acceptable rating level Percentage of roads seal coated out of total requiring such work Average quality assurance measures achieved on completion of maintenance resurfacing (e.g., average smoothness) Year-to-year change in the average service life of different types of maintenance work on different categories of highways Citizen perceptions of road condition based on public opinion surveys Average time to respond to citizen complaints	Ties maintenance accomplishments to changes in road condition and level-of-service goals A reliable, repeatable, and commonly used method for measuring roughness Easy to collect, but considerable engineering knowledge required to correlate with maintenance outcomes, quality, or needs Relates pavement condition to level-of-service goal Compares accomplishments to needed work Measures on-site work quality; quality assurance/control is becoming increasingly important in road work Indicates whether maintenance work is longer lasting Measures perceptions of users Measures responsiveness to concerns of road users

EFFICIENCY	Ratio of inputs to outputs:
	  Average unit dollar cost for labor, equipment, and material for particular types of repair such as average labor-hours per mile of street resurfaced
	Measures related to outcomes/quality:
	  Number of miles maintained in a "satisfactory" or better condition per dollar of expenditure by road category (i.e., PSI > 2.5)
	  Number of miles improved to or maintained at PSI > 2.5 per dollar of expenditure by road category
	  Comparison of performance measures for in-house and contract labor by maintenance activity
		Measures efficiency in a widely used and easy-to-compute manner
		
		Relates productivity to changes in road condition and level-of-service goal
		
		Relates productivity to quantitative level-of-service goal
		
		Helps determine whether different types of maintenance should be contracted out

EXPLANATORY DATA	Weather (degree days, freeze-thaw cycles) Terrain (flat, rolling, mountainous) Type of road (flexible, rigid) Traffic volume and percentage of trucks (or equivalent single-axle loads) Average time or distance to work sites Lane miles of agency maintenance responsibility by road type Pavement age distribution Other unusual work circumstances	Helps explain exceptional or unusual values of performance indicators

*The recommended indicators presented in this exhibit are illustrative. They are intended to serve as a starting point for use in the development of a comprehensive set of SEA indicators for external reporting of an entity's results of operation.

This exhibit does not provide illustrations of indicator disaggregation or of comparison data such as trends, targets, or other comparable entities. Both disaggregation and comparison data are, however, important aspects of SEA reporting.

one is judging cost performance for the same number of miles of road.

It is strongly recommended that maintenance agencies jointly develop level-of-service goals with public officials who have budget responsibility. Other interested members of the public should also participate. In this way, a reasonable consensus can be developed concerning the desirable or acceptable condition in which roads should be maintained. Also, level-of-service goals can serve as a benchmark for the accomplishment of different types of maintenance work.

As the role of the private sector grows in road maintenance, it will be increasingly important to compare the cost of performing maintenance work in-house to contracting with a private firm. Agencies should seek competitive bids to use as a basis for comparison. Where the same type of work is being performed both in-house and by contractors, then inputs, outputs, quality indicators, and measures of productivity and efficiency can potentially be compared.

Explanatory Data

It is important for appropriate explanatory data to be reported along with SEA indicators. Explanatory data are particularly useful in explaining SEA significantly above or below norms a government is using or to account for failure to achieve goals and objectives.

Explanatory data are necessary to make full sense of comparisons. If the "number of lane miles of maintenance resurfacing" declined from one year to the next, what is the reason? Reduced productivity, a drop in funding, inflation in road maintenance costs, an unusually long winter, equipment breakdowns, heavy turnover of personnel, or work on roads with much higher traffic, trucks, and loads? Explanatory data concerning these and other factors, such as terrain and absenteeism, can help explain unusual variations in SEA indicators.

If SEA measures are found to be unreliable year after year because of various extenuating circumstances, then the agency should attempt to devise a new set of measures that will more reliably communicate to external audiences the agency's service efforts and accomplishments.

The governments to which we talked and from which we received budget documents and other literature almost never include explanatory data information when reporting SEA data. This information gap should be filled.

Verifiability of Statistics Produced by Indicators

SEA indicators should be as accurate as possible. Thus, there should be ways to check the data that underlie the SEA measures. Verifiability can be enhanced if the following occurs:

- Field data is checked for accuracy before entry into the computer.
- The original data concerning inputs—labor, equipment, material, and time—are retrievable for at least three or four years.
- Information for maintenance management systems, pavement management systems, accounting systems, and fiscal reporting use the same data and are fully coordinated. Reporting periods should be identical and, where relevant, accounts should balance to the dollar both within and between systems.
- Ratings of rideability and distress are repeatable. A random sample of road sections should be double-checked periodically to ensure accuracy.
- Road roughness equipment is calibrated to ensure annual and geographical comparisons are meaningful.
- Sample data for SEA measures are statistically sound.

Notes

1. *The Status of the Nation's Highways: Conditions and Performance,* report of the Secretary of Transportation to the U.S. Congress (Washington, D.C.: U.S. Government Printing Office, June 1987).

2. American Association of State Highway and Transportation Officials, *AASHTO Maintenance Manual 1987* (Washington, D.C.: AASHTO, 1987).

3. See, for example:
   City of Cincinnati, *The Public Works Story,* 4th ed., January 1987.
   City of Winston-Salem, North Carolina, *Annual Budget Program 1984-85.*
   City of Alexandria, Virginia, *FY 1987 Budget.*
   City of Dallas, "General Description of the Street Inventory," memorandum to Councilman Craig Holcomb, November 5, 1986.

City of Dallas Street and Sanitation Services Department, "Street Maintenance Issue Paper," July 26, 1985.

City of Portland, Oregon, "Report by the Office of the City Auditor," February 1988.

Mississippi House of Representatives, Legislative Service Office, "Report to the Fiscal Affairs and Government Operations Committee of the Southern Legislative Conference," October 5, 1987, 1-2.

New York City Department of Transportation, *Street Smart: A Plan to Improve & Equalize Street Smoothness Conditions in New York City,* March 1988.

New York State Department of Transportation, "The Pavement Condition of New York's Highways: 1984," December 1984.

Pennsylvania Department of Transportation, "Districts' Parallel Activities to Those in Bureau of Maintenance," quarter ending December 1987.

4. Donald R. Anderson, *Maintenance Management Systems,* National Cooperative Highway Research Program Synthesis of Highway Practice, Report 110 (Washington, D.C.: Transportation Research Board, National Research Council, October 1984).

5. R. Kulkarni et al., *Maintenance Levels-of-Service Guidelines,* NCHRP Report 223 (Washington, D.C.: Transportation Research Board, National Research Council, June 1980).

6. C. L. Monosmith et al., "Pavement Management at the Local Level," briefing document for meeting at Turner Fairbank Highway Research Center, April 3, 1988.

7. 23 CFR Part 626, FHWA Docket No. 87-16.

8. K. J. Feighan et al., "Estimation of Service Life and Cost of Routine Maintenance Activities," in *Highway Maintenance Planning,* Transportation Research Record 1102 (Washington, D.C.: Transportation Research Board, National Research Council, 1986), 13-21.

Calculating Compensation Costs

Marvin Friedman

"Compensation" consists of both salaries and/or wages and fringe benefits. It encompasses all forms of wage payments (including, for example, bonuses, commissions, and incentive payments) as well as the cost to the employer of all types of fringes.[1] Obviously, the higher-paid, senior employees in the bargaining unit tend to enjoy higher compensation, while the compensation of those at the opposite end of the salary and seniority spectrums tends to be lower.

For bargaining purposes, the most relevant statistic is the unit's average compensation or, more specifically, its *weighted* average compensation. The weighted average compensation (hereafter "average compensation" or, simply, "compensation") is merely an expression of how much it costs the employer, on the average, for each person on the payroll. It is this figure which presumably will be increased through negotiations.[2]

Although precision in computing these compensation costs depends very much on detailed data usually available only in the employer's payroll records, it is possible to develop some reasonably accurate approximations even without such detailed information.

Indeed, the ability to do so may be quite important in making judgments as to whether a settlement proposal is or is not satisfactory. Moreover, an awareness of the concepts and techniques that are involved in these computations can prove invaluable in carrying out the bargaining dialogue or in dealing with a third-party neutral.

Reprinted from *The Use of Economic Data in Collective Bargaining* (Washington, D.C.: U.S. Department of Labor, 1978.)

These computations, it must be remembered, are not performed simply to engage in a mathematical exercise. The reason for seeking out this type of information is its usefulness at the bargaining table.

The value of salaries and fringe benefits must be known so that the value of any bargaining offer or settlement can be judged. Logically, therefore, the base compensation costs as of the point in time of negotiations—or, more accurately, immediately prior to the receipt of any increase—must be known.

The information that is needed in most cases in order to compute compensation costs is (a) the salary scales and benefit programs, (b) the distribution of the employees in the unit according to pay steps, shifts, and length of service, and (c) for purposes of some medical care programs, the employees' coverage status. If this information is in hand, just about all but one item of compensation can be readily computed.

The sole exception is the cost of the overtime premium. Overtime is apt to vary widely from week-to-week or month-to-month. Consequently, the data for any one pay period are an inadequate gauge where overtime is concerned. Simply by chance, it may cost the employer more one week than the next. It is common practice, therefore, to cost-out the overtime premium by averaging the cost of that benefit over the prior 12 months.

So far as the other elements of compensation are concerned, however, it is not necessary to study a full year's experience. With salaries, vacations, holidays, etc., the costs can be based on a snapshot taken at a fixed point in time on the basis of the provisions in the current collective bargaining agreement and the current distribution of the employees in the bargaining unit. That snapshot of compensation costs should be made as of the time the parties are at the bargaining table.

The purpose of this essay is to provide guidance on how to perform those computations, as well as the computations to determine the cost—the value—of an *increase* in compensation. The development of such compensation information gives the parties a basis for weighing the value of any particular wage and fringe benefit package.

Before the value of cost impact of any increase in compensation—whether in salaries, fringes, or both—can be gauged, the first step is to develop the base, or existing, compensation figure. A pay increase of $500 per employee, for example, means something different for a bargaining unit whose existing salary and fringe benefit cost per employee amount to $20,000 per year than for a unit whose compensation is $10,000. In the latter case, it represents an increase of 5 percent, but on a base of $20,000 it amounts to only $2^1/_2$ percent. Thus, the base compensation figure is essential in determining the percentage value of any increase in compensation.

In order to demonstrate the computation methods for arriving at the base compensation figure, a Sample Bargaining Unit has been constructed and certain levels of employment, salaries, fringe benefits and hours of work have been assumed (Exhibit 1).

Exhibit 1: *Sample Bargaining Unit*

(a) Employment and Salaries

Classification	Number of Firefighters	Salary
Probationary		
Step 1	5	$10,100
Step 2	10	11,100
Private	65	12,100
Lieutenant	15	13,500
Captain	5	14,500
	100	

(b) Longevity Payments

Longevity Step	Number of Firefighters	Longevity Pay
Step 1	20 Privates	$ 500
Step 2	10 Privates	1,000
Step 2	15 Lieutenants	1,000
Step 2	5 Captains	1,000

(c) Hours of Work

The scheduled hours consist of one 24-hour shift every three days (one on; two off), or an average of 56 hours per week and a total of 2,912 hours per year.

(d) Overtime Premium

All overtime hours are paid at the rate of time-and-one-half. The Sample Bargaining Unit is assumed to have worked a total of 5,000 overtime hours during the preceding year.

(e) Shift Differential

The shift differential is 10 percent for all hours between 4 p.m. and 8 a.m. However, 10 members of the unit work exclusively on the day shift, from 8 a.m. to 4 p.m.

(f) Vacations

15 employees—(probationers) 5 shifts
35 employees—(privates) 10 shifts
50 employees—(all others) 15 shifts

(g) Holidays

Each firefighter is entitled to 10 paid holidays and receives 8 hours pay for each holiday.

(h) Clothing Allowance

$150 per employee per year.

(i) Hospitalization

Type of Coverage	Number of Firefighters	Employer's Monthly Payment
Single coverage	15	$20.00
Family coverage	85	47.00
	100	

(a) Pensions

The employer contributes an amount equal to 6 percent of the payroll (including basic salaries, longevity, overtime and shift differentials).

COMPUTING BASE COMPENSATION

On the basis of the foregoing information on employment, salaries, and benefits, we are now in a position to compute, for the Sample Bargaining Unit, its average base compensation—in essence, the cost of compensation for the average employee. (See Exhibit 2.)

The combined average salary cost and average longevity cost amount to $12,630 per year. On an hourly basis, this comes to $4,337 ($12,630 ÷ 2,912).

It can be seen from the overtime-cost calculations (Exhibit 3) that the half-time premium is worth $108.43 per year on the average, while the straight-time portion is worth $216.85. This means, of course, that total pay at straight-time rates amounts to $12,846.85 ($12,630 plus $216.85) per firefighter.

Exhibit 2: *The Cost of Compensation for an Average Bargaining Unit Employee*

(a) Average Straight-Time Salary

(1) Classification	(2) Number of Firefighters	(3) Salary	(4) Weighted Salaries (2) × (3)
Probationary			
Step 1	5	$10,100	$ 50,500
Step 2	10	11,100	111,000
Private	65	12,100	786,500
Lieutenant	15	13,500	202,500
Captain	5	14,500	72,500
	100		$1,223,000

Average Annual Basic Salary =
$1,223,000 ÷ 100; or $12,230 per year

(b) Longevity Pay

(1) Longevity Step	(2) Number of Firefighters	(3) Longevity Pay	(4) Total Longevity Pay (2) × (3)
Step 1	20	$ 500	$10,000
Step 2	30	1,000	30,000
			$40,000

Average Annual Longevity Pay =
$40,000 ÷ 100;* or $400 per year

*Since the unit is trying to determine its average base compensation—that is, all the salary and fringe benefit items its members receive collectively—the total cost of longevity pay must be averaged over the entire unit of 100.

Exhibit 3

(c) Average Cost of Overtime

Overtime work for the Sample Bargaining Unit is assumed to be paid for at the rate of time-and-one-half. This means that part of the total overtime costs is an amount paid for at straight-time rates and part is a premium payment.

	(1) Annual Cost	(2) Number of Firefighters	(3) Average Annual Cost (1) ÷ (2)
Straight-time cost ($4.337 × 5,000 overtime hours)	$21,685.00	100	$216.85
Half-time premium cost (1/2 × $21,685.00)	10,842.50	100	108.43
Total overtime cost	$32,527.50		$325.28

Exhibit 4

(d) Average Cost of Shift Differential

The Sample Bargaining Unit receives a shift differential of 10 percent for all hours worked between 4 p.m. and 8 a.m. But 10 members of the unit who work in headquarters are assumed to work hours that are not subject to the differential. This leaves 90 employees who receive the differential.

Since the differential is paid for hours worked between 4 p.m. and 8 a.m., it is applicable to only two-thirds of the normal 24-hour shift. It, therefore, only costs the employer two-thirds of 10 percent for each 24 hours. That is the reason for column (5) in the following calculation. Each employee receives the differential for only two-thirds of his 24-hour tour.

(1) Classification	(2) Number on Shift Pay	(3) Salary	(4) 10% of Column (3)	(5) .667 of Column (4)	(6) Total Cost (2) × (5)
Probationary					
Step 1	5	$10,100	$1,010	$ 674	$ 3,370
Step 2	10	11,100	1,110	740	7,400
Private					
Longevity-0	35	12,100	1,210	807	28,245
Longevity-1	17	12,600*	1,260	840	14,280
Longevity-2	7	13,100*	1,320	880	6,160
Lieutenant	12	14,500*	1,450	967	11,604
Captain	4	15,500*	1,550	1,034	4,136
	90				$75,195

Average Annual Cost of Shift Differential = $75,196 ÷ 100,** or $751.95 per year

*Basic salary plus longevity pay.

**Since the unit is trying to determine its average base compensation—that is, all the salary and fringe benefit items its members receive collectively—the total cost of the shift differential must be averaged over the entire unit of 100.

Exhibit 5

(e) Average Cost of Vacation

Vacation costs for the unit are influenced by (a) the amount of vacations received by the employees with differing lengths of service, and (b) the pay scales of those employees.

(1) Classification	(2) Number of Firefighters	(3) Hourly Rate*	(4) Hours of Vacation**	(5) Total Vacation Hours (2) × (4)	(6) Total Vacation Cost (3) × (5)
Probationary					
Step 1	5	$3.468	120	600	$ 2,080.80
Step 2	10	3.812	120	1,200	4,574.40
Private					
Longevity-0	35	4.155	240	8,400	34,902.00
Longevity-1	20	4.327	360	7,200	31,154.40
Longevity-2	10	4.499	360	3,600	16,196.40
Lieutenant	15	4.979	360	5,400	26,886.60
Captain	5	5.323	360	1,800	9,581.40
	100				$125,376.00

Average Annual Vacation Cost = $125,376 ÷ 100; or $1,253.76 per year

* Derived from annual salaries (including longevity pay), divided by 2,912 hours (56 hours × 52 weeks). The 10 firefighters who do not receive shift differential would be on a regular 40-hour week and would, therefore, have a different hourly rate and vacation entitlement. The impact on cost, however, would be minimal. It has, therefore, been disregarded in this computation.

**Since each firefighter works a 24-hour shift, the hours of vacation are arrived at by multiplying the number of work shifts of vacation entitlement by 24 hours. For example, the figure of 120 hours is obtained by multiplying 5 shifts of vacation × 24 hours (one work shift).

Exhibit 6

(f) Average Cost of Paid Holidays

Unlike vacations, the number of holidays received by an employee is not typically tied to length of service. Where the level of benefits is uniform, as it is with paid holidays, the calculation to determine its average cost is less complex.

In the Sample Bargaining Unit, it is assumed that each firefighter receives 8 hours of pay for each of his 10 paid holidays, or a total of 80 hours of holiday pay:

(1) Average Annual Cost of Paid Holidays = $346.96 (80 hours × $4.337 average straight-time hourly rate), or

(2) Total Annual Cost of Paid Holiday hours per year = 8,000 (80 hours × 100 employees)

Total annual cost of paid holidays = $34,696.00 (the unit's average straight-time hourly rate of $4.337 × 8,000 hours)

Average annual cost of paid holidays = $346.96 (34,696.00 ÷ 100 employees)

Exhibit 7

(g) Average Cost of Hospitalization

(1) Type of Coverage	(2) Number of Fire-fighters	(3) Yearly Premium Cost to Employer	(4) Total Cost to Employer (2) × (3)
Single	15	$240	$ 3,600
Family	85	564	47,940
	100		$51,540

Average Annual Cost of Hospitalization = $51,540 ÷ 100; or $515.40 per year

(h) Other Fringe Benefits

(1) Pensions cost the employer 6 percent of payroll. The payroll amounts to $1,370,723 (salary cost—$1,223,000; longevity cost—$40,000; overtime cost—$32,528; and shift differential cost—$75,195). Six percent of this total is $82,243 which, when divided by 100, yields $822.43 as the average cost of pensions per firefighter, per year.

(2) The yearly cost of the clothing allowance is $150 per firefighter.

As the recapitulation in Exhibit 8 indicates, total compensation—salary plus fringes—for each firefighter averages $16,795.78 per year.

Once having determined the base compensation costs, it is now possible to compute the value—or cost—of any increase in the items of compensation. The methods used to make these computations are essentially the same as those used to compute the base compensation data.

Before proceeding to that exercise, however, a general observation about the computation of base compensation should be made. Since the purpose is to produce an average *total* cost per employee—whether by the hour or by the year—it follows that the objective must be to capture and include in the computation, for each item of compensation, the full amount of the employer's expense. This is why accurately maintained payroll records are desirable. Among other things, such records can help to resolve what might otherwise be protracted debates over approaches to the costing-out process on certain complicated benefit programs.

One such item that comes to mind is paid sick leave. Many paid sick leave programs permit the employee to accumulate unused sick leave. Suppose, for example, the employees are allowed five paid sick leave days each year, with the opportunity to "bank" the unused days and, upon separation or retirement, to receive pay for one-half of the days in the "bank."

Exhibit 8: *Average Annual Base Compensation for the Sample Bargaining Unit*

(a) Straight-Time earnings	**$12,846.85**
Basic salary	$12,230.00
Longevity pay	400.00
Overtime	216.85*
(b) Fringe Benefits	**$3,948.93**
Overtime premium	$108.43
Shift differential	751.95
Vacations	1,253.76
Holidays	346.96
Hospitalization	515.40
Clothing allowance	150.00
Pension	822.43
(c) Total	**$16,795.78**

*This is only the straight-time portion of overtime pay. The premium portion appears with the fringe benefits.

With such a program, it is likely that not all of the employees in the unit would use all five days each year. It would be incorrect, however, to cost-out sick leave on the basis of the days actually taken each year since, at some subsequent point, there would be partial reimbursement for the unused days. Further complicating matters is the fact that the employee's rate of pay at the time the reimbursement takes place will very likely be higher than it is when the unused days are put in the "bank." Obviously, there is no way of knowing what that future rate of pay will be, so there is no way to determine now how much those "banked" days will be worth at the time of reimbursement.

One way to cost out the unit's paid sick leave in any year may be simply to charge everyone with five days. Needless to say, this may misstate the true cost and may generate controversy and debate.

Such disputes may be avoided if the actual total dollar cost of the sick leave program for the year can be derived. To do this, however, it would be necessary to have the dollar costs for each piece—that is, in our example, the cost of the days used in the year plus the cost of the reimbursements made in the year—in order to produce a total annual cost. That total, divided by the number of employees in the unit or by the number of hours worked by the unit during the year, would then yield the cost per employee or per hour for this particular benefit.

In a case such as the sick leave program cited, the availability of dollar amounts reflecting total annual costs would, as mentioned earlier, help to forestall controversy over the procedure to be used for costing out the benefit. And this approach would be consistent with the basic concept that is involved in costing out the other elements of employee compensation. That approach, as was also mentioned earlier, seeks to capture and include in the computation the full amount of the employer's expense for each item of compensation.

COMPUTING THE COST OF INCREASES IN ITEMS OF COMPENSATION

In order to demonstrate how to cost-out any increases in compensation, it will be assumed that the Sample Bargaining Unit negotiates a settlement consisting of the following package:

- An increase of 5 percent in basic salaries;
- Two additional shifts of vacation for all at the second step of longevity;
- An improvement in the benefits provided by the hospitalization program, which will cost the employer an additional $4.00 per month for family coverage and $2.50 for single coverage.

The cost of this settlement—that is, the amount of the increase in compensation that it represents—would be computed in the manner presented below, starting first with the cost-impact of the salary increase. As will be noted, the objective of the computation is to find the *average* cost of the increase—that is, the cost per firefighter, per year.

(a) *Increase in Cost of Salaries.* The increase in average annual basic salary ($0.05 \times \$12,230$) is $611.50. The cost of longevity pay does not increase. This is because longevity increments for the unit are fixed dollar amounts. If these payments were based on a percentage of salary—that is, if they were linked to the pay scales—then the cost of the longevity payments would also have risen by 5 percent. However, as a fixed dollar amount, these payments remain unaffected by the increase in basic salaries.

As a result, the increase in the unit's total average salary ($12,230 in basic salary plus $400 in longevity) is, in reality, not 5 percent, but only 4.8 percent ($611.50 \div \$12,630$).

This difference is important because of the way in which pay increases impact on the cost of fringe benefits. This is commonly referred to as the "roll up." As salaries increase, so does the cost to the employer of such fringes as vacations, holidays, overtime premiums, etc. This increase in cost comes about even though the benefits are not improved.

Some fringes, however, are not subject to the roll up. This is the case with respect to those fringe benefits that are not linked to pay rates. Examples of this type of fringe benefit include shift differentials that are stated in cents-per-hour (in contrast to a percentage of salary), a flat dollar amount for clothing allowance, and most group insurance programs.

(b) *Cost Impact of the "Roll up."* The increase in average straight-time pay (basic salary plus longevity pay) of the Sample Bargaining Unit was shown to be 4.8 percent. This means that the average cost of every benefit linked to salary will likewise increase by 4.8 percent. In our example, therefore, the average cost of compensation will go up by

$611.50 per year in salaries, plus however much this adds to the costs of the fringe benefits as a result of the roll up.

But there is more. For our example, it is also to be assumed that the Sample Bargaining Unit will gain a vacation improvement—two additional shifts at the second step of longevity—and an improved hospitalization program.

The employer's contribution for the hospitalization program of the Sample Bargaining Unit is a fixed dollar amount and is, therefore, not subject to any roll up. Thus, we need in this instance be concerned only with the costing-out of the improvement in that benefit.

This is not the case with the vacations. Here the cost-increase is double-barreled—the cost of the improvement *and* the cost of the roll up.

None of the other fringe benefits of the Sample Bargaining Unit will be improved. Consequently, so far as they are concerned, we need only compute the increases in cost due to the roll up. The fringes which fit this category are overtime premiums, holidays, sick leave, shift differentials, and pensions.

As is indicated in Exhibit 9, column (3)—the added cost due to the roll up—is obtained by multiplying the base (pre-settlement) cost by 0.048. Obviously, if shift differentials and/or pensions were based on a set dollar (or cents) amount (instead of a percentage of salary), there would be no roll up cost associated with them. The only increase in cost that would result in such a situation would be associated with an improvement in the benefit item.

Having performed this computation, we can now begin to see the impact of the roll up factor. As a result of the increase in pay, the four fringe benefit items will together cost the employer an additional $107.83 per firefighter, per year.

(c) Increase in Cost of Vacations. As noted earlier, the vacation improvement of two shifts—48 hours (2 shifts × 24 hours)—is to be limited to those whose length of service is equal to the time required to achieve the second step of longevity in the salary structure. Thus, it will be received by 30 members of the unit—10 privates, 15 lieutenants, and 5 captains.[3]

The first step in the computation is to determine the cost of the *new* benefit under the *existing* (old) salaries—that is, before the 4.8 percent pay increase (see Exhibit 10).

Exhibit 9

(1) Fringe Benefit	(2) Base Average Annual Cost*	(3) Roll Up Factor	(4) Increased Cost (2) × (3)
Overtime			
Straight-time	$216.85	0.048	$ 10.41
Premium	108.43	0.048	5.20
Shift differential	751.95	0.048	36.09
Holidays	346.96	0.048	16.65
Pensions	822.43	0.048	39.48
			$107.83

*See Exhibits 2-8 for derivation of these costs.

Exhibit 10

(1) Number of Firefighters	(2) Hours of Increased Vacation	(3) Total Hours (1) × (2)	(4) Existing Hourly Rates*	(5) Cost of Improvement (3) × (4)
10 Privates	48	480	$4.499	$2,159.52
15 Lieutenants	48	720	4.979	3,584.88
5 Captains	48	240	5.323	1,277.52
				$7,021.92

*See Exhibit 5 for derivation of hourly rates.

The calculation thus far reflects only the additional cost of the vacation improvement based on the salaries existing *prior* to the 4.8 percent pay raise. In other words, if there had been no pay increase, the vacation improvement would result in an added cost of $7,021.92. But there was a pay increase. As a result, the base year vacation costs—including now the added cost of the improvement—must be rolled up by the 4.8 percent factor. Every hour of vacation—the old and the new—will cost 4.8 percent more as a result of the pay increase (Exhibit 11).

By adding the two "new" pieces of cost—$7,021.92, which is the cost of the improvement, and $6,355.10, which is the cost due to the impact of the wage increase—we obtain the total increase in the cost of vacations. It amounts to $13,377.02. In order to figure the *average* cost, this total must be divided

Exhibit 11

(1) Classification	(2) Existing Vacation Costs*	(3) Increase in Cost**	(4) Adjusted Base Costs (2) + (3)	(5) Roll Up Factor	(6) Increased Cost from Roll Up (4) × (5)
Probationary					
Step 1	$ 2,080.80	—	$ 2,080.80	0.048	$ 99.88
Step 2	4,574.40	—	4,574.40	0.048	219.57
Private					
Longevity-0	34,902.00	—	34,902.00	0.048	1,675.30
Longevity-1	31,154.40	—	31,154.40	0.048	1,495.41
Longevity-2	16,196.40	$2,159.52	18,355.92	0.048	881.08
Lieutenant	26,886.60	3,584.88	30,471.48	0.048	1,462.63
Captain	9,581.40	1,277.52	10,858.92	0.048	521.23
	$125,376.00	$7,021.92	$132,397.92	0.048	$6,355.10

*The base (or existing) vacation costs are from Exhibit 5.
**From data in preceding table.

by the number of firefighters in the Sample Bargaining Unit. The increase in the average cost of vacations, therefore, is—

$13,377 ÷ 100, or $133.77

Had the vacation improvement been granted across-the-board, to everyone in the unit, the calculation would have been different—and considerably easier. If the entire unit were to receive an additional 48 hours of vacation, the total additional hours would then be 4,800 (48 hours × 100 employees). These hours would then be multiplied by the unit's old average straight-time rate ($4.337), in order to arrive at the cost of the additional vacation improvement which, in this case, would have come to $20,817.60 (4,800 hours × $4.337). And, in that case, the total cost of vacations—that is, the across-the-board improvement, plus the impact of the 4.8 percent salary increase—would have been computed as follows:

(a) Roll up of old vacation costs = $ 6,018.05
 ($125,376 × 0.048)

(b) Cost of vacation improvement = $20,817.60

(c) Roll up cost of improvement = $ 999.24
 ($20,817.60 × 0.048)

These pieces total to $27,834.89. When spread over the entire Sample Bargaining Unit, the increase in the average cost of vacations would have been $278.35 per year ($27,834.89 ÷ 100 employees).

This latter method of calculation does not apply only to vacations. It applies to any situation where a salary-related fringe benefit is to be improved equally for every member of the unit. An additional paid holiday would be another good example.

(d) *Increase in Cost of Hospitalization.* In this example, it has been assumed that the Sample Bargaining Unit has negotiated as part of its new package an improvement in its hospitalization programs. As with most hospitalization programs, the one covering this unit is not linked to salaries.

This improvement, it is assumed, will cost the employer an additional $4.00 per month ($48 per year) for family coverage and $2.50 per month ($30 per year) for single coverage. Thus, based on this and previous information about the breakdown of employees receiving each type of coverage, the calculation of the increase in hospitalization costs is as shown in Exhibit 12. The unit's average hospitalization cost will be increased by $45.30 per year ($4,530 ÷ 100 employees).

Exhibit 12

(1) Type of Coverage	(2) Number Covered	(3) Annual Cost of Improvement	(4) Total New Cost (2) × (3)
Single	15	$30	$ 450
Family	85	48	4,080
			$4,530

THE TOTAL INCREASE IN THE AVERAGE COST OF COMPENSATION

At this point, the increase in the costs of all the items of compensation which will change because of the Sample Bargaining Unit's newly negotiated package has been calculated. All that is left is to combine these individual pieces in order to arrive at the total increase in the unit's average cost of compensation. This is done in the tabulation which appears as Exhibit 13.

As the recapitulation shows, the average increase in salary costs amounts to $621.91 per year, while the average increase in the cost of the fringe benefits (including *new* benefit costs, as well as *roll up* costs) comes to $276.49, for a total increase in average annual compensation of $898.40 per firefighter, per year. That is the total annual cost of the settlement per firefighter.

There remains one final computation that is really the most significant—the *percent* increase that all of these figures represent. The unit's average base compensation per year was $16,796. The total dollar increase amounts to $898. The percent increase, therefore, is 5.3 percent ($898 ÷ 16,796) and that is the amount by which the unit's package increased the employer's average yearly cost per firefighter.

COMPUTING THE HOURLY COST OF COMPENSATION

The increase in the cost of compensation per *hour* will be the same. The approach to the computation, however, is different than that which was used in connection with the cost per year. In the case of the hourly computation, the goal is to obtain the cost per hour of *work*. This requires that a distinction be

Exhibit 13: *Increase in Average Annual Cost of Compensation for Sample Bargaining Unit*

(a) Straight-Time Earnings	$621.91
Basic salary	$611.50
Longevity pay	
Overtime (straight-time portion)	10.41
(b) Fringe Benefits	**$276.49**
Overtime premium	$ 5.20
Shift differential	36.09
Vacations	133.77
Holidays	16.65
Hospitalization	45.30
Clothing allowance	
Pensions	39.48
(c) Total Increase in Average Annual Cost of Annual Compensation	**$898.40**

drawn between hours worked and hours paid for. The difference between the two is leave time.

In the Sample Bargaining Unit, for example, the employee receives an annual salary which covers 2,912 regularly scheduled hours (56 hours per week, times 52). In addition, he works an average of 50 hours of overtime per year. The sum of these two—regularly scheduled hours and overtime hours, or 2,962—are the total hours paid for.

But they do not represent hours worked, because some of those hours are paid leave time. The Sample Bargaining Unit, for example, receives paid leave time in the form of vacations and holidays. The number of hours actually worked by each employee is 2,600 (2,962 hours paid for, minus 362 hours of paid leave).[4]

The paid leave hours are, in a sense, bonuses—hours paid for, above and beyond hours worked. Thus, in order to obtain the hourly cost represented by these "bonuses"—that is, the hours of paid leave—the annual dollar cost of these benefits is divided by the annual hours *worked*.

It is the same as if we were trying to compute the per-hour cost of a year-end bonus. The dollar amount of that bonus would simply be divided by the total number of hours worked during the year.

So it is with *all* fringe benefits, not only paid leave. In exchange for those benefits the employer receives hours of work (the straight-time hours and the overtime hours). Consequently, the hourly cost of any fringe benefit will be obtained by dividing the annual cost of the benefit by the annual number of hours *worked*. In some instances that cost is converted into money that ends up in the employee's pocket, as it does in the case of fringe benefits like shift differentials, overtime premiums, and clothing allowances. In other instances—such as hospitalization and pensions—the employee is provided with benefits in the form of insurance programs. And in the case of paid leave time—holidays,[5] vacations, sick leave, etc.—the return to the employee is in terms of fewer hours of work.

The average annual costs of the fringe benefits of the Sample Bargaining Unit were developed earlier in this [selection] in connection with the computations of the unit's average annual base compensation. They appear in column (2) below.

In order to convert the costs of those fringe benefits into an average hourly amount, they are divided by 2,600—the average hours worked during the year by each employee in the unit. As can be seen, the hourly cost of all fringe benefits amounts to $1.518. (See Exhibit 14.)

In addition to the fringe benefit costs, compensation includes the basic pay. For our Sample Bargaining Unit this is $12,630 per year (average salary plus average cost of longevity payments). On a straight-time hourly basis, this comes to $4.337 ($12,630 ÷ 2,912 hours). Even with the straight-time portion for the year's overtime included ($216.85), the average straight-time hourly rate of pay will, of course, still remain at $4.337 ($12,846.45 ÷ 2,962 hours).

A recapitulation of these salary and fringe benefit cost data produces both the average *annual* base compensation figure for the Sample Bargaining Unit and the average *hourly* figure:

	Yearly	Hourly
Earnings at straight-time	$12,846.85 ÷ 2,962	= $4.337
Fringe benefits	3,948.93 ÷ 2,600	= 1.519
Total compensation	$16,795.78	$5.856

As indicated, on an annual basis, the average compensation cost comes to $16,795.78, a figure that was also presented earlier in this [selection]. And on an hourly basis, the average compensation of the unit amounts to $5.856.

Essentially the same process is followed if the *increase* in compensation is to be measured on an hourly (instead of an annual) basis.

The 5 percent pay increase received by the Sample Bargaining Unit would be worth 21 cents ($12,230 × 0.05 = $611.50; $611.50 ÷ 2,912 = $0.21). The annual increase in the unit's fringe benefit costs per firefighter—$276.49 for all items combined—works out to 10.6 cents per hour ($276.49 ÷ 2600 hours).

Together, these represent a gain in average compensation of 31.6 cents per hour, or 5.4 percent ($0.316 ÷ $5.956). This is one-tenth of a percentage point off from the amount of increase (5.3 percent) reflected by the annual data—a difference due simply to the rounding of decimals during the computation process.

Notes

1. Technically, employee compensation may also include the cost of legally required employer payments for programs such as social security, unemployment compensation, and workers' compensation. These items are disregarded in this analysis.
2. It is also referred to as the "base" compensation—that is, the compensation figure against which the cost of any settlement will be measured in order to determine the value of the settlement.

Exhibit 14

(1) Fringe Benefit	(2) Average Annual Cost	(3) Average Hours Worked	(4) Average Hourly Cost (2) ÷ (3)
Overtime premium*	$ 108.43	2,600	$0.042
Shift differential	751.95	2,600	0.289
Vacations	1,253.76	2,600	0.482
Holidays	346.96	2,600	0.133
Hospitalization	515.40	2,600	0.198
Clothing allowance	150.00	2,600	0.058
Pensions	822.43	2,600	0.316
	$3,948.93		$1.518

*Includes only the premium portion of the pay for overtime work.

3. In costing out an improvement in vacations, the computation should cover the cost impact in the first year *only*. There is no need to be concerned with the impact in subsequent years when, supposedly, more and more employees become eligible for the improved benefit. For computational purposes, it must be assumed that the average length of service in the unit remains constant. This constancy is caused by normal personnel flows. As the more senior staff leave because of retirement or death, the staff is replenished by new hires without any accumulated seniority. Thus, for this type of computation, it must be presumed that the proportion of the workforce which benefits from the improved vacation will be constant year after year.

It should be noted that an improvement in vacations (or any other form of paid leave) that is offset by corresponding reductions in on-duty manning does not represent any increase in cost to the employer.

4. Each firefighter receives 80 hours in paid holidays per year. The average number of hours of vacation per year was derived as follows:

15 firefighters × 120 hours (five 24-hour shifts)	=	1,800 hours
35 firefighters × 240 hours (ten 24-hour shifts)	=	8,400 hours
50 firefighters × 360 hours (fifteen 24-hour shifts)	=	18,000 hours
		28,200 hours

This averages out to 282 hours of vacation per firefighter (28,200 ÷ 100) which, together with 80 holiday hours, totals 362 paid leave hours.

5. Typically, of course, firefighters do not receive time off, but are paid an extra day's pay for working a holiday.

Budgeting Capital Outlays and Improvements

A. John Vogt

A medium-sized city recently spent $4.9 million to increase treated water storage capacity and to replace water lines. A fast-growing metropolitan city is spending $12.6 million for improvements to thoroughfares and intersections. A nearby county will spend $42 million in bond proceeds to build new schools over the next five years, and the principal city in that county will spend about $6 million to buy raw land for a new landfill. A small rural county is spending $45,000 to acquire and install a new microwave radio system for its emergency medical services program and another $86,000 for personal computers and other equipment for county administrative offices. These expenditures, different in nature and amount, are alike in one way—they are all capital expenditures.

This article will examine the elements involved in planning and budgeting capital outlays and improvements and develop a model of capital budgeting for state and local governments. Whereas we have a well-defined model for operating budgeting in the public sector, this is not the case with capital budgeting—a truth made evident in that while many states require their local governments to have annual operating budgets and prescribe specific steps for preparing that budget, far fewer states require a special process for local government budgeting of capital expenditures. Similarly, while we have numerous books and manuals on operating budgeting which portray a fairly uniform process, we have few books and manuals on capital budgeting, and their treatment of the process and techniques varies greatly. Moreover, most of these latter books and manuals typically cover only one phase or aspect of capital budgeting, such as capital improvement programming, borrowing to finance capital improvements, or quantitative methods for evaluating capital project proposals.

The model of capital budgeting developed in this article consists of three stages: planning, budgeting, and implementation, and it shows how different techniques and approaches like capital programming fit into each stage and the entire capital budget process.

First, however, we will define capital outlay, discuss what capital outlays and projects should be reviewed and approved in a separate capital budget process, and consider why a special process or set of procedures have evolved in many jurisdictions for capital budgeting.

WHAT IS A CAPITAL OUTLAY?

Capital outlays are different from other expenditures. Capital outlays are durable—that is, they yield benefits for many years, or they result in the acquisition of property that has a long life. Many capital outlays do not recur each year, and irregular intervals of time elapse between periodic replacements. Capital outlays are also typically expensive, requiring large expenditures compared with most ongoing current expenditures.

Two formal definitions of capital outlay are available in the literature. One is from economics, and it

---

A. John Vogt is professor of publc finance and government, Institute of Government, The University of North Carolina at Chapel Hill.

gives a broad meaning to the concept. The other is from accounting, and it provides a more restricted definition.

Economics states that a capital outlay is any expenditure that will produce benefits in future years or for at least more than one year, whereas a current expenditure yields benefits for only the current year.[1] Under this definition, whether the capital outlay results in the acquisition of specific property is irrelevant. Thus, even advertising expenditures made to attract new industry to a state or community, which accounting practices would charge to a current account, would be considered to be capital expenditures because they are made to obtain benefits or revenues in future years. This is clearly a broad conception of capital outlay.

Accounting, on the other hand, defines a capital outlay as an expenditure of significant value that results in the acquisition of or an addition to a fixed asset.[2] "Significant value" can be $100, several hundred dollars, or $1,000 or more, depending on the size of the jurisdiction. If an item costs less than the significant dollar amount, the expenditure for it is an operating outlay even though it would otherwise qualify as a capital outlay. The term *fixed asset* refers to tangible property that is held or used for a long period of time or at least more than one year. "Fixed" as used here does not mean immobile; thus an automobile is commonly classified as a fixed asset.

The major difference between these two definitions from accounting and from economics is whether a fixed asset is acquired. Economics says that any outlay that produces future benefits, whether or not a fixed asset is acquired, is a capital outlay. To qualify as a capital outlay under the definition from accounting, however, an expenditure must produce future benefits and result in the acquisition of a fixed asset or add to an existing one. Indeed, it is through the use of the fixed asset that the future benefits are realized.

The definition from accounting is the one generally used in government financial practices, and that is the meaning intended for capital outlay in this article. The major categories of capital outlay under this definition follow:

1. Land. This blanket term includes land; legal, brokerage, and other expenses incidental to the purchase of land; and land-preparation costs.

2. Buildings. This designation refers to permanent structures for housing persons or property, and equipment or furnishings that are fixed or attached to such structures. The costs for legal, architectural, and engineering services related to building construction are also classified here.

3. Improvements other than buildings. Examples in this category are streets, bridges, tunnels, and water or sewer lines.

4. Unattached equipment or furnishings. Included here are trucks, automobiles, furniture, and other equipment that is used for more than one year or fiscal period.

What Capital Outlays Belong in the Capital Budget?

Not all capital outlays should be included and reviewed in the capital budget process. The annual or biennial operating budget is the best place for capital outlays that will not involve a great deal of money. These expenditures typically are for unattached equipment and furnishings, small parcels of land, and small construction projects. A dollar cutoff that ranges from $1,000 to as much as $100,000 or so (depending on the size of the jurisdiction) serves as the instrument for deciding which capital outlays are large enough to place in the capital budget. Thus while the accountant for a large city would probably record an expenditure of several thousand dollars for mowing equipment as a capital outlay, the budget officer of that jurisdiction would probably include and review such an expenditure in the operating budget; the item would be classified under "capital outlay" or "permanent property" in the operating budget.

The capital budget should also not include capital outlays that recur each year, even though the total outlay or outlay per item is above the dollar cutoff for determining which capital outlays belong in the capital budget. For instance, a large city may have a capital budget with a dollar cutoff of $50,000; a capital item that will cost over $50,000 is included in the capital budget, and a capital item that costs less than $50,000 is placed in the operating budget. The city may be replacing one fire department pumper truck each year, at a current cost of $220,000 per year. This expenditure is for a long-lived capital asset, and it is more than $50,000; and on this basis, the expenditure for the fire trucks should be placed in the capital budget. However, since the expenditure occurs each year, it should be placed in the operating budget. The operating budget is able to finance an annual capital outlay as readily as annual operating expenditures for salaries, fringe benefits, supplies, etc. The capital budget therefore should be reserved for capital outlays that are costly, i.e., above a specified dollar cutoff, and that do not recur each year.

Some say that the capital budget should include *all* extraordinary, unusual, or large nonrecurring expenditures, and not just those that result in the acquisition of a fixed asset. They argue that all of these expenditures, whether current or capital, draw on the jurisdiction's capital resources and therefore should be evaluated together in the capital budget process. Examples of expenditures like this would be a one-time extra Medicaid payment of $2 million by a medium-sized county or $75,000 spent by a small city for a management improvement study. The former is clearly not a capital outlay. The latter could qualify as a capital outlay under the economist's but not the accountant's definition of capital outlay. The danger of putting large operating expenditures that do not recur each year into the capital budget is that if the capital budget is financed with long-term debt, this practice opens the door to financing current expense items—those that benefit only the current year—with debt proceeds that are paid back in the future. Debt to be repaid in the future should be used to finance only outlays that produce benefits in the future—or better still, the accountant would say, to finance only capital or fixed assets that will last or be used for many years into the future.

WHY CAPITAL PLANNING AND BUDGETING?

Why would a local government establish a special process or set of procedures for making and implementing capital outlay decisions? The first reason is the sheer magnitude of many capital outlays, especially for the construction of buildings or improvements. Much money is at stake in these decisions, and a government should try to make sure that these decisions are the right ones and that the money is not wasted.

Because capital outlays are often so large, the decisions of government to undertake them can shape the most basic features of a community. For example, a school board's decision to locate a new high school on the north side of a city can speed major new development there and indirectly slow growth in other parts of the city. Moreover, the consequences of a capital outlay decision usually extend well into the future. In other words, the impact of the decision may be irreversible for as long as the useful life of the facility or equipment acquired with the outlay. Thus, when a city builds a new city hall in a particular style and at a specific site, the city probably will have to live with that decision, whatever its merits, for perhaps 30 or 40 years. Similarly, if a small town buys a new fire truck, it has committed itself to the technology represented by the new truck's capabilities for probably a decade or so.

Another reason for capital budgeting arises because the same capital outlay decisions do not recur each year. In the operating budget, expenditures recur each year and officials have the current year's experience to guide them in making decisions for the coming year, which reduces the risk of error in these decisions. On the other hand, major capital outlay decisions do not recur every year, and officials do not have the previous years' experience to guide them in making these decisions. The consequent risk of error is much higher for these decisions, which is a good reason to set up a separate process for capital budgeting to assure that major capital decisions are fully considered before they are approved and funded.

Since capital outlay decisions are frequently financed in whole or in part with debt, the risk of default in debt financing is another reason for having special procedures for making these decisions. Moreover, when it commits its government unit to debt financing, the governing board this year binds future governing boards to pay annual principal and interest installments on the debt. In other words, the present governing board exercises authority over those that follow it—a fact that obliges the board to take great care in making capital outlay and financing decisions.

Capital planning and budgeting helps a community provide for the orderly replacement and development of public facilities. To maintain the quality and efficiency of public services like water and sewer systems, public transportation, schools, or recreation, the facilities involved must be replaced or upgraded periodically. Moreover, new buildings or equipment are usually needed to meet growth in service demand. Both replacement and new capital needs must be taken care of within the limited capital resources of a community. A capital budget process helps achieve this purpose—not by lessening the need for new or replacement facilities or by increasing the resources to meet capital needs but by setting priorities to meet the most pressing needs first, by submitting projects to several analytic stages to eliminate poor or very low-priority projects, by carefully scheduling approved projects, and by providing financial projections to help a community avoid overextending itself in meeting capital needs.

CAPITAL PLANNING AND BUDGET PROCESS

What is a capital budget process? How does it work? The model of capital budgeting presented here divides the process into three stages:

1. Planning stage
   - Classification and initial analysis of capital requests.
   - Ranking capital requests into priority. Although this ranking is tentative and will be reviewed and most probably revised later on in the process, decision makers should begin to think about the community's most pressing capital needs at this initial stage of the capital budget process.
   - Preparation of a capital improvement program (CIP) that schedules capital requests for approval, funding, and implementation over a 5- to 10-year future planning period.
   - Forecast of financial resources that will be available to fund capital requests over the same planning period spanned by the CIP.
2. Budget stage
   - Project evaluation. This is a feasibility study that precedes the decision whether to undertake a capital project or buy a capital item. If the project or item is of major size, the study is likely to be contracted out to an architect or engineer. Project evaluation, whether done by in-house staff or contracted, may involve the use of quantitative analysis.
   - Selection of financing for capital requests. Such financing can come from operating revenues, debt proceeds, capital reserves, and other sources.
   - Approval of capital requests and appropriating money to fund them.
3. Implementation stage
   - Acquiring, managing, and investing the revenue available to fund capital requests.
   - Buying equipment, land, and other capital assets.
   - Designing, contracting for, and supervising construction projects.

All three stages with their steps constitute a full capital budget process. We should note here that the appearance of a capital or fixed-asset statement in a local unit's budget does not mean necessarily that the unit has a separate process for making capital expenditure decisions. A statement in the budget documents can be used to show what expenditures are capital and how much of the budget they take. Many jurisdictions use such a statement in their budget books without having either a full-fledged or even a partial capital budget process. Such a process implies that decisions on proposed capital outlays are treated differently in the review and approval process from decisions on current operating expenditures.

CAPITAL PLANNING: IDENTIFICATION AND INITIAL ANALYSIS OF REQUESTS

Identification and initial analysis occurs when the need for a capital outlay is recognized and the request to meet the need is first made. If a government has no CIP or other type of long-range capital plan, most capital requests probably will be formulated and made shortly before the final decision must be made on whether to approve the request. However, we place "identification and initial analysis of requests" as a step in the planning stage to suggest that capital needs should be identified several years ahead of the time when decisions to meet those needs have to be approved and funded. This permits a governmental unit to have a planning stage in its capital budget process and to carefully plan individual capital requests.

The initial analysis of capital requests includes several steps: (1) deciding whether particular requests are in fact capital and whether they belong in the capital budget or in the operating budget; (2) determining that each request is a practical way of meeting the need in question; (3) determining that all expenditures that should be charged to a capital request are counted; (4) analyzing the capital expenditures for each request and estimating the impact that each will have on the operating budget; and (5) beginning to consider what source or sources of financing should be used to fund each request.

CAPITAL PLANNING: ESTABLISHING PRIORITIES

Few, if any, organizations have sufficient resources to meet all of their capital needs. Only some requests can be funded at any one time. Because capital needs or requests compete with one another for limited resources, a critical question to ask about any one request is how great the need for it is compared with the need for other requests. To answer this question, the requests must be ranked into priority. Such ranking occurs throughout the capital budget process as capital needs are assessed and reassessed. However, a preliminary ranking should be made in the planning stage before the capital improvement program (CIP) is proposed. The CIP allocates the costs for capital requests among the years of the CIP planning period, and costs allocated to the first few years of the planning period are presumed to have a higher priority than those allocated to the latter years. Thus some sort of priority setting has to occur before the CIP is prepared.

There are different approaches to priority setting. Decision makers can simply rank capital requests from high to low on the basis of their judgment about the relative need for each request. Or they can first establish categories of capital need and then examine the requests and allocate them among the categories. An established priority ranking system for capital construction projects might have the following categories, ranging from high to low priority:

1. Repairs or construction to ensure the safety of persons or property.
2. Construction to complete projects previously authorized.
3. Major renovations or additions to provide fuller use of existing facilities.
4. New facilities to reduce overcrowded conditions or relieve obsolescence.
5. New facilities to meet increases in demand.
6. New facilities to provide for improvements in programs.
7. New facilities for new programs or services.

The ranking categories of this system favor renovation and repair projects over new facilities to accommodate program expansion or new programs. However, officials could just as easily devise another system with different categories or different priorities among the categories.

Some governments have used a two-dimension rating system for ranking capital requests. With a two-dimension system, two types of priorities are established, the categories for each are ranked and assigned a numeric score, and the scores for the categories from one dimension are multiplied by the scores for the categories from the other dimension to produce a matrix of ratings like that shown in Figure 1. The two dimensions used for the matrix are degree of urgency and priority of function, and the categories for each from high to low are as follows:

Degree of Urgency

1. Legislation: Required by legislation or regulation of federal or state government.
2. Hazard: Removes an obvious or potential hazard to public health or safety.
3. Efficiency: Replaces equipment or a facility that is obsolete, or would be too costly to repair, or maintains and better utilizes existing equipment and facilities.
4. Standard of service: Maintains or provides existing standard of service in developed areas, or provides comparable standard of service in newly developed areas.
5. Economic advantage: Directly benefits the city's economic base by increasing property values or other revenue potential.
6. Increased service: Expands or increases a service or improves a standard of service.
7. New service or convenience: Makes possible a new service or increases convenience or comfort.

Priority of Function

1. Protection of persons and property: police, fire, rescue, inspections, etc.
2. Environmental health: water, sewer, sanitation, public health, etc.
3. Heritage and cultural: education, libraries, etc.

Figure 1: *Two-Dimension Rating Matrix for Capital Proposals*

Urgency	Function							
	Protection 1	Environmental Health 2	Heritage and Cultural 3	Housing 4	Transportation 5	General Maintenance 6	Recreation 7	General Government 8
1 Legislation	1	2	3	4	5	6	7	8
2 Hazard	2	4	6	8	10	12	14	16
3 Efficiency	3	6	9	12	15	18	21	24
4 Standard of service	4	8	12	16	20	24	28	32
5 Economic advantage	5	10	15	20	25	30	35	40
6 Increased or improved service	6	12	18	24	30	36	42	48
7 New service or convenience	7	14	21	28	35	42	49	56

Source: This model is adapted from the matrix used by the City of Durham, North Carolina.

4. Housing: public housing, rehabilitation of housing, etc.
5. Pedestrian and vehicular transportation: street construction and maintenance, mass transit, parking, etc.
6. General maintenance of city-owned property.
7. Recreation: parks, athletic programs, etc.
8. General government: office facilities, central services, etc.

Using a matrix like the one in Figure 1, decision makers can rank capital requests by assigning each a rating from the matrix. A low rating from the matrix indicates a high priority and vice versa.

A priority ranking or rating system is a useful device in capital budgeting because it provides a common framework for decision makers to rank requests. It is particularly helpful to decision makers in ranking medium-priority requests. The high- and low-priority requests are likely to be readily apparent, but the "correct" ranking among requests that fall in the middle may not be so clear-cut. The major problem in using a priority ranking or rating system lies in selecting the categories, setting them into priority in a way that satisfies different decision makers, and then staying with these categories during the ranking process. A ranking or rating system is not likely to work if the decision makers disagree significantly about the priorities, or if the categories are changed to accommodate individual requests.

CAPITAL PLANNING: THE CAPITAL IMPROVEMENT PROGRAM

The capital improvement program (CIP) is at the heart of the planning stage of the capital budgeting process. As already mentioned, a CIP lists capital projects and outlays that a government expects to undertake. Most CIPs extend 5 to 7 years into the future. A forecast period much shorter than this does not allow enough time for planning major projects. While some CIPs extend as much as 10 years or even longer, requests made for years that far into the future are likely to be based on "guesswork" rather than serious planning.

The essential feature of a CIP is the apportionment of capital expenditures among the years covered by the CIP. On the CIP summary form in Figure 2, the column designated "Prior Year's Expenditures" is used for capital projects that are now under way. The column "Coming Budget Year" lists capital expenditures that will be incurred in the upcoming year. These expenditures can be for projects in process or for projects or outlays that are in the final stage of review in the current year's CIP. The latter projects and outlays will be funded either in the capital budget or the coming year's annual budget, or else postponed to a later year in the CIP or dropped altogether. The columns on the CIP form for the planning years show forecasted expenditures for projects in process, projects getting under way in the budget year, or projects or outlays scheduled to start in one

Figure 2: *Capital Improvement Program*

Project and Project Elements	Total Project Expenditures	Prior Year's Expenditures	Coming Budget Year	Planning Year One	Planning Year Two	Planning Year Three	Planning Year Four	Planning Year Five	Years beyond CIP Period

of the planning years. The column for years beyond the CIP is for the expenditures of projects that get under way in the CIP planning period but carry beyond that period before the projects are finished.

The CIP is conceived of as an annual process, and most jurisdictions that use the CIP repeat it each year. Annual repetition provides for a recurring assessment of capital needs and updates the CIP every year to account for new needs. Use of a CIP presumes that capital needs are foreseen and requests will be placed in the CIP in one of the distant planning years. Then the requests are reviewed each year when the CIP is repeated. When the requests that survive reach the budget year, they are approved and funded, rejected, or perhaps postponed another year. Of course, not all capital needs can be recognized five or six years ahead of the time when the final decision to approve or reject them must be made. Some will have to be approved and funded almost immediately upon first request. However, if this happens for many requests, the CIP loses much of its value as a planning tool.

In simple form, a CIP may be no more than a list prepared by the administration that shows future capital outlays by year. However, in both content and process, a CIP usually evolves into something more elaborate, especially for medium-sized or large local governments. In a more elaborate CIP process, requests are subjected to review by different public bodies or officials. A planning agency or citizen's group often makes one review. This review evaluates each request in terms of need, conformity to the comprehensive development plan (if there is one), and whether alternatives are available to the request. The planning agency may hold public hearings on the capital requests. The chief executive officer of a jurisdiction also reviews capital requests for the CIP. This review considers the feasibility of requests, ranks the requests into priority if this has not already been done, and compares the total dollar cost of all the requests with the financial resources available for capital purposes over the period covered by the CIP. The governing or legislative body or a committee thereof makes a final review of CIP requests. More public hearings may be held at this stage, with popular feelings on projects weighed against need, financial feasibility, and other factors. When its review is finished, the governing board can stop here, or it can adopt a formal resolution approving the CIP. This latter course is recommended by most authorities, since it formalizes the CIP process. However, such a resolution typically neither commits funds to a project nor gives the go-ahead to start construction or to make a purchase. The resolution is basically a statement of governing board intent.

As this description of the CIP process suggests, the total time required for CIP preparation, review, and approval may span three or more months for large local governments and perhaps a month or two for small local governments. An important question with regard to timing is whether the CIP process should occur before, simultaneously with, or after the annual budget process. In one city with a July 1–June 30 fiscal year, the CIP process starts in early fall and is completed in February when the annual budget process begins. Thus, the CIP is one factor that sets the stage for the annual operating budget in that city. The other factor is a five-year projection of annual operating needs. Without such a projection, preparing the CIP before the annual operating budget runs the risk that capital plans will be formulated without regard for program or annual operating needs. Probably the best timing is to proceed with the CIP and annual budget process simultaneously. The inherent difficulty in such a schedule is that each process requires much work, in both preparation and review, and doing both together is very difficult in practice.

CAPITAL PLANNING: FINANCIAL PROJECTIONS

Financial projections are undertaken to provide an estimate of the financial resources available for capital outlay purposes for the same period that the CIP covers. Such projections are important because having a CIP without knowing about available financing sources in effect proposes capital decisions without regard for a jurisdiction's ability to fund the decisions.

Projecting the financial resources available for capital outlays means that future operating needs are also projected. Because capital outlays are frequently financed with current revenue and because debt source payments must be made from such revenues, the resources available for capital outlays cannot be predicted realistically without also forecasting how much revenue operating needs are likely to absorb in the future.

At least four general projections are involved in predicting resources available for capital outlay purposes: annual operating revenue and expenditures, outstanding debt, annual debt-service payments, and intergovernmental aid and grants.

Projections of annually recurring revenue are usually based on past trends in existing revenue sources.[3] In looking at the trends, natural growth must be distinguished from growth resulting from changes in a revenue or tax base or rate enacted by the legislative body or governing body. Since revenues from individual sources usually grow at different rates, projections are better based on the individual trend for each major revenue source followed by summation than on the total revenue trend. If changes in revenue classifications have been made during the trend period, past classifications must be adjusted to make them consistent with existing ones. Finally, in making the projections, existing revenue sources and tax rates are assumed to continue through the planning period, but then the trends, as carried into the future, must be adjusted for changes in fiscal conditions or decisions that will affect revenues during that period.

Two major local operating revenue sources are the property tax and revenue from water-sewer systems. Projection of future revenue from the property tax must consider existing property valuation, future building activity, any revaluation or annexation that will occur during the planning period, the assessment ratio if property is not assessed at market value, and the expected collection rate. When water-sewer operations are self-supporting, cost is the best base for projecting revenue from them. This involves predicting the number of water-sewer customers (by category if applicable), the average consumption per customer, and cost per unit of consumption, e.g., 1,000 gallons, at the expected level of consumption. Information on these variables can then be combined in a formula to calculate the amount of revenue that must be secured to cover costs.

As with operating revenues, the projection of operating expenditures should be based on historic trends and adjusted for conditions expected to prevail in the planning period. The expenditures are ordinarily grouped by fund, department or function within each fund, and major line-item classes within each department or function. Only a few general line-item classes need to be used: salaries, fringe benefits, contractual services, supplies, permanent property, and contributions to individuals, organizations, or other governments. Adjustments to historic expenditure trends in anticipation of future decisions and developments should consider salary and wage increases likely to be awarded in the future; changes in fringe benefits; inflation on contractual services, operating supplies, and permanent property; the probable addition or deletion of positions to meet changes in workload requirements; and new positions for improvements in services or new services slated for the planning period.

If operating revenues exceed operating expenditures in a particular year, the sum can be transferred to the capital budget to finance capital improvements and outlays. Or it could be left in an operating fund balance. Such a balance usually serves as an operating reserve to meet unforeseen operating expenditures. But operating fund balances may sometimes be built up to amounts greater than needed for this purpose and then drawn down to finance capital projects and outlays. The financial projection should therefore also forecast operating fund balances during the planning period.

Projecting outstanding debt and annual debt service is important for capital planning purposes because state and local governments issue bonds, and other types of long-term debt to finance major capital improvements. If the improvements in question are for general government functions, the debt often takes the form of general obligation (G.O.) bonds. Such bonds are backed or secured by a government's unlimited taxing power. For local governments, the term "unlimited taxing power" generally refers to the local unit's legal authority to levy property taxes without limit as to rate or amount to make debt service payments on the bonds.

Many states have constitutional or statutory debt provisions that restrict the amount of G.O. debt that local government can issue to some percentage of that unit's assessed or appraised valuation for property tax purposes. For example, North Carolina limits a city or county's outstanding and authorized but unissued G.O. debt to 8 percent of the appraised value of the unit's property that is subject to taxation.[4] The 8 percent limit does not apply to revenue bonds (bonds backed solely by the net earnings of a public enterprise) or G.O. bonds for self-supporting municipal or county utilities. The 8 percent limit is one benchmark for determining how much G.O. debt a local government in North Carolina can safely borrow. However, it is an *outside* limit; most localities in the state try to keep their outstanding G.O. debt within 3 percent of appraised valuation[5] so that they can sell their bonds at low interest rates.

The ratio of outstanding debt to appraised valuation is often a less than adequate measure or boundary of safety in borrowing because real property is appraised for tax purposes only at widely spaced intervals in many states (in North Carolina once every eight years). Also, when property is appraised it is often valued at varying percentages of market value depending on local appraisal practices. As a result, appraised (and assessed) values diverge from true market value depending on state property tax laws and local appraisal practices.

Local government debt for general public improvements may take the form of lease-purchase agreements or certificates of participation (COPs). Lease-purchase agreements are popular methods of financing the acquisition of equipment, such as computers, fire trucks, sanitation vehicles, etc. Under a lease-purchase agreement, a government unit acquires possession and use of (if not title to) the equipment and agrees to make annual periodic payments over a term of from several to usually 5 years or so to pay for the equipment. The annual payments cover the original cash price of the equipment plus interest on whatever portion of the cash price is outstanding. Once the annual lease payments are complete, the government owns the equipment free of lien. COPs are shares in long-term, i.e., 10 to 20 years or more, lease-purchase agreements to finance major facilities or equipment. COP financing is for projects so large that one lessor or investor is unable to provide all of the financing required for the project. Certificates of participation in the financing are created and sold or marketed, much like G.O. bonds are sold to the public.

Both lease-purchase and COP financing are secured by the property being financed rather than by future taxing power. If a local government fails to make one or more payments on a lease-purchase agreement or COP financing, the recourse of the lessor or investors is to take possession of the equipment or facility being financed. The lessor or investors may not compel the unit to levy taxes to continue the lease-purchase or COP payments. Because of this, lease-purchase or COP debt usually does not require approval by the voters in a referendum, nor is it typically subject to statutory or constitutional debt limits. However, lease-purchase and certificate of participation debt for general public improvements as well as any local government debt that must be repaid from general revenues, rather than from revenues of a self-supporting enterprise or from specially earmarked revenues, should be added to general obligation debt in forecasting the future debt capacity of a local government.

Certain indicators or ratios are available to help determine the boundaries of safety in general obligation, lease-purchase, certificate of participation, and other types of borrowing for general or non–self-supporting improvements. One is the ratio of annual debt service payments on such debt to general fund and other operating fund expenditures for governmental purposes. Nearly all local government debt for general public improvements is repaid in serial maturates. That is, a portion of the debt is retired or paid back each year, usually over a period of up to 20 or 25 years. Annual debt service payments include the amount of debt retired that year plus interest at a specified rate on the amount of debt outstanding for the year. A rough rule of thumb is that annual debt service payments on G.O. bonds and other non–self-supporting debt should not exceed 15 to 20 percent of annual operating expenditures.[6] Conservative jurisdictions try to hold debt service to 10 to 15 percent or less of such expenditures. Future annual debt service on G.O. bonds or other debt to finance a proposed capital facility can be added to the schedule of debt service on existing outstanding debt and the sum divided by projected operating expenditures to determine whether future operating budgets will be able to make the future debt service payments without strain.

Another measure for determining the boundary of safety in borrowing is outstanding debt, including G.O. bonds, for general public improvement or non–self-supporting purposes in relation to population, i.e., debt per capita.[7] The limit for this ratio applicable to a specific local government should depend on growth prospects and the general economic characteristics of the locality.

Debt limitations for revenue bonds and other forms of self-supporting debt are usually stated in terms of a coverage ratio. Coverage is the ratio of net earnings to annual debt service for the enterprise or facility to be financed with the revenue bonds. Net earnings equal operating revenues less operating expenses, depreciation excluded. Since net earnings are the major (and often sole) security for the bonds, investors will require a coverage ratio in excess of 1.0 for projects to be financed with revenue bonds. The ratio required by investors varies by the type of enterprise financed with the bonds.[8]

Although intergovernmental aid and grants can be a significant source of financing for some local governmental capital projects, forecasting the availability of such aid and grants is problematic. Such aid and grants are subject to frequent reductions because of federal and state budget problems and changes in federal and state government administrations. Even for the aid or grant programs for which this does not occur, legal and administrative provisions governing the distribution of the aid often change, making forecasts of such aid difficult. Potential intergovernmental aid and grants should be considered but seldom counted on in a forecast of financial resources available for funding future capital outlays and projects.

CAPITAL BUDGETING: PROJECT EVALUATION

Project evaluation refers to a detailed and often technical study of a capital outlay proposal, and it is usually done late in the planning stage or early in the budget stage. It is the study that a locality does (or has done) just before it decides finally whether to commit funding to a capital outlay or project. As such, it relates more to capital budgeting than to capital planning.

Project evaluation can be conducted by in-house staff or contracted out. If the project is large and involves technical considerations, part or all of the evaluation will be contracted out to an architect or engineering consulting firm. The purpose of evaluation, no matter who does it, is to help determine the need for and/or economic viability of the project. For capital construction, the study is also likely to involve the preparation of general plans and specifications.

The methods or techniques for project evaluation range from approaches that rely on informed judgment to sophisticated quantitative analysis. Informed judgment is the simplest of all evaluation methods, yet, it can be reliable. It is most applicable when the outlay being considered is relatively modest in scope and not too complex and when the priorities among competing or alternative outlay proposals are fairly clear. It generally involves consulting with manufacturers and those who will use the facility or equipment and visiting other jurisdictions that have a similar facility or piece of equipment.

Quantitative techniques can be used for project evaluation when a project will generate a stream of revenue over the period of its useful life. Government activities or projects that produce revenue are those financed in significant part with user fees—for example, water-sewer systems and, increasingly, solid waste operations. Quantitative analysis can also be used to evaluate a capital project or piece of equipment that generates a stream of savings over the period of its useful life. For example, a municipality may be renting privately owned office space, and the question arises whether the cost of a new city office building will be compensated for in whole or part by the savings in private office rentals (less annual maintenance cost on the city hall) by having the city-owned facility.

Various economic techniques can be used to evaluate capital projects.[9] One technique used in the private sector is to calculate the payback factor—that is, the number of years required before the annual net cash revenue from a project recoups the original capital outlay or investment. The payback method is simple and also, when capital funds are lean, it favors projects that return income or capital to the locality quickly. Its disadvantages are that (1) it fails to consider net revenue after the investment has been recouped; and (2) it values revenue in different years equally. Because of the risk associated with the future, this year's revenue should be valued higher dollar for dollar than revenue next year and revenue next year more than revenue two or more years from now.

A second economic technique that can be used for project evaluation in the public sector is the present-value method, which considers the time value of money. This method (1) lists all net cash revenues or savings for each year over the useful life of a project; (2) discounts the annual net revenues or savings to the present, using a chosen interest rate; and (3) compares the total present worth of net revenues or savings with the original capital investment. If the present worth of the future annual net revenues or savings exceeds the investment, the project is presumably economically viable. The present-worth method is considered superior to payback because it considers annual revenues or savings over the full useful life of a project and takes into account the time value of money. But present worth is more difficult to compute than payback, and it assumes the ability to forecast receipts and costs far into the future. It also presents the problem of having to select an appropriate discount rate. Possible rates for discounting are the rate at which a government can borrow money, the rate it can earn by investing idle cash, or the rate that private citizens could earn if the money were kept and invested by them.

Another problem with the present value method (shared by all economic analysis techniques) is that it gives undue emphasis to benefits that can be quantified. The capital outlays or projects of local government usually have important nonmonetary benefits, and when economic analysis is used for project evaluation, nonmonetary benefits and costs are too often neglected by decision makers.

CAPITAL BUDGETING: PROJECT FINANCING

In the capital planning process, financial projections are made to set long-term capital needs within the expected level of available funding. The principal financial issue at the budgetary stage is what source(s) of financing should be selected to fund individual capital requests and how heavily a government should rely on each alternative funding source for the whole of its capital budget. A capital request can be financed by one or a combination of several sources, including operating revenue, debt proceeds, capital reserves or fund balances built up from prior years' revenue, equipment-purchase revolving funds, special assessments, other charges to property, and intergovernmental aid or grants.

The use of operating revenue to finance capital outlays or projects is commonly called pay-as-go financing. The capital budgets of some local governments are financed entirely or mainly on a pay-as-go basis. Such pay-as-go funding is practical only when a government spends more or less the same amount for capital purposes each year or when a local government is not growing very much. Pay-as-go financing is most commonly used to finance equipment purchases, land acquisition, and modest construction and remodeling projects.

The advantages of pay-as-go financing for capital outlays are that (1) it encourages responsible spending by requiring the same officials who approve projects or outlays also to raise the revenues to pay for them; (2) it avoids paying the interest charges that are involved with debt; and (3) it avoids the accumulation of large, fixed debt service payments in the operating budget.

Debt, in the form of G.O. or revenue bonds, lease-purchase agreements, or COPs is a second general method for financing capital projects, which is designated pay-as-use because the financing comes ultimately from annual debt service payments made while the capital facility or equipment is being used. Pay-as-use financing is commonly employed when the project is very large relative to the community's resources and when the project need not be replaced for many years, e.g., a city hall or sewerage treatment plant. Pay-as-use financing is also necessary in communities that are growing rapidly. Such communities typically face substantial and rather immediate needs for public facilities that can be provided only through borrowing. Pay-as-use financing may often be involved in annexation, in which extending municipal services to a new area requires new public facilities. Equipment acquisitions and remodeling or modest construction projects are least likely to be financed with debt.

Debt or pay-as-use financing for capital projects has several advantages. First, through annual debt service payments spread over the useful life of a project, the users of a project are charged for its costs plus interest. Second, in a period of inflation, pay-as-use financing enables a locality to borrow dear or expensive dollars and pay back with cheaper ones. Third, when operating revenue or reserves are used to finance capital projects, the projects may have to be delayed until the funds are accumulated. Pay-as-use financing enables a capital need to be met more immediately. Finally, although borrowing carries an interest cost, the use of operating revenue for capital projects has a corresponding opportunity cost, which is equal to the rate of return that the locality or its citizens could have earned by investing the current revenue rather than allocating it to finance the capital project.

Capital outlays or projects can also be financed with money accumulated in one or more capital reserve funds.[10] Once a reserve is established, monies can be accumulated in it by periodic appropriation from the operating budget, interest earnings on money accumulated in the fund and invested, and other sources. When needed, money is drawn from the reserve to pay for a project or outlay. Thus the timetable for reserve financing of capital outlays is opposite that for debt financing. In reserve financing, annual installment payments are made before the capital item is acquired, while in debt or pay-as-use financing, the annual debt service payments are made after acquisition.

Capital reserve financing is feasible for purchases of land and major equipment items. It can also be used for building projects of modest scope or to accumulate funds to match debt, or intergovernmental grant proceeds for large construction projects. Capital reserve financing is often not practical to accumulate 100 percent of the funds required for a major construction project. The need for such a project cannot be seen far enough ahead to accumulate sufficient money to finance the project.

As already mentioned, some governments build up operating fund balances to amounts greater than needed as operating reserves and the balances are then drawn down to finance capital projects or outlays. The use of operating fund balances in this way is similar to capital reserve financing of capital requests. The difference is that local law often requires that money placed in a capital reserve be used only for capital purposes. On the other hand, money that is accumulated and held in fund balance generally may be used either for operating expenditures or for capital projects and outlays. This is a problem in building up and counting on "excess" operating fund balances to finance future capital outlays. The money being accumulated from year to year in this way can be drawn off very easily to finance operating expenditures rather than the capital project or outlay for which it was originally intended. Moreover, taxpayers sometimes object to the accumulation of large balances in operating funds. They may not understand that the money is being held for future capital purposes.

A revolving internal service fund can also be used to finance equipment purchases. Such a fund is first established by transferring seed money from the general fund, but thereafter it is financed by annual rental charges to the line departments that use the equipment purchased and owned by the fund.

Special assessments are levied on property to finance specific improvements or services that benefit the property. Street-paving, curb and gutter, sidewalks, and water-sewer and other utility-line extensions are improvements for which special assessments are often charged.[11] Special assessments are supposed to be levied in proportion to the benefit that accrues to each property from a project, but as a practical matter, each benefiting property shares in a project's cost generally in the proportion that its area or front footage bears to the area or front footage of all property that benefits from the project. Still, property owners seldom pay the full cost of a project financed with special assessments. The governmental unit usually pays part of the cost because the community as a whole presumably benefits from most any project for which special assessments are levied. Special assessments are generally not levied, until after a project is complete and the costs for it are known, and benefiting property owners usually have the option of paying special assessments either in a lump sum or in installments plus interest over a multiyear period. If a large project extends over many years and is divided in phases, installment payments resulting from assessments levied for work done in the earlier years of a project can be used to help finance the project in later years.

Special assessments are one type of charge to private property to finance the cost of public improvements serving that property. Impact or facility fees are another.[12] Such fees are payments made by developers or builders to defray the costs of providing public infrastructure necessitated by or associated with new development or building. Impact or facility fees are generally set in terms of a standard measure such as number of dwelling units or bedrooms per development. They are usually paid at the time that a new development is approved or as it is being built, and they can be used to finance both infrastructure located in or near new development for which the fees are paid (neighborhood water and sewer lines or local streets, etc.) and general public facilities serving the new development and also other parts of the community (e.g., a new central water or sewer treatment plant or a new law enforcement center serving an entire community). Impact or facility fees may not be levied on new development in excess of the costs associated with the portion new general public facilities necessitated by the new development. While special assessments are most often levied after the project being financed with the assessments is complete, impact fees are often levied in advance or in anticipation of the projects to be built with the impact fee revenue. In these cases, authorizing legislation typically requires the impact fee revenue to be placed in a reserve fund until the intended project is begun.

Intergovernmental aid or grants were once a major source of financing for local government capital projects. Today, they are far less significant. We have already discussed the problems of projecting intergovernmental aid or grants in capital planning. A question to resolve at the budget stage of the capital budgeting process concerning intergovernmental aid or grants available for capital purposes is whether the availability of such outside money should raise the priority of a request or move up the funding timetable for it. If a project is scheduled for implementation sometime in the future and a grant becomes available for the current year to finance part of the project's cost, this is reason enough in most cases to proceed with the project ahead of schedule. On the other hand, the availability of a grant should not lead a government to undertake a project that it would not otherwise approve if the project entails significant capital or future operating costs for the government.

CAPITAL BUDGETING: AUTHORIZATION OF CAPITAL OUTLAYS

The third step in the budgetary phase of the capital budget process is the authorization of capital requests and the appropriation of money for the requests. This is usually done by the governing body, but occasionally a legislative or governing body provides a lump sum of money for capital requests for the year and delegates the authority to approve and fund individual requests to administrative officials or to a committee composed of legislative or governing body members and administrative officials. The usual vehicles for capital project authorization and appropriations are listed here:

1. The annual or biennial budget ordinance or bill.
2. A capital projects ordinance that provides funding for all capital requests approved in a year—these requests can come forward from the capital improvement program; or a series of separate capital projects ordinances that are enacted throughout the year for individual capital requests.
3. One or more bond orders approved by the governing board and perhaps by the voters.

Each method of authorizing capital outlays has advantages and disadvantages. Authorization in the annual or biennial budget helps assure that capital expenditure decisions are coordinated with operating budget decisions. Moreover, because annual or biennial budget authorization is only for a year or two at a time, it provides for periodic review of projects in process or under construction.

The disadvantages of authorizing capital outlays in the annual or biennial budget apply mainly to large multiyear projects. One is the incongruity of authorizing a project only a year or two at a time when in fact contracting and spending for the project and construction occur over several years. A more difficult problem is that authorizing capital outlays in the annual operating or biennial budget can cause that budget to fluctuate erratically, so that confusion arises as to the amount of the operating budget. Also, it can camouflage substantial growth in the operating budget. For example, a major increase in the operating budget can be obscured by the completion of a capital project and its removal from the annual or biennial budget in the same year.

The disadvantages of capital outlay authorization in the annual or biennial budget are addressed or overcome by using a capital projects ordinance.[13] This type of ordinance, whether comprehensive and embracing all projects to be authorized in a year or broken into separate ordinances for individual projects, continues in force until the projects or acquisitions are built or completed. In other words, the authorization and the money appropriated by such an ordinance do not lapse at the end of a fiscal year if not contracted or spent. Second, by authorizing capital projects separately from operating ones, current expenditures and the benefits flowing from them are matched more readily with annual revenues. Large capital outlays with benefits that occur in future fiscal years are segregated, and this helps decision makers and the general public to determine precisely what the operating budget is and to identify and deal with changes and increases in that budget from year to year.

The disadvantages of relying on a capital projects ordinance to authorize capital outlays lie, first, in deciding whether all capital outlays or only those that are above a certain dollar level or of a specific nature—for example, those involving construction—will be authorized through such an ordinance. Presumably, small or recurring capital outlays would be authorized in the operating budget, while major nonrecurring capital outlays would be approved by projects ordinances. Second, if a capital projects ordinance is passed at a different time from the annual or biennial operating budget, capital decisions may be reached without giving adequate regard to their effect on annual operating needs. Finally, enacting capital project ordinances for individual projects or outlays may foster a fragmented approach to capital decision making, each capital outlay being evaluated on its own merits but without regard to any priorities among different capital needs.

An approved bond order authorizes a jurisdiction to issue bonds to finance a capital request or project.[14] Passage of the bond order is often tantamount to authorizing a project, although officials can still choose not to issue the bonds and thereby block or postpone the project. In some jurisdictions, no further authorizing action or capital appropriations are necessary after the bond order has been passed. In other jurisdictions, the local governing body has to appropriate bond proceeds previously authorized by a bond order in the annual or biennial budget or in a capital projects ordinance before the bond proceeds can be spent. In these instances, the authorization process has two steps.

IMPLEMENTING THE CAPITAL BUDGET

The last step in the capital planning and budget process is implementation. Failure here can put all the plans and financial arrangements made in the earlier stages of the process down the drain. Key facets of capital budget implementation are management and investment of the revenue available to finance a project, equipment purchases, and design and construction of buildings or improvements.

Management of revenue proceeds available for capital outlay purposes usually requires an investment plan. A locality may have revenue accumulated to finance a project well before the revenue must be spent. On a construction project, bond proceeds are typically issued at the start of the project—usually just after the bids for construction are received, while the proceeds are spent throughout the construction process. This means that idle funds are available that can be invested during construction. A plan should be formulated for investing these funds so that they become available in cash in the appropriate amounts to meet payments to vendors and contractors when the payments are due, to provide investment income to offset interest paid on the bonds during construction, and to minimize rebates or penalties paid to the federal government because of arbitrary regulations.[15]

Two important factors in implementing equipment purchases are timing and bid procedures. When major equipment purchases are financed from current revenue, the purchases are often timed to coincide with the period of greatest revenue in-flow from operating sources. Unlike expenditures for salaries and supplies that must be made regularly throughout the year, equipment purchases can usually be made when a government chooses. Making them when revenue in-flow is large eases a jurisdiction's cash-flow problem.

Equipment purchases must also be made according to the applicable purchasing laws. For example, in North Carolina any piece of equipment that costs $20,000 or more must be purchased according to formal bid procedures that involve public advertisement and submittal of sealed bids.[16] Moreover, any equipment that costs between $5,000 and $20,000 must be purchased using informal bid procedures, i.e., bids secured by telephone or in a similar manner.[17]

Implementing capital outlay decisions that involve construction is more complex. First, if the project is of any magnitude, an architect or engineer is usually employed to draw up plans and specifications. State law often requires that this be done when the cost of the project exceeds a certain amount[18] and, legal requirements aside, securing an architect usually pays off in avoiding costly construction mistakes. Architects are not usually selected by formal bidding. They are generally chosen through a request for proposal process or negotiation focused initially on design considerations. Architects are usually paid on a sliding scale, which starts with a flat fee plus a percentage of the project's cost, ranging from 3 or 4 to 12 percent, depending on the size of a project. Some governments employ one architect to draw the preliminary design for a project, and a second to do the final blueprints and specifications and to supervise construction. In reviewing architectural proposals and plans, local officials must balance high construction costs and low maintenance costs later versus low construction costs and high maintenance costs later.

Implementing a construction contract and supervising construction under a contract for a capital project carry special concerns. First, state law typically requires that any contract involving an estimated expenditure above a certain amount (e.g., $50,000 in North Carolina[19]) be let through formal bid procedures. Second, separate contracts may be required for different types of construction—general construction, electrical, plumbing, etc.[20] Third, a performance bond or the equivalent is often required on any construction project. This bond protects the government financially from the contractor's failure to complete his work. A retainage provision written into the contract has a similar effect. Such a provision allows a locality to hold back a portion, usually 5 to 10 percent, of each month's payment to the contractor for work done during the month and construction materials delivered to the site. This money is not paid to the contractor until construction is complete and is satisfactory to the locality. Finally, during construction, the work done should be inspected frequently, daily if possible, by either the architect or the government's own engineer or building inspector.

CONCLUSION

We might ask here whether a particular town, city, or county, should establish special procedures or a separate process for capital planning and budgeting. But the actual experience of local governments in making capital outlay decisions indicates that this would be an inappropriate question. Most governments of any size already use some of the steps that are described here as elements of capital budgeting. State legal provisions require the performance of some steps, especially those having to do with project authorization and implementation, and some of the other steps simply represent commonsense approaches to planning and carrying out capital outlay decisions.

Therefore, perhaps the better questions to ask are whether the individual procedures that a government has for making capital expenditures should be pulled together into a coordinated capital budget, and whether other missing elements or procedures—for example, a capital improvement program or long-range financial forecast—should be added to form a more complete process for capital budgeting. Some of the criteria that will help a government answer these questions go back to the reasons cited for capital budgeting at the beginning of the article. Thus the more the following conditions hold, the more likely a government is to benefit from having a separate and more complete capital budget process: (1) the unit faces large capital needs requiring the expenditure of substantial amounts of money; (2) meeting these needs is likely to shape or alter the basic features of the community; (3) debt will be required to meet at least some of the needs; and (4) other procedures will probably not guarantee that the needs are met in an orderly and fiscally sound manner.

Notes

1. G. David Quirin, *The Capital Expenditure Decision* (Homewood, Ill.: Richard D. Irwin, Inc. 1967), 1-2.
2. Government Finance Officers Association, *Government Accounting, Auditing and Financial Reporting* (Chicago: GFOA, 1994), 330.
3. See Charles D. Liner, "Projecting Local Government Revenue," *Popular Government* 43, no. 3 (Spring 1978), 32-38, for a summary of revenue forecasting that is based on historical trends. [Ed. note: Liner's article is included in this volume, pp. 183-91.]
4. N.C. Gen. Stat. §159-55.
5. The ratio of outstanding debt to appraised valuation of taxable property for all North Carolina cities and counties is maintained by the Department of the State Treasurer, State of North Carolina.
6. Standard & Poor's Corporation, *Municipal Finance Criteria* (New York: Standard & Poor's Corp., 1994), 23.
7. Debt per capita as one measure or limit of safety in borrowing as illustrated in Moody's Public Finance Department, *North Carolina Counties: Comparative Analysis General Obligation Bonds* (New York: Moody's Investors Service, 1991).
8. *Municipal Finance Criteria*, 65-134, provides a good discussion of rating criteria for revenue bonds.
9. For a discussion of payback, present worth, and other quantitative methods for evaluating capital projects, see National Association of Accountants, *Financial Analysis Techniques for Equipment Replacement Decisions* (New York: National Association of Accountants, 1965); and A. John Vogt and Lisa A. Cole, *A Guide to Municipal Leasing* (Chicago: GFOA, 1983), 115-46. [Ed. note: See articles 9 (Miller) and 28 (Chapman) in this volume.]
10. The use of capital reserve financing is discussed by Alan Walter Steiss, *Local Government Finance: Capital Facilities Planning and Debt Administration* (Lexington, Mass.: Lexington Books, 1975), 105-7.
11. The use of special assessments by local governments is explained in Glenn W. Fisher, *Financing Local Improvements by Special Assessments* (Chicago: Municipal Finance Officers Association of the United States and Canada, n.d.), 59.
12. Impact and facility fees are discussed in Joni L. Leithe with Mathew Montavon, *Impact Fee Programs: A Survey of Designs and Administrative Issues* (Chicago: Government Finance Officers Association, 1990).
13. North Carolina municipalities and counties can appropriate money for capital outlays either in the annual budget ordinance or in a separate capital projects ordinance. See N.C. *Gen. Stat.* §159-13, -13.2.
14. See, for example, N.C. *Gen. Stat.* §159-54.
15. Terence P. Burke, *Guide to Arbitrage Requirements for Governmental Bond Issues* (Chicago: GFOA, 1992). Also see Burke, *1994 Supplement to Guide to Arbitrage Requirements for Governmental Bond Issues*.
16. N.C. *Gen. Stat.* §143-129.
17. N.C. *Gen. Stat.* §143-131.
18. See, for example, N.C. *Gen. Stat* §133-1.1.
19. N.C. *Gen. Stat.* §143-129.
20. See, for example, N.C. *Gen. Stat.* §143-128.

Capital Financing: A New Look at an Old Idea

Ronald Chapman

Capital budgeting within local government has not received the serious attention it deserves by practitioners or academicians. Theoretically, municipal capital budgeting involves the preparation of cost and revenue estimates for all proposed projects, an examination of the need for each, both politically and economically, and a choice of those worthy of capital investment.

In reality, few municipalities use financial decision-making tools when evaluating capital projects. Instead, they rely too heavily on political considerations to determine which, if any, capital investment is worthwhile.

Political considerations are needed. Often they are valuable decision-making tools. With respect to capital budgeting, they should enter the picture after the proposed capital investment has been financially tested using traditional capital financing approaches. This will ensure the investment is truly good for the municipality.

Three traditional business techniques are available for local governments to use in order to reach these decisions. Each will be briefly described. The reader can judge which one would best fit his or her situation.

Reprinted by permission of *American City and County* magazine. This article appeared in *Practical Financial Management: New Techniques for Local Government,* edited by John Matzer, Jr. (Washington, D.C.: International City Management Assoc., 1984), 141-47.

The techniques have been modified some to fit the municipal government environment. They include: payback period, rate of return on average investment, and discounted cash flow.

The simple payback method evaluates the time required to recover the capital investment through net annual cash flow savings. These are the monies the municipality expects to save by making the capital investment minus expected expenditures.

For example, suppose the municipality is evaluating the purchase of a $100,000 computer system expected to have a gross annual savings of $50,000 and an annual operating cost of $15,000. The net annual cash flow savings is $35,000 ($50,000 minus $15,000).

To fully utilize this method, the municipality must determine the total investment required to purchase the capital asset. In the example, the municipality has received open competitive bids for a computer with the lowest bid being $100,000. For our purposes, we will assume the lowest bid is offering the better package.

Second, the municipality must determine the expected life of the asset. Also for this purpose, we will adopt the traditional life of five years for high technology assets.

The payback period (PP) can then be determined by dividing the annual investment (I) by the net annual cash flow savings (AS) as follows:

$$I/AS = PP$$
or
$$\$100,000/\$35,000 = 2.86 \text{ years}$$

A further refinement of this method takes into account the expected life of the asset in determining actual savings. The expected life (*EL*) minus the payback period equals the remaining asset life:

$$EL - PP = RL$$

The remaining life is multiplied by the annual savings (*AS*) to determine the actual savings (*aS*) or

$$RL \times AS = aS$$

To determine the payback period and actual savings, apply this composite formula:

$$I/AS = \text{Payback period}$$

while

$$(EL - PP) \times AS = aS$$

A word of caution. The payback method does not address the time value of money. It should only be applied where the annual savings flow evenly.

This approach becomes more useful the further into the future the municipality is predicting. Where future predicting is extreme and interests are unpredictable, this method is superior. For comparative purposes, the project with the shortest payback period is generally considered the best.

The second technique, rate of return on average capital investment, is calculated by dividing the net annual savings by the average investment in the capital asset. It assumes the municipality depreciates its assets each year. Also, a sum equal to the yearly depreciation in a capital replacement fund should be invested to ensure available replacement revenue at the end of the asset's useful life. If this is not practiced, don't use this technique as it does not address the time value of money.

In our earlier example, the municipality estimated its net annual savings to be $35,000 through investing $100,000 in a computer system. The average investment method assumes each year's depreciation will reduce the book value of the asset by $20,000. The formula looks like this:

$$\frac{I \text{ (initial investment)}}{EL \text{ (expected asset life)}} = \text{Annual depreciation}$$

Consequently, the municipality assumes it will have a $100,000 book value the first year of investment (*FI*) and a $20,000 book value the last or fifth year (*LI*). Therefore, the municipality will have an amount invested equal to the computer system book value each year, or an average investment (*AI*) of $60,000. This is calculated as follows:

$$\frac{FI + LI}{2} = AI$$

or

$$\frac{\$100{,}000 + \$20{,}000}{2} = \$60{,}000$$

Once the average investment is determined, the rate of return on average investment (*RI*) may be calculated by dividing the net annual savings (*AS*) by the average investment (*AI*) as follows:

$$AS/AI = RI$$

or

$$\$35{,}000/\$60{,}000 = 58.3\%$$

Whether a return on average investment of 58.3 percent is good or not relates to other municipal investments. Such a return is better than 12 percent, but not as good as 75 percent. Therefore, a basic rule may be applied. If the return on average investment is higher than current investment returns on invested capital, and the net annual savings represent uniform savings, the investment opportunity should be seriously considered.

The third technique, discounted cash flow, when compared with amounts to be invested, offers a better means of selection.

A Central American saying "a bird in hand is worth a thousand flying" resembles our "a bird in the hand is worth two in the bush," only more so. The first maxim places a higher value on money in hand today over future promises.

Present-day interest rates provide a typical example. In fact, interest rates represent a ratio of exchange between today and tomorrow.

The higher the value placed on today, the higher the present day interest. In other words, how much will the principal be worth in year *n*? This may be determined using this formula:

$$F = P(1 + i)^n$$

where *F* is the sum at the end of year *n*, *P* the principal, *i* the interest rate, and *n* the number of years invested.

On the other hand, discounting is compounding interest in the reverse. With the present value concept, a future sum of money discounted at an appropriate interest rate determines its equivalent present sum. It looks from the future back to the present. It asks what is present value (PV) of future sum invested for years n, at interest i, compounded annually? The formula works like this:

$$PV = \frac{F}{(1 + I)^n}$$

or

$$PV = F(1 + i)^{-n}$$

Adopting the discounted cash flow or present value model to municipal budgeting is an excellent way to evaluate investments with uniform and nonuniform net annual cash flow savings. It works equally well for phased capital investments. Here's a look at each of these.

When a municipality makes a capital investment, it expects to secure from it a stream of future savings or net annual savings. Normally, it should not invest in the capital asset unless the annual savings discounted to present dollars are sufficient to return the amount invested, plus a satisfactory return on investment. The return sought should equal present investment earnings. This uniform discounted cash flow method is shown in Table 1.

The table shows that the capital investment of $100,000 in a computer system with a net annual savings of $35,000 will recover the initial investment. It will also result in a 10 percent annually compounded return on investment. Moreover, it produces an added $32,650 positive net present value. If the municipality considers this return a good investment, the system should be purchased.

Using this method, several investment opportunities can be compared. If each has the same initial investment and risk, the one having the highest positive net present value is preferred.

Often the municipality must select between two or more investment opportunities with varying investments required and nonuniform net annual savings. Here again, the discounted cash flow method is the best to use.

Assume, for example, the municipality has three capital projects to choose from: A, B, and C. Project A requires an initial investment of $80,000 and has net annual savings of $35,000, $35,000 and $35,000.

Table 1: *Uniform Discounted Cash Flow Method*

n Years	F Net Annual Savings	(1-i) Present Value of $1 at 10%	P Present Value of Annual Savings
1	$35,000	.909	$31,815
2	35,000	.826	28,910
3	35,000	.751	26,285
4	35,000	.683	23,905
5	35,000	.621	21,735
Total present value			$132,650
Amount to be invested			100,000
Positive net present value			**$ 32,650**

Project B requires an initial investment of $80,000 and has a net annual savings of $40,000, $30,000, and $25,000. Project C requires an initial investment of $50,000 and has net annual savings of $10,000, $15,000, and $20,000.

To determine which asset is the better investment, the discounted cash flow method should be applied to each project as shown in Table 2. In this case, AS equals the net amount cash flow savings, Factor the discounted rate (10 percent annually) and PV the present value of AS.

In Table 2, capital projects B and C result in a negative net present value. They should be rejected. Project A, on the other hand, has a return on investment of 10 percent, plus an added return of $7,010. This makes it the better investment.

All capital investments cited were assumed to have no salvage value at the end of their expected life. If a salvage value is present, the cost analysis remains the same. The salvage value is added to the last year's net annual savings prior to the present value calculation.

Suppose the municipality is investigating the purchase of a new computer system with an initial investment of $50,000. Further investments would require outlays of $100,000 and $125,000 in years two and three. Also, assume the net annual cash flow savings are $75,000, $100,000, and $125,000 in years one through three. Present value calculations for this project are presented in Table 3.

Using this table, we can see the capital project has a total present value savings of $244,650, a total present value investment of $223,544, and a net present value of $21,106. Assuming a 10 percent return on investment is desirable, the municipality should go forward with the project.

Table 2: *Nonuniform Discounted Cash Flow Method*

	Project A			Project B			Project C		
Period	AS	Factor	PV	AS	Factor	PV	AS	Factor	PV
1	$35,000	.909	$31,815	$40,000	.909	$36,360	$10,000	.909	$ 9,090
2	35,000	.826	28,910	30,000	.826	24,780	15,000	.826	12,390
3	35,000	.751	26,285	25,000	.751	18,755	20,000	.751	15,020

Table 3: *Phased Discounted Cash Flow Method*

	Annual Cash Flow Savings Discounted by 10%			Phased Investment Discounted by 10%		
Period	AS	Factor	PV	AS	Factor	PV
1	$ 75,000	.909	$68,175	$ 50,000	1.000	$50,000
2	100,000	.826	82,600	100,000	.909	90,900
3	125,000	.751	93,875	100,000	.826	82,644

Total PV (savings) $244,650
Total PV (investments)   223,544
Net PV $ 21,106

The phased investment plan requires the same 10 percent discounting as is used in annual cash flow savings. This reduces the total required investment to its present value.

In phased investment projects, the total investment is not required in the initial stage. Therefore, the amounts required in years two and three must be discounted to their respective present values.

For example, suppose a planned investment equal to $100,000 is to be made in the second period. The municipality only needs to invest $90,900 at 10 percent interest today to realize $100,000 at the end of one period.

The initial investment in period one is never discounted because it already reflects present value. As a result, when discounting phased investments this formula should be applied to all except the initial investment:

$$PV = \frac{F(n-1)}{(1+i)}$$

or

$$PV = F(1+i)(n-1)$$

Of the three techniques, discounted cash flow often produces the better decision-making data. However, the payback period and return on investment methods should be used instead where interest rates cannot be accurately predicted.

In reality, the discounted cash flow analysis places each proposed project on an equal footing.

The assessing of current budget impact is important in this era of cutback management. This is especially true when one assumes future years will not produce large and lavish budgets.

In the final analysis, the chief executive must ask if the project is financially proven; does the municipality have the current finances needed to invest in the project; and, if the project is not financially proven and the municipality does not have the current resources available, are the political factors important enough to tip the scales in favor of the project?

If the decision is made on purely political factors, the chief executive is like a blind man leading the blind. He simply has no idea of the present or future impact the project might have on the budgetary structure. As the saying goes: "A bird in hand is worth a thousand flying."

PART 2
EXECUTION

29 Introduction

Part 2 of this collection of articles examines activities involved in administering—or executing—the budget. Implementing a budget requires frequent referral to the adopted budget as necessary budget adjustments are made to accommodate changing needs or demands. Implementation also requires cash—at a flow to match demands. Therefore, a set of financial operations must be managed, including the capacity to borrow money, to manage risks, and to purchase the lowest and best items. Attention also must be given to financial and administrative controls, especially those directed toward assuring that the accounting system can provide data for managerial decision making. Reporting practices provide background on how financial and other data serve various needs; auditing provides accountability.

BUDGET IMPLEMENTATION

Following through on the exact plans embedded in the budget assumes that events follow plans. If revenues do not materialize as planned or spending escalates beyond the expected path, the budget quickly becomes dated, requiring change. John Forrester and Daniel Mullins label the need for midyear budget adjustments as "rebudgeting." Their survey of municipal rebudgeting experience is valuable for its ability to specify the terms of stimulus for within-year change, the types of transfers and adjustments possible, and the rebudgeting process itself. They find that technical needs not politics force adjustment, with cities using "rebudgeting to marginally adjust programs and to meet management needs in a changing environment."

Just because an item has been budgeted does not mean that a liability to pay for it can be incurred. Many governments require a two-step process before an individual obligation (such as filling a position, signing a contract, or approving a purchase order) can be made against the treasury: It must be shown that (1) there is a specific part of the budget allocation that can be cited as authority and (2) there is cash to pay the bill. Meeting the first criterion is dependent upon an approved budget, resulting in a tracking number to assign to a planned expenditure. The second criterion, however, has less to do with the budget than with cash in the bank.

Liquidity is the availability of cash, and it is a fundamental requirement for any ongoing enterprise. Monitoring the flow of cash identifies periods of excess cash (more than needed to meet immediate needs) and illiquidity (cash insufficient to meet demands). Aman Khan's, "Cash Management: Basic Principles and Guidelines," offers an introduction to the topic. Cash management is the estimation of future cash flows, and a monthly or daily cash budget is the basic tool.

Astute managers invest excess cash, which results in added revenues without tax increases. As with most areas of public budgeting and finance, state laws often govern investment of idle cash, also called working capital. For instance, investments earned from monies retained in some earmarked account might be restricted for use only in that account. Further, certain investment instruments—such as common stock—almost always are off limits for governments (except for pension funds where there is an ability to buy and hold the investment through economic cycles). The investment debacle that led to the voluntary bankruptcy of Orange County, California, in late 1994 revealed what a stunning impact cash management practices can have on the life of an organization.

DEBT MANAGEMENT

This section introduces methods to carry out the financing plan of the governmental unit, debt management. Governments must nurture their capacity to pay for borrowed funds. Rationing this debt capacity requires an understanding of capital markets, debt instruments, and choices.

Debt is a fiscal option available to most local governments. Borrowing money makes sense when financing large, costly capital improvement items that are to be paid for over a long period of time. Debt is even an option for smoothing cash imbalances, if the borrowed funds are repaid by year-end. The consequences of using short-term debt to cover budget shortfalls, such as the financial emergencies in New York and Cleveland in the 1970s, provide lessons that officials should not forget, however.

By defining debt as the "current use of future revenue," Michael Zino conveys what is at stake. In "The Development of a Planned Debt Policy," he shows why it is important to determine debt capacity thresholds in concert with capital plans. Moreover, W. Bartley Hildreth isolates the choices facing debt issuers, revealing strategies for obtaining the lowest cost of capital for the desired repayment schedule, in the article "State and Local Governments as Borrowers." In addition, he identifies the relationships between the numerous parties involved in borrowing money.

Investors in governmental debt instruments look to third-party assessments (ratings) of the government's likelihood of default, or nonpayment of principal and interest when due. This is termed credit analysis. Historically, higher bond ratings result in lower borrowing costs (with cost measured as the interest rate charged for renting the money for the term of the loan). Two firms, basically similar in credit analysis methods utilized, are the major providers of this service to investors: Moody's Investors Service and Standard and Poor's (S&P) Corporation.

In "Municipal Finance Criteria," Standard and Poor's offers key insights into the bond rating process, especially for general obligation and tax-supported bonds. Included are descriptions of the rating process, information needs, and clues on credit quality indicators. Similarly, "The Fundamentals of Revenue Bond Credit Analysis" by Moody's Investors Service examines various enterprise operations that rely on revenue bonds and notes. "Because the revenue bond is secured by a narrow stream of revenues, as opposed to the all-encompassing general obligation pledge, the scope of the enterprise system producing that single stream of revenues becomes a paramount factor in credit analysis."

Issuers sell debt to investment banking firms, called underwriters, who in turn sell the debt instruments to the ultimate investors (either individual or institutional purchasers). A critical decision facing public officials is whether or not to offer the bonds to any underwriter or group of underwriters willing to offer the lowest cost (termed a competitive sale) or to enter into an arrangement with a selected underwriter for a negotiated sale. Advantages and disadvantages of these options as well as recommendations are discussed in "Competitive versus Negotiated Sale of Debt" by the California Debt Advisory Commission (CDAC).

Complicating the decision on how to conduct a debt sale is the fact that competitive sales do not always lead to a cheaper cost of borrowing. In a negotiated sale, a major cost component is the underwriter's compensation for marketing the local government's bonds and "the underwriting spread is ... the difference between the price at which an underwriter purchases bonds from an issuer and the prices at which the bonds are resold to investors." A second paper from the CDAC, "Understanding the Underwriting Spread," illustrates both its calculation and negotiation.

Financing a project requires an analysis of options. If a project is not funded on a pay-as-you-go basis, one of several forms of indebtedness is possible. In "Techniques to Lower Municipal Borrowing Costs," Manly Mumford provides a simple comparison of methods. He helps to demystify the methods used in making financial decisions.

Instead of financing projects through use of long-term bonds, many governments have turned to lease financing. Another CDAC paper, "Types and Purposes of Lease Financing," reviews the types of tax-exempt leases. "A government gains flexibility from tax-exempt leasing because a transaction can be arranged quickly, and therefore it can adapt to unusual or unique circumstances requiring the acquisition of assets in an expedited manner," the authors maintain.

OPERATIONS

Asset management involves the procurement of goods and services and the protection of physical and financial reserves. Purchasing and risk management systems illustrate two management systems employed to meet these challenges. Plus, managing a local government pension system with its large impact on budgets requires an understanding of how cash is accumulated to meet future liabilities.

Governments purchase an amazing array of items, from land and fire trucks to paper and pencils. As Charles Coe notes in "Government Purchasing": "The goal of any purchasing agency should be to have lively competition, not just in prices, but in the competence of vendors, in the quality of the goods and services bought, and in the ability of vendors to make timely deliveries. Active competition, of course, results in lower prices and higher quality products and services." He suggests ways to achieve more competition and professionalism in purchasing.

Buying the lowest-priced item is not, however, always the "best buy" because the cost of owning an item includes the item's acquisition, operation, and maintenance costs. In his discussion, "Life-Cycle Costing," Roderick Lee shows what it takes to do a life-cycle cost analysis, a critical tool for effective purchasing decisions.

Local governments neglect, at great risk, the financial implications of having inadequate insurance coverage, poor control of worker's compensation claims, and overly generous employee benefit plans. By paying closer attention to risk management principles, governments can identify and adequately handle these and other programs that could lead to financial loss.

"Advantages of a Risk Management Program" by Miller and Hildreth, offers an introduction to this long-neglected area of financial liability. Risk management and its liability protection program are based on four principles: identification, measurement, control, and finance. With its concern for loss prevention and control, risk management serves to unite the activities of safety, insurance, and some elements of employee benefits under one responsibility function. Better management of risks can result in cost savings.

Pension obligations arise from extending retirement benefits to employees and show up as a budget line-item. A retirement system achieves financial strength when current assets cover the long-term value of benefit obligations. Hildreth and Miller address a range of issues in "Pension Policy, Management, and Analysis." Even a governmental unit that does not operate its own retirement system but is part of a state-controlled one is influenced by the pressures facing pension administrators.

ACCOUNTING

While accounting data are the "currency" of any control system, the overall accounting system serves as a data collection, storage, and format system for managers. That is, various records dealing with the receipt of money (e.g., property bills, court fines, license fee receipts) and its disbursement (e.g., payroll sheets, vouchers) must be organized and recorded in a way that gives decision makers an understanding of the organization's financial condition. Thus, the manner in which the financial accounting system is constructed and operated says much about the manager's ability to answer financial questions.

Gloria Grizzle's "Fund Accounting: An Introduction for Public and Nonprofit Organization Managers" reviews applicable Generally Accepted Accounting Principles (GAAP) and the basics of double-entry bookkeeping. Grizzle also shows how to interpret illustrative financial reports that record assets, liabilities, and fund equity (the balance sheet) and revenues and expenditures (akin to a business firm's "income statement").

Managerial accounting, in contrast to financial accounting, focuses on internal costs, revenues, and volumes of service. Managers planning to use efficiency and effectiveness measures for a service need to know its cost structure. In "Managerial Accounting," James Sorensen, Glyn Hanbery, and A. Ronald Kucic offer a practical guide to doing cost analysis. They show how to find the fixed and variable cost elements, the precursor to doing break-even analysis. Bolstering an understanding of the process is David Ammons' companion example in "Identifying Full Costs of a Program."

REPORTING

Communicating the government's financial profile to interested persons is important. Financial statements can be prepared and issued not just at fiscal year-end, but also periodically during the year. Interim reports fulfill an internal need for financial status measurement while end-of-year reports are key documents for external dissemination. Unlike the business model, there is no simple bottom-line measure that encapsulates all the financial decisions of governments. Contributing to the confusion is that governmental financial statements do not consolidate all operations into one statement of financial position, resorting instead to combined reporting by fund type—namely the general, special revenue, debt service, capital projects, proprietary, and fiduciary fund types.

One measure that analysts quickly look for in a financial statement is the level of unreserved fund balance. In his article, Ian Allan states: "(F)und balance is the cumulative difference of all revenues and expenditures from the government's creation. It can be considered to be the difference between fund assets and fund liabilities, and can be known as fund equity." A fund balance can be reserved (and thus not available for later use) and unreserved ("expendable available financial resources"). To many in government finance, the key financial planning decision is the level of unreserved fund balance. Allan expertly clarifies how to interpret fund balance designations in "Unreserved Fund Balance and Local Government Finance."

Is there any hope in trying to read and interpret the full scope of financial statements? Yes, but first one must gain a basic understanding of governmental accounting concepts, such as those provided in the earlier selection by Grizzle. Building upon that knowledge, Price Waterhouse & Company, in "Understanding Local Government Financial Statements," dissects a financial statement, grounding many accounting concepts with specific examples.

Financial statement analysis is simplified greatly by calculating ratios of important variables. This is all the more critical since there is not one single measure to which one can turn. What are some of the most important indicators? Ken Brown offers "The 10-Point Test of Financial Condition." One value of this easy-to-use assessment tool for smaller cities is that the results can be compared to a yearly set of data maintained by the Government Finance Officers Association of the United States and Canada. Furthermore, Karl Zehms shows how to compare a city's financial condition to that year's comparison group in "Proposed Financial Ratios for Use in Analysis of Municipal Annual Financial Reports."

Who needs governmental financial literature, reports, or statements? A variety of people have some interest in the operation of a particular governmental unit. While elected officials, managers, and employees have perhaps the most direct personal interest, citizens (the owners, so to speak) also have a vested interest, however unarticulated it may be. Even some outsiders—investors in a government's debt—have an interest. Financial communications must, therefore, respond to various users' needs. Are these needs all the same? No. While state auditors might want detailed data to check on local compliance, citizens may want nothing more than a brief summary. Investors, however, will likely demand specialized information.

ACCOUNTABILITY

The budgetary system can be viewed as a way to hold public officials and managers accountable for the manner in which the public's tax dollars are allocated and spent. Auditing has evolved as a formalized approach for dealing with the accountability question, but it covers more than rechecking accounting entries.

The U.S. General Accounting Office (GAO) has adopted a body of "Government Auditing Standards" that are relied upon by independent auditors of local government. It is therefore advisable for public officials and managers to understand their features. In addition to the traditional *financial audit,* the GAO calls for *performance audits* (program and economy and efficiency audits). Given the attention on service quality and performance, this expanded scope should benefit taxpayers.

What is involved in the actual audit process? A guide for local officials in the state of Massachusetts, "The Municipal Audit: Choice and Opportunity," provides a summary of the audit sequence. Fundamentally, the selection demonstrates why elected officials should involve themselves in choosing an auditor and in monitoring the audit itself, and how officials might pursue this responsibility to achieve some of the benefits of having an independent audit.

Upon receipt of an audit, it is incumbent on managers and officials to follow up on any audit recommendations. Not only is it a waste of money to let recommendations sit on the shelf unfulfilled, but it fosters a poor image (if not liability) when a problem arises in the future that implementation of a prior audit recommendation could have prevented. Richard Brooks and David Pariser, in "Local Government Accountability and the Need for Audit Follow-Up," discuss the relationship between accountability and audit follow-up systems.

SUMMARY

As this collection of articles demonstrates, formulation and execution of the local government budget are based on assumptions, knowledge, and skills. This reader highlights critical concepts and practices that might enable budget participants to understand and better use the budget-making authority of local governments. Moreover, the approach taken here has attempted to reveal how budgeting can be integrated with features of debt management, operations, accounting, auditing, financial reporting, and evaluation.

Budget Implementation

Rebudgeting: The Serial Nature of Municipal Budgetary Processes

John P. Forrester and Daniel R. Mullins

The term 'annual' is unfortunate. It has distracted attention from the real issue to a defense or criticism of the year as a specific unit of measure for budgetary purposes (Sundleson 1935, 253).

The annual or biannual budget has been the presumed standard time frame for governmental budgeting. It is used by the federal government as well as by state and local units. To preserve the concept of the annual budget, legislative bodies and executives have implemented strategies that try to cushion the budget from political pressures and economic uncertainty. Ironically, these same strategies may also provide the means for altering the budget throughout the fiscal year. Our objective in this article is to explain why municipal governments make such changes, or more simply, why they *re*budget.

Rebudgeting is what governments do to revise and update the adopted budget during the course of the fiscal year. As a continuation of the annual budgetary process, rebudgeting should be a means by which cities can meet the varied and even conflicting objectives of budgeting, including continuity and control, change and accountability, and flexibility and predictability (Wildavsky 1988). Over the short term, emphasis may shift as fiscal needs change.

However, over the longer term, such as over the course of a fiscal year, what might at first be perceived as competing objectives become compatible (Lyden 1975). In this vein, the approved budget can truly become *"the basis for* the financial plan for the operations of each agency during the fiscal year" (Office of Management and Budget 1989b, 95, emphasis added). As a living financial plan, the budget must be dynamic. It must offer the capacity to manage the unforseen without sacrificing the control and accountability ingrained in the budget during pre-execution (Pitsvada 1983).

If the budget is the basis for a living financial plan, then modifying or remaking the budget within a year may be a way of bringing about change (Wildavsky 1988; Caiden and Wildavsky 1974). Rebudgeting may be used to make the budget more responsive to the needs of budget participants and to the environment. For instance, if rebudgeting is, like budgeting, a process for coordinating activities, disciplining officials, and mobilizing the support of interest groups (Wildavsky 1988, 7), then the process may be infused with politics, providing a means for the legislature and its committees, the executive, and the bureaucracy to renegotiate their agendas (Draper and Pitsvada 1981). Or, if the process is guided more by technical matters, the range of players may be limited to auditors and controllers, with little input from interest groups (Rubin 1990). The salience of various actors may depend on the reason(s) for rebudgeting.

The need for change does not necessarily sound "the death knell for the annual budget" (Wildavsky 1988, 202-3), rather, it underscores the importance

---

Reprinted from *Public Administration Review* 52, no. 5 (1992): 467-73. By permission of Public Administration Review © by the American Society for Public Administration (ASPA), 1120 G Street N.W., Suite 700, Washington, D.C. 20005. All rights reserved.

of the annual budget as the take-off point for rebudgeting by laying the ground rules for a continuous process. It indicates that, like annual budgeting, rebudgeting reflects spending "commitments made at different times" (Wildavsky 1988, 12). Evidence indicates that a comprehensive understanding of the budget requires that the analytical focus shift from annual and one-shot to subannual and serial, and that it include, for instance, supplemental and deficiency budgets, updates, executive impoundments, and other possible revisions. All can act as critical safety valves (Axelrod 1988; Wildavsky 1988) for the living budget, cushioning it from dilemmas unforeseen during the regular approval process. Or they may reflect the misplacement of entrenched procedures and rules, despite desired budget purposes. A budget that reflects these changes may be most appropriately described as *annualized,* not as annual.

In short, rebudgeting may be an integral component of a serial budget that takes its cue from the initial budgetary process. It may be a way to tune up the original budget by redressing objectives shortchanged in the initial effort (Rubin 1990). It may also be a way for departments and agencies to work with the budget office to more effectively accomplish policy objectives. By examining rebudgeting and how it fits into the budgetary cycle, local governments might be

DATA AND METHODOLOGY

Data were collected by surveying officials in 91 U.S. central cities in December 1990, selected at random from the universe of central cities in the United States with populations under 1,000,000 (of which there are 517). A total of 59 officials from 49 (54 percent) of the 91 cities returned completed surveys. We received responses from two officials in 10 of the cities. Seventy-six percent of these were appointed officials. Completed questionnaires were received from representatives of the mayor's office in 16 cities (13 were mayors), representatives of the city manager's/administrator's office in 21 cities (17 were city managers/administrators), and officials in the finance or budget office in 20 cities (15 were finance directors and budget officers).

Respondents from the 59 completed surveys were grouped as follows. Respondents classified as representing the office of the mayor included 13 mayors, 1 deputy mayor, 1 executive officer to the mayor, and 1 administrative assistant to the mayor. Respondents classified as representative of the city manager's/administrator's office included 17 managers/administrators, 3 assistant city managers, and one assistant to the city manager. Respondents from the finance and budget office category included 6 finance officers/directors, 8 budget directors/finance and management division administrators, 1 controller, 2 assistant finance/budget directors, 3 senior financial/budget analysts. One respondent did not indicate his/her position with the city, and another was not classifiable within these categories. Fifty percent of the respondents had more than 10 years of experience with the city, and fewer than 22 percent had less than 5 (the average was 12 years, 11 months). Generally, we report the findings without singling out the particular classes of respondents identified above, because results from contingency table analyses indicated that respondents tended to be consistent with each other.

We conducted contingency table statistical analyses on all questions by categories of respondents (mayor's office, city manager's/administrator's office, finance director's office). The results indicated that where differences were statistically significant, the disparity was one of magnitude rather than direction. The one exception was that 53 percent of the city manager's/administrator's office respondents said that the midyear process favors the influence of the city administration, whereas only 25 percent of the mayor's office respondents and 18 percent of the finance/budget director's office respondents felt that way. This may suggest that managers and administrators see the mid-year adjustment process as a means for exercising their authority and power over budgetary matters. This is very reasonable since these administrators likely see themselves as responsible for taking discretionary actions to assure a balanced budget; whereas the offices of the mayor and the finance director may see the changes as reflecting primarily technical adjustments (since political decisions are made during the regular budgetary process). The cities represented had budgets ranging from $14 million to $1.4 billion. Half had budgets in excess of $100 million.

in a better position for managing the annualized budget. Our objective is to further understand rebudgeting by examining within-year budgetary changes at the municipal level.

EVIDENCE FROM THE EXPERIENCES OF LOCAL OFFICIALS

We have tapped the experiences of municipal decisionmakers regarding their exposure to rebudgeting. In doing so, we surveyed city mayors, administrators, and finance officers regarding their views on the nature of midyear budget adjustments.

The average population of the cities for which officials responded was 159,000. The largest was nearly 900,000 and the smallest, 25,000. The median was 93,000. Sixteen of the cities were organized under the mayor-council form of government, while 33 represented the city manager form. Responses were received from all regions of the country, with 17 of the cities located in the north central region, 16 in the South, 9 in the West, and 7 from the Northeast. Although respondents came from a random sample of large central cities, it is not clear how generalizable the findings are to a broader universe of U.S. cities.

Process and Restrictions

Our interest is in alterations in the budget that require formal approval of the legislative body, especially midyear adjustments outside the previously agreed-upon levels of administrative discretion, and in the level of administrative discretion available, as it may greatly influence the need to resort to formal adjustments. To comprehend the adjustments, one must understand their administrative context. Although substantively meaningful, background levels of administrative discretion are implicit in the agreements and the setting of the original budget.

Restrictions on Administrative Discretion. The vast majority of cities surveyed restricted the ability of city administration to reallocate funds within and between functions without explicit approval of the legislative body. Alternatively, legislatively allowable midyear adjustments covered a broad range. The process and products emerging from the space between the level of discretion afforded the administration and that assigned the legislative body was the focus of this research. Table 1 outlines the physical dimensions of this space. Administrative adjustments that would transfer resources between funds were heavily restricted, with prohibitions on such transfers existing in 87 percent of the cases. Likewise, transfers between functions within the same fund were prohibited in 67 percent of the cities. Alternatively, transfers between categories of expenditures within a function (e.g., transfers from personal services to materials and supplies within the police function) were allowed in 82 percent of the cities, while 84 percent permitted transfers between objects of expenditures within categories of a function. These findings suggest that administrative flexibility was allowed as long as it did not shift the overall expenditure priorities of the budget. Midyear adjustments which could alter these priorities usually required council approval. As such, these adjustments were available to the city council in more than 90 percent of all cases.

Constraints on administrative discretion tend to be stated in the city charter, the annual appropriations ordinance, or state law, rather than administrative rules/procedures. Rarely can they be altered through administrative means, and, to the degree local authority may relax them, it requires council approval (Table 2).

Table 1: *Within-Year Discretion for Making Budget Adjustments (Percentage)*

Budget Adjustment	Administratively Permitted	Legally Permitted
Transfers between funds	13 (7)	91 (50)
Transfers between functions	33 (18)	93 (51)
Transfers between categories	82 (46)	96 (53)
Transfers between objects	84 (47)	94 (50)
Increases in total expenditures	11 (6)	91 (50)
Decrease in total appropriations		96 (50)

Note: Numbers in parentheses indicate number of respondents.

Table 2: *Authority to Alter Administrative Discretion (Percentage)*

	Authority to		
Site of Authority	Decrease Discretion	Increase Discretion	Both
Legislative body	9 (5)	21 (12)	43 (24)
Mayor	7 (4)	2 (1)	5 (3)
City administrator	4 (2)	2 (1)	13 (7)
Finance officer	4 (2)	2 (1)	5 (5)

Note: Numbers in parentheses indicate number of respondents.

Expenditure Controls. To further assure the adherence of departments to the priorities established in the budget, many cities reportedly relied on a variety of expenditure budgetary controls. Of the cities surveyed, 93 percent used formal encumbrance systems and 91 percent used formal monthly or quarterly expenditure reviews to minimize the need for rebudgeting. Yet 22 percent of the respondents used formal allotments (i.e., budgeted funds parcelled out to departments on a quarterly or other basis) to control agencies.

Adjustment Process. The city council may receive requests for midyear budget adjustments from the mayor, individual council members, the city administrator, or department heads. The majority (69 percent) of responding cities relied on the city administrator or manager to make adjustment requests; only 24 percent relied on the mayor (Table 3). This process of communicating the request was consistent with the procedures for bringing the original budgetary requests to the city council in most communities. For 82 percent of the cities, if midyear adjustments were to occur, only a simple majority vote of the council was required. The public, however, tended to have little effect on midcourse corrections; although 94 percent of the communities were required to hold public hearings on the original budget proposal, less than 40 percent were required to do so for budget adjustments. Of the cities that did, more than 40 percent indicated that they were not on a par with hearings on the original budget.

The Actors in Rebudgeting

Actors that may affect rebudgeting range from local council and administrative officials to program clients, taxpayer groups, and the general public. Sixty-six percent of respondents suggested that the city manager saw transfers and appropriation adjustments as fairly routine, and 63 percent felt the council considered them routine. Although viewed as a rather routine process, the roles of actors varied considerably between actors and relative to their involvement in the original budget-setting process.

Actor Involvement. Respondents were asked how active they felt actors were in initiating or resisting budget adjustments, compared to their role in determining the original budget. Table 4 indicates the percent of respondents that judged actors to be at least moderately active in the budget or adjustment process. All actors were judged to be less involved in the adjustment process than in setting the original budget. Of the governmental actors, high-level administrators were the primary actors in establishing the original budget, followed by the city council and mayor. Actors outside the government tended to be much less active in determining the original budget. Here, program clients (37 percent) and taxpayer groups (25 percent) are judged most active.

In comparing the original budget process to the process for budget adjustments, one sees a striking

Table 3: *Process for Midyear Adjustments That Require Action or Approval of Legislative Body (Percentage)*

Procedure	Affirmative
Adjustment proposed by mayor	24 (14)
Adjustment proposed by city administrator/manager	69 (40)
Other	5 (3)
Simple majority approved by council	82 (45)
Super majority approved by council	18 (10)
Hold public hearings on original budget	94 (49)
Hold public hearings on proposed adjustments	38 (22)
Adjusted hearings equivalent to budget hearings	59 (10)

Note: Numbers in parentheses indicate number of respondents.

Table 4: *Percent of Respondents Judging Actor to Be At Least Moderately Active*

Site of Authority	Authority to		
	Original Budget	Initiating Adjustments	Resisting Adjustments
Mayor	82 (45)	41 (22)	35 (19)
City council	89 (49)	32 (17)	42 (23)
City administrator/manager	96 (45)	85 (40)	48 (23)
Department heads	100 (54)	80 (43)	26 (13)
Program/project directors	81 (42)	54 (28)	18 (9)
Program clients	37 (19)	10 (5)	10 (5)
Taxpayer groups	25 (13)	4 (2)	12 (6)
Business groups	19 (10)	4 (2)	10 (5)
General public	15 (8)	2 (1)	12 (6)

Note: Numbers in parentheses indicate number of respondents.

decline in the level of involvement of both city officials and the general public. Based on order of magnitude, the decline in public activity surrounding the initiation of adjustments was much greater than that for public officials. The public, however, played a more active role in resisting adjustments. Higher-level administrative officials were, once again, in leadership positions surrounding the initiation of midyear adjustments and were augmented by a relative increase in the influence of program directors. Following these administrative officials in influence were the mayor and city council. However, their level of involvement was only one-half to one-third what it was in the normal budget process. The leadership focus for resisting midyear adjustments tended to lie primarily with the city administrator/manager followed by the city council and mayor.

Actor Influence. Respondents were also asked whether the adjustment process, compared to the original budget process, favored any actors at the expense of others. When respondents perceived a shift in influence, the city administration was most often considered the beneficiary (33 percent), followed by the legislative body (23 percent), program clients (21 percent), and specific departments (19 percent). The increased influence of clients appeared limited to the identification of a previously unknown need to which the legislative body was sympathetic and to the allocation of unexpected additional intergovernmental revenues.

The Stimulus for Rebudgeting in U.S. Cities

The experiences of city officials were further explored along three categories of rebudgeting stimuli. These included adjustments required (1) *managerial necessity* stemming from the technical complexity of estimating needs and resources and the level of restrictions placed on management decisionmaking, (2) *environmental pressures* because of changes in the external environment within which services were delivered, and (3) *political concerns* emanating out of the political nature of public sector resource allocation decisions.

Managerial Necessity. Rebudgeting may be necessary because of managerial or administrative difficulties in planning for the activities of the nation's urban centers. These may include, at a minimum, the following three factors. First, rebudgeting may occur to counter administrative rules or regulations that excessively narrow the ability of department heads or administrators to adjust their budgets to fluctuations in the service environment. Second, rebudgeting may arise because of a need to modify inaccurate expenditure estimates. Finally, cash flow may be very erratic, enough to require increasing expenditures for priority items based on greater than anticipated revenues or reducing expenditures when revenues are less than anticipated.

The experiences of city administrative officials regarding the importance of managerial necessity as an explanation for rebudgeting are summarized in Table 5. Respondents were asked to indicate for the adjustments initiated by administrators and for those initiated by legislators how often each of the reasons was involved in stimulating budget adjustments. They were asked to rate that involvement as "almost never," "sometimes," "frequently," or "very often." Table 5 shows the percentage of respondents that indicated a stimulus was "sometimes," "frequently," or "very often" a factor.

Managerial necessity, overall, was much more important as a stimulus for administratively initiated adjustments than for legislatively initiated ones. Of the specific factors considered, consistent with the above findings, difficulty in accurately estimating

Table 5: *Stimuli for Within-Year Budgeting (Percentage)*

Basis of Stimulus	Administrators		Legislators	
	Sometimes	Frequently	Sometimes	Frequently
Managerial Necessity				
Administrative discretion	22 (11)	29 (14)	23 (11)	8 (4)
Estimating need	45 (23)	31 (16)	25 (12)	8 (4)
Estimating revenue	40 (20)	20 (10)	17 (8)	11 (5)
Environmental Pressures				
Resource fluctuation	34 (16)	11 (5)	23 (10)	2 (1)
Need fluctuation	35 (17)	4 (2)	20 (9)	0 (0)
Mandate	40 (19)	8 (4)	30 (13)	2 (1)
Political Concerns				
Redress	37 (19)	2 (1)	42 (20)	6 (3)
Symbolism	12 (6)	2 (1)	11 (5)	2 (1)
Drift	10 (5)	0 (0)	11 (5)	0 (0)
Administrative politics	21 (10)	4 (2)	9 (4)	2 (1)

Note: Numbers in parentheses indicate number of respondents.

expenditure needs was most significant. Forty-five percent of the respondents indicated that it was sometimes a factor in administratively initiated adjustments, and 31 percent said that it was at least frequently at work. Functions most susceptible to difficulties in estimating need included police services, because of unexpected events necessitating the payment of overtime and additional services; capital projects, because of shifts in priorities, underestimated costs, or estimates being made far in advance of the project; growth-related needs, and needed repairs of both plant and equipment, because of breakdowns; and sanitation, water, and utilities, because of weather-induced shifts in demand and growth.

Restrictions on administrative discretion and difficulties in estimating revenues were also important. For instance, 51 percent of respondents indicated that excessive administrative restrictions were at least sometimes evident in administration-initiated adjustments, and 31 percent indicated the same for legislative-initiated cases. Narrative comments suggested several reasons for the importance of restriction on discretion. They included internal and external conditions such as public safety restrictions set at the state level through state laws or as restrictions placed on the receipt of intergovernmental funds; intergovernmental restrictions on the use of grants for parks and recreation services, sanitation and sewerage, and capital projects; and collective bargaining restrictions due in union contracts settled after the adoption of the original budget. Some functions which were "controllable," such as parks and recreation and street repair services, and "large" departments (such as police and public works, which could absorb freezes) also acted as reserves in the event of reduced discretion and environmental pressures in other functions. Regarding revenue estimating difficulties, respondents suggested that health services and planning and code enforcement were affected because their funds were determined largely by other governments or the economy. Other functions that might be rebudgeted because of difficult-to-predict revenues included housing and community development, parks and recreation, police services, and courts. Some respondents suggested general administrative functions and capital projects as the first targets to replace lost revenues.

Environmental Pressures. Rebudgeting might also arise from changes in the external environment within which services were delivered. We considered three environmental pressures: (1) environmental resource fluctuation from unanticipated economic decline or expansion, legal exposure, or significant changes in state or national grant programs; (2) environmental need fluctuation from large, unanticipated shifts in demand for services; and (3) environmental mandate from action required by the state or national governments or the courts (e.g., state-ordered increases in the financing of housing programs or court determinations in challenges to property values or federal pollution abatement requirements).

As with managerial necessity, environmental pressures affected adjustments initiated by administrators more than those initiated by legislators. The most important of these was the environmental mandate, followed by resource fluctuations and need fluctuations. The importance of mandates tended to revolve around the city's physical and legal environment. Sanitation and sewerage, as well as solid waste collection and disposal, were frequently offered as functions requiring adjustments due to revisions in state and national environmental regulations. Public safety was also suggested to be susceptible to changes in state criminal law and changes in fire-safety standards. Resource fluctuations, like problems in estimating revenues, emerged primarily from uncertainties surrounding functions heavily dependent on intergovernmental revenues, such as health services and capital projects. Additional problems arose for public transit because of changes in fuel prices and for solid waste disposal because of increases in tipping fees. Environmental need fluctuations emerged out of rather extreme conditions and, as such, were less likely to impact budget adjustments; however, when they occurred, they could have a substantial impact. Economic downturns often created emergencies that required the response of public safety and public assistance. Extremes in weather also taxed public services from water systems (for breakage of mains) to storm and sanitary sewers (from too excessive water intake), and public safety services (for emergency services).

Political Concerns. Rebudgeting might also emerge out of political aspirations regarding the public budget. Four political scenarios were considered: (1) political redress as individuals or groups from the public attempted to counter losses experienced during the normal budgetary process; (2) political symbolism as adjustments made to counteract decisions taken during the normal budget process for symbolic rather than substantive reasons (e.g., restoring cuts); (3) political drift as adjustments were stimulated because political priorities had changed since the budget was adopted; and (4) administrative politics as administrators stimulated adjustments to lessen losses or expand in a more favorable political climate.

Political concerns, with the exception of administrative politics, showed comparable levels of activity between administration and legislator initiated adjustments. By far the most active of these in midyear budget adjustment motives was political redress. Administrative politics were of moderate importance only for administratively initiated adjustments and political symbolism and drift were only of the most modest influence. Political redress and administrative politics appeared to be active in numerous functional areas. Housing and community development, and neighborhood capital and recreation projects, especially, were susceptible to the lobbying efforts of neighborhood groups for funding of projects omitted from the original budget. Street and highway repair services were often adjusted midyear if revenues allowed (i.e., they functioned as residual or marginal projects which could be brought on-line if demands emerged and resources allowed). Human service programs were susceptible to lobbying efforts by external human service agencies and were often expanded to address existing need if resources permitted. Public safety services were involved because of the high levels of public support for the services provided and a perception by some cities that they were generally "under budgeted." Administrative personnel could be active in mobilizing this external support.

Overall, as a category, managerial necessity appeared to be the most active stimulus for both administration-initiated and legislative-initiated adjustments, followed by environmental pressures and political concerns. Individually, however, political redress appeared to be the single most important factor in legislator-initiated adjustments and estimating need was by far the most important for administration-initiated adjustments.

Control, Management, and Planning

Respondents were also asked to comment on the effect of rebudgeting on the ability of administrators or legislators to control, manage, or plan city operations. Control is the process of assuring that resources are spent for the purposes appropriated and do not exceed the amount authorized. Management is the process of assuring that resources are used effectively and efficiently in carrying out activities. Planning is the process of determining both the goals and objectives of public policy and the mobilization of resources to achieve them.

Control. Respondents overwhelmingly felt that the midyear adjustment process did not adversely affect administrators' control over expenditures. Often this was because the midyear adjustments were generally small (e.g., less than 10 percent of the original budget). Rather, respondents said that the added review stimulated by the adjustment process and the documentation required for adjustments might even have enhanced the level of overall control. Although most impressions were similar for legislative control, some respondents suggested this process might slightly derail the council through responding to community and neighborhood pressure and providing an opportunity to patronize. Even so, the requirement of council approval seemed to reassure fiscal control. More than one respondent indicated that requests for midyear correction might have negative implications for future budgets; this might be considered a form of control in and of itself.

Management. Many respondents suggested that the midyear process augmented management by providing the marginal changes necessary to aid in the achievement of programmatic goals and objectives. Some suggested that the need for adjustments, itself, communicated clear information regarding a manager's performance. Respondents felt that midyear adjustments had no significant effect on the legislative body's ability to manage; as they accurately pointed out, management was not the role of that body.

Planning. Several respondents suggested that planning was a continuous process and that the added flexibility of midyear adjustments allowed for adaptations, reflecting the nature of this process. The vast majority felt that these adjustments improved planning by allowing the budget to respond to changing needs. Some, however, cautioned that adjustments might symbolize less than the most thorough advance planning and, more importantly, a tendency for legislatively initiated adjustments to chart off in directions somewhat at cross-purposes to overall planning efforts. In this sense, the midterm adjustment could also reflect a breakdown in planning.

Is the Annual Budget Cycle Too Long?

Finally, respondents were asked if the annual cycle of their budget was too long. Ninety percent of them answered "No." In the context of the midyear process, many suggested that, like planning, budgeting could be viewed as a continuous process. The budget plan must be flexible enough to meet new demands and priorities. The annual budget cycle was not felt to inhibit this. In fact, some respondents pointed out that a cycle of "less than a year would not permit good planning." Given such comments, a caveat was offered that, for planning purposes, any midyear adjustments "must be measured and evaluated against the formally adopted annual budget."

DISCUSSION

As evident from the above, participants saw rebudgeting as an extension of the normal budgetary process. The budgeting environments were similar; however, the interaction of rebudgeting on its environment was somewhat different, as was the role and influence of the actors. Administrative officials usually initiated rebudgeting. This might be at the expense of the legislative body and the general public, because administrative officials controlled the flow of information, and shaped the midyear agenda, and midyear changes were generally limited. The process itself tended to be less visible than the original budget process because the impact of adjustments on policy was unclear and because public participation was not encouraged. When the public participated, however, it generally resisted proposed adjustments. The legislative body appeared to be more reactive in this process. Although department heads and program directors were involved less in rebudgeting than in regular budgeting, they apparently used this process to recoup losses from the normal budgetary process. The flow of information and the reduced role of the legislative body also suggested that the site of checks on midyear increases lay predominantly with higher-level city administration and in the potential ramifications of requested increases on budget successes in successive years. This process's likely result, then, was to increase the influence of administrative actors.

Administrative actors entered the process primarily out of managerial necessity and environmental pressures, although political redress and administrative politics also served as motivations. Legislators, less frequently active, entered the process in a less predictable manner, yet they tended to be disposed toward funding increases. Environmental pressures, managerial necessity, and political concerns were all active but at lower levels.

It also appeared that different functions were variably susceptible to midyear adjustments. Functions which, for environmental or managerial reasons, were more volatile received greater attention (e.g., public safety, capital projects); those for which expenditures were more controllable often provided the resources for adjustments when fund balances were insufficient. Moreover, in general, distributive and development services received more attention than did redistributive. This was true except in the more limited cases of political redress and symbolism, but even here, neighborhood specific, distributive services, were heavily represented. Finally, although many adjustments were motivated by need, this appeared to be less important for needs-based (social service) functions. They depended on fluctuating intergovernmental revenue and on the availability of new resources.

CONCLUSIONS

Rebudgeting and budgeting, as components of a serial process exhibit many of the same characteristics. Rebudgeting, however, also has unique qualities. Although rebudgeting may not significantly reorient public policies, it may offer a hedge against uncertainty and therefore rationalize budgeting in uncertain times. During periods of revenue and expenditure uncertainty, rebudgeting may be used to tune up policies, requiring more attention to rebudgeting and its effects on policy. If volatility declines, the need for rebudgeting may decline as well. The universal presence of some environmental uncertainty, however, engenders it with value.

Irrespective of the existing environmental characteristics, adjustments to the rebudgeting process intended to open up the process and increase its formality might bring it more in line with the values expressed in the normal budgetary process. To formalize the process, however, might impede its flexibility and utility as a midyear correcting process, perhaps even divert attention away from the annual cycle and, as respondents said, away from planning. As they saw it, midyear budgeting yields marginal changes to agreed-upon budget policy priorities. Also, to open the process may resurrect old policy battles. Restricting the openness of rebudgeting may be a fair balance to the openness of the regular budget process. The check that these alterations do not lead too far astray is found in the process for establishing the succeeding annual agreements.

Rebudgeting, at least at the local level, appears to be primarily technically driven. Political concerns are present in this process, but evidence suggests that cities use rebudgeting to marginally adjust programs and to meet management needs in a changing environment. As such, it is an extension of the managerial and planning dimensions of budgeting. In communities experiencing more dramatic adjustments midyear, the political motivations and ramifications may become more pronounced. The conditions under which this takes place are questions requiring additional consideration. Doing so awaits further analysis.

References

Axelrod, Donald. 1988. *Budgeting for Modern Government*. New York: St. Martin's Press.

Caiden, Naomi, and Aaron Wildavsky. 1974. *Planning and Budgeting in Poor Countries*. New Brunswick, N.J.: Transaction.

Draper, Frank, and Bernard Pitsvada. 1981. "Limitations in Federal Budget Execution." *Government Accountants Journal* 30 (Fall): 23.

Lauth, Thomas P. 1988. "Mid-Year Appropriations in Georgia: Allocating the 'Surplus'." *International Journal of Public Administration* 11: 531-50.

Lyden, Fremont J. 1975. "Control, Management, and Planning: An Empirical Examination." *Public Administration Review* 35 (November/December): 625-28.

Office of Management and Budget, Executive Office of the President. 1989a. "Mid-Session Review of the Budget." Washington, D.C.: U.S. Government Printing Office.

Office of Management and Budget, Executive Office of the President. 1989b. "The United States Budget in Brief." Washington, D.C.: U.S. Government Printing Office.

Pitsvada, Bernard T. 1983. "Flexibility in Federal Budget Execution." *Public Budgeting & Finance* 3 (Summer): 83-101.

Rubin, Irene. 1990. *The Politics of Public Spending: Getting and Spending, Borrowing and Balancing*. Chatham, N.J.: Chatham House Publishers, chap. 6.

Sundleson, J. Wilner. 1935. "Budgetary Principles." *Political Science Quarterly* 50: 236-63.

Wildavsky, Aaron. 1988. *The New Politics of the Budgetary Process*. Glenview, Ill.: Scott, Foresman and Company.

31 Cash Management: Basic Principles and Guidelines

Aman Khan

Like all financial organizations, local governments have become increasingly concerned in recent years with the management of their assets, especially those related to idle cash. Local governments receive most of their tax revenue during two or three short periods in the year, leaving substantial cash available to them for short-term investment. An effective cash management program can very easily remedy the general problems of cash flow, idle cash balance, and investment.

There are three principal motives that provide justification for a government to develop effective programs for managing its cash and other liquid assets: (1) transaction motive—to make sufficient cash available on a timely basis to pay for all government programs and activities; (2) precautionary motive—to provide for contingencies requiring sudden and unforeseen expenditures; and (3) speculative motive—to maximize income through the identification and investment of cash, not immediately required, into securities paying the highest interest rates. An ideal cash management program of a local government, responding to the transaction and precautionary objectives, would seek to maximize this interest earning, subject to a wide range of constraints such as bank requirements, compensating balance, and government policies.

This may seem ambitious, requiring time and effort on the part of the local government. Nonetheless, a sound cash management program has significant fiscal payoffs—it lowers debt service and generates additional income. To the extent that such payoffs are realized, they represent money which could be used to create additional local programs or enrich existing ones, reduce taxes or further other community goals and objectives. This article discusses in a systematic fashion a number of activities and presents some guidelines that are important to the development of a sound cash management program for a local government. These activities are (1) preparing a cash budget, (2) managing cash flows, (3) determining bank relations, (4) understanding the legal framework, (5) identifying optimal cash balance, and (6) developing investment strategies.

CASH BUDGETING

The first and foremost step in making cash management decisions is to estimate future *cash flows,* i.e., cash receipts and disbursements, usually for a quarter, based either on weekly or monthly data. Without these estimates, a government has no way of telling how much money is needed for its operations and how much money will be required to support its future growth. To develop a cash budget, say, at the end of a fiscal year in August, a cash manager (or the person responsible for cash management) would need to complete the estimates for September, October, and November. This would be followed by preliminary estimates for every following month for the rest of the fiscal year. At the end of September, the cash manager would refine the estimates for October, November,

---

Aman Khan is associate professor in the Public Administration Program, Department of Political Science, Texas Tech University.

and December, and the process would continue. The advantage of this repeated updating is that it ensures greater accuracy and precision in the estimates. Since cash flows constantly change, estimates should be constantly updated to provide a basis for more objective cash budgeting.

The preparation of a cash budget is not a difficult task once the information on a government's operating budget is known. There are four simple steps in the actual preparation of a cash budget. These steps are (1) estimate cash receipts (inflows), (2) estimate cash disbursements (outflows), (3) subtract the outflows from inflows to ascertain excess (or shortage) of funds, or *net cash flow*, and (4) add this balance to previous month's closing balance (*beginning balance* for current month) to obtain the projected total cash balance. Exhibit 1 presents a sample format of a local government cash budget.

As it becomes apparent from these steps, the most important aspect in the construction of a cash budget is to be able to estimate cash receipts and disbursements. There is no single method that can best estimate these receipts and disbursements, although there is a bewildering array of techniques one can use ranging from simple average to exponential smoothing to more complex Box-Jenkins, depending on how familiar one is with these methods and the quality of cash flow data available or maintained by a government. However, four methods are suggested here for their simplicity and ease of application. These are (1) interview adjustment method, (2) constant average method, (3) simple moving average, and (4) trend-line projection.

Interview Adjustment Method. This is the simplest of the four methods and requires no formal estimation. To apply the method, simply list cash re-

Exhibit 1: *A Sample Cash Budget Format*

Cash Flow	Monthly Series			Forecast Period			
	June (1)	July (2)	August (3)	September ...	October ...	November ...	Etc.
Cash receipts (inflows)							
Tax revenue							
Property taxes							
(Local) Sales taxes							
(Local) Income tax							
Nontax revenue							
Charges and fees							
State and federal aid							
Miscellaneous							
Total inflows:	[ ]	[ ]	...	...	...	...	[ ]
Cash disbursements (outflows)							
Salaries/Wages							
Materials and supplies							
Debt service							
Benefit payments							
Any other							
−Total outflows:	[ ]	[ ]	...	...	...	...	[ ]
Change in cash balance							
= Net cash flow	[ ]	[ ]	...	...	...	...	[ ]
+ Beginning balance[a]	[ ]	[ ]	...	...	...	...	[ ]
= Closing balance	[ ]	[ ]	...	...	...	...	[ ]

[a] This can also be presented at the very beginning of the table, in which case the total cash receipts will include the *beginning balance*, say, for the month of June (which is the *closing balance* for May) and the total inflows for that month. The *change in cash balance* will simply be the difference between total receipts and total disbursements. The closing balance for June will then become the beginning balance for July and so on.

ceipts and disbursements for the current month and then have interviews with the agency or department heads to adjust the data to include expected changes in the coming months. Finally, compare these receipts and disbursements for each month to determine when excess or deficit cash balance will occur.

Constant Average Method. This method is the least complex among the time-series methods. It is calculated on the basis of percentage changes from one period to the next and is extremely suitable for situations where there is not too much fluctuation in the data. To determine the forecast value of any one period, say, the sales tax receipts for next month, one simply needs to assume that they are equal to actual sales tax receipts of the current month, plus the average of the percentage changes experienced up to that month or period times the current receipts. However, like most simple time-series methods, the constant average is based on the *naive* assumption that there is no cause-and-effect relationship between the forecast variable and the environment; it simply says that the value of a forecast variable is the same as the past, plus an adjustment based on the average of past data. The constant average method can be formally expressed as

$$F_{t+1} = F_t + [(\% \text{ Change Average}) \times F_t]$$

where F_t is the value of the forecast variable F at time t; F_{t+1} is the value at time $t+1$; and, in general, F_{t+i} is the future value of F at i ($i = 1, 2, \ldots, n$).

Simple Moving Average. Used primarily for short-term forecasting such as cash budgeting, this method consists of taking cash receipts and disbursements for a given number of months (weeks), usually between three and six, calculating the arithmetic average and then using that average as the forecast for the next month (week). The term moving average is used because as the new cash receipt and disbursement data become available, a new average is computed by dropping the oldest one from the average and including the newest one. The new average is then used as the forecast for the next month or week. Thus, the number of data points from the series used in the average is always constant and includes the most recent information. This method is expressed as

$$F_{t+1} = (F_t + F_{t-1} + F_{t-2} + F_{t-3} + \ldots + F_{t-n+1})/n$$

where F_{t+1}, as before, is the value of the forecast variable F at time $t+1$; F_{t-i} is the past value of F at period i ($i = 1, 2, \ldots, n$); and n is the total number of periods.

Trend-Line Projection. This method represents a continuous movement in the direction of time series. The trend line, the heart of this method, is calculated by using a simple procedure called *least square*. The least-square method produces a straight line that minimizes the sum of the squared deviations from the line and the actual data representing past receipts and disbursements. It provides estimates of two parameters, *intercept and slope*, that allow one to calculate future trend values. In fact, it is the slope that represents the direction and level of change in time series for each period of time. The slope can be negative or positive, but remains constant for each period. However, to apply the trend-line projection method, one would need as a rule of thumb at least 10 data points, i.e., 10 months (weeks) of receipts and disbursements. Formal expression of the trend-line method is

$$F_t = a + bT + e$$

where F is the same as before; T is the explanatory trend variable, time; a is the intercept; b is the slope; and e is an error term.

MANAGEMENT OF CASH FLOWS

Since the seventies, two factors have significantly influenced the cash management practices of local governments: one is the interest rate and the other technology. During the late seventies and to some extent in the early eighties, interest rates were quite high, raising the opportunity cost of holding cash and forcing the cash managers to search for better ways to manage cash. At the same time, new technologies, particularly electronic transfers, offered alternatives to deal with cash transactions more efficiently than ever before. Although most cash management activities are performed jointly by a government and its banks and other depositories, the cash manager is ultimately responsible for its cash management program. A cash manager can significantly affect the cash management decision by undertaking such measures as (1) synchronizing cash flows, (2) using float, (3) accelerating collections, and (4) controlling disbursements.

Synchronizing Cash Flows. Just like individuals, a government can improve its forecasts so that its cash receipts will coincide with cash outflows which, in turn, will reduce transaction balances to a minimum. The synchronization will allow a government to use regular *billing cycles* throughout the month, especially for certain types of activities such as utility enterprises, since these activities arrange to bill the users of their services on a regular basis. This will further help to reduce their cash balances, decrease bank loans, and lower interest expenses.

Using Float. In the broadest sense, *float* refers to the difference between the balance a government has in its checkbook and the balance in its bank's records. The difference, called *net float,* represents the time it takes for the checks issued by a government to clear and the time it takes for the checks received and deposited by the government to clear. If the government clears on average more checks with amounts that are larger than the amounts for the average number of checks it issued, it will have a positive net float, called *disbursement float.* The reverse is called *collection float.* Net floats can produce a considerable amount of savings for governments, depending upon where the depositories are located. With electronic transfers becoming commonplace and the Federal Reserve imposing increasing restrictions on time-clearance, float may disappear as a viable option in the near future.

Acceleration of Receipts. Cash managers have always searched for ways to improve the collection of receivables such as taxes. Collection involves reducing the time between when the residents in a particular jurisdiction receive the bill and when they make the payment. A standard procedure for improving the collection process is to provide a return envelope with the bill. If necessary, governments can and should offer early payment discounts or penalties for late payment or even advance the date of payment, barring legal restrictions. Another method, perhaps as old as cash management practice itself, is to have all payments made to the government mailed directly to the bank or to a post office *lock-box* controlled by the bank. Payments can be immediately deposited, thereby increasing the cash availability or reducing collection float. Although efficient in speeding up collections, the lock-box system can result in the government's cash being spread around many different banks. An alternative would be to mobilize funds from decentralized locations into one or more central cash pools to allow for economies of scale in cash management.

Controlling Disbursements. Control of disbursements is the exact opposite of acceleration of receipts. Efficiency in cash management can result only if both inflows and outflows can be effectively managed through disbursement control. The cash manager can easily build up cash flows by timing the payments of bills to be paid only when they become due (unless contingent upon early payment). Payments can also be made late in the day so that the funds stay in the bank account for the remainder of the day. Alternatively, the government can set up several disbursement accounts, all with zero-dollar balance on which checks are written. These accounts usually have a central account in the major bank, called *lead bank.* When checks are presented to these *zero-balance accounts,* funds are automatically transferred from the central account, thus reducing the amount of idle cash balance. In the event the central account has a negative balance, it could be replenished by borrowing from the bank against a line of credit, or by borrowing in the commercial paper market, or by selling T-bills from the portfolio of marketable securities.

A more recent, but frequently used method of optimizing payment is to use wire-transfer. Wire-transfer is a real-time method of transferring funds from one bank to another using Federal Reserve account balances. With a wire transaction, the payor's account is debited and the payee's account is credited the same day. Transaction information flows through a computer network residing in the Fed's 12 district banks. These transfers, for which the lead bank usually charges a city an amount equal to the cost of transfers, significantly contribute to the cash-flow management of the government by minimizing the float.

BANK RELATIONS

Bank relations of a government represent the keystone of its cash management program. It is through the banking system that a government implements its regular cash transactions such as collecting its receivables, paying its bills, investing its idle cash balances, and carrying out other functions vital to its financial affairs. Local government cash managers should be concerned with several aspects of their relationships with banks and the services provided by them. These include (1) selection of banks, (2) compensation for services, (3) consolidation of bank accounts, and (4) reviewing bank relationships.

Selection of Banks. Selecting the right bank or depository is by far the most crucial element of bank relations. Most local governments tend to conduct their business with one major bank which handles most of their daily transactions. Which bank a local government should regularly do business with must depend on a number of factors. For instance, in selecting a bank, the cash manager must carefully analyze not only the government's banking needs but also the latter's capabilities to meet them. Typically, the decision to use a particular bank is subject to two major considerations. First, the bank which a government would primarily use should be conveniently located. Although the local government may select banks outside the community for certain services, the lead bank should be located within easy reach to enhance personal contact, ease of deposits, and so on. Second, the lead bank should be able to provide the necessary services required by the government. The cash manager, if necessary, should invite several banks and other financial institutions interested in being considered as authorized depositories to provide information concerning their various services and fees. In addition to the lead bank, the government should use one or more banks for short-term investments. This would substantially reduce the dependency on the lead bank for services.

Compensation for Services. Governments frequently pay for the banking services they receive through a service charge based on a practice called *compensating balance.* A service charge is a monthly fee imposed on the quantity of services rendered by a bank, such as number of checks processed, number of accounts reconciled, etc. Compensating balances, on the other hand, are funds a government purposely leaves or is expected to leave on its deposits with the banks to enable them to cover the cost of handling its checking accounts, maintaining a line of credit for its use, or performing other functions required by the government in managing its finance. Banks also rely on the float to pay for part of their own costs.

In many instances, however, it becomes difficult to get a bank to openly discuss its costs or a minimum compensating balance. This usually happens if a government already has large holdings in the bank, or if there are not too many banking facilities in and around the community. In such a situation, it is important that the cash manager keeps the environment competitive by regularly reviewing the costs and services offered by other banks as well as the lead bank.

Consolidation of Accounts. Governments, in general, tend to maintain a large number of bank accounts, which often works as a constraint on the investment of excess cash. They should try to reduce the number of accounts through consolidation, whenever possible. Consolidation of accounts can be easily accomplished, once the lead bank has been decided, by combining many small balances which by themselves do not have any investment potential. There are several advantages to consolidation. First, it affords the *pooling* of cash into one or a few accounts in order to maximize investment opportunities and to smooth out cash flows. Second, it generates a much greater volume which, in turn, allows for investment in larger denominations. Third, it simplifies bank reconciliation since checks are written on a small number of accounts. Finally, it helps achieve an effective use of manpower.

Reviewing Bank Relationships. For a government whose banking needs call for frequent services and dealing with more than one bank, a recurring challenge is how to tell which bank is giving it the best services. One way of resolving this problem is to size up these banks through personal contacts with their key officials. Traditionally, this has been the *forward approach* among cash managers, and many, perhaps out of habit, rely greatly on it for judging the quality of services provided them. From time to time, however, it may be necessary for the government to make an effort to look at the financial soundness of its banks and other depositories. The review can be carried out regularly once or twice a year, but should involve a detailed analysis. A more casual approach would be to occasionally read the banks' annual reports or scan their interim balance sheets as they appear in the business press.

THE LEGAL FRAMEWORK

Conventional literature tends to ignore or undermine the role of legal framework in cash management. Many local governments get into unforeseen financial predicaments for failing to keep abreast of the legal limitations that surround their cash management programs. A good example is a small local government in Pennsylvania that some years back borrowed twice the amount from a local bank it frequently transacted with than it was legally allowed to borrow under Pennsylvania law at the time. Upon discovering the mistake some months later, the community was forced to return the balance with an additional cost for holding the cash for the duration of the time. Unfortunately, neither the community nor the bank knew of the existence of such laws in the state. Although the laws that govern cash management are seldom stated in a simple and straightforward manner, it is important that the government has a firsthand knowledge of these laws and regulations before making any cash management decision. There are at least two situations where a government should be aware of the legal limitations: borrowing and investing funds.

Borrowing. There are occasions when short-term borrowing is preferable to paying bills out of cash earmarked for other purposes. For instance, governments engage in short-term borrowing in anticipation of revenue, to meet the emergencies due to budget shortfall, and in anticipation of the issuance of bonds for capital projects. The instruments of short-term borrowing have different terminologies. The more general titles are bank loans, tax anticipation notes, revenue anticipation notes, bond anticipation notes, etc. However, these notes could be issued in anticipation of one, two, or all three situations. Although most governments frequently resort to this practice, there are limits as to when and how many of these notes can be issued by a local government. As a general rule, they should frequently check with government charters and other legal documents and guidelines.

Investing Funds. Most governments have options to invest funds in a variety of government and government-approved securities and other portfolios. Some governments, especially those that are small, may have restrictions as to where they may or may not invest. On occasion, local governments may be required to combine their accounts or join with other governments by combining their accounts for the purposes of enhancing investment opportunities. Such decisions provide the legal authorization for local governments to enter into pooling arrangements with other governments or to pool their own funds for investment purposes, so long as a clear audit trail is maintained.

OPTIMAL CASH BALANCE

Optimal balance is the minimum amount a government must maintain at any given time without incurring the possibility of either running a surplus or having a shortage of cash. Determining this cash position is probably one of the most difficult tasks facing a cash manager because of its inexact nature, although several procedures now currently exist that can offer suitable guidance as to how one should identify this position. One simple rule of thumb is to hold a certain number of days' outflow of cash as minimum balance. This may be one or two weeks' cash disbursements. If, for instance, the average weekly cash outflow of a local government is $450,000, then this amount would be the 'ideal' balance the government must maintain, with residual cash invested in marketable securities. Whenever the cash balance falls below this level, securities should be sold to restore the balance. On the other hand, any buildup in cash above this balance must be invested.

Other rules of thumb based on cash outflow patterns can be easily devised. In the case of most local governments, forecasts of cash needs are usually accurate, so the prospect of unexpectedly running out of cash is not real. Consequently, rules of thumb could provide useful operating procedures for cash management. Particularly for smaller governments, the added effort and expense of more sophisticated models may not be justified on the grounds of possible benefits. Still, certain models are available which may permit a more accurate analysis of the costs and benefits associated with various levels of cash. Two such models, one by Baumol and the other by Miller-Orr, are briefly discussed here.

The Baumol Model. One of the most widely discussed models for determining the optimal cash balance was the inventory approach suggested by William Baumol. Baumol was the first to notice that cash balances are in many respects similar to inventories and that the well-known Economic Order Quantity (EOQ) inventory model can be used to establish an *optimal* balance similar to optimal inventory. Baumol's model assumes (1) that the government uses cash at a steady and predictable rate, say, $500,000 per week; (2) that its cash inflows from operations also occur at a steady and predictable rate, say, $450,000 per week; thus (3) producing a net cash outflow, which also occurs at a steady rate of $50,000 per week.

If, according to this illustration, the government is to start at Time 0 with a normal cash balance of C=$200,000 and if its outflows exceeded its inflows by $50,000 per week, then (1) its cash balance would drop to 0 at the end of Week 4, and (2) its average cash balance would be C/2=$200,000/2=$100,000. That means, at the end of the fourth week, the government would need to replenish its cash balance, either by borrowing or by selling securities. If C were to be much larger than $200,000, say $300,000, then the cash supply would last for two additional weeks and the government would not have to replenish the cash balance after Week 4 by borrowing or by disposing of some of its securities. Since there is a transaction cost involved when a government borrows or sells, it makes sense to have a much larger cash balance than $200,000 to keep the transaction costs lower, but this will increase the size of the idle balance along with the opportunities lost from interest income that could have been earned from investing the additional $100,000.

This situation is analogous to the classical EOQ model and Baumol uses the same inventory expression, with some differences for the variables, to determine the optimal cash balance:[1]

$$C^* = \sqrt{\frac{2bT}{i}}$$

where b is the fixed cost per transaction of transferring funds from marketable securities to cash or from cash to securities, T is the total amount of cash needed for transaction for a given period, i is the opportunity cost of holding cash or, to put it simply,

---

1. The model can be easily derived from a simple cost function (P), given by the following expression:

Total Cost = $f(b, T, i, C, v)$

where b, i, T are described as above; v is the variable cost per transaction; and C is the normal cash balance. Given this, the total cost (P) of cash management consists of transaction cost (fixed as well as variable) plus a holding (opportunity) cost. That is,

Total Cost = Transaction Cost + Holding Cost
= [Fixed Transaction Cost + Variable Transaction Cost] + Holding Cost

$$P = [\frac{T}{C}(b) + vT] + \frac{C}{2}(i)$$

$$= bTC^{-1} + vT + \frac{iC}{2}$$

Now, to determine the optimal cash balance, one only needs to differentiate P with respect to C and set the derivative equal to 0, which then gives the famous square root formula that yields the optimal balance:

$$\frac{dP}{dC} = -bTC^{-2} + \frac{i}{2} = 0$$

$$C^2 i = 2bT$$

$$C^* = \sqrt{\frac{2bT}{i}}$$

The last expression is the Baumol model for determining optimal cash balances.

the interest rate on marketable securities, and C^* is the optimal cash balance. To illustrate its use, suppose $b = \$50$; $T = \$1,000,000$ for the year; and $i = 10\% = 0.10$. Then,

$$C^* = \sqrt{\frac{(2)\,(\$50)\,(\$1,000,000)}{0.10}} = \$31,623$$

Therefore, the government should borrow or sell securities in the amount of \$31,623 when its cash balance approaches 0, thus bringing its balance back to the optimal level. From this expression, one could easily find the total number of transactions per year by simply dividing T by C^*: \$1,000,000/\$31,623 = 31.62 (rounded to 32) or 32/52 weeks = 0.62 a week. The government's average cash balance for the period will be $C^*/2$ = \$31,623/2 = \$15,812. There are a couple of points worth mentioning about these results. First, the optimal cash balance does not necessarily increase with transactions. For instance, if the need for cash were to increase, for whatever reasons, say, by 100 percent from \$1,000,000 to \$2,000,000, the average cash balance would increase by 41 percent, from \$15,812 to \$22,361. This would suggest that there are economies of scale in holding, as given by the information in this particular example. Second, there is a positive relationship between transaction costs, b, and the optimal balance, provided everything else remains the same. That is, if b goes up, so will the optimal balance, and vice versa.

The Miller-Orr Model. One of the weaknesses of the Baumol model is that it is too simplistic. For instance, the very assumption of steady, predictable cash inflows and outflows does not provide any scope for uncertainty. The Miller-Orr model offers an alternative by considering uncertainty or random fluctuation in the *daily* (as opposed to weekly or monthly) net cash flows. Their model assumes that the distribution of this cash flow is approximately normal (bell-shaped). That is, each day, the net cash flow could be higher (H), or lower (L), or equal to an expected value, Z (theoretical optimal), drawn from this distribution. If it is higher, that is, when the cash balance reaches H, then H-Z amount should be transferred from cash to marketable securities. Alternatively, when the cash balance reaches L, Z-L amount should be transferred from marketable securities to cash.

The following presents the formal expression for their model:

$$Z = \left[\frac{3b\sigma^2}{4i}\right]^{1/3} + L$$

and

$$H = 3\left[\frac{3b\sigma^2}{4i}\right]^{1/3} + L$$

Furthermore, the average cash balance is given by

$$Z^* = \left[\frac{4Z - L}{3}\right]$$

where Z = optimal cash balance; H = upper limit; L = lower limit; b = fixed transaction cost; i = opportunity cost on a daily basis; σ^2 = variance or the sum of the squared deviations of net daily cash flows; and Z^* = average cash balance. To illustrate, suppose L is \$0; and b is \$50 as before; i is given by 0.10/365 since 10 percent per year must be converted to a daily rate; and the σ^2 of daily net cash flows is 100,000. Now, substituting these values into the model expressions would produce Z = \$2,392.14; H = \$7,176.42; and an average cash balance (Z^*) of \$3,189.52.[2] There are several caveats to this model that are worth noting here. First, the optimal balance is not halfway between the upper and lower limits, as one would tend to believe from these expressions. Second, the optimal cash balance increases with both b and σ^2, but decreases with a larger value of i (meaning that it becomes more costly to hold cash). Third, the lower limit does not necessarily have to be 0 because of the compensating balance requirements and also because of the fact that most governments would prefer to have a margin of safety. Finally, the model, although it works much better than rules-of-thumb practices, has a tendency to produce less than optimal results when one has to deal with several different types of securities at the same time.

Recently, computer models such as Monte Carlo simulation have been used to determine the optimal cash balance. These models generate a series of expected values which can be used to determine, with varying degrees of confidence, whether or not there will be a surplus or shortage of cash. In some sense, cash management simulation models can be re-

---

2. Rounding differences will produce slightly different results.

garded as an extension of the Miller-Orr model, since they all focus on uncertainties, expected values, and other statistical considerations.

INVESTMENT STRATEGIES

Once the optimal cash balance has been determined and it has been found that there is a surplus of cash, the cash manager can begin to decide how to invest and where to invest this surplus. It is important that the cash manager has a good knowledge of the investment market and, in particular, of the securities of the federal government as well as those of the government approved financial institutions. Exhibit 2 presents a sample of investment instruments available to governments. The cash manager must decide from this portfolio the best possible investment or a combination of investments for the program.

However, before being able to make any investment decision, the cash manager must develop a set of strategies that will ensure a safe and profitable investment for the government. At a minimum, the following must be given the most serious attention when deciding on the best possible investment strategies: (1) yield, (2) liquidity, (3) transferability, (4) maturity, and (5) safety.

Yield. To start with, the manager must aggregate as large a sum as possible. Decreasing the number of banks, consolidating the accounts, making some pooling arrangements with other local governments, or even contributing to state pools (those organized by the states on behalf of their local governments), if available, will contribute to this. The larger the amount available for investment, the greater will be the return. As a general rule, the manager must shop around for instruments with the highest *yield*. This is a good strategy if the market is stable. Since historically high-yielding instruments have been known to have greater risks or volatility, caution should be exercised in participating in this type of venture. Both timing and knowledge are extremely critical here.

Liquidity. One of the oldest, but still a useful strategy is to purchase securities (such as T-bills, CDs, or more easily convertible Money Market Funds) maturing each week or daily in amounts sufficient to cover the disbursements projected for that week. When the investments come due, part of the proceeds are placed in demand deposit accounts and part are invested in overnight instruments (such as repurchase agreements) to mature on subsequent days as checks are presented for payment.

Transferability. A more aggressive strategy would call for the cash manager to pay continual attention to movements in the investment market. For instance, in a tight market, short-term rates would increase faster than the rates on different types of securities, thereby increasing the interest differential, called *spread,* between various instruments. The cash manager must take advantage of this differential by *swapping* the low-yielding instruments for the high-yielding ones. Conversely, when the market is soft and interest rates are down, these differentials may narrow, thus making it attractive to swap back.

Maturity. Another strategy is to take advantage of the well-known *yield curve* (that compares interest rates to time to maturity) to determine the type of maturities the government should maintain at any given point in time. When, for instance, the yield curve is sloping upward, very short maturities are often suggested, even though the funds may not be needed at maturity. This will allow for the opportunity to *roll over* by investing the proceeds from maturing obligations in similar securities. On the other hand, when the yield curve is sloping downward, longer-term maturities should be preferred, even though some of the securities have to be liquidated (usually in the secondary market) rather than held until maturity.

Exhibit 2: *Examples of Investment Instruments*

Type of Security	Typical Maturity at Time of Issue	Denomination ($Minimum)
Nongovernment issues		
Commercial savings	Instant	None
Savings institutions	Instant	None
Money market mutual funds	Instant	$500
Repurchase agreements	Overnight	Varies
Time deposits	30 days	$1,000
Certificates of deposits	Up to 1 year	$10,000
Commercial paper	3-270 days	$1,000
Banker's acceptance	30-180 days	Varies
Government issues		
U.S. treasury bills	91 days to 1 year	$10,000
U.S. treasury notes	3-10 years	$5,000
U.S. treasury bonds	Up to 30 years	$500

Safety. Finally, there are many more strategies that a cash manager could devise that would best serve the interest of the government. However, one of the important underlying considerations in designing a strategy is to recognize the fact that the highest interest rate is not always the best rate, especially when public funds are concerned; safety should be a vital primary consideration. Prudent judgments must be used to minimize risks and loss potential without sacrificing yield. This, in turn, will ensure financial stability resulting from sound investment decisions.

CONCLUSION

This article has presented a brief, but systematic discussion of the various factors that are important in developing an effective cash management program. The principles and procedures suggested here are simple but, nonetheless, would require the supervision of trained personnel to efficiently manage such a program. Financial limitations often impose major restrictions upon personnel programming in most governments. They impose even more serious restrictions upon small communities where the number of full-time employees is small and where the finance officer has little, if any, staff assistance.

Yet, while it is frequently not so dramatically evident, the need for cash management personnel is just as pressing in these communities as in their larger neighbors. There are several ways in which these communities could compensate for their cash management personnel. First, the government could hire, on a part-time basis, a professional cash manager responsible for its financial management in general and the cash management program in particular. Second, the government could get in touch with other governments to share the experience or contract with an outside consultant (at a minimum fee) for advice and assistance in gathering data and to help it develop its own program. Finally, where staff additions are impossible, the responsibilities of the cash management program could be assigned to a member of the existing administrative structure, who is interested in the program and can devote time to it. Additionally, arrangements can be made to train the employee.

Needless to say, overcoming these problems is a must if a government intends to develop and maintain a sound cash management program. This is vitally important since the effectiveness of the program would depend on the quality of decisions made by those who are a part of the program. These decisions must concern not only the ends the local governments seek, but also the plans for achieving them and the operations necessary to support them.

References

Baumol, W.J. "The Transactions Demand for Cash: An Inventory Theoretic Approach." *Quarterly Journal of Economics* 66 (November 1952): 545-56.

Miller, G. "Cash Management." In *Local Government Finance: Concepts and Practices,* edited by J.E. Peterson and D.R. Strachota. Washington, D.C.: Government Finance Officers Association, 1991, 241-62.

Miller, M.H., and D. Orr. "A Model of the Demand for Money." *Quarterly Journal of Economics* 80 (August 1966): 413-35.

Schwartz, E. "Inventory and Cash Management." In *Management Policies in Local Government Finance,* edited by J.R. Aronson and E. Schwartz. Washington, D.C.: International City Management Association, 1985, 342-63.

Steinberg, H.I. "Cash Management for Local Government." *Governmental Finance* 4 (November 1975): 5-10.

Debt Management

The Development of a Planned Debt Policy

Michael Zino

Debt can be viewed as the current use of future revenue. Obviously, no prudent government contracts today to spend the full amount of its projected future revenue. In fact, a prudent government would be discerning, in general, in committing future revenues to pay for capital spending.

Sound budget management requires a government to design the availability and use of present and future revenues so that it can provide on a recurring basis both for high priority operational services in its expense plan and, in its capital plan, for affordable capital services that meet its need for a modern infrastructure. The development of a planned debt policy is essential to ensuring that financing decisions and capital program objectives both lie within a jurisdiction's fiscal and economic capacity and are consistent with operating budget priorities.[1]

A functioning debt policy serves as a bridge that rationally connects expense budget decisions and capital program goals, and it should provide confidence that a government's decisions on the use of debt are consistent with its financial resources and its long-term capital plans. Such a policy should at a minimum include

1. an examination of statutory debt limit restrictions and debt capacity thresholds;
2. a presentation of capital program goals and commitments, and a projection of future debt and debt service costs;
3. a rationale or strategy for using pay-as-you-go financing and undertaking the refunding of existing debt; and
4. a clear written statement detailing the established debt policy, as well as a schedule that will be followed for updating the policy on a regular cycle.[2]

DETERMINING CAPACITY AND THRESHOLDS FOR DEBT

Local governments generally fund the major portion of their capital program needs through the use of two instruments: general obligation bonds, backed by the full faith and credit of their taxing authority; and revenue bonds, backed by the income generated by specific related projects. The use of general obligation bond financing has typically been limited by caps imposed by states on the amount of general obligation debt that can be outstanding, while revenue bonds have been limited by restrictions on the uses for which the bonds could be issued. Therefore, a rational first step in developing a planned debt policy is to determine the amount of debt that can be issued under existing statutory debt limit restrictions for the current year and for an appropriate number of future years. The forecast of a future statutory debt limit should cover, at a minimum, a period of years that would provide sufficient lead time to rationally adjust capital program plans and debt issuance requirements should such an adjustment become necessary.[3]

Reprinted from *Municipal Finance Journal* 15, no. 1 (1994): 75-84. By permission of Panel Publishers, a Division of Aspen Publishers, Inc., 36 West 44th Street, New York, N.Y. 10036.

Once the amount of debt permitted to be issued under statutory debt limit restrictions is established, the municipality must determine if it has the ability or desire to support the maximum level of debt permitted. This can only be accomplished if appropriate measures of debt capacity have been decided upon, and thresholds or limits that are affordable have been determined.

In developing a debt policy, it is exceedingly important that the debt burden placed on the operating budget and the local economy be accurately measured and completely understood. The measures of debt burden chosen and the limits established should serve to both guide and control future borrowing decisions. Clearly, the municipality must be prepared to present the rationale for its decision to support the debt burden it expects to undertake. Such rationale should be based on a thorough review of the historical relationship that has existed between debt and debt service levels, and measures of both economic and budget capacity.

The limits set for debt burden should include the impact of both general obligation and revenue bond financing undertaken by or directly for the benefit of the municipality. This is important because future resources used to repay revenue bonds must be generated by the local economy and, even though the debt and debt service are not part of the municipality's budget, the use of these resources by the public sector is quite real and will ultimately affect the competitive position of the municipality.

The determination of appropriate threshold levels for debt and debt service costs will indeed represent a crucial decision because it will control both the future size of a jurisdiction's capital program as well as its ability to support alternative competing high priority services provided through its expense budget. The choice of debt burden measures and the determination of limits should seek to assure the following objectives:

1. Adequate capacity to issue new debt to meet capital needs in future years will be preserved.
2. Sufficient expense budget resources will remain available after the payment of debt service to fund other high priority services at acceptable levels.
3. The competitive position of the local economy will not be eroded by an unsustainable debt service burden.

Examples of three possible measures of debt burden for which thresholds could be established to meet these objectives are presented below.[4]

Percentage of Outstanding Principal Maturing within Ten Years

An average maturity schedule for capital projects is one in which about 50 percent of the debt is retired in 10 years.[5] A schedule that is faster or slower has profound effects on the balance between debt service and current services in the operating budget. A faster maturity schedule could be considered prudent only if it does not place excessive pressure on the operating budget and the local economy. For example, the continued sale of bonds with maturities shorter than the useful life of the projects being financed would result in current taxpayers bearing a disproportionate share of the cost of facilities that will also benefit future taxpayers. Such an approach could be justified only if, after the payment of debt service costs, sufficient resources remained in the operating budget to provide the desired level of services, and the resources raised to pay for both the operating services and debt service costs did not place an undue burden on the local economy.

Alternatively, a slower maturity structure raises other concerns, discussed in a recent article on debt policy: "Longer debt, or debt with retirement back-ended to the later maturities, tends to keep the debt burden longer, at a time when additional debt may have to be stacked on for big ticket items, such as a replacement of water mains or new schools." The same article further states, "A more rapid debt redemption schedule creates additional borrowing capacity—as debt is paid off, new debt becomes more affordable."[6] Clearly, debt with a longer maturity structure is attractive, because stretching out the redemption of principal reduces debt service payments and frees budget resources for other purposes. However, this benefit must be measured against the diminished capacity to incur new debt in the future to satisfy what will likely be a continuing and largely undiminished need to rebuild and maintain a municipality's infrastructure.

Given the fact that a municipality's creditworthiness and future capital capacity will be enhanced by raising the lower boundary for this threshold, serious consideration should be given to the 50 percent guideline, considered to be an average for issuers, endorsed by the Standard and Poor's Corporation.[7]

Debt Service as a Percentage of Tax Revenues

Tax revenues represent that portion of a municipality's revenue budget over which it has the most discretion. At the same time, it is the portion of the revenue budget most vulnerable to economic decline. Establishing an appropriate target for an upper limit on the proportion of tax revenues that will be needed to pay debt service costs, therefore, would help ensure that, when revenues fall, sufficient resources would be left over after paying debt service to be able to fund a core group of high priority expense budget programs. Establishment of such a threshold would be an important contribution to recurring budget balance, which is centered on the capacity to sustain stable delivery of basic operating services during economic downturns. The amount of debt service one is obligated to pay even when revenues decline during an economic downturn is a critical limitation on the ability to sustain basic services.

Determining an upper limit for debt service costs that is consistent with recurring budget balance is a judgmental endeavor. The limit would be expected to change over time to reflect changes in the municipality's expense and capital priorities or perceived economic capacity. However, an established threshold that is reviewed on a periodic basis as part of an overall written debt policy should help ensure that sufficient lead time will be available to make orderly adjustments in operating and capital plans should they become necessary due to economic fluctuations.

General Obligation and Public Authority Debt Service as a Percentage of Personal Income

The fact that debt service on revenue bonds issued by public authorities is not included in municipal budgets highlights the need to integrate fully direct public authority debt service costs into a comprehensive debt policy. A reasonable approach for accomplishing this objective is to establish an upper limit for the combined total of general obligation and direct public authority debt service costs as a percentage of local personal income.

The sale of revenue bonds by public authorities provides numerous advantages, one of which is diversification in the type of debt issued and, as a consequence, the potential for lower interest rates on general obligation bonds sold by the municipality. However, unless a rational threshold is established for the combined total of general obligation and direct public authority debt service costs, the long-term competitive position of the local economy will be left unprotected and it would not be clear when the debt service burden was in danger of becoming excessive.

PRESENTATION OF CAPITAL PROGRAM PLANS AND COSTS

After deciding upon threshold levels for an affordable and acceptable debt burden, a long-term capital plan needs to be developed. It should be based upon a priority ranking of projects so that it may be sized to fit within the established thresholds. A disparity between financial resources available and the cost of capital facilities desired would be assumed to exist. Criteria established for choosing among projects in various functional areas should be fully disclosed and discussed publicly. In this regard, whenever feasible, cost-benefit analysis should be used to evaluate and select projects. The use of cost-benefit analysis is particularly well suited for deciding among discretionary capital expenditures in areas such as housing and economic and port development.

The development of the capital plan should also take into consideration the expected cost of maintaining capital assets. Spending on maintenance will determine the need to replace the assets on an accelerated basis and, as a result, will have a direct impact on how much debt capacity will be available to pay for new assets rather than replace assets that deteriorate prematurely.

The capital plan should be presented in a form that provides a timetable for when contracts will be entered into, when expenditures will take place, and when financing will be required. The type of information that will be needed to develop an adequate debt policy statement will at a minimum require

1. a presentation of amounts of capital contracts anticipated to be entered into on an annual basis in each functional area within the capital program;
2. a projection of the annual amount of capital spending expected to result from capital contracts that will have to be financed over the period covered by the capital program; and
3. a forecast of annual future levels of outstanding debt and debt service costs expected to result from the financing required to be undertaken to implement the capital program.

The projections of outstanding debt and debt service costs resulting from the completion of a capital strategy obviously must fall within the previously established debt burden thresholds after including debt expected to be issued by both the municipality and public authorities to meet capital program objectives. With the establishment of, and agreement on, affordable limits for outstanding debt and debt service costs, the implementation of capital program goals should proceed with predictability, consistency, and certainty. This should occur because with the adoption of a formal debt policy a jurisdiction's capital program plans should lie within its fiscal and economic capacity and should be consistent with its other operating budget priorities.

DEVELOPING A UNIFIED PAY-AS-YOU-GO AND REFUNDING STRATEGY

Assuming projected levels of capital spending generate debt and debt service costs that fall within established defensible thresholds, the use of pay-as-you-go financing and the issuance of debt for refunding purposes could be strategically integrated into the framework of a cohesively planned debt policy. The goal of a unified pay-as-you-go and refunding strategy would be to help ensure that an affordable capital plan that exists harmoniously within a structurally balanced budget is implemented in a consistent and predictable fashion. The likelihood of this objective being achieved would increase if a strategy is developed and implemented to help ease the impact of economic cycles on both the expense and capital budgets, without compromising their ability to support operating and capital programs planned for future years.

Generally, refunding outstanding debt should enhance the likelihood that capital program goals will be accomplished as planned. Obviously, opportunities to reduce debt service costs by refunding existing debt with new debt at lower interest rates are desirable because costs are reduced and resources are released for other uses. However, refundings could also be used to postpone principal redemptions and add to future debt-service costs. These refundings take future revenues from other uses, and over the long term are likely to result either in reduced operating services or in reduced future capital spending in order to remain within established thresholds for debt and debt service levels. Such refundings are sometimes viewed in a positive way from a short-term budgetary perspective, but are troublesome when considered from a long-term capital planning perspective.

Working under the assumption that debt and debt service payments are within the limits for affordability established in the municipality's debt policy statement, the refunding of bonds to stretch out principal payments and provide budget relief could be used as a legitimate means of easing the debt service burden and providing some budget flexibility during periods of economic contraction, as tax revenues decline. However, during periods of economic expansion, when tax revenues exceed forecasts, pay-as-you-go contributions to the capital program should then be made in amounts equal to the amount of budget relief provided by refunding during the economic contraction. Such a strategy would preclude the use of refunding to provide budget relief by stretching out principal payments during periods of economic expansion, even if the growth in debt service is proportionately greater than the growth in tax revenues being generated by an economic recovery. The objective of such a strategy would be to have a neutral impact on the debt burden over time, and in the process help to assure that planned initiatives in both expense and capital programs are undertaken as scheduled.

Therefore, to the extent refunding is used to stretch out debt, the negative impact of the refunding would have to be offset by the use of pay-as-you-go financing at appropriate times to fund a portion of the municipality's capital program requirements. If the amount of pay-as-you-go financing were equal to the operating budget savings provided by stretching out debt, both future debt capacity and debt service expenditures would be largely unaffected by refunding actions. Thus, a unified pay-as-you-go and refunding strategy could provide both flexibility in the operating budget and stability in the capital budget at the same time that it would have a relatively neutral impact over time on the municipality's budget and debt capacity.

WRITING A DEBT POLICY STATEMENT

The development of a formal debt policy can make a positive contribution to sound budget management and the implementation of a long-term capital plan.

However, to be effective, that policy must be reduced to a clear and simply written document. Such a document should at a minimum address four major areas of concern:

1. The rationale for threshold levels of outstanding debt and debt service payments deemed to be affordable within the expense budget as well as supportable by the local economy.
2. The long-term operating budget impact expected to result from the level of financing projected to be undertaken.
3. The approach expected to be used to accommodate both the future debt service burden projected to exist as well as the cost of other high priority expense budget needs.
4. The use of pay-as-you-go financing and refunding to help assure the completion of the capital program as planned.

This approach would permit an opportunity for review, debate, and ultimately agreement on a debt policy that would be supported by elected officials and the public. For example, if the capital plan provided modern school buildings but required reallocation of operating budget resources to pay higher debt service costs and employ fewer teachers, it would seem likely that a significant review of alternatives as well as a debate on the merits of the proposal would ensue.

Committing a debt policy to writing is particularly important when the expanded size of the capital program results in a future relative debt service burden that is expected to require an increasing share of local resources. Increasing the relative share of budget resources required to pay debt service costs is always a difficult and controversial decision. It becomes much more difficult when the increased resources must come from existing programs rather than tax increases. Nevertheless, a thoroughly informed choice is critical if support for the choice is to be sustained.

Once a debt policy is formulated and adopted, a review of the policy should be undertaken on a recurring but not frequent basis. An annual or even biennial review might prove to be sufficient. Although the implementation of a debt policy is incremental and sufficient flexibility should be permitted, substantial diversions from the policy should be promptly acknowledged and explained if the credibility of the policy is to be established and maintained.[8]

BENEFITS OF A WELL THOUGHT-OUT AND PLANNED POLICY

The adoption and integration of a debt policy into the budget and planning process may prove to be a difficult and laborious task. The benefits, however, are numerous and the current environment is propitious. A planned debt policy aids in the development of a budget that is structurally balanced. Future levels of debt expected to result from capital and refunding decisions could be shown to be affordable, and a clear strategy would exist to accommodate such costs within future budgets. This would reduce the need to ratchet back the capital program, which is generally a disruptive process and not a very effective one for obtaining budget relief in the short-run. The implementation of the capital program would proceed with more certainty and predictability, which should be viewed positively by investors and citizens alike.

The municipality would have a formal policy approach that, during periods of economic contraction, would warrant reducing the debt service burden imposed on its expense budget by stretching out principal on outstanding debt. Simultaneously, the negative impact of refunding its debt would be offset by its explicit commitment to use operating budget resources instead of debt to meet a portion of its capital program needs during periods of economic recovery. The relatively neutral long-term impact on the debt structure would eliminate the need to downsize the capital program to accommodate the added costs resulting from refunding, while at the same time providing budget relief to soften the impact of service reductions during a period of cyclical economic decline.

The existence of a debt policy would ensure that a formal construct exists for analyzing and reviewing decisions that would affect the municipality's debt structure and the future burden it will place on the budget and the local economy. Potential changes in existing local laws to permit a longer maturity structure on new debt could be reviewed within a more meaningful framework. For example, municipal issuers on average retire about 50 percent of the principal on outstanding debt in 10 years, which quickly creates additional capacity to issue new debt. A knowledgeable decision about lengthening the maturity structure of debt, and as a result slowing the retirement of debt and reducing future debt issuance capacity, can only be made if rational and defensible thresholds for future debt burdens have been considered and determined within the framework of an agreed-upon debt policy.

A formal debt policy would likely engender improved credit ratings and increased market access as credit analysts conclude that the municipality's capital program is affordable and manageable during both economic expansions and contractions. Credit analysts generally recognize the development of a formal debt policy and its integration into the budget and capital planning process as a commitment to sound debt management, and they usually reward such a commitment with a positive judgment about credit quality. Moreover, with the adoption of a planned debt policy, government officials can recognize and address potential credit concerns well before underwriters, credit analysts, and investors begin to react negatively and drive up the cost of borrowing. The opportunity to effectively manage the combined consequences of financing, operating, and capital decisions will likely prove to be a significant contribution resulting from the adoption of a formal debt policy.

Notes

1. A detailed discussion on debt policy is presented in the December 1991 staff report of the New York State Financial Control Board in the section entitled "The Development of a Planned Debt Policy."
2. Given the fact that our main focus will be on the long-term consequences of capital and financing decisions, we have limited our review of debt policy primarily to its relevance to the issuance of long-term debt. However, we recognize and endorse the concept that a complete debt policy statement should also address the use of short-term debt and the government's need to limit its refinancing risk by setting reasonable limits on the use of short-term debt.
3. The forecast of a statutory debt limit for a period that covers a minimum of 5 years would under normal circumstances be sufficient when debt is issued solely for capital purposes. However, when debt is issued for both capital and refunding purposes, the time horizon should be increased and a forecast period covering at least 10 years would be more appropriate.
4. A detailed discussion of thresholds for debt and how they could be applied in the city of New York is presented in the March 1992 staff report of the New York State Financial Control Board in the section entitled "Debt Policy and Thresholds for Debt."
5. This guideline for debt maturity can be found in a Standard and Poor's publication entitled "Debt Ratings Criteria" in the section on general obligation debt.
6. Richard Larkin and James Joseph, "Developing Formal Debt Policies," *Government Finance Review* 7 (August 1991): 11-14.
7. The useful life of the projects being financed is a significant factor in determining the length of the maturity for the bonds sold and, therefore, it is possible to justify a guideline below 50 percent. However, the justification for establishing an alternative should be presented as part of a formal debt policy statement.
8. Formal written debt policy statements have been developed by the city of Pittsburgh and the city of Baltimore.

State and Local Governments as Borrowers: Strategic Choices and the Capital Market

W. Bartley Hildreth

State and local governments issue securities to obtain financing for publicly desired projects or activities. A borrower's optimum economic goal is to obtain the lowest cost of capital over the desired repayment schedule. The role of the government's chief financial officer is to design appropriate strategies to achieve this goal within a context of changing market conditions, debt structures, and influences on borrowing choices.

Once considered staid and consistent, state and local government debt instruments—collectively known as municipal securities—now are market-driven decisions. Municipal securities are structured in terms of maturity, denomination, interest (coupon) rate and other features to attract particular investor groups, such as mutual funds. Debt offerings are timed to meet market opportunities, not just the local financing agenda. Further, the security backing the debt is less the full taxing power of the borrower than the ability of an enterprise project to generate revenues to cover debt costs. Taken together, these, and other, practices reveal a dynamic financing arena compounding the search for funds.

Municipal securities have long enjoyed two distinctive qualities—their tax-exempt status and an absence of restrictive federal regulations. Both qualities are now threatened. Unique among investment options, municipal securities pay interest that is traditionally exempt from the U.S. income tax. Although Congress has restricted the tax exemption for certain types of uses over the last two decades, it was not until the U.S. Supreme Court's *South Carolina v. Baker* (1988) decision that it became clear that the Congress, not the Constitution, remains the benefactor of the federal income tax exemption. What Congress grants, it can take away. Although a deceptively simple statement on the surface, it means that Congress can avoid federal income tax losses (also known as tax expenditures) by further curbing or eliminating the tax-exempt nature of municipal securities. This could help generate funds to offset some of the federal budget deficit, but it would do so by abolishing a domestic market dedicated to financing programs and projects approved by state and local governments.

Limited federal regulatory oversight, another hallmark of the municipal market, is threatened also. While corporations face a web of securities laws, issuers of municipal securities have enjoyed little federal interference, short of an issuer committing fraud in a debt offering. The Securities and Exchange Commission (SEC), spurred by the $2.25 billion Washington Public Power Supply System (WPPSS) default, has turned its attention to the municipal market. Recently, SEC rules have been clarified to state that it is unlawful for investment banking firms to participate in most municipal debt offerings without first investigating the issuer's disclosure documents. The SEC is prohibited by the Tower Amendment of 1975 from *directly* regulating issuers. By

---

Reprinted from *Public Administration Review* 53, no. 1 (1993): 41-49. By permission of *Public Administration Review* © by the American Society for Public Administration (ASPA), 1120 G Street N.W., Suite 700, Washington, D.C. 20005. All rights reserved.

placing the regulatory burden on the investment banking community, it is understood, and expected, that the effective burden rests with the governmental debt issuer and the adequacy of the issuer's disclosure documents. As a result of the SEC actions, national standardization of disclosure documents is in the offing.

This article reviews the municipal finance literature and practices to isolate the behavior of issuers. I first review the market behavior of issuers—specifically, differences in terms of the capacity to borrow and the costs of borrowing—and then discuss strategies appropriate to these market concerns. In the second part of the article, the focus is on issuer strategies relative to individuals or groups with a formal stake in state and local debt financing. Once public executives recognize these market features, they can adopt active financial management strategies to exploit the market on behalf of their taxpayers.

THE BEHAVIOR OF ISSUERS

Governmental jurisdictions are *not* created equal in their ability to borrow or in their cost of borrowing. As political scientist Sbragia (1983, 98) notes, the market is not a "redistributive or compensatory mechanism," rather it rewards the strong and greatly penalizes the weak. As a result, two basic issuance behaviors are observable. First, some issuers borrow more than other issuers. Second, some issuers borrow at lower costs than others.

The Capacity to Borrow

An issuer's capacity to borrow is neither absolute nor static. Rather, debt issuance varies, as tempered by incentives and disincentives. Incentives are based on the need for funds to secure physical assets that will enhance public services while also advancing political agendas and exploiting capital market opportunities.

A leading incentive to borrow arises from a preference to spend. The focus is on what can be purchased or constructed with the capital—physical assets such as buildings, highways, facilities, and other infrastructure items. Whereas capital improvement needs vary by jurisdiction, a series of recent studies document the nation's infrastructure needs (for example, National Council on Public Works Improvement 1988; Office of Technology Assessment 1990).

Unmet needs represent a borrower's appetite for capital, if available on the right terms. Plus, the argument that public infrastructure investments have a positive influence on private productivity is the subject of a growing body of research (Cuciti 1991, for example).

Financing a project over time through borrowing overcomes the lack of sufficient up-front capital, a second incentive to borrow. An issuer could husband slack resources by foregoing immediate consumption in order to build a "savings" account. Few governmental entities finance capital improvements out of savings, however. Rather, most jurisdictions use one-time or yearly flows. An immediate and one-time infusion of capital results from external borrowing. In contrast, proceeds from an earmarked tax permit continual restocking of a capital investment account. The charter of Akron, Ohio, for example, dedicates for capital improvement purposes 27 percent of the yearly proceeds from the local income tax. Assured of a yearly base of financial support, capital improvement needs are further enhanced with bond proceeds and other revenue sources, especially federal and state project grants.

Third, borrowing engenders political capital. According to public-choice theory, politicians seek to maximize their self-interest, or reelection probability. The trade currency, political capital, is facilitated by the stock of funds generated from borrowing. In fact, current federal tax law encourages state and local governments to expend bond proceeds quickly, measured in months, thus stripping issuers of the option to borrow at low tax-exempt rates and then invest the bond proceeds in higher yielding taxable investments while delaying expenditure of bond funds—termed arbitrage. Furthermore, being able to construct new facilities, with repayment stretched out over several decades, creates a sort of fiscal illusion. This helps to explain the propensity for capital projects to become a "porkbarrel," or the trading of votes to support projects in various districts. Public choice theory postulates strong incentives to create debt. Research on governors and their propensity to issue debt confirms that debt issuance occurs in time to bolster reelection efforts (Baber and Sen 1986).

Exploiting a changing market constitutes a fourth incentive to borrow. Outstanding debt normally imposes a fixed debt-service cost on the issuer based on factors present at the time of borrowing. Market conditions change; contemporary and prospective views of the market may provide an opportunity to achieve interest savings beyond that found in the original issuance. One method requires calling in old debt at the earliest possible date, using proceeds generated from new debt issued at lower rates. Yet the original debt may contain provisions prohibiting the issuer from redeeming the security prior to its stated maturity, thus negating such a call. Issuers circumvent call restrictions by advance refunding—where funds generated by new debt (at lower rates) are placed in escrow to pay the old debt service as it comes due, not early as with a call. In recent years, debt refunding has accounted for one-fifth or more of the total volume of new bond issues (*Bond Buyer* 1991).

A listing of disincentives to borrow must include legal, political, and economic factors. Leading the list is the legal or structural limit, expressed either in absolute or relative terms. At first glance, it may seem that an absolute prohibition on borrowing is clear (either it is allowed or it is not), but exceptions are possible. For example, the state of Indiana is prohibited from issuing general obligation debt yet it enters the capital markets by having several statutory authorities finance infrastructure and economic development projects on its behalf.

A relative limit permits borrowing, but only up to a certain level. Debt ceilings require issuers to ration their debt appetite. For local governments, a typical ceiling is expressed as a percentage of the assessed value of property within a jurisdiction's boundaries. Issuers circumvent these limits by borrowing against project revenue-generation capability, expected streams of earmarked taxes (e.g., a sales or gasoline tax), or agreements to pay yearly lease payments equal to the debt service on a public-use facility.

To have excess legal capacity to borrow means little if political hurdles are not overcome, a second disincentive to borrow. Gaining approval for a particular debt issuance requires governing-body support, and, where applicable, voter approval and state validation. Navigating these hurdles requires a combination of consensus decision making, careful timing, skilled marketing, and legal preciseness. Generally, voter approval is the most uncertain of the legal hurdles that must be addressed.

Third, an economic disincentive to borrow is the obvious requirement to pay back the borrowed funds, with interest. With a diversified, growing local economy, issuers can borrow against a future, larger tax base. In contrast, some jurisdictions face liquidity problems in handling current spending, much less repaying past borrowing or incurring more long-term obligations. This is especially a problem if no new taxes are levied to support the new borrowing or the tax base is not diversified or growing. This burden to repay requires prospective borrowers to temper their debt creation activities. Confirmation that issuers perform some capital rationing and control is the fact that no general obligation bonds are known to have defaulted since the Great Depression (Davidson 1991). The widespread fiscal stress of state and local governments in the early 1990s warrants careful monitoring, however. Of course, this does not convey much, if anything, about the cost of debt.

The Cost of Borrowing

The market behavior of issuers is characterized by a second phenomenon: some issuers borrow at lower costs than other issuers. Why? Although a quick (and incorrect) answer is that the credit rating assigned to the issue greatly determines the interest rate, the rating is really more the result than the cause. Besides, the yields of individual tax-exempt bonds are determined by many variables, including many outside the issuer's control (Cook 1982). This article focuses on issuer experience, bidding competition for its debt, frequency, and market competition.

First, debt issuers benefit from market experience. Bland (1985) demonstrates that up to a point, the more experience a municipality has with debt financing, the more likely the municipality will generate interest rate savings. He places the upper limit to this benefit of experience at four prior sales within a ten-year period.

Second, state and local governments benefit from more competition for their bonds. As demand for an issuer's securities increases, the issuer's cost of borrowing declines (Cook 1982).

Third, the frequency of the borrowing can impact borrowing costs. One strategy calls for frequent market entries. Lennox Moak, the dean of municipal finance, advocated sales of identical security at intervals of not less than six months (Moak 1982, 161). Consistent with this advice, a study of the secondary market for New York City debt concluded that the city should "establish itself as a seasoned and reliable issuer" (Financial Control Board 1984, 4). A contrasting view emerges from a study of smaller jurisdictions (Bland 1984) in which infrequent issuers gained interest rate savings. The greatest savings accrued to two groups—infrequent issuers borrowing less than half a million dollars and infrequent issuers borrowing large amounts. Based on the research, Bland (1984) advises issuers to delay entry into the market until various needs are bundled into a larger, omnibus debt package.

Fourth, an issuer receives a penalty for timing a sale in conflict with other issuers, especially those selling larger amounts. When competitive bids are due at or near the same time for more than one issue within a broad market, issuers are likely to receive fewer bids than might otherwise be the case. This exacerbates some issuers' problems since research reveals that lower rated bonds tend to receive fewer bids, and the bids received have less dispersion (or range) in rates, resulting in higher borrowing costs (Cook 1982).

Although the credit rating services point out that the debt issue determines the rating, higher credit ratings are associated with lower borrowing costs. In addition to designing the bond structure, an issuer has choices in how and when it will sell its bonds, factors that also influence the cost of borrowing.

RELATIONSHIPS AND STRATEGIES

Given the fact that most state and local governments can borrow funds under specified circumstances and that their needs vary, opportunities exist for some jurisdictions to adopt deliberate capital market strategies. Identifying debt issuance strategies by following the debt issuance process (i.e., identifying the need, structuring the offering, gaining approval, selling the debt, etc.) is one approach. An alternative approach, and the one adopted here, tracks issuer strategies for dealing with the various participants in the debt issuance process.

Strategic management is premised on purposeful behavior and the recognition that others can have an effect on organizational results (Hildreth 1989). This premise is bolstered by several lines of thinking. Interest group theory holds that public decisions are influenced by an often shifting set of interested parties. Network political economy, as recently extended into state and local debt issuance by Miller and Hildreth (1988), posits that the various participants involved in a borrowing may have conflicting goals and that results of this team effort may differ from the expectations of a single team member, such as the issuer. This highlights the need to explore in more detail the financing perspectives of each debt issuance participant, such as the executive in charge of the public treasury. Applying Freeman's (1984) stakeholder model of strategic management, government finance executives must deal actively with individuals or organizations who can influence, or be influenced by, achievement of the jurisdiction's objectives. This approach follows the public management school of thinking by assessing debt management choices from the executive's viewpoint, in this case the chief financial officer. Therefore, this article attempts to define the need for purposeful behavior on the part of the issuer relative to key participants in capital acquisition. Employing the term participants instead of stakeholders is not meant to signify significant differences in concept, rather it is to follow standard terminology in the debt issuance domain.

STRATEGIES FOR DEALING WITH PARTICIPANTS

The municipal market works because of the interactions of various participants. A state or local government, as an issuer, sells a debt instrument or security to an underwriter (also called an investment banker), who then resells the security to an investor (also known as a bondholder). The investor, therefore, loans capital to an issuer; in return, the issuer agrees to pay the investor an agreed-upon interest rate (usually semiannually) and, upon maturity, to repay the principal.

Several other participants enter into the debt process. A paying agent (or trustee) serves as the conduit for the flow of interest and principal payments between the issuer and the investor. A bond counsel advises the issuer on how to meet all legal requirements to borrow and provides a legal opinion to the investor that the debt instrument meets state and local laws and federal tax law standards. Many governments employ financial advisors to assist in defining capital needs and in structuring and completing the deal. Early in the process, citizens may have to approve the planned borrowing. A state oversight board may have to give its approval. If the issuer desires anything more than local bidders or private placement, private credit rating firms must have an opportunity to pass judgment on the probability of debt repayment.

The issuer has an opportunity to influence each participant's actions and decisions. A review of research and practice will help isolate issuer behaviors.

Issuers

Issuers face many institutional and market hurdles in the borrowing process. A market penalty is assessed for poor timing, as discussed earlier. Most issuers face a lag time (often measured in months) between a decision to borrow and the actual date of borrowing, especially if voter approval is required and the issue is competitively offered for sale. To elude these structural hurdles, issuers utilize several avoidance strategies.

First, to sidestep the hurdles imposed on general obligation borrowing, issuers turn to revenue bonds. During the 1980s, revenue bonds constituted over 65 percent of the yearly dollar volume of municipal bonds. By the first half of 1992, revenue bonds had fallen back to pre-1980 levels but still exceeded the issuance of general obligation bonds. Revenue bonds, to a much greater extent than general obligation bonds, may serve as a strategic tool for municipalities facing fiscal strain or limits (Sharp 1986). This is consistent with the extensive expansion of special districts and other statutory authorities—often termed off-budget entities—empowered to issue revenue bonds without placing at direct risk the taxing capacity, or full-faith-and-credit guarantee. In fact, many off-budget entities serve as "conduits," defined as a governmental issuer of securities with an ultimate credit source being a private profit-making or nonprofit organization (Zimmerman 1991). The revenue bond market segment also represents municipalities borrowing in anticipation of future revenue flows (such as collections from nonproperty tax sources such as sales taxes); debt backed by planned, but not guaranteed, lease payments (including certificates of participation); and, other creative security arrangements.

Second, creative debt instruments help issuers take advantage of changing market demands. For instance, where future interest rates are expected to be higher, investors demand a premium to tie up their money in maturities of 20 to 30 years. Issuers who are unwilling to pay the price to sell these long securities can instead sell shorter maturities. Instruments such as variable rate securities allow issuers to borrow long but at near short-term rates.

In many instances, issuers have the authority to sell yearly bond anticipation notes (BANs) as a source of interim financing for capital projects during the construction period. Upon project completion, the expected strategy is to convert the capital financing from short-term notes (BAN) into long-term bonds. Issuers may deviate from this expected conversion strategy. Given that short-term rates are historically lower than long-term rates and that on occasion (such as the early 1980s) long-term rates hover in the double-digits, short-term financing seems sensible, even for completed projects as long as the tax laws permit such practices.

One manifestation of this economic environment is that issuers may roll-over BANs year after year to avoid the long-term market, where allowed by law, such as in Ohio. The intended strategy is to wait out the market. However, the more times BANs are rolled over, the more difficult it is for an issuer to obtain interest rate reductions sufficient to offset the accumulated, capitalized interest costs.

A contrary strategy is that by delaying entry into the long-term market, the borrower accrues interest cost savings. As noted earlier, Bland (1985) found evidence supporting this delayed entry strategy. However, his study did not take into account the situation where the prospective *bond* issuer may be incurring and capitalizing interest costs during the delay period by issuing *notes*. Delay imposes costs, not just benefits (Choate 1980).

To be successful, issuers must gain a competitive advantage over other issuers. This is best reflected in the timing of the sale or in the pricing of the offering. As might be expected, timing finesse is easier to accomplish if the choice is negotiated pricing rather than announcing and, after a specified number of days, holding a competitive auction.

Issuers using competitive auctions must be willing to terminate the sale at the last minute by rejecting all bids if the market undergoes a significant change in direction. A highly elastic relationship exists between increases in interest rates and the volume of issuer cancellations and delays (U.S. General Accounting Office 1983). Market conditions can be systemic to all markets or peculiar to the municipal market. Instances of market volatility include legislative consideration to tax interest payments of municipal bondholders in 1968, tax reform initiatives in early 1986, stock market disruptions in 1989, and war news in 1991. A long-set auction consummated at the time of volatility in the market may quickly close favorable windows of opportunity to borrow, resulting in higher than expected borrowing costs. Either canceling a sale at the last minute or rejecting all bids is a serious step. Compelling reasons may exist for proceeding with a sale, especially if the time required to restart the issuance process is long, imposing still further uncertainty and risk.

Traditionally, state and local governments give notice of their plans to issue securities weeks ahead of time, specifying the date and time when bids to purchase are due. New York's Local Finance Law (Section 58.00(2)) breaks with tradition by permitting its municipal corporations to announce to the market a 30-day window within which the auction may be made. Within this period and with 48 hours notice, the municipal corporation can set the time and date for the auction. Alternatively, the issuer can set a time and date for the auction and retain the option to make a change in time and date if done at least 48 hours prior to the time originally scheduled. The new schedule has to be with 48 hours notice, too. These options permit a borrowing jurisdiction to time its auction with more sensitivity to market conditions, a hallmark of negotiated sales.

Investors

Historically, an issuer had little interest in knowing who actually held its securities, for several reasons. First, issuers sell the security to the underwriter, who then markets them to investors. As a result, the issuer does not deal directly with investors at the sale nor does the issuer know the pool of likely investors, especially individual investors. The common view of the market holds that underwriters serve as salesmen to get a product of demand (by the investor) from a supplier (an issuer) and, in the process, make a transaction profit (measured in fractions of the total value) by linking the buyer with the seller.

A second reason for an issuer's historical inattention to investors is due to the fact that even after the sale, issuers could not find out, even if they inquired, who actually owned the securities. Until 1982, municipal bonds were negotiable instruments, meaning that the last holder could redeem the security with little fear of contrary evidence of ownership. As a result, the issuer had no record of all investors in its securities. The Tax Equity and Fiscal Responsibility Act of 1982 changed the rules, however. Now all municipal securities over one year in maturity must be registered. Although not mandatory for previously issued securities, the investment banking community has responded by converting bearer securities into registered form whenever the securities are traded or come into the possession of institutional investors.

Because issuers are more prone to take an interest in their investors if they know their names, new strategies are possible. Issuers now develop debt issuance plans based on current and prospective investors' interests because the segmentation of the municipal market means investor clienteles are different for short- and long-maturity bonds (Poterba 1986). Tax-exempt mutual funds, for example, need a stock of relatively short-term maturities. Tax-exempt bond funds also are major buyers of municipal securities. The growth of holdings by individuals and mutual funds combined was steady, and pronounced, into the 1990s.

New financial products, such as "minibonds," allow governmental jurisdictions to alter this bifurcated relationship between issuers and investors. A minibond is a small denomination debt instrument (in $100 or $1,000 units) sold directly to customers. This type of product appeals to retail customers, allowing the borrowing government to attract investors it might otherwise be unable to attract.

A more involved investor relations program can help issuers. Some issuers develop strategies to appeal directly to institutional investors, perhaps attempting to offset the perceived, overly critical, bond rating agencies. Issuers attempt to convey that their credit is stronger than the bond ratings might otherwise suggest. Basically, an issuer seeks to let institutional investors know that it is attentive to the needs of large investors.

Recognizing their market strength, representatives of institutional investors (such as mutual fund companies and insurance firms) along with market analysts from investment banking firms have initiated efforts to require debt issuing jurisdictions to enhance the disclosure of information that might influence the pricing and trading of bonds in the secondary market (that is, after a bond has been issued but before it matures). A key step in this movement is to get issuers to certify that they will satisfy these continuing disclosure concerns, under the implicit threat that this segment of the investor community will not buy the bonds otherwise (Ciccarone 1992). This is important to an issuer because a shrinkage in demand means the cost to issue debt will rise, all other things being equal.

Underwriters

Investment banking firms underwrite the purchase and resale of the securities. Underwriters, as they are called, provide issuers with informed market access because most U.S. state and local issuers tend to rely on outsiders to gauge the market's interest in their securities. Issuers can use competitive auctions to ensure that the bids received from underwriters reflect current market assessments. The overwhelming evidence reveals that competitive bidding promotes more efficient market pricing, meaning that an issuer's interest costs decline as the number of bidders increase (Cook 1982).

A negotiated sale is one where the issuer selects an underwriter to conduct the debt issuance. This segment of the market has grown to almost 75 percent of all financings. A long line of research indicates that issuers pay an interest rate premium to negotiate the sale rather than to offer it for competitive sale (Cook 1982). Bland shows, however, that an *experienced issuer* (measured by prior market entries) can use negotiation to achieve an interest rate comparable to competitive bid rates (Bland 1985). This finding holds up only if there is little bidding competition, calculated at three bids. So, if the experienced issuer expects more than three bids, then a competitive sale is likely to result in the lowest cost; if the experienced issuer expects no competition for the bonds, then a negotiated sale is less costly. For first-time or very infrequent debt issuers, Bland's advice is to sell "bonds through competitive bidding in order to avoid the heavy penalty placed on inexperience if negotiation is used" (237).

Competitive auctions as practiced in the United States means the underwriter individually or in a group (called a syndicate) bids for all the bonds in the offering. Inzer and Reinhart (1984) suggest that issuers should change this practice and allow the underwriter to bid on parts of the offering, not just the whole offering. This change would allow underwriters to select the optimal bonds for their clients.

For this tiered-bidding system to work, however, the issuer would have to assume the risk of having no bidders for particular maturities, resulting in less than the desired amount of proceeds from the sale. To mitigate this result, the issuer would need flexibility in the amount to be offered at each maturity. By accepting more uncertainty, including the exact amount of debt proceeds, Inzer and Reinhart postulate that the issuer should receive lower interest costs, all other things considered. Two recent Nevada bond sales tested the tiered-bidding theory with favorable results. In 1989, the State of Nevada offered $48.7 million in three distinct series of maturity, with separate bids required on each. Interest savings of $36,000 were achieved when two underwriting syndicates bought different parts versus the cost if the syndicate winning two had also won the third series (Lamiell 1989). A Nevada school district used a similar sales structure in 1990, lowering its borrowing cost by more than $160,000 (Walters 1990).

Financial Advisors

A financial advisor, if employed, serves as an issuer's impartial consultant on structuring and selling securities. When an issuer auctions general obligation bonds, the services of a financial advisor are in addition to those of the underwriter. With negotiated sales, the underwriters have the responsibility to optimize debt structure and pricing, both from an issuer's and the underwriter's standpoint. This reduces, but does not entirely eliminate, the need for an independent financial advisor.

Financial advisors press for long-term, comprehensive debt strategy consultations not just the traditional transaction-driven service based on each debt issuance. Issuers utilize financial advisors to "work-out" financial difficulties (such as Cleveland's note default and the recurring fiscal problems in Detroit and Philadelphia) and to enhance market perceptions (such as Boston's multi-year strategy of redefining its economic image). The visibility of financial advisors was most strikingly demonstrated in Philadelphia where, in 1991, a locally based, but nationally known, financial advisor campaigned, but was defeated, in a bid for election as mayor. His failed campaign emphasized his skills in municipal finance. After the election, the victorious mayoral candidate quickly appointed the (defeated) financial advisor's firm to spearhead a review of city finances and to serve as its ongoing financial advisor. By working with the issuer to advance broad fiscal agendas, financial advisors expand their scope of services.

Independent financial advisors seek to segment their industry, separating themselves from investment banking firms providing financial advisory services. A new national association of independent financial advisory firms is dedicated to enhancing the level of professional credentials of its members and to marketing to issuers the need for independent financial advisors. An issuer has to realize net economic benefits from such advice (savings in borrowing costs to offset fees paid to financial advisors) or the total cost of issuance increases as financial advisory fees are combined with the underwriter's cost, bond rating agency fees, bond counsel fees, and other transaction expenses.

Bond Counsels

A bond counsel plays a critical role in an issuer's attempt to obtain underwriter and investor interest in an issue. When tax laws are uncertain, bond counsels hesitate to issue an opinion on the tax-exempt status of bonds. As the events of early 1986 demonstrated, the market expects a bond counsel to help screen out unacceptable risks. In early 1986, the U.S. Senate held without action the House-passed tax reform bill that included a retroactive effective date of January 1, 1986, along with significant limits on debt issuance and use of bond proceeds. The market demanded assurances that issuers would comply with current law, proposed law (that in the House bill), and potential law (that which had not yet been voted upon). Needless to say, bond lawyers hesitated to take such a step toward unknown accountability. Because of those tax-law uncertainties, many issuers were unable to take advantage of an otherwise favorable interest rate market.

Bond counsel expertise enhances an issuer's financial agenda. A bond counsel can point out seemingly small nuances in the law permitting the desired public purpose to be debt financed. Whether the goal is to further a joint public-private capital investment venture or to provide street lights in nonincorporated areas of a county, presumed legal restrictions are prone to new interpretations and tests.

When a debt issue is embedded in trouble, the bond counsel can be part of the problem as well as part of the solution. As bond counsel of record on a bond issue facing imminent technical or actual default, the bond counsel faces the potential of a liability suit by bondholders, as those associated with the WPPSS defaulted bonds found out. If a troubled debt issue is dealt with early enough, the bond counsel can serve as a powerful ally in designing a remedy. Given that the bond counsel is at risk too, it can work to the issuer's advantage. Because the major bond counsel firms are also some of the more prominent legal firms in a particular state, if not the region or nation, their influence runs throughout the various seats of power. For an issue facing troubled times, bond counsel efforts to secure interlocal, state, and/or federal legislation or assistance can rebound to the jurisdiction's benefit.

Trustees

A paying agent, generally a financial institution, is selected by the issuer to receive and disburse coupon and principal payments to bondholders. For revenue bonds, however, the same, or a different financial institution, enters into a more complicated legal duty on behalf of bondholders, serving as a fiduciary to ensure that the issuer follows all bond indenture requirements.

Although all is fine as long as the debt issuer pays principal and interest as specified, the trustee's role expands as trouble looms. In scenarios concerning troubled revenue bonds, the trustee must take care to act as if the assets were his own—a fiduciary role (Sawicki 1985). In such cases, the trustee weighs the consequences of asserting remedial powers, such as to assume management of the debt-financed project or to "pull the plug"—that is, to declare the bonds due and payable immediately. In such a situation, an issuer may attempt to position the trustee so that the trustee's success depends upon a cooperative relationship with the issuer instead of the adversarial one envisioned by the remedial powers provisions of the indenture.

By the nature of their position, trustees often detect a change in a debt issuer's repayment status before many others, especially bondholders. A trustee's duty is to report to current (registered) bondholders. By design this gives sellers of the outstanding bonds a market advantage over buyers because of information asymmetries. To counter this secondary market problem, the trustee industry group (a part of the American Banking Association) encourages its members to provide broad market disclosure of significant events or developments, not just provide the information to current bondholders.

Credit Rating Agencies

Credit rating agencies are paid by the debt issuer to provide an assessment of its risk of nonpayment of borrowed funds. More practically, rating agencies serve as *de facto* gatekeepers to the broad municipal bond market. For inexperienced or inadequately qualified issuers, either the expected or the actual decision of credit raters can effectively bar an issuer's market entry. Thus, bond ratings are not sought by all debt issuers. Some issuers acknowledge their negative market qualities and rely upon local investors (e.g., local banks), not the broad market of investors. For example, private-purpose revenue bonds, small-sized general obligation bonds, public purpose revenue bonds, and short-term notes often are placed with local investors. If an issuer desires or needs access to the national, or even regional, public market of investors, then an investment-quality rating (the top four rating levels, "Baa" or higher) is necessary. The rating is necessary for both the initial offering of the debt as well as throughout the life of the debt, if the issuer expects any secondary market for that or any future debt issue.

Although credit rating agencies are unlikely to acknowledge their role as market gatekeepers, issuers follow behavioral patterns that substantiate this observation. The hurdle of achieving an investment-quality credit rating leads to at least two observable sets of behavior by issuers: to attempt to *influence* the rating process and/or to *avoid* the rating process, or a part of it.

Avoidance of the credit ranking process appears uninviting for all but the smallest issuers. Although a quarter of all municipal bonds are unrated, the total dollar volume of such bonds makes up less than 10 percent of the entire municipal bond market (Petersen 1989). This means there are numerous small dollar-sized bond issues that avoid the rating process.

With two private rating services dominating the market, a second avoidance strategy is to have a single rating, either to avoid a rating agency perceived to be overly critical or merely to stand on the basis of one rating. As to the preference for one credit rating service over another, the two dominant bond rating services enjoy similar dollar volume market shares (Petersen 1989). Furthermore, to assume that one rating saves money is contrary to research that suggests that a second rating lowers an issuer's borrowing cost, even if the ratings are different (Hsueh and Kidwell 1988). In fact, while only about 40 percent of new issues carry ratings from *both* Moody's and Standard & Poor's, this group represents almost 70 percent of the total dollar volume of the municipal market (Petersen 1989).

An issuer has a third option, avoiding a direct rating on its credit quality, in essence, by leasing the credit of a higher-rated institution. Credit enhancement takes the form of bond insurance or a letter of credit facility, whereby a third party guarantees debt service. Bondholders gain added security from the third-party guarantor's credit. Bond insurance also offers economic benefits to issuers (Quigley and Rubinfeld 1991). Research indicates that issuers expecting a rating below the second highest rating class ("Aa") should consider credit enhancement (Reid 1990). As might be expected then, the market for credit enhancement services has grown in recent years (*Bond Buyer* 1991).

Most debt issues carry a bond rating, either their own or a borrowed credit. In fact, a three-year study of debt concluded that only one in ten issues (amounting to 2 percent of the dollar volume) did not enjoy a credit rating either directly or indirectly. Those without some form of credit rating were small issues, averaging 1 million dollars in size (Petersen 1989, 25, 28).

A fourth avoidance behavior is to sell a short-term note to local investors without a rating. The issuer preserves the option to request a rating at some later point, especially at the time of conversion into a bond. An advantage of rolling over the yearly note for several years is that it offers the jurisdiction time to take steps to position itself in a better credit light. Yet rating agencies now assign ratings to notes and look upon increasing amounts of short-term debt in negative terms.

Avoidance of bond ratings may be in the best interests of small governments, for several reasons (Sullivan 1983; Palumbo and Sacks 1987). First, for small-sized bond issues, the fee to obtain a bond rating is a cost of issuance that may not be adequately recovered in interest savings. Second, small governments are unlikely to receive high bond ratings, especially for general obligation bonds. Higher bond ratings are associated with larger-dollar-sized amounts and larger-sized population centers. Thus, small and rural governments face systematic adverse market assessment of credit worthiness (Palumbo & Sacks 1987). Yet in an odd twist, small, rural governments do not have to overcome as much investor suspicion as those borne by a larger jurisdiction. Unlike larger debt issuers who rely on a national investor base, small government bonds often are bought locally; these local investors must trust their own assessment of the debt issuer's credit quality. Thus, a small government may avoid a bond rating and still obtain a reasonable rate of borrowing because local investors know that government's capabilities (Sullivan 1983, 110).

An issuer attempts to *influence* the bond rating decision by enhancing its arguments and the security of the planned issue. Measures to enhance the security backing an issue range from obtaining a third-party guarantee to tightening the financial package, such as putting more up as collateral (e.g., an earmarked sales tax plus sewer user fees for a revenue bond). A guarantee can take the form of a standby letter of credit (primarily for short-term borrowing), a state program (as in Texas where the oil-land-enriched Permanent Fund guarantees local school district borrowings), or private bond insurance. Although a third-party guarantee results in the highest credit rating (an automatic "Aaa" rating in most cases), it does not guarantee that the issuer will borrow at levels commensurate with the highest rating (Bland 1987; Reid 1990).

To enhance its credit quality arguments, an issuer has to document the political, financial, and managerial control necessary to achieve effective public services. This is achieved through such actions as tight financial controls, protection of fund balances, adoption of generally accepted accounting principles (GAAP), adherence to strong financial disclosure practices, and maintenance of political consensus. These steps represent an issuer's preventive or preemptive strategy for dealing with bond rating agencies. That is, issuers attempt to anticipate, and then implement, the more obvious fiscal management policies and practices that credit analysts consider indicators of strong management quality (Doppelt 1985). Generally, actions taken to influence an issuer's credit standing are also effective fiscal management. However, as Detroit was recently told by Moody's Investors Service, strong fiscal management will not offset the negative credit implications of the lack of viable private economic activity (Peirog 1992). Strong economic activity and diversification are the keys to a high bond rating (Loviscek and Crowley 1990).

As part of an enhancement strategy, issuers seek to maintain close contact with the rating agencies to foster harmonious relations and timely disclosure of relevant information. To help advance the spirit of continuous disclosure, issuers share with rating analysts news that could be interpreted as having either positive or negative impact on credit quality. This nurturing of a relationship is very noticeable in the tendency of governors and mayors to visit the raters and to recognize the political, as well as financial, importance of debt strategies, given the credit raters' ability to issue a locally perceived negative or positive signal, as retold by the local media.

Voters, Monitors, and Controllers

Issuers with a requirement to obtain voter or state approval for debt issuance can attempt to influence or avoid some, or all, of these barriers. Voters tend to approve bond elections, at least in terms of a national aggregate trend (*Bond Buyer* 1991). Notwithstanding historical approval trends, some issuers cannot obtain voter approval despite repeated attempts. Needless to say, each bond approval referendum requires a particular marketing campaign. An effective strategy for voter approval tends to be built around a highly perceived, but justified, need coupled with a political-style campaign to motivate citizens to vote for the proposal within a political environment of fiscal trust and accountability.

Issuers show a propensity to avoid onerous debt hurdles, if possible. This is reflected in efforts to (1) use less-encumbered financing sources or (2) take steps to remove some of the restrictions. One opportunity arises when the restrictions on issuing revenue bonds are less than those for general obligation bonds. For example, Louisiana local governments must obtain voter approval for general obligation bonds but not for sales-tax-backed revenue bonds; as a result, revenue debt outstanding is significantly higher than general obligation debt. The incentive to utilize revenue bonds is intense in such situations.

Another issuer strategy is to circumvent debt limits. Often this can be accomplished by using "off the debt schedule" financing, such as lease-purchase deals, certificates of participation (COP), or loans from statutory authorities (i.e., a state-created financial conduit agency that issues revenue bonds to generate proceeds to loan to other governmental jurisdictions).

California local governments became major users of COPs because of Proposition 13 restrictions. This innovation spread widely across the country. As the recession of the early 1990s accelerated, investors in COPs grew nervous as public officials publicly questioned the requirement to continue appropriating funds to repay the COPs, knowing that investor comfort in the bonds comes from the issuer's agreement, but not legal requirement, to appropriate yearly funds to repay the investors. This concern was well founded given the 1991 COP default by the Richmond (California) Unified School District and the state's belated questioning of the legality of such borrowing.

Some issuers have two sets of general obligation debt issuance powers. One is greatly restricted in dollar amounts but requires only the governing body's approval—termed unvoted debt in Ohio, for example. The other requires voter approval but has a high ceiling of available borrowing power—termed voted debt in Ohio. Public officials prefer, of course, the flexibility associated with debt merely requiring the approval of the governing body. Thus, one strategy is to carefully select certain projects for placing before the voters, those more attractive and characterized by political consensus. The unvoted debt capacity is reserved for projects where timing is of the essence or the likelihood of voter approval is more suspect. Rationing within the unvoted-debt capacity becomes a significant fiscal strategy. Effective management of the unvoted-debt capacity requires the imposition of internal capital hurdle rules to avoid depleting the slack capacity too quickly.

In summary, issuers adopt strategies to circumvent debt monitors, including the voters. The problem with this behavior is that public officials focus more on how to manipulate state and local debt restrictions than on effective strategies for matching capital needs to the market and the price for borrowed funds (Sbragia 1979; Peterson 1990). In the end, such debt strategies may prove successful, but the issuer may pay the price in significant interest rate differentials whether it is due to delay, issuance of revenue bonds, or other factors.

CONCLUSION

This article suggests that issuers of state and local government securities have an optimum capital goal —to obtain the lowest cost of capital over the desired repayment schedule—and that this goal is achieved through strategic choices. I discussed strategies built around the phenomena that issuers differ in their capacity to borrow and in borrowing costs. I also reviewed selected strategies for an issuer to manage its own financial agenda in the municipal market. Some issuer strategies have the benefit, if successful, of generating interest rate savings while other strategies have less precise economic benefits for the issuer. The research on debt strategies is sporadic at best. More empirical work is required.

While this article is only an exploratory discussion of issuer strategy, one point seems to emerge: issuers should follow deliberate capital strategies instead of allowing capital decisions to evolve out of inattention, being unduly swayed by others in the debt issuance process, or incremental decision making. A mistake in this management area stays with the community for many years to come, as long as the debt is outstanding.

References

Baber, William R., and Pradyot K. Sen. 1986. "The Political Process and the Use of Debt Financing by State Governments." *Public Choice* 48, no. 3: 201-15.

Bland, Robert L. 1984. "The Interest Savings from Optimizing Size and Frequency of Participation in the Municipal Bond Market." *Public Budgeting and Finance* 4 (Winter): 53-59.

———. 1985. "The Interest Cost Savings from Experience in the Municipal Bond Market." *Public Administration Review* 45 (January/February): 233-37.

———. 1987. "The Interest Cost Savings from Municipal Bond Insurance: The Implications for Privatization." *Journal of Policy Analysis and Management* 6, no. 2: 207-19.

Bond Buyer. 1991. *1991 Yearbook*. New York: Thomson Publishing Corporation.

Choate, Pat. 1980. *As Time Goes By: The Costs and Consequences of Delay*. Columbus, Ohio: Academy for Contemporary Problems.

Ciccarone, Richard A. 1992. "Municipal Disclosure: A Question of Intentions." *Municipal Finance Journal* 13, no. 1 (Spring): 68-71.

Cook, Timothy Q. 1982. "Determinants of Individual Tax-Exempt Bond Yields: A Survey of the Evidence." *Federal Reserve Bank of Richmond Economic Review* (May/June): 14-39.

Cuciti, Peggy. 1991. "Infrastructure and the Economy: Serious Debate in the Profession." *Municipal Finance Journal* 12, no. 4 (Winter): 73-81.

Davidson, R. B. 1991. "A Framework for Analyzing Municipal Quality Spreads." *Municipal Finance Journal* 12, no. 3 (Fall 1991).

Doppelt, Amy. 1985. "Assessing Municipal Management." *Standard and Poor's Creditweek*, March 4.

Financial Control Board. 1984. *The Performance of New York City Bonds in the Secondary Market*. New York: New York State Financial Control Board.

Freeman, R. Edward. 1984. *Strategic Management: A Stakeholder Approach*. Boston: Pitman Publishing.

Hildreth, W. Bartley. 1989. "Financing Strategy." In Jack Rabin, Gerald J. Miller, and W. Bartley Hildreth, eds., *Handbook of Strategic Management*. New York: Marcel Dekker, 279-300.

Hsueh, L. Paul, and David S. Kidwell. 1988. "Bond Ratings: Are Two Better Than One?" *Financial Management* 17, no. 1 (Spring): 46-53.

Inzer, Robert B., and Walter J. Reinhart. 1984. "Rethinking Traditional Municipal Bond Sales." *Governmental Finance* 13 (June): 25-29.

Lamiell, Patricia. 1989. "Around the Nation: Nevada." *The Bond Buyer* (January 24): 24.

Loviscek, Anthony L., and Frederick D. Crowley. 1990. "What Is in a Municipal Bond Rating?" *The Financial Review* 25, no. 1 (February): 25-53.

Miller, Gerald J., and W. Bartley Hildreth. 1988. "The Municipal Debt Financing as a Network Political Economy: Network Stability and Market Efficiency." Paper presented at the Annual Meeting of the American Political Science Association, Washington, D.C., September.

Moak, Lennox L. 1982. *Municipal Bonds: Planning, Sale and Administration*. Chicago: Municipal Finance Officers Association.

National Council on Public Works Improvement. 1988. *Fragile Foundations: A Report on America's Public Works*. Washington, D.C.: Government Printing Office.

Office of Technology Assessment, Congress of the United States. 1990. *Rebuilding The Foundations: A Special Report on State and Local Public Works Financing and Management*. Washington, D.C.: Government Printing Offices.

Palumbo, George, and Seymour Sacks. 1987. *Rural Governments in the Municipal Bond Market*. Washington, D.C.: Economic Research Service, U.S. Department of Agriculture.

Peirog, Karen. 1992. "Mayor of Detroit Protests Moody's Ba1 Downgrade, Citing Unfairness." *The Bond Buyer* (July 20): 1, 25.

Petersen, John E. 1989. *Information Flows in the Municipal Bond Market: Disclosure Needs and Processes*. Washington, D.C.: Government Finance Officers Association.

Peterson, George E. 1990. "Is Public Infrastructure Undersupplied?" In Alicia H. Munnell, ed., *Is There a Shortfall in Public Capital Investment?* Boston: Federal Reserve Bank of Boston, 113-30.

Poterba, James M. 1986. "Explaining the Yield Spread between Taxable and Tax-Exempt Bonds: The Role of Expected Tax Policy." In Harvey S. Rosen, ed., *Studies in State and Local Public Finance*. Chicago: University of Chicago Press, 549.

Quigley, John M., and Daniel L. Rubinfeld. 1991. "Private Guarantees for Municipal Bonds: Evidence from the Aftermarket." *National Tax Journal* XLIV, no. 4, pt. 1 (December): 29-39.

Reid, Gary J. 1990. "Minimizing Municipal Debt Issuance Costs: Lessons from Empirical Research." *State and Local Government Review* 22, no. 2 (Spring): 64-72.

Sawicki, Theodore J. 1985. "The Washington Public Power Supply System Bond Default: Expanding the Preventure Role of the Indenture Trustee." *Emory Law Journal* 34: 157-99.

Sbragia, Alberta. 1979. "The Politics of Local Borrowing: A Comparative Analysis." Paper published by Center for the Study of Public Policy, University of Strathclyde, Glasgow, Scotland.

―――. 1983. "Politics, Local Government, and the Municipal Bond Market." In Alberta Sbragia, ed., *The Municipal Money Chase: The Politics of Local Government Finance*. Boulder, Colo.: Westview Press, 67-111.

Sharp, Elaine B. 1986. "The Politics and Economics of the New City Debt." *American Political Science Review* 80, no. 4 (December): 1271-88.

South Carolina v. Baker. 1988. 485 U.S. 505.

Sullivan, Patrick J. 1983. "Municipal Bond Ratings: How Worthwhile Are They for Small Governments?" *State and Local Government Review* 15, no. 3 (Fall): 106-11.

U.S. General Accounting Office. 1983. *Trends and Changes in the Municipal Bond Market as They Relate to Financing State and Local Public Infrastructure*. Washington, D.C.: General Accounting Office.

Walters, Dennis. 1990. "Around the Nation: Nevada." *Muniweek* (October 15): 32.

Zimmerman, Dennis. 1991. *The Private Use of Tax-Exempt Bonds: Controlling Public Subsidy of Private Activate*. Washington, D.C.: Urban Institute Press.

Municipal Finance Criteria

ROLE OF RATINGS

Over the years, Standard & Poor's Corp. credit ratings have achieved wide investor acceptance as easily usable tools for differentiating credit quality. Issuers range from public corporate utilities such as Commonwealth Edison Co. to conglomerates such as ITT Corp. To these are added municipal issuers such as New York City and Anchorage, Alaska, foreign governments such as Japan and Finland, and foreign corporations such as Nippon Telegraph & Telephone Public Corp. and Imperial Chemical Industries PLC of England. Issuers sell bonds with varying security pledges and seniority, and also issue debt that is insured, structured, or complex in various other ways. Ratings published by S&P provide a single scale to compare among this array of different debt instruments.

The value of a rating emanates from the validity of criteria and reliability of judgment and analysis of S&P's professional staff. S&P's criteria are regularly communicated through *CreditWeek Municipal*, *CreditWeek*, and *CreditWire*—S&P's electronic ratings dissemination service. The credibility of ratings also requires objectivity. S&P's objectivity results from not investing for its own account, not serving as an underwriter, financial advisor, or manager of funds, and being independent of the issuer's business.

Excerpted from *Municipal Finance Criteria* (New York: Standard & Poor's Corp., 1993), 2, 4-5, 9-10, 12-14, 18-25. By permission of S & P.

S&P operates with no government mandate, subpoena powers, or any other official authority. As part of the media, S&P simply has a right to express its opinions in the form of letter symbols. Recognition as a rating agency relies on investors' willingness to accept its judgment.

Investors' Use of Ratings

To use credit ratings properly, one should first understand what a rating is and is not. The rating performs the isolated function of credit risk evaluation, which is one element of the entire investment decision-making process.

A credit rating is not a recommendation to purchase, sell, or hold a particular security. A rating cannot constitute a recommendation as it does not take into consideration other factors, such as market price and risk preference of the investor. Moreover, because S&P receives confidential information from issuers, S&P believes it would be improper to recommend the purchase or sale of rated bonds. Rating agencies that do publish "market" recommendations may forego management contact, relying exclusively on publicly available data.

A rating is not a general-purpose evaluation of an issuer. For example, an issuer's 'AA' rating may be based primarily on a specific security or third-party support underlying the obligation.

Although many probing questions are asked the issuer at various stages of the rating process, S&P does not perform an audit, nor does it attest to the authenticity of the information provided by the issuer and upon which the rating may be based. Ratings can be changed, withdrawn, or placed on CreditWatch as a result of changes in, or unavailability of, information.

Ratings do not create a fiduciary relationship between S&P and users of the ratings; there is no legal basis for the existence of such a relationship.

Issuers' Use of Ratings

It is commonplace for municipal issuers to structure financing transactions to reflect S&P's credit criteria so they qualify for higher ratings. However, the actual structuring of a given issue is the function and responsibility of an issuer and its advisors. S&P is the recipient and user of materials prepared by those in a position to attest to such materials' accuracy and completeness. Although S&P will react to a proposed financing, publish papers outlining its criteria for that type of issue, and interpret and make evaluations available to an issuer, underwriter, bond counsel, or financial advisor, S&P does not function as an investment banker or financial advisor. Adoption of such a role ultimately would impair the objectivity and credibility that are vital to S&P's continued performance as an independent rating agency.

RATING DEFINITIONS

Long-Term Debt

An S&P corporate or municipal debt rating is a current assessment of the creditworthiness of an obligor with respect to a specific obligation. This assessment may take into consideration obligors such as guarantors, insurers, or lessees.

The debt rating is not a recommendation to purchase, sell, or hold a security, as it does not comment on market price or suitability for a particular investor.

The ratings are based on current information furnished by the issuer or obtained by S&P from other sources it considers reliable. S&P does not perform an audit in connection with any rating and may, on occasion, rely on unaudited financial information. The ratings may be changed, suspended, or withdrawn as a result of changes in, or unavailability of, such information, or for other circumstances.

The ratings are based, in varying degrees, on the following considerations:

1. Likelihood of default—capacity and willingness of the obligor as to the timely payment of interest and repayment of principal in accordance with the terms of the obligation.
2. Nature and provisions of the obligation.
3. Protection afforded by, and relative position of, the obligation in the event of bankruptcy, reorganization, or other arrangement under the laws of bankruptcy and other laws affecting creditors' rights.

Investment Grade

AAA. Debt rated 'AAA' has the highest rating assigned by S&P. Capacity to pay interest and repay principal is extremely strong.

AA. Debt rated 'AA' has a very strong capacity to pay interest and repay principal and differs from the highest rated issues only in small degree.

A. Debt rated 'A' has a strong capacity to pay interest and repay principal although it is somewhat more susceptible to the adverse effects of changes in circumstances and economic conditions than debt in higher rated categories.

BBB. Debt rated 'BBB' is regarded as having an adequate capacity to pay interest and repay principal. Whereas it normally exhibits adequate protection parameters, adverse economic conditions or changing circumstances are more likely to lead to a weakened capacity to pay interest and repay principal for debt in this category than in higher rated categories.

Speculative Grade

Debt rated 'BB', 'B', 'CCC', 'CC', or 'C' is regarded as having predominantly speculative characteristics with respect to capacity to pay interest and repay principal. 'BB' indicates the least degree of speculation and 'C' the highest. While such debt will likely have some quality and protective characteristics, these are outweighed by large uncertainties or major risk exposures to adverse conditions.

BB. Debt rated 'BB' has less near-term vulnerability to default than other speculative issues. However, it faces major ongoing uncertainties or exposure to adverse business, financial, or economic conditions which could lead to inadequate capacity to meet timely interest and principal payments. The 'BB' rating category is also used for debt subordinated to senior debt that is assigned an actual or implied 'BBB-' rating.

B. Debt rated 'B' has a greater vulnerability to default, but currently has the capacity to meet interest payments and principal repayments. Adverse business, financial, or economic conditions will likely impair capacity or willingness to pay interest and repay principal. The 'B' rating category also is used for debt subordinated to senior debt that is assigned an actual or implied 'BB' or 'BB-' rating.

CCC. Debt rated 'CCC' has a current identifiable vulnerability to default, and is dependent upon favorable business, financial, and economic conditions to meet timely payment of interest and repayment of principal. In the event of adverse business, financial, or economic conditions, it is not likely to have the capacity to pay interest and repay principal. The 'CCC' rating category also is used for debt subordinated to senior debt that is assigned an actual or implied 'B' or 'B-' rating.

CC. Debt rated 'CC' typically is applied to debt subordinated to senior debt which is assigned an actual or implied 'CCC' debt rating.

C. The rating 'C' typically is applied to debt subordinated to senior debt which is assigned an actual or implied 'CCC-' debt rating. The 'C' rating may be used to cover a situation where a bankruptcy petition has been filed, but debt service payments are continued.

CI. Debt rated 'CI' is reserved for income bonds on which no interest is being paid.

D. Debt rated 'D' is in payment default. The 'D' rating category is used when interest payments or principal payments are not made on the date due even if the applicable grace period has not expired, unless S&P believes that such payments will be made during the grace period. The 'D' rating also will be used upon the filing of a bankruptcy petition if debt service payments are jeopardized.

Plus (+) or minus (–). The ratings from 'AA' to 'CCC' may be modified by the addition of a plus or minus sign to show relative standing within the major rating categories.

c. The letter 'c' indicates that the holder's option to tender the security for purchase may be canceled under certain prestated conditions enumerated in the tender option documents.

p. The letter 'p' indicates that the rating is provisional. A provisional rating assumes the successful completion of the project financed by the debt being rated and indicates that payment of debt service requirements is largely or entirely dependent upon the successful timely completion of the project. This rating, however, while addressing credit quality subsequent to completion of the project, makes no comment on the likelihood of, or the risk of default upon failure of such completion. The investor should exercise his own judgment with respect to such likelihood and risk.

L. The letter 'L' indicates that the rating pertains to the principal amount of those bonds to the extent that the underlying deposit collateral is federally insured, and interest is adequately collateralized. In the case of certificates of deposit, the letter 'L' indicates that the deposit, combined with other deposits being held in the same right and capacity, will be honored for principal and pre-default interest up to federal insurance limits within 30 days after closing of the insured institution or, in the event that the deposit is assumed by a successor insured institution, upon maturity.

*Continuance of the rating is contingent upon S&P's receipt of an executed copy of the escrow agreement or closing documentation confirming investments and cash flows.

N.R. Not rated.

Debt obligations of issuers outside the United States and its territories are rated on the same basis as domestic corporate and municipal issues. The ratings measure the creditworthiness of the obligor but do not take into account currency exchange and related uncertainties.

Bond investment quality standards: Under present commercial bank regulations issued by the Comptroller of the Currency, bonds rated in the top four categories ('AAA', 'AA', 'A', 'BBB', commonly known as investment-grade ratings) generally are regarded as eligible for bank investment. Also, the laws of various states governing legal investments impose certain rating or other standards for obligations eligible for investment by savings banks, trust companies, insurance companies, and fiduciaries in general.

Rating Outlooks

An S&P rating outlook assesses the potential direction of an issuer's long-term debt rating over the intermediate to longer term. In determining a rating outlook, consideration is given to any changes in the economic and/or fundamental business conditions. An outlook is not necessarily a precursor of a rating change or future CreditWatch action.

Positive indicates that a rating may be raised.

Negative means a rating may be lowered.

Stable indicates that ratings are not likely to change.

Developing means ratings may be raised or lowered.

N.M. means not meaningful.

Notes

An S&P note rating reflects the liquidity factors and market access risks unique to notes. Notes due in three years or less will likely receive a note rating. Notes maturing beyond three years will most likely receive a long-term debt rating. The following criteria will be used in making that assessment:

- Amortization schedule—the larger the final maturity relative to other maturities, the more likely it will be treated as a note.
- Source of payment—the more dependent the issue is on the market for its refinancing, the more likely it will be treated as a note.

Note rating symbols are as follows:

SP-1. Strong capacity to pay principal and interest. An issue determined to possess a very strong capacity to pay debt service is given a plus (+) designation.

SP-2. Satisfactory capacity to pay principal and interest, with some vulnerability to adverse financial and economic changes over the term of the notes.

SP-3. Speculative capacity to pay principal and interest.

Commercial Paper

An S&P commercial paper rating is a current assessment of the likelihood of timely payment of debt having an original maturity of no more than 365 days. Ratings are graded into several categories, ranging from 'A' for the highest quality obligations to 'D' for the lowest. These categories are as follows:

A-1. This designation indicates that the degree of safety regarding timely payment is strong. Those issues determined to possess extremely strong safety characteristics are denoted with a plus sign (+) designation.

A-2. Capacity for timely payment on issues with this designation is satisfactory. However, the relative degree of safety is not as high as for issues designated 'A-1'.

A-3. Issues carrying this designation have an adequate capacity for timely payment. They are, however, more vulnerable to the adverse effects of changes in circumstances than obligations carrying the higher designations.

B. Issues rated 'B' are regarded as having only speculative capacity for timely payment.

C. This rating is assigned to short-term debt obligations with a doubtful capacity for payment.

D. Debt rated 'D' is in payment default. The 'D' rating category is used when interest payments or principal payments are not made on the date due, even if the applicable grace period has not expired, unless S&P believes such payments will be made during such grace period.

Variable-Rate Demand Bonds

S&P assigns "dual" ratings to all debt issues that have a put option or demand feature as part of their structure.

The first rating addresses the likelihood of repayment of principal and interest as due, and the second rating addresses only the demand feature. The long-term debt rating symbols are used for bonds to denote the long-term maturity and the commercial paper rating symbols for the put option (for example, 'AAA/A-1+'). With short-term demand debt, S&P's note rating symbols are used with the commercial paper rating symbols (for example, 'SP-1+/A-1+').

RATING MUNICIPAL DEBT

The municipal debt rating process is depicted in Figure 1. In view of the complexity and documentation involved in the rating process, issuers requesting ratings should allow three to four weeks before the sale date for preparation and release of a rating decision. For first-time ratings, or when a field trip is indicated, an additional one or two weeks may be required. For frequent borrowers—those issuing debt more than once in 12 months and having a rating history at S&P—there is a shorter time frame for new issues. Without all necessary documentation, a rating conclusion is not possible.

As part of the rating process, meetings with issuers' representatives are often useful and sometimes required. To establish a new rating, a meeting with management is recommended, either at S&P's offices

Figure 1: *S&P's Municipal Debt Rating Process*

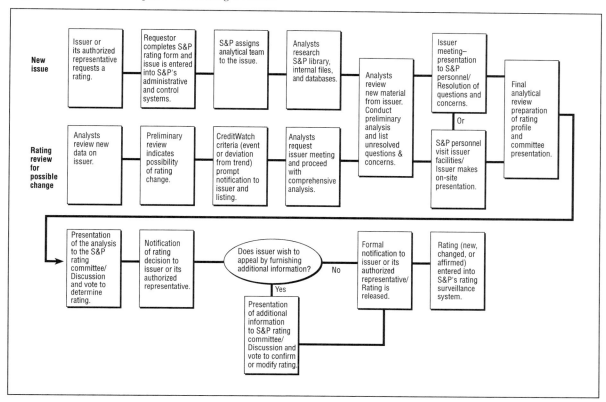

or at the issuer's site. Such meetings give the issuer an opportunity to make a presentation and provide a framework for exchanging views—all best accomplished through personal contact. S&P is represented at such meetings by a minimum of two staff members, at least one being a member of the issue committee. Representatives of the issuer should include only those who can make a constructive contribution to the flow of information and dialogue; too large a delegation results in an overly laborious and unwieldy meeting which becomes counterproductive. Also, to assure productivity, all textual documentation should be received by S&P one week prior to the meeting.

RATING SURVEILLANCE

Municipal debt ratings remain in effect as long as current information is furnished regularly or until the next sale of debt secured on a par with an outstanding debt rating (the exception is private placement ratings, which represent only a current credit assessment). Data needed regularly include annual financial reports, budgets, capital planning, zoning, or land use changes, changes in major local taxpayers and employers, and federal and state aid programs. For revenue-producing projects under construction, progress reports and engineering updates are also part of S&P's ongoing information needs. In lease rental financings where the lease payment is dependent upon timely completion and/or acceptance of the project by the lessee, S&P requests a copy of the certificate of completion. Failure to supply the above information on a timely basis will necessitate a withdrawal of the rating, since all ratings must be supported by adequate facts.

Also, should an issuer sell a parity obligation on which S&P has an outstanding rating and not request a rating for the new issue, the new issue will not be rated and S&P reserves the right to withdraw outstanding ratings. Changes in rating status are published regularly in S&P's weekly credit publications, *Credit-*

Week, and *CreditWeek Municipal,* and electronically in the Municipal Finance section of *CreditWire.* Comprehensive ratings are available in S&P's *Municipal Bond Rating Handbook* (published monthly), or can be obtained by calling S&P's Rating Information Desk at (212) 208-1527. For larger, market-sensitive issues, rating changes are disseminated immediately through the public news media.

When an issuer has a long-term debt rating and sells notes for which no rating is requested, documentation for the note sale is required to maintain the long-term rating; note sale documentation often contains information significant to long-term credit factors. Failure to provide such documentation may result in a withdrawal of the long-term rating. Special informational requirements for short-term debt may include updated cash flows and credit draws.

Surveillance is part of S&P's ongoing rating process. Ratings are reviewed on a periodic basis. S&P determines whether to review certain ratings more frequently by evaluating their financial or economic base history, or new trends prompting a listing on CreditWatch.

RATING CHANGES

As a result of the surveillance process, it sometimes becomes apparent that the condition of an issuing entity is changing, requiring reconsideration of the outstanding debt rating. When this occurs, the analyst makes a preliminary review, followed by a comprehensive analysis, including communication with management and a presentation to the rating committee. The rating committee evaluates the matter, arrives at a rating decision, notifies the issuer, and publishes the rating. The process is the same with a new issue.

Reflecting this surveillance, the timing of rating changes does not necessarily depend upon the sale of new debt issues.

From time to time, S&P may consider an issuer's appeal of a rating decision, after the rating committee has deliberated and notified the issuer of the debt rating and rationale for assignment. In a rating appeal, the only information that will be considered will be new additional information, or submission of revised action plans that specifically address the areas of credit concern cited in the rating rationale. In that regard, new information regarding debt factors will carry no weight in a rating appeal if S&P's concerns focus on economic trends or budgetary and financial operations.

ISSUER MEETING

Issuers frequently inquire about what takes place during a meeting with S&P and how best to prepare for it. The chief purpose of the meeting is to establish a forum in which S&P and the issuer can exchange information.

This discussion takes place either in S&P's New York headquarters or at the issuer's location. The S&P analysts involved become familiar before the meeting with the issuer's preliminary official statement and supporting documents.

Normal procedure at the meeting is for the issuer to make a 10-15 minute introductory statement highlighting the more important features of the submitted documents. S&P then poses questions designed to clarify or supplement the data already advanced.

S&P (and hopefully the issuer) tries to allocate time toward the end of the meeting for discussion of any relevant points not covered routinely by the agenda. One caveat: S&P prefers that the key public officials and only a few necessary representatives participate. If more information is necessary, S&P can follow up by phone.

INFORMATION NEEDS

Municipal Credit

Rating information needs for specific types of issues have been detailed earlier in this article. The following data primarily encompass general obligation and revenue issues, and represent a general overview of the types of information that should be submitted to S&P for rating applications. S&P's files should contain the following information with respect to any municipal entity requesting a debt rating:

- Last three annual audit reports
- Current budget document
- Current capital improvement program
- Official statements for new financing
- Planning document
- Zoning or land-use map
- Cash flow statement, in case of interim borrowing

- Statement of long- and short-term debt with annual and monthly maturity dates as appropriate
- Indication of appropriate authority for debt issuance (S&P's files should contain documentation of charter, constitution, or law concerning debt issuance)
- Interest rate swap agreements (terms and documentation, including counterparty risk)
- Statement concerning remaining borrowing capacity plus tax rate and levy capacity
- Statement regarding sources and allocation of funds for project being financed
- Description of project being financed
- Will additional funds be required to complete project? If yes, where will funds be derived from and under what conditions?

The nature of the security for the debt should be concisely but accurately defined.

If the debt is guaranteed by another party, full credit review of the other party must be done unless S&P has a current rating for that party.

S&P must be able to measure credit impact potential of guaranteed or debt service reserve make-up provision debt upon obligor. A full schedule of such commitments must be in S&P's file.

Issuer's range and level of services and capacity to provide such services must be documented. Such data would cover the type of government, the relationship with other governments, and areas of shared responsibilities.

The manner in which principal officials are chosen and the authority and method by which policy and program decisions are made must be described.

Information with respect to recent additions or losses of major industrial, commercial or governmental entities, or other employers or major taxpayers must be provided.

In enterprise financing, a description of the location and general character of the principal facilities should be supplied. Is project land owned or leased by issuer?

Indicate any lease obligations, their nature and term.

Engineering and/or feasibility report. How many of such reports on the project under review were done? If such reports were not done, what are the reasons?

In enterprise financings, the service area and monopoly, or competitive nature of service in the area, should be described.

Ten-year trend of customers and five-year forecast by categories of major revenue producers should be included. Issuer should do the following:

- List 10 leading customers by revenues and usage.
- List any governmental program providing an important part of enterprise revenues.
- Indicate party responsible for rate determination and whether it is subject to outside review.
- List sources and availability of raw materials essential to present and proposed operations of an enterprise.
- Describe status of licenses, permits, and franchises required to be held by enterprise, including Environmental Protection Agency, environmental impact, and the like.
- Indicate status of labor relations.
- Describe debt trend for last 10 years, long- and short-term, including lease-rental obligations, guaranteed debt, and other contingent debt.
- Provide 10-year trend of assessed values with basis of assessment noted.
- Provide 10-year trend of net direct debt ratios per capita plus true value and income where available.
- Provide statement of debt remaining authorized and unissued.

Description of issuer's accounting practices and any deviation from generally accepted accounting principles should be in S&P's files. Any accounting change in the last three years and the impact thereof upon financial results as reported should be explained.

For enterprises, the major revenue and expenditure categories should be indicated for 10 years and current budget as well as most recent 12-month period available. Issuer should supply the following:

- Key balance sheet data for three years. Fund balances and year-end adjustments should be noted.

- 10-year trend on annual debt service as a percent of expenditures.
- 10-year trend of special tax if issue is payable from such tax.

Issuer's property valuation and assessment procedure, tax collections, enforcement, and changes in such policy in last five years should be described.

Priority of tax claims of issuer over other indebtedness of taxpayer should be described.

Five-year trend of valuations by category—industrial, commercial, utility, and residential—should be supplied.

Issuer should indicate status of borrowing against delinquent taxes and policy regarding write-offs on such taxes.

Issuer should describe borrowing for operating expenses and deficits in last five years, other than revenue anticipation notes or tax-anticipation notes against current revenues.

Issuer should indicate whether debt service in past five years has been met through loans from other governments, including source, amount, and any commitment to repay.

Issuer should provide description of any legislation or procedures—federal, state, or otherwise—which would apply to the issuer in case of a financial emergency.

Issuer should indicate whether consultants on engineering, feasibility, and the like were employed on a contingent basis and if so, the nature of such a basis. Issuer should also indicate if any such person was or is connected with the issuer as underwriter, financial adviser, bondholder, member of governing body, or employee.

S&P's files also should contain the following:

- Statement regarding any pending litigation affecting status of debt, governmental structure, or fiscal condition of issuer
- Statement regarding status and funding of public employee pension funds
- For revenue bonds, the bond resolution, trust indenture, and lease if appropriate
- For hospitals, historical and projected occupancy and utilization for five years
- Necessary approvals and accreditations
- Detail of third-party payers
- Evidence of community support

ACCOUNTING AND FINANCIAL REPORTING

S&P's Policies

An integral part of S&P's municipal rating process is the timely receipt and analysis of financial statements certified by independent certified public accountants, or appropriate state or local auditing agencies.

Improved, timely, and standardized financial accounting and reporting have become increasingly important to participants in the municipal marketplace, including issuers, analysts, underwriters and investors, as well as the Congress and state legislatures. S&P's position on this subject is as follows:

Although S&P does not and cannot perform an audit function, S&P's rating process can and must consider the type and quality of reporting and accounting standards being used by the issuers under review.

The Governmental Accounting Standards Board (GASB), based in Norwalk, Conn., is the standard setter for governments.

Financial Reporting

The financial crises of the mid-1970s in New York, Cleveland, Chicago, and other entities led to, among other things, demands for full disclosure, generally accepted accounting principles (GAAP) for governments, enhanced accountability, and improved financial management and information systems. Now better financial reporting is enhancing the management process as administrators recognize previously neglected or overlooked costs. As a result, voters also become better informed about the scope and cost of government.

According to GAAP. All financial statements submitted to S&P, either in connection with a rating request for a bond sale or for a review, are expected to be prepared in accordance with GAAP. Where legal requirements for recording transactions differ from GAAP, the accounting system employed should make provision for both. In the preparation of general financial statements, GAAP must take precedence.

These statements should be independently audited, either by a certified public accounting firm or a qualified independent state or local agency on a timely basis, i.e., no later than six months after the fiscal year-end. The audit should include the auditor's opinion, as well as comprehensive disclosure notes covering such items as the the following:

- Summary of significant accounting policies (fund accounting, encumbrances, reserves, investments, and others)
- Any departures from GAAP that materially impact results
- Status of pension plans
- Lease obligations if applicable
- Contingent liabilities (compensated absences —such as vacation, sick leave, and sabbatical leave)
- Any pending litigation

Also, although not part of the audit itself, the auditor's management letter is an extremely useful document as it points out any weaknesses or deficiencies in financial and/or management controls. If such a management letter exists, it should be furnished to S&P; if none exists, a written statement to that effect should be provided.

The basis of accounting employed refers to the time when revenues, expenditures/expenses, transfers, and the relative assets and liabilities are recognized in the accounts and reported in the financial statements. They relate specifically to the timing of the measurements being made on either the cash or accrual method. Under the cash basis of accounting, revenues and transfers *in* are not recorded until cash is received, and expenditures or expenses and transfers *out* are recorded only when cash is disbursed.

Under the accrual basis of accounting, most transactions are recorded when they occur, regardless of when cash is received or disbursed. Items not measurable until cash is received or disbursed are accounted for at that time in both commercial and governmental accounting, as may be items whose measurements would be approximately the same under either basis or which are immaterial.

The absence of financial reports prepared in accordance with GAAP is considered a negative factor.

A rating is not provided if the report is not timely or is substantially deficient in terms of reporting. Each issuer is expected to advise S&P immediately of any material changes in, or additions to, any information contained in the previously mentioned documents.

Where cash-basis accounting is modified to account for liabilities and/or encumbrances, S&P considers such modifications, which may serve to lessen the negative impact on the financial reporting considerations in the rating process.

Other pronouncements. Some of GASB's more recent pronouncements include guidance for governmental colleges and universities, accounting for operating leases, disclosure of information on post-employment benefits other than pension benefits (e.g., healthcare or life insurance benefits), deposits with financial institutions, and investments, including repurchase agreements.

Major Accounting Problems

Two of the most difficult and controversial subjects confronting GASB continue to be pension accounting and the basis of accounting. Among the issues raised in pensions, besides disclosure, are the going concern versus termination, valuation of assets, and the determination of proper funding levels based upon salary progression and the related valuation to the liability. The subject basis of accounting includes a possible change in the modified accrual standards towards full accrual. For governments now on a full cash basis, full accrual is likely to present significant reporting problems and related explanations. Other issues include the depreciation of fixed assets, and accounting and reporting standards regarding budgets.

S&P will support further advancements in GAAP for governments. It is vital that municipal analysts encourage acceptance and support the effort to make their work more credible and promote the ultimate efficiency of the marketplace.

TAX-BACKED DEBT

Since their first use in the United States by New York City around 1812, general obligation (G.O.) bonds secured by property taxes have been regarded by many as the safest possible investment next to U.S. Treasury bonds. There are many reasons for their reputation: for decades such bonds were routinely secured by the full faith and credit of municipalities, backed by the entire amount of taxable property within these communities, and subject to an unlimited tax rate. The proceeds were generally used for schools and other capital projects with an uncontroversial public purpose. The repayment record was good. Although 4,770 municipalities defaulted on $2.85 billion of debt between 1929 and 1933, most of these defaults were cured by the 1940s, an enviable record compared to banks and corporations. While the default rate of municipal bonds in general remains extremely low (averaging less than 1 percent of issues since 1940), the credit characteristics of G.O. bonds are becoming more complicated. This is due in part to the changing nature of federal, state, and local financial relationships.

When the discrete three-tier system of government finance—federal, state, and local—was replaced with today's "marble-cake" system after World War II, governmental flows of funds became much more complicated. Federal mandates for social change led to complex patterns of transfer payments and overlapping fiscal responsibilities and obligations. In addition, self-perpetuating municipal authorities with debt-issuing and taxing ability proved to be very popular and spread across the country. During the 1960s, mounting property tax bills and a broad new social agenda helped boost the popularity of revenue bonds, which could be issued without a vote and did not create a lien on peoples' homes. The volume of new revenue bond issues first exceeded that of G.O. issues in 1976. Over the last 30 years, tax-backed G.O. issues dropped to about 30 percent from near 70 percent of new issue volume.

Another reaction to rising property taxes was outright revolt, as in California's Proposition 13 in 1978, which limited total public debt to 1 percent of the full cash value of the property tax base and severely limited tax increases. Three years later, voters in Massachusetts passed Proposition $2^1/_2$, which limited debt in that state to 2.5 percent of property value and imposed other restrictive conditions. More ominous still is the mounting pressure on municipal budgets caused by rising demand for social services in the face of federal cutbacks. The Bridgeport, Conn., invocation of Chapter 9 bankruptcy in 1991 made many in the municipal marketplace feel uneasy, since numerous state and local governments are struggling with deficits. Many market participants and investors remember 1975, when New York City demonstrated to holders of its notes that it would default rather than withhold essential government services.

As strong as a tax-backed G.O. pledge is, it is not an absolute guarantee of repayment. In fact, some investors are starting to view the dedicated revenue stream from a government enterprise operation, derived from charges for services and outside of property tax restrictions, as perhaps a more flexible and reliable security. This view is debatable, since the security behind revenue bonds is affected by changing supply and demand conditions for specific municipal services, as well as by trends in delivery systems. Nevertheless, tax-backed bonds clearly are coming under stress. During 1991, Standard & Poor's Corp. lowered more G.O. ratings than it raised. In 1992, when the number of upgrades exceeded downgrades, the dollar volume of downgrades was greater. In contrast to this, municipal utility bonds saw more upgrades than downgrades during these years.

The Variety of Tax-Backed Debt

G.O. bonds generally are regarded as the broadest and soundest security among tax-backed debt instruments. One factor that accounts for this strength is that they create a link between public and personal debt: a homeowner unable to pay his property taxes will forfeit his house just as surely as if he could not pay his mortgage, and an unlimited-tax G.O. pledge would enable a trustee to invoke *mandamus* to force the issuer to raise the tax rate as much as necessary to pay off the bonds.

Property-tax supported bonds have other strengths as well: the property tax tends to be a steady and predictable revenue source for municipalities, and when a vote is required to issue them, bondholders have some indication of taxpayers' willingness to pay. On the other hand, it always has been an unpopular tax. The value of real property is not necessarily linked to household income and, therefore, to the ability to pay property taxes. Also, property assessment is not always done in a consistent fashion and is slow to respond to changes in economic value. In 1932, property taxes provided local governments with 97 percent of their total revenues. Today, the aggregate figure is closer to 80 percent, and the specific percentage now varies greatly by type of municipal entity. While cities and towns have been shifting to more reliance on sales taxes, income taxes, and various fees and charges, counties and school districts remain very reliant on the property tax. Political and legal barriers to raising property taxes, combined with fewer federal and state dollars flowing to local governments, have put considerable pressure on the general funds of all types of issuers. The inability to raise needed revenues has serious credit implications; issuers need flexibility to deal with future problems.

Beyond these general strengths and weaknesses, however, there is an enormous variety of credit characteristics among G.O. bonds. For example, there are unlimited and limited tax G.O.s. Some issuers of limited tax G.O.s are well below their taxing limits, while others are tight against theirs, with little flexibility to react to emergencies. Depending on the location, some issuers need a vote of the people to authorize G.O. bonds. Some G.O. bonds are issued by cities which currently levy no property tax at all; while certain others may be unlimited tax bonds, but are supported almost entirely by one taxpayer in financial difficulty, like a local factory. Ratings are a convenient way to differentiate among bonds which may, on the surface, appear equally safe.

Moral obligation bonds fall short of a full faith and credit obligation. Bondholders must rely on a best-efforts pledge of the issuer (generally a state) to seek appropriations when needed. S&P can rate moral obligation bonds if certain requirements are met. One, the issuer covenants to maintain a debt service reserve fund equal to the maximum annual debt service requirement. Two, if the amount in the debt service reserve fund falls below this level, a notification process is engaged, culminating in the request for an appropriation to restore the fund to its required level. If the necessary funds, notification procedures, and legal requirements are in place, moral obligation bonds can be rated as high as one full category below an issuer's G.O. rating.

Leases are another special form of tax-backed debt. For these obligations, timely payment of principal and interest usually depends on continuing appropriations by the issuer. Because lease payments are not binding on future legislatures or councils, leases are generally not considered "debt" under issuers' technical, legal definitions. In fact, issuers often resort to issuing lease debt to avoid the need for the popular vote usually required to issue G.O. bonds. On the other hand, for some issuers lease debt is the only practical source of capital for infrastructure improvements either because of difficult voting hurdles or outright constitutional prohibition against the use of G.O. debt. In the case of tax-backed, general-fund supported leases, there is always some risk that appropriations will not be continued, especially if the project financed by the lease is no longer considered needed or usable. Even when the lease payments are being appropriated, these monies usually come only from what is currently available in the issuer's general fund. In the event of inadequacy, no trustee can force the issuer to raise taxes to pay off a lease obligation. For these reasons, lease debt is rated lower than the corresponding G.O. debt of an issuer. In rating lease obligations, S&P places a lot of emphasis on the legal covenants, which protect investors in the event of damage to the project, and on the essentiality of the project to the ongoing operations of the issuer. As budgets tighten, lease debt has come increasingly under fire by taxpayers.

Tax and revenue anticipation notes (TRANs) are short-term obligations of an issuer, due within one to three years of the date of issuance, and often used for annual cash flow borrowing. The source of payment is often tax revenues attributable to the current fiscal year, but the timing of these revenues and note payments varies considerably from state to state and issuer to issuer. With short-term notes, the rating focus is not so much on long-term regional economic trends as on patterns and trends in the issuer's annual cash flows. Sometimes an issuer with a mediocre economic profile can achieve S&P's highest note rating, 'SP-1+', because demonstrated, available cash provides excellent coverage on the note payment dates. Although arbitrage opportunities were severely reduced by changes in the federal tax code, tighter budgets are driving more and more government issuers to the short-term market for operating cash.

Special districts come in a wide variety of forms and powers. Their obligations are generally "tax-backed," but investors must be aware that special taxing districts' ability to levy taxes is often severely restricted. California's Mello-Roos districts, for example, can levy property taxes, but not ad valorem property taxes. Often the tax levied is an amount set according to the type or size of parcel or structure, and frequently there is a limit on the total amount of tax revenue a district can generate. Mello-Roos districts that are large, already developed, and mainly residential can have credit characteristics similar to those of G.O. bonds. Others may be little more than raw land, and their bonds highly speculative in nature.

Tax increment districts can tax growth in property value over a designated base year, usually up to a limit set by their authorizing resolutions. Depending on how much existing property, already on the tax rolls, covers the maximum annual future debt service requirement, tax increment bonds can be rated investment grade. In addition to current coverage, a variety of legal covenants controlling future debt issuance and dilution of the increment stream by tax-sharing agreements also will help determine the safety—and, therefore, the rating—of these bonds.

Often used for redevelopment of deteriorated downtown areas, tax increment bonds can have good ratings if the size of the project area is significant and there is good diversity among taxpayers. When the existing property in the district does not currently generate enough tax revenue to cover the future annual maximum debt service—or the value of the property is low relative to the debt it supports—bondholders face the risk that the projected development in the district may not proceed as planned. Additionally, if a small number of taxpayers in the district pay a significant percentage of the total tax, and the excess coverage is not enough to compensate for their loss, interruption of debt service payments due to bankruptcy is a real possibility.

Finally, not all special district bonds are backed by real estate. The much-publicized defaults of certain special districts in Colorado involved G.O. debt of those districts, but, unlike the case with California Mello-Roos bonds, bondholders had no recourse to the underlying property in the event of difficulty. When underestimated development costs created an intolerable tax burden on properties within these districts, the owners walked and the districts went bankrupt. Unrated special district debt often implies speculative debt, and investors should exercise caution.

In the following section, S&P examines in detail the security features, rating approach, and documentation requirements for these various types of tax-backed debt.

GENERAL OBLIGATION DEBT

When a state or municipal issuer sells a G.O. bond, the issuer pledges its full faith and credit to repay the financial obligation. Unless certain tax revenue streams are specifically restricted, the G.O. issuer frequently pledges all of its tax-raising powers. Typically, local governments secure the obligation with their ability to levy an unlimited ad valorem property tax; state governments, which have a different tax structure, usually pledge unrestricted revenue streams like sales or income taxes.

G.O. bonds remain essential financing instruments of tax-supported capital projects. Since the 1970s, however, the increasing popularity of revenue bonds has reduced the dominance of G.O. financings in the municipal market. The reasons underlying the relative shift are many, but leading these developments are

- the attractiveness of financing capital projects through user fees rather than broad-based taxes,
- the limited legal and practical capacity of governments to carry larger debt burdens, and
- continuing market innovations, which favor revenue bond insurance.

Although the Tax Reform Act of 1986 dampened G.O. bond market growth for several years, G.O. debt issuance has rebounded steadily from its previous low in 1987. By 1992, G.O. bond new issue volume grew to $81.5 billion, representing 35 percent of the total new issue municipal bond volume. In comparison, 1987 G.O. bond new issue volume was $30.8 billion, or 29 percent of total new issue volume.

The capacity and willingness of municipal governments to repay their G.O. debt can be assessed by examining four basic analytical areas:

- Economy
- Financial performance and flexibility
- Debt burden
- Administration

Economic Base

The economic base is the most critical element in determining an issuer's rating and incorporates both local and national economic factors.

The foundation of a community's fiscal health is its economy. Financial growth prospects and volatility of major revenue sources are dependent on the performance of the local economy. Economic conditions also influence the affordability and range of services delivered by a government in such categories of expenditures as social welfare, education, health care, and public safety.

Demographics

Population analysis extends over a four-decade span. The local population base is profiled in terms of age, education, labor skills and competitiveness, and wealth and income levels. Demographic analysis also considers the impact of annexations and the effect of migration patterns.

Tax Base

The initial focus is on size, structure, and diversity. The tax base's composition is reviewed to identify proportionate contributions from residential, commercial, and industrial tax revenue sources. To determine the degree of concentration, the leading taxpayers are profiled and assessed for their direct and indirect effects on the local economy. Significant changes in the tax base are analyzed to determine whether the causes are structural or cyclical.

Composition of Output and Employment

Diversity and growth of the economy and employment base are prime considerations in evaluating the strength of the economy. Economic factors examined include

- composition by employment sector—manufacturing, trade, construction, services, government, and agriculture;
- concentration in major employers or reliance on particular industries;
- employer commitment to the community—importance of local facilities and employees to the overall strategy of local employers, business development plans, age of plant, and industry prospects;
- employment trends and quality of the local labor force; and
- regional economic patterns to assess relative gains in employment and income growth.

Farm sector. To monitor the economic trends that will be challenging rural municipalities and agricultural-based economies, S&P reviews international trade developments, trends in U.S. farm policies, natural resource endowment, and local crop and livestock production. Since many agricultural communities frequently rely on property tax collections, trends in farm bankruptcies, agricultural prices, and land utilization have relevance in monitoring farm belt fiscal performance. (See Exhibit 1.)

Exhibit 1: *Early Signs of Farm Belt Stress*

> Presence of one or more of these conditions could signal a weakening of a rural municipality's credit quality:
> - Falling commodities prices for area's major cash crops or livestock
> - Declining government target price and/or loan rate for major cash crop
> - Rising average farm debt/equity ratios
> - Lack of alternate employment in immediate area
> - Increasing foreclosure rate or loan renegotiations on farm mortgages
> - Rising rate of bank failures
> - Dwindling population
> - Decreasing property and land values
> - Declining personal income

Manufacturing sector. S&P analyzes the nature of manufacturing enterprises, the diversity of their output, and the cyclical influences of the leading manufacturing employers on total employment and income patterns. Industries with strong growth potential are viewed more positively than those experiencing overcapacity and increased competition. Where industries are facing strong international competition in unit labor costs, corporate success might be more appropriately measured by continuing gains in production and investment in plant and equipment.

Service sector. Many communities with manufacturing-based economies have sought to replace lost manufacturing jobs with service sector employment. The replacement of what are usually high-income manufacturing positions with lower-paying service sector jobs may be of limited benefit. The quality of service employment and the industry's growth prospects are key to evaluating service sector development.

Comparative Criteria

Specific comparisons of the general factors just outlined are made with available economic data. Where appropriate, these data also are compared with Metropolitan Statistical Area (MSA) data—for example, wealth and income levels. Historical trends and their likely development are much more valuable than data comparisons for a specific point in time.

Sources

Since economic data for many governments below the county level are limited, S&P relies on issuers to provide some data for its economic analysis. Greater consistency in methodology is available from data produced by federal and state economic agencies, including the U.S. Departments of Commerce, Labor, and Agriculture, the Federal Reserve Bank, and private economic consulting firms. Labor departments in each state and universities that maintain state economic models also are valuable sources of economic data. S&P does not make its own economic forecasts for a local economy. Internal and external information sources are utilized to understand local economic risks and judge the credibility of tax revenue projections.

Summary

Generally, those communities with higher income levels and diverse economic bases have superior debt repayment capabilities. They are better protected against sudden economic shocks or unexpected volatility than other communities. Nevertheless, a strong economy does not always ensure a strong ability to meet debt payments.

Financial Indicators

Financial analysis involves the following areas:

- Accounting and reporting methods
- Revenue and expenditure structure and patterns
- Annual operating and budgetary performance
- Financial leverage and equity position
- Budget and financial planning
- Contingency financial obligations, such as pension liability funding

An analysis of these factors will present a clear indication of the financial strengths and weaknesses of an issuer. This analysis will also provide the framework for judging capacity to manage economic, political, and financial uncertainties.

Accounting and Reporting

The first important variable in judging financial performance is the method of accounting and financial reporting. Based on the guidelines of generally accepted accounting principles (GAAP), S&P assesses the fairness and comparability of financial reports. Emphasis is placed on the governmental funds, i.e., general, debt service, and special revenue funds, under the modified accrual basis of accounting. Further, Governmental Accounting Standards Board (GASB) interpretations of accounting rulings are considered in evaluating the organization of funds, accruals, and other financial reporting methods.

GAAP reporting is considered a credit strength, and the ability to meet the Government Finance Officers Association's (GFOA) Certificate of Conformance reporting requirements also is viewed favorably. Enhancing public disclosure is a government's Comprehensive Annual Financial Report (CAFR), which should include significant financial data and various statistical data to supplement the accounting statements.

Issuers are expected to supply adequate and timely financial reports. Financial reports prepared by an independent certified public accountant are preferred. Lack of an audited financial report prepared according to GAAP could have a negative impact on an issuer's rating since the quality of financial reporting may be considered suspect. In cases of extremely strong financial performance or consistently strong cash flow history, non-GAAP financial reporting may be given positive consideration. If financial reports are prepared by state agencies or other internal government units, S&P is interested in any deviation from GAAP standards and the independence of the auditors preparing the reports. A copy of the management letter which accompanies an independent audit is requested, along with the issuer's response to any cited problem areas.

Current Account Analysis

Current account analysis includes an examination of operating trends focusing on the structure of revenue and expenditure items, primarily within the general fund and debt service funds. If other funds are tax-supported or include revenues related to general government purposes, they also have relevance in developing a complete understanding of financial performance.

Revenue analysis. Diverse revenue sources are preferable as they can help strengthen financial performance. While property taxes tend to be among the most stable revenue sources, the failure or inability to levy taxes on nonresidential economic activity can represent a lost opportunity. The increasing use of fees not only creates a new revenue stream, but places the burden for municipal services on the users of the services. Although a balanced composition of revenues gives an issuer the flexibility to meet all its financial obligations, it does not protect against general economic decline. For example, if a government's tax collections are dependent on several major revenue sources, the direct and indirect effects of an economic downturn can be broad enough to affect revenue performance significantly.

S&P reviews the composition of the municipalities' revenue stream and the stability of major revenues, such as

- property, sales, and income taxes;
- user charges;
- intergovernmental aid; and
- investment income.

These revenue sources are examined over a three-to-five-year period. S&P will review unusual patterns in revenue performance that could lead to significantly different financial performance in the future.

Expenditure analysis. Similarly, expenditure composition and stability are analyzed in the context of revenue patterns. Large expenditure items are identified and examined to determine if continued expenditure growth could endanger existing services or require additional taxing efforts. To the extent that certain spending items are extraordinary or nonrecurring, their effect on long-term financial performance is discounted.

Balance sheet analysis. The balance sheet examination focuses on liquidity, fund balance position, and the composition of assets and liabilities. In S&P's consideration of appropriate fund balance levels, several variables are important:

- The volatility and patterns of the tax revenue stream
- The predictability of government spending
- The availability of unencumbered reserves or contingency funds
- The ability of public officials to sustain a strong financial position

The fund balance position is a measure of an issuer's financial flexibility to meet essential services during periods of limited liquidity. S&P considers an adequate fund balance to be a credit strength.

Transfers. The effect of any revenue transfers among other governmental and capital funds is considered in the review of financial performance. When the general fund and/or debt service fund is supported by interfund transfers, S&P reviews the policy guidelines and historical transfer practices. Deterioration in revenue transfers that represents a deviation from past policy could be viewed as a sign of fiscal stress.

Short-term financing. The analysis of financial performance takes into account the role of short-term financing and its implications. As available cash balances decrease, cash flow difficulties can become more prominent. Nevertheless, conservative financial strategies and management practices can enable an issuer to minimize cash flow problems.

In reviewing an issuer's cash management and investment practice, S&P considers the types of investments, security precautions, and uses of investment income.

S&P is interested in the long-term fiscal strategy, the risks inherent in such a strategy, and the monitoring systems used to measure performance against financial objectives. One measure of financial management strength is the review of financial results against original expectations. Variances between budget and actual results are indicative of management's financial planning capabilities, particularly when considered over a period of time. Assumptions behind the projections used in budget development and planning are extremely valuable and form the basis of discussions with the managerial team.

Pensions and Other Long-Term Liabilities

The management of pension fund and other long-term financial obligations is having an increasingly meaningful impact on financial performance and position. While meeting unfunded accrued liabilities should be a high-priority objective, the task is often clouded by the variations in calculating future asset and liability values.

Recent GASB rulings regarding appropriate methods for rates of return on investments are designed to standardize pension fund reporting for the public sector. In view of current limitations and lack of standardization in valuation studies, no system-by-system comparative analysis can be employed. Despite these uncertainties, S&P believes that the financial management team should undertake measures to address these obligations. Failure to contain the growth of unfunded pension liabilities endangers the government's ability to meet its long-term debt obligations.

Other long-term contingent liabilities—such as accrued sick leave and vacation pay—should be included at least as a footnote within the financial statements. It is considered a strength if a reserve fund is established to cover some or all of such costs.

Insurance risk management for governmental issuers has become increasingly complex. In light of the difficulties in ensuring sufficient coverage under traditional insurance programs, S&P is interested in the types of coverage and, where self-insured programs exist, the amount of insurance reserves set aside to meet claims.

Debt Factors

The analysis of debt focuses on the nature of the pledged security, the debt repayment structure, the current debt servicing burden, and the future capital needs of an issuer. Accelerated debt issuance can overburden a municipality, force the reduction of necessary services, and consequently lead to lower ratings. Alternatively, a low debt profile may not be a positive credit factor, since it may indicate underinvestment in capital facilities.

Investment in public infrastructure is believed to enhance the growth prospects of the private sector. Neglecting critical capital needs may impede economic growth and endanger future tax revenue generation. Although some capital projects are discretionary and can be deferred in difficult economic periods, the failure to maintain existing facilities can create a backlog of projects. Eventually, when the backlogged projects are funded, the cost may prove burdensome to future taxpayers.

In difficult fiscal situations where municipalities face operating deficits, some entities choose long-term financing of accumulated deficits as a solution. S&P believes the "bonding out" of financial problems is not a permanent cure and may complicate the ultimate resolution of the crisis.

Type of Security

A G.O. pledge takes various forms that provide different degrees of strength.

Unlimited ad valorem property tax debt, secured by a full faith and credit pledge, usually carries the strongest security. However, during a period of fiscal stress, debt service competes with essential services, such as police and fire protection.

Limited ad valorem tax debt, or a limited tax pledge, carries legal limits on tax rates that can be levied for debt service. S&P views this type of security more as a means to limit debt issuance than as a strict cap on revenues available to retire debt. In a limited tax situation, the tax base's growth and the economy's health are often more significant credit factors than the limited source of payment. In fact, a limited tax bond can be rated on par with unlimited bonds if there is enough margin within the tax limit to raise the levy or if other tax revenues are available for debt service.

Double-barreled bonds are secured by an enterprise system's revenues, such as water or sewer user charges. They also carry a full faith and credit pledge, but taxing power is used only if the enterprise's revenues are insufficient. S&P's approach is to review both security pledges.

A well-run enterprise system can enhance the general government's credit by making substantial financial contributions to the general fund. In contrast, a troubled utility can threaten the integrity of the general fund.

Credit implications may be positive when the enterprise has

- a solid track record of self-support, i.e., no reliance on tax revenues;
- covenants to maintain rates; and
- other provisions that would work to prevent a potential fiscal drain upon the general fund.

G.O. bonds are considered self-supporting when the enterprise can pay debt service and operating expenses from its own operating revenues. Such a self-supporting enterprise could utilize the full faith and credit support of a municipal government without diminishing the credit quality of the government's G.O. debt.

Special assessment bonds may have speculative characteristics, since economic and financial risks can be concentrated in relatively small parcels of property. Some of these credit concerns can be allayed if the bonds are on parity or have a senior lien on ad valorem property taxes or other legal protections. Low project risk and economic incentives for timely repayment, and low project risk also can mitigate concerns.

A moral obligation pledge occurs when an issuing entity relies on another to make up any deficiency in the debt service reserve fund. That pledge is non-binding and most often given by a state to the debt of its agencies or authorities. The promise of a government to appropriate money to the debt service reserve fund usually enhances the creditworthiness of the issuing authority.

Maturity Schedule

The maturity schedule can become important in some circumstances. Prudent use of debt dictates that the debt's term matches the useful economic life of the financed facilities. For example, 3-year bonds issued to finance police cars would be appropriate, while 15-year bonds would be viewed negatively.

An average maturity schedule for capital projects is one in which 25 percent of the debt rolls off in 5 years and 50 percent is retired in 10 years. A faster maturity schedule may be desired to avoid increased interest costs; however, it can place undue strain on the operating budget.

Debt Limitations and Needs

S&P looks for realistic debt limitations that permit the issuer to meet its ongoing financing needs. A city near its debt limit has less flexibility to meet future capital needs but, more importantly, may be unable to borrow money in the event of an emergency. Restrictive debt limitations often result in the creation of financing mechanisms that do not require G.O. bond authorization or voter approval.

S&P examines the community's future financing needs. Municipalities should regularly review their critical capital needs and schedule capital improvements for the project's life cycle. The history of past bond referendums is one indication of the community's willingness to pay for such improvements.

S&P also measures the debt burden against a community's ability to repay. Three indicators of that ability are

- the tax base,
- the wealth and income of the community, and
- total budget resources.

In general, a debt burden is viewed as high when debt service payments comprise 15 percent–20 percent of the combined operating and debt service fund expenditures. This benchmark will vary with the structure of government and the level of services an issuer provides.

Administrative Factors

As municipal operations expand and become more complex, an understanding of the organization of government is a prime necessity. The powers of a municipality establish the entity's ability to plan for changes in the political, economic, and financial environment, and the capacity to respond in a timely fashion. The entity's degree of autonomy is affected by home rule powers, as well as both legal and political relationships between state and local levels of government.

The range and growth potential of services provided by the issuer also are examined in relation to the capacity to provide such services. The ability of officials to make timely and sound financial decisions in response to economic and fiscal demands can depend on the tenure of governmental officials and frequency of elections. The background and experience of key members of the administration are important considerations if they affect policy continuity and ability to reformulate plans.

Documenting the Planning Goals

Adherence to long-range financial plans is considered a reflection of good forecasting and planning. To clarify and communicate these plans, long-range financial planning goals and objectives should be documented. Income statement and balance sheet projections should be part of the planning documents. The ability to make accurate short-range forecasts, in order to ensure the availability of funds for seasonal and other short-range requirements, is of prime importance. Financial objectives should be closely aligned with projections included in the operating budget to reflect future operating and capital budget growth.

Financial Management

Financial management is a major factor to be considered in the evaluation of state and local government creditworthiness. Past performance against original plans, depth of managerial experience, and risk preferences of key leaders all have an impact on the bottom line.

Major aspects of financial management include

- economic analysis and revenue forecasting,
- tax policies,
- governmental accounting practices,
- financial strategies, and
- debt management.

Increasing attention is being paid to risk management policies. Risk management analysis includes investigating the adequacy of insurance coverage for accidents, health, and potential lawsuits for public officials liability.

Annual Budget

An operating and capital budget, along with at least three years of financial audits, are required documentation in the debt rating process. S&P views the budget as an expression of administrative capability and intent.

Timeliness of budget adoption is a factor in considering the efficiency of the budget-formulation process. In contrast, late budgets are a hindrance to planning and can be indicative of political or administrative difficulties.

A sound budget plan should anticipate risk elements that lie outside of administrative control, such as the uncertainty of economic performance and potential effects on major revenue sources. The administration is expected to present a realistic budget and exhibit willingness to address necessary intrayear revenue and expenditure changes to meet fiscal targets. Continuous budget surveillance should be maintained to identify problem areas and enable timely budget adjustments.

Capital Improvement Program

As part of the debt rating process, S&P requires a well-documented capital improvement program (CIP). Necessary components of this plan include

- the outlook for capital needs,
- the flexibility to modify the program in difficult economic periods, and
- the ability to finance investment through operating surpluses.

Since the reliance on long-term debt can have burdensome consequences on a government's budget, the ability to identify and use other operating funds for capital purposes can be a financial strength. The discussion of historical construction management experience also can carry implications on a government's ability to meet its budgetary constraints and project completion schedule.

Benefits Statement

A pension and employee benefits policy statement, explaining the degree of participation by both employer and employees and describing appropriate actuarial methods and assumptions, should be made available to S&P. A discussion of funding contributions and investment guidelines is important. Periodic actuarial reports and a review of the financial position of the program by independent professionals should also be submitted to S&P.

In cases where bonds are issued to fund the unfunded portion of the employee retirement pension obligations, the impact of the additional debt on the existing governmental debt will be considered. Reflecting the limited comparability of actuarial studies, no system-by-system comparison analysis is undertaken. Provided the same actuarial standards are applied, the analytical focus will be on the trend of unfunded liabilities, the benefits package, contributions, and investment rates.

Property Tax Administration

Administrative factors analyzed by S&P include the issuer's property valuations and assessment trends, changes in assessment ratios, and assessment procedures. S&P looks at the valuations by assessment categories—industrial, commercial, utility, and residential—and how the assessment ratio applies to the different classes of properties. Property tax administration is also analyzed by focusing on tax rates, levies, collection rates on both a current and a total basis (which includes delinquencies), and delinquent tax collection procedures, which are examined over a 10-year period. Tax due dates and delinquency rates are noted for their possible cash flow effects. An administration's taxing flexibility is an important rating factor if delinquencies run at a high level.

Labor Settlements and Litigation

The labor environment—relationships between employer and employees and recent wage and salary increases—should be part of the financial management discussion. Full disclosure of the nature and implications of labor disputes, if any, also should be included.

If a municipality faces litigation that may prove onerous, contingency plans are considered to assess the government's financial flexibility. The focus will include insurance coverage and the budgetary implications of these potentially large liabilities.

State Ratings

The approach to rating the G.O. bonds of states is similar to that of local government units. State governments have sovereign powers and therefore possess unique administrative and financial flexibility. These options and how they are exercised will affect the creditworthiness of a state's G.O. bonds. Conversely, the states' functional responsibilities are more extensive than those of local units, increasing the likelihood of expenditure pressures.

Sovereignty Tested

Although most states have broad powers to establish their own tax structures and expenditure responsibilities, these sovereign characteristics can be limited. State constitutions—and voter referendums enshrined in these constitutions—can dictate tax or spending policies. For example, California's Proposition 98 mandates spending levels for primary, secondary, and community college education. Proposition 98's mandates limit alternative expenditure allocations. Colorado's Amendment 1, which strictly limits how much revenue the state can collect and spend, is another example.

Many states failed to respond in a timely manner to the financial pressures that stemmed from regional or national recessions. The failure to react to the changing economic environment led to reductions in G.O. bond ratings. Massachusetts' sharp credit deterioration in 1989 was based, in part, upon its lack of timely financial decision making and on S&P's concern about the commonwealth's willingness to adhere to sound fiscal policies. California's record budget delay in 1992 and its flawed budget solutions contributed to that state's ratings decline. These states, among others, failed to employ their sovereign powers in a manner consistent with their rating levels.

State/Local Relationships

States' relationships with their localities continue to evolve. Successful legal challenges to some states' funding of primary and secondary education have bolstered state aid to schools—most notably in Kentucky and Texas. Reliance on state aid by local governments grew in states such as California and Massachusetts as property tax limitation measures restricted local revenue growth. Budgetary pressures at the state level, however, may be reversing this trend as states pare local assistance. While downloading responsibilities to local governmental units can ease a state's financial burden, these actions can weaken credit ratings of local governments unless accompanied by new local revenues or mandate relief.

S&P's G.O. worksheets for states include all of the factors considered in any G.O. rating. These factors are grouped under four broad categories. The discussion below highlights areas of difference between state and local ratings.

Economic base analysis is the most critical element of the rating process. As with local governments, the economic condition of a state defines its ability to generate tax revenue, perform its functions, and repay debt. A state's economy is generally more diverse than that of a local unit. It encompasses urban, rural, and suburban communities.

The creditworthiness implication of this difference between states and local units can be both positive and negative. The larger nature of the state's economic base may avoid the problems of employment or tax base concentration, low income levels, and economic dependency on a neighboring community that can exist for local units. But the state's greater diversity can leave it more vulnerable to downturns in a larger variety of industries. A state must find a method to handle effectively the diverse economic performance of the various areas within its boundaries.

Financial factors. Since many states can unilaterally establish funding levels for certain local programs (such as education), they have a greater degree of control over expenditure levels. Funding levels are usually statutorily, not constitutionally, determined. However, the political reality is such that once a certain funding level has been established, it may be difficult to change. Nevertheless, states enjoy considerable discretion in establishing or changing disbursement dates and funding levels for state assistance. States also enjoy flexibility in setting and modifying tax rates and their collection dates. These discretionary powers can immediately and favorably influence a state's cash flow, as well as its fiscal condition.

Debt considerations. States generally issue a wide variety of tax-supported debt in addition to G.O. debt. Such issues include authority debt that is secured by state lease rental payments, subject to appropriation; moral obligation debt; and debt secured by specific taxes, such as the sales tax.

When S&P examines the debt burden of a state, it looks not only at the direct G.O. debt but also at these other types of debt and at all obligations incurred as local government debt. A calculation is then made of the S&P Index, which is per capita total debt divided by per capita personal income. The index yields a measure of the debt burden relative to the income level. It also can be used as a balancing indicator, since states differ in their relationships with local governments. Some states issue a great deal of G.O. debt for local purposes (roads, schools, and the like), and others very little, leaving these functions to the local units. The S&P index evens out these jurisdictional variations.

To deal with timing differences between receipts and disbursements, some states enter the short-term debt market because of prohibitions against—or limitations on—interfund borrowing. Others utilize the maximum interfund borrowing and then issue short-term debt as necessary. S&P looks at both internal and external liquidity supports to assess the effect of the alternative used on creditworthiness.

Administrative factors are as important to state creditworthiness as they are to local governments. Tax structure, or the ability of a state to benefit from the economic activity within its boundaries, is an important rating factor. So is the degree of flexibility existing in this structure, both legally and politically. Expenditure pressures and disbursement schedules also are important, as state officials deal with the needs of a wide variety of local communities.

For many states, the voter initiative process and its effects are becoming increasingly important. When decisions about specific tax levels and spending allocations are placed in the hands of the electorate, state managers have reduced flexibility to respond to changing economic or financial situations.

35
The Fundamentals of Revenue Bond Credit Analysis

In his book *The Power Broker,* Robert Caro partly attributes the success of Robert Moses' empire of potent public agencies to the attention given the minutiae of the authorizing legislation and the indentures for various revenue bonds. The indentures for these revenue bonds, which were issued to fund the construction of bridges, highways and other public projects throughout New York, allowed excess toll revenues to flow annually back to the issuing agency and provided Moses with substantial financial muscle that could be applied to numerous other capital projects. Moses' success illustrates that the essential legal nature and structure of a revenue bond, its pledged revenues, flow of funds, events of default, and all other characteristics, are not generic. Rather, revenue bonds tend to be unique, developed for particular financing situations, and, as a result, each creates a distinct legal universe. This fundamental aspect of the revenue bond distinguishes it from a general obligation bond, and the understanding of this distinction is key in assessing its creditworthiness. A revenue bond credit analysis must be attuned to the particular situation and the specific set of legal parameters created in each indenture. Since revenue bonds by definition are dependent on a particular revenue, the source, context, and variability of that revenue are paramount considerations.

While revenue bonds have been in use since the 1930s, they were considered fairly radical financing instruments. Only in the past several decades have they become relatively common. In contrast to the all-encompassing general obligation pledge, the revenue bond pledges repayment from a single source of revenues. As these revenues are often derived from a single facility, whose construction and subsequent use may pose risks, revenue bonds required various legal protections such as reserve funds, rate covenants, and additional bonds tests. This association with risk is not unfounded. Although municipal bond defaults in the United States have been very infrequent, project revenue bonds such as those of the Washington Public Power Supply System and large toll road undertakings such as the Chesapeake Bay Bridge and Tunnel or the Calumet Skyway, have been among the largest.

Revenue bonds became more common since the 1930s, particularly with the advent of national environmental legislation beginning in the late 1960s when conditions for receipt of federal pollution abatement grants encouraged the use of revenue bond financing. Since then, environmental issues, whether relating to air quality, water pollution, sewage, storm drainage, or solid waste, have continued to drive much of the public finance revenue bond market. Over this period, the municipal enterprises set up to operate water, electric, or sewer operations have grown and matured, and demonstrated their long-term reliability.

Adapted, by permission, from *Moody's on Revenue Bonds: The Fundamentals of Revenue Bond Credit Analysis* (New York: Moody's Investors Service, Inc., 1992).

REVENUE BOND CREDIT RATINGS

As with the credit assessment of any debt obligation, a credit evaluation of a revenue bond involves a judgment about the issuer's willingness and ability to pay. In general, the narrower pledge of revenue bonds tends to result in lower credit ratings than general obligation bonds. Indeed, only 0.6 percent of the revenue bonds rated by Moody's Investors Services have ratings that are in the two highest rating categories, *Aaa* and *Aa1*, as compared with almost 3.0 percent for general obligation bonds. Conversely, a greater portion of revenue bonds bear "below investment grade" ratings (that is, ratings below *Baa*)—2.2 percent compared with 0.8 percent for general obligation bonds. On the other hand, many revenue bonds are strong enough to achieve a high quality rating of *Aa*. Some 9.4 percent of revenue bonds are rated *Aa* by Moody's, a figure which compares favorably with the 9.1 percent of general obligation bonds with the same rating.*

In some instances a revenue bond, particularly one issued for a purpose that is integral to municipal operations, can be equal in credit quality to a general obligation from the same issuer. After all, the same citizens, whether they are paying through property taxes or user charges, are supporting the debt. Occasionally, the revenue bond is the stronger of the two securities as a result of the enterprise system's insulation from the political process, including the ramifications of voter resistance to property tax increases. A revenue system's ability to enforce payment for services is related to this insulation. Whereas a repossession and tax sale of property can be highly politicized and take years, a water or electric system will terminate service in a month or two following a nonpayment notice. Even for nonessential enterprise systems, payment enforcement is strong. For example, access to a stadium or toll bridge requires payment up front.

So as some general government credits weaken because of limited revenue-raising powers and the rise in the cost of mandated social services, the enterprise systems serving that same area often can remain financially stable because of the independence and strength of their revenue-raising systems.

---

*All figures cited exclude ratings based on credit enhancements.

Municipal Enterprise Definitions

Balance Sheet Components and Ratios	
Net fixed assets	Fixed assets less accumulated depreciation.
Net working capital	Net current assets and net assets of all funds and accounts not devoted to debt service.
Long-term debt	Gross long-term debt plus the current portion of long-term debt.
Net funded debt	Long-term debt plus accrued interest payable less the balance in both the Debt Service Reserve Fund and the Debt Service Fund.
Debt ratio (%)	Net funded debt divided by the sum of net fixed assets plus net working capital.

Income Statement Components and Ratios	
Gross revenue and income	Operating revenue plus non-operating revenue.
Operating and maintenance expenses	Operating and maintenance expenses net of depreciation, amortization, and interest requirements.
Net revenues	Gross revenue and income less operating and maintenance expenses.
Operating ratio (%)	Operating and maintenance expenses divided by total operating revenues.
Net take-down (%)	Net revenues divided by gross revenue and income.
Debt service coverage (x)	Net revenues divided by principal and interest requirements for year.
Debt service safety margin (%)	Net revenues less principal and interest requirements for year divided by gross revenue and income.

ESSENTIALITY VERSUS DISCRETIONARY USE: THE VITAL QUESTION OF DEMAND

Because the revenue bond is secured by a narrow stream of revenues, as opposed to the all-encompassing general obligation pledge, the scope of the enterprise system producing that single stream of revenues becomes a paramount factor in credit analysis.

Specifically, the relationship between a revenue bond and the local economic base depends on the need for the enterprise itself as well as that enterprise's extent and importance. This may effectively place a ceiling on the creditworthiness of the bond, which other factors, such as debt level and structure, or financial performance, may not be able to raise. Thus, a bond secured by the net revenues of an essential, citywide enterprise such as water supply can be as strong as the citywide economy itself, because the absolute need for water ensures usage of that system. Therefore, the flow of water system net revenues will mirror the performance of the citywide economy. If the economy is thriving, the creditworthiness of the revenue bond may be very high indeed, subject to other factors such as the system's physical condition, capital needs, debt load, financial operations, and management.

The citywide water system may be contrasted with several other examples. A bond secured by the net revenues of a convention center, for instance, is only tenuously linked to the city economy. While everyone within the city may use the convention center, this use is entirely discretionary, and depends on such variables as the attractiveness of the center's shows and exhibitions, and the cost of admission. Thus, the demand for a convention center is likely to be very difficult to predict with any degree of accuracy, and will exhibit much greater elasticity than will the demand for the water system's essential service.

Similarly, a parking revenue bond is subject to discretionary and price-sensitive usage, but, unlike the convention center, a parking system composed of only a few garages would not even be available to the larger city economy. The economic base of a parking system may consist only of the few square blocks within walking distance of the garages, and may have very little to do with the city's larger economy. The credit analysis in this case becomes as specific as that for a real estate transaction. In addition to price elasticity and the vagaries of the several-square-block economy, the parking revenue flow is also subject to a third variable—that of competition. The parking garage faces competition from street and lot parking as well as from other garages. Among the other facilities that are subject to competitive pressures of varying geographic extent are airports, ports, universities and colleges, toll bridges and highways, and health care facilities. The several large toll facility revenue bond defaults mentioned earlier all resulted from significantly weaker-than-forecast demand that resulted in part from competition from nontoll highways.

Relative Demand for Revenue Bond-Financed Services and Facilities

Essential	Important but Demand-Sensitive	Discretionary, Nonessential
Public power	Toll bridge, highway	Convention center
Water	Mass transit	Parking facility
Sanitary sewer	University	Stadium
Storm drainage	Commercial airport	Marina
Solid waste disposal	Major hospital	General aviation airport
	Nonpotable water supply	Golf, tennis, skating facilities, etc.
	Seaport	

FEASIBILITY STUDIES

Because the issue of demand is such an important variable for the creditworthiness of any revenue bond, a new revenue financing (as opposed to a refunding) is typically accompanied by a feasibility analysis that addresses the reasonableness of demand forecasts and the projected revenue flows. Demand forecasting may be relatively simple for well-established and essential infrastructure systems for which demand has been clearly demonstrated within a given service area, unless the financing involves a major new extension of service. For more discretionary and nonessential enterprises, however, much greater depth of forecast analysis is typically required, including elasticity and sensitivity studies. In the case of facilities such as ports and hub airfields, the demand largely depends on private transportation operators, air carriers and shipping lines, and the analysis must extend to these industrial sectors.

Feasibility studies typically include information that ranges from data on the physical and engineering aspects of a project, to economic and operational concerns, including estimates of operating revenue and expenses, which are of critical importance. Whether the feasibility study speaks to technical feasibility, financial feasibility, or both, credit analysts must carefully consider the comprehensiveness of the data and the assumptions behind it, since feasibility studies vary widely in scope and quality. The conclusion that a project is feasible offers no assurance of the ultimate financial success and long-term credit quality of the bonds issued to finance the capital project under consideration.

A well-structured feasibility study encompasses more than the likely users of the enterprise service, projections of consumption, a conclusion about the issuer's ability to pay, and debt service coverage. Key components to look for in a feasibility study include the following:

1. A project overview, including a description of the purpose and scope of the project proposed, cost estimates and contingencies, future financing requirements, and sources of funding.
2. A description of the existing facilities or system, if any, in both physical and operating terms.
3. A project construction schedule, including any future financing and construction required.
4. A definition of major financial and operating policies, including key conditions, assumptions, laws, policies or other factors that will affect operations or the conduct of business.
5. An analysis of the project's demand or needs survey, including a discussion of competitive issues, where appropriate. The analysis might include comparison with other similar systems in operation.
6. An analysis of both historical and anticipated operating trends.
7. An analysis of historical and anticipated revenue and expenditure trends.
8. An evaluation of the customer base and user trends.
9. Debt service requirements.
10. Estimates of future rates and charges required to provide sufficient revenue.
11. Socioeconomic and demographic considerations that will allow a determination of whether projected increases in rates could be absorbed.
12. A discussion of revenue and expenditure performance under the indenture that may differ from GAAP (Generally Accepted Accounting Principles).
13. A reconciliation of revenues and expenditures between GAAP and indenture accounting.
14. A discussion of the derivation of rates and charges under the ordinance or other agreements.
15. A comparison to costs at competing facilities.
16. A description of the methodologies and assumptions employed in preparing the study.
17. Conclusions and recommendations.

There have been numerous cases over the years of unrealistic performance expectations and flawed projections. In some cases, this can be directly attributed to the quality of the study's preparation. Erroneous, overly optimistic assumptions may be made or insufficient attention paid to key variables. Sources of information may be questionable, or inadequate effort may be put into analyzing the historical experience of the particular industry or enterprise. Since it is rare to see a study that does not endorse the feasibility of a project, careful scrutiny and a healthy skepticism are critical to an effective evaluation of a study's results.

NET VERSUS GROSS REVENUE: OPERATIONS AND THE MATTER OF LEGAL PLEDGE

If an enterprise system is a legally closed or self-contained one, as defined by its own indenture, it is typically also a closed system in terms of financial operations. It executes its services, pays its employees and its suppliers, maintains its plant and vehicles, and funds its capital needs out of the charges imposed for the services it provides. It typically has no taxing power and no revenue-raising ability not directly linked to its basic role of service provider. Unlike many other municipal operations that issue debt, an enterprise system closely approximates the workings of a business and may make in-lieu-of-tax payments to the related local general government, as many businesses do. Long-term credit quality thus depends on the continued, businesslike operation of the enterprise to provide services and generate revenues.

For these critical reasons, the use of a gross revenue pledge, wherein debt service payments are made before payment of operating and maintenance (O&M) costs, does not provide any meaningful improvement in credit quality over a net revenue pledge, wherein debt service is paid after O&M costs. In either case, a net revenue analysis is necessary because of the direct relationship between credit quality and the long-term viability of the enterprise itself. It should be noted that "long-term viability" extends well beyond the matters of annual O&M and debt service to include the condition of plant and related capital needs, the retention and protection of rate-making flexibility, managerial quality and stability, and other attributes of a truly businesslike enterprise operation.

COVERAGE AND OTHER MEASURES OF RESILIENCE

Traditional revenue bond credit analysis has often focused on debt service coverage as a primary indicator of credit quality, with the highest coverage of annual debt service by annual system net revenues equated with the highest credit quality. In certain of the generic, nonessential or demand-sensitive enterprise systems described above, relatively high levels of coverage are in fact desirable because they can offset various exogenous events affecting demand that are simply too difficult to predict with any accuracy. Such events might be the construction of a successful competing convention center or parking garage by a private developer, or international labor or trade agreements that alter the economics of steamship companies.

On the other hand, in certain enterprise systems, the revenue and legal structure can render debt coverage virtually meaningless as a credit factor. For most airport revenue bonds, for example, the basic flow of funds is governed primarily by the set of airport/air carrier operating agreements that exist outside the bond indenture itself. In many cases, these agreements stipulate that air carriers cover all airport operating expenses and debt service up to the covenanted amount, and no higher. The resulting 125 percent annual debt service coverage thus demonstrated by most large airports reveals very little of these airports' relative ability to repay debt.

While the coverage-limiting, external funds flow dependence of airports is not typical of many essential service public enterprise systems, too much can be made of debt service coverage at the expense of other, very relevant issues. Such issues include service area economy, price or cost of service, condition of plant, and the overall efficiency and quality of system management. The legislative or legal ability of most enterprise systems to raise rates quickly is also critical, and is an important difference between many municipal enterprises and private utilities, which are more often subject to regulatory rate review. In this sense, long-term credit quality can be seen as a measure of resilience, or the ability of the enterprise system to respond to reasonably foreseeable events while continuing to operate the system and pay debt service.

While many of these factors are not directly quantifiable, there are useful analytic ratios, such as operating ratios and net take-down, that are not related to debt service. The operating ratio expresses operating expenditures as a percentage of operating revenue, and essentially measures the comfort margin between annually recurring costs and revenues. An enterprise system that must rely on nonrecurring, nonoperating revenues, such as investment income or water/sewer connection fees linked to building permit activity, is thus a potentially weak credit. The net take-down measures the overall net annual profitability of the system, or net revenue as a percentage of gross system earnings. Both ratios can be compared across types of systems to test for aberrations or unusual patterns from year to year which could reveal either stability or vulnerability.

EVALUATING DEBT LEVELS AND STRUCTURE

For most enterprise systems, debt levels are likely to look high relative to those for tax-supported debt of the same issuer. This is because the scope of an enterprise system's assets cannot compare to wealth encompassed in a tax base. A commonly used measure for evaluating the relative debt load of an enterprise system is the "debt ratio," a figure calculated by dividing a system's debt (net of debt reserves and other debt service funds) by its fixed assets and working capital. The debt ratio reflects the system's reliance on debt financing relative to its assets and also assesses its capacity to support additional debt. Because the capital needs of different types of enterprises vary widely, they need to be judged by separate standards. For example, airports tend to have more complex and extensive capital needs relative to their assets than water or sewer systems. Not surprisingly, a typical debt ratio for an airport is more than twice that for a water and sewer system (57 percent versus 27 percent).* Some revenue systems have debt ratios approaching 100 percent. This is not necessarily a negative credit factor if the system is well managed and its capital plans are reasonable.

---
*Moody's Investors Service Public Finance Department, 1992 Medians, Selected Indicators of Municipal Performance. See exhibit below for selected indicators of enterprise performance.

Debt structure can be as important as debt levels. In general, long-term fixed rate debt instruments that have lives no longer than the projects being financed are appropriate. These instruments allow annual debt service costs to be predictable and to occur over a time period when users are getting maximum benefit from the respective project. Debt structures that involve heavy reliance on short-term instruments, such as bond anticipation notes and variable rate obligations, subject the issuer to fluctuating market conditions, and can make planning, forecasting, and rate-setting more difficult. The ability to handle short-term and variable rate debt depends on the extent of the system's cash reserves, the sophistication of management, and the ease with which user charges can be raised when needed.

Exhibit: *Enterprise Performance Medians*

- The following medians, derived during 1991, convey various measures of performance and earning capability that are common to revenue-producing enterprises. These medians are valuable in assessing an enterprise's financial strengths and weaknesses relative to other similar enterprises.
- Ratios derived from the income statement provide measures of profitability (operating ratio and net take-down) and debt-servicing capacity (coverage and safety margins). Coverage levels demonstrate both current and prospective debt repayment ability while safety margins denote additional levels of protection. The debt ratio, which is calculated from the balance sheet, signifies the enterprise's reliance on debt financing and its capacity to support additional debt.
- The medians are intended to serve as broad indicators only. Significant deviation from the median is not necessarily an indicator of credit quality and may, in fact, highlight a significant event or unusual characteristic of the enterprise (i.e., start-up operation, system expansion or restructuring, or abnormal weather).

Selected Municipal Enterprise Medians

	Electric Distribution Systems	Electric Generation and Transmission	Airports
Operating ratio (%)	88.20	76.30	54.00
Net take-down (%)	14.50	29.10	49.80
Debt service coverage (x)	2.99	2.29	1.71
Debt service safety margin (%)	11.00	15.60	21.40
Debt ratio (%)	32.90	50.40	56.95

	Water	Sewer	Water and Sewer
Operating ratio (%)	64.60	62.40	63.00
Net take-down (%)	41.70	44.40	42.10
Debt service coverage (x)	2.20	2.07	2.18
Debt service safety margin (%)	19.10	24.60	19.40
Debt ratio (%)	32.10	29.90	26.80

EVALUATING MANAGEMENT

Since each enterprise faces challenges that can vary greatly, it is difficult to devise a standard by which to evaluate management. However, an analyst must determine to what extent management dictates the direction of the enterprise, as this is an important facet of credit assessment. Management's ability to interact with political, natural, and regulatory forces without severely compromising its agenda is key to the analyst's assessment.

Management proficiency should be assessed not on the characteristics of any individual or any group of individuals but rather according to the practices and philosophies that are institutionalized within the enterprise's organization. Analyzing practices, such as budgeting techniques, methodologies for capital planning, construction management programs, and responsiveness to regulatory pressures are good indicators of management's effectiveness.

More often than not, an organization that has institutionalized strong managerial programs also displays a historically stable and cohesive relationship between the board and administrative staff. At times, however, effective management can be undermined when relationships between these parties become politically charged, as might be the case with an election pending. Determining the nature of these relationships requires a good degree of analytical judgment. Review of the board's voting records, campaign issues of a recent election, attendance levels at public hearings, and coverage by local print media can often add insight into the assessment of managerial cohesiveness.

PROTECTION PROVIDED BY BOND COVENANTS

Since the legally pledged security for revenue bonds is a limited one, the market has historically demanded that additional legal protections be built into the documents as a condition of purchasing these bonds. Strong legal covenants in and of themselves cannot guarantee strong debt security. The underlying fundamentals—a satisfactory customer base, good finances, manageable debt levels, etc.—must be present for debt to be well secured. Bond covenants can require certain debt service coverage levels, but if there is lower-than-expected demand for the project's services and the system cannot raise adequate revenues, the system will be unable to meet the coverage requirement.

Because of the inherent limitations of legal covenants in preventing a default and the generally successful track record that revenue bonds have demonstrated, bond covenants have tended to become less stringent over time. Nevertheless, they continue to play an important role for three reasons. First, revenue bond covenants can provide bondholders with some protection in helping to avert a bankruptcy or default. Second, they can provide bondholders with remedies in the event that a bankruptcy or default does occur. Finally, bond covenants tend to promote more prudent management by creating certain ground rules for financial operations. The weaker and riskier the enterprise, the greater the need for strong legal protections to promote financial discipline and diffuse the potential for default.

In addition to the pledge of revenues (net versus gross) discussed earlier, among the legal protections typically found in bond documents are provisions for the debt service reserve fund, rate covenant, flow of funds requirements, additional bonds test, investment limitations and, with some financings, a mortgage of the underlying asset.

Debt Service Reserve Fund

Historically, the debt service reserve fund, financed from bond proceeds at a level equal to maximum annual debt service, served two functions: (1) it bought time for a workout to prevent a default in the event of a catastrophe or some occurrence that could lead to a shortfall in pledged revenues to pay the debt; and (2) it served notice that, in the event the reserve fund had to be tapped to pay bondholders, serious and timely actions would be taken (a "tripwire" use). While these functions are still valuable, the debt service reserve fund has been reduced in importance by provisions of the 1986 Tax Reform Act which reduced the maximum funding of a debt service reserve fund to 10 percent of the issue size, and by a growing recognition that for strong issuers, the likelihood of the debt service reserve fund being needed was minimal. However, the fund is still important as a security feature for weak systems or for project financing where adverse developments cannot be shared over an entire system.

Rate Covenant

The rate covenant is a legal pledge whereby the obligor agrees to set rates and charges at a level sufficient to generate adequate funds to cover operating costs and debt service. The purpose of the covenant is to ensure that rates and fees are set high enough to ensure that debt service payments will be met, even in the event of a major shortfall in revenues or unplanned increase in expenditures. Initially, rate covenants provided for substantial coverage (net revenue would be required to cover debt service by a minimum of 1.5-2.0 times). More recently, however, they have become much less stringent, sometimes only calling for 1.0 times coverage. Even though the typical rate covenant has weakened, for most enterprise systems actual coverage is usually higher, often by a significant amount, than the legally required minimum.

Flow of Funds

The "flow of funds" requirements reflect the process by which monies are allocated to the various funds held under the trust indenture. Typically, revenues are deposited as received into a general revenue fund, from which funds flow out, in the following order:

1. to pay operations and maintenance costs
2. debt service
3. to replenish the debt service reserve fund if for any reason it becomes depleted
4. to fund a depreciation or maintenance fund
5. to fund contingencies or a rate stabilization fund

One key analytic issue is whether funds may flow totally out of the system—for example, to a parent government to pay overhead expenses or general obligation debt supported by a subordinate claim on revenues—or must be retained within the system ("open" and "closed" loops, respectively). There are obvious benefits to bondholders of retaining funds within the system, either as working capital or to finance "pay-as-you-go" capital projects, rather than issuing additional debt. At the same time, if the enterprise system needs to generate sufficient funds to pay general obligation bonds, that may be beneficial to holders of revenue debt that has a senior claim on the net revenues of the system.

A related point is that, because funds flow first to pay senior lien debt, senior lien obligations will often be of higher credit quality than the same system's junior lien revenue debt. It should be noted, however, that the credit distinction between senior and junior lien bonds is unlikely to be large, since an enterprise system must generate enough revenues to remain an ongoing concern and to cover all its obligations.

The deposit of all system revenues to a "lock box" held by the revenue bond trustee can be beneficial in ensuring that all monies pledged to bondholders flow through the trustee. Similarly, the inclusion of a rate stabilization fund, whether in an open- or closed-loop system, may provide additional security to bondholders by reducing the need for rate increases under adverse economic conditions or other undesirable circumstances.

Additional Bonds Test

The additional bonds test requires the issuer to demonstrate that the revenue stream is sufficient to pay both the old and the new debt as a condition to new issuances. This test is intended to ensure that future debt issuance does not reduce bondholder security by placing too high a burden on the revenue stream. Some years ago, tests required that an enterprise's actual historical net revenue cover several times the maximum annual debt service on both old and new bonds. Gradually, however, required coverage levels began to decrease as the market became more comfortable with revenue bonds, and the detrimental effects of unnecessarily high debt coverage requirements were recognized. Required coverage levels began to decrease and various special adjustments could be made to demonstrate sufficient coverage. In addition, a variety of other debt instruments, such as variable rate demand obligations, commercial paper, and subordinate lien bonds, were often not readily susceptible to treatment under a conventional test and thus were not made subject to the test. These various factors, in turn, served to undermine the importance of the classical test, rendering it very weak, if not meaningless in some cases. However, the additional bonds test, if it is a "true" and reasonable test, can help promote appropriate debt management and can be a favorable credit factor, particularly for weaker systems or those that are growing very rapidly.

Investment Limitations

Investment limitations on monies held under the revenue bond trust indenture are particularly critical for stand-alone project financings. In the absence of a refunding or the issuance of additional completion bonds, the inability to complete the project will preclude the generation of revenues to pay bondholders. In the case of a system with existing revenue-generating capacity these concerns are somewhat mitigated, since debt service costs can be spread over the system through rate increases until additional funds can be found. Nonetheless, prudent investment is always desirable. In order to allay any concerns about default risk related to investments, investments should be limited to U.S. Government securities or federal agencies, highly rated corporate or municipal debt, highly rated asset-backed investments, and repurchase/reverse repurchase agreements with rated counterparties and structural protections that meet counterparty bankruptcy concerns. The ability to avoid market rate risk by matching investment maturities with expected needs should not be overlooked, even for a revenue bond supported by system revenues rather than project revenues.

Mortgages

Historically, revenue bond legal documents incorporated, for the bondholder's benefit, a grant to the trustee of a mortgage on the property or facility being financed. This was instituted ostensibly to increase bondholder security in the event of a default. Currently, many municipal market participants place little analytic weight on this provision. This reflects the belief that enforcement of the legal remedy, i.e., foreclosure on the public facility, would probably be precluded as a matter of public policy, if the property or facility were deemed essential to the public safety or welfare. In the case of a 501 (c)(3) borrower, such enforcement might not be precluded as a postdefault remedy. However, the nature of the financed facility might limit its ready disposal without a significant loss to bondholders. More important, however, is that any such remedy would only be exercisable after the occurrence of a default.

Recent Changes in U.S. Bankruptcy Code

Revenue bondholders should benefit from recent changes in Chapter 9 of the U.S. Bankruptcy Code in the event that the issuer of their bonds files a petition for bankruptcy. First, the risk to bondholders that debt service payments could be disgorged as voidable preferences was eliminated by the abolition of the concept of preference for municipal bonds and notes. Second, possible delays in bondholder payment under the "automatic stay" provision (section 362[a]) to trustee-held debt service payments has been eliminated for holders of bonds supported by "special revenues," which would include most, if not all, revenue bondholders. Finally, the lien on system revenues possessed by bondholders is not extinguished postbankruptcy, as would be the case in a corporate or other bankruptcy filing. These changes are beneficial to bondholders, but are applicable only in postbankruptcy, whether or not there has been a default on the actual bonds.

TYPES OF ENTERPRISE SYSTEMS

In evaluating a revenue bond, the credit analyst must first decide whether the debt is issued for a "simple" or "complex" system. While most revenue bonds reflect the pledge and operations of a "simple" single enterprise, the financing of very large facilities, such as power plants, central sewage treatment complexes, or water systems, is often done as a joint effort by several individual enterprise systems. Many smaller cities, for example, might pool their resources to build an otherwise unaffordable plant. This is typically achieved through the workings of a joint action or joint powers agency (JPA), which adds a level of legal and administrative issues to the credit analysis. These issues include such elements as the oversight power of the administering authority, the nature of the individual participant's payment as a form of parity net revenue pledge or simple operating payment, and the specific commitment of the various participants to make up any shortfalls in the payments of others, such as through a step-up provision. A single issuer pledging the revenues of a combined or multiple utility system represents a variation of the complex system. An analysis of each of the component systems is appropriate with such an issue.

Whether simple or complex in nature, each enterprise system must be evaluated in light of the technical, regulatory, and operational issues that are particular to its industry. Following is a brief discussion of some of the unique analytical concerns for different types of enterprises.

ENTERPRISE SYSTEMS THAT PROVIDE ESSENTIAL SERVICES

Water and Sewer

Many of the key issues for water and sewer systems involve compliance with environmental mandates, most notably the Clean Water Act. Meeting federal and state standards on issues such as secondary and tertiary treatment of sewage is often costly and complicated. Moreover, in the process of meeting these mandates, many older, urban sewer enterprises need to address problems stemming from the fact that they have combined systems for storm and sanitary sewers. Because separating the two functions is expensive, municipalities tend to look for alternatives, such as building retention facilities or developing methods to keep potential overflows within sewer lines for longer periods. Arranging for sludge disposal is also a growing problem. It should be noted that while most systems are grappling with making improvements to meet environmental mandates, the paramount issue for other systems, such as those in California, is the procurement of an adequate water supply. In these cases, an assessment of the quality and sufficiency of the potential water source will be a key credit concern.

Credit assessment of water and sewer debt has taken on new dimensions with changing financing trends. Major water and sewer problems initially involved large urban systems, most of which issued their own debt. In recent years, however, there has been a proliferation of debt issues for smaller systems and consequently, an increase in pooled financings for water and sewer purposes. Additional credit issues have been introduced by the replacement of federal grant programs with state revolving funds (SRFs), backed in part by the revenues of water and sewer systems. For pooled financings and SRFs, credit analysis must focus on the operations of the individual water and sewer system participants as well as on the structural characteristics of the pool.

Public Power

Many of the key analytic concerns for public power involve the type of system (generation, transmission and/or distribution), the nature and source of the power supply; and the ability of the system to meet baseload and peak demand in the most cost-effective way. Generating systems typically have greater capital needs than distribution systems. However, they also have more control over their power supply as well as the ability to enhance revenues by selling excess power. The credit quality of debt sold by generating systems reflects the value of their power relative to that of other providers, including investor-owned utilities. In contrast, the credit quality of distribution systems reflects the nature and structure of their power purchase contracts. In either case, electric systems operate in a more competitive environment than water and sewer system enterprises, which must be taken into account in the rate-setting process.

A key determinant of rates for electric enterprises is the cost of their fuel sources relative to alternatives. Changes in the economic and regulatory climate can make an enormous difference in the analysis of the relative strengths of various fuel sources. Oil and gas were considered cheap until the Arab oil embargo, and are now again relatively inexpensive. Nuclear power was originally seen by many as a cost-effective way to provide massive amounts of new energy, but has obvious safety and environmental concerns, highlighted by the incident at Three Mile Island. Currently, reliance on coal, particularly low sulfur coal, is an advantage, since such power plants can more easily comply with Clean Air Act standards.

A final key analytic concern for many large power systems is the nature of the contracts between the JPA and its participants. "Take-or-pay" contracts, in which each participant must pay whether or not it receives service, are stronger than "take-and-pay" contracts, (in which each participant only pays for service received). It should be noted, however, that while take-or-pay contracts have been upheld in some states, such as Massachusetts, they remain untested in most states. Of course, if the power project is not economically viable, there will be more incentive by participants to find legal means to negate their obligations.

Solid Waste/Resource Recovery

The creation of resource recovery facilities is a step in the evolution of solid waste disposal from a concern to a full-blown enterprise. Only a few systems have so matured. Major credit issues for resource recovery facilities include the choice of technology, political difficulties in siting facilities, the role of the vendor in project design, and construction and operation. Issues of technology and politics have rendered most single-facility approaches obsolete in favor of a more flexible "system approach" including the use of landfills and other alternatives to mass burn and other resource recovery facilities. The flow of funds is usually a key credit issue and typically, the general government must be willing to provide "deep pockets" to cover operating deficits until the facility is self-supporting.

Storm Water/Flood Control

This type of enterprise debt reflects the recognition and growth of an essentially new utility. While storm drainage had generally been addressed as part of street and road operations, the extensive suburbanization of development in the 1980s and the consequent problems with increased storm water runoff have made it a broader concern. Storm water utilities mix land-use controls and planning with "hard" construction, such as channels, catch basins and the like, with "soft" measures, such as the preservation and maintenance of swales, ravines, and other natural drainage features. An interesting credit aspect of a storm water/flood control system is the adaptation of the traditional revenue bond to a system providing a service that, although essential, reflects nonmetered "consumption." The problem of how to charge users fairly for the storm water system has typically been solved through the generation of a "runoff coefficient," similar to a user fee, for each parcel of property, which assesses that property's contribution to the storm water problem based on parcel type, size, and amount of paving. This type of assessment is dependent on a systemwide master plan and represents an approach similar to that of a user fee, but it has been used effectively for some systems.

SYSTEMS THAT PROVIDE IMPORTANT BUT DEMAND-SENSITIVE SERVICES

Airports

A key market issue in the analysis of general airport revenue bonds (GARBs) is the mix of origin-and-destination (O&D) traffic versus that derived from hubbing activities. The facility's economic base is generally a more significant credit consideration for airports that have a high proportion of O&D traffic, while the health of the dominant air carrier(s) will carry more weight in an airport devoted primarily to hubbing. Also key to evaluating an airport's credit position is an assessment of the extent of flexibility afforded through airline operating agreements. An airport generates substantial revenue from a variety of sources including concessions, parking, ground transportation, and building and ground rentals. However, these revenues may or may not accrue to the direct benefit of the airport, depending on the way they are handled in the airport's rate-making methodology.

The degree to which an airport exercises control over its gates and other facilities has become an extremely important credit factor. More than any other element, gate control determines whether or not an airport can access its passenger market and take advantage of any resilience within its rates and charges should the failure of a dominant carrier threaten a disruption in operations. If the airport does not have control over its gates, that is to say, if the gates are exclusively leased by carriers with preferential or usage-based clauses, in a worst-case scenario, it could be a bankruptcy court and not the airport administration, that determines gate utilization. Because of consolidation among airlines and reduced competitiveness, which has led to the more frequent domination of individual airports by single carriers, an airport's debt ratings may be closely linked to the fortunes of a dominant carrier. This relationship is further determined by a variety of factors, including the role that the airport and its market play in the air carrier's overall operations, and the degree of the air carrier's commitment to that facility.

Seaports

Seaports are similar to airports in that operating revenues depend on external private entities, which in this case are steamship companies, as well as a host of specialized firms related to shipping, such as freight forwarders, brokers, and insurers. As with air transportation, shipping is an industry heavily influenced by competition from other transportation modes, shifts in international trade patterns and tariffs, and changes in the costs of labor and fuel. Any of these factors could determine whether the cheapest sea freight route to the United States from Singapore is via an Atlantic or Pacific port, which directly affects utilization at those particular facilities. One important trend is the shift by container freight operators to larger vessels that make fewer stops, in the interest of reducing costly stays in ports. Given that container freight is the high-value activity for a port, as opposed to bulk or break-bulk freight, competition to attract shipping companies is becoming intense. One final, salient issue from the perspective of credit quality is that many port operations enjoy heavy state subsidies, and are therefore not comparable to pure port revenue systems.

Toll Roads and Bridges

For toll roads and bridges, the issue of competitive demand, often within a very localized geographic area, is paramount. Some of the municipal market's major revenue bond defaults—the West Virginia Turnpike, the Calumet Skyway, and the Chesapeake Bay Bridge and Tunnel—resulted from underestimations of traffic growth related to the competition from other roads. As a result of the inability to control competing modes and facilities, new toll systems are generally considered to be very risky. As a result, most recent toll bond issues involve the funding of relatively minor extensions or improvements to large and well-established systems, wherein debt service coverage from existing operations is ample.

Mass Transit

Given the often substantial capital needs of transit systems, as well as the cost of operations, fare-box revenues alone rarely, if ever, provide adequate funds to allow the transit system to be self-supporting. However, because mass transit is critical to the smooth functioning of the local economy, particularly in larger cities, transit systems often receive sizable federal and/or state grants. In many cases, mass transit systems that issue debt derive subsidies from local sales tax revenues. While the credit analysis of these systems must examine overall operations and systemwide net revenues, the debt is essentially special tax-supported, as opposed to revenue, debt.

Higher Education

Analytic distinctions for university and college bonds are twofold: first, whether the bonds have a broad revenue pledge such as tuition and fees, or a narrow one such as dormitory rents; and second, whether the institution is public or private. For a public university, trends in state aid, the place of higher education on the state's list of competing priorities, and the state's own financial position are important credit considerations. For a private university, more weight would be given to other factors, such as the size of the endowment, debt-to-asset ratios, and the competitiveness of tuition levels.

Competition for applicants is a top concern for both public and private institutions, as demographics shift and baby boomers no longer provide a swelling body of potential students. Consequently, colleges across the country are becoming more sophisticated in marketing themselves, and in offering scholarships and other financial incentives to prospective students. Credit analysis of university bonds must address how effective these strategies are and their impact on the university's finances, particularly given cutbacks in federal research grants and fluctuations in private and corporate contributions. For many private universities and colleges, effective management of endowments is also a key financial concern. Tightening finances are worsened in some instances by the university's connection with a hospital, which itself may be strapped due to the competitive forces and reimbursement challenges in the health care industry. Generally, the larger and more prominent universities have continued to do well, despite some financial tightening. The most vulnerable institutions are the smaller, private ones that have limited resources and lack a national or even statewide prominence.

Health Care

Because of concern over rapidly rising health care costs, the various payers of hospital bills (government programs such as Medicare and Medicaid, and private health insurers) have been aggressively attempting to limit payment increases to hospitals. In addition, a number of states have established rate-setting commissions or budget review procedures, which tend to further limit hospital revenues. As a result of these factors, revenues are not keeping pace with costs at many hospitals, and consequently some institutions are experiencing serious financial problems.

The health care industry is extremely competitive. Hospitals must compete for patients, for doctors and other skilled personnel, and for new medical technologies. This competition is of particular concern in many areas of the country where there remains an overcapacity of hospital facilities. Nevertheless, overall utilization of hospitals is likely to stay relatively strong due to the important nature of health services and the aging of the American population.

Tax-exempt hospital revenue bonds are issued on behalf of a wide variety of hospitals, from large teaching institutions affiliated with prestigious medical schools, to small rural hospitals that serve sparsely populated, often poor, areas. The manner in which the reimbursement climate and demand for health care services affects any individual institution will depend on its specific mix of services, its particular niche in the market, and how effectively it deals with changes in its revenue and cost structures. Ultimately, some hospitals will gain at the expense of others. Greater operating efficiencies, more consolidations, and additional hospital closures and bankruptcies are likely to be characteristics of this industry for some time to come.

SYSTEMS PROVIDING DISCRETIONARY SERVICES

Convention Centers

Convention centers are typically built to promote economic development. Indeed, activity stemming from large conferences held at such facilities can be a boom to the local economy. As costly, nonessential-service providers, however, convention centers and similar facilities are rarely if ever self-supporting. Consequently, bonds are usually serviced by a variety of hotel/motel and other sales taxes that supplement income from the operation of the facility itself.

Key to the success of a convention center is a strategic decision about the facility's "mission," for example, whether it will accommodate large trade shows and compete nationally, or host smaller conferences and compete regionally. Location is also key, as a convention center is most likely to thrive in a community that is seen by conventioneers as a desirable place to visit. Proximity to an adequate number of hotels and motels, as well as to retail and recreational facilities, is equally critical. In addition, the facility must be competitive in terms of cost, accessibility, and convenience.

As a result of the frequent need for accompanying commercial development, competition from similar facilities in the region and/or nation, and the vulnerability of demand to overall economic conditions, convention centers, and related facilities are very risky ventures. Since the enterprise is unlikely to be self-supporting, the credit analyst will need to analyze trends in the related hotel, motel, and amusement tax revenues in order to determine whether projected revenues from these sources will be adequate to pay debt service and operations and management.

Parking

The location of the parking facility and the level of existing competition are critical factors in evaluating parking revenue bonds. Because a parking garage serves a relatively restricted service area, it is imperative that the analysis include a thorough evaluation of that area and the activities likely to generate a flow of traffic. Business closings, fuel shortages, or other unanticipated economic events can have sharp or sudden effects on parking demand. A relatively positive credit scenario is presented by parking garages that are part of a diverse, municipally owned system, pre-lease a significant portion of their available spaces, encounter limited competition from private competitors, and possess a reasonable degree of elasticity in their rate structure. Garages that are stand-alone facilities, are positioned in a highly competitive environment, or that suffer from an inability to raise rates should be considered cautiously. A record of timely rate review and revision, an adequate record of maintenance provision, and appropriate hazard-insurance levels speak to quality of management and are positive credit factors.

Golf Courses, Ice Rinks, and Other Recreation Facilities

Bonds sold for golf courses, ice rinks, and other recreational facilities are among the riskiest municipal securities because they are stand-alone, nonessential facilities with very narrow revenue streams. Demand can fluctuate greatly for such facilities, depending on weather conditions, economic circumstances, and consumer preferences. Such facilities should have adequate hazard insurance, and the bonds sold on their behalf should have strong legal protections.

CREDIT OUTLOOK FOR ENTERPRISE SYSTEMS

The credit outlook for any individual revenue bond depends on the strength and interplay of the various credit factors: the economy, financial performance, debt, management, and legal structure. As a class, however, revenue bonds, particularly those issued for essential services, have been improving in credit quality. As essential service enterprise systems are usually segregated from municipal general funds, their revenues are largely shielded from diversions to help pay for municipal programs that have suffered decreases in federal and state aid. In addition, although the revenue streams of these systems are narrowly defined, the process by which rates can be raised is usually far easier than bolstering general purpose revenues for a municipality in today's tax-defiant environment. Thus, the narrowly defined agenda of an enterprise system can provide an advantage in the political arena.

The single focus of such enterprise systems also tends to facilitate management. Although these systems are often vulnerable to the forces of nature and regulatory change, on the whole they have demonstrated remarkable long-term reliability. For example, California's major water utilities' credit ratings remain as strong as they were in predrought days. The track record of these utilities proves that they can endure periods of hardship.

The future challenge for these systems will be their ability to adapt to ever-increasing levels of regulatory pressure. Until recently, consumer rates for enterprise system services such as sewage treatment have been kept relatively low by expanding customer bases as well as by generous federal grant programs for pollution control. As customer base expansion slows and federal grant programs continue to disappear, however, these enterprise systems will have to confront their customers with the real costs of increased regulatory demands.

Despite such challenges, the credit quality of the debt of many of these systems is likely to remain stable or to improve. Mature enterprise systems that provide essential services and have a long track record of successful operations are increasingly likely to have debt that is equivalent in credit quality to bonds secured by the general obligation pledge of the same municipality.

36 Competitive versus Negotiated Sale of Debt

INTRODUCTION

While one may quibble with the notion that the decision to sell debt through the negotiated or competitive process is "the most important decision an issuer can make," this issue clearly represents one of the most controversial topics in public finance today. The controversy extends back to the mid-1970s, when more and more issuers began to select the negotiated method as the preferred way of selling bonds. This shift has been attributed to several factors, including the increasing utilization of revenue bonds instead of general obligation bonds; the volatile interest rate environment of the late 1970s and early 1980s; and the emergence of innovative financing options and products. The last factor is particularly relevant to California, where the restrictions imposed by Proposition 13 in 1978 led to the development of new financing techniques.

Most bond industry professionals would agree that neither the competitive sale nor the negotiated method of sale is ideal for *all* bond issues. The appropriate method of sale should be determined on a case-by-case basis after evaluating a number of factors related to the proposed financing, the issuer, and the bond market. The challenge for public issuers, then, is to properly identify how the relevant decision factors apply to their proposed bond issues. This *Issue Brief* on the two principal methods of selling public debt is designed to help issuers conduct such a systematic evaluation of their proposed bond issues. It is intended to provide general guidelines for public issuers, particularly those who are infrequent participants in the bond market.

COMPETITIVE UNDERWRITING

Competitive underwriting is the method of bond sale in which the issuer sells its bonds to the underwriter offering the lowest bid meeting the terms of the sale. In a competitive underwriting, the issuer, typically with a financial advisor or investment banker, conducts all the origination tasks necessary for the bond offering. These tasks include structuring the maturity schedule, preparing the official statement, verifying legal documents, obtaining a rating, securing credit enhancement, and timing the sale. The issuer then advertises the sale of the bonds in advance of the specified sale date through a Notice of Sale (NOS). The NOS contains relevant information on the proposed issue and the criteria by which the bonds will be awarded. At the specified date, time, and venue, the issuer opens all bids and awards the right to purchase the bonds to the underwriter with the best bid based on the criteria specified in the NOS.

Advantages

Competitive environment. The issuer's ultimate goal in a financing is to protect the public's interest by obtaining the lowest possible interest cost. Consequently, the most compelling argument in favor of a competitive sale is that the competition among underwriters

---

California Debt Advisory Commission, Issue Brief No. 1 (Sacramento: CDAC, September 1992). Reprinted by permission of CDAC.

provides the incentive for keeping the effective interest cost as low as possible. Under the competitive bid process, market forces determine the price.

Historically lower spreads. While the gross underwriting spreads (management fee, expenses, underwriting fee, and takedown) between competitive and negotiated bond sales have been narrowing over the past decade, competitive underwriting is still generally viewed as the best means of reducing underwriting costs. While one may argue that equating spreads is an *apples versus oranges* comparison and that any advantage in spread should be weighed against other costs of the financing, data since 1982 indicate that competitive issues hold an edge in terms of lower underwriter fees paid on general obligation and revenue bond issues.

Open process. The other positive feature of competitive sale is that the issuer generally avoids allegations of unfairness or impropriety in the selection of the underwriter because the bonds are sold through a public auction.

Disadvantages

Risk premium. Underwriters bidding on a competitive sale have no guarantee of being awarded the bonds. Thus, underwriters cannot be expected to conduct the same level of pre-sale marketing (canvassing prospective investors before the sale) as in a negotiated sale. To compensate for uncertainty about market demand, underwriters may include a hedge or a risk premium in their bids, which can show up either in the spread or the reoffering scale. The amount of the risk premium, however, should also be weighed against the total cost of the financing.

Limited timing and structural flexibility. An issuer's ability to make last-minute changes is limited by the competitive sale process. With regard to timing, competitive bidding entails a 15-day lag between the time documents are completed and the actual sale date, due to legal notice requirements. Hence, the issuer's ability to speed up the sale process, if necessary, is restricted. While a Notice of Sale can be structured to allow for postponement of a competitive sale and subsequent reoffering with a minimum of two days prior notice, the competitive sale process remains less flexible than its negotiated counterpart.

In addition, the competitive sale restricts the issuer's ability to adjust major structural features, such as final maturity and call provisions, to match the demand realized in the actual sale process. Again, while a properly structured NOS can increase the flexibility of competitive sale by allowing for changes in the size of the issue (within certain parameters), principal maturity amounts, and the composition of serial versus term bonds, a negotiated sale still holds the advantage if flexibility in structuring is of paramount consideration.

Minimum issuer control over underwriter selection and bond distribution. In competitive underwriting, the bonds are sold to the underwriter submitting the best bid, based on the NOS criteria. The issuer exerts little influence over which underwriting firms actually purchase the bonds and how these bonds are ultimately distributed. For example, the issuer's ability to ensure that regional firms are included in the underwriting syndicate of a large issue, or that a portion of the bonds are sold to certain types of investors (e.g., retail or regional investors) is limited. In competitive sale, market forces determine the distribution of the bonds. This lack of control, however, should only be disadvantageous to the extent that the issuer is interested in influencing the composition of the underwriting team or the distribution of the bonds.

NEGOTIATED UNDERWRITING

In a negotiated sale, the terms of the purchase are subject to negotiation between the issuer and the underwriter. Whereas the issuer accepts or rejects the underwriter bids in a competitive sale, the issuer can and is expected to negotiate with the underwriter over the price of the bonds and the spread in a negotiated sale.

In a negotiated sale, underwriter selection is one of the first steps taken by the issuer. Because the issuer selects an underwriter without fully knowing the terms under which that underwriter is willing to purchase the bonds, the issuer's selection is based on other criteria, which generally include the underwriter's expertise, financial resources, compatibility, and experience. Once the underwriter is selected, both the underwriter and the issuer participate in the origination and the pricing of the issue. A financial advisor or another investment banking firm will often represent the issuer's interest in a negotiated sale.

Advantages

Assistance in originating the issue. While the underwriter's primary role in a negotiated sale is as the purchaser of the issue, the underwriter can also assist the issuer in performing origination tasks such as preparing the official statement, making presentations to rating agencies, and obtaining credit enhancement—in essence, "one-stop shopping." Some issuers, however, prefer to engage a financial advisor or another investment banking firm for assistance in a negotiated sale. In a competitive sale, the issuer performs the origination tasks or pays for these services separately.

Effective pre-sale marketing. Because the underwriter in a negotiated offering is assured the right to purchase the bonds, the underwriter can conduct more effective pre-sale marketing than in a competitive sale. By developing information about market demand for the bonds, the underwriter can reduce inventory risk, presumably leading to a lower risk premium in the pricing. Pre-sale marketing is especially important for issuers who have not developed a reputation among investors or whose securities are not widely held among investors.

Timing and structural flexibility. Another advantage of negotiated underwriting is flexibility—the ability to sell the bonds at any time and to change the structure of the issue in response to changing conditions. Although the issuer may announce a negotiated sale date, this date is considered a target and can be changed if deemed necessary (because of a large supply of similar securities or unfavorable interest rate movements, for example). Similarly, negotiated underwriting allows the issuer the flexibility to adjust the structure of the issue up until the time of sale to meet either the issuer's or the investors' needs.

Influence over underwriter selection and bond distribution. In a negotiated sale, the issuer exercises more influence over underwriter selection and bond distribution. The choice of the underwriter in a negotiated sale is based on a variety of criteria which may target certain types of underwriting firms and establish distribution goals. Issuers trying to reach certain market sectors may be able to negotiate with the underwriter to allocate the bonds accordingly. Again, this type of control should only be relevant to issuers wishing to include certain firms in the underwriting syndicate or wanting to make sure that certain types of customers receive a portion of the bonds.

Disadvantages

Lack of competition in the pricing. In a negotiated sale, the bond pricing is less subject to the rigors of competition, as the underwriter obtains the exclusive right to purchase the bonds in advance of the pricing. Unless the issuer is vigilant during the pricing, the interest rates may be structured to protect the profit margin of the underwriter, not to keep the issuer's borrowing costs as low as possible. Although some underwriters may exercise restraint in the pricing to protect their reputation and promote future business, issuers should take the responsibility to obtain market information on comparable transactions at the time of the pricing.

Elements of spread open to wide fluctuation. While underwriters in a negotiated sale can provide an array of financial services which are in addition to the actual underwriting of the bonds, issuers should not lose sight of the fact that these services come at a price. Insofar as the cost of these services will be paid for as part of the underwriting spread (versus a flat fee), some issuers may not be fully aware of the compensation that is being provided for such services, or whether they actually need all the services being provided. Thus, the chances for wide fluctuations in spread between comparable deals is greater in a negotiated environment. The negotiated sale process demands increased scrutiny on the part of the issuer to keep spreads reasonable.

Appearance of favoritism. Because underwriter selection is based on quantitative *and* qualitative factors, negotiated sales can be subject to allegations of impropriety. Issuers must be prepared to defend their underwriter selection criteria, as well as their ultimate cost of borrowing, to avoid the appearance of impropriety.

COMPETITIVE VERSUS NEGOTIATED: DECISION FACTORS

While it is impossible to develop a fail-safe formula to follow for making a decision on the appropriate method of sale, issuers can make informed decisions by conducting a systematic review of certain factors on a case-by-case basis. These factors can be classified under **issuer characteristics**, including *market familiarity, credit strength,* and *policy goals;* and **financing characteristics**, including *type of debt* *instrument, issue size, complexity of the issue, market conditions,* and *story bonds.*

Issuer Characteristics

Market familiarity. Attracting sufficient investor and underwriter interest is critical to the success of any bond issue. The frequent issuer is at an advantage in terms of attracting market interest insofar as the market is already familiar with its credit quality. Although the trend is toward greater disclosure for all issuers, generally, the market does not require as much information from frequent issuers as it does from infrequent market participants. Consequently, the infrequent issuer should consider the extent to which pre-sale marketing—which may be more effective under the negotiated sale—is necessary for the success of its bond sale.

Credit strength. Everything else being equal, the higher the credit quality of the issue and the issuer, the less likely there will be a need for negotiation. Because of the steady demand for high quality municipal bonds, issuers with a strong credit position can fare well in competitive bidding. Consequently, issuers should consider the competitive sale for issues rated A and above. Weak issuers may not attract sufficient market interest to induce competition and, consequently, may benefit from the more effective education process offered by the negotiated sale.

Policy goals. As noted earlier, issuers will find that the competitive bid process does not provide them much influence over the composition of the underwriting syndicate or the distribution of bonds. Moreover, some have argued that the competitive sale process screens out minority-owned, women-owned, or other small firms that do not have the resources to compete with more established underwriters.

In a negotiated sale, smaller firms will often have a better chance of being included in an underwriting syndicate, though there is no guarantee that smaller firms will be allocated bonds. To the extent that issuers believe that influencing the composition of the underwriting syndicate and the distribution of bonds are worthwhile policy objectives, they may be better served by the negotiated sale. When issuers choose negotiated sale for these reasons, however, they should clearly specify the rationale and criteria for the selection of underwriters and the allocation of bonds to avoid any appearance of impropriety.

Financing Characteristics

Type of debt instrument. The market responds to familiar or well-known debt instruments and, likewise, tends to be apprehensive about innovations. An issuer using a relatively new debt instrument may have to familiarize the market with the security features of the instrument. The negotiated sale is invariably more conducive to this education process. However, insofar as the market has the ability to rapidly absorb information regarding new debt instruments, "innovative" instruments can quickly become mainstream. Thus, as the market becomes more familiar with a particular debt instrument, the need to educate market participants on the nuances of the instrument will diminish. Everything else being equal, more familiar instruments will be better suited to competitive sale.

Issue size. The size of the bond issue influences both the level of investor interest and the market's ability to absorb the issue. The general rule is that if the issue is either too small or too large, the issuer should consider negotiating the sale. A very small issue will probably not attract any attention in the market without a concerted sales effort. A very large issue, on the other hand, may not easily be absorbed by the market. Therefore, effective pre-sale marketing activity—offered by the negotiated sale—becomes necessary.

Complexity of the issue. It is convention in the public finance industry that "plain vanilla" issues (i.e., those which are readily accepted and understood by underwriters and investors) lend themselves to the competitive bid process. Consequently, bonds which are structured to include features such as variable rates, put features,* or interest rate swaps, may be more appropriate for negotiated sale.

Market conditions. During periods of interest rate stability, the need for flexibility in the timing of the sale is not particularly critical. Conversely, the timing of the sale is very critical in an unstable or volatile market, especially when there is a need to bring an issue to the market in a few days. In such cases, the flexibility inherent in a negotiated sale can be indispensable. For example, refunding issues which are motivated by the desire to capture the sav-

---

*A "put" feature grants the bondholder the right to require the issuer or a specified third party to purchase the bonds at a certain time(s) prior to maturity.

ings offered by lower interest rates, and which may be susceptible to even minor fluctuations in market rates, may be better served by the timing flexibility offered by the negotiated sale.

Story bonds. In some cases, an issue faces market difficulties because it is associated with unusual events or conditions. For instance, issues linked to a previous default, litigation, or other adverse circumstances may be difficult to place. By the same token, issues or structures which are not familiar to the market may require added explanation. These issues are sometimes referred to as "story bonds," because in order to develop sufficient market interest, the issuer has to "tell a story," or explain why the bonds are actually sound investments. Issuers of story bonds, such as Mello-Roos bonds, can benefit from the more effective pre-sale marketing opportunities offered by the negotiated sale. Nevertheless, bonds which may require an explanation, such as the bonds sold by the city of Los Angeles to finance a court-ordered judgment against the city, can be sold successfully in a competitive sale if the market is familiar with the issuer and the credit security is particularly strong.

ALTERNATIVE APPROACHES

Issuers who find that the traditional approaches outlined in earlier sections do not completely meet their financing needs, may want to consider one or more of the alternative approaches described below.

Conducting Competitive Bidding within the Legal Framework of a Negotiated Sale

Issuers who prefer the competitive pricing environment offered by the competitive sale but, for one reason or another, can ill afford the 15-day notice requirement, may want to consider an approach that offers both the flexibility of the negotiated sale and the competition in the pricing of the competitive sale. Under this approach, the issuer utilizes the legal framework of the negotiated sale, allowing the acceleration of the sale process. However, instead of negotiating the price and interest rate of the issue with just one underwriter, the issuer solicits bids from all interested underwriters and awards the right to purchase the bonds to the lowest bidder, thereby maintaining a competitive environment in the pricing. A disadvantage with this approach is that it does not provide the flexibility to make last-minute or unanticipated changes in the structure of the issue.

Infusing Competition in the Negotiated Sale Process

More often than not, competition among underwriters produces lower costs and higher levels of service. Thus, it is important that issuers who plan to use the negotiated sale consider employing a competitive process for the selection of their underwriter. The use of a request for qualifications (RFQ) or request for proposals (RFP) to solicit interest requires potential underwriters to compete against one another on the basis of cost and services offered.

There are at least two ways the issuer can infuse competition into the underwriter selection process. One way is to establish an underwriting pool, similar to the one developed by the State Treasurer's Office, from which underwriters for all negotiated issues will be chosen. The issuer should select pool underwriters based on responses to an RFQ in order to determine those who are qualified to take the issuer's bond offerings to the market. Another method is to issue an RFP requiring interested underwriters to outline their proposals for taking a specific bond offering to the market. Either way, issuers should consider the quality and level of service offered, not just costs, when selecting the underwriter.

"Unbundling" Financial Services

Issuers who do not need the full range of services offered by a financial advisor or investment banker, and who are concerned about costs, may want to consider "unbundling" financial advisory services—hiring a financial advisor or investment banker only for certain portions of the sale. For example, in a negotiated sale, the issuer can hire a financial advisor or another investment banking firm to assist in the bond pricing, but not in preparing the bond documents. By splitting the services in this way, the issuer can lower the costs of financial advisory services, while receiving needed assistance on a particular element of the bond sale process.

RECOMMENDATIONS

The following recommendations are intended to assist issuers not only in choosing an appropriate method of sale, but also in reducing issuance costs.

Participate in All Aspects of the Bond Issuance

Issuers should never forget that it is their responsibility to protect the public trust by selling their bond issues at the lowest possible interest cost. The members of the financing team are merely agents of the issuer. Therefore, issuers should take an active part in all the decisions related to the sale of their bonds: the selection of the underwriting method; the selection of the financing team; the marketing of the bonds; and the investment of the bond proceeds. While not all issuers are experts in municipal finance, they should not be shy about asking their financing team members critical questions.

Moreover, it is important that issuers who choose the negotiated sale do not relegate the responsibility to obtain the best pricing for the issue to the underwriter. Personal and trustworthy relationships, notwithstanding, the underwriter's fiduciary responsibility ultimately lies with its investors. And because the investors' and the issuer's interests are not necessarily complementary, the responsibility for looking out for the issuer's interests during the pricing should remain with the issuer.

Assess the Level of Demand for the Issue

Naturally, a competitive sale will not be successful if it does not produce real competition. While as a technical matter, two bids are necessary to generate competition, three or more bids will generally ensure the issuer that the bid price of the bonds approximates the price of comparable securities being issued at the same time. (A notable exception is the State of California, which customarily receives only two bids on its general obligation bond sales and is still able to secure competitive prices for its bonds.) If the issuer determines that a competitive sale will generate only one bid, a negotiated sale may be preferable.

Focus on the Total Cost of the Financing

The spread is but one component of the total cost of the financing. While it is an important cost factor, concentrating negotiations on the spread at the expense of the interest rate pricing can prove counterproductive to the issuer's goal of keeping the total financing cost as low as possible. Conversely, focusing on the interest rates without considering other costs of borrowing, such as underwriter spread and financial advisory fees, can be equally deceiving. The key is to consider the total cost of financing when evaluating a particular debt issue.

When in Doubt, Hire a Financial Advisor

Negotiated bond sales customarily require a greater deal of skill on the part of the issuer than competitive sales. In order to evaluate the financial terms offered by the underwriting syndicate, the issuer must be able to identify how the market is pricing similar transactions. An issuer lacking the expertise to undertake such an analysis negotiates from a position of weakness. In such cases, the issuer should consider hiring a financial advisor or another investment banking firm to assist in some or all aspects of the financing. Similarly, an issuer lacking the expertise to perform the origination tasks necessary to prepare an issue for competitive sale or to evaluate the bids once they are submitted, may also benefit from the services of a financial advisor or an investment banker.

Evaluate the Method of Sale for Every Issue

It is very important that issuers evaluate the method of sale for each bond issue. Issuers should avoid becoming too comfortable with a particular approach. Each time an issuer comes to market, it should be with the knowledge that the method of sale has been thoroughly evaluated.

Understanding the Underwriting Spread

INTRODUCTION

One of the issuer's primary goals in any public debt offering is to borrow needed funds at the lowest possible cost. Inevitably, this entails not only obtaining favorable interest rates, but also holding other borrowing costs to a minimum. A major cost component of public debt issuance is the underwriter's compensation, which usually takes the form of the *underwriting spread*. While the amount of the underwriting spread will vary significantly depending on the characteristics of (1) the issuer, (2) the project, and (3) the financing, a general discussion of its components can prove valuable to an issuer evaluating proposed underwriting spreads.

The amount of the underwriting spread poses more of a concern to issuers offering debt through negotiated rather than competitive sale. In a competitive sale, the bonds are awarded to the underwriter offering the lowest qualifying bid (combined interest and spread), regardless of the level of underwriting spread which is imbedded in the bids. For instance, an underwriting firm with a superior distribution network might be able to offer the lowest bid even while setting the underwriting spread at a higher level than its competitors. By contrast, a negotiated sale requires the issuer and the underwriter to agree on the terms and conditions of the bond sale. These negotiations focus on the interest rate pricing and on the other major cost factor in the sale of bonds: the underwriting spread. Because the underwriter has obtained the exclusive right to purchase the bonds, the issuer cannot rely on competition between underwriters to keep the underwriting costs down. Consequently, it is critical that issuers become familiar with the various components which make up the underwriting spread.

THE UNDERWRITING SPREAD

The underwriting spread is defined as the difference between the price at which an underwriter purchases bonds from an issuer and the price at which the bonds are resold to investors. Bonds are generally offered in $5,000 increments. Spreads, however, are typically quoted in dollars per $1,000 bond. Thus, if an underwriter purchases a $1,000 bond from the issuer at $990 and reoffers it to investors at the face value, the underwriting spread is $10, or 1 percent. If the underwriter purchases bonds at par or at a premium, the underwriting spread is earned by reoffering the bonds to investors at a higher premium. Hence, if an underwriter purchases a $1,000 bond from the issuer at the full face value, the bonds could be reoffered at $1,010 to generate a spread of $10, or 1 percent. The underwriting spread compensates the underwriter for certain services rendered and is the source of underwriting profits.

Small issues generally require only one underwriter to distribute the bonds. Consequently, one underwriter assumes all the risks of the transaction and receives all the profits from the reoffering of the

---

California Debt Advisory Commission, Issue Brief No. 2 (Sacramento: CDAC, March 1993). Reprinted by permission of CDAC.

issue. Large issues, however, often require the purchase and selling power of an underwriting *syndicate*. A syndicate is a group of underwriters convened to collectively purchase and reoffer an issue. Syndicate members share the liability of, and the profits from, the purchase and the resale of the issue. Generally, a syndicate is headed by a *senior manager* (and *co-senior managers,* if any) who usually negotiates with the issuer, signs all contracts on behalf of the syndicate, and allocates the bonds among the syndicate members. A syndicate may also have *co-managers* who assist the issuer in preparing the issue for the sale.

In an underwriting syndicate, the senior managers typically take on the highest share of the underwriting liability. Accordingly, they receive the highest share of the syndicate profits. The senior managers are followed by the co-managers in terms of level of liability and share of the profits. The remaining members of the syndicate typically assume the smallest share of liability and profits. In addition to, or in lieu of, a syndicate, the underwriter may opt to form a *selling group*. A selling group consists of dealers and brokers brought together to help sell bonds. They do not share the underwriting risk and, consequently, do not receive a share of the syndicate profits.

THE FOUR COMPONENTS OF THE SPREAD

As indicated earlier, the spread is where the underwriter recoups the costs of providing investment banking services and derives its profits. The four components of the spread are **management fee, expenses, underwriting fee**, and **takedown**. While it is customary for the underwriting spread to be quoted as a percentage of the issue size, some components of the spread, such as the management fee and certain expense items, can be quoted in fixed terms, irrespective of the issue size.

Management Fee

The management fee compensates the underwriter for the investment banking services provided to the issuer, above the amount of compensation earned from other components. In the case of an issue underwritten by a syndicate, the management fee is paid to the senior manager (and co-senior manager, if any) for managing the affairs of the syndicate. Depending on the conditions agreed upon by the syndicate and the issuer, a management fee may also be paid to the co-managers for providing services to the issuer. Some of the services covered by the management fee are as follows:

- Development of a financing plan and a maturity schedule best suited to the needs of the issuer. These activities may be conducted in coordination with the financial advisor.
- Origination and marketing tasks such as preparation of bond documents, rating agency presentations, and circulation of disclosure information.
- Assessment of market conditions and advice on the timing of the sale.
- Preparation of reports on the post-sale results of the transaction.

The management fee can vary significantly from one transaction to another depending upon the time and effort expended by the underwriter.

Expenses

This component of the spread reimburses the underwriter for out-of-pocket costs incurred in the course of the sale. The biggest expense item is usually the underwriter's counsel fee. In addition, travel expenses can be a significant expense item, especially if the underwriter does not have an office located near the issuer or access to necessary professional expertise in the vicinity of the issuer. Other expense items include advertising and printing costs, computer services, bond clearance, communications (phone, FAX, courier, messenger services), Municipal Securities Rulemaking Board fees, and California Debt Advisory Commission fees.

Underwriting Fee

Because the underwriter cannot always be certain that all of the issuer's bonds will be readily purchased by investors, the underwriter may charge a fee to cover the possibility that some of the bonds may have to be reoffered at a lower price or taken into the underwriter's inventory. The size of the fee is directly related to the market risk involved. In a strong and stable market, characterized by an abundance of buyers, all the bonds may already be presold. In this instance, the underwriting fee can be waived because the underwriter's risk has been eliminated.

Takedown

The takedown is the biggest and perhaps the most confusing component of the spread. Essentially, the takedown is a sales commission paid to the underwriter. In order to obtain the most favorable interest rates, the issuer has to provide the underwriter's sales force sufficient incentive, in the form of the takedown, to work hard at finding investors willing to accept the lowest rates.

In effect, the takedown functions as a discount from the listed reoffering price given to the firm that sells the bond to the investor. The takedown consists of two parts: the *concession* and the *additional takedown*. [Note that the term "additional takedown" does not refer to an amount *in addition* to the takedown. Rather, it refers to a subcomponent of the takedown.] Apportioning the takedown between the concession and the additional takedown is basically a convention that provides an incentive for *nonmember firms* to sell bonds. If a syndicate member sells the bonds directly to investors, that firm receives a discount equal to the sum of the concession and the additional takedown, or the *full takedown*. When a nonmember firm sells the bonds, it takes down the bonds from the syndicate *at the concession*—at a discount equal to the concession—and reoffers them to investors at the listed reoffering price. The remaining portion of the takedown, the additional takedown, stays with the syndicate as profit.

Each maturity in a bond issue carries a separate takedown. Generally, the takedown bears an inverse relationship to credit quality and a direct relationship to the length of principal maturities. For example, a triple-B credit maturing in 10 years typically will have a higher takedown than a triple-A credit of the same maturity because a lower rated bond is more difficult to market. In addition, bonds which mature in the 20th year will normally have a higher takedown than bonds from the same issue which mature on the first year because short maturities are usually more marketable than long maturities. Because the takedown varies among different maturities within the same bond issue, the *average takedown*—the average of the takedowns for each maturity in the issue—is often used when discussing the total spread.

AN ILLUSTRATION OF UNDERWRITING SPREAD

For a more concrete understanding of the underwriting spread, consider the following illustration of a hypothetical $10 million negotiated serial bond issue. Leaving the interest rate pricing aside for the purposes of this discussion, assume that the underwriter offers to purchase the issue for $9.9 million with a plan to reoffer it to the public at par or face value—leaving a $100,000 underwriting spread.

Table 1 breaks down the underwriting spread of $10 per $1,000 bond. (The spread figures used in this illustration were chosen for ease of calculation only and may not reflect current or historical spreads.) Of this amount, $1.50 per $1,000 bond (a total of $15,000 for the issue) is designated as the management fee, paying for such services as developing the debt service schedule and obtaining a rating. If this issue is being underwritten by a syndicate, the management fee also compensates the senior underwriter for negotiating with the issuer, allocating the bonds, and confirming customer orders. Another $1.50 per $1,000 bond (a total of $15,000) is designated reimbursement for the underwriter's expenses such as bond counsel fee, travel, and printing.

Table 1 also shows that the underwriting fee is 75 cents per $1,000 bond, or $7,500 for the entire issue. Remember, the underwriting fee compensates the underwriter for the possibility that it may not be able to sell all the bonds at the listed reoffering price. The presence of a $7,500 underwriting fee suggests that at least some portion of the bonds remains unsold at the time of the sale. Essentially, this amount serves as the hedge for the syndicate in the event that

Table 1: *Hypothetical Underwriting Spread, $10 Million Issue*

Components	Amounts per $1,000 bond	Percentage of Issue	Total for Issue
Management fee	$ 1.50	0.150%	$ 15,000
Expenses	1.50	0.150	15,000
Underwriting fee	0.75	0.075	7,500
Average takedown	6.25	0.625	62,500
Concession	(3.75)	(0.375)	(37,500)
Additional takedown	(2.50)	(0.250)	(25,000)
Total Spread	**$10.00**	**1.00%**	**$100,000**

the remaining bonds cannot be sold at par. However, if the underwriting syndicate manages to sell all the bonds at par, it keeps this amount free and clear. Considered part of the syndicate profits, this amount will be divided among the members of the syndicate based on the proportion of each member's participation (share of the liability) in the underwriting. Say, for example, that this issue is being underwritten by a six-member syndicate consisting of two senior managers with 25 percent participation each ($2.5 million liability each), two co-managers with 15 percent participation each ($1.5 million liability each), and two members with 10 percent participation each ($1 million liability each). The $7,500 underwriting fee will be divided according to their liability, with each of the senior managers receiving $1,875 (25 percent), each co-manager receiving $1,125 (15 percent), and each member receiving $750 (10 percent).

The average takedown for this issue is $6.25 per $1,000 bond or $62,500 for the entire bond issue. Of that amount, $3.75 represents the concession and $2.50 represents the additional takedown. As noted in the previous section, however, the average takedown is a figure used mainly for general discussion purposes. The takedown of the bonds actually varies by maturity. To fully understand the mechanics of the takedown, it is necessary to look at each maturity in the issue.

Takedown Distribution

Table 2 shows the 10 maturities of the hypothetical $10 million serial bond issue, as well as the takedown for each maturity. As indicated earlier, members of the syndicate take down the bonds at the full takedown—at a discount equal to the sum of the concession and the additional takedown. For instance, the 1995 maturity carries a full takedown of $1/4$ of 1 percent ($1/8$ concession + $1/8$ additional takedown) or $2.50 ($1.25 concession + $1.25 additional takedown) for every $1,000 bond. Hence, if firm A, which is a member of the syndicate, takes down a $1,000 bond from the 1995 maturity, it would pay the syndicate $997.50 ($1,000 – $2.50) for the bond and reoffer the bond to investors at par (the listed reoffering price). A firm that is not a member of the syndicate, however, purchases or takes down the bonds from the syndicate at the reoffering price less the concession. Hence, for the 1995 maturity, nonmember firm B would receive a $1/8$ of 1 percent ($1.25 concession) discount for every $1,000 bond it takes down. This means that firm B would purchase a $1,000 bond from the syndicate at $998.75 ($1,000 – $1.25) and reoffer it to investors at par. The syndicate, in turn, would retain $1/8$ of 1 percent ($1.25 additional takedown) for every $1,000 bond in the 1995 maturity sold by a nonmember firm as part of its profits. This amount will eventually be divided among the syndicate members based on their participation, in the same fashion as the underwriting fee.

As an example of the variation of the takedown between maturities in the same issue, compare the total takedown for the 2003 maturity with the total takedown for the 1995 maturity. The $11.25 per $1,000 bond total takedown for the 2003 maturity is

Table 2: *Hypothetical Takedown by Maturity, $10 Million Issue,* (per $1,000 bond)

Maturities	Amounts	Coupon Rates	Prices/ Yields	Conc./Add TD (fractions)	Conc./Add TD (dollar amounts)
1994	$1,000,000	4.65	100	$1/8 + 1/8$	$1.25 + $1.25
1995	1,000,000	5.15	100	$1/8 + 1/8$	1.25 + 1.25
1996	1,000,000	5.30	100	$1/8 + 1/8$	1.25 + 1.25
1997	1,000,000	5.50	100	$1/4 + 1/8$	2.50 + 1.25
1998	1,000,000	5.65	100	$3/8 + 1/4$	3.75 + 2.50
1999	1,000,000	5.80	100	$1/2 + 1/4$	5.00 + 2.50
2000	1,000,000	5.90	100	$1/2 + 1/4$	5.00 + 2.50
2001	1,000,000	6.05	100	$1/2 + 1/4$	5.00 + 2.50
2002	1,000,000	6.15	100	$5/8 + 1/2$	6.25 + 5.00
2003	1,000,000	6.25	100	$5/8 + 1/2$	6.25 + 5.00

significantly higher than the $2.50 per $1,000 bond total takedown for the 1995 maturity. The profit margin for the longer maturity is obviously bigger. Thus, if a syndicate member sells bonds from the 2003 maturity, it would receive a discount from the listed reoffering price (par) equal to $11.25 ($6.25 concession + $5.00 additional takedown) for every $1,000 bond taken down versus $2.50 for every $1,000 bond taken down from the 1995 maturity. A nonmember firm taking down bonds in the 2003 maturity would receive the $6.25 (concession) discount from par for every $1,000 bond versus $1.25 for every $1,000 bond from the 1995 maturity.

NEGOTIATING THE UNDERWRITING SPREAD

The breakdown of underwriting spread just shown is for illustrative purposes only. It is not intended to represent an ideal spread distribution. Actual spreads vary between issues due to differences in credit quality, maturities, debt service payment sources, tax status, and a host of other factors. Two issues of the same size sold at the same time will not necessarily have the same spread. Two issues with the same spread will not necessarily have the same distribution of spread among component parts. The following section offers suggestions for negotiating proposed underwriting spreads.

Setting Spread Parameters in the RFP

One approach used by some issuers to control costs, while retaining the flexibility to adjust the spread to reflect the underwriter's performance in the sale, is to set spread parameters in the Request for Proposals (RFP). Under this approach, the issuer requires underwriters to indicate an estimate for each component of the spread in their responses to the RFP. Given that the takedown and underwriting fee are closely tied to the interest rate pricing which occurs much later, it is sometimes unrealistic to expect a concrete estimate for these two components. However, the issuer can obtain fairly sound estimates for the management fee and expense components. To hold the underwriters true to these estimates, the issuer specifies in the RFP that the estimates will be considered as bids and the selected underwriter's bids will function as caps for the management fee and expense components. Thus, while the issuer may want to leave final spread negotiations until closer to the sale date, it can set the parameters for at least the management fee and expense components of the spread based on the underwriter responses to the RFP.

Management Fee

When negotiating the management fee, issuers should consider the level and the quality of the services provided by the underwriter. An underwriter that helps the issuer structure a complex offering might merit a higher management fee. However, for a straightforward issue, the management fee is often waived or nominal. If financial advisory tasks such as developing the financing plan, structuring the issue, and obtaining a rating are performed in-house or by a financial advisor, the issuer should also seek a waiver or nominal management fee.

Expenses

It is important that issuers hold underwriters accountable for expense reimbursements. At the outset, the issuer and the underwriter should identify which expenses are eligible for reimbursement. The issuer should require the underwriter to provide a line-item listing of reimbursable expenses, including underwriter's counsel fees. Issuers should not be shy about asking underwriters for explanations of questionable items.

Underwriting fee

Issuers should not agree to pay any underwriting fee unless, during the pricing process, there is evidence of the risk that the underwriter cannot sell all the bonds at the listed reoffering price. Hence, when negotiating the underwriting fee, issuers should monitor the progress of the bond orders. If the underwriter receives orders for a significant portion of the bonds by the end of the initial order period, the issuer should look for a nominal, if any, underwriting fee. If all of the bonds have been presold to investors during the initial order period, the underwriter faces no inventory risk and should not be paid an underwriting fee. Issuers should also be aware that some managers are willing to commit their capital to a successful sale, even if it means underwriting a portion or all of the issue. Thus, issuers should always explore the possibility of waiving the underwriting fee at the outset of the negotiations for every offering.

Takedown

Obtaining orders at market rates while paying the lowest possible takedown is the issuer's challenge. However, a singleminded pursuit for the lowest takedown without regard to the interest rate pricing, would not necessarily serve the issuer's interest. The takedown provides an incentive for the sales force to aggressively market competitively priced bonds. If the takedown is set too low, there is less motivation for the sales force to find investors willing to accept the issuer's rates. Thus, when maturities are *undersubscribed* (not receiving sufficient orders) during the initial order period, the issuer should recognize that it may be able to generate adequate orders for some of the undersubscribed maturities by increasing the takedowns, rather than raising the rates. If the issuer insists on keeping the takedowns at low levels, the only option would be to raise the rates to generate sufficient orders for the undersubscribed maturities. On the other hand, when maturities are *oversubscribed* (receiving more orders than there are bonds available) during the initial order period, the issuer should not be shy about pursuing reductions in the interest rates or the takedowns for those maturities.

Techniques to Lower Municipal Borrowing Costs

Manly W. Mumford

Before the adoption of the laws and regulations governing the investment of tax-exempt bond proceeds in taxable obligations (the "arbitrage laws"), a city could often earn more interest than it paid on unnecessarily borrowed funds by investing in government bonds at a yield higher than the yield on its own bonds. Those days are gone. As a result of the restrictions on investment yield in the Internal Revenue Code, with minor exceptions, a city cannot obtain and keep the same net return on tax-exempt borrowed money that it pays out. Even though a city may invest at nearly the same yield as that which its lenders receive, it cannot recoup costs of issuance (other than credit enhancement charges) by investing at or above that yield. So the first order of the day is to determine whether, how much, when, and how to borrow. This article discusses methods of reducing borrowing costs in the absence of countervailing arbitrage profits.

DON'T BORROW

You don't have to pay interest on money you don't borrow. The phrase "pay as you go" has been used to suggest that a city should not borrow at all, but pay for its public improvements out of current funds. Such a notion appeals to taxpayers who compare the total principal and interest to be paid on a bond issue with the total cost of a project; the former can be twice the latter. It does not appeal to taxpayers who compare this year's tax bill with last year's.

In theory, a city could establish a revolving fund into which money would be deposited each year and invested without regard to the arbitrage laws. When public improvements were needed, the city would withdraw sufficient money from this fund. I know of a few municipal utility operations that work this way; but I know of no general-purpose governments that operate this way. Perhaps this disparity exists because the people who run cities are elected, while most of those who run utility operations are not; more likely, it stems from a more relaxed public attitude toward utility bills than toward taxes: taxpayers do not like the notion of accumulating a large surplus to pay for future improvements not yet identified, but utility rate payers are more likely to consider the practice a sound business decision.

As a matter of governmental philosophy, the practice of borrowing for large projects has the benefit of causing the generation of people who use the project to pay for it. To pay for a new public library out of current taxes places the burden on this year's taxpayers, nearly all of whom will be gone before the end of the library's useful life. Payments on a bond issue for that library will be made by future taxpayers, including some yet to be born, who will comprise its principal users.

BORROW LESS

When borrowing is unavoidable, it is best to borrow as little as possible (despite the feelings of those who

---

Reprinted from *Municipal Finance Journal* 12, no. 3 (1991): 13-31. By permission of Panel Publishers, Inc.

regard the bond issues on which they work as monuments to themselves—the bigger the better).

One technique for borrowing as little as possible is to apply the funds that would be used to pay the first installments of principal to the payment of project costs. Exhibit 1 demonstrates this technique: the $4,315,000 that would otherwise be used to pay the first three years' principal saves $438,500 in interest that would otherwise fall due on a $50,000,000 bond issue. (If this amount of interest were to be capitalized, the size of the bond issue would have to be correspondingly increased.) This technique has value in the case of bonds, such as utility revenue bonds, that are paid from the same source as the money used to pay for the improvements. In the case of bonds payable from property taxes, however, non-borrowed payment of project costs often must be made from the general fund, while the payment of principal and interest on the bond issue is made from a special tax; thus the $4,315,000 may reduce by a like sum the amount that can be expended from the general fund for other purposes during those three years.

In addition, the city benefits from the fact that this unborrowed $4,315,000 can be invested—with no restrictions on yield or requirements for rebate under the arbitrage laws—until spent. It might occur to a finance director to hold such general fund money until the last payments fall due under a construction contract, investing it at the highest yield available, while using bond proceeds to pay the first payments to come due. Before doing so, the finance director should consult with counsel to consider the effect of Section 1.148-8T(e)(1) of the arbitrage regulations: "If an investment is allocated to more than one source, all payments and receipts with respect to the investment shall be allocated ratably to each source." Further, if, under prevalent market conditions, the city cannot find short-term investments bearing a yield as high as the yield on its long-term bonds, the absence of yield restriction or rebate requirement is of little value.

BORROW LATER

Use Funds On Hand First

Every month for which the delivery of a bond issue is postponed (without lengthening the life of the issue) is a month by which the issue is shortened and for which the city need pay no interest. Thus, to the extent that funds on hand (such as the general fund money mentioned in the previous section) are used to make early payments under a construction contract and the delivery of a bond issue is correspondingly delayed, the interest on the entire issue is eliminated for the period of that delay. Under most market conditions, a shorter average life means a lower average interest rate. There is always a risk that the market may get worse for the issuer during this delay, but there is also the possibility that it will improve. Absent some peculiar factor (such as a maximum voted interest rate that cannot be met if the market worsens), a city might proceed on the assumption that the risk and the possibility cancel each other out.

Because expenditures on a project generally follow a rough bell curve (low at the beginning, high in the middle, and low at the end of the construction period) the temporary use of a relatively small amount of funds on hand at the beginning can have a relatively large effect in postponing the time when borrowed money must be spent. Exhibit 2 shows that the early expenditure of $4,118,336 in current funds in anticipation of bond proceeds can postpone for nine months the need to borrow the $50,000,000 project cost. Under the debt service schedule in Exhibit 1, the interest accruing on the issue of $50,000,000 for that period would have been $2,536,144. Yet a city bears some risk in going ahead with a project before issuing the bonds to complete it: If, for example, litigation prevents the delivery of the bonds after the city has spent general fund money and has entered into contracts to be paid with bond proceeds, a sudden inability to issue bonds could be embarrassing. Another consideration is that contractors may choose not to submit their lowest possible bids on a project before the bond proceeds are in the bank because of the risk that bond proceeds may not be available when payments fall due. In most cases, after the necessary bond referendum has passed, any substantial risk of this nature should be foreseeable.

An issuer that postpones a bond issue may qualify under Internal Revenue Code Section 148(f)(4)(iv), which exempts excess yield on investments in the construction fund from rebate, by shortening the time between the issuance of the bonds and the expenditure of the bond proceeds. This exemption may apply if

1. various percentages of the proceeds of a construction bond issue are spent no later than provided in this section,

Exhibit 1: *Apply to Project Costs Funds Conventionally Used for First Three Installments of Principal*

	Conventional Bond Issue					Revised Bond Issue				
Year	Principal	Rate (%)	Interest	Debt Service	Year	Principal	Rate (%)	Interest	Debt Service	Paid Directly
1	$ 1,370,000	5.00	$ 3,381,525	$ 4,751,525	1			$ 3,165,775	$ 3,165,775	$1,370,000
2	$ 1,435,000	5.00	$ 3,313,025	$ 4,748,025	2			$ 3,165,775	$ 3,165,775	$1,435,000
3	$ 1,510,000	5.00	$ 3,241,275	$ 4,751,275	3			$ 3,165,775	$ 3,165,775	$1,510,000
4	$ 1,585,000	5.50	$ 3,165,775	$ 4,750,775	4	$ 1,585,000	5.50	$ 3,165,775	$ 4,750,775	$ 0
5	$ 1,670,000	5.50	$ 3,078,600	$ 4,748,600	5	$ 1,670,000	5.50	$ 3,078,600	$ 4,748,600	$ 0
6	$ 1,760,000	5.50	$ 2,986,750	$ 4,746,750	6	$ 1,760,000	5.50	$ 2,986,750	$ 4,746,750	$ 0
7	$ 1,860,000	6.00	$ 2,889,950	$ 4,749,950	7	$ 1,860,000	6.00	$ 2,889,950	$ 4,749,950	$ 0
8	$ 1,970,000	6.00	$ 2,778,350	$ 4,748,350	8	$ 1,970,000	6.00	$ 2,778,350	$ 4,748,350	$ 0
9	$ 2,090,000	6.00	$ 2,660,150	$ 4,750,150	9	$ 2,090,000	6.00	$ 2,660,150	$ 4,750,150	$ 0
10	$ 2,215,000	6.50	$ 2,534,750	$ 4,749,750	10	$ 2,215,000	6.50	$ 2,534,750	$ 4,749,750	$ 0
11	$ 2,360,000	6.50	$ 2,390,775	$ 4,750,775	11	$ 2,360,000	6.50	$ 2,390,775	$ 4,750,775	$ 0
12	$ 2,510,000	6.50	$ 2,237,375	$ 4,747,375	12	$ 2,510,000	6.50	$ 2,237,375	$ 4,747,375	$ 0
13	$ 2,675,000	7.00	$ 2,074,225	$ 4,749,225	13	$ 2,675,000	7.00	$ 2,074,225	$ 4,749,225	$ 0
14	$ 2,860,000	7.00	$ 1,886,975	$ 4,746,975	14	$ 2,860,000	7.00	$ 1,886,975	$ 4,746,975	$ 0
15	$ 3,065,000	7.00	$ 1,686,775	$ 4,751,775	15	$ 3,065,000	7.00	$ 1,686,775	$ 4,751,775	$ 0
16	$ 3,280,000	7.50	$ 1,472,225	$ 4,752,225	16	$ 3,280,000	7.50	$ 1,472,225	$ 4,752,225	$ 0
17	$ 3,525,000	7.50	$ 1,226,225	$ 4,751,225	17	$ 3,525,000	7.50	$ 1,226,225	$ 4,751,225	$ 0
18	$ 3,790,000	7.50	$ 961,850	$ 4,751,850	18	$ 3,790,000	7.50	$ 961,850	$ 4,751,850	$ 0
19	$ 4,070,000	8.00	$ 677,600	$ 4,747,600	19	$ 4,070,000	8.00	$ 677,600	$ 4,747,600	$ 0
20	$ 4,400,000	8.00	$ 352,000	$ 4,752,000	20	$ 4,400,000	8.00	$ 352,000	$ 4,752,000	$ 0
TOTAL	$50,000,000		$44,996,175	$94,996,175		$45,685,000		$44,557,675	$90,242,675	$4,315,000

$90,242,675 Debt Service, Revised Issue
 4,315,000   Paid Directly
$94,557,675 Total
($94,996,175) Debt Service, Conventional
($ 438,500) Saving

2. all but a reasonable retainage of not over 5 percent is spent within two years after the issuance of the bonds, and
3. the retainage is spent within three years of issuance.

Whether this exemption has any value for an issuer depends on whether short-term investments that bear a yield higher than the yield on the bond issue can be found.

Exhibit 2: *Hypothetical Drawdown Schedule*

Month	Expenditures	Cumulative
1	$ 200,000	$ 200,000
2	$ 239,535	$ 439,535
3	$ 286,884	$ 726,419
4	$ 343,593	$ 1,070,012
5	$ 411,512	$ 1,481,524
6	$ 492,857	$ 1,974,380
7	$ 590,281	$ 2,564,662
8	$ 706,964	$ 3,271,625
9	$ 846,711	$ 4,118,336
10	$1,014,083	$ 5,132,419
11	$1,214,539	$ 6,346,958
12	$1,454,620	$ 7,801,578
13	$1,742,159	$ 9,543,737
14	$2,086,536	$11,630,273
15	$2,498,987	$14,129,260
16	$2,992,969	$17,122,229
17	$3,584,597	$20,706,826
18	$4,293,174	$25,000,000
19	$4,293,174	$29,293,174
20	$3,584,597	$32,877,771
21	$2,992,969	$35,870,740
22	$2,498,987	$38,369,727
23	$2,086,536	$40,456,263
24	$1,742,159	$42,198,422
25	$1,454,620	$43,653,042
26	$1,214,539	$44,867,581
27	$1,014,083	$45,881,664
28	$ 846,711	$46,728,375
29	$ 706,964	$47,435,338
30	$ 590,281	$48,025,619
31	$ 492,857	$48,518,476
32	$ 411,512	$48,929,988
33	$ 343,593	$49,273,581
34	$ 286,884	$49,560,465
35	$ 239,535	$49,800,000
36	$ 200,000	$50,000,000

One provision of state law that creates a trap for the unwary provides that a contract with a public body is unenforceable unless, when the contract is made, the funds to pay it are in hand. See, for example, *Crystal City Independent School District, Appellant v. Bank of Dallas,* 727 SW 2d 762 Court of Appeals of Texas, Fifth District (1987).

Reimburse Internal Borrowing

One method of postponing borrowing without depriving the issuer of access to the funds used to pay the early installments due under the construction contract is to advance the money from an account that will not need it until after the bonds are issued. This account may be reimbursed, subsequently, from bond proceeds. Before implementing this practice, the issuer should do the following:

1. Make sure that reimbursement of sums advanced from such an account is one of the purposes for which bond proceeds can be spent under state law and under the bond documents.
2. Adopt a resolution (such as an inducement resolution common in conduit financing) of the governing body showing that the advance is made in anticipation of the proceeds of an identified bond issue to be delivered in the future.
3. Make sure that all requirements of the pertinent regulations proposed by the Department of the Treasury and the Internal Revenue Service have been or will be complied with. These government agencies may promulgate regulations designed to prevent issuances of tax-exempt bonds that ostensibly are for the purpose of reimbursing advances, but that actually are for buying high-yield investments.

If the account from which an advance is made can be invested at a higher yield than that of the bonds, the advance of funds appears to lose rather than save money; but if the result of the advance is to postpone the issuance of the entire bond issue (without extending maturities), then the amount of money saved includes not only the amount of the advance, but also the interest on the entire bond issue for the time of the postponement.

An additional advantage of waiting until a project is wholly or partly completed before issuing bonds lies in Code Section 148(f)(3)(B). This Section makes it unnecessary to rebate excess yield on investments of bond proceeds that are invested for a temporary period of not more than six months pending completion of the project.

Case Law. There is a body of case law that sheds light on the reimbursement of expenditures from bond proceeds. *Chapin v. Town of Lincoln,* 217 Mass. 236, 104 NE 745 (Sup Jud Ct 1914) affirmed an injunction against the issuance of bonds to reimburse expenditures on a water system made without evidence of intent to reimburse from bond proceeds. *Winterfield v. Town of Palm Beach,* 455 So 2d 359 (Fla Sup Ct 1984) affirmed the validation of a voted bond issue when part of the proceeds were to be used to reimburse prior expenditures under circumstances that indicated an intent to reimburse. *Manning v. Fiscal Court of Jefferson County,* 405 SW 2d 755 (Ky Ct App 1966) and *White v. City of Hickman,* 415 SW 379 (Ky Ct App 1967) involved the issuance of industrial development bonds by political subdivisions to pay for factories located therein; *Manning* held void bonds to reimburse the factory owner after the factory was built without the promise of such financing; *White* upheld reimbursement of sums expended in reliance on an expectation of such financing, as did *State v. Kemp,* 151 SE 2d 680 (W Va Sup Ct App 1966) and *Nuessner v. McNair,* 157 SE 2d 410 (SC Sup Ct 1967). *Wilson v. Board of County Commissioners,* 273 Md 30, 327 A 2d 488 (Ct App 1974) upheld reimbursement of funds spent by a corporation for pollution control purposes before the effective date of the act authorizing the bonds. The fact that the more liberal cases involved conduit financing should not be disregarded. It is predictable that a state court will be more relaxed in a case involving conduit financing than in a case involving conventional financing; the need to protect the right of the taxpayer to bear none but those debts incurred for a lawful purpose disappears when the user of the facilities provides all the money to pay the bonds.

Treasury (IRS) Regulations have recently been proposed, as Sections 1.103-17 and 1.103-18 to prevent the issuance of tax-exempt bonds ostensibly to reimburse advances but really to buy high-yielding investments. In general, these regulations require (1) that the issuer formally declare its intent to reimburse an expenditure; (2) that the declaration be made within two years before the expenditure; (3) that a reimbursement allocation of bond proceeds be made after the expenditure is made but not later than one year after the latter of the date of expenditure or the date that property acquired is placed in service; and (4) that the economic life of property acquired by the expenditure is at least one year.

It is possible for cities to direct the payment of project costs from funds other than those earmarked for capital expenditures without incurring undue attention from the IRS or the state courts. The municipality should take the precaution of making such payments only in anticipation of a specifically designated bond issuance on which the city has already taken some sort of official action. If, however, the advance comes from a fund earmarked for capital expenditures that is expected to return a higher yield than that of the bonds, the response from the IRS may be quite different. Regardless of the city's intentions when the advance is issued, the fact that the bond proceeds are invested at a higher yield after being used to reimburse the advance is likely to generate unwelcome attention from the Service.

Bond Anticipation Notes

One way to postpone a bond issue is to issue bond anticipation notes, payable from bond proceeds and running for a year or two pending the delivery of the definitive bond issue. Since they are short-term instruments, these notes generally bear a lower interest rate than long-term bonds. Bond anticipation notes would be issued more frequently if the issuer could be sure that interest rates on long-term bonds would not rise during the interim. In one case, a city accustomed to paying 3 or 4 percent interest in the 1960s decided to issue bond anticipation notes when interest rates rose to 5 percent. The city planned to pay the anticipation notes from proceeds of bonds it would issue when long-term rates returned to 4 percent; but the rates failed to meet the city's expectations and it had to issue 6 percent bonds to retire the notes. Bond anticipation notes have the disadvantage of forcing the issuer to issue bonds—or to roll the notes over (if permitted by law)—at a time or under conditions that the issuer might wish to avoid. If a city wants to take temporary advantage of the lower interest rates available for short-term borrowing, it should consider issuing floating-rate bonds and retaining the right to fix the permanent rate in the future.

FLOATING-RATE DEBT

Although business corporations that issue bonds (whether or not through political subdivisions acting as conduits) are active in issuing floating-rate instruments of indebtedness, municipalities tend to pursue this practice less aggressively when borrowing on their own behalf. Usually a floating-rate obligation bears interest at a lower rate than a fixed-rate obligation issued at the same time; if market rates subsequently rise, the floating rate may exceed the yield of the fixed-rate obligation; if market rates fall, the floating rate drops far below the yield of the fixed-rate obligation and the issuer gets a windfall.

Bond dealers offer a variety of floating-rate bond issues to suit different market conditions. Variations may include differences in the method of determining the rate, in the period during which a rate remains constant, and in the conditions, if any, under which the issuer can fix a permanent rate or under which a holder can require a third party to purchase the bonds ("put bonds").

One important reason why cities may choose not to issue floating-rate bonds is that under a floating rate, the issuer's interest payments during the ensuing year cannot be accurately predicted. This uncertainty causes problems for a city's preparation of its annual budget and determination of its tax levy or utility rate structure. State laws can also raise obstacles to the issuance of floating-rate bonds, particularly if they impose maximum legal rates of payment or if they require the bonds to be voted under a proposition that fixes a maximum interest rate. Utility revenue bonds are typically issued under documents that permit the issuance of additional bonds on a parity, if adjusted historical earnings exceed some multiple (usually 1.25) of future debt service on the outstanding and new parity bonds. This test is hard to meet when the issuer can't tell what its future annual interest cost will be. Another impediment in the issuance of floating-rate bonds is that the fee charged by the bank that writes a letter of credit to support a liquidity facility (whether or not it constitutes a "guaranty" under Temporary Regulations Section 1.148-3T(b)(12) pertaining to arbitrage bonds) for "put" bonds may not be payable from taxes levied to pay bonds. Such obstacles tend to discourage competition in the bond market, for only the ingenious and industrious persist in surmounting them.

Budget and Tax Levy

An issuer of floating-rate bonds can budget for the floating rate of the bond by setting a maximum rate above which the interest on the bond may not float. The budget is calculated to assume that maximum rate; any money left over in the interest account because of a lower rate during a given year remains in the account to reduce the following year's budget. In the following year, the issuer again assumes that the interest will be at its maximum all year long. This procedure can require a high first year's budget for interest, so any payment of principal may be omitted from that year's debt service schedule. See Exhibit 3a.

There is an alternative that can provide the issuer budget a constant amount for debt service every year; this constant amount is sufficient to cover interest at the maximum permitted rate with little budgeted for principal. Each year, the finance director is directed to call for the redemption of as many bonds as possible with the amount in the debt service fund that exceeds what is required for interest payments. Exhibit 3b shows that such a provision has a compounding effect: each year's redemptions diminish the amount of principal on which interest will be paid in all future years. The market does not welcome long-term bonds that are immediately redeemable, but the issuance of such bonds at a modest discount coupled with a par call should counteract any resulting hostility: a holder whose 20-year bond is redeemed at the end of one year would get a higher than market yield.

Another approach is to schedule serial bonds to mature annually in amounts less than the issuer believes will be retired and to redeem additional bonds prior to maturity in direct order of maturities so that an investor buying a 10- or 20-year bond will not be taken out in the first few years.

Put Bonds

The floating-rate bonds that bear the lowest rate of interest are usually "put" bonds. These are bonds that can be tendered to an agent for purchase at par at regular intervals. To ensure the availability of funds for such purchases, a bank writes a letter of credit to the agent to confirm sufficient funds for the purchase of all tendered bonds. A bond dealer undertakes to remarket the tendered bonds under an agreement with the issuer under which the dealer will set

Exhibit 3a: *Budget Fixed Amount for Debt Service on Variable-Rate Bonds and Apply Unused Amounts to Reduce Next Year's Tax Levy* (Assume that the maximum permitted interest rate is 10 percent.)

Year	Maturing Principal	Effective Rate (%)	Interest	Princ. + Int. ($5,000,000 fixed amount)	Year-End Bonds Outstanding	Carryover	Tax Levy	Present Value @ 7.00%
					$50,000,000			
1	$ 0	6.90	$ 3,450,000	$ 3,450,000	$50,000,000	$1,550,000	$ 5,000,000	$ 4,672,897
2	$ 1,335,000	7.20	$ 3,600,000	$ 4,935,000	$48,665,000	$ 65,000	$ 3,450,000	$ 3,013,364
3	$ 1,430,000	7.00	$ 3,406,550	$ 4,836,550	$47,235,000	$ 163,450	$ 4,935,000	$ 4,028,430
4	$ 1,530,000	6.70	$ 3,164,745	$ 4,694,745	$45,705,000	$ 305,255	$ 4,836,550	$ 3,689,781
5	$ 1,640,000	7.50	$ 3,427,875	$ 5,067,875	$44,065,000	($ 67,875)	$ 4,694,745	$ 3,347,288
6	$ 1,755,000	7.20	$ 3,172,680	$ 4,927,680	$42,310,000	$ 72,320	$ 5,067,875	$ 3,376,939
7	$ 1,875,000	6.50	$ 2,750,150	$ 4,625,150	$40,435,000	$ 374,850	$ 4,927,680	$ 3,068,711
8	$ 2,005,000	5.50	$ 2,223,925	$ 4,228,925	$38,430,000	$ 771,075	$ 4,625,150	$ 2,691,879
9	$ 2,150,000	6.20	$ 2,382,660	$ 4,532,660	$36,280,000	$ 467,340	$ 4,228,925	$ 2,300,255
10	$ 2,300,000	6.60	$ 2,394,480	$ 4,694,480	$33,980,000	$ 305,520	$ 4,532,660	$ 2,304,175
11	$ 2,460,000	7.00	$ 2,378,600	$ 4,838,600	$31,520,000	$ 161,400	$ 4,694,480	$ 2,230,314
12	$ 2,630,000	7.40	$ 2,332,480	$ 4,962,480	$28,890,000	$ 37,520	$ 4,838,600	$ 2,148,396
13	$ 2,815,000	7.80	$ 2,253,420	$ 5,068,420	$26,075,000	($ 68,420)	$ 4,962,480	$ 2,059,253
14	$ 3,015,000	7.90	$ 2,059,925	$ 5,074,925	$23,060,000	($ 74,925)	$ 5,068,420	$ 1,965,621
15	$ 3,225,000	8.00	$ 1,844,800	$ 5,069,800	$19,835,000	($ 69,800)	$ 5,074,925	$ 1,839,386
16	$ 3,450,000	7.00	$ 1,388,450	$ 4,838,450	$16,385,000	$ 161,550	$ 5,069,800	$ 1,717,317
17	$ 3,690,000	6.00	$ 983,100	$ 4,673,100	$12,695,000	$ 326,900	$ 4,838,450	$ 1,531,729
18	$ 3,950,000	5.90	$ 749,005	$ 4,699,005	$ 8,745,000	$ 300,995	$ 4,673,100	$ 1,382,602
19	$ 4,225,000	5.50	$ 480,975	$ 4,705,975	$ 4,520,000	$ 294,025	$ 4,699,005	$ 1,299,314
20	$ 4,520,000	5.00	$ 226,000	$ 4,746,000	$ 0	$ 254,000	$ 4,451,975	$ 1,150,475
TOTAL	$50,000,000		$44,669,820	$94,669,820			$94,669,820	$49,818,126

Note that in years 6, 14, 15, and 16 a levy over $5,000,000 is required by higher-than-anticipated effective rates in the immediately preceding years combined with the fixed maturity schedule. Negative carryovers represent temporary borrowing to meet current debt service.

the rate of interest until the next tender date at the lowest rate at which the bonds can be sold at par. Although the letter of credit is primarily considered an assurance of liquidity, the bank does take a credit risk when it agrees to provide funds for the agent to buy them at par. The holder may tender bonds because he or she is dissatisfied with the newly set rate, needs the invested money for some other purpose, or doubts the credit of the issuer. Thus the bank's fee is likely to be substantial. Courts have not yet faced the question of whether a special tax dedicated to the payment of bonds can be used to pay such a fee; the question has been covered by statute in Arizona under Arizona Revised Statutes Section 9-529 C, which provides specific authority for political subdivisions to employ various practices common to put bond and other variable-rate financing.

Most of the floating-rate municipal bonds that have been issued comprised conduit financing: the money to pay the interest on them comes from business corporations. Since the Tax Reform Act of 1986, there have been fewer of these issues, so the supply of variable-rate bonds available on the market is likely to decline. This will result in increased demand for such paper, especially to feed tax-exempt money market funds; political subdivisions that issue this type of bond will find the interest they must pay attractively low compared to other tax-exempt rates.

Public Sale of Floating-Rate Bonds

Many states have enacted laws that require their bonds of their political subdivisions to be sold at advertised public sales. Typically, the winning bidder is the one that bids the lowest interest cost for an is-

Exhibit 3b: *Budget Fixed Amount for Debt Service on Variable-Rate Bonds and Apply Amounts Not Needed for Interest to Redeem Bonds*

Year	Effective Rate (%)	Available for Debt Service ($5,000,000 fixed amount)	Interest Paid	Bonds Retired	Year-End Bonds Outstanding	Carry-over	Tax Levy	Present Value @ 7.00%
					$50,000,000			
1	6.90	$ 5,000,000	$ 3,450,000	$ 1,545,000	$48,455,000	$5,000	$ 5,000,000	$ 4,672,897
2	7.20	$ 5,005,000	$ 3,488,760	$ 1,515,000	$46,940,000	$1,240	$ 5,000,000	$ 4,367,194
3	7.00	$ 5,001,240	$ 3,285,800	$ 1,715,000	$45,225,000	$ 440	$ 5,000,000	$ 4,081,489
4	6.70	$ 5,000,440	$ 3,030,075	$ 1,970,000	$43,255,000	$ 365	$ 5,000,000	$ 3,814,476
5	7.50	$ 5,000,365	$ 3,244,125	$ 1,755,000	$41,500,000	$1,240	$ 5,000,000	$ 3,564,931
6	7.20	$ 5,001,240	$ 2,988,000	$ 2,010,000	$39,490,000	$3,240	$ 5,000,000	$ 3,331,711
7	6.50	$ 5,003,240	$ 2,566,850	$ 2,435,000	$37,055,000	$1,390	$ 5,000,000	$ 3,113,749
8	5.50	$ 5,001,390	$ 2,038,025	$ 2,960,000	$34,095,000	$3,365	$ 5,000,000	$ 2,910,046
9	6.20	$ 5,003,365	$ 2,113,890	$ 2,885,000	$31,210,000	$4,475	$ 5,000,000	$ 2,719,669
10	6.60	$ 5,004,475	$ 2,059,860	$ 2,940,000	$28,270,000	$4,615	$ 5,000,000	$ 2,541,746
11	7.00	$ 5,004,615	$ 1,978,900	$ 3,025,000	$25,245,000	$ 715	$ 5,000,000	$ 2,375,464
12	7.40	$ 5,000,715	$ 1,868,130	$ 3,130,000	$22,115,000	$2,585	$ 5,000,000	$ 2,220,060
13	7.80	$ 5,002,585	$ 1,724,970	$ 3,275,000	$18,840,000	$2,615	$ 5,000,000	$ 2,074,822
14	7.90	$ 5,002,615	$ 1,488,360	$ 3,510,000	$15,330,000	$4,255	$ 5,000,000	$ 1,939,086
15	8.00	$ 5,004,255	$ 1,226,400	$ 3,775,000	$11,555,000	$2,855	$ 5,000,000	$ 1,812,230
16	7.00	$ 5,002,855	$ 808,850	$ 4,190,000	$ 7,365,000	$4,005	$ 5,000,000	$ 1,693,673
17	6.00	$ 5,004,005	$ 441,900	$ 4,560,000	$ 2,805,000	$2,105	$ 5,000,000	$ 1,582,872
18	5.90	$ 2,970,495	$ 165,495	$ 2,805,000	$ 0	$ 0	$ 2,970,495	$ 878,862
19	5.50	$ 0	$ 0	$ 0	$ 0	$ 0	$ 0	$ 0
20	5.00	$ 0	$ 0	$ 0	$ 0	$ 0	$ 0	$ 0
TOTAL		$88,012,895	$37,968,390	$50,000,000			$87,970,495	$49,694,977

sue of predetermined size. This standard does not work in the sale of floating-rate bonds, because the rates of interest to be borne by the bonds throughout their lives can be determined only for the initial period; after that it is impossible to tell whether one scheme or another will produce the best rate. The only way to circumvent this problem is to require all bidders to accept the same predetermined floating-rate plan: a restriction that would prevent bond dealers from utilizing their best plans.

There is an as yet untried technique that may be workable. It entails that a city determine in advance the debt service (including bank and fixed-maximum remarketing agent fees) to be paid each year for the life of the bonds; then the city advertises on the basis that the winning bidder will be the one that offers to buy the greatest principal amount of bonds payable from that debt service. The bidder can utilize whatever combination of fixed-rate bonds, floating-rate bonds, and zero coupon bonds the bidder deems expedient. Although the city will not know the exact amount of its issue until the bonds are sold, it has a good estimate beforehand from its financial advisor, and it knows for certain what its debt service will be. Often the size of a bond issue is determined not by how much money the city needs for a single capital project of a determined size (since most cities have large numbers of projects to undertake when they can get the money to pay for them) but by how much debt service can be paid each year.

Caps and Floors

Almost any floating-rate measure used by a city will have to include a cap, or maximum rate of interest, on the bonds to protect the city against egregious rises in interest rates generally. The cap may be legally required by statute or by virtue of a stated maximum rate in the notice of election; it may be required by practical consideration such as the budgetary and other constraints mentioned previously. Although there is no legal reason to include a floor beneath which a floating interest rate will not fall, under certain market conditions such a floor helps to sell the bonds under more favorable terms than would otherwise be available; the risk that the cap will reduce an investor's return compared to the return in another market is offset by the possibility that the floor will keep the return above that which could be gotten elsewhere. The investor might then choose to trade the risk against the possibility in some other market by employing hedging techniques familiar to large banks and money managers.

Commercial Paper

Unlike most bonds, commercial paper is issued as a succession of series of instruments. Each series comprises instruments that run for periods that are not necessarily all the same length, depending on the judgment of the placement agent. No period exceeds 270 days. The paper is not sold to an underwriter, but is placed by a placement agent who judges the market at the time of marketing and sets one or more maturities and interest rates that he or she believes will provide the best borrowing opportunity for the issuer. Any instruments that are not retired at maturity are rolled over into new series. Interest rates for this type of paper are low, but issuing it entails delegating to the marketing agent a substantial amount of authority in setting maturities and interest rates, which may conflict with a statutory duty of the governing body to exercise its own judgment in determining maturity and interest rates. (In the case of commercial paper, such delegation would be necessary since city councils are overburdened enough without having to meet at irregular intervals to set maturities and interest rates every time a series of commercial paper is rolled over.) However, where state law permits its issuance, commercial paper can be a useful tool for some types of financing if the issuer can afford the risk that the paper may become marketable only at a higher interest rate than what the issuer is willing to pay. Commercial paper is sometimes used in conduit financing for business corporations, but cities seldom issue it for their own purposes. One possible use of commercial paper by cities may be as a means to finance current expenditures in anticipation of taxes and other revenues, thus enabling a city to coordinate the maturities with the receipt of tax collections.

At present, the availability and cost of the letters of credit needed to assure the liquidity and security of put bonds and commercial paper are less encouraging than in the past because of the current difficulties in the banking industry. A general improvement in the banking business should make such tools more attractive.

ZERO COUPON BONDS

A long-term bond that pays interest only at maturity or early redemption is called a zero coupon bond (sometimes called a capital appreciation bond). Generally, the redemption feature requires the issuer to pay the accreted value of a zero coupon bond (plus redemption premium if applicable) on redemption prior to maturity.

Under some market conditions (most notably a large difference between low short-term and high long-term rates), the inclusion of zero coupon bonds in the longer maturities of an issue can provide considerable savings for the issuer. If the issuer is willing to give up the right to call the zero coupon bonds for redemption prior to maturity (thus making it impossible to substitute lower interest rate bonds if the market improves), investors will accept a lower than market yield in exchange for the right to lock in perceived high yield (comprising yield on the principal plus yield on reinvested interest, compounded semiannually). Such bonds are popular with individual investors trying to save money for the college educations of their children; several states, including Illinois, have been successful in marketing zero coupon bonds as "college bonds" and selling them to this market.

It is not always economically worthwhile for a city to close off its option to call the long-term zero coupon bonds for redemption prior to maturity, however. In addition to giving the issuer the right to substitute lower interest rate bonds, the redemption feature provides an opportunity for amending covenants. The city must weigh the likelihood of such needs against the possible gains to be realized.

Even if an issuer decides to keep the redemption feature, however, the use of zero coupon bonds in the longer maturities is often advantageous in itself, because it diverts money from the payment of early interest on the long-term bonds to the retirement of additional principal in those early years, thus enlarging the proportion of short-term, low-interest bonds. Exhibit 4 compares a conventional $50,000,000 20-year

Exhibit 4: *Comparison of Conventional $50,000,000 Issue with One Containing Zero Coupons in Last Five Maturities* (Substitute (*i*) zero coupon bonds for last 5 years' debt service and (*ii*) additional principal and interest for interest payments on long-term conventional/bonds.)

Year	Original Principal	Additional Principal	Rate (%)	Interest	0 Percent Bonds Maturity Value	0 Percent Bonds Present Value	New Debt Service	Original Debt Service	Difference
0.5		$ 285,000	5.0	$ 1,352,838			$ 1,637,838	$ 1,690,763	($ 52,925)
1.0	$ 1,370,000	$ 290,000	5.0	$ 1,345,713			$ 3,005,713	$ 3,060,763	($ 55,050)
1.5		$ 300,000	5.0	$ 1,304,213			$ 1,604,213	$ 1,656,513	($ 52,300)
2.0	$ 1,435,000	$ 305,000	5.0	$ 1,296,713			$ 3,036,713	$ 3,091,513	($ 54,800)
2.5		$ 315,000	5.0	$ 1,253,213			$ 1,568,213	$ 1,620,638	($ 52,425)
3.0	$ 1,510,000	$ 320,000	5.0	$ 1,245,338			$ 3,075,338	$ 3,130,638	($ 55,300)
3.5		$ 330,000	5.0	$ 1,199,588			$ 1,529,588	$ 1,582,888	($ 53,300)
4.0	$ 1,585,000	$ 335,000	5.5	$ 1,191,338			$ 3,111,338	$ 3,167,888	($ 56,550)
4.5		$ 345,000	5.5	$ 1,138,538			$ 1,483,538	$ 1,539,300	($ 55,762)
5.0	$ 1,670,000	$ 355,000	5.5	$ 1,129,050			$ 3,154,050	$ 3,209,300	($ 55,250)
5.5		$ 365,000	5.5	$ 1,073,363			$ 1,438,363	$ 1,493,375	($ 55,012)
6.0	$ 1,760,000	$ 375,000	5.5	$ 1,063,325			$ 3,198,325	$ 3,253,375	($ 55,050)
6.5		$ 385,000	5.5	$ 1,004,613			$ 1,389,613	$ 1,444,975	($ 55,362)
7.0	$ 1,860,000	$ 400,000	6.0	$ 994,025			$ 3,254,025	$ 3,304,975	($ 50,950)
7.5		$ 410,000	6.0	$ 926,225			$ 1,336,225	$ 1,389,175	($ 52,950)
8.0	$ 1,970,000	$ 420,000	6.0	$ 913,925			$ 3,303,925	$ 3,359,175	($ 55,250)
8.5		$ 435,000	6.0	$ 842,225			$ 1,277,225	$ 1,330,075	($ 52,850)
9.0	$ 2,090,000	$ 445,000	6.0	$ 829,175			$ 3,364,175	$ 3,420,075	($ 55,900)
9.5		$ 460,000	6.0	$ 753,125			$ 1,213,125	$ 1,267,375	($ 54,250)
10.0	$ 2,215,000	$ 475,000	6.5	$ 739,325			$ 3,429,325	$ 3,482,375	($ 53,050)
10.5		$ 490,000	6.5	$ 651,900			$ 1,141,900	$ 1,195,388	($ 53,487)
11.0	$ 2,360,000	$ 505,000	6.5	$ 635,975			$ 3,500,975	$ 3,555,388	($ 54,412)
11.5		$ 520,000	6.5	$ 542,863			$ 1,062,863	$ 1,118,688	($ 55,825)
12.0	$ 2,510,000	$ 540,000	6.5	$ 525,963			$ 3,575,963	$ 3,628,688	($ 52,725)
12.5		$ 555,000	6.5	$ 426,838			$ 981,838	$ 1,037,113	($ 55,275)
13.0	$ 2,675,000	$ 575,000	7.0	$ 408,800			$ 3,658,800	$ 3,712,113	($ 53,313)
13.5		$ 595,000	7.0	$ 295,050			$ 890,050	$ 943,488	($ 53,437)
14.0	$ 2,860,000	$ 615,000	7.0	$ 274,225			$ 3,749,225	$ 3,803,488	($ 54,263)
14.5		$ 635,000	7.0	$ 152,600			$ 787,600	$ 843,388	($ 55,788)
15.0	$ 3,065,000	$ 660,000	7.0	$ 130,375			$ 3,855,375	$ 3,908,388	($ 53,013)
15.5		$ 0	7.5		$ 685,000	$ 218,806	$ 685,000	$ 736,113	($ 51,113)
16.0		$ 0	7.5		$ 3,960,000	$1,219,202	$ 3,960,000	$ 4,016,113	($ 56,113)
16.5		$ 0	7.5		$ 560,000	$ 166,181	$ 560,000	$ 613,113	($ 53,113)
17.0		$ 0	7.5		$ 4,085,000	$1,168,413	$ 4,085,000	$ 4,138,113	($ 53,113)
17.5		$ 0	7.5		$ 425,000	$ 117,167	$ 425,000	$ 480,925	($ 55,925)
18.0		$ 0	7.5		$ 4,215,000	$1,120,020	$ 4,215,000	$ 4,270,925	($ 55,925)
18.5		$ 0	8.0		$ 285,000	$ 66,775	$ 285,000	$ 338,800	($ 53,800)
19.0			8.0		$ 4,355,000	$ 981,118	$ 4,355,000	$ 4,408,800	($ 53,800)
19.5			8.0		$ 120,000	$ 25,994	$ 120,000	$ 176,000	($ 56,000)
20.0			8.0		$ 4,520,000	$ 941,466	$ 4,520,000	$ 4,576,000	($ 56,000)
TOTAL	$30,935,000	$13,040,000		$25,640,450	$23,210,000	$6,025,143	$92,825,450	$94,996,175	($2,170,725)

$30,935,000 Original Principal
13,040,000 Additional Principal
6,025,143 0% Bonds
$50,000,143 Principal Proceeds

bond issue with an issue that contains zero coupon bonds in the last five annual maturities. In the latter case, the diversion of debt service in years 1 through 15 results in saving over $100,000 per year in debt service, even though in both cases all bonds of the same maturity bear the same rate of interest. The conventional issue bears a yield of 7.08038 percent per annum, whereas the issue containing the zero coupon bonds yields 6.7890278 percent, a spread of nearly 30 basis points.

Exhibit 5 assumes that a city has issued a zero coupon bond that has a maturity value of $1,000,000

Exhibit 5: *Assume That 20-Year Zero Coupon Bond Is Refunded at End of 10th Year*

Year	Accreted Value @ 8.00000%	Refunding Issue in Year 10				Future Value in Year 20 @ 5.83135%
		Principal	Rate (%)	Interest	Total	
0.0	$ 208,289					
0.5	$ 216,621					
1.0	$ 225,285					
1.5	$ 234,297					
2.0	$ 243,669					
2.5	$ 253,415					
3.0	$ 263,552					
3.5	$ 274,094					
4.0	$ 285,058					
4.5	$ 296,460					
5.0	$ 308,319					
5.5	$ 320,651					
6.0	$ 333,477					
6.5	$ 346,817					
7.0	$ 360,689					
7.5	$ 375,117					
8.0	$ 390,121					
8.5	$ 405,726					
9.0	$ 421,955					
9.5	$ 438,834					
10.0	$ 456,387					
10.5	$ 474,642				$ 14,888	$ 14,868	$ 25,702
11.0	$ 493,628	$ 35,000	5.0	$ 14,868	$ 49,888	$ 83,687
11.5	$ 513,373			$ 14,013	$ 14,013	$ 22,840
12.0	$ 533,908	$ 40,000	5.5	$ 14,013	$ 54,013	$ 85,546
12.5	$ 555,265			$ 12,913	$ 12,913	$ 19,872
13.0	$ 577,475	$ 40,000	5.5	$ 12,913	$ 52,913	$ 79,122
13.5	$ 600,574			$ 11,813	$ 11,813	$ 17,163
14.0	$ 624,597	$ 45,000	6.0	$ 11,813	$ 56,813	$ 80,209
14.5	$ 649,581			$ 10,463	$ 10,463	$ 14,353
15.0	$ 675,564	$ 45,000	6.0	$ 10,463	$ 55,463	$ 73,929
15.5	$ 702,587			$ 9,113	$ 9,113	$ 11,802
16.0	$ 730,690	$ 50,000	6.0	$ 9,113	$ 59,113	$ 74,393
16.5	$ 759,918			$ 7,613	$ 7,613	$ 9,309
17.0	$ 790,315	$ 50,000	6.5	$ 7,613	$ 57,613	$ 68,455
17.5	$ 821,927			$ 5,988	$ 5,988	$ 6,913
18.0	$ 854,804	$ 55,000	6.5	$ 5,988	$ 60,988	$ 68,417
18.5	$ 888,996			$ 4,200	$ 4,200	$ 4,578
19.0	$ 924,556	$ 60,000	7.0	$ 4,200	$ 64,200	$ 67,998
19.5	$ 961,538			$ 2,100	$ 2,100	$ 2,161
20.0	$1,000,000	$ 60,000	7.0	$ 2,100	$ 62,100	$ 62,100
TOTAL		$480,000		$171,313	$651,313	$852,848

and bears a yield of 8 percent compounded semi-annually. The city has received a price of $208,289 for this bond and determines to refund this bond at the end of the 10th year, when the accreted value has reached $456,387 and market rates have declined to those shown in the example. The size of the refunding bond issue is calculated as follows:

Accreted value:	$456,387
2 percent premium:	9,128
2.5 percent costs:	11,936
Rounding:	2,549
Issue size:	$480,000

The total principal and interest on that refunding bond issue (if issued as current interest bonds) would be $651,313; the future value of those payments compounded semi-annually at 5.83135 percent per annum (the combined yield on the refunding bonds) would be $852,848 at the end of year 20, resulting in a savings measured at $147,152 future value in that year. If, instead of making the zero coupon bond subject to redemption, the issuer could borrow the same $208,289 by issuing a non-callable zero coupon 20-year bond in the maturity amount of $852,848 (thus yielding 7.17395 percent per annum compounded semiannually), doing so would effect the same future value savings as exercising the redemption option in year 10 and issuing refunding bonds at the interest rates shown in the example. If the initial zero coupon bond is part of an issue that advance refunds bonds issued after 1985, it cannot be advance refunded with tax-exempt bonds under Code Section 149(d)(3)(A); only a current refunding of the zero coupon bond can be accomplished, and then only when it is redeemable under its terms or with consent of the holder. However, if it is issued for new money, the bond can probably be advance refunded if interest rates fall to levels low enough to make such refunding worthwhile before the first redemption date. This opportunity for an advance refunding would increase the value of an option to redeem the bond, and should be considered in determining how much reduction in yield justifies issuing a nonredeemable bond.

CONCLUSION

Each of the techniques described in this article—not borrowing, borrowing less, borrowing later, floating rates, and zero coupon bonds—is useful in certain circumstances. The question of when to use each of these techniques is one for experienced financial experts; none of the techniques is a substitute for sound judgment based on experience and study. Nevertheless, when used appropriately, any one of them can save enough money to make its use worthwhile.

Types and Purposes of Lease Financing

This article reviews different types of tax-exempt leases in which state and local governments participate. It discusses how the different types of leases are structured, who is involved in them, and how cash flows within them.

A review will also be presented of master leases and lease pools—arrangements that help lessees acquire, on a single financing, assets of different types or that permit two or more lessees to combine their financing needs in one transaction. Figures (flowcharts) that depict the flow of funds will complement this discussion.

State and local agencies can participate in different types of leasing arrangements that range from operating leases—where they have use but not ownership of the property (these leases are not tax-exempt) —to variations on tax-exempt financing leases, all of which lead to property ownership. This discussion does not examine operating leases except for comparison with tax-exempt leases.

The primary distinction among tax-exempt leases is their packaging—whether they are small, privately placed transactions (usually for equipment) or whether they are sold to investors through certificates of participation (COPs). The principal distinction among certificated leases is whether they are sold to a limited number of investors or publicly distributed on the retail securities market.

Regardless of the source of funding, the flow of funds for a typical tax-exempt lease is fairly straightforward. Once the lessee has selected the asset and the cost is known, the financing can be arranged. The lessor funds the asset cost to be paid either directly to the vendor/contractor or to an escrow for later disbursement. The lessor may act as investor and make the funds available itself or raise them from among other investors (either individuals, banks, credit companies, corporations, etc.). The lessee makes its regular payments either to the lessor, the trustee or another assignee. Title to the asset will pass to the lessee either at the outset of the lease or at its conclusion, based upon the legal requirements of each transaction.

As the name implies, tax-exempt leases involve interest components calculated at tax-exempt rates. The lessee, as ultimate owner of the leased asset, has the advantage of lower interest payments and the investor earns tax-exempt income. This contrasts with operating leases in which governments obtain use of an asset over the lease term but ownership stays with the lessor. Interest on operating leases, although not always separately stated, is taxable to the lessor and is, therefore, computed at higher rates.

A municipality enters into a tax-exempt lease to finance the purchase of equipment or the purchase or construction of real property. Among the types of assets that can be lease financed are the traditional equipment needs—such as computers, telephones, firetrucks, automobiles, and garbage trucks—and real estate projects such as jails, administration buildings, and waste-to-energy facilities. However, financed assets, in a few cases, have included less traditional

---

California Debt Advisory Commission, *Leases in California: Their Form and Function* (Sacramento: CDAC, 1991), 1-21. Reprinted by permission of CDAC.

items such as computer software, systems integration and building maintenance.

The term of the financing is generally equivalent to the useful life of the asset being financed. Hence, few equipment leases extend beyond 7 to 10 years but real property leases may exceed 20 years. For instance, police vehicles are usually financed for 2 to 3 years, while computers, telecommunications systems, and firetrucks are financeable for 5 to 7 (and, perhaps, 10) years. Buildings generally can be financed for 20 years while it may be possible to finance some environmental facilities (wastewater, solid waste, etc.) for up to 30 years.

WHY LEASE?

The value of leasing to governments is that it serves as an alternative to bond financing and can be an essential part of a capital improvement program to supplement the issuance of bonds. A government gains flexibility from tax-exempt leasing because a transaction can be arranged quickly and, therefore, it can be adapted to unusual or unique circumstances requiring the acquisition of assets in an expedited manner.

Among the reasons that governments participate in tax-exempt leases are that

- they provide 100 percent financing of asset cost;
- they spread out the cost of equipment or facilities over the assets' useful lives;
- the short useful lives of certain assets do not justify bond financing;
- selling bonds, including obtaining voter approval, can be time consuming and, given the time value of money, may increase the acquisition cost;
- equipment leases are relatively simple to complete and allow governments to obtain their equipment quickly;
- the bond market may not be an option because the lessee has no bond rating or market experience, or the lessee is unable to have a bond referendum approved;
- they offer the opportunity to preserve cash for other projects or activities for which leasing is not an alternative; and
- they do not require voter approval.

Tax-exempt leases also may be referred to as municipal leases, installment sales, lease-purchase agreements, conditional sales, and lease-to-ownership agreements.

NON-APPROPRIATIONS AND ABATEMENT PROVISIONS

The difference between a bond or note and a lease is that in most instances a tax-exempt lease is not legally considered debt because of the non-appropriations or abatement provision found in leases. The non-appropriations provision states that in the event that future years' lease payments are not appropriated, the lessee can terminate the lease without being in default and without obligation to make further lease payments. The lessee, however, must return the asset. Under the statutes of most states (and upheld by courts in at least 30 states), the effect of the non-appropriations language is to make lease payments operating, rather than capital, expenses.

As protection for the investors, most non-appropriations leases also contain a non-substitution provision which states that following a non-appropriation, the lessee, for a specified period, cannot substitute like equipment or contract for services that the leased asset would have provided. They also contain covenants requiring best efforts by the lessee to request funding of lease payments in future fiscal periods and a confirmation of the essential use of the equipment being funded.

As a result of the perceived risks of non-appropriation, tax-exempt leases are arranged for essential assets—those assets regularly used in the day-to-day operations of the lessee. In the view of investors, rating agencies, and credit enhancement providers, it is less likely that a lessee will non-appropriate for an asset on which it relies to perform an essential function (i.e., a computer that keeps tax rolls and handles all other accounting functions.)

In California, however, many tax-exempt leases are structured with abatement clauses that allow lessees to stop rental payments if they do not have use of the leased asset. These clauses may allow or call for abatement of all rents or may permit proportionate abatement of an amount of rents applicable to that portion of the asset(s) not available for use. This provision may be in addition to a non-appropriation provision but more likely replaces it. California courts have ruled that abatement leases do not legally constitute debt. Further, they have held that such leases can be executed for multiyear periods, can have rental payments payable from any legally available source, and can have stronger default provisions. To protect investors from abatement risks, many of these leases require the lessee to purchase rental interruption insurance to supplement the usual requirement of property and casualty insurance.

The market perceptions of non-appropriations and abatement leases differ. In general, an abatement lease, particularly when supported by rental interruption insurance, is viewed as a less risky investment because the lessee is obligated to budget for and make its lease payments. Lease payments can be terminated without a default if the lessee is denied use of the asset. On the other hand, a non-appropriations lease allows the lessee to terminate a lease, without being in default, if it should non-appropriate for lease payments.

TYPES OF LESSORS

To understand tax-exempt lease arrangements, it also is helpful to know the types of participants who act as lessors for such transactions. Tax-exempt leasing dates back at least to 1954 when the federal tax courts first began to determine how the interest portion of lease payments made by a governmental unit would qualify as exempt from federal income tax. At that time, tax-exempt leasing generally involved transactions between a lessee and an equipment vendor. By treating part of the lease payment as tax-exempt interest, the vendor could be more competitive in its lease rates to governmental customers and presumably could sell more equipment.

As early as 1970, lease brokers, who traditionally facilitated taxable lease transactions, began to provide their services to the tax-exempt lease market. The lease broker is typically an organization that specializes in assisting vendors or lessees in locating investors to fund the sale/purchase of assets. Throughout the early and mid-1970s, the typical client (investor) of the lease broker was an institution, such as an insurance company or bank, with some brokers or investment bankers selling small leases directly to wealthy individuals. The lease broker gradually became more sophisticated and created both lessor companies and brokerage (or lease placement) companies. Sometimes these affiliated companies have different names which make the involvement of the lease broker's affiliates less apparent to lessees and investors.

Starting in the late 1970s, institutional investors began to participate directly in the structuring of tax-exempt lease transactions and now actively solicit transactions among lessees. These types of investors are typically large finance companies which are often affiliated with corporate conglomerates (e.g., General Electric Credit Corporation, IBM Credit Corporation) or subsidiaries of major commercial banks. In addition, captive credit companies (which only finance assets that their affiliates produce) have also increased their activities in tax-exempt leasing.

Finally, with the enormous growth of tax-exempt leasing that occurred in the 1980s, a new financing source joined the list of participants. This is the individual investor represented by an underwriter who primarily sells tax-exempt leases through the certificate of participation format. Although underwriters can and do sell some transactions on a private placement basis, their greatest contribution is in the retail distribution of COPs to large numbers of individual investors. The availability of retail market distribution has contributed greatly to the increased volume of tax-exempt leases. However, underwriters generally cannot act as lessors. Therefore, another group of lessors—including nonprofit corporations, joint powers authorities, and other special authorities—have developed to facilitate large underwritten transactions.

With this brief introduction to tax-exempt leases and lessors, the next sections discuss different types of leasing arrangements, why and how they are structured, who participates in them, and the flow of funds.

TYPES OF LEASES

Privately Placed Tax-Exempt Leases

Although the general terms and conditions of most tax-exempt leases are similar, some structures are more complex than others and involve more participants. The simpler leases generally include fewer participants, tend to be for relatively small dollar volume acquisitions, and are sometimes termed "middle market" transactions.

The first lease structure reviewed is of the simpler (usually smaller) leases which are collectively referred to as privately placed tax-exempt leases. The label "privately placed" refers to the fact that the leases ultimately are sold privately to a few investors and frequently are sold to a single investor as a single lease.

Because there are no reporting requirements either nationally or in most states, the annual number of privately placed leases is unknown but is thought to be quite high. At the same time, however, the total dollar volume is estimated to be low, particularly in relation to the dollar volume of certificates of participation.

The typical privately placed lease involves a lessee that wants to acquire property (usually equipment but sometimes real property) with a relatively low dollar cost. The dollar amount of each lease can run from $10,000 to $5,000,000 or sometimes even more. However, most privately placed leases usually are for less than $1,000,000.

Privately placed leases are used to finance capital assets in many states around the country. In California, these leases have either abatement or non-appropriations provisions. However, in most other states, privately placed leases contain non-appropriations provisions.

Lessees seek their financing either competitively or through negotiated bids. This decision may be dictated by state or local laws that require competition. Some lessees may choose to negotiate the financing in order to expedite the process or because the transaction size is too small to interest or warrant an extensive bidding process or is too time consuming to warrant any resulting savings.

Most lessees enter into a privately placed lease when they need equipment and they do not have the cash to pay outright or they are unable to or do not want to use bond proceeds for the purchase. Generally, the lessee selects the asset needed and solicits proposals for its acquisition. It may ask the vendor to state a purchase price that includes a lease rate or to provide both a cash purchase price and a calculation of what lease payments would be.

However, many lessees will solicit vendor prices for the asset acquisition only and will independently seek lease financing rates from third-party companies and financial institutions accustomed to investing in tax-exempt leases. This permits the lessee to obtain the most cost-effective price as well as financing cost. Many vendors do not specialize in financing their products and, as a result, either will offer to finance at high rates (and serve as the investor) or will introduce a third-party lessor/investor. In the latter situation, the involvement of the vendor as lease broker tends to drive up the financing cost. Lessees also may benefit from separating asset acquisition from financing bids by potentially broadening the equipment supplier market. This occurs because some vendors cannot or do not offer financing and would be excluded from bidding on a combined sales and finance package.

The two primary categories of privately placed tax-exempt leases are described below.

Vendor-Financed Leases

As its name implies, the vendor-financed lease involves a vendor of equipment handling the financing of the leased asset. In this type of lease, the vendor usually acts as lessor and investor and holds the lease for its full term. Alternatively, the vendor may assign the lease to one or more subsequent investors. The vendor/lessor is responsible for providing the leased asset—both its manufacture and its financing. Usually, no funds are required in a vendor-financed lease until the asset is delivered and accepted, at which time lease payments commence from the lessee to the vendor/lessor.

The primary incentive to the vendor/lessor is usually to accommodate the sale of the assets it manufactures. If the vendor retains the lease as an investment, the vendor will also receive tax-exempt interest from the future lease payments. If the vendor assigns the lease to other investors, the vendor may receive a broker's fee from the new investor, adding another layer of cost to the financing. Many vendor/lessors, however, do assign leases to investors without making an additional financing profit. In these cases, the vendor provides the financing to its customers as a service, presumably to encourage future sales of its products.

The vendor-financed lease is usually the easiest and quickest to document. It typically involves a single (often preprinted form) lease between the vendor/lessor and the lessee. The lessee will be expected to provide an opinion of its counsel that the lease is valid and binding and that the lessee has complied with the bidding and procurement statutes. A separate bond or tax counsel opinion is generally not required. Since the vendor is typically the initial lessor, an escrow of funds to assure payment of the acquisition price is unnecessary and rarely found in these transactions. Figure 1 presents a flow chart of this sample transaction.

Third-Party Financed Leases

In a third-party financed lease, someone other than the vendor assumes the responsibility of providing or arranging the financing of the leased assets. The third party may be a direct investor or a lease broker, either of whom usually acts as lessor, although occasionally the vendor may continue as lessor. The difference between a vendor/lessor in a vendor-financed lease and a vendor/lessor in a third-party financed lease is the level of financing responsibility the lessor assumes.

In the simplest form of a third-party financed lease, the lessor leases to the lessee who accepts the asset from the vendor, following which the lessor pays the vendor and the lessee makes lease payments to the lessor. After the lessee has selected the asset and the lease financing is documented, the vendor is authorized to deliver the asset. If the leased asset is not accepted in its entirety at the time the lease is funded, some or all of the purchase price may be placed in an escrow account. In such cases, the services of an escrow agent/trustee will be required. The escrow agent holds the lease proceeds until the lessee accepts the asset and authorizes the escrow agent to pay the vendor.

A third-party financed lease generally takes more time to document than a vendor-financed lease, frequently three weeks or longer. The lessee will be required to provide the same type of legal opinion as required for a vendor-financed lease. However, the third party may also require a separate opinion of tax counsel concerning the tax-exempt treatment of the interest portion of the lease payments under federal and state income tax laws.

The various parties in this case benefit from the transaction in different ways. The lessee finances its assets at tax-exempt interest rates without incurring debt. The vendor benefits from the sale of its product. The third-party lessor/investor earns a profit from receiving tax-exempt income or, where it assigns the lease to investors, from a "spread" in the financing rate it receives from the lessee and the rate at which it obtains money from investors. For instance, in a lease in which the third-party lessor assigns its interests to another party, the lessee may be paying an interest rate of 7.5 percent and the lessor may find an investor willing to fund the transaction at a tax-exempt yield of 6.75 percent. The spread of .75 percent is the lessor's gross profit and the new investor becomes the beneficiary of tax-exempt income. The lessor's gross profit is reduced by any closing costs (legal fees, etc.) to achieve its net profit. Usually the smaller the dollar volume of the lease, the larger the spread to compensate the participants to the transaction. The actual dollar margins will depend on the size of the financing, the terms of the lease, and the payment frequency. For example, to receive 1 percent of margin (or gross profit) on a three-year lease with monthly payments in arrears, the lessor will require an interest rate spread of approximately .67 percent (67 basis points); to achieve the equivalent margin, for a lease with a five-year term, the spread is reduced to .42 percent (42 basis points). Similarly, a monthly payment structure will provide less margin to the lessor than quarterly payments due to the present value of cash flows.

Figure 2 outlines the flow of activities in a typical third-party financed lease.

Certificates of Participation

A popular form of lease packaging involves a certificate of participation (COP). A COP is a variant of a lease financing in which the lease is divided by the lessor into individual units sold separately to investors. More precisely, a COP is a security (issued in a form similar to a municipal bond) that evidences the undivided fractional interest the investor holds in a particular lease and, as appropriate, a security in-

Figure 1: *Vendor-Financed Lease Purchase*

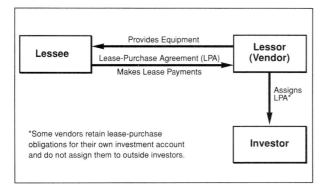

Figure 2: *Third-Party Financed Lease Purchase*

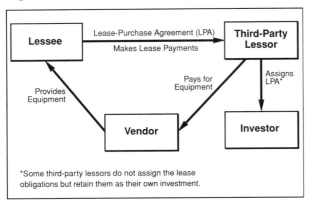

terest in the rental to be paid and the assets being financed. The number of parties, the documentation, and the cash-flow patterns mirror those of a bond sale. COPs also can have as many structural variations as bonds.

The volume of COPs increased significantly in the 1980s with governments in California accounting for the vast majority of those transactions. By example, the California Debt Advisory Commission (CDAC) reported in 1988 that 165 COPs were issued in that state for a total dollar volume of more than $2.2 billion. Standard & Poor's Corporation reported for the same period that, nationally, it rated more than $3.5 billion of tax-exempt leases, with leases by California governments representing 47.1 percent of that total. The primary reason for the high volume of COPs in California is the impact of several legislative referenda (including Proposition 13 and the Gann initiative) that severely limit property taxes as a source of revenue to governments in the state and require a two-thirds majority voter approval for any general obligation debt financing. Decreased revenues have led, quite naturally, to a leveraging of that revenue to lease financing.

COPs are used for all types of assets but have been widely used for large real property purchases. The distinction between a COP and a privately placed transaction is that COPs are generally sold to more than one investor. Although they may be sold privately to sophisticated investors, they frequently are sold publicly, through broker-dealers, in an underwritten transaction to a diverse group of investors.

A COP is more complex than a privately placed lease. While the underlying lease has the same contractual features (non-appropriation or abatement, essentiality, etc.), the transaction requires more time to organize and involves more participants.

The participants in a COP transaction include the governmental lessee, the lessor, the vendor(s), and an underwriter who will solicit investors. Many COP transactions also require a trustee. The trustee acts on behalf of the multiple investors primarily to collect rent from the lessee and to disburse it to the respective investors. In some transactions, the trustee also holds the acquisition funds in an escrow account until payment to the vendors or contractors is required. Finally, the trustee has a duty to act for the investors' interest if the lessee defaults, abates, or non-appropriates on the lease. The trustee may also be substituted by a paying agent or escrow agent.

Most of the parties will be represented by counsel and a bond or tax counsel will participate to render the opinion that the transaction is tax exempt. Other participants may include the credit rating agency analysts (if the transaction is to be rated) and representatives of the credit enhancement provider (if it is to be enhanced). The enhancer will also be represented by counsel. Of course, lessee's counsel will be involved during the preparation and negotiation of the documents.

COPs are or may be structured with a nominal lessor that may be a nonprofit corporation, a private entity, a joint powers authority, or another special agency. This structure typically involves a trustee who receives the proceeds of the COPs sale and to whom the lessor assigns the duties to disburse the proceeds to the vendor(s), the collection of lease payments, and the disbursement of principal and interest payments to the certificate holders.

COPs can be sold competitively or on a negotiated basis. If competitive, the lessee, usually assisted by special counsel and a financial advisor, prepares the documents, issues the official statement, takes bids on a specified date, and awards to the lowest bidder. When negotiated, the underwriter works closely with the lessee in structuring the transaction and preparing the documents, including the official statement; the pricing is negotiated between the underwriter and the lessee. In a negotiated transaction, the lessee may be in a position to bring its COPs to market at an advantageous time relative to interest rate volatility. In addition, negotiation sometimes allows the lessee to market more complicated COPs to specialized investors (those who understand the lease document and the risks of non-appropriation or abatement). On the other hand, the competitive sale of COPs assures open bidding among a wide source of underwriters and, for straightforward transactions, may produce the lowest interest cost.

One way in which a COP structure may differ from that of a bond is that COPs may call for a debt service reserve fund that may mitigate the risks of non-appropriation or abatement. In this case, COPs are funded for more than the asset cost to provide for the debt service reserve account. In accordance with the 1986 Tax Reform Act, reserves from bond or lease transactions may not exceed 10 percent of the initial offering.

COPs are generally sold through an official statement that describes the transaction, the sources of repayment, and the general economic, financial, and demographic trends of the lessee. Like bonds, COPs may be rated. They may also have credit enhancements to offset the investment risks of non-appropriation or abatement. COPs are traded in established securities markets, and for public offerings are typically sold in $5,000 denominations.

Figure 3 shows the typical way in which funds and responsibilities flow in a COP transaction.

Lease Revenue Bonds

Lease revenue bonds in some instances are the equivalent of COPs except the word "bond" may make them more acceptable in the financial marketplace. For example, if a building authority issues revenue bonds to finance the construction of a jail or office buildings and then leases that facility to another state agency, the underlying lease most likely will contain the same language and provisions common to the tax-exempt leases previously discussed. Therefore, a revenue bond relying on the pledge of the lease payments has similar risks as a COP. Lease revenue bonds also are not treated as debt for state law purposes, either under the "lease" exception (discussed in another part of the publication from which this article was excerpted) or under the special revenue exception to debt limitations.

Figure 3: *Certificate of Participation (COP)*

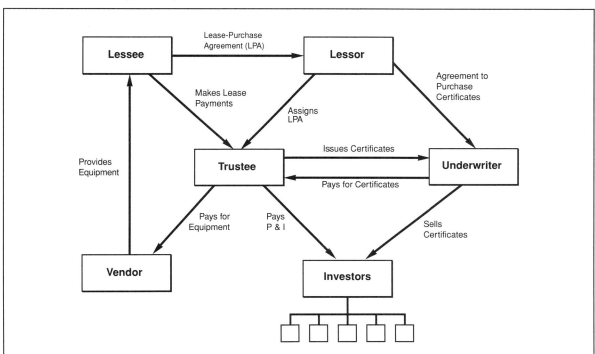

However, many lease revenue bonds will also be supported by a specific pledge of the income derived from the leased asset. For example, the lease of a wastewater treatment facility by an improvement authority to a municipal sewer utility would likely contain a pledge of net sewer fees charged by the utility to its customers. This type of lease revenue bond is principally evaluated on the strength of the pledged revenue stream and not primarily on the other provisions of the lease.

In California, issuers of lease revenue bonds (also called enterprise leases) include non-profit corporations, joint powers authorities, redevelopment agencies, and parking authorities. In other states, other types of governmental entities can issue these bonds as long as they are supported by project revenues.

Lease revenue bonds involve similar parties with similar roles as already reviewed above in the discussion on COPs.

Master Leases, Lease Lines of Credit, and Lease Pools

Master Leases

A master lease can provide governmental lessees with many economies and efficiencies. By entering into such an arrangement, a lessee is able to acquire various pieces and types of real and/or personal property from different vendors over a period of time under one lease contract. In addition to the benefits of working with one set of documents for multiple acquisitions, the lessee does not have to seek financing each time a new acquisition occurs. Frequently, master leases are arranged to consolidate outstanding leases or to coordinate the leasing activities of many agencies within one government.

The flow of funds of a master lease will mirror either that of a third-party financed lease or a COP (except that a trustee or paying agent is usually involved to hold funds and disburse to vendors as appropriate). The primary difference between a master lease and other tax-exempt leases is that there generally is more than one vendor and there may be more than one user. Frequently, a primary lessee in a master lease (such as a state purchasing bureau) may sublease the assets to other qualified municipal agencies.

When a master lease involves assets to be used by many agencies within one government, an additional set of agreements may be required, depending on the authority of the central governmental unit acting as lessee in the master lease. The central lessee may simply be authorized by statute to act on behalf of all agencies or it may require the agencies to specifically authorize its actions. If an authorization document is needed, it could be in the form of a sublease agreement incorporating all the provisions of the master lease, or it could be a simple memorandum of understanding committing the user agencies to abide by the terms of the master lease.

Figure 4 outlines the master lease transaction which typically occurs when operating departments of a governmental unit request a central purchasing or finance office (the "primary lessee") to lease assets to serve each department's unique needs. The primary lessee enters into a lease with a lessor who generally assigns the lease to a trustee who issues certificates of participation to an underwriter. The underwriter sells the COPs to investors and deposits those proceeds (less commission) with the trustee for payment to vendors after delivery and acceptance of assets by the operating departments. The primary lessee is responsible for collecting rents from the operating departments and remitting these to the trustee, who in turn pays the investors.

Many master leases with non-appropriations provisions are structured as "all or nothing" leases to enhance their security value. In other words, if a lessee chooses to non-appropriate, it must non-appropriate all assets acquired under the master lease. With this restriction, the risk of non-appropriation is minimized.

Lease Lines of Credit

Many master leases are also organized as lines of credit with the interest rates set by formula as the funds are needed. At the point at which funds are drawn down, the rate is fixed pursuant to an index or continues to float on an index. As a result of this structure, lessees know or can calculate the cost of financing from the outset and are assured that their costs are competitive and reflect current interest rates.

Lease lines of credit are normally provided directly by investors or some lease brokers who arrange to provide the requisite financing on demand whenever the lessee receives assets under the program. The line of credit lessor agrees to pay vendors

Figure 4: *Master Lease Agreement*

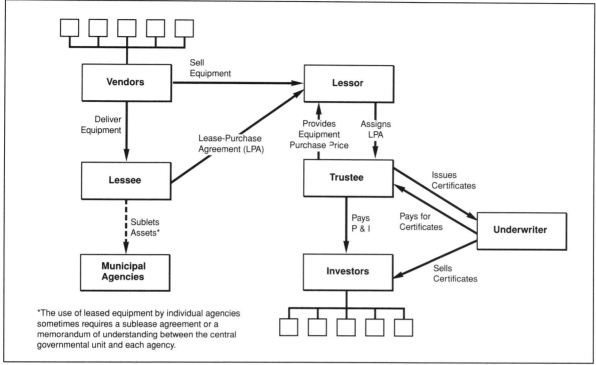

identified by the lessee as and when assets are delivered and accepted. Specific assets are not identified when the line is negotiated; however, an understanding is reached during the negotiation of the documents as to the types of assets and the useful lives that are acceptable. When each asset or group of assets is paid for, a schedule is added to the lease to identify the asset, the financing term, and the applicable payments.

A lease line of credit frequently does not involve a trustee or paying agent because the line provider acts both as lessor and investor. A trustee or paying agent may be used if a subsequent sale to multiple investors is anticipated.

Lease Pools

In the last several years, some state associations have sponsored tax-exempt lease pools. In California, for instance, the County Supervisors Association, the California School Boards Association, the California Special Districts Association, and the Association of Bay Area Governments have set up lease pools for their members. Similar programs have been set up by the Florida School Boards Association and the Utah School Boards Association.

These lease pools typically are organized with a subsidiary of the sponsoring organization acting as nominal lessor and usually involve a group of separate leases to several lessees. The pools are organized and sized to respond to the lease needs of the member governments. In active programs, lease pools may be financed annually or more frequently.

A lease pool will always involve a trustee to receive lease payments from multiple lessees and disburse them to the investors. The trustee will issue COPs representing undivided interests in all leases in the pool. An investor assumes a portion of the risk associated with each lease. However, since each lease is legally a separate obligation, the risks of nonappropriation or abatement are limited to the specific lessee; the different lessees are not responsible for the obligations of other lessees.

A credit enhancement in the form of a liquidity letter of credit can be of particular benefit to lease pools that involve a number of different lessees. Because of the differing levels of creditworthiness among the lessees in a pool, a liquidity letter of credit can contribute to its marketability by providing a uniform level of credit to the lessees and assuring investors of prompt payment.

Because of their complexity and the larger number of lessees in lease pools, bond counsel and other special counsel will assist in the preparation of documents to assure their compliance with federal tax and securities laws. In addition, each lessee's counsel will be involved in the transactions.

CONCLUSION

In summary, the roles of the different participants to a lease transaction are outlined in Exhibit 1. As the prior discussion reveals, these parties may or may not be in all leases, they may play more than one role, and they may play different roles.

While the size of transactions and the sources of funding may vary, the underlying leases are very similar. Lessees select the lease packaging that best fits their needs—whether it is a vendor-financed transaction for a small equipment purchase or a publicly sold COP that will finance a new city hall. The flow of funds and responsibilities in these transactions may differ in their complexity as may the number of parties involved but the result is the same. A government has acquired an asset and has not incurred debt but has undertaken a payment obligation. The investors receive tax-exempt income and have a secured interest in an asset that they hope never to possess.

Exhibit 1: *Tax-Exempt Leasing: Participants and Their Roles*

Who	Role
Lessee	Governmental unit that uses the leased asset, makes periodic payments of principal and interest, and gains ownership of the asset at some point during the transaction. The lessee chooses the asset and financing source.
Lessor	Party that may provide the funds and act as investor or that may assign its interest in the leased property to another party. If a nominal lessor, it acts as a conduit to acquire the asset for resale to the lessee. The lessor may be the vendor/contractor, the investor, or a public or private third party.
Vendor/ Contractor	Party that provides the asset to the lessee. These parties are selected by the lessee and perform according to lessee specifications.
Underwriter	Original purchaser of COPs (from the lessee or escrow agent) with the intent to resell the certificates to investors.
Assignee	Party to whom lessor assigns its rights and interests in the leased asset.
Credit Rating Agency	Provides the credit rating to some lease transactions.
Credit Enhancement Provider	Party that protects the investors against risks of non-appropriation abatement or default by providing a financial guaranty.
Trustee/ Escrow Agent	Usually a financial institution that provides administrative services, through an escrow or trust agreement, for the benefit of the parties to the lease including, among other services, the safekeeping of proceeds, and holding physical possession of title documents for the leased asset. Depending on the structure, the lessee or lessor pays trustee fees which, depending on the transaction, may be assessed annually or are paid at lease commencement.
Financial Advisor	Consultant who provides assistance in the structure, timing, terms, and other topics concerning new or existing leases.

Operations

 # Government Purchasing: The State of the Practice

Charles K. Coe

I. INTRODUCTION

Governments purchase over $500 billion of goods and services, which constitutes about 20 percent of the gross national product. Because of the large sums involved, purchasing goods and services is a large part of any government's operations. Professional and progressive purchasing procedures reduce the cost of government; but the converse is equally true, shoddy practices result in waste and excessive costs. The seemingly constant stream of stories about slipshod defense contracting bears witness to this point.

Government purchasing differs from private purchasing in several distinctive ways. First, businesses purchase privately with only the buyer deciding on the vendor—a choice that can be made on the basis of price, convenience, or on personal considerations such as friendship or family ties. Governments, in sharp contrast, must conduct all of their dealings in the public eye, subject to strict legal guidelines. Secondly, governmental purchasing often is more subject to social and political strictures. For example, states and localities sometimes require that particular goods be bought locally or that preferences be given to minorities or the handicapped. Finally, because of the market mechanism, private sector purchasing is generally more professional. The bottom line, the amount of profit, is sharply reduced by incompetent purchasing such as delays in receiving goods, stock unnecessarily tied up on inventory shelves, and by the absence of vendor competition. Given the increasing pressure of international competition, the private sector has improved its purchasing procedures. Thus, private purchasing managers in general are better trained than public managers. Furthermore, firms are more likely to have state-of-the-art computerized purchasing and inventory control systems.

While private sector purchasing may be better than public purchasing, governmental purchasing has made very significant advancements over its history. Governmental purchasing has gone through four stages (CSG, 1989: 101). In the 1800s the emphasis was on contracts for public works. The chief concern was protecting taxpayers against fraud and favoritism. Purchasers were exclusively technicians who needed little educational preparation.

Centralization of purchasing into a single department marked the second stage. The adoption of the income tax and then the outbreak of World War II caused the federal expenditures to grow greatly. Greater control over purchasing was needed. It was highly inefficient to allow agencies to do their own purchasing. Centralized purchasing demanded that purchasing officials be better trained and operations be more sophisticated.

World War II signaled the third stage of purchasing. Huge amounts of supplies had to move throughout the world, and vast amounts of military weapons and equipment needed to be built in a short time frame. Consequently, purchasing became more sophisticated. For example, computers were first introduced to make acquisitions and schedule construction projects.

Reprinted from *Handbook of Comparative Public Budgeting and Financial Management,* edited by Thomas D. Lynch and Lawrence L. Martin (New York: Marcel Dekker, Inc., 1993), 207-23. By permission of the publisher.

Purchasing is now in its fourth stage. Even greater expertise is now required because governments must make intelligent decisions about purchasing a wide range of technologically sophisticated equipment and systems such as communications systems, computer hardware and software, telephone systems, CATV, and telecommunications networks. Further, governments are faced with other new challenges including a heightened sensitivity to ethical conflicts, the selection of professional services, and decisions about whether to privatize services.

II. THE STATE OF THE PRACTICE

The challenges now facing governments are indeed great. A cost-conscious and tax-shy public wants governments to be more efficient, which is a clarion call for more purchasing competition, more innovation, higher ethical standards, and for better trained purchasing officials. What is the state of the practice? How well are governments responding to the challenges of the 1990s? The report card is mixed. While marked improvements are being made in some areas, progress is slow in other critical aspects of purchasing management. Let us examine the state of the practice of governmental purchasing.

A. Education and Training

Unfortunately, most governmental purchasing officials must learn their craft only on the job through experience, not through any structured education (CSG, 1989: 101). While on-the-job knowledge is indeed valuable, it should be complemented by formal training and instructional programs; yet relatively few such programs are offered at any level of government. The private sector, driven by the bottom line, recognizes the need; but unfortunately government mostly does not. In 1981, 275 colleges and universities offered courses in purchasing, but these were for industrial purchasing. The opportunity to receive a degree in public purchasing is virtually nonexistent (CSG, 1989: 101).

Outside the academic environment, however, some progress has been made. In 1978 the National Institute of Government Purchasing (NIGP) joined the National Association of Purchasing Managers (NAPM) to create a Universal Public Purchasing Certification Council and program. The NIGP offers seminars throughout the country to certify purchasing officials as a Certified Public Purchasing Officer (CPPO) or as a Professional Public Buyer (PPB). These programs offer a good, basic understanding of purchasing and buying, but participation in them is generally restricted to larger governments that can afford the tuition and travel cost. As of 1990 there were about 600 CPPOs and 1,000 PPBs, which is commendable, but still only a small fraction of the total number of government purchasing officials in cities, counties, schools, states, and colleges and universities. Furthermore, while both certification programs are very useful, they cannot prepare the purchasing officer for the very specific purchasing laws and regulations of each state. Thus, each state should have a training program to complement the NIGPs. Such a program would emphasize state law and be geared to those smaller local jurisdictions that cannot afford to send people to the NIGP. Ideally, these programs would certify purchasing officials as does the NIGP. Unfortunately, however, North Carolina is the only state to have such a program, which is operated by the Institute of Government at the University of North Carolina at Chapel Hill.

In addition to training by the NIGP or other agencies, governments themselves provide formal training; however, the frequency of such training is very slim. In 1982 state purchasing officials reported that only 12 states provide special training for new employees; moreover, only five states have any training programs for their entire purchasing staff. At the local level, the picture is the same; only 9 percent of cities and 13 percent of counties have any training programs (CSG, 1989: 102).

When we compare the salaries of private sector purchasing officials to their public sector counterparts, it is not surprising, considering the general lack of professional training by governments, that public officials lag far behind. The General Accounting Office found that the salaries for the federal positions of Buyer I to Buyer IV in the federal government range from 29 percent to 38 percent behind salaries paid to comparable private sector employees (GAO, 1987: 19).

Further, the salaries paid to purchasing officials generally are quite low, considering the range of responsibilities and expertise required. For example, a 1989 survey reports that the salaries of 22 percent of purchasing officials are less than $20,000; another 55 percent have salaries less that $28,000 (NIGP,

1989: 9). Moreover, this survey significantly underreported smaller jurisdictions of less than 50,000 population which undoubtedly have even lower wages.

The lack of training and low pay at the local level are due in part to organizational reasons. In small cities, counties, and schools, purchasing is just one of many responsibilities that the finance director or clerk has. As governments get larger, they create a purchasing office, typically under the supervision of the finance director whose background is in accounting not purchasing. Thus, finance directors sometimes are simply not aware of the cost savings and economies that result from state-of-the-art purchasing. City and county managers and school superintendents need to recognize the importance of the purchasing and inventory functions and ensure that salaries are high enough to attract and retain professionals. To provide for autonomy and professionalism, top managers of large, local jurisdictions should consider splitting purchasing from the finance director and put purchasing under the direct supervision of an assistant manager for operations.

B. Federal Purchasing

The history of federal purchasing reflects a longstanding concern on the part of the President and Congress to have economical and efficient operations. In 1792 Congress authorized the Treasury and War Departments to make purchases for the federal government. In 1809 the Procurement Act required that formal advertising be used in purchasing, and over the years, rules were established for bidding and for military purchases. In 1949 the General Services Administration (GSA) was created to purchase for all agencies except Defense, NASA, Energy, and the Energy Research and Development Agency. GSA sets standards for purchases, issues long-term contracts, and stores supplies.

As the federal government grew in size, maintaining tight accounting control over purchasing became more problematic. Numerous studies and reports have centered on how to improve purchasing. Numerous actions have also been taken by both Congress and the Executive Office to shore up glaring deficiencies. In 1974 the Office of Federal Procurement Policy (OFPP) was set up to coordinate and improve the efficiency of purchasing. In 1976 the Federal Acquisition Institute (FAI) was created to train procurement personnel and conduct research to improve purchasing practices. The Financial Integrity Act of 1982 requires ongoing evaluations of the internal control and accounting systems that protect federal programs against fraud, waste, abuse, and mismanagement. In 1984 the Federal Competition in Contracting Act was passed to increase competition within departments and narrow the justification for sole source contracting. Finally, in 1987 the Director of Office and Management administratively appointed a Chief Financial Officer (CFO) for the federal government and for each department and agency.

Despite the intense interest in improving purchasing and financial management generally, progress generally has been slow. For example, the OFPP encountered widespread resistance from Congress, defense agencies, and other agencies (Walsh and Leighland, 1989: 487). Moreover, GAO finds that, while the Financial Integrity Act has resulted in modest progress towards tighter controls over financial transactions, the results are considerably less than what Congress intended (GAO, 1989: 3). To back up this assertion, the GAO cites examples of purchasing problems (GAO, 1989: 20-21):

- In 1988 the Naval Security and Investigative Command reported instances of procurement fraud, conflict of interest, and bribery.
- After spending over $30 billion on the B-1 bomber, it does not work as planned.
- GSA has serious internal control weaknesses such as its incomplete analysis of the range of alternatives for satisfying federal telecommunication requirements.

GAO also notes considerable shortcomings in the area of property control (GAO, 1989: 30-31). The federal government has over $450 billion in property, plant, and equipment, or about 40 percent of the government's total reported assets. Yet GAO repeatedly takes federal agencies to task for their poor control over these valuable assets. For example, the Army has no accounting system to control fraud, waste, and abuse to the $2 billion in government material furnished to contractors. Moreover, the amount of unneeded inventories in stock grew from approximately $10 billion in 1980 to about $29 billion in 1988.

GAO also cites numerous instances of poor inventory control in agencies other than Defense. For example, for over 18 years the GAO has reported inadequate internal controls over personal property located at about 260 foreign posts and 21 domestic cities. This condition exists because the State Department does not follow regulations.

Interestingly, while improvements should indeed be made to Defense contracting, Defense is more competitive than the private sector in one way. In fiscal year 1986 Defense competitively bid 82 percent of its contracts compared to 56 percent by businesses (Williams and Bakhshi, 1988: 32). However, because large weapons systems are difficult to bid competitively, only a slightly higher dollar amount of purchases were bid competitively by Defense.

Though Defense receives more bids than the private sector, a great deal of waste and fraud nevertheless exists in federal purchasing and inventory management. What can and should be done to tackle this problem? GAO recommends that OMB develop and implement a long-range, government-wide financial management improvement plan (GAO, 1990: 24). The hope is that a plan would result in a coordinated and integrated system and would provide direction and continuity when leadership changes occur. Any real hope for success, however, depends on sufficient resources being available for implementation (GAO, 1990: 25).

C. Achieving More Competition

At the heart of purchasing is competition. The goal of any purchasing agency should be to have lively competition, not just in prices, but in the competence of vendors, in the quality of the goods and services bought, and in the ability of vendors to make timely deliveries. Active competition, of course, results in lower prices and higher quality products and services. To this end, most governments stipulate a dollar limit over which competitive, sealed bids must be taken with public notice and opened in public. Most jurisdictions require that bids be awarded to the "lowest responsible bidder." In all but a few cases, this is synonymous with the lowest bidder. The qualification, "responsible," is included to reject vendors with a past history of poor performance or vendors that cannot meet bid requirements.

Below the dollar bid limit, established either by law or policy, statutes usually require that purchases be based on a system of informal bidding or quotes. Usually, the government must receive a specified number of informal bids or quotes before making a purchase. Having a process of informal bidding becomes more important as bid limit amounts are raised, which has been the case in many states (CSG, 1989: 24) and local units (NIGP, 1989: 18).

Although rules requiring bids and procedures for informal quotes indeed ensure a healthy measure of competition, competition is nonetheless sometimes constrained by laws, by improper purchasing procedures, and by the anticompetitive practices of bidders. Let us examine each.

1. Laws Limiting Competition

Some states and local jurisdictions limit competition by only buying from vendors in their geographic area. As early as 1954, state purchasing officials opposed such in-state preference statutes. Nonetheless, 12 states still have in-state preference laws, requiring that a specific percentage of state contracts be awarded either to bidders located in the state or to firms that produce goods within the state (CSG, 1989: 26). The typical level of preference is 5 percent. Research shows that preference laws increase state expenditures by about 3 percent per capita over what would be expected (CSG, 1989: 27). Moreover, at least three-quarters of the states have statutes extending some preference to state firms usually in the case of tied bids. States should eliminate any in-state preferences laws.

Many local jurisdictions also limit competition with a "keep the money at home" mentality (NIGP, 1989: 13). Ten percent of cities legally require that goods be bought locally, and 37 percent do not have a legal requirement but do so administratively. Nine percent of counties have similar legal restrictions and 33 percent do so administratively. Localities give preference to local vendors because they contribute to the local economy in the form of taxes and outside firms do not. This practice, however, usually results in excessive costs. Instead of a blanket local preference policy, local jurisdictions should determine exactly how much taxes would be lost and only give preference in those few cases where lost taxes are greater than savings gained through competition (for a formula to calculate this difference, see Coe, 1989: 100).

Competition is further limited by policies that give preference to small or disadvantaged businesses. In 1961 Congress legislated that "a fair portion" of federal funds be awarded to small businesses. If a firm obtains a federal contract over a certain amount, it must make a "best effort" to place orders with small subcontractors for a specific percentage of the total contract. Fifty-three percent of federal agencies and states either legally or administratively have percentage preferences for small or disadvantaged businesses as do about 32 percent of cities and counties (NIGP, 1989: 14). In these instances, legislators have determined that the goals of encouraging small businesses and of promoting social equity are more important than the goal of efficiency through paying the lowest possible cost.

Another way governments limit competition is by requiring purchase of certain goods made only in America. Congress passed the Buy American Act to ensure that the United States maintains its ability to produce several "essential" goods. The Act specifies that a contract be awarded to a domestic supplier provided that its price is not over a given percentage greater than that offered by the foreign vendor. A total of 52 percent of federal agencies and states use buy American provisions as do 42 percent of cities and counties. These policies are seen by economists as counterproductive because they, like tariffs, in the long run make American businesses less competitive and ultimately increase prices.

2. Improper Purchasing Procedures

Sometimes governments conduct purchasing procedures that limit competition. Often, these actions are simply due to ignorance of more suitable methods. Improper practices are continued because "We have always done it this way." For example, traditionalism sometimes stands in the way of selecting professional services competitively. Historically, professional services—such as those rendered by auditors, fiscal advisors for bond issues, architects and engineers, banks, and lawyers—were not acquired competitively. That is, governments simply negotiated a price and a contract for services with a particular firm and did not inquire of other firms. In the case of consulting engineers, the charge was a percentage of construction costs based on a formula devised by the American Society for Professional Engineers.

In the last 10 years, however, there has been a notable trend toward more competition. Governments more often seek from firms competitive proposals in which price is one factor considered. With respect to the selection of consulting engineers, the Environmental Protection Agency has led the way by requiring that competitive price proposals be sought by cities and counties that receive EPA grants to improve their sewage treatment systems. Likewise, the Government Finance Officers Association (GFOA) calls for competition in the process of selecting outside auditors to audit financial records.

Experience shows that price competitive procedures can result in lower prices. Model contracts are available to design Requests for Proposals (RFPs) and contracts for the services of fiscal advisors (Petersen and Watt, 1986), banks (Miller, 1986), consulting engineers (Coe, 1979), and auditors (Gauthier, 1989). Nonetheless, some governments are reluctant to seek competition either for political reasons or because they fear change.

Despite the cost advantages of competition, governments should be careful when purchasing professional services. Cost should not be the principal factor considered; instead, most important is the firm's ability to do a professional job as demonstrated by past experience. The obvious danger, however, is that elected officials may feel pressured into taking the lowest proposal even though that firm may be less able to provide a professional product. Because goods are selected almost always on the basis of the lowest cost, officials may feel intense pressure to not award a contract for professional services to a higher costing firm, even though that firm has a demonstrably better track record. To help governments resist this temptation and to understand the arguments for and against competition, the NIGP has prepared an excellent handbook on the purchasing of professional services (Zemansky, 1987).

Another purchasing practice limiting competition is what is known as "back door selling" which occurs when vendors cultivate favor among agency personnel who use their products. Suppliers may try to gain favor by financial enticements such as gifts, bribes, kickbacks, and expense paid trips to the vendor's home office. Most often, however, the sales representative simply gains an edge by being helpful in supplying technical data and by becoming a close friend. Consequently, agency officials become sold on a particular vendor's items and design the purchasing specifications so that only the favored supplier can meet them. Determining the frequency of "back door selling" is not possible, but clearly it does happen. For example, 41 state purchasing officials indicate that they are aware of such practices taking place in their state (CSG, 1989: 158).

Other purchasing practices may limit competition as well. For example, paying invoices slowly discourages vendor competition and often precludes participation by small businesses that need a steady cash flow to survive. Moreover, competition is limited when a jurisdiction mutually agrees with a contractor to extend a contract. Finally, most favored customer stipulations restrict competition by requiring that contractors not offer to other clients prices lower than those quoted to the government.

3. Anti-Competitive Practices by Bidders

Though an infrequent occurrence, competition is restricted by vendors themselves in two ways. First, firms may resort to collusive bidding. For example, they may rotate low bids among each other or may allocate business by geographical location or territory. Second, firms may submit identical bids because a manufacturer agrees with his distributors on a set price, or because competitors agree on charging one price within a geographic zone.

Collusive bidding often is especially hard to detect. Unlike governmental decisions that must be made in the public arena, suppliers' decisions to act in restraint to trade are made secretly. Two handbooks that explain how to counter anti-competitive practices are *Government Purchasing and the Antitrust Laws* (1977) and *Impediments to Competitive Bidding* (1963).

III. ADVANCES IN THE FIELD OF PURCHASING

Notwithstanding the need to increase training, to reform federal purchasing, and to achieve greater competition, the field of purchasing has made some very significant strides especially during the 1970s and 1980s. A singular development was the publication of the Model Procurement Code by the American Bar Association (ABA). The NIGP and the National Association of State Purchasing Officials (NASPO) find much to commend the code but have some reservations about parts that do not reflect accurately state and local experience (CSG, 1989: 12). All parties agree, however, that the code has increased the public's awareness and interest in improving governmental purchasing.

The code recommends that purchasing policy be separated from purchasing operations. The policy functions should be carried out by a central policy office, located preferably as a separate entity in the executive branch. The policy office can be headed by an official under the chief executive or by a board. The policy office should issue purchasing regulations and conduct research and training.

On the other hand, actual day-to-day purchasing should be headed by a chief procurement officer with at least eight years purchasing experience.

The code is used as a guide. States and local jurisdictions adapt it to their own local conditions. By 1988, 13 states had passed bills based on the model code. Some states, like Georgia, adopted only parts of the code. Bills were also being drafted or are under consideration in six other states (Lemov, 1988: 97). At the local level, a survey of larger local jurisdictions indicates that 29 percent have adopted the model code (NIGP, 1989: 4).

Only a few of the 13 states that have adopted the model code have mandated that their local jurisdictions adopt the code. New Mexico requires that all but home rule cities adopt the law, and South Carolina and Virginia mandate that local jurisdictions enact procurement ordinances consistent with the state code.

A. An Increased Ethical Awareness

Purchasing is potentially an ethical minefield because large sums of moneys are involved. At one extreme, bribery, kickbacks, and fraud can occur. Such instances are relatively uncommon but do occur. For example, in a recent New York scandal, 106 municipal officials were offered bribes and 105 accepted them (Lemov, 1988: 96). Furthermore, scandals in Defense contracting are an unfortunate occurrence.

Governments have taken various actions to curb such abuses. Reaction has been especially intense at the federal level. In 1986 Congress enacted the Anti-Kickback Act, which provides civil and criminal penalties for kickbacks between subcontractors and contractors. The law also spells out the fine points on bribery, illegal gratuities, outside income, kickbacks, conflicts of interest, and 47 different forms of contract fraud. The law is a maze, and as a consequence, the General Services Administration teaches a course on ethics to federal purchasing officials (Johnston, 1989).

At the state level, various actions have been taken as well. Codes of ethics have existed in states since the early 1900s. However, not until the 1970s did conflict of interest laws become common due to numerous scandals. Between 1974 and 1984, 45 states enacted new conflict of interest provisions or revised existing ones (Walsh and Leighland, 1989). Additionally, states have adopted the model code or use it as a guide. The code eliminates any possible errors of judgment due to vague or non-existent policies and procedures. The code prescribes very specific and comprehensive rules for organizing procurement offices, for soliciting and handling bids, and for dealing with protests about contracts. The code also has very specific ethical prohibitions against purchasing agents accepting any gifts, favors, or meals.

The publication, *Ethics and Quality Purchasing* (Zemansky, 1988), is helpful to those looking for guidance in the area of purchasing ethics. This handbook contains the *NIGP Code of Ethics,* samples of model city ordinances on ethics, and typical ethical dilemmas faced by purchasing agents and other managers. Without clear and specific guidelines, what constitutes ethical behavior is murky. For example, can a purchasing agent accept insignificant items like a desk calendar from suppliers? Can an employee accept a lunch from a supplier when business is discussed? Should managers be able to resign and use their expertise to help businesses that contract heavily with the government? The answers to these and other such ticklish questions should be clearly spelled out in the law or in a written procedures manual.

B. Innovative Purchasing Techniques

The field of purchasing is becoming more sophisticated on two fronts. First, smaller local units are adopting professional procedures that larger jurisdictions have used for some time. In this vein, smaller jurisdictions are making real progress with respect to inventory management and to cooperative purchasing. Second, governments of all sizes are adopting new and advanced techniques such as performance purchasing, value engineering, computerization, total cost purchasing, faxing, commodity coding, and life-cycle costing. Let us discuss each of these improvement areas.

1. Inventory Management

Inventory control has long been a deficient area of governmental purchasing. For example, the typical governmental inventory only turns over three times per year (NIGP, 1989: 8). That is, the inventory's annual sales divided by the average monthly inventory on hand is three times. Inventory turns in the private sector vary with the industry but generally are seven or higher. This means that governments are tying up in their inventories excessive amounts of cash that could be invested or used for other purposes. One empirical study documents this fact (Reid et al., 1984). Moreover, even with such sizable inventories on hand, sometimes critical parts or supplies are not available when needed.

One reason for this problem is that the inventory function often is performed by operating departments not by central purchasing. Central purchasing has more expertise in inventory management, and it makes sense to centralize all purchasing functions. This is the trend at the state level. Twenty-three states report that inventory and property disposal are now more often a function of central purchasing (CSG, 1989: 169).

A second reason why inventory control has been slack is that, until the 1980s, inexpensive software was not available to manage inventories. To order the optimal amount and minimize stock on shelf, the economic order quantity (EOQ) method must be used. EOQ is based on the relationship between the cost of placing an order, an item's annual usage, and the cost of carrying the item in the inventory. Furthermore, this method calculates the optimal re-order point and a safety margin for each item of stock. Considering that a typical inventory has a large number of items in stock, these formulae must be automated.

Historically, large governments have had the programming staff to develop inventory management software to make such calculations; however, small local jurisdictions did not have programmers. However, since the mid-1970s a wide variety of off-the-shelf inventory management software has been written. It is available at an inexpensive price and can be operated on personal and mini-computers. Consequently, many small local jurisdictions are now implementing inventory control systems and this trend will continue.

2. Cooperative Purchasing

Governments can cooperatively purchase with each other in three ways. First, two or more jurisdictions can combine their requirements into a single request for bids either for goods or for services. Second, one government may operate a warehouse and allow one or many governments to buy from the warehouse. For example, schools buy and stock large inventories of office and maintenance supplies. Schools can allow cities and counties to take advantage of the lower unit costs of these goods by permitting them to buy out of the school inventory. Finally, cooperative purchasing most commonly happens when local jurisdictions buy goods on state contracts. States buy large amounts and commonly obtain significantly lower unit prices than local jurisdictions. Only five states (Florida, Hawaii, Kansas, North Dakota, and Vermont) do not permit local jurisdictions to purchase on state contract (CSG, 1989: 167-68). Further, 45 states formally or informally help local units with mailing lists, specifications, and similar information.

Cooperative purchasing results in substantial savings. Savings of at least 10 percent are reported by 80 percent of cities and counties (NIGP, 1989: 7). Moreover, 43 percent of federal and state agencies report savings of more than 15 percent. And in the case of some goods, the savings are greater than 30 percent.

Despite the obvious cost advantages of cooperative purchasing, about a third of larger local governments do not do it (NIGP, 1989: 7). The percentage of nonuse is undoubtedly higher in small sized local units. Why? The biggest constraint is a "keep the money at home" attitude on the part of local elected officials. Local jurisdictions do not purchase on state contract because they think that goods and services bought from suppliers in their jurisdiction will contribute to the tax base. This is true. The empirical question, however, is how much taxes are gained versus dollars lost on purchases not made cooperatively? A method is available to make such a determination (Coe, 1989) and to work out the often delicate political aspects of implementation (Singer, 1988). However, despite these aids and the obvious economic advantage, key business officials sometimes place such intense political pressure on local elected officials to buy locally so that the "money is kept at home."

In addition to buying on state contract, there is a growing trend toward local jurisdictions co-purchasing (Lemov, 1988: 96). For example, 27 towns in Connecticut jointly accept bids on 12 items, such as chlorine, gasoline, paint, and fertilizer. Moreover, local jurisdictions band together to purchase services cooperatively. For example, 40 cities in Allegheny County, Pennsylvania, share six street sweeping machines and three catch-basin cleaning machines; ten cities in Georgia jointly employ someone to test their wastewater treatment plants; and three cities in Maryland jointly purchase computer hardware and software.

Cooperative purchasing is also being considered between states. In-state preference policies complicate this arrangement; nonetheless, a number of possibilities are being examined. For example, Florida, Georgia, and Alabama are considering joining to buy long-distance telephone services at cheaper rates.

3. Performance Purchasing

A growing trend exists to purchase based on overall performance not just on lowest price. Performance purchasing looks at factors other than just price. Compared to five years ago, 44 states report that they are more frequently taking into account the cost of supplies, energy, parts, warranties, maintenance, and other costs of owning and operating a product in determining the low bidder (CSG, 1989: 144).

Performance purchasing requires that performance specifications be used. The specifications aim at purchasing goods that are both economical and efficient. Performance purchasing looks at whether prospective products have characteristics that will result in more efficient operations. The efficiency of each brand can be determined from technical data required to be submitted as part of the bid process. Sometimes central purchasing must use outside expert knowledge to assess technical data.

An aspect of performance purchasing is Life Cycle Costing (LCC), which considers the total cost of ownership of a commodity or building. In addition to the initial acquisition cost, LCC accounts for the cost of using and of disposing of commodities. The rationale behind LCC is that, while the initial cost of a product may be greater than a competing good, the cost of ownership may be less because, over its useful life, it is less expensive to operate or maintain. LCC is used for such energy-consuming items as any motorized vehicle, air conditioners, water heaters, pumps, typewriters, lamps, and copying machines. LCC is also used to decide what types of buildings to construct based on a building's energy usage over its useful life.

Because of the oil shortage of the early 1970s, LCC and other energy preserving practices were very common. However, as the energy crisis abated, LCC became less frequent, which is unfortunate because LCC is such an effective cost-savings measure.

Historically, governments have not made full use of LCC because of the political problem sometimes caused when awarding bids that are not the lowest. Another reason for nonuse is that smaller governments are not able to develop the very technical specifications needed to purchase energy-consuming goods. Top managers should address the political obstacle by clearly documenting to elected officials and to the citizenry the substantial savings that result from LCC. Regarding specifications, in the 1970s the federal government subsidized several states' development of LCC specifications. Governments wishing to use LCC should acquire specifications from the states of North Carolina and Connecticut, which have specifications for over 40 items.

4. Value Engineering

Value engineering is a method of analyzing a product or service so that its function can be performed at the lowest possible overall cost without sacrificing quality. Achieving the lowest cost may require redesigning or eliminating components by using different, new, or more efficient technology. Value engineering can be used during a project's design phase or during its construction. The federal government conducts value engineering on defense projects, highway construction, and water resource projects. Moreover, the Environmental Protection Agency (EPA) requires that value engineering be done during the design phase of wastewater treatment projects costing more than $10 million. An explanation of the EPA approach illustrates both the process and benefits of value engineering.

During the design phase, a local jurisdiction that has received an EPA grant over $10 million must form an independent team of professionals. EPA guidelines recommend that these professionals have expertise in design, sanitary, structural, electrical, and mechanical engineering. Next, the local jurisdiction briefs the team on the project's purposes, requirements, capacities, cost, and other specifics. The value engineering team then studies the project's plans and specifications to identify and evaluate alternatives that will accomplish the project at less cost or more efficiently. The local jurisdiction then reviews and assesses proposed changes and incorporates them into the final design. EPA reports that from 1977-1983, value engineering resulted in net savings of $400 million on 273 projects (GAO, 1985: 13).

After the project is designed, value engineering during construction takes advantage of a contractor's expertise. An incentive clause is included in the bid package and the subsequent contract. If the contractor proposes cost-savings measures, and the owner agrees to the proposal, a contract change order is processed specifying the revised construction measure, the reduction in contract price, and the contractor's share of any savings. EPA does not require value engineering during construction; thus, it is much less prevalent. Nonetheless, where performed, value engineering during construction results in very large cost savings (GAO, 1985: 7).

The use of value engineering will increase. The General Accounting Office (GAO) strongly urges that value engineering be conducted on EPA-funded wastewater treatment projects costing $10 million or less and that EPA funds be able to be used to pay for the cost of the value engineering team (GAO, 1985: 13). Furthermore, GAO strongly promotes the use of value engineering in all federal agencies that have construction projects.

5. Computerization

When asked to cite the single change or improvement most benefiting their department, state purchasing agents most often referred to computerization (CSG, 1989: 171). Computers are used for a wide variety of functions. We have already referred to the inventory system. Another very useful purpose is to maintain an inventory of how much, how often, and from whom commodities have been bought. Data on usage patterns, current and future market conditions, warehouse capacities, and inventory levels are used to determine whether particular items can be bought more advantageously either as an individual purchase or in great volume. Moreover, automation is used to maintain vendor history files, generate bid lists, and track purchase orders.

The NIGP has developed purchasing software that will operate on personal computers. One valuable aspect of this package is its commodity coding system. Governments buy thousands of different items. Large governments have names of bidders frequently numbering more than 8,000. To ensure a good response from bidders, the bidders list needs to be coded into major commodity classifications. The extent to which major commodity classes are subdivided depends on the nature of the item and the responses received to bid solicitations. The NIGP software has a classification coding system that increases the likelihood of an excellent bidder response.

A total of 23 percent of governments use the NIGP commodity code; 37 percent use some other coding system; and 40 percent do not have a bid classification system (NIGP, 1989: 5).

6. Other Purchasing Enhancements

According to purchasing officials, the most significant productivity improvement available to the purchasing unit since the advent of the personal computer and the creation of the NIGP software is the use of facsimile machines (NIGP, 1989: 19). Facsimile machines are used for a variety of functions:

Use by Facsimile Machines	Percent of Use
Accept request for quotations	77
Accept sealed bids	18
Accept bid bonds	12
Keep bids confidential	71

Apparently, purchasing departments are encountering few problems using facsimile machines for these purposes. Only 6 percent of the respondents say it has created any purchasing problems. Only 7 percent indicated that "junk" messages are a problem. More governments (21 percent), however, have requested a legal opinion on the use of it for bidding, and 14 percent have established a written policy on the use of facsimile machines.

Another trend that will certainly continue to increase is the use of operational recycling programs. Many states and local units are passing mandatory recycling legislation. Governmental jurisdictions buy recycled products, collect materials for recycling, operate drop-off centers, and pick up recycled materials. A total of 43 percent of governments operate such a recycling program (NIGP, 1989: 20). Purchasing departments often take the lead in awarding recycling contracts and in purchasing recycled goods.

IV. SUMMARY

Governmental purchasing is both an opportunity and a challenge. Strengthening purchasing and inventory management will reduce the cost of government while ensuring that the most appropriate goods and services are available to operating departments. For this to become a reality, however, government must provide more training to purchasing officials and must pay wages that attract professionals.

The future can only bring increased demands on the purchasing profession. New and heightened standards of ethical behavior exist for all public managers. The seemingly harmless, insignificant gift from a thankful vendor now is a risky offering. Moreover, the public should increase its demand for better and more cost-efficient services. And yet resistance to new taxes will increase as international business competition squeezes American industry. At the heart of any government is the purchasing function. Sophisticated technology—including computers, new software, and facsimile machines—now aids the purchasing manager. The ultimate challenge is to use this technology to its fullest while ensuring as much competition as possible and efficient procedures and policies.

References

Coe, Charles. (1989). *Public Financial Management,* Prentice-Hall, Inc., Englewood Cliffs, New Jersey.

Coe, Charles. (1979). *Getting the Most from Professional Services: Consulting Engineer,* Institute of Government, University of Georgia, Athens, Georgia.

(CSG) The Council of State Governments. (1989). *State and Local Government Purchasing* (3d ed.), Iron Works, Pike, Kentucky.

(GAO) U.S. General Accounting Office. (1990). *Financial Management,* Washington, D.C.

(GAO) U.S. General Accounting Office. (1989). *Financial Integrity Act,* Washington, D.C.

(GAO) U.S. General Accounting Office. (1987). *Procurement Personnel: Information on the Procurement Workforce,* Washington, D.C.

(GAO) U.S. General Accounting Office. (1985). *Greater Use of Value Engineering,* Washington, D.C.

(GAO) U.S. General Accounting Office. (1977). *Government Purchasing and the Antitrust Laws,* National Association of Attorneys General, Washington, D.C.

(GAO) U.S. General Accounting Office. (1963). *Impediments to Competitive Bidding,* Council of State Governments, Iron Works, Pike, Kentucky.

Gauthier, Steven J. (1989). *Audit Management Handbook,* Government Finance Officers Association, Chicago, Illinois.

Johnston, David. (1989). Boning up on new ethics of procurement. *New York Times,* May 23.

Lemov, Penelope. (1988). Purchasing officials push new techniques to get more for their money. *Governing:* 40-43, 45-47.

Miller, Girard. (1986). *Investing Public Funds,* Government Finance Officers Association, Chicago, Illinois.

(NIGP) The National Institute of Governmental Purchasing. (1989). *Results of the 1989 Procurement Research Survey,* Falls Church, Virginia.

Petersen, John E., and Watt, Pat. (1986). *The Price of Advice,* Government Finance Officers Association, Chicago, Illinois.

Reid, Richard A., Huth, Case, and Bryson, Donald N. (1984). Inventory cost determination: A public sector challenge. *Journal of Purchasing and Materials Management. 20:* 27-31.

Singer, Jerry. (1988). *Purchasing Management,* International City Management Association, Washington, D.C.

Walsh, Annette H., and Leighland, James. (1989). Designing and managing the procurement process. In *Handbook of Public Administration,* J. L. Perry (ed.). Jossey-Bass, San Francisco, pp. 483-98.

Williams, Robert F., and Bakhshi, V. Sagor. (1988). Competitive bidding: Department of Defense and private sector practices. *Journal of Purchasing and Materials Management. 24:* 29-35.

Zemansky, Stanley D. (1987). *Contracting Professional Services,* National Institute of Governmental Purchasing, Falls Church, Virginia.

Zemansky, Stanley D. (1988). *Ethics and Quality Public Purchasing,* National Institute of Governmental Purchasing, Falls Church, Virginia.

Life-Cycle Costing
Roderick C. Lee

Local governments are consumers and, like individual consumers, frequently purchase the cheapest of several similar items performing the same function, believing that the lowest-priced item is the "best buy." Sadly, however, this is not always true, because the cost of owning an item includes more than its purchase price. Life-cycle costing is a technique increasingly used in business and government to determine the total cost of owning an item, including costs associated with the item's acquisition, operation, and maintenance. The technique accounts not only for the purchase price of the item but also identifies hidden costs of ownership. This discussion describes the life-cycle approach to costing, suggests when the use of this technique is most appropriate, and offers a simple formula for calculating the lifetime cost of owning an item.

WHEN TO APPLY THE TECHNIQUE OF LIFE-CYCLE COSTING

Life-cycle costing can be applied to many local government purchases but is most frequently used to determine the lifetime costs of moderately expensive, energy-consuming equipment, including motor vehicles, climate control systems, data processing equipment, and lighting systems. Table 1 illustrates how life-cycle costing can be used to compare two 15-horsepower electric motors. Based solely on the purchase price, the motor offered by vendor A seems less expensive than the motor offered by vendor B. However, motor A has a higher rate of energy consumption (18.64 kilowatts/hour) than motor B (13.98 kilowatts/hour). As shown in the table, motor A will actually cost $5,292 more than motor B over their lifetimes, assuming equal maintenance costs.

The underlying concepts of life-cycle costing may also be used to strengthen performance standards in bid specifications. The specifications should call for the bidders to provide all of the technical information necessary to project life-cycle costs. While it may be helpful to give a reference brand name to act as a guideline to potential bidders, care should be taken to avoid preempting the competitive process. Along with the bid invitations, the manager or local government purchasing agent should require each potential supplier to submit documentation regarding an item's expected energy consumption rate, the anticipated useful life of the item, and the duty cycle (how much use it is expected to get over a one-year period).

PREPARING A LIFE-CYCLE COST ANALYSIS

Three cost factors and salvage value are core elements of a life-cycle cost analysis. The three cost factors are acquisition costs, lifetime maintenance costs, and energy costs. The acquisition costs of an item include its purchase price and transportation and installation costs. The acquisition costs should also reflect discounts in the purchase price and credit for trade-in equipment. An item's projected lifetime maintenance

---

Reprinted from David N. Ammons, *Administrative Analysis of Local Government: Practical Application of Selected Techniques* (Athens: Carl Vinson Institute of Government, University of Georgia, 1991), 100-105.

Table 1: *Example of Life-Cycle Costing*

Life-Cycle Cost	Motor from Vendor A	Motor from Vendor B
Bid cost	$600	$900
Duty cycle	1,000 hrs./yr.	1,000 hrs./yr.
Life	15 years	15 years
Efficiency rating	60%	80%
Energy consumption (kilowatts/hour)	18.64	13.98
Energy costs (kwh consumption rate × $.08/kwh × 15,000 hours)	$22,368	$16,776
Life-cycle cost (bid cost + energy cost)	$22,968	$17,676
Life-cycle cost difference ($22,968 − $17,676) = $5,292		

Source: League of California Cities, *A Guide to Life Cycle Costing: A Purchasing Technique That Saves Money* (Sacramento: League of California Cities, December 1983), 2. Reprinted by permission of the League of California Cities.

and energy costs are the anticipated costs for keeping the item in operable condition and for energy consumed in operating the item. The fourth factor, fundamental to the analysis, is salvage value: how much can the local government recoup by selling the item at the end of its projected life? Adding the three cost factors and subtracting the salvage value provides a simplified version of the life-cycle cost of an item (Fig. 1).

Calculating life-cycle costs based solely on acquisition costs, maintenance and energy costs, and salvage value may be sufficient for most analyses. However, for especially large or otherwise significant purchases managers may find it useful to examine, when applicable, seven other costs associated with ownership. These are

- *failure costs* including downtime, production losses, and rental costs;
- *training costs* for personnel training in equipment usage, including tuition, time away from job, meals, transportation, and lodging;
- *consumable supply costs* arising from an item's use;
- *storage costs* for the item or for repair parts;
- *secondary costs* for disposal of by-products associated with the item's use (Such costs may be positive or negative—for example, waste heat can be used to reduce energy consumption in colder months, reducing overall costs.);
- *labor costs* or the wages and benefits for employees engaged in the operation of an item; and
- *money costs* including interest paid for loan to purchase item or interest forgone on money that could be invested elsewhere if not tied up in equipment purchases.

The following example demonstrates the use of a life-cycle costing formula that considers acquisition cost, maintenance and energy consumption costs, salvage value, and two other cost factors: failure cost and labor cost.

Figure 1: *Formula for Life-Cycle Costing*

The basic life-cycle cost formula is

life-cycle costs	= **acquisition cost + lifetime maintenance costs + lifetime energy costs − salvage value**

Where

acquisition costs	= purchase price + transportation cost + installation cost − trade-ins and discounts,
lifetime maintenance costs	= anticipated costs of keeping the item in operable condition,
lifetime energy costs	= energy consumption rate × cost of energy × duty cycle × life of the item, and
salvage value	= anticipated worth at the end of the item's projected life.

The components of the lifetime energy costs are

energy consumption rate	= rate at which energy is consumed (kilowatts/hour),
cost of energy	= dollars per energy unit (cents per kwh),
duty cycle	= annual number of hours item is used (number of hours in use per day × number of days in use), and
life	= length of time until item is replaced (number of years in use based on the duty cycle).

For example, the formula for determining the energy cost of an electric typewriter would be

(number of kilowatts/hour) × (cents/kwh) × (number of hours in use/year) × (number of years) = energy cost.

Source: Adapted from League of California Cities, *A Guide to Life Cycle Costing: A Purchasing Technique That Saves Money* (Sacramento: League of California Cities, December 1983), 3-4. Adapted by permission of the League of California Cities.

♦ Lindsey, Virginia

The city of Lindsey, Virginia, plans to purchase a new 1.25 cubic yard crawler/crane, dragline, and clamshell for its water and sewer department. The machine is expected to operate 2,000 hours per year for five years.

Competitive bids were received from three vendors proposing equipment with purchase prices ranging from $24,000 to $28,000 (Table 2). Despite the purchase price advantage of equipment offered by vendor A, the city's purchasing agent and director of Water and Sewer are recommending that the city accept bid C. While bid C's acquisition price is the highest of the three bids, the life-cycle cost of the crawler/crane offered in bid C is $37,800 lower than that of bid A and $14,900 lower than that of bid B.

Table 2: *Applying Life-Cycle Costing*

	Bid A	Bid B	Bid C
Purchase price (bid)	$ 24,000	$ 26,000	$ 28,000
Less trade-in on present unit	2,000	2,200	1,800
Acquisition cost	22,000	23,800	26,200
Energy cost[a]	30,000	25,000	20,000
Maintenance cost[b]	30,000	19,000	15,000
Failure cost[c]	6,000	3,800	3,000
Labor cost[d]	60,000	55,000	50,000
Less expected resale value[e]	5,000	6,500	9,000
Life-cycle cost	143,000	120,100	105,200

Source: Adapted from Stanley D. Zemansky, "Life-Cycle Cost Procurement," in Joseph T. Kelley, *Costing Government Services: A Guide for Decision Making* (Washington, D.C.: Government Finance Officers Association, 1984), 128. Adapted by permission of the Government Finance Officers Association.

[a] The energy costs for all bids were calculated using a one dollar per gallon fuel cost. The machine in Bid A was estimated to consume 30,000 gallons over the five-year period. The machines in Bid B and Bid C were estimated to consume 25,000 and 20,000 gallons over the period, respectively.

[b] Maintenance costs for all bids were based on cost records of similar machines used by the city of Lindsey.

[c] Anytime the machine is not available for work, renting back-up equipment would be necessary. Records indicate rental equipment is 20 percent of each machine's maintenance cost.

[d] Each machine would require approximately the same operator's salary for regular operations, but employees are sometimes required to work overtime when a machine is out of service during normal working hours.

[e] Resale values were based on average sale prices as a percent of original price at used equipment auctions for five-year-old crawler/cranes of the proposed makes.

VARIABILITY OF RELEVANT FACTORS

This example illustrates the variety of characteristics of significance to the life-cycle costs of a particular piece of equipment. For other items, a different set of cost factors may be more significant. For example, a life-cycle cost analysis for microfiche readers for county libraries and court systems might be especially concerned with the useful life of the readers, the duty cycle, and energy costs. The local administrator will also want to know about failure rates and service costs, the availability of parts and prompt service in the event of a breakdown, and the degree of specialized training needed to service the readers.

Requiring the use of a carefully designed bid worksheet approved by the local government can assure that all information needed for calculating life-cycle costs will be uniformly secured from all bidders. Comprehensiveness and uniformity of information will permit a more direct and complete comparison of bids.

LIMITATIONS OF LIFE-CYCLE COSTING

While life-cycle costing can be a useful tool for local governments, it has its limitations. The technique requires local government managers to accumulate detailed information about the various costs associated with a potential purchase. Some of that information, including energy consumption and other product performance data, may be supplied by the manufacturers and sellers of equipment. Local government managers should attempt to get complete documentation from manufacturers and sellers regarding all claims made for their products. The remedies available to governments that have been deceived by false vendor claims depend on the conditions specified in the purchase contract and whether or not the information was presented in a deliberately misleading or inaccurate manner.

Local government managers attempting to use life-cycle costing will find that they often can be much more accurate in their projections if they are maintaining good performance records for their own equipment. Much of the cost information related to maintenance, downtime, rental and storage charges, and other pertinent expenses may be based, in part, on the government's previous experience with those cost factors for identical or similar equipment or on the experience of other local governments that have used the particular model in question. As such, the adequacy of the technique is linked in most cases to the availability of useful information.

Life-cycle costing can be applied to many types of local government purchases. However, the information requirements and the additional time required to use the technique may make its application impractical in some cases. Local government managers may wish to prioritize the items selected for life-cycle costing.

Finally, a frequent problem in applying life-cycle costing in local governments is the question of legal authority for basing purchasing decisions on life-cycle costs rather than simply on purchase price. While several local governments, such as Baltimore, Maryland, have adopted life-cycle costing as a major component of the decision-making process for purchasing equipment, many others assume, often incorrectly, that they have no choice other than awarding the bid to the vendor with the lowest purchase price. In reality, many regulations specify award to the "lowest and best bid," language that appears to leave the door open for consideration of factors other than price tag. Life-cycle costing does not eliminate the lowest bid concept; rather, it applies the concept to a greater range of costs. Local government managers who wish to use life-cycle costing should make themselves aware of applicable legal requirements in their particular community.

Suggestions for Further Reading

Brown, Robert J., and Rudolph R. Yanuck. *Life Cycle Costing*. Atlanta, Ga.: Fairmont Press, 1980.

Gecoma, Richard M., Arthur B. Mohor, and Michael G. Jackson. *Energy Efficient Purchasing for Local Governments*. Athens: Institute of Government, University of Georgia, 1980.

League of California Cities. *A Guide to Life Cycle Costing: A Purchasing Technique That Saves Money*. Sacramento: League of California Cities, December 1983. Reprinted as, "Life Cycle Costing." In *Practical Financial Management: New Techniques for Local Government*, edited by John Matzer, Jr. Washington, D.C.: International City Management Association, 1984.

"Life Cycle Costing Saves Money for Albuquerque." *Public Works* 115 (June 1984): 100.

Malan, Roland M., James R. Fountain, Jr., Donald S. Arrowsmith, and Robert L. Lockridge II. "Analysis." In *Performance Auditing in Local Government*, 139-67. Chicago: Government Finance Officers Association, 1984.

Winslow, R., B. Morrow, R. Carbone, and E. Cross. *Life-Cycle Costing for Procurement of Small Buses*. Washington, D.C.: U.S. Department of Transportation, 1980.

Wubbenhorst, Klaus L. "Life Cycle Costing for Construction Projects." *Long Range Planning*, 19 (August 1986): 87-97.

Zemansky, Stanley D. "Life-Cycle Cost Procurement." In Joseph T. Kelley, *Costing Government Services: A Guide for Decision Making*, 115-39. Washington, D.C.: Government Finance Officers Association, 1984.

Advantages of a Risk Management Program

Gerald J. Miller and W. Bartley Hildreth

INTRODUCTION

Governments today face severe risks. The risks include property damage and loss; liability claims for damage to others' property, for government agents' implementation of unconstitutional policies, and for antitrust law violations; death or sickness of employees; and losses in productivity due to nonexistent or poorly planned pension programs. Facing uncertainty, government managers must confront, even manage, these potential losses.

Risk management provides a means or a strategy to protect governmental resources against accidental or anticipated losses. As a "planned" approach, risk management uses systematic analysis, often based on statistical or probability rules, to identify areas of potential loss, evaluate their potential severity and frequency, control or eliminate potential risk exposures, and provide the means to finance those losses which do occur (Valente 1980).

The body of knowledge dealing with the management of risks developed as insurance programs to protect property against theft, fire, and flood. These early programs have evolved into broader management principles with programs specifically tailored to government activities.

Organizations began using the term risk management to describe a systematic approach to dealing with potential losses only recently. However, the risk management profession is older than the term "risk manager" or "risk management," having evolved from the insurance office.

Although the terms "risk management" and "insurance management" are often used interchangeably, there is a fundamental difference. Risk management is broader than insurance management in that it deals with both insurable and uninsurable risks and the choice of the most appropriate techniques for dealing with these risks.

Risk management also differs from insurance management in philosophy. Instead of the traditional focus in which an insurance buyer simply tried to get the most insurance for the least money, risk management emphasizes the reduction of risks and their costs by the most appropriate techniques. Insurance management involves techniques other than insurance, such as loss prevention and noninsurance, but these other techniques are generally considered primarily as alternatives to insurance. Under the risk management concept, insurance is viewed as simply one of several approaches for dealing with the risks the organization faces.

Our purpose in this essay is to describe the principles of risk management which underlie a loss prevention program and which command systematic examination and disposal of potential losses. In a first section, we describe four principles which guide the vast majority of programs. Then, in the second section, we show why the government should assign

---

Gerald J. Miller is associate professor of public administration, Graduate Department of Public Information, Rutgers-The State University of New Jersey, at Newark; W. Bartley Hildreth is Regents Distinguished Professor, Hugo Wall School of Urban & Public Affairs, Wichita State University.

responsibility to deal directly with potential losses—usually to a risk manager, who coordinates organization effort.

LOSS PREVENTION PROGRAM PRINCIPLES

The four principles which constitute a liability prevention program are identification, measurement, control, and finance. The process of risk management begins with the identification of possible threats to the public treasury, or simply, unanticipated or anticipated losses. These possible losses can then be measured in terms of how often they occur and how severely at each frequency. Among these possible losses, some the organization can avoid and others it can reduce, either in frequency or severity. Of the remainder, the organization may choose to retain some losses, finding them frequent enough and/or not severe enough to choose to transfer. Some, however, evade prediction and may have catastrophic impact, in which case the organization may choose to buy insurance in one form or another.

The process, of course, gets implemented both through the organization and through its management. The organization depends upon the size and complexity of the risks faced, often requiring a risk manager dealing with the problem full-time. Whether a delegate of the chief executive officer supervises the implementation of the risk management program or not, the management of the organization effort follows three basic steps: constructing rules and procedures to guide the program, training organization members, and monitoring organization performance.

We will expand the discussion of each of the elements in the risk management process in subsequent sections.

Identification of Risks

Risk identification is the process of isolating and analyzing potential sources of accidental loss. To the public organization, loss could be classified as that occurring to property or capital, such as damage to buildings or losses due to liability suits, or that occurring to people, such as death or accident, or the risk of economic insecurity after retirement. In all cases, assets of the jurisdiction are jeopardized. In response to these potential losses, managers now design property loss and liability prevention, life insurance, safety, and pension programs.

Risk identification is the first step in the design process. Initially, the manager's effort includes investigation, analysis of data, and classification of risks. Investigators attempt to find out what the potential losses are and where they lie. Surveys and questionnaires, examination of financial records, and study of operations flow charts usually constitute the means of investigation (Head and Horn 1985).

Analysis of risks requires one to determine what potential losses loom largest or most frequent. Data generated during investigation suggest the frequency but give no reliable estimate of severity. Gaining knowledge of just how large a loss can be requires the perspective of other organizations. Therefore, analysis of risks necessitates an in-depth study based on a broad perspective.

Measurement of Risks

Based on identification and analysis, a manager can classify risks by measuring and evaluating them. A public official must determine the probability and financial impact of potential losses. In other words, how likely is a loss and how severely could the loss affect the budget? Not only should the information about one type of loss be identified, but public officials should also weigh the probability and severity of each type against others. Both the probability and financial impact of losses may be determined by maintaining complete and accurate records on the number and kinds of losses sustained in the past, both in the organization and in other governmental units.

What should one know? Liability suits provide one example. In this case, useful information might include the official sued, the management practice in question, the amount of the court judgment paid, attorneys' fees and other costs such as court costs, and the length of time spent by the official's professional and support staffs defending the suit. Making this difficult to interpret is the low number of suits encountered by all but the largest governments. Other governments' experience can provide a fuller perspective. Similar data requirements apply to the risks associated with an employee's death, disability, and loss of income at retirement.

Control of Risks

Not only must a public official identify and measure risks, he or she must also attempt to manage and control organizational practices which could lead to losses and to select methods of handling anticipated or accidental losses. In fact, control is the most important step in risk management. This effort encompasses all government activities and requires establishing, implementing, monitoring, and updating policies and procedures related to those practices identified as risks. Four suggested approaches are (1) avoiding risks, (2) reducing them, (3) retaining some, and (4) transferring others.

Avoid the Risk

Public officials can forego activities involving risk. Earlier identification of risky programs or activities can aid decision making. The nature of government programs, however, forestalls adequate use of avoidance. Few activities required of a public official can actually be avoided; therefore, careful scrutiny of legal requirements should precede efforts to avoid a particular activity. Moreover, all public officials want to provide a variety of facilities and services to citizens, even though some of these facilities and services can result in loss.

A city-owned swimming pool is one example. Adequate recreation facilities hallmark the policies of most public officials. Yet, the provision of swimming pools carries with it a number of potential losses. Inadequate security for the facility in winter months may result in destruction. Little regard for safety and supervision in summer months may lead to accidents and then liability suits. Providing the pool at all represents a desire to serve the community; however, no legal requirement necessitates a city's undertaking the responsibilities and the risks. Therefore, decision makers must balance the desire to provide services that improve the quality of life of citizens against the chance of financial loss.

Consider also safety of employees. Clearly, a safety program can isolate hazardous jobs or tasks, and, through conscientious implementation, the program can minimize the number of activities in which accidents occur. Yet, many risks will remain. For example, employees involved in police, fire, and military matters involuntarily face quite risky situations. In these areas, risk reduction may help.

Reduce the Risk

Officials' own efforts can reduce the probability of loss. Consider three available methods. First, carefully crafted policies and procedures can guide officials' actions as well as those of public employees, especially in high-risk activities. Development and implementation of sound policies and procedures in these exposure areas can provide employees and officials with uniform guidelines.

Personnel administration, licensing decisions, and equipment operation provide examples. Policies can state explicitly how new employees get selected without bias, even to specification of procedures such as forms and action steps taken in handling job applications. Similar steps can state qualifications for a particular license, and procedures can prescribe hearing requirements in reviewing and deciding whether a particular applicant is qualified. Finally, safety guidelines can provide employees the wherewithal to reduce accidents while operating automobiles or construction machinery, and preventive medical checkups of employees might allow supervisors to remove the worker from potential disability-provoking work requirements.

Second, officials can follow sound management principles, such as adequate training and supervision of employees, to reduce risks. Thus, policies in force are made part of the required training materials, and supervisors can inspect employees' work from time to time to ensure their compliance.

Third, clarifying responsibilities within the organization can often reduce risk. For example, having several different people responsible, in part, for one task increases risk. By consolidating functions or delimiting roles, managers can fill specialized jobs with highly skilled individuals. Such clear definition of work might prevent neglect or accident.

Retain the Risk

While public officials have avoided some risks and reduced the probability of others, they may retain many other risks through government assumption of financial losses. Research in risk management suggests guides for retaining risks. The guides rest on the notion of frequency and severity of losses, a classification yielded by the original investigation and measurement of risks. There are four possible outcomes:

a. Low frequency, low severity
b. Low frequency, high severity

c. High frequency, low severity
   d. High frequency, high severity

Risks that fall within categories a, c, and d could be retained and budgeted for, avoided, or reduced. Greene and Serbein (1978) argue that only risk category b—low frequency, high severity—be transferred. Decisions about the amount to set aside for retained risks would, of course, also depend on the data generated by an identification and measurement of potential losses. A public entity can assume the financial consequences of a potential risk, absorbing the loss in the operating budget when the loss occurs. "Going bare," as absorbing a loss is called, would pertain, if ever, only to a low frequency, low severity risk.

A second method requires use of both organizational and outside resources. The public entity can assume either a small or large part of the loss, leaving the remainder to insurance coverage. The small loss retention results when the government assumes some in-kind services or the deductible on an insurance policy. For instance, the small loss situation may allow the government to reimburse officials for attorneys' fees and court costs should they be sued for actions taken in the performance of their jobs. Policies can also hold that the government's attorney defend officials if they are confronted with a personal liability suit. In these cases, the government entity will pay for what can be small losses, leaving court judgments to insurance. Workers' compensation claims can be covered by funds equal to probable losses and set aside systematically. Also, governments can retain larger deductibles with insurance contracts, resulting in possibly lower insurance premiums.

The large loss retention is arranged through government funds used with catastrophic insurance coverage. Government indemnity illustrates the use of government funds and perhaps insurance coverage. Indemnity may emanate from state provision of local government liability, or simply from allowing injured citizens to sue the government. State laws follow two basic approaches to indemnification—open-ended and closed-ended (U.S. Advisory Commission on Intergovernmental Relations 1978).

Open-ended approach to indemnification. "Open-ended" indemnification suggests broad government responsibility for losses to citizens. This approach provides that the government is liable for all activities, unless an act is specifically excluded. For example, state law may provide for open-ended liability except in specified instances generally relating to essential government functions such as legislative, judicial, and executive actions; taxing; inspections; and licensing. Liability of employees and the government is "merged" by such laws; the governmental unit must defend the employees and pay any judgment if the employee was acting within the scope of his or her powers.

Most important, such laws limit the amount of liability, establish procedures for bringing claims against a government, and authorize broad powers for governmental accounting units to insure themselves against liability cases. In this case, the "open-endedness" creates a potential high frequency, high severity condition. To reduce the effects associated with the "high-high" condition, the government can share or partially transfer the risk. The government could pay part of the amount of any judgment, leaving all above to an insurance company.

Closed-ended approach to indemnification. "Closed-ended" liability narrowly defines indemnity. This approach provides for the exclusion of suits against governments except in certain instances. Under such laws, governments are immune except for damages caused by a public vehicle or a dangerous condition in public property. Limits are often placed on the amount of liability.

Such an approach may yield a low frequency, high severity risk. The result would depend, as always, on the judicial interpretations of the law. If a large loss were probable, the deductible for almost total insurance coverage could represent some attempt to retain losses.

Retention of losses can require a self-insurance program. A self-insurance program systematically handles all of the functions of an insurance agency, but normally at a lower cost than the premiums paid to insurers. Thus the government accounts for amounts set aside to cover losses; measures the probability of losses; and administers adjusting, legal work, and payment for losses. The benefits gained from self-insurance are also measured against the costs in determining which losses to retain through self-insurance. Those losses that the local government can handle by itself at lower cost than insurance can be self-insured. Others can be transferred (Governmental Accounting Standards Board 1989).

Prohibitive expense is not the sole reason for self-insuring. Insufficient insurance policy limits, insurance policy exclusions and deductibles, and unavailability of insurance expertise may necessitate a conscious and well-planned effort to create organization capacity to absorb losses.

Transfer the Risk

In deciding how to control risks, public officials may buy insurance after they have eliminated all other methods—avoiding, reducing, or retaining risks—as either impractical or impossible. Insurance for public employees and officials increasingly interests managers concerned with the uncertainty of the world in which they operate.

Two methods of insurance have gained wide acceptance: commercial insurance and public entity risk pools.

Commercial insurance. Using private companies to insure risks has traditionally served cities well in areas such as property damage and employee life and health. The area of liability, however, poses problems. Industry-wide conditions change, insurance firms exit the municipal market, liability laws change, and premiums escalate to levels that exceed local budget plans.

What should one consider in purchasing insurance? Analysis of coverage, service, and cost yield particularly pertinent information to guide choice. First, the analysis of coverage expressed by an insurance contract yields answers to whether one is getting the coverage desired—has the coverage desired, in fact, been obtained?—and whether the obligations of buyer and insurer are clear. Various kinds of insurance policies cover various risks, and many authorities can assist in selecting the appropriate form (Greene and Serbein 1978). However, all insurance policies have four common features (Betterly 1967: 9-85):

1. *Declarations* include names, location, amount, term, and premium. These should be checked for accuracy. Failure to properly name the insured or to designate the correct address has been the basis for more than one lawsuit by an unsatisfied insured.
2. *Insuring agreements* state what is covered. Although usually expressed positively, they do include limitations sometimes more significant than the exclusions. Be sure to clarify any ambiguity.
3. *Exclusions* are a necessary part of any insurance contract, but the type of exclusions and the number of them constitute significant points of comparison between two or more proposals.
4. *Conditions* include standard clauses required by statute, plus basic provisions common to a species of policy. Usually they can be broadened in favor of the insured, and such amendments may be necessary so that the insurance will do what the buyer intended.

Public entity risk pools. Governments can form risk pools to which several entities contribute and from which claims are paid, taking on characteristics of an insurer. For example, each jurisdiction contributes regularly and assumes a set deductible amount in case of a claim.

The decision concerning commercial insurance or risk pools depends upon the cost of each, of course. However, the risk pool may sometimes be the only choice for risk transfer, given general economic conditions and the market conditions of the insurance industry.

Risk Finance

Budgeting and shrewd purchasing policies for insurance coverage clearly underlie a risk management program. Even more, self-insurance and interlocal risk pools illustrate the government's need to connect financial planning and risk management. Risk funding requires setting aside funds to meet losses arising out of those uncontrolled risks that cannot be eliminated or transferred. If local or state law requires the government to assume certain losses in which insurance may incur prohibitive expense, prudent management dictates that public officials budget for the contingency.

The accounting methods have real importance in any risk financing plan (Governmental Accounting Standards Board 1989). In other words, how should risks that the organization retains be controlled? Public entity risk pools are similar to commercial insurance firms and, therefore, are perhaps best viewed as an enterprise fund. An internal service fund provides another accounting method. This fund —a self-insurance fund—charges operating funds an amount equivalent to premiums based upon the identified and measured risks. The internal service fund aids managers in capturing the total cost of the risk management program and facilitates allocations of cost back to the various operating funds.

The self-insurance set-aside may also be accounted for through the General Fund. This arrangement generally allows greater managerial flexibility, although the commingling of funds prevents segregation of the true costs of the risk management program.

As enticing as self-insurance sounds, the local government must be able to handle the financial necessities of such a fund without curtailing normal service activities or placing its assets in jeopardy. Similar comments, of course, apply in funding insurance schemes, especially in times of rapidly escalating fees. The watchword is prudent management of financial resources.

ADMINISTERING THE RISK REDUCTION PROGRAM

What does risk management require? Common sense supported by careful planning and supervision can result in sound management. Aided by systematic effort on all officials' parts, a risk management program can successfully reduce the threat of liability.

There are four major steps in setting up a risk management program:

1. Establish a management policy with local government goals in preventing and controlling risks, and organize risk management units, assigning responsibility to a risk manager on the local government staff.
2. Review and amend policies, procedures, and practices which create potential risks and isolate chronic risks in the organization.
3. Increase awareness among officials and employees of liability risks through memoranda and training.
4. Monitor officials' and employees' compliance with management policies and procedures and the risk management program through observations of on-the-job behavior and through citizen feedback.

Policy and Organization

Public officials guide the management of risks with dictates, adopting and announcing management policy that sets out the broad designs of the loss prevention and reduction program. Despite this logic, policymaking more often gets honored in its breach.

Formal policy may not guide a program in many cities, but a government concerned about liability risks must provide a coordinating unit responsible for risk management. Cities, again, have yet to emphasize organization, unlike their state counterparts and private business.

Implementation of a risk management program is normally assigned to a professional risk manager, a practice especially noticeable in private sector organizations. The risk manager's office may report to or form part of a finance or personnel office or stand free of other staff departments, reporting only to the chief executive officer. The office, in any case, usually has staff status, associated with the chief executive.

Centralization or decentralization of structure varies. Basically, a risk manager must not only support individual departments in their risk management programs but also provide specialized expertise for elected or appointed officials on risk management aspects of new or existing policies.

The scope of duties given the risk manager may differ. A major part of the risk manager's responsibility is insurance management, but employee benefits often get added. Most important, the risk manager coordinates the managerial aspects of risk prevention.

Implementation

After organizing the unit, risk managers must seize the early initiative by following at least three major steps: constructing sound practices for dealing with areas that create potential risks or ones chronically creating loss; training employees in these new rules and procedures; and monitoring compliance with the procedures so that early indicators of system failure or recidivism surface quickly and lead to corrective action.

The first ingredient is the construction of rules and procedures to define what may be done and how losses can be prevented. Initially, this may involve a survey to find out how the problem areas are currently being handled. It might be useful to evaluate current policy in light of other organizations' perspectives, legal trends, and other indicators such as citizen complaints. In such managerially important areas as personnel administration, for example, this would involve validated selection instruments and appropriate affirmative action procedures. Similarly, the due process rights of employees deserve special attention. When considering discipline or dismissal actions, local government officials should practice caution. Rash action in cases of employee misconduct should be tempered with thorough investigation and application of penalties consistent with past cases.

In each case, the risk manager and other public officials scrutinize the problems that create losses and attempt to deal with them reasonably and systematically. Whether the effort to be made by the official goes toward solving a problem, meeting a demand, or trying to comply with court orders, he or she must clearly determine what the object of the regulation will be and address it with applicable and reasonable rules. This step is crucial because all procedures, training, and monitoring will by definition be based on the efforts to grapple with this problem.

Comprehensive, on-going training, the second step, provides a special opportunity. Through training, risk managers can address safety, life/health, and liability questions constructively. Training programs can be instituted to familiarize employees with established policies and procedures conforming to safety standards and those complying with the law. Using case studies or actual court cases to outline potential risks, employees get special warning of the specific areas that can result in accidents or damage suits.

Two types of programs can be designed: one for skill updating and another for new employees. In each program the basic rules and procedures gain visibility and employees learn to use these rules and procedures with more facility.

A variety of training methods may be employed in the two programs, of course. For example, role-playing exercises efficiently illustrate the dynamics of safety and liability situations and provide experience in decision making under these constraints. The approach has met with success in providing experiential training to a wide cross-section of public administrators. A by-product of training sessions such as these could well be the identification of previously undetected risks, adding an unexpected feedback element to the first step of constructing and reviewing rules and procedures.

Complementing this effective, but incidental, feedback will be the process of monitoring. Monitoring systems will help officials to check employees' performance, gain internal organization feedback, and govern the implementation of policies. Monitoring employees' compliance will strengthen the training process, demonstrate unclear training methods, reveal gaps in understanding, and isolate individuals who cannot comprehend the risks being taken. Internal organization feedback can help change managerial practices before their inadequacy leads to disruption, loss, or even litigation. Finally, monitoring the effect of policies and procedures will permit policymakers to adapt rules to the needs of clientele and point out unfair ways of dealing with problems.

CONCLUSIONS

The most positive implications of the legal challenges to management are the creation or encouragement of fair and effective management practices where none existed before and the recognition of risks and plans to deal with them. Thus, objective rulemaking and fair procedures in applying them, rigorous and continual training, and constant monitoring of the effects of both rules and training can help. Moreover, following risk management principles can do more. As a result, no exotic remedies are called for in response to court judgments, legislative actions, and other risk threats. Rather, just and sound managerial approaches can control the challenge to public officials today.

References

Betterly, G. "Risk management." 1967. In *Handbook of business administration*. H.B. Maynard, ed. Chicago: McGraw-Hill.

Governmental Accounting Standards Board. 1989. "Accounting and financial reporting for risk financing and related issues (GASB-10)." Washington, D.C.: GASB.

Greene, M.R., and Serbein, O.N. 1978. *Risk management*. Reston, Va.: Reston Publishing Company.

Head, G.L., and S. Horn. *Essentials of the risk management process*. 1985. Malvern, Pa.: Insurance Institute of America.

U.S. Advisory Commission on Intergovernmental Relations. 1978. *Intergovernmental Relations* (Winter).

Valente, P. *Directory of risk management practices*. 1980. Washington, D.C.: International City Management Assoc. (ICMA).

Wasserman, N., and D.G. Phelus. 1985. *Risk management today*. Washington, D.C.: ICMA.

Pension Policy, Management, and Analysis

W. Bartley Hildreth and Gerald J. Miller

The employee benefit package of nearly all full-time government employees includes a form of post-retirement income protection, better known as a pension program. Whether the pension program is administered locally or by the state, or by the U.S. social security system, governmental jurisdictions face significant yearly appropriations to cover the employers' contributions to these employee retirement programs. Inattention to the purposes and management of pension programs can lead to poorly planned benefit packages, insufficient funding precipitating plan insolvency, and/or wasted appropriation of increasingly scarce public funds.

To provide a fuller understanding of public pension management, this article explores distinguishing characteristics and major controversies. First, the purposes of pension programs are outlined. Then, public pension systems' development and administration are sketched. Attention then turns to general but key features of pension benefits. Different ways of financing pension plans (such as pay-as-you-go and actuarial funding) are reviewed along with ways in which pension systems have an impact on public budgeting. Investment strategy, including socially beneficial investment, is noted. The closing section focuses on such issues as control, regulation, and reform of public pension plans.

W. Bartley Hildreth is Regents Distinguished Professor, Hugo Wall School of Urban & Public Affairs, Wichita State University; Gerald J. Miller is associate professor of public administration, Graduate Department of Public Information, Rutgers-The State University of New Jersey, at Newark.

PURPOSES

Pension systems benefit both the employee and the employer: economic and social needs of the employee are addressed and the personnel management objectives of the political jurisdiction are supported. Viewed from an *economic security* perspective, pensions systems can allow an accumulation of income to provide for retirement, disability, and/or income to survivors in case of death. While pension programs are often regarded as postretirement income, members generally receive disability and survivor's benefits, too.

Personnel management objectives are served by pension systems. One of the initial reasons for such public sector programs was the need to supplement the public employee's low salary. Further, retirement systems were considered a means to foster a career system, with retirement benefits serving as compensation for a long public service career. Plans have therefore been constructed which grant increased benefits to members of organizations who hold long-standing seniority.

Military, police, and firefighter pensions systems have been developed to meet somewhat different personnel management goals. Because uniformed work requires great personal risks, it is essential that members of such units maintain a high level of physical stamina and capacity to respond to rapidly developing events. This set of needs clashes with the normal aging process and the time it takes to build up the tenure that is associated with adequate accumulation of pension contribution. The uniformed services, as a result, typically offer incentives for their members to retire early, opening up opportunities to make the transition into a second career at a relatively early age. Often, a person making such a move will have sufficient time in a second occupation to qualify for another pension. Such opportunity to earn two retirement checks is often referred to negatively as "double-dipping," yet both are earned in compliance with all laws.

ADMINISTRATION

With approximately 9,000 public employee retirement systems (Zorn 1991) in existence, and with many covering specialized groupings within a state or a municipality—such as law enforcement, judges, or elected tax assessors—it is understandable that there are varying administrative arrangements and benefit programs. Fundamental differences exist between the administration of a public pension system and that of a private program (McCollum and Mundt 1976). A private system is managed according to company policy with basic ground rules, or standards, established by federal law. In contrast, legislative policymakers generally have direct control over a public pension system. Legislative control often implies that benefits, funding, investment, and other pension management issues depend on politically inspired change, often without due consideration of the consequences. For example, granting police officers liberalized vesting privileges might be followed by demands for comparable features for other occupational groups. This phenomenon, called "leapfrogging," often occurs without adequate fiscal analysis of even the first benefit expansion.

While most public pension systems are locally administered, there are those who contend that centralized, state-administered management is preferable. Cost efficiencies, uniform benefits, maximum investment yield, and effective management and control serve as rationale for consolidation.

Consolidation also creates problems. For example, since extensive locally administered plans can lead to varying benefit levels across a state, such programs encourage increases in employee salaries in jurisdictions that are low paying prior to consolidation to allow those employees to achieve a level of comparability with all other jurisdictions following consolidation. Costs are therefore spread across the entire "consolidated" membership. The effort to gain uniformity through consolidation results in smaller-plan members actually receiving more benefits than before—a plus for smaller-plan members which places greatly increased budget demands on their employers (Tilove 1976).

Under what conditions should a state-administered consolidation program be pushed as a reform? Although there is no single test, several criteria seem reasonable. First, when the size of the employee group is small and relatively stable, in a community with limited growth and resource potential, arguments favor consolidation. Basic requirements of a pension system include an ability to spread the liability across as large a workforce as possible. When a workforce is small and unlikely to grow, members could not gain the benefits found, perhaps, in larger plans.

Second, when locally administered plans develop financial problems the particular state government may be able to offer relief. State-administered plans or general monitoring programs often emerge in an effort to bring some systematic disclosure or resolution of financial problems.

Given the above conditions which are conducive to consolidating pension programs, what factors prolong fragmentation? First, members of a locally administered pension system usually have an interest in retaining control over their own program. While members might not have a major impact on particular benefits, a locally administered plan theoretically allows more individuals to influence decision making. In addition, local policymakers fear the loss of local autonomy to state legislatures.

Even under statewide consolidation, proliferation of plans according to occupational groups occurs. For example, fire and police groups typically press for continued segregation of their plans from other groups' programs. By so doing, occupational groups can pinpoint their demands for benefit changes without having to worry about extending similar benefits to other work groups.

BENEFITS

Consideration of a plan's objective and its design raises profound issues for pension system operations.

Objective

Disputes rage over the objective of a retirement program. One view holds that retirement benefits should not total more than full pay at retirement. Another view supports the constant-standard-of-living concept: that to maintain approximately the same standard of living that beneficiaries had immediately preceding their retirement, benefits must be indexed to increases in the cost of living, usually to the consumer price index. Grants of postretirement income indexed to changes in the cost of living are widely sought by employees. Indexing, however, results in a dramatic increase in benefit costs. While public employee pension programs might adhere to the above objectives, many private sector employees receive less protection from economic insecurity. Despite the apparent illogic, taxpayers with little or no protection for their own retirement often permit their taxes to subsidize government workers with better retirement benefits. A benevolent attitude could, of course, account for this phenomenon. Another explanation is that voters simply are not fully informed about the variance between their own status and that of the public worker (Tilove 1976; Winklevoss and McGill 1979).

Design

Benefit designs are not uniform for all public pension systems. While pension plan administrators may use model plans to gauge their efforts, the fact that public plans are designed by politically motivated policymakers yields a state of affairs where benefits often lack a coherent pattern. Four key design problems involve the use of employee contributions, the compensation basis, vesting concerns, and social security issues.

Contributions

Public pension plans are built on the accumulation of employer as well as employee contributions. Public pension plans enjoy generally higher benefits than their private sector counterparts because of this joint contribution by both the public employer and the employee. In addition, public plans establish benefit levels irrespective of the contributions for a particular employee—termed a defined benefit plan. Private plans, in contrast, generate benefits in direct relationship to the employee's individual contributions, and earnings on those assets, since employers do not make contributions to most plans—termed a defined contribution plan.

Compensation-Based Benefit Formula

Most public employee retirement systems compute benefit levels based on the final salary, averaged over the last few work years, with the actual method depending upon the particular plan. A three-year average salary tends to be a favorite approach, but this can be defined as the average of the highest three years of participating service. This practice can lead to perverse behavior, depending upon the rules. If permitted, selling unused leave days and cashing-in on lax overtime rules in the last year can greatly inflate the wage base upon which future benefits are calculated. Unless tightly controlled, such systems provide major incentives to abuse compensation programs, thereby unnecessarily inflating benefit levels for years into the future.

Benefit levels are seldom based solely on a flat percentage of the compensation base. Instead, a unit-benefit formula is followed, meaning that a selected percentage amount (such as 1.5 percent) is multiplied by the number of years of creditable service (years of employment). For example, under a 1.5 percent unit rule, an employee with 30 years of creditable service would have his or her yearly pension benefits set at 45 percent (1.5 times 30) of the compensation base. Some public pension plans, especially those for police and firefighters, often use a two-step percentage to calculate pension benefit accumulations, with the lower rate (say 1.5 percent) used for the first 10 years and a higher rate (2 percent) applied to the remaining work years (Zorn 1990).

Vesting

Public pension systems, like private plans, establish a date on which the employee acquires rights to the plan's stated benefits, although benefits will be claimed at a later, agreed-upon retirement age. The appropriate vesting date is a major pension policy decision. For example, vesting policy can adversely limit employee movement. If employees perceive an overriding financial disadvantage in leaving a job only because they will not receive all the benefits of contributing to their pension plan, they will certainly experience frustration, loss of commitment, and other problems with which managers must deal. In the private sector, vesting periods are mandated by the Employee Retirement Income and Security Act

(ERISA). Short of similar national regulation of public pension systems, one approach is for statewide, uniform vesting privileges to encourage at least intrastate portability of pensions and, therefore, employee mobility (Munnell and Connolly 1979).

Social Security and Public Pensions

While private employers must participate in the federal Old Age, Survivors and Disability Insurance, better known as the social security program, state and local governments have had the option of whether or not to join. The vast majority of public employees, however, participate in social security (Zorn 1990). A byproduct of the public plan is some degree of integration of benefits, by adjusting benefits to reflect eventual social security coverage (Zorn 1990). Of those public employees whose employers do not participate in the social security system, many eventually gain social security coverage. For instance, firefighters enjoy work schedules that allow them to "moonlight" in a second career, deriving an income to enable them to pay into and qualify for subsequent social security benefits.

FINANCIAL POLICIES AND ANALYSIS

Pension programs can follow an actuarial-based reserve funding approach or use a pay-as-you-go method. A reserve funding program involves use of an actuarial plan to provide a systematic schedule of contributions based on long-term needs. On the other hand, a pension program financed by existing members and employer appropriations to cover current expenses (such as benefits, refunds, and administrative expenditures) is referred to as a pay-as-you-go plan. Pay-as-you-go programs are generally in disfavor and violate generally accepted accounting principles (GAAP). Tilove notes:

> Pay-as-you-go arrangements encourage irresponsibility—the grant of benefits without recognition of the cost—and expose employees to the hazards of disappointment if the jurisdiction financing the system loses its ability to pay or if the taxpayers revolt against the ultimately high costs. (1976, 348).

Despite such analyses, pay-as-you-go is an all too frequent means of financing public pension plans. What accounts for the staying power of pay-as-you-go plans? One probable reason is that pay-as-you-go plans typically require lower annual appropriations than do the fully funded plans.

Private plans illustrate the goal of full funding. ERISA requires a fully funded system for private pensions systems. This law was designed to keep private employers from abandoning businesses, and thus pension systems, leaving pension plan members without recourse or economic security. Unfortunately, this goal has fallen short, with a bankrupt firm's employee pension obligation being covered by premiums to an insurance fund paid by other firms' employees.

The financial strength of a public retirement system is the degree to which current assets are estimated to cover the long-term value of benefits. Many public pensions systems, however, end up with an unfunded pension obligation—where the present value of all future benefits exceeds the present value of all assets, including expected future contributions (U.S. General Accounting Office 1992). Actuarial estimates of future contributions are based on assumptions regarding potential investment returns, projected rate of inflation, demographic composition of the covered workforce, mortality and disability rates, and expected career paths (Roeder 1987; Tilove 1976).

Given the importance of tracing a pension plan's actuarial accrued liability, a growing pension benefit obligation is one negative trend (as shown in Table 1). Another way of looking at the unfunded pension obligation is as a percentage of the net assets available for benefits. Following this measure over a period of years indicates whether the pension system is becoming financially stronger or weaker (with a greater percentage representing a stronger system). Since benefits are tied to payroll, and inflation affects both, another common measurement ratio is pension benefit obligation as a percentage of the payroll of all covered employees. The lower the number, the stronger the system, with a fully funded (no pension benefit obligation) pension system having a zero coverage ratio. These indicators are part of the pension disclosure requirements to meet generally accepted accounting principles (Governmental Accounting Standards Board 1986).

Several commentators have advanced the idea that using a fully funded system for government pension plans is questionable (Bacon 1980; Tilove 1976).

Table 1: *Funding Analysis of the City of Brightside Public Employee Retirement System (in millions)*

Fiscal Year	(1) Net Assets Available for Benefits	(2) Pension Benefit Obligation	(3) Percentage Funded (1)/(2)	(4) Unfunded Pension Benefit Obligation (2)–(1)	(5) Annual Covered Payroll	(6) Unfunded Pension Benefit Obligation as a Percentage of covered payroll
19X1	$300.0	$378.6	79.2	$78.6	$111.1	70.7
19X2	$313.4	$402.2	77.9	$88.8	$114.1	77.8
19X3	$327.9	$421.0	77.9	$93.1	$122.6	75.9
19X4	$348.1	$441.9	78.8	$93.8	$136.9	68.5
19X5	$380.4	$475.3	80.0	$94.9	$145.4	65.3

The argument holds that governmental units enjoy seemingly perpetual life and access to tax resources. In fact, taxpayers might be concerned if current tax receipts were put into a funded reserve and not used for the benefit of current taxpayers. Besides, annual contributions would have to increase manyfold in order to get state and local public employee pension funds rapidly into compliance with ERISA standards.

Still, a fully funded pension plan seeks to avoid the situation of one group of taxpayers pushing off the payment liability to another taxpaying generation.

BUDGET ISSUES

The budgetary impact of retirement programs in the public sector is enormous. Employer payments for employee pension and social security programs make up roughly one-half of the budgeted benefit dollar.

Public employers' contributions to the pension funds of their employees are mostly funded from general taxes, not earmarked ones. Since numerous public services are also funded from these taxes, pension contributions have to compete with other spending programs for tax dollars. Pension contributions have been funded by other arrangements, too. In some communities, voters have approved dedicated property tax levies to partially cover pension plan contributions.

Can pension contributions be cut during austerity efforts? In many instances, pension funding is a mandatory appropriation. Written into some state constitutions as a contractual obligation, pension benefits cannot undergo arbitrary cutbacks. Still, efforts to delay the employer's contribution have proven successful (but very contentious) in some cases. Plus, employers contributing less than the actuarially required amount leads to plan underfunding.

Another sleight-of-hand method used to reduce employer contributions involves manipulation of the assumptions upon which future estimates of the plan are built. For example, by raising the assumed rate of earnings on the fund's assets (interest earnings), lower pension costs result—almost miraculously. In such a manipulation, a 1 percent increase in the assumed investment return rate, holding other assumptions constant, could result in a 20 to 25 percent reduction in the required annual contribution. Higher investment earnings, then, mean that the employer has to contribute less to maintain the same employee benefit structure.

Pension assets remain an attractive source for cash-poor politicians. Several jurisdictions actually have used pension system receipts to finance other annual operations (U.S. Advisory Commission on Intergovernmental Relations 1973; Tax Foundation, Inc. 1976). Policymakers have expanded public pension benefits in times when salary increases have been politically unappealing. As governments seek to streamline the workforce and reduce spending, efforts to "call back" some of the most costly, liberalized benefits take center stage. Employee unions fight such attempts. And, in fact, efforts to scale back existing benefit levels raise questions about the keeping of explicit or implied contractual obligations to employees about pension programs. Still, changes in the fiscal environment of governments (including voter resistance to higher taxes) force such discussion.

INVESTMENT

The investment of employee and employer pension contributions helps increase the value of the pension fund's assets. High investment yields reduce the need for increases in contribution levels. Poor investment decisions, however, can result in a loss of principal, if not a loss of opportunity as gains realized are lower than alternative investments might have yielded.

Public sector pension programs have historically operated with severe limits on investment opportunities. In recent decades, investment flexibility has emerged with prudent investment policy guiding action. Not only can money be placed in fixed income securities, such as U.S. securities, and high-quality domestic corporate bonds, but other classes have gained wide acceptance, such as foreign bonds, equity ownership through stock in foreign and domestic publicly traded firms (i.e., the stock market), and private partnership interests in real estate development.

Portfolio managers are frequently asked to make socially beneficial investments. Their advocates argue that these investments achieve both important public policy goals and economic security of public employees. Social investments defy pat characterization. Examples of economically targeted investments include requirements to invest in local development projects, to fund venture capital pools designed to spur small businesses or minority-owned firms, or to engage in other things that might help stimulate the local community, even at a lower investment yield than available in the national market.

While economically targeted investment is politically appealing, questions arise about adopting such policy for pension investment. Members and beneficiaries of the plan might question the reasonableness of having pension dollars steered to help solve the fiscal problems of some local endeavor. To follow a social investment strategy requires examining the alternatives in terms of risks and returns. Even cautious corporate pension funds see value in some economically targeted investments (Hawthorne 1993).

Pension plans develop asset allocation policies to cover their choice of investments. First, acceptable asset classes are developed, based on return expectations given the risk of such investments. Limits, by classes, are set by the governing board of directors. Then, the focus turns to the management of funds within each class. An operating premise is that by diversifying its investments, a pension system can avoid placing too much emphasis on one area of investment (Miller 1986).

Pension assets are often assigned, under contract, to several external investment managers who then implement the board-selected investment strategies. Therefore, a very careful selection and monitoring process must be utilized to ensure that the external investment manager(s) produces the desired results (McKenzie 1989).

CONTROL

Three types of controls are important when considering public employee retirement systems: management, financial, and political. First, management control extends from a strong board of directors that monitors policy directives to the professional staff charged with efficient management of the retirement system. The board of directors, usually made up of member representatives and others, has authority to implement legal requirements. The board's direction to the professional staff involves assessing actuarial assumptions, handling investments, constructing appropriate accounting systems, processing claims effectively, and reporting plan results.

Financial stability is essential for continuity and to meet expectations of members. This goes beyond an adequate accounting system to the entity's financial reputation. A major change has been the movement by public pension systems to follow generally accepted accounting principles (GAAP). This gives policymakers and taxpayers consistent reporting regarding the fiscal condition of the pension system, especially changes in the unfunded pension liability. Since pension liabilities are considered a negative credit element by municipal bond rating agencies, large unfunded liabilities can hinder the jurisdiction's capital acquisition program. For example, bond market disclosure documents that do not reveal pension funding conditions (such as unfunded accrued liability) can lead to investor suspicion that the issuer has something to hide or does not understand the pension plan. The result of such management inattention can adversely affect the cost of capital.

As has already been discussed, political control also affects pension plans. Actions by *state* legislators to liberalize pension benefits of *local* employees affect local taxpayers unfavorably. This results from having benefit-setting policy separated from the responsibility to implement such policies (Bleakney 1972).

REGULATION AND REFORM

As noted earlier, ERISA dictates private sector pension management practices. Attempts to construct a federal regulatory framework for public employee pension systems have not been very successful, due partly to constitutional questions (U.S. House of Representatives 1978). Governors and legislators tend to push for state-level, rather than federal, control over local plans (see National Governors' Association 1978). In lieu of direct state-administration, state oversight commissions help monitor local pension plans (Salomone 1989). But, despite these efforts, calls continue for more effective "fail-safe" monitoring systems (Munnell and Connolly 1979; U.S. Advisory Commission on Intergovernmental Relations 1973).

SUMMARY

This article has outlined the key features of pension administration and policy and the challenges it faces. Understanding the purposes and design of pension programs helps the manager assess the consequences of benefit changes, for instance. In contrast, pension *mis*management results from inadequate attention to the interrelationships among and between the pension system and the government's financial and management needs.

References

Bacon, A. R. 1980. A note on selecting the appropriate pension funding method for localities. *Public Administration Review* 40: 265-69.

Bleakney, T. P. 1972. *Retirement systems for public employees.* Homewood, Ill.: Richard D. Irwin, Inc.

Governmental Accounting Standards Board. 1986. *Disclosure of pension information by public employee retirement systems and state and local governmental employers* (GASB5). Norwalk, Conn.: GASB.

Hawthorne, F. 1993. Social investing gets down to business. *Institutional Investor XXVII* (September): 98-104.

McCollum, W. J., and Mundt, B. M. 1976. Philosophy and equity of municipal pension plans. *Management Controls* 23: 101-4.

McKenzie, C. 1989. Evaluating pension fund investment managers. *Public Management* 71 (February): 8-9.

Miller, G. 1986. *Investing public funds.* Chicago: Government Finance Officers Association.

Munnell, A. H., and Connolly, A. M. 1979. *Pensions for public employees.* Washington, D.C.: National Planning Association.

National Governors' Association. 1978. *Public pension reform: An overview.* Washington, D.C.: National Governors' Association.

Roeder, Richard G. 1987. *Financing retirement system benefits.* Chicago: Government Finance Officers Association.

Salomone, A. W. 1989. Public Employee Retirement Commissions. *Public Management* 71 (February): 5-7.

Tax Foundation, Inc. 1976. *Employee pension systems in state and local government.* 1976. New York: Tax Foundation, Inc.

Tilove, R. 1976. *Public employee pension funds.* New York: Columbia University Press.

U.S. Advisory Commission on Intergovernmental Relations. 1973. *City financial emergencies.* Washington, D.C.: Government Printing Office.

U.S. General Accounting Office. Letter to House Select Committee on Aging from associate director (HRD-93-9R), December 3, 1992.

U.S. House of Representatives, Committee on Education and Labor. 1978. *Pension task force report on public employee retirement systems.* Washington, D.C.: Government Printing Office.

Winklevoss, H. E., and McGill, D. M. 1979. *Public pension plans: Standards of design, funding and reporting.* Homewood, Ill.: Dow Jones-Irwin.

Zorn, P. 1990. A survey of state retirement systems covering general employees and teachers. *Government Finance Review* (October): 25-29.

―――. 1991. *Public employment retirement systems and benefits.* In J. E. Petersen and D. R. Strachota, eds. *Local government finance: Concepts and practices.* Chicago: Government Finance Officers Association, 369-91.

Accounting

Fund Accounting: An Introduction for Public and Nonprofit Organization Managers

Gloria A. Grizzle

Accounting provides information that supports the budgeting process during both the formulation and execution phases. During execution it provides a control mechanism to keep spending within the amount appropriated and prevent deficit spending. In doing so, it classifies and summarizes revenues and expenditures. These data on actual revenues and expenditures can then help the manager develop the organization's budget request in future budget cycles.

Keep in mind three documents when considering the relationship of accounting to budgeting—the budget document itself, the set of financial accounts, and the financial reports. The adopted budget document shows the amounts and the sources of the revenues that are expected and the spending authorized. The set of accounts records these planned revenues and expenditures and the actual financial transactions as they occur. The financial reports then summarize all the financial transactions that took place and were recorded in the set of accounts.

Financial reports are the end products of the accounting system. A manager needs some understanding of the language and processes of accounting in order to make good use of the information contained in these reports. This article first introduces the manager to the authorities who decide what constitutes principles of good practice in governmental accounting. It then explains the accounting process that is based upon these principles and leads the reader through an interpretation of illustrative financial reports.

THE AUTHORITIES

In accounting, a system of rules or conventions has gradually evolved into a set of principles that guide good practice. A principle must satisfy two basic requirements set by the American Institute of Certified Public Accountants. First, it must be generally accepted and followed by organizations. Second, an organization must consistently follow the principle from one fiscal period to another.

For over 50 years, the Governmental Accounting Standards Board and its predecessors have made pronouncements that are authoritative for state and local governments. Its predecessors include the National Committee on Municipal Accounting, the National Committee on Governmental Accounting, and the National Council on Governmental Accounting. These pronouncements have been published in the *Governmental Accounting and Financial Reporting Standards*, published jointly with the Government Accounting Research Foundation of the Government Finance Officers Association. Since 1979, the Financial Accounting Standards Board has assumed the responsibility for accounting and reporting standards for nonprofit organizations that are neither state nor local governments. Both the Governmental Accounting Standards Board and the Financial Accounting Standards Board operate under the auspices of the Financial Accounting Foundation.

Gloria A. Grizzle is professor and director, Askew School of Public Administration and Policy, Florida State University.

The principles for governmental accounting were codified by the National Council on Governmental Accounting and its successor organization, the Governmental Accounting Standards Board.[1] Following these principles provides a common basis of understanding when we read the financial statements of different governmental units. The next several sections introduce the reader to principles important for governmental accounting.[2]

THE ACCOUNTING PROCESS

Accounting includes recording, summarizing, interpreting, and communicating the results of the financial transactions of an organization or individual. This same general process applies to many diverse types of organizations; for example, an industrial firm like General Motors, the local chapter of the American Society for Public Administration, a city government, a farmers' cooperative, a household. A *financial transaction* may be defined as an economic event that is measured in dollars and recorded in the accounts of an organization or individual. Paying an employee for the work that he or she has done is one example of a financial transaction. Collecting property tax from a home owner and buying a computer are other examples. Another part of the definition of accounting consists of the ways that we can operate upon these financial transactions. We can analyze them, record them, summarize them, interpret them, and communicate the results.

An accountant first records each financial transaction in a book called a *journal*. A journal is a chronological record of transactions that shows the names and the classification numbers of the accounts each transaction affects, the amount of change in each account, and a brief explanation of the transaction.

The information put into the journal is transferred to a book of accounts. This book or group of accounts is called the *ledger*. An *account* is a sorting device or classification system for collecting transactions that affect similar assets, liabilities, expenses, or revenues. For example, one account might contain all the organization's expenditures for payroll and another might contain expenditures for travel. A manager using the journal to find out how much the organization had spent on travel during the year would need to go through the entire chronological listing of transactions and pull out each transaction that included spending for travel. Having a group of accounts in a ledger means that the expenses are already classified by account. By simply looking at the travel account in the ledger, the manager can see all the spending on travel that has taken place during the year.

Exhibit 1 summarizes what an accountant does with financial transactions. In analysis, the accountant takes each financial transaction and decides which accounts the transaction affects. The effect for each account is quantified in dollars and then recorded in the form of an entry to the journal. The accountant then transfers the information from a journal entry to a ledger account in a process called *posting*.

At the end of the fiscal period, all the transactions are summarized, first in the form of a trial balance and second in the form of financial statements—the balance sheet, revenue and expenditure report, and change in fund balance statements. In the interpretation stage, the accountant would analyze the changes in the organization's financial position during the fiscal period and perhaps perform additional analyses, such as cash flow analysis, variance analysis, and break-even analysis. The final step in accounting is communicating the results of the accounting

Exhibit 1: *What an Accountant Does with Transactions*

Analyze		For each financial transaction, decide which accounts to debit and which to credit and in what amount.
Record	Journalize	For each transaction, record the results in a journal.
	Post	For each account affected by a transaction, record the changes in that account.
Summarize	Trial Balance	Balance each account and close out temporary accounts.
	Financial Statements	Prepare a balance sheet and revenue and expenditure report.
Interpret		Analyze changes in the organization's financial position and perform additional analyses.
Communicate		Publicize information about the financial operations of the organization, e.g., through an annual financial report.

work. Here the accountant would publicize information about the financial operations of the organization—perhaps through an annual financial report.

Funds

In governmental accounting, all financial transactions are organized within several funds. The National Council on Governmental Accounting gives a rather long definition for *fund:*

> A fund is a fiscal and accounting entity with a self-balancing set of accounts recording cash and other financial resources, together with all related liabilities and residual equities or balances, and changes therein, which are segregated for the purpose of carrying on specific activities or attaining certain objectives in accordance with special regulations, restrictions or limitations.[3]

There are several key points to consider in this definition of fund. The first point is that the fund is a group of accounts segregated for certain purposes. Second, the financial transactions related to these purposes will be recorded in accounts of this fund. And third, these accounts must be self-balancing and must include all the financial resources, liabilities, and equities for those purposes.

There are seven fund types:

1. *General fund:* used to account for revenues that are not allocated to specific purposes. These general-purpose revenues include sources such as the income tax, sales tax, property taxes, licenses, and permits. The general fund is also used for the expenditures that these revenues finance.
2. *Special revenue fund:* like a general fund except it is used to account for a revenue earmarked for a specified purpose or purposes. One county government, for example, earmarks a mill of property tax revenues to be used to provide emergency medical services. A transportation fund for which the gasoline tax is earmarked for road construction and maintenance is another example of a special revenue fund.
3. *Enterprise fund:* used to account for self-supporting activities that render services primarily for the public on a user-charge basis. Examples of such services might be a parking garage, an electricity plant or a water utility, a hospital, a civic center, garbage or trash pickup.

Think now about how a service gets funded from the general fund versus a special revenue fund or an enterprise fund. The garbage collection activity, for example, could have its financial transactions recorded in any one of these funds, depending upon its funding source. If a user's charge is levied that covers the cost of garbage collection, then that activity is a self-supporting enterprise and the revenues and expenses for garbage collection would be recorded in the enterprise fund. If, on the other hand, garbage collection, along with a variety of other general governmental services, is paid for from local property taxes or other general-purpose revenues, the garbage collection activity would be in the general fund and not in the enterprise fund. Finally, if a special tax that is not a user charge is earmarked for garbage collection (say, for example, that a two-mill property tax is levied), then garbage collection expenditures would be recorded in a special revenue fund.

4. *Internal service fund:* accounts for service activities that are performed for units within the organization on a cost-reimbursement basis. Examples might be a central motor pool and garage, central printing, or centralized purchasing. The distinction between the internal service fund and the enterprise fund is that enterprise funds have services that are rendered primarily for the public on a user-charge basis, but internal service funds have services that are rendered internally to other units of the organization. Both, however, are termed proprietary funds.
5. *Debt service fund:* used to account for the payment of interest and principal on long-term general obligation debts, but only on long-term general obligation debts that are not paid from special assessments and that are not issued for and serviced primarily by a government enterprise fund. There are three kinds of such long-term debts: (1) a term, or sinking fund bond, (2) a serial bond, and (3) notes or time warrants that mature over a year after they are first issued.

6. *Capital projects fund:* used to account for all the resources that are used in acquiring capital facilities, except for those facilities that are financed by special assessment funds and enterprise funds. Street paving or street lighting projects might be examples. State and municipal office buildings are other examples.
7. *Trust or agency fund:* used to account for assets which are received by the government in the capacity of trustee or agent. With these funds, the organization has a fiduciary responsibility for assets that it does not own. Examples are pension and retirement systems, or an endowment that has been made to a university when only the income from it can be spent.

While each fund is a separate self-balancing set of accounts, monies may flow from one fund to another. Common interfund transfers include short- and long-term loans, payments for services, and subsidies. Exhibit 2 illustrates several transactions that may take place between a city's General Fund and its internal service and enterprise funds. The Central Motor Pool Fund charges each city department that uses the cars in the motor pool. This cost, for those city departments whose funding is through the General Fund, shows up as an expenditure in the General Fund and as a revenue in the Central Motor Pool Fund. The Electric Fund also charges each city department that uses electricity. For those departments funded through the General Fund, this cost is an expenditure in that fund but a revenue to the Electric Fund. In this example, the General Fund revenues are insufficient to fund all its expenditures and the Electric Fund makes a profit. A part of this profit is transferred out of the Electric Fund into the General Fund to subsidize the services provided through this fund. Finally, the bus system operates at loss, and the General Fund subsidizes the mass transit operation by a transfer from that fund to the Mass Transit Fund.

Because of these flows between funds, one cannot simply total the expenditures or revenues of all the city's funds to determine how much it is spending or receiving. To do so would be double counting part of the revenues and expenditures.

Classification of Accounts

A schedule that lists all the accounts and gives their codes is called a *chart of accounts*. Each fund would have its own chart of accounts. Exhibit 3 diagrams the general types of account. *Proprietary* accounts show the actual financial position and operations of

Exhibit 2: *Monies Flow among the Funds*

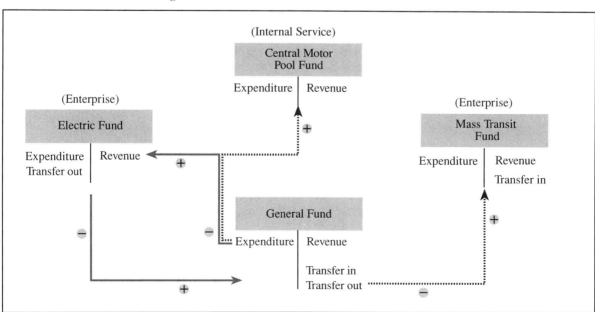

an organization. There are two types of proprietary accounts. *Real* accounts are those that actually appear on the balance sheet. *Nominal* or temporary accounts are closed into the fund balance at the end of the year and do not appear on the balance sheet.

Real accounts include assets, liabilities, and fund balance. *Assets* are the valuable things that the organization has, such as cash, investments, equipment, buildings, and land. *Liabilities* are the claims against these assets by others. Examples of liability accounts are accounts payable, vouchers payable, and notes payable. *Fund Balance* represents what is left after the claims against the organization are subtracted from the valuable things that the organization has.

Nominal accounts include revenue and expenditure accounts. *Revenue* accounts represent either an increase in assets or a decrease in liabilities with a corresponding increase in the organization's fund balance. Examples of revenues are service charges, property taxes, sales taxes, grants, and fines. *Expenditure* accounts represent the charges incurred by the organization that result in either a decrease in assets or an increase in liabilities with a corresponding decrease in the organization's fund balance. Expenditures may be classified by object, such as salaries, travel, contractual services, rent, and supplies.

Budgetary accounts—appropriations, estimated revenues, encumbrances, and allotments—show the budgetary status of the organization. *Appropriation* accounts show the amount the organization's legislative body has authorized the organization to spend for certain purposes during a specified period of time. *Estimated revenue* accounts show the amount of money the organization expects to collect or accrue during a specified period of time.

An *encumbrance* is an obligation that is chargeable to an appropriation for which part of the appropriation has been reserved. The encumbrance account is paired with an off-setting account called *reserve for encumbrances*. These accounts have several purposes. They act as a control to prohibit a unit from overspending its budget. Second, they help a manager to pace spending so that the expenditures will equal appropriations at the end of the fiscal year. Third, they can keep the manager from losing funds appropriated to the organization when goods and services are ordered but cannot be received before the end of the fiscal year.

Exhibit 3: *Types of Account*

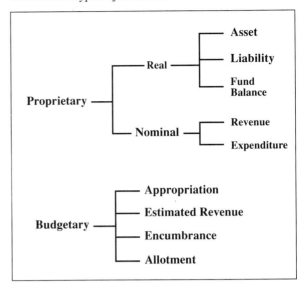

The last type of account is the allotment. An *allotment* is the amount of an appropriation that the organization is authorized to spend for a certain purpose for some part of a fiscal year. Allotments are generally made for each quarter of the year. When there is a revenue shortfall, the budget office can avoid a deficit by making allotments that are less than the amount of the appropriation in order to keep spending within the amount of actual revenues received.

Bases of Accounting

A basis of accounting governs how one matches revenues and costs for a fund during some specified time period, such as a fiscal year. The authorities for governmental accounting recommend that the full accrual basis be used only for enterprise, internal service, and some trust and agency funds (i.e., those funds for which spending generates income and therefore makes looking at a fund's net income sensible). The modified accrual basis is to be used for all other fund types.

Both the accrual and the modified accrual methods require that revenues be recognized and recorded in the journal when they are earned and that expenditures be recognized and recorded when the good or service is received. The modified accrual method results in a more conservative statement of the fund's financial position because it recognizes when earned only those revenues for which the amount can be determined in advance, the collection is legally enforceable, and the collection will occur during the fiscal year or shortly thereafter.

Another basis, the cash basis, records revenues only when the government receives the money and expenditures only when the payments are made. Therefore, the cash basis of accounting does not provide full disclosure of the financial condition of the fund when there are unpaid bills or uncollected revenues. For this reason, the authorities recommend never using the cash basis.

Basic Accounting Equation

In order to understand financial statements and discuss the financial implications of financial transactions, the manager needs a basic understanding of the effects of financial transactions on the accounts. All transactions can be described in terms of their effects on what is known as the "basic accounting equation."

The basic accounting equation is

Assets = Liabilities + Fund Balance.

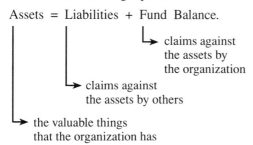

This equation contains the real accounts that appear on the balance sheet. Assets will always equal liabilities plus fund balance because the accounting system is based upon the dual principle. For every transaction recorded, the accountant makes a change in at least two accounts that affect this equation. This equation is subject to algebraic manipulations. For example, assets minus liabilities equal fund balance.

Using the hypothetical county of Prosperity as an example, let's consider the effect of several different kinds of financial transactions on this equation for its general fund (Exhibit 4). At the beginning of the fiscal year, the county had cash on hand of $1 million and did not owe anyone. It therefore had assets of $1 million and, under the dual principle of accounting, an offsetting fund balance of the same amount that represents the county's own claim against those assets.

On July 15, the county levied a franchise tax amounting to $10 million. It did not receive the cash on that date; it merely levied the tax. The county now had two types of asset—the cash in its bank account and another asset called "taxes receivable," representing the county's claim for the taxes that it would collect in the future. The county's fund balance, then, increased to $11 million because it had a claim of $1 million against the cash in the bank and another $10 million against the taxes receivable.

On July 20, the county obtained a short-term loan from a bank in the form of a tax anticipation note amounting to $5 million. Again, following the dual principle, the effect of this transaction on the basic accounting equation was twofold: It increased the amount of cash the county had on hand (an asset) and increased the claim the bank had against the county for repayment of the loan (a liability).

On July 31, the county used $4 million of the cash to pay its employees. This transaction's effect was to reduce both the asset cash and the fund balance by this amount.

On August 15, the county received $8 million from franchise taxes it had previously levied. This transaction increased the balance in one asset account, cash, and decreased the amount in another asset account, taxes receivable.

On August 20, the county repaid the loan to the bank. This transaction reduced the balance in an asset account, cash, and reduced the balance in a liability account, notes payable. As you can see from Exhibit 4, each transaction maintained the equality of assets to liabilities plus fund balance.

The expanded accounting equation adds revenues and expenditures to the basic accounting equation:

Assets = Liabilities + Fund Balance −
Expenditures + Revenues

Revenues and expenditures are really subsets of the fund balance. At the end of the accounting period, these accounts will be closed out and their balances transferred to the fund balance account. As in the basic accounting equation, the expanded accounting equation that includes revenues and expenditures requires that assets equal liabilities plus fund balance. An expenditure account has a debit balance. When closed out into the fund balance account, an expenditure will therefore decrease the fund balance.

Exhibit 4: *Effect of Transactions on the Accounting Equation*

July 1—At the beginning of the fiscal year, the county has cash on hand of $1 million.

Assets	=	Fund Balance
Cash		
$1,000,000		$1,000,000

July 15—The county levies a $10 million franchise tax.

Assets	=	Fund Balance
Cash + Taxes Receivable		
$1,000,000 + $10,000,000		$11,000,000

July 20—The county borrows $5,000,000 from a bank.

Assets	=	Liabilities + Fund Balance
Cash + Taxes Receivable		Notes Payable + Fund Balance
$6,000,000 + $10,000,000		$5,000,000 + $11,000,000

July 31—The county pays its employees salaries of $4,000,000.

Assets	=	Liabilities + Fund Balance
Cash + Taxes Receivable		Notes Payable + Fund Balance
$2,000,000 + $10,000,000		$5,000,000 + $7,000,000

August 15—The county receives $8 million of the franchise tax.

Assets	=	Liabilities + Fund Balance
Cash + Taxes Receivable		Notes Payable + Fund Balance
$10,000,000 + $2,000,000		$5,000,000 + $7,000,000

August 20—The county pays back the $5 million it borrowed from the bank.

Assets	=	Fund Balance
Cash + Taxes Receivable		
$5,000,000 + $2,000,000		$7,000,000

That is why the expenditures have a negative sign in the expanded accounting equation. A revenue, on the other hand, normally has a credit balance that, when closed into the fund balance account, would increase the fund balance. Revenues therefore have a positive sign in the expanded accounting equation. The expanded accounting equation shows the revenues and expenditures on the right-hand side of the equation because they are a part of the fund balance.

Expanded further, the accounting equation includes the budgetary accounts:

Assets = Liabilities + Fund Balance −
Estimated Revenues + Appropriations +
Revenues − Expenditures − Encumbrances +
Reserve for Encumbrances

Like the nominal accounts, the budgetary accounts are closed into the fund balance account at the end of the fiscal period, and the same logic applies to the signs given them in the accounting equation. When closed into the fund balance account, estimated revenues and encumbrances decrease the fund balance. Appropriations and the reserve for encumbrances, on the other hand, increase the fund balance.

ANALYZING FINANCIAL TRANSACTIONS

Analyzing transactions consists of two parts. First, an accountant decides which accounts a transaction affects and whether each account is increased or decreased. Second, he or she applies the rules of debit and credit to determine the effect of the increases or decreases on the account balance.

The concept of debit and credit is so simple that people get confused by it. Forget about anything you have ever heard about what the words "debit" or "credit" mean and stick to the simple definitions as they are used in the language of accounting. A debit means to make an entry on the left-hand side of the account. That is all it means: make an entry on the left-hand side of the account. A credit means to make an entry on the right-hand side of the account.

Exhibit 5 summarizes the rules for debiting and crediting accounts. These rules place the balance in each account on the same side as the real accounts appear on the basic equation. Assets appear on the left-hand side of the equation. All asset accounts normally have a debit balance, meaning that the balance is found on the left-hand side of the account. Increase an asset account by debiting the account; decrease an asset account by crediting it.

Liability accounts are on the right-hand side of the equation, and they normally have a credit balance. Increase a liability account by crediting it, and decrease it by debiting it. The fund balance account is also on the right-hand side of the accounting equation, and the accountant increases its balance by crediting it and decreases it by debiting it.

Recall that revenue and expenditure accounts are temporary accounts whose balances are closed out at the end of each fiscal period. Because their balances are transferred into the fund balance account, these accounts do not appear on the balance sheet. Revenues serve either to increase assets or decrease liabilities. Therefore, revenues have a credit balance, and the accountant increases this balance by crediting it and decreases it by debiting it. Expenditures, on the other hand, serve either to decrease assets or increase liabilities. Expenditure accounts therefore have a debit balance, and the accountant increases an expenditure account's balance by debiting it and decreases it by crediting it.

After analyzing a transaction, an accountant records the results as an entry in the journal. The journal entry states the accounts that are affected and in what amount. The debited accounts are listed first and the amounts entered in the left-hand column. The credited accounts are listed second and the amounts entered in the right-hand column. The transactions are listed in chronological order and dated. For each transaction, a short explanation of the transaction appears beneath the names of the accounts. Exhibit 6 summarizes the typical sequence of journal entries for a governmental organization.

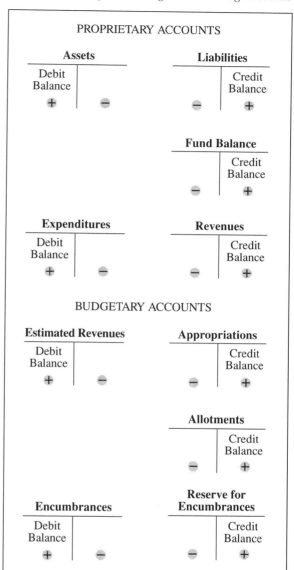

Exhibit 5: *Rules for Debiting and Crediting Accounts*

To illustrate the analysis of transactions for proprietary accounts, the following transactions assume the modified accrual basis of accounting is being used to account for general fund transactions for Prosperity County in the state of New Hope.

October 1: The county commission levies a property tax in the amount of $18 million. Because collection of this tax is enforceable and the amount is known, the accountant recognizes the revenue at the time of the levy even though the money has not been collected.

446 / BUDGET EXECUTION: ACCOUNTING

	Debit	Credit
Taxes Receivable	18,000,000	
Revenue		18,000,000

October 10: The county borrows $1 million from a bank to pay its bills until its citizens pay their property taxes. The accountant recognizes the cash as an asset along with an offsetting liability to repay the loan.

Cash	1,000,000	
Notes Payable		1,000,000

October 12: The county receives a bill of $3,000 for telephone service. The accountant recognizes the expenditure when the bill is received and the liability is recognized even though the bill is unpaid.

Expenditures	3,000	
Vouchers Payable		3,000

October 15: Several citizens pay their property taxes, amounting to $9,000. The accountant prepares a journal entry that exchanges one asset, taxes receivable, for another asset, cash.

Cash	9,000	
Taxes Receivable		9,000

October 17: The county comptroller writes a check to pay for the telephone bill received October 15. The accountant prepares a journal entry that reduces the cash balance and writes off the liability for the telephone bill.

Vouchers Payable	3,000	
Cash		3,000

October 18: The county payroll for the first half of the month is $500,000. The accountant prepares a journal entry that recognizes the county's liability to its employees and the expenditure at the same time, even though checks have not been written.

Expenditures	500,000	
Vouchers Payable		500,000

October 28: The comptroller prepares employees' paychecks and distributes them. The accountant writes off the liability and reduces the balance in the cash account.

Vouchers Payable	500,000	
Cash		500,000

Exhibit 6: *Sequence of Journal Entries for the General Fund (Modified Accrual Basis of Accounting)*

Record the budget as adopted by the legislative body.	Estimated Revenues Appropriations
Record allotments at the beginning of each allotment period.	Appropriations Allotments
Record revenues when they are billed.	Taxes Receivable Revenues
Record collections of revenues as they are received.	Cash Taxes Receivable

Encumber accounts as commitments to spend are made.	Encumbrances
	    Reserve for
	    Encumbrances

Record expenditures when the liability is incurred.	Reserve for Encumbrances
	    Encumbrances
	Expenditures
	    Vouchers Payable

Write off the liability when bills are paid.	Vouchers Payable Cash

At the end of the fiscal period, close out the non-real accounts.	Revenues
	    Estimated Revenues
	Appropriations
	    Allotments
	    Expenditures
	    Encumbrances

At the end of the fiscal period, the ending balances for the real accounts would appear on the balance sheet. The revenues would appear in a statement comparing actual revenues with estimated revenues. Expenditures would appear in a statement comparing expenditures and encumbrances with authorizations. The following transactions illustrate how the accountant prepares journal entries for the budgetary accounts.

October 1: The county commission adopts the budget for the fiscal year. The accountant prepares a journal entry that shows the amount of revenues estimated to be received and the amount of the appropriation. Recall that for every transaction debits must equal credits. In this example, revenues are estimated to be higher than the appropriation. The difference between the estimated revenues and the appropriation is credited to the fund balance.

Estimated Revenues	48,923,825	
Appropriations		48,620,000
Fund Balance		303,825

October 1: The budget office makes the allotment of funds that all the county's departments can spend during the first quarter of the fiscal year. The accountant prepares a journal entry that makes that portion of the appropriations allotted available to the departments for spending.

Appropriations	12,000,000	
Allotments		12,000,000

October 3: The purchasing office issues a purchase order for four personal computers for the planning department. The accountant sets up a memorandum account to track orders not yet received and to prevent the planning department from entering into an obligation to spend more funds than allotted to it. The memorandum account is not a liability but a reminder that by issuing the purchase order, the county is committed to incur a liability when it receives the computers.

Encumbrances	6,200	
Reserve for Encumbrances		6,200

October 16: The computers are delivered to the county along with a bill in the amount of $6,150. The accountant first writes off the encumbrance for the amount originally encumbered. Second, the accountant prepares a journal entry that recognizes the expenditure and the liability to pay for the computers. Frequently the actual amount of the bill will be different from the amount of the purchase order. The encumbrance account is always reduced by the same amount it was encumbered, not by the amount of the liability incurred.

Reserve for Encumbrances	6,200	
Encumbrances		6,200
Expenditures	6,150	
Vouchers Payable		6,150

In a real accounting system, the revenues would be separated into different revenue accounts according to the source of revenue. The authorities recommend that expenditures be classified by character, organizational unit, object of expenditure, and program or activity. Character identifies whether the expenditure is for a current expense, capital outlay, or debt service.

FINANCIAL REPORTING

One can judge the financial condition of an organization by examining its financial statements. A manager can also use revenue and expenditure statements during budget execution to control spending and to prepare the next budget request. While the balance sheet prepared at the end of the fiscal year may be more useful to people outside the organization who want to assess the organization's financial condition, the interim revenue and expenditure statements are more useful to the manager during budget execution.

The authorities consider four annual financial statements to be essential in presenting an organization's financial condition. The first of these, the balance sheet, presents the balances in the real accounts. Its purpose is to show the organization's financial condition as of a certain date by properly classifying and disclosing assets, liabilities, and fund balance. It is divided into two sections. The first section lists the assets in order of liquidity (i.e., how easily they can be converted into cash). Thus, cash is always listed first. The second section lists the liabilities and fund balance accounts. As in the basic accounting equation, the total asset account balances must equal the total balances of the liabilities and fund balance accounts.

Exhibit 7 presents a balance sheet for Prosperity County.[4] The principle of full disclosure requires that financial statements present information on the financial position of the organization in a way that is not misleading to the reader of the financial statements. As mentioned previously, the cash basis of accounting violates this principle because a balance sheet prepared on the cash basis does not disclose liabilities or revenues that have been earned but not collected.

Another required report is the analysis of change in fund balance. As its name indicates, this statement explains the reasons for the changes in the fund balance account during the year. Three kinds of change are most likely to appear on an analysis of change in a fund balance statement. First is a difference between actual revenues and actual expenditures during the fiscal period. Revenue receipts are added to the fund balance and expenditures are deducted from it. Outstanding encumbrances are also deducted. Third, reserve accounts established during the fiscal period are deductions from fund balance, and reserve accounts written off are additions to the fund balance. Other things being equal, an organization with a small fund balance must be more careful to ensure that expenditures do not exceed revenues than an organization with a large fund balance. If the fund balance is large enough, it can act as a cushion to absorb excess spending over revenues during times of unexpected revenue shortfalls. Without such a cushion, the organization must make midyear reductions in spending to avoid running a deficit. A fund with a negative fund balance is one whose liabilities exceed assets.

A third annual financial report is the statement of revenue—estimated and actual. Exhibit 8 shows this statement for Prosperity County. The purpose of this statement is to indicate how accurate the revenue forecasts are. Having this statement helps to prevent consistent underestimation or overestimation of certain revenues from year to year. If a manager finds a significant difference between actual revenues and estimated revenues, he or she should ask two questions about it: Is the difference favorable or unfavorable? What caused the difference? Thinking about the reasons for these differences is important for forecasting future revenues.

The last of the four essential annual financial reports is a statement of expenditures and encumbrances compared with authorizations. Exhibit 9 shows this statement for one department in Prosperity County. This statement shows to what extent the organizational units have stayed within the amounts that were authorized for them. It too provides the manager useful information for budget preparation because it provides annual expenditures for each function, activity, and object of expenditure. These expenditures can serve as a basis for estimating future spending needs.

Two essential interim statements are the statement of actual and estimated expenditures and the statement of actual and estimated revenues. Usually, a manager would get each of these statements on a monthly basis. They are similar to their annual counterpart statements of revenues and expenditures, with the exception that the interim statements show expenditures to date rather than total expenditures, or revenues to date rather than total revenues. These collections or expenditures to date are compared to estimates to date to see the amount that is over or

Exhibit 7: *Balance Sheet for Prosperity County*

General Fund Fiscal Year Ended June 30, 1995	
Assets	
Cash	$1,700,094
Investments	2,809,800
Taxes Receivable	690,400
Due from Other Funds	382,610
Due from Other Governments	543,762
Total Assets	**$6,126,666**
Liabilities and Fund Balance	
Liabilities	
Vouchers Payable	$1,438,211
Contracts Payable	76,432
Due to Other Funds	237,018
Total Liabilities	$1,751,661
Fund Balance	
Reserved for Encumbrances	67,481
Unreserved	4,307,524
Total Fund Balance	$4,375,005
Total Liabilities and Fund Balance	**$6,126,666**

Exhibit 8: *Statement of Revenue for Prosperity County—Estimated and Actual*

General Fund Fiscal Year Ended June 30, 1995			
Revenues	**Estimated**	**Actual**	**Variance**
Property Taxes	$17,905,000	$17,184,494	(720,506)
Utility Taxes	9,063,000	9,042,365	(20,635)
Franchise Taxes	7,112,000	7,835,875	723,875
Licenses and Permits	1,318,592	1,363,369	44,777
Fines and Forfeitures	765,000	861,746	96,746
Intergovernmental	6,685,408	6,765,040	79,632
Service Charges	2,063,558	2,302,423	238,865
Interfund Service Charges	4,011,267	5,717,048	1,705,781
Total	48,923,825	51,072,360	2,148,535

Exhibit 9: *Statement of Expenditures and Encumbrances Compared with Authorizations*

Prosperity County Park and Recreation Department—General Fund Fiscal Year Ended June 30, 1995					
Division	Expenditure	Encumbrance	Total	Budget	Variance
Park Center	$1,192,572	$1,658	$1,194,230	$1,194,230	$ 0
Recreation	951,010	5,027	956,037	947,713	18,676
Athletic Fields	164,068	0	164,068	164,763	695
Golf Course	115,218	0	115,218	115,305	87
Swimming Pools	320,105	0	320,105	329,772	9,667
Administration	121,626	206	121,832	121,842	10
Total	$2,864,599	$6,891	$2,871,490	$2,900,625	$29,135

under expectations. Each manager would receive similar reports detailing expenditures by activity or object of expenditure for each organizational unit or program under his responsibility.

One thing a manager wants to see on a statement of actual and estimated expenditures is whether some activities or objects are in danger of being overspent. If so, the manager should take action to hold spending within the appropriation or allotment. If the allotment for some objects appears too small to last the year, while other object accounts seem more than adequate, the manager may want to initiate requests for a series of transfers from one account to another. If, for example, the salary account for temporary employees is being overspent and the salary account for permanent employees has a surplus due to unfilled positions, the manager may want to transfer some funds from the permanent salary account to the temporary salary account. The manager may be required to seek authorization for transfers from a higher authority.

Another thing the manager may do to keep spending within the allotment is reduce the level of expenditures. For example, if the travel account balance is running low, the manager may prohibit the staff from traveling except in emergency situations. A still more drastic measure is to freeze the accounts for some objects of expenditure. Common examples would be to not fill any vacancies in positions that occur for the remainder of the year, to not purchase any equipment, and to prohibit all travel. As the fiscal year draws to a close, these account balances need to be checked frequently. During the last month of a fiscal year, the manager may receive these statements more frequently, perhaps once a week or daily.

MEASUREMENT FOCUS

While the basis of accounting relates to when the accountant measures and records financial transactions, measurement focus relates to what the accountant measures. One focus presents information about the flow of financial resources and the other focus presents information about the flow of economic resources. The difference between the two foci lies in how one accounts for spending.

Funds using the modified accrual basis of accounting use the flow-of-financial-resources focus. The accountant records resources as expenditures at the time he or she recognizes the liability for them, no matter how much the resource cost or how long it will last. Thus, long-lasting resources, such as buildings, land, and equipment, are recorded as expenditures when purchased. That means that these purchases do not appear on the balance sheet as assets. They appear as expenditures on the statement of expenditures and encumbrances compared with authorizations. Similarly, the accountant does not record long-term liabilities in the fund (long-term liabilities and assets are not simply ignored, instead, they are recorded in a group of accounts separate from the fund).

Exhibit 7 is an example of a balance sheet prepared using the flow-of-financial-resources focus. The purpose of the balance sheet when using this focus is to tell the reader what monies are available for spending—i.e., assets minus liabilities. The purpose of the expenditure statement is to publicly account for spending in compliance with the legally adopted budget.

Funds using the full accrual basis of accounting use the flow-of-economic-resources measurement focus. Under this focus, expenses rather than expenditures are recorded. The accountant records expenses when the resources are consumed, not when they are purchased. When resources are purchased but not immediately consumed, the accountant records the resources as assets. As the asset is used, the accountant records the portion consumed as an expense and reduces the asset account balance by that amount. At the end of a fiscal period, the amount of the asset consumed or used up during that period appears as an expense on the revenue and expense statement. The amount not consumed appears as an asset on the balance sheet. For example, a building would be depreciated over its useful life. Each year, the financial statements would show the net value (cost minus accumulated depreciation) on the balance sheet and depreciation as an expense on the revenue and expense statement.

Similarly, the accountant records all long-term liabilities, such as bonds issued, in the fund instead of in a separate group of accounts. This focus permits a fund's expenses to be subtracted from its receipts to determine the profit or loss. The balance sheet tells the reader the amount of capital or equity the fund has—i.e., assets minus liabilities. That is why the full accrual basis and the flow-of-economic-resources measurement focus are recommended for enterprise and internal service funds.

What constitutes the most appropriate measurement focus and accounting basis is a controversial area. In 1990, the Governmental Accounting Standards Board issued a statement on this subject that altered financial reporting effective with fiscal periods that began after July 15, 1994. This statement required accruing additional revenues and expenditures in those funds that have used the modified accrual basis and flow-of-financial-resources focus. In 1993, it was announced that the Board had delayed implementation of this statement indefinitely.

SUMMARY

The accounting process is generally the same for both private-sector and governmental organizations. Accounting for governments and nonprofit organizations, however, includes some features especially designed to provide good stewardship of the public's funds. Except for enterprise, internal service, and some trust and agency funds, no attempt is made to match costs to revenues in order to determine the profit. Instead, governmental accounting places more emphasis upon controlling spending through using the budgetary accounts—appropriations, allotments, and encumbrances. Several important principles of fund accounting covered in this paper are recapitulated here:

1. All financial transactions are quantified in dollars and recorded in journals.
2. Assets always equal liabilities plus fund balance.
3. Financial transactions are posted from the journal to the accounts. Funds are self-balancing sets of accounts segregated for the purpose of carrying on specific activities or attaining certain objectives. There are eight fund types: general, special revenue, enterprise, internal service, debt service, special assessment, capital projects, trust or agency.
4. The basis for matching revenues and costs should be either modified accrual or full accrual, depending upon the type fund.
5. Four annual financial statements are essential—the balance sheet, the statement analyzing changes in fund balance, the statement comparing actual revenues with estimated revenues, and the statement comparing expenditures and encumbrances with authorizations. The two essential interim statements are the statement of actual and estimated revenues and the statement of actual and estimated expenditures.
6. Revenue accounts should be classified by fund and source.
7. Expenditure accounts should be classified by fund, by function, by organization unit, by activity, by character, and by principal class of objects.
8. Financial statements must present information on the financial position of the organization in a way that is not misleading to the reader of the financial statements.

These principles represent good practice as recommended by the authorities. Some state and local laws prescribe accounting practices that deviate from one or more of these principles. In such cases, the organization should follow the law. For example, the law may require that revenues be accounted for on a cash basis even though the principles require revenues to be accounted for on a modified accrual basis. When legal requirements are inconsistent with the generally accepted accounting principles, organizations sometimes prepare two sets of reports, one set conforming to the principles and the other to legal requirements.

Notes

1. *Codification of Governmental Accounting and Financial Reporting Standards* (Chicago, Ill.: Copublished by the Governmental Accounting Standards Board and the Government Accounting Research Foundation of the Government Finance Officers Association, 1987).

2. The reader interested in a more in-depth, but still easily understandable, treatment of this subject may consult Paul E. Glick, *A Public Manager's Guide to Government Accounting and Financial Reporting*, Financial Reporting Series No. 10. (Chicago, Ill.: Government Finance Officers Association, 1990).

3. *Governmental Accounting, Auditing and Financial Reporting* (Chicago, Ill.: Government Finance Officers Association, 1988), 11.

4. The reader interested in seeing illustrations and interpretation of the full set of annual and interim financial reports for different fund types may consult Paul E. Glick, *How to Understand Local Government Financial Statements: A User's Guide*, Financial Reporting Series No. 6 (Chicago, Ill.: Government Finance Officers Association, 1986).

Managerial Accounting

James E. Sorensen, Glyn W. Hanbery, and A. Ronald Kucic

NATURE OF MANAGERIAL ACCOUNTING

Every manager faces two difficult questions:
 Are we doing what we ought to be doing?
 How well are we doing what we do?

Today's complex environment gives neither easy nor clearcut answers to these questions. The first question requires the formulation of long-term objectives and the translation of these objectives into plans. Planning requires choosing alternatives which best meet objectives and then evaluating the expected outcomes of those alternatives. Tools such as budgeting become the managerial accounting link to planning when budgets reflect the targeted plans of managers.

How well the organization is doing is easier to assess than whether objectives are appropriate. Efficiency and effectiveness are two measures of achievement. Efficiency is the accomplishment of objectives at minimum cost; effectiveness measures how well objectives have been achieved. Managerial accounting contributes to efficiency analysis. Cost behavior, contribution margin analysis, differential analysis, flexible budgeting, and budget variance analysis are the bywords of managerial accounting.

Managerial accounting analyzes internal costs, revenues, and volumes of services. Financial statements outline resource flows (e.g., revenues and expenses) and stockpiles (assets); managerial accounting deals with the specifics and dynamics of these flows and stockpiles. Key internal reports include budgets and cost-finding which reveal relationships between volume of service, expenses, revenues, cash flows, and unit of service costs, and give managers organizational control.

UNDERSTANDING COST BEHAVIOR AND COST CLASSIFICATIONS*

Organization costs can behave in numerous and complex ways depending on contemplated or actual volumes of service. One of the most important guides in financial management decision making is an understanding of cost behavior—how total costs change in relation to changes in the volume of activity.

Expense and Cost

Assets are the resources or service potentials an organization consumes; assets can be obtained by expenditure or commitment to future expenditure. When the asset's service potential is released, the asset becomes an expense. Some expenditures such as salaries are classified directly as expenses; the service potential has been consumed because they are paid after the services have been performed. The cost method values an asset by measuring the outlay (typically cash) made by the firm to obtain the asset or service; other possible methods of valuation, such as fair market value, are not widely used. Because cost-finding analysis involves

---

Adapted from *Accounting and Budgeting Systems for Mental Health Organizations*, Series FN, no. 6 (Washington, D.C.: National Institute of Mental Health, 1983), 21-27, 142-43.

*Material in this section is adapted from National Institute of Mental Health (1975).

the tracing of expired assets and other expenses to the services or products created by the organization, the process should be called "expense-finding," but popular use equates cost with the expiration of an asset (an expense), and the term "cost-finding" is widely used. In this discussion the terms will be used interchangeably, but the term "expense" is implied.

Classification of Expenses

Expense behavior is subject to various influences. Usually, total expense of an organization or its subunits varies with the volume of activity. Several types of expenses may make up the total expense. Variable expenses are expected to fluctuate, in total, in direct proportion to some measure of activity such as the number of patients in beds or number of patient visits; expenses such as food or medications in inpatient or partial hospitalization program elements may vary with the daily census. Some expenses may be step-variable, varying over a wide range of activity but not in direct proportionality. Professional labor expenses, for example, behave in step-fashion; there is a practical limit to the number of patients a psychiatric social worker can serve before another person must be added to the staff. Fixed expenses are a constant total amount regardless of the level of or fluctuations in the volume of activity. Salaries of administrators, rent, and depreciation expenses are fixed expenses.

The relationships of variable, step-variable, and fixed expenses are shown in Figure 1.

An example of the relationships between fixed, variable, and step-variable or semivariable expenses in a hypothetical outpatient program is shown in Table 1. The table also shows the effects of service volume changes on these expenses.

In Table 1 the fixed expenses total the same amount at both levels of service; an increase in service volume caused no change in this range. The change in volume of outpatient visits, however, reduced the expense per visit because the fixed expense was spread over more visits. Fixed expenses remain the same in total, but the fixed expense per unit of volume decreases as volume increases and increases as volume decreases.

Variable expenses such as supplies and medications are assumed to be purely variable; that is, varying in proportion to the change in volume. In Table 1, for example, they increase by 20 percent as volume increases by 20 percent. The result is a unit expense that does not change with a change in volume. The total expense changes in the same direction as volume and by the same percentage.

Semivariable expenses, in total, change in the same direction and in relatively the same percentage as volume. Semivariable expenses are approximately the same per unit, usually tending to be slightly lower per unit as volume increases significantly.

Figure 1: *Analysis of Expense Behavior*

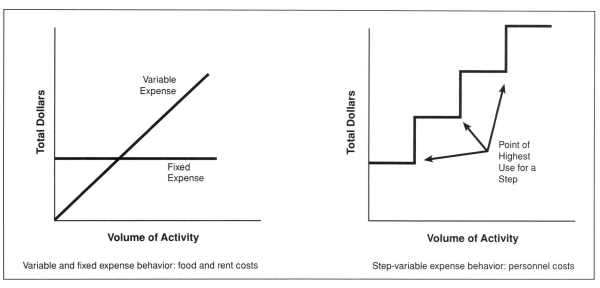

Table 1: *Types of Expense for an Outpatient Program at Two Different Volumes of Visits*

	Number of Outpatient Visits			
	5,000		6,000	
Type of Expense	Total Expense	Per Visit Expense	Total Expense	Per Visit Expense
Fixed	$150,000	$30.00	$150,000	$25.00
Variable	5,000	1.00	6,000	1.00
Step-variable	2,500	.50	2,700	.45
	$157,500	$31.50	$158,700	$26.45

Examination of the expenses of the outpatient program shows a total amount increase (from $157,500 to $158,700) as expected, but not in the same percentage as the change in volume. As a result, the total unit expense per visit declines, primarily because of the greater use of fixed resources.

The behavior of per unit expense is different from the behavior of the total expense. Variable per unit expenses are constant on a per unit basis but variable in total, while fixed expenses are variable on a per unit basis (depending on the volume of activity), but constant in total. Semivariable expenses change both per unit and total as volume fluctuates. These relationships are shown in Figure 2.

Expense behavior helps analyze rate-setting and determine the financial desirability of specific services or programs. Distinguishing between average, variable, and fixed expenses is important in a decision to add or drop a service. Dropping a service may reduce some variable and fixed expenses, but most fixed expenses cannot be avoided. Eliminating a service may increase the average expense of the remaining services since the fixed expense previously allocated to the deleted service is now allocated to the remaining services. Adding a service could cause the opposite effect: original services would show lower expense since some of their fixed expense would be allocated to the newly formed service. Adding or dropping a service usually requires identification of affected expenses. Incremental or decremental analysis of the budget is required because examination of "average" expenses is insufficient.

BREAKEVEN ANALYSIS—CRITICAL TOOL FOR NOT-FOR-PROFIT ORGANIZATIONS

Breakeven analysis helps mental health managers translate programs and program changes into staff workload requirements while maintaining financial viability. Equation technique, contribution margin technique, and graphic technique are prevalent breakeven analysis approaches.

Figure 2: *Behavior of Total and Per Unit Expenses*

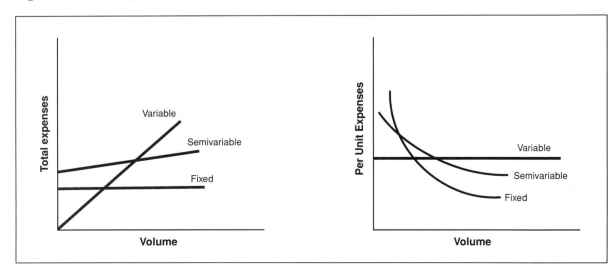

Equation Technique

The most general form of breakeven analysis is an expression of the income statement:

Revenues = Variable expenses (x) + Fixed expenses + Overrecovery of expenses

where

x = Number of units of service to be delivered to break even.

Assume that outpatient service expenses and rates are as follows:

	Per Hour	Percent of Rate
Standard billing rate:	$25	100
Variable expenses per hour	5	20
Contribution to fixed expenses	$20	80
Fixed expenses:		
Staff salary and fringe	$ 50,000	
Facility expenses	20,000	
Total fixed	$170,000	
Hours of outpatient service to be provided	?	
Revenue dollars to break even	?	

In equation form: To break even (assuming no under- or overrecovery),

$25x = \$170,000 + \$5x + \$0$
$25x - \$5x = \$170,000 + \$0$
$20x = \$170,000$
$x = 8,500$ visits.

(Proof: $8,500 \times \$25 = \$212,500$
$\$170,000 + \$5 (8,500) = \$170,000 + \$42,500 = \$212,500$)

An alternative approach is to solve for the breakeven revenue dollars required to cover the fixed expenses and the variable costs expressed as percentage of revenue (in the illustration, the variable cost percentage is 20 percent of the billing rate), thus

If x = billable revenues to break even, then
$x = \$170,000 + .2x$
$x - .2x = \$170,000$
$.8x = \$170,000$
$x = \$212,500.$

(Proof: $\$212,500 - [\$170,000 + (8,500 \times \$5)] = 0$
$\$212,500 - (\$170,000 + \$42,500) = 0$
$\$212,500 - \$212,500 = 0$

Contribution Margin Technique

Perhaps an easier approach is the contribution margin technique. Every unit of service generates a contribution margin (or marginal increase), which is the excess of standard billing rate over the variable expense for a unit of service.

$$\text{Breakeven in units} = \frac{\text{Fixed expenses + Expense overrecovery}}{\text{Contribution margin}}$$

$$\text{Breakeven in revenue dollars} = \frac{\text{Fixed expenses + Expense overrecovery}}{\text{Contribution margin ratio}}$$

Outpatient service:

$$\text{Breakeven in units} = \frac{\$170,000 + 0}{20} = 8,500 \text{ units of service}$$

or

$$\text{Breakeven in revenue} = \frac{\$170,000 + 0}{.8} = \$212,500 \text{ in revenue dollars}$$

Graphic Technique

The graphic approach is a straightforward and commonsense five-step procedure.

1. Plot the revenue line (viz., units of service times rate).
2. Determine the fixed cost and plot with a dotted line.
3. Determine the variable costs at two or more levels of volume and place the costs on top of the fixed costs; in other words, determine the total costs at two or more levels of volume.
4. Connect the dots to identify the total expense line.
5. Identify breakeven point in units of service and in dollars.

Making the graph as shown in Figure 3 identifies activity levels that underrecover and overrecover expenses.

SENSITIVITY ANALYSIS

What if fixed expenses like rent or salaries change? What if the contribution margin (e.g., variable costs) changes? What if a cost overrecovery must finance

Figure 3: *Graphic Technique for Breakeven Analysis*

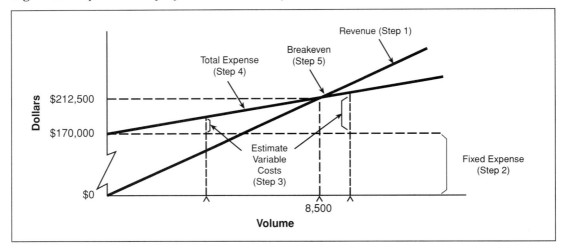

service expansion or offset underrecovery in another service? What happens to the breakeven volume if several changes are instituted at the same time, such as adding new staff (an increase in fixed expenses) and increasing variable expenses such as travel costs? Each of these questions poses the question of sensitivity. How sensitive is the solution to variations in one or more of the key factors?

Multiple Changes in Key Factors

The breakeven analysis model helps the manager assess the effects of varying combinations of variable and fixed-cost factors. For example, suppose the director wishes to improve the delivery of outpatient services by

- adding two new permanent staff members at $30,000 per year,
- providing an overrecovery cushion of $10,000,
- maintaining the $25 per visit current standard rate, and
- decreasing the average cost of medications per visit by $1.

Using the contribution margin model, the financial implication of the proposed change is as follows:

$$\text{Breakeven in units of service} = \frac{\text{Fixed costs} + \text{Changes in fixed costs} + \text{Desired overrecovery cushion}}{\text{Contribution margin in \$} + \text{Decrease in variable expenses}}$$

$$= \frac{\$170{,}000 + \$30{,}000 + \$10{,}000}{\$20 + \$1}$$

$$= \frac{\$210{,}000}{\$21}$$

$$= 10{,}000$$

The combined effect is to move the level of activity from 8,500 units of service to 10,000, an increase of 1,500 units. The analysis highlights the consequences of the decisions: Can 1,500 patient visits be generated? If not, what is the impact of eliminating the overrecovery cushion? ($170,000 + $30,000 ÷ $21 = 9,524 visits.) Eliminating the cushion reduces the level to 9,524 visits or 476 fewer than the original proposed 1,500 increase. What if the standard fee is raised to $30 (increasing contribution by another $5) and no overrecovery cushion is planned? Assuming that the $1 decrease in medication costs is still possible,

$$\text{Breakeven} = \frac{\$170{,}000 + 30{,}000}{\$20 + 1 + 5} = \frac{200{,}000}{26} = 7{,}692 \text{ visits.}$$

By increasing the fee, decreasing variable expenses, and adding new staff, the required number of visits is now 808 fewer (8,500 − 7,692 = 808) than required under current operating conditions.

Cost Recovery/Volume Chart

The contribution margin model can be simplified into a cost recovery/volume (CV) chart which highlights the impact of volume changes on under- or overrecovery. The total revised contribution margin of raising or not raising the standard fee, adding new staff, decreasing variable cost, and adding or not adding an overrecovery cushion are shown in Figure 4.

If the chart shows several services, shifts in the mix of services can be plotted to reveal effects on cost under- or overrecovery. Cost-volume over-/underrecovery is an analytical framework and a tool for exploring optional decisions. The analysis makes several simple assumptions.

- Revenues and expenses are linear.
- Expenses may be classified into fixed and variable categories; total fixed expenses do not vary with changes in volume; total variable expenses vary directly with volume.
- Efficiency and productivity are unchanged over time.
- The relative mix of services in the revenue function, if it comprises several services, remains constant.

One of management's important responsibilities is the analysis of cost-volume- and over/under cost recovery. While many mental health program managers are not yet familiar with these techniques, knowledge of cost behavior and volume-cost-over-/underrecovery provides a valuable insight into planning and controlling operations, both short- and long-term.

EXTENDING TO A MULTISERVICE SETTING

Most service delivery settings offer several services. The following illustration of a hypothetical single service CMHC extends to multiple service settings.

As shown in Table 2 the service X contribution percentage is 40 percent while service Y is 80 percent. The service mix ratio is 9 to 1 (viz., 1,000 of X, 9,000 of Y). In total, the weighted average contribution percentage is 67.69 percent ($220,000 ÷ $325,000 = 67.69 percent); thus, for every revenue dollar roughly two-thirds is contribution margin. Dividing the total fixed costs by the weighted average contribution margin percentage gives an estimated breakeven in dollars.

$$\text{Multiservice breakeven} = \frac{\text{Total fixed costs}}{\text{Weighted average contribution margin percentage}}$$

$$\$295{,}464.61 = \frac{\$200{,}000}{.6769}$$

If services are actually rendered in the planned 9 to 1 ratio at the planned rates and costs, the center would break even when $295,464 of revenues are billed and eventually collected.

Figure 4: *Cost Recovery/Volume Chart*

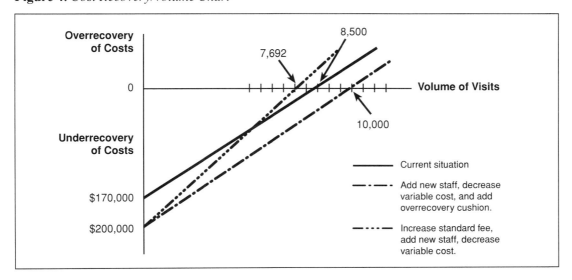

Table 2: *Deriving Contribution Margins for a Hypothetical CMHC Providing Two Services*

	Service X			Service Y			Total		
	Units	Rate	Total	Units	Rate	Total	Units	Rate	Total
Revenues	1,000	$100	$100,000	9,000	$25	$225,000	10,000	$32.50	$325,000
Variable costs	1,000	60	60,000	9,000	5	45,000	10,000	10.50	105,000
Contribution margin	1,000	$ 40	$ 40,000	9,000	$20	$180,000	10,000	$22.00	$220,000
Contribution margin percent	$40,000 ÷ $100,000 = 40%			$180,000 ÷ $225,000 = 80%			$220,000 ÷ $325,000 = 67.69%		

Note: The center's fixed costs are $200,000.

ADVANTAGES OF THE CONTRIBUTION MARGIN APPROACH

The advantages of the contribution margin approach are that it facilitates the cost-volume-recovery analysis with single or multiple changes in revenue, costs, and recovery factors; helps trace the financial effects of redesigning, pricing, promoting, adding, or diminishing various services; permits calculation of required minimum unit or revenue volumes by dividing fixed expenses by the contribution margin or the contribution margin ratio; and helps identify the most efficient use of fixed, given resources through the use of contribution to fixed expenses.

COST DISTINCTIONS FOR PLANNING AND CONTROL

Fixed and variable costs can be subdivided into committed and discretionary costs and engineered and discretionary variable costs, respectively.

Committed and Discretionary Costs

Fixed costs measure the capacity for delivering services and performing administration or research and reflect the capability for sustaining a planned volume of activity; fixed costs are divided into committed and discretionary costs.

Committed fixed costs are costs of physical equipment and the bases of the organization, such as rent, insurance, property taxes, and key personnel. Generally, these costs are affected by long-run forecasts that, in turn, indicate long-run capacity needs. Committed costs are the least responsive to short-run variation in volume of activity.

Discretionary fixed costs, also called managed or programmed costs, are the costs of periodic (usually yearly) allocation decisions by top management regarding the maximum level of expenditure permitted. They do not have demonstrable or easily identified relationships between inputs (e.g., costs) and output (e.g., services). Examples include research, staff training, professional development, and advertising. In hardship periods these expenditures could be reduced for short periods of time in direct contrast to the committed cost. Management often believes in the value of a discretionary program even if the consequences are difficult to evaluate.

Engineered and Discretionary Variable Costs

Variable costs are of two types: engineered and discretionary. Engineered variable costs have an explicit, specified physical relationship to a selected measure of activity. Efficiency is defined as the optimum relationship between the inputs and outputs. A mental health center that attempts to develop workload standards and to monitor the productivity of staff is using the concept of engineered costs.

Discretionary variable costs describes only a few variable costs. Medication costs, for example, may vary if the clinician prescribes generic instead of brand name drugs.

When management is looking for areas of cost reduction in the short run, discretionary fixed and discretionary variable costs are the first candidates for review. Cuts into committed fixed costs probably would impair service delivery as well as the quality of care; slashes in engineered variable costs undoubtedly would affect quality of care. Cost classification helps locate the type of costs that can be altered in the short run without seriously affecting service delivery system. However, discretionary expenditures such as staff training and building repairs cannot be postponed indefinitely without negative consequences.

DIFFERENTIAL COSTS AND REVENUES

In many decisions, comparisons of options are confused by the introduction of irrelevant costs or revenues. Examining only those costs or revenues which are incremental (or decremental) and differential between the alternatives helps clarify the options. Only costs expected to change because of a decision should be considered; only changes which reveal differences between options are valuable in decision making. The following data for a hypothetical CMHC illustrates differential costs and revenues. The CMHC operates three direct services and contracts the rest. The data in Table 3 are for its most recent year.

If every service should carry its own weight, the alcoholism counseling center's $14,000 loss is a major problem; discontinuing this service would increase outpatient services revenues by $5,000 but have no effects on use of other services or total assets. The vacated space would be idle or added to administrative office space, but separable fixed expenses could be avoided by not operating the Alcoholism Center. In reaching a decision on whether to drop this service, the data appearing in Table 4 could be used.

In this particular example, discontinuing a losing service would actually increase losses from breakeven to $6,000. If the incremental and differential costs and revenues had been considered, the analysis would have resulted in the decision to retain alcoholism services. This is illustrated in Table 5.

Table 4: *Effects of Discontinuing Alcoholism Service on the Financial Statement of the Hypothetical CMHC in Table 3*

	Outpatient	Consultation and Education	Total
Revenues	$54,000	$31,000	$85,000
Separable fixed expenses	5,000	4,000	9,000
Variable expenses	5,000	2,000	7,000
Subtotal	10,000	6,000	16,000
Contribution margin	$44,000	$25,000	$69,000
Committed fixed			[75,000]
Net Loss			[6,000]

Table 5: *Effect on Net Income of Decision to Discontinue Alcoholism Services for Hypothetical CMHC*

	Decision	
	Keep	Discontinue
Revenues–Alcoholism Center	0	[15,000]
Outpatient	0	+ 5,000
Net	0	[10,000]
Avoidable fixed expenses	0	3,000
Avoidable variable expenses	0	1,000
Subtotal	0	4,000
Change in contribution margin	0	[6,000]

Table 3: *Revenue and Expense Report for a Hypothetical CMHC Providing Three Services*

	Outpatient	Consultation and Education	Alcoholism Counseling Center	Total
Revenues	$49,000	$31,000	$15,000	$95,000
Separable fixed expenses	5,000	4,000	3,000	12,000
Joint fixed expenses allocated equally	25,000	25,000	25,000	75,000
Variable expenses	5,000	2,000	1,000	8,000
Net income (loss)	14,000	0	[14,000]	0

The negative change of $6,000 in contribution margin is also the new loss experienced by discontinuing the service. Costs common to both decisions are excluded since they would offset (e.g., fixed expense is constant). This illustration also points out the danger in using average and/or allocated costs from cost-finding in situations where cost behavior is appropriate.

EXTENDED ANALYSIS OF COST BEHAVIOR (Appendix)

Importance to Budget Process

Cost behavior and cost classification can be confusing, but several short-cut approaches offer useful insights into the cost behavior of almost any mental health organization. Cost behavior is how costs change in relation to changes in the volume of activity. Without a knowledge of cost behavior certain management tools such as cost-volume-profit analysis cannot be used. The entire budget process, from master budget, to flexible budgets and variance analysis, depends on an understanding of how costs behave as the volume of services changes. This appendix presents basic tools for analyzing cost behavior.

Mixed Costs

Expenses often contain both fixed and variable components, and are called mixed costs, an example of which would be the charge for a rental car. The car rental fee is x dollars per day plus y cents per mile driven. The fixed portion cannot be avoided if the car is rented for a day, but the variable portion is directly proportional to a measure of activity, viz., miles driven.

Separation of Mixed Costs. A variety of techniques separate mixed costs into fixed and variable components. The most common ones in ascending order of sophistication are account analysis, high-low method, scatter diagram, simple regression, and multiple regression.

Account analysis compares all expenses for two or more periods and makes a judgment about fixed and variable behavior. The high-low method provides a mathematical technique for separating costs into variable and fixed components. Its short-cut approach provides a good starting point for more detailed cost analysis. Scatter diagrams plot cost data against time for many periods. If a straight-line relationship is apparent, a line can be fitted to the points, and the fixed and variable components can be determined.

Regression techniques provide a statistically valid method for assessing cost behavior. Simple regression is for relationships assumed to be one to one and if the cost behavior is thought to be a function of a single variable. Separating the fixed and variable components of utility costs as a function of the number of patient contacts is an example of the use of simple regression. Multiple regression is used if the behavior of a given cost element is thought to be a function of two or more variables (analyzing utility costs as a function of both patient contacts and the season of the year, for example).

The High-Low Method. This technique, while less accurate than the regression methods, is simpler and easier to use and is illustrated here. By plotting two points, one representing a cost at a time when it was high and one representing it when it was low, for an actual or expected range of activity, a straight line can be fitted between the points. The function then can be extended backward to intersect the vertical axis, thus identifying the fixed portion of the total cost. The variable portion is determined from the slope of the line.

The same analysis can be accomplished with the following formulas:

1. Variable rate = $\dfrac{\text{Change in total mixed cost}}{\text{Change in activity volume}}$

2. Fixed costs = Total mixed cost less variable component at a given level of activity volume

3. Formula for estimating costs:

Total cost = Fixed costs + variable cost at given level of activity volume

An an example of the use of the high-low method, the technique is applied to an outpatient service with the following data:

Volume of Activity during Last Year	Number of Client Visits per Month	Costs (Including Personnel)
High month	1,000	$26,000
Low month	600	24,000

Note: This appendix is adapted from Sorensen and Hanbery (1978).

Using an equation approach, it is possible to separate the variable rate and fixed costs in these data. The resulting data are:

Variable rate = $\dfrac{(\$26{,}000 - \$24{,}000)}{1{,}000 - 600} = \dfrac{\$2{,}000}{400} = \$5$ per visit

Fixed cost = $\$24{,}000 - (\$5 \times 600)$
= $\$24{,}000 - \$3{,}000$
= $\$21{,}000$

or

Fixed cost = $\$26{,}000 - (\$5 \times 1{,}000)$
= $\$26{,}000 - \$5{,}000$
= $\$21{,}000$

Figure 5 shows a graphic approach to an analysis of these costs.

With the cost formula presented earlier, costs can be estimated at varying levels of activity. If, for example, the number of visits was 730, the estimated cost would be $24,650, calculated as follows:

Total cost = Fixed costs + Variable cost (Number of visits)
= $\$21{,}000 + \$5\,(730)$
= $\$21{,}000 + \$3{,}650$
= $\$24{,}650$

The high-low method works for all types of costs—fixed, variable, and mixed. If a cost is purely fixed, it will not change between periods; hence, the variable component will be zero. If a cost is purely variable, the fixed component will be zero, and the total cost will equal the variable component at a given level of activity.

Figure 5: *Example of an Application of the High-Low Method of Separating Fixed and Variable Costs in an Outpatient Setting*

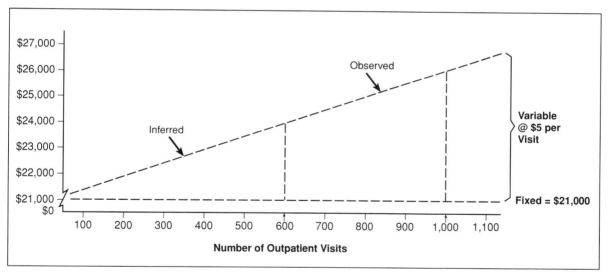

Identifying Full Costs of a Program

David N. Ammons

Local governments tend to understate the cost of individual programs or activities in much the same manner that most of us would underestimate, say, the annual cost of operating our own automobiles.[1] In our estimates, we would probably include the cost of gasoline and oil; we might also include our monthly payments or some appropriate component of the initial purchase price if we bought the car outright. But unless we were very careful, most of us would slip up somewhere. We might forget to distribute the down payment over the life of the car or we might neglect to include interest charges. We might forget to include insurance premiums, the charge for the extended warranty, repair charges, the cost of tires, the new paint job, the tag fee, the charge for an operator's license, parking fees, or fines for occasional speeding tickets. Each of those costs is directly associated with the operation of a vehicle: omitting any would understate expenses. Other related expenses such as the cost of a garage and driveway, in the case of homeowners, might not be eliminated by a decision to sell the car and use public transit; but in a full accounting of related expenses, they should be included on a pro rata basis as well.

Understating the cost of a program or activity in local government is rarely the product of deliberate deceit. More often, it is simply the result of overlooking expenses that are related to a program, though sometimes only indirectly, but budgeted elsewhere or allocated in a previous fiscal year.

Unless all expenses associated with a program are identified, the cost of that program will be understated and comparisons with similar programs offered by other entities, or even comparisons over time in a single jurisdiction, will be inaccurate and misleading. Incomplete estimates of program costs are especially troublesome when jurisdiction decisionmakers are considering major program changes or service delivery alternatives.

♦ Barrow, Maine

The city council of Barrow, Maine, had just adopted the budget for the upcoming year, and the budget director and her assistant were relaxing in her office, celebrating the high points and commiserating over the low points of the previous months. Suddenly, the budget director interrupted the conversation with what seemed a strange question.

"What kind of a budget would you say we have?"

"A program budget," the budget analyst responded.

"A program budget?"

"Yes. Sure. We call them 'activities,' but each page describes a program and reports all of its costs."

"*All* of its costs?"

"Yeah. I think so."

The budget director shook her head. "On three occasions in the last five years, we've invited contractors to submit bids to contract for the delivery of some service we're doing in-house. We didn't award any of

---

Reprinted from David N. Ammons, *Administrative Analysis for Local Government: Practical Application of Selected Techniques* (Athens: Carl Vinson Institute of Government, University of Georgia, 1991), 84-92.

those bids because they were never any cheaper than our budgeted figures for doing the work ourselves. Why is it that we're always reading about the savings from contracting and other forms of privatization and yet we're zero for three? I think we're underreporting our costs."

"What costs do you think we're missing?" asked the budget analyst.

"Well, I'm not sure we're including all the costs of employee benefits with each program. I suspect that we're understating the costs of operating our vehicles and allowing the city garage to absorb some of that. Some of the costs of the finance department, the personnel department, and other administrators here at city hall should be allocated to the various programs that benefit from the services they provide. I'll bet that we also badly understate various overhead costs associated with our facilities. We don't even charge building rental."

"Building rental? The city owns these buildings. Why should a department have a rental charge?"

"The building wasn't free. Some form of rental or depreciation would more accurately reflect the costs of providing a particular program."

DETERMINING FULL COSTS

The budget director and budget analyst continued to discuss various costs that might be missed in the current budget format and cost comparisons. By the end of their conversation, the list was rather long, and the budget analyst had offered to explore the matter more systematically.

A review of available reference materials provided little help until the budget analyst discovered a workbook for evaluating refuse collection options.[2] Using that workbook as a model, he developed five worksheets for identifying the costs of a selected local government program or activity.

Worksheets

Personal services—salaries, wages, and fringe benefits—are a major expense in most local government programs. Worksheet 1 calls for

1. the identification of all positions directly engaged in the selected program or activity;
2. the staffing of each such position in full-time equivalents (e.g., if the employee works 20 hours per week year round, the full-time equivalent [FTE] is 0.5; if the position is filled by a seasonal employee working 40 hours per week for three months, the FTE is 0.25);
3. estimation of the percentage of each employee's time on the job *spent on the selected program* (e.g., a full-time employee devoting 20 hours per week to the program would have 0.5 recorded in this column, as would a 20-hour per week employee devoting 10 hours to the program);
4. notation of annual salary or wages for each position on a full-time basis (or the average if several employees engaged in the program have the same title); and
5. the product of columns 2, 3, and 4. The sum of column 5 plus total overtime payments for the program captures the salaries and wages of personnel directly engaged in the program.

Worksheet 2 addresses fringe benefit costs. The person-years devoted to the program and covered by specified benefits are multiplied by the cost per person-year for those benefits to derive total fringe benefit costs.

Worksheet 3 addresses other operating expenses. Common expenses such as supplies, building expenses, vehicles, equipment, insurance, and contractual services are identified on the form, but many programs have unusual expense items that should also be identified and included in the total.

Capital items and internal services deserve special attention in calculating program expenses. The costs of acquiring and maintaining buildings and vehicles, for example, often are not reflected in the budget of the program that benefits from their use. The building may have been constructed years ago with resources from the sale of bonds, the debt service for which is budgeted in another activity. Automobiles assigned to the program may have been purchased last year, with this year's budget showing no acquisition costs whatsoever. The expense of maintaining buildings and vehicles may be reflected only in the budgets of the internal service departments responsible for those maintenance activities. In such cases, program expenses are understated, making the program appear less costly than it actually is.

Worksheet 1: *Salaries and Wages of Personnel for Selected Program/Activity*

Titles of Positions Directly Engaged in Selected Program/Activity[a] (1)	Number of Employees (in full-time equivalents) (2)	Fraction of Time on the Job Spent on Selected Program/Activity (3)	Annual Expenditure per Person-Year($) (4)	Total (2) × (3) × (4) (5)
_____	_____	_____	_____	_____
_____	_____	_____	_____	_____
_____	_____	_____	_____	_____
_____	_____	_____	_____	_____
_____	_____	_____	_____	_____
_____	_____	_____	_____	_____
_____	_____	_____	_____	_____
_____	_____	_____	_____	_____
_____	_____	_____	_____	_____
_____	_____	_____	_____	_____
_____	_____	_____	_____	_____
_____	_____	_____	_____	_____
_____	_____	_____	_____	_____
_____	_____	_____	_____	_____

Total Overtime Payment for Selected Program/Activity[b]: $ _____

Total Salary and Wage Costs: $ _____

Source: Adapted from Columbia University, Public Technology, Inc., and the International City Management Association, *Evaluating Residential Refuse Collection Costs: A Workbook for Local Government* and *Worksheet Supplement* (Washington, D.C.: Public Technology, Inc., 1978). Adapted by permission of Public Technology, Inc.

[a] Include supervisory and support personnel (e.g., secretaries, clerks, custodians) from the same department.

[b] For overtime figure, see budget or financial records.

A more accurate statement of program expenses would assign proportionate capital and maintenance expenses to the programs that derive benefits from those facilities and equipment. Various options exist for determining reasonable assessments. Annual costs for building "rental," for example, may be based on the program's proportionate share (based on square footage) of the annual debt service requirements—principal and interest—to retire the bonds sold to finance construction of the building. Vehicle "rental" may be based on a depreciation schedule or annual contributions to a Vehicle Replacement Fund in amounts sufficient to have enough money available to purchase a replacement vehicle when the current vehicle is no longer serviceable. Similarly, maintenance assessments should be based on actual costs or a proportionate share of general maintenance expenses.

Worksheet 2: *Fringe Benefit Costs for Selected Program/Activity*

Benefit (1)	Person-Years Devoted to Program/Activity That Are Covered by Specified Benefit[a] (2)	Expenditure per Person-Year($) (3)	Total (2) × (3) (4)
Social Security			
Insurance:			
A. Health and hospital			
B. Dental			
C. Life			
D. Disability			
E. Worker's compensation			
F. Unemployment compensation			
Retirement fund			
Uniforms and cleaning			
Safety equipment (e.g., gloves, shoes, etc.)			
Longevity or bonus pay			
(Other)			
		Total Fringe Benefit Costs:	$

Source: Adapted from Columbia University, Public Technology, Inc., and the International City Management Association, *Evaluating Residential Refuse Collection Costs: A Workbook for Local Government* and *Worksheet Supplement* (Washington, D.C.: Public Technology, Inc., 1978). Adapted by permission of Public Technology, Inc.

[a] Full-time equivalent (FTE) of employees who are engaged at least partially in the selected program and who are entitled to benefit coverage multiplied by the fraction of their time spent on that program.

Finally, consideration should be given to cost recovery if the program provides services for which funds are received to defray operating expenses.

Worksheet 4 provides for the tabulation of overhead costs—a program's proportionate share of the expense of various administrative and support services provided by other departments of the local government. The city manager's time, for example, is divided among the various programs of the local government. Similarly, the personnel department provides services on an organization-wide basis. Each program derives benefits from those services and is spared the trouble and expense of performing various functions itself. It is only proper that a proportionate share of the costs of overhead agencies be borne by the various programs of the local government on some proportionate basis. The basis used on this worksheet is the ratio of salary and wages for the selected program to salary and wages for the entire local government work force. The assumption—an imperfect one, at best—is that a program that includes 10 percent of the local government's payroll probably also receives about 10 percent of the benefit of the city manager's office, the finance department, the city clerk's office, and other overhead agencies.

Worksheet 3: *Other Operating Expenses for Selected Program/Activity*

Category (1)	Total Annual Expenses (2)	% Applicable to Selected Program (3)	Total (2) × (3) (4)
Supplies			
_____	_____	_____	_____
_____	_____	_____	_____
Other	_____	_____	_____
Building expenses			
Telephone	_____	_____	_____
Utilities	_____	_____	_____
Rent[a]	_____	_____	_____
Maintenance	_____	_____	_____
Other	_____	_____	_____
Vehicles			
Rent[a]	_____	_____	_____
Operation[b]	_____	_____	_____
Maintenance[b]	_____	_____	_____
Other equipment	_____	_____	_____
_____	_____	_____	_____
_____	_____	_____	_____
Insurance	_____	_____	_____
_____	_____	_____	_____
_____	_____	_____	_____
Contractual services	_____	_____	_____
_____	_____	_____	_____
_____	_____	_____	_____
Other operating expenses	_____	_____	_____
_____	_____	_____	_____
_____	_____	_____	_____
		Subtotal	_____
		Less Cost Recovery[c]	_____
		Total	_____

Source: Adapted from Columbia University, Public Technology, Inc., and the International City Management Association, *Evaluating Residential Refuse Collection Costs: A Workbook for Local Government* and *Worksheet Supplement* (Washington, D.C.: Public Technology, Inc., 1978). Adapted by permission of Public Technology, Inc.

[a] If the local government is renting office space and vehicles for this program, those amounts should be entered here. If the local government possesses its own program facilities and vehicles, it is still appropriate to enter "rental" of some kind (perhaps based on annual allocations for replacement, on a depreciation schedule, on debt service, or on market rates) rather than to imply that they are "free."

[b] Fuel, parts, and maintenance expenses should be recorded here, except when such expenses would duplicate previous entries (e.g., if repair personnel are listed on Worksheet 1, labor charges should not be repeated here).

[c] Consideration of cost recovery (i.e., reimbursement or other receipt of funds from service recipients) is especially important when it is available with one program option but unavailable with others. Fairness of comparison among multiple programs or options will demand uniform treatment of program receipts, whether labeled "cost recovery" and reported in the budget as an expenditure reduction or labeled "general revenue" and having no such effect on reported program expenditures.

Worksheet 4: *Overhead Costs for Selected Program/Activity*

Name of Overhead Agency	Salaries and Wages	Expenses Other Than Salaries, Wages and Fringe Benefits
Mayor/Manager		
Fin., comptroller, budget, treas.		
Clerk		
City attorney		
General services		
Data processing		
Purchasing		
Personnel		
City council		
....		
....		
Total:	_____ (A)	_____ (B)

(C) =

Overhead adjustment: total salary and wages for selected program (Worksheet 1) ÷ salary and wages for entire city work force

                                (C)   (C)

Total overhead salaries
(A) × (C) = (D)   _____ (D)

(E) =

Fringe adjustment: fringe benefits for selected program (Worksheet 2) ÷ total salaries and wages for selected program (Worksheet 1)

                                (E)

Fringe benefits for above
(A) × (E) = (F)   _____ (F)

Other overhead costs for selected program/activity
(B) × (C) = (G)   _____ (G)

Total Overhead Costs: _____
                              (D) + (F) + (G)

Source: Adapted from Columbia University, Public Technology, Inc., and the International City Management Association, *Evaluating Residential Refuse Collection Costs: A Workbook for Local Government* and *Worksheet Supplement* (Washington, D.C.: Public Technology, Inc., 1978). Adapted by permission of Public Technology, Inc.

Worksheet 5 combines the figures from the other four worksheets to arrive at a cost summary for the program. That total may differ substantially from the amount listed for the activity in the local government's annual budget. It provides a much improved basis for comparison of program costs with those of other jurisdictions, assuming their costs are similarly developed, and for consideration of service delivery options.

Worksheet 5: *Cost Summary for Selected Program/Activity*

Total personnel salaries and wages from Worksheet 1	_____
Total fringe benefits from Worksheet 2	_____
Other operating costs from Worksheet 3	_____
Total overhead costs from Worksheet 4	_____
Total Cost	$ _____

Source: Adapted from Columbia University, Public Technology, Inc., and the International City Management Association, *Evaluating Residential Refuse Collection Costs: A Workbook for Local Government* and *Worksheet Supplement* (Washington, D.C.: Public Technology, Inc., 1978). Adapted by permission of Public Technology, Inc.

UTILITY OF FULL-COST IDENTIFICATION

A true program budget reports all of the costs associated with a given program. A basic premise of such a system is that full cost reports will help policymakers in their deliberations regarding needs, priorities, and options. Systems that presume to report full costs but fail to do so are deceptive and may contribute to ill-advised decisions.

Unless they have identified the full costs of a program, officials are unable to answer some very basic questions: How much are we paying for this service? What is the cost per unit of service? How does our cost compare with that of other jurisdictions? How does the cost of this service compare with the costs of various other services offered by our city or county government?

If basic questions are tough to answer without full cost information, answers to more complex questions are especially elusive: How much money could be saved by making service delivery changes? Could money be saved by contracting for service delivery? How much?

The use of the worksheets offered in this discussion provides a means of addressing both the basic and more complex questions with a considerable degree of accuracy. When identifying full costs for purposes of evaluating contract service options, however, care should be taken to identify those costs that will not be eliminated even with a decision to contract for a particular service. For example, in most cases, many of the expenses of the various overhead agencies would not be reduced appreciably, if at all, by eliminating an in-house program; the costs would simply be redistributed to other programs. Similarly, the expenses of a building owned by the local government but no longer inhabited by the in-house program would simply be shifted to the new occupant allowed to expand into those premises. Although such expenses are legitimate components of program costs, they should be carefully weighed when considering service delivery alternatives. Ignoring the fact that some costs may continue could lead local government decisionmakers to contract for services under an erroneous assumption that they would be saving money. The result could actually be greater total expenses rather than less.

Notes

1. Savas examined budgets and actual costs in 68 jurisdictions and discovered actual costs 30 percent greater than the figures shown for various services on their budget pages. See E.S. Savas, "How Much Do Government Services Really Cost?" *Urban Affairs Quarterly* 15 (September 1979): 23-42.
2. Local governments desiring to identify the costs associated with their in-house residential refuse collection program may wish to examine the worksheets designed specifically for that objective. Columbia University, Public Technology, Inc., and the International City Management Association, *Evaluating Residential Refuse Collection Costs: A Workbook for Local Government* (Washington, D.C.: Public Technology, 1978).

Suggested for Further Reading

Columbia University, Public Technology, Inc., and the International City Management Association. *Evaluating Residential Refuse Collection Costs: A Workbook for Local Government* and *Worksheet Supplement*. Washington, D.C.: Public Technology, 1978.

Friedman, Marvin. "Calculating Compensation Costs." In *Budget Management: A Reader in Local Government Financial Management*, edited by Jack Rabin, W. Bartley Hildreth, and Gerald J. Miller, 116-27. Athens, Ga.: Carl Vinson Institute of Government, University of Georgia, 1983. Reprinted from *The Use of Economic Data in Collective Bargaining*. Washington, D.C.: U.S. Department of Labor, 1978.

Kelley, Joseph T. *Costing Government Services: A Guide for Decision Making*. Washington, D.C.: Government Finance Officers Association, 1984.

Reporting

Unreserved Fund Balance and Local Government Finance

Ian J. Allan

Local governments in the United States are operating in an increasingly difficult fiscal environment which has been made worse by the effects of an economic slowdown. Of particular concern to many finance officers has been a decrease in revenues from economically sensitive sources, which has led to budget shortfalls and deficits. Compounding problems in local revenue collection are similar problems occurring at the state level which, in some instances, have resulted in cutbacks in state aid to localities.[1]

A number of actions can be taken by local governments seeking to improve their chances of avoiding financial difficulty during periods of sluggish or negative economic growth. Those actions include the following:

- The use of budgetary/expenditure controls, such as the establishment of an allotment system that would require the careful planning of all departmental expenditures and budget office approval of spending plans, or the limiting of departmental expenditures to amounts less than that budgeted (95%, for example).
- The use of contingent spending and tax rules that would make levels of spending and tax increases contingent upon the amount of revenues collected during the fiscal year.
- The use of other budgetary controls including restrictions on travel and budgetary transfers,

deferral of purchases of goods and services, and a hiring freeze.
- The use of unreserved fund balance resources or monies held in a fund established specifically for contingencies (such as a budget stabilization or "rainy day" fund).

The first two are anticipatory mechanisms which can be used to minimize the chances of budget shortfalls developing during a fiscal year. The latter two are options available to finance officers after a financial problem has developed. While all represent useful tools in difficult fiscal times, this paper will focus on the use of unreserved fund balance resources for contingencies.[2]

Sufficient levels of unreserved fund balance (or monies set aside in a budget stabilization fund) can ensure the continued orderly operation of government and provision of services to residents and the continued stability of the tax structure. Local governments that have built up sufficient levels of unreserved fund balance can avoid or reduce budget cutbacks and tax increases if budget shortfalls develop during a fiscal year. The maintenance of fiscal stability is a particularly important factor considered by credit rating agencies in their evaluation of the creditworthiness of local government debt, with instability potentially leading to a credit downgrade and increased borrowing costs.

The purpose of this paper is to discuss the significance of unreserved fund balance to local governments, and provide guidance to those finance officers concerned about the possible effect of a sluggish

---

Reprinted from *Research Bulletin* (Washington, D.C.: Government Finance Research Center, Government Finance Officers Association, November 1990), 1-8. By permission of GFOA.

economy (or other external influences) on their government's financial condition. The development of a policy that establishes the appropriate level of unreserved fund balance for a government, a difficult task, will also be discussed. Complicating this issue is the existence of some confusion over what is meant by the term "fund balance," and the fact that there is no nationally uniform standard regarding the appropriate level of unreserved fund balance that local governments should maintain. There is also a paucity of literature and other information on the use of unreserved fund balance or other financial resources for contingencies, with much of it devoted to the establishment of budget stabilization or "rainy day" funds at the state level.

WHAT IS FUND BALANCE?

Prior to discussing the issues related to the establishment of an adequate level of unreserved fund balance for contingencies, it is important to define what is generally meant by fund balance. Fund balance does not refer to cash balance, nor is it the difference between revenues and expenditures. Rather, fund balance is the cumulative difference of all revenues and expenditures from the government's creation.[3] It can also be considered to be the difference between fund assets and fund liabilities, and can be known as fund equity.[4]

For accounting purposes, a distinction is often made between reserved and unreserved fund balance. Reserved fund balance consists of portions of fund balance that are either legally restricted to a specific future use or are not available for appropriation or expenditure. Legally restricted portions of fund balance include "fund balance-reserved for encumbrances" and "fund balance-reserved for debt service." The portion(s) of fund balance that is not available for appropriation or expenditure represents assets that are *not* considered "expendable available financial resources." Reserved fund balance is often further broken down into several categories based on the purpose of the monies held. Exhibit 1 shows typical fund balance accounts.

Unreserved fund balance is often subdivided into designated and undesignated portions. The former reflect tentative management plans for future financial resource use, such as the replacement of equipment.[5] Other designations include "for contingencies" and "for appropriation in future years." Undesig-

Exhibit 1: *Typical Fund Balance Accounts*

- Reserved for advances to other funds
- Reserved for debt service
- Reserved for encumbrances
- Reserved for endowments
- Reserved for fixed assets held for resale
- Reserved for inventories
- Reserved for noncurrent loans receivable
- Reserved for prepaid items
- Reserved for disability
- Unreserved
- Unreserved, designated (for specific purposes)
- Unreserved, undesignated

nated portions of unreserved fund balance represent expendable available financial resources that can be used to meet contingencies and working capital requirements.

The emphasis of this discussion will be on the level of unreserved fund balance that local governments maintain in their general fund for contingencies and which is available for use in the event a government experiences financial difficulty. The general fund is singled out because it contains the bulk of monies appropriated for general government operations. Most governments seeking to set aside financial resources for contingencies assign them to the general fund's unreserved fund balance, either in the "unreserved, undesignated" account or in the "unreserved, designated for contingencies" account.[6] Some local governments create a separate fund for contingencies or financial emergencies, such as a budget stabilization or "rainy day" fund. The creation of such a fund will be discussed later in this paper.

WHY IS AN UNRESERVED FUND BALANCE NECESSARY?

Two important goals of local governments are the maintenance of a stable tax and revenue structure and the orderly provision of services to residents. Such stability is necessary to maintaining or improving the jurisdiction's credit standing, but can be threatened by uncertainty emanating from a number of areas; foremost is economic uncertainty.

Economic Uncertainty

Determining how well the local or regional economy will perform and its subsequent impact on local government finances is one of the more difficult tasks facing the finance officer. Changes in economic activity affect both the revenue structure and government spending, with the effects varying from jurisdiction to jurisdiction. Of critical importance to governments attempting to maintain fiscal stability is that the growth in revenues continues to match or exceed the growth in expenditures.

The finances of governments that are dependent on economically sensitive revenues, such as general sales or income taxes, will be more affected by a downturn in the economy than governments that are dependent on more stable tax sources, such as the real property tax. The former are more likely to benefit from the maintenance of an adequate level of unreserved fund balance. Governments that are dependent on the real property tax may also be affected by an economic slowdown, however, particularly if the market value of real estate and assessed values decline. In addition, economic downturns may also contribute to the loss of major taxpayers in some jurisdictions, severely depressing local revenue collections.

In some cases, governments have little control over the factors that affect expenditures. This is particularly true of governments responsible for entitlement programs such as public welfare services, expenditures which quite commonly increase dramatically during economic downturns. In addition, the impact of inflation on local government costs is often hard to anticipate.

Other Forms of Uncertainty

While the health of the economy often has the major effect on local government finances, other forms of uncertainty must also be taken into consideration, such as the following:

- Unanticipated changes in the tax and spending policies of federal and state governments. Changes in federal and state tax policies can have an impact on local governments, which must compete for increasingly scarce tax revenues. Similarly, changes in federal and state spending policies can impact local governments, particularly if reductions in spending force local governments to increase their own spending to make up for the loss in federal or state monies.
- The imposition of mandates by federal and state governments, which often have uncertain economic and financial impacts on local governments.
- Court decisions that result in unexpected local expenditures, such as court-mandated improvements to correctional facilities or the invalidation of a major revenue source that requires a government to return revenues already collected.
- Limitations on a government's taxing and spending powers as the result of the passage of voter referendums.
- Financial impacts of labor agreements, particularly those stemming from binding arbitration.
- Unanticipated expenditures resulting from natural disasters.
- Unforeseen increases in energy costs.
- Unexpected capital expenditures resulting from water main breaks, bridge collapses, etc.
- Extraordinary employee overtime costs.
- Errors in revenue and expenditure estimation due to the difficulty in identifying the turning point in the business cycle.
- Unexpected variations in a government's cash flow that necessitate the use of short-term borrowing if sufficient monies are not available to cover shortfalls.

Although there is more maneuvering room in some budgets than others, particularly when it is possible to defer purchases of goods and services, all finance officers should accept the fact that uncertainty exists and hedge against it through the development and use of adequate levels of unreserved fund balance.

The adequacy of a jurisdiction's unreserved fund balance will depend to a great extent upon an accurate assessment of the uncertainty it faces. Such an assessment will include an examination of past experiences, including an analysis of cash flows that looks at revenue collection and spending patterns. Without such a review, and without adequate resources to deal with financial emergencies, budget cutbacks and tax increases during a fiscal year may become a real possibility, and credit ratings may be threatened.

Why Not Maintain an Unreserved Fund Balance?

Arguments for the establishment and maintenance of adequate levels of unreserved fund balance for contingencies reflect financial management imperatives. This perspective often finds itself under attack from taxpayer advocates and proponents of greater government spending who may oppose the establishment and maintenance of any level of unreserved fund balance, but whose views contribute to the debate over the appropriate level and uses of unreserved fund balance.

Taxpayer advocates argue that when the government establishes an unreserved fund balance it is attempting to hoard monies that it does not need, resulting in higher than necessary tax burdens. They argue that monies should remain in the taxpayers' hands until needed to pay for services and that if surpluses exist, they should be returned to the taxpayer through tax cuts and tax refunds. Resources should be accumulated prudently, kept only for specific purposes in formally created reserve funds, with little or no unreserved fund balance. This view is commonly expressed during periods of rapid increase in the market and assessed value of real property, particularly if property tax rates are not lowered and property tax bills increase significantly.

Spending advocates argue that when a government allocates financial resources to unreserved fund balance it is hoarding monies that would be better spent on some public good or service. While this viewpoint could be expressed at any time, it is more likely during periods of fiscal uncertainty, especially when cutbacks in key programs are threatened.

ESTABLISHING A FUND BALANCE POLICY

All governments should have a policy that accurately reflects their financial objectives. These objectives encompass a wide range of activities, from raising revenues through specific forms of taxation to adequately accounting for assets and liabilities and investing public funds. Such policies should be in written form, and subject to review by elected officials on a regular basis.

As part of their comprehensive financial policy, local governments should have a formal policy regarding the level of unreserved fund balance that they wish to establish and maintain for contingencies and other purposes. An important reason for developing such a policy is to provide the taxpayers with an explanation of why financial resources have been set aside and the conditions under which such resources will be expended. This policy should cover all fund balance accounts. This paper, however, limits its focus to those accounts used for contingencies.

A government's fund balance policy should address

- setting aside financial resources for contingencies;
- allocating financial resources to unreserved fund balance (or a budget stabilization fund);
- utilizing unreserved fund balance resources; and
- determining the appropriate size of unreserved fund balance (or budget stabilization fund).

Some governments have included a statement regarding the level of financial resources that they will set aside for contingencies in the Summary of Significant Accounting Policies (SSAP) or the letter of transmittal accompanying the government's Comprehensive Annual Financial Report (CAFR). These policy statements along with the jurisdiction's comprehensive financial policy should be reviewed and updated on an annual basis to reflect current economic and financial conditions.

Setting Aside Financial Resources for Contingencies

Local governments committed to setting aside financial resources to hedge against economic and other forms of uncertainty can choose among the following options:

- the fund balance of the general fund
- a fund established specifically for budget stabilization or "rainy day" purposes
- other funds

General Fund

The general fund provides the simplest and most direct way of setting aside financial resources for contingencies. Allocating such resources to the general fund's unreserved fund balance makes clear the jurisdiction's policy regarding the establishment and maintenance of financial resources for contingencies. The main problem with this approach is that allocations to unreserved fund balance are readily identifiable and represent an attractive pool of monies that taxpayer advocates will eye for tax cuts and that spending advocates will eye for spending increases. The major questions facing finance officers adopting this approach will be

- How can monies not be earmarked for something and be unavailable? and
- Under what circumstances can these monies be utilized?

From an accounting perspective, it is preferable that financial resources set aside for contingencies be assigned to unreserved fund balance or a fund established specifically for that purpose. Resources allocated to unreserved fund balance should be either "designated for contingencies" or maintained as an "unreserved, undesignated" balance. That has not stopped some finance officers from assigning such resources to some of the reserved fund balance accounts. This practice may result in the development of misleading financial statements, however.

Budget Stabilization Funds

A number of governments, particularly at the state level, have established special funds for the purpose of guarding against such negative effects of an economic downturn as revenue shortfalls and increased expenditure demand, which can lead to operating budget deficits. At present, 35 states have established budget stabilization or "rainy day" funds to guard against these effects.[7] The availability of monies in such a fund can minimize the need for tax and spending changes during the fiscal year.

The proliferation of budget stabilization funds among state governments is primarily due to their sensitivity to economic downturns. Some local governments are also sensitive to economic downturns, particularly those dependent on general sales and income tax revenues and those with economically sensitive expenditure structures.

Budget stabilization funds are not without their problems, some of which include

- lack of sufficient funding;
- discretionary deposit methods that have resulted in little or no money going into the funds; and
- withdrawal of monies for reasons unrelated to budget problems.

Other Funds

Finance officers interested in the indirect approach to setting aside financial resources for contingencies have utilized a variety of funds, including self-insurance funds and claims reserve funds. The use of other funds represents the least obvious method of developing adequate levels of resources for contingencies. The other funds approach has sometimes resulted in abuses of proper accounting standards and procedures, however.

It is important to note that there is no economic difference between the general fund, budget stabilization fund, and other funds alternatives. Total cash position will be the same, as will the amount available for use during a budget crisis and the amount withheld from current spending or for tax reduction. There are other differences among the three approaches, however. Budget stabilization funds, for example, will almost always require the passage of enabling legislation prior to their creation, while the other two alternatives would not. This is a major drawback to the use of budget stabilization funds.

The other drawback to the budget stabilization approach is the high visibility of financial resources set aside in a fund established specifically for contingencies (also a problem for the general fund approach), which represents a tempting pool of monies to both taxpayer and spending advocates, a fact that underscores the need for a formal fund balance policy. Finally, the other funds approach is less desirable than the other two approaches because it is an indirect method of setting aside financial resources for contingencies and, in some cases, has resulted in abuses of accepted accounting standards and procedures.

Allocating Financial Resources to Unreserved Fund Balance

While decisions related to the establishment of an unreserved fund balance have often been left to the discretion of the finance officer or executive, this is a decision which could benefit from greater formality. A mechanism can be established through which financial resources can be set aside for contingencies. This mechanism must be clearly identified and explained in the jurisdiction's financial/fund balance policy. Options available to local governments include

- formulas that determine unreserved fund balance amounts (typical formulas include: 1-3 month's operating expenditures, or unreserved fund balance as a proportion of annual operating expenditures, such as 5 percent);
- requirements that a portion of any operating surplus be deposited into unreserved fund balance; and
- dedication of revenues from a specific source, such as the real property tax, to the establishment of an adequate level of unreserved fund balance.

The assignment of financial resources to unreserved fund balance or a budget stabilization fund is most often done during good economic times for use in bad times.

Utilizing Unreserved Fund Balance Resources

It is important that criteria be developed to guide the use of financial resources set aside for contingencies, whether those resources have been allocated to unreserved fund balance or to a fund established specifically for that purpose. Of critical importance are two questions:

- Under what circumstances should unreserved fund balance resources be utilized?
- Who should make the decision regarding their use?

In response to the first question, the primary reason for the use of unreserved fund balance resources is to alleviate unanticipated short-term budgetary problems, such as revenue shortfalls or budget deficits. These problems are often uncovered during routine analysis of a government's cash flow patterns. Returning to the two major goals of local government financial management, the resources should be utilized to stabilize the tax structure and ensure the orderly provision of services to residents. It would not be appropriate to use these resources in an attempt to solve long-term financial problems, which should be dealt with in other ways.

Often, the decision on whether to use financial resources set aside for contingencies is a political one, determined by spending needs or the desire to maintain tax stability. These decisions are typically made by the executive or the legislative body. In this case also, a mechanism must be established for determining when those resources should be used. A number of methods are available, including

- supplemental appropriation of the resources to correct revenue shortfalls or budget deficits;
- executive orders requiring the transfer of resources to operating accounts;
- formula disbursement of the resources to various operating accounts; and
- automatic appropriation or transfer in case of budget shortfalls.

Determining the Appropriate Size of Unreserved Fund Balance

Determining the appropriate size of unreserved fund balance (plus monies set aside for contingencies in other funds) is one of the more formidable tasks facing local government finance officers and elected officials. Clearly, what is an adequate level of unreserved fund balance for one jurisdiction, given its particular financial and economic characteristics, may not be adequate for another. In this section, the following will be discussed:

- the computation of an unreserved fund balance ratio
- the use of unreserved fund balance as an indicator of financial condition
- the determination of the appropriate size of unreserved fund balance

Unreserved Fund Balance Ratio

Prior to discussing the issue of the appropriate size of unreserved fund balance, the concept of the unreserved fund balance ratio should be introduced. This ratio is important because it is often used as a measure of a government's financial health. The first step in the computation of this ratio is the determination of what financial resources are available to meet contingencies. In some jurisdictions, this amount will be equal to the resources contained in the general fund's unreserved fund balance account. In other jurisdictions, resources contained in other places, such as a budget stabilization fund, should be considered for inclusion.

In computing the unreserved fund balance ratio it is important to exclude the legally restricted portions of fund balance (that reserved for encumbrances, and for debt service) and those resources reserved for other purposes. It is not critical that resources "designated" for specific purposes in unreserved fund balance be excluded from this calculation, as the designations reflect only tentative plans for use, although it may be appropriate to do so.

The amount of resources available for contingencies is then compared with annual operating expenditures (for the general fund in this case).[8] The resultant ratio (or a variant thereof) is often used by the credit rating agencies and other analysts in measuring financial condition.

Unreserved Fund Balance as an Indicator of Financial Condition

Because of the importance of unreserved fund balance to the credit rating agencies' evaluation of a local government's creditworthiness, it is appropriate to discuss their views regarding the subject. The rating agencies' primary concern is that governments have an adequate level of financial resources to ensure the timely payment of principal and interest on their outstanding debt.

Of particular importance to the credit rating agencies are the size of "fund balance" (resources available for contingencies) and the trend in the size of fund balance.[9] A fund balance that decreases in size from year to year is sometimes seen as a problem and as an indicator of fiscal weakness. A small fund balance (under 5 percent of annual operating expenditures) could also be looked upon negatively if the government has experienced financial difficulties in the past due to external factors, such as a slump in the economy. A fund balance deficit would be looked upon very negatively since it clearly indicates that a government has had prior difficulty balancing its budget and is in a weakened position to deal with future financial problems.

In the following paragraphs, the views of the major credit rating agencies regarding the subject will be presented. Although Moody's Investors Service, Standard & Poor's Corporation, and Fitch Investors Service take similar approaches to the issue of adequate fund balance, there are differences among them.

Moody's: The Moody's analyst is interested in measuring control, or the ability of the government to call forth and manage financial resources so that debt obligations can be met in full and on time. The availability of adequate financial resources that can be used to address unforeseen contingencies adds to an issuer's control.

Although a "fund balance" that equals 5 percent of budgeted expenditures is deemed prudent by the Moody's analyst, the appropriate level of fund balance will vary from jurisdiction to jurisdiction. The level of fund balance that an analyst would like to see is directly related to the likelihood of the government being forced to call upon these resources. A fund balance below 5 percent of budgeted expenditures may not adversely affect an issuer's credit position if the lower amount is justified by a long-term trend of annual operating budget surpluses. On the other hand, a larger fund balance may be necessary in jurisdictions with economically sensitive revenues and expenditures that are not easily forecasted.[10]

S&P's: S&P's considers an adequate level of "fund balance" to be a credit strength because the level of fund balance measures the flexibility of an issuer to meet essential services during transitionary periods. While S&P's considers 5 percent of annual operating expenditures to be an adequate level of fund balance for some governments, it may not be for others. Of particular importance to the S&P analyst is the maintenance of a stable level of fund balance over time; sudden, sharp decreases in fund balance levels are generally looked upon unfavorably.

The S&P analyst takes into account several variables when evaluating fund balance size: the cash flow of an issuer (i.e., tax collection practices v. spending patterns); other reserves or contingency funds available to meet unforeseen expenses; and the philosophy of government officials and the community toward large government revenue surpluses.[11]

Fitch: Fitch, which recently began to rate general obligation bond issues, offered the following statement describing its approach to the issue of adequate "fund balance":

> An unreserved fund balance provides a government with available resources in the event of unforeseeable occurrences, budget variances or for cash flow purposes. Most analysts look to a fund balance of about 5 percent of revenues as a prudent level to allow for a reasonable degree of error in budget forecasting or other occurrences within the definition of a casual event.

Fitch believes this is a reasonable benchmark recognizing that the appropriate level may vary according to needs. For instance, a municipality that relies on a large percentage of its taxes collected late in the fiscal year may need higher balances for cash flow requirements. Also, a locality which possesses a cyclical economic base may be more susceptible to wider budget swings requiring a larger and more liquid contingency. Conversely, an entity with a more even flow of receipts throughout the year, which has good capabilities in accurate budget forecasting and monitoring, may not need as large a balance. Fitch places less emphasis on actual fund balance level, but rather stresses longer term financial balance and management. In the long run, the fundamental economic, capital and financial management factors more heavily influence credit quality and ratings.[12]

Size of Unreserved Fund Balance

Traditionally, two methods have been used by finance officers in determining the appropriate size of unreserved fund balance:

- allocating financial resources equal to a percentage of annual operating expenditures
- allocating financial resources equal to a certain number of months' operating expenditures

A common standard of measuring unreserved fund balance (or resources available for contingencies) holds that an amount equal to 5 percent of annual operating expenditures is sufficient to guard against the effects of most types of uncertainty. To some extent, this standard has been supported by the credit rating agencies.

Other governments utilize a different method of measuring the adequacy of resources available for contingencies. This method involves the establishment of an unreserved fund balance equal to a certain number of months of operating expenditures. While the equivalent of one month's operating expenditures (equal to 8.3 percent of annual operating expenditures) appears to be widely used, two to three months or more is not uncommon.[13]

In both cases, the method utilized should be incorporated in the jurisdiction's financial policy. Again, this will help to ensure that all concerned are aware of why the resources have been set aside.

It should be made clear that while these standards are in use by a large number of governments, they will not be appropriate for all. One of the reasons why there is no nationally uniform rule for use in measuring the amount of resources available for contingencies is that all governments are different in terms of their economic and financial characteristics. Instead of a rigidly defined standard that dictates what level of financial resources local governments should maintain for contingencies, it is more appropriate for those governments to make their own decisions about whether to set aside more or less resources based on their assessment of the uncertainty that they face.

Is there a level of unreserved fund balance that is considered to be excessive? An informal standard that is utilized by some governments holds that an unreserved fund balance in excess of 10 percent of annual operating expenditures should be examined carefully.[14] The general feeling is that if an unreserved fund balance is in excess of 10 percent, there should be some notion as to what the resources will be used for. For governments facing a high degree of uncertainty, however, an unreserved fund balance in excess of 10 percent of annual expenditures may not be high enough.

What level of unreserved fund balance should a local government maintain? The level established should be directly related to the degree of uncertainty which it faces; the greater the uncertainty, the greater the financial resources necessary. Each government must evaluate the degree of risk that it faces on an annual basis and make a decision as to the level of financial resources that it wishes to maintain for contingencies. This evaluation will involve an analysis of past experiences, including an examination of cash flows, and an estimate of the degree of uncertainty currently faced by the government in question.

As a general rule, local governments should maintain an amount equal to 5 percent of annual operating expenditures. This should satisfy some of the credit rating agencies' concerns regarding the adequacy of resources available for contingencies.[15] Those governments facing greater uncertainty should maintain a higher level of unreserved fund balance. Those governments that maintain an unreserved fund balance above 10 percent of annual operating expenditures should be able to provide appropriate justification for maintaining that level. This, in turn, will satisfy the concerns of those analysts who consider an unreserved fund balance in excess of 10 percent to be unwarranted.

Like many other things in government finance, the determination of the appropriate level of unreserved fund balance that should be maintained for contingencies is an art, not a science. Past experience can be used as a guide, with particular attention paid to the following:

- Governments with more volatile revenue structures (such as those dependent on general sales tax revenues) will need a larger unreserved fund balance than others to provide the same stabilization result.
- Governments dependent on one or two major revenue sources may need a larger unreserved fund balance if those revenues are sensitive to the effects of the business cycle.
- Those governments with greater ability to defer purchases can operate with a smaller unreserved fund balance than governments which do not have such ability.[16]
- Larger governments, which typically possess broader and deeper tax bases, may be able to function with a smaller unreserved fund balance than other governments.
- Governments with consistent operating surpluses may not need a large unreserved fund balance.
- Governments with occasional or frequent operating deficits will need a larger unreserved fund balance.
- Governments with uneven cash flows can minimize the need for short-term borrowing by maintaining a larger unreserved fund balance.
- Governments with economically sensitive expenditure structures (i.e., those governments with large public welfare responsibilities) will need a larger unreserved fund balance.

CONCLUSION

Finance officers concerned about the possible effects of an economic downturn (or other external influences) on their government's financial condition should consider the development of a sufficient level of unreserved fund balance that can be used for contingencies. Sufficient levels of unreserved fund balance can help to ensure the continued orderly operation of government and provision of services to residents and the continued stability of the tax structure. The maintenance of such stability is a particularly important factor considered by the rating agencies in their evaluation of the creditworthiness of local government debt, with instability potentially leading to a credit downgrade and increased borrowing costs.

Determining what level of unreserved fund balance to maintain is a difficult task. Because of differences in the economic and financial characteristics of local governments around the country, no nationally uniform standard exists regarding the level of unreserved fund balance that local governments should maintain. Instead, each government must assess the degree of uncertainty which it faces and make a decision as to the level of financial resources it wishes to maintain for contingencies.

As economic conditions worsen, a growing number of local governments will find themselves in an increasingly difficult financial position. Those governments that have recognized the economic uncertainty facing their governments, and that have had the foresight to develop adequate financial resources in response to this uncertainty, will be much better able to deal with the consequences of a slowing economy than those who have not.

Notes

1. During FY90, 20 states—up from 8 in FY89—were compelled to reduce the size of their adopted budgets. Marcia Howard, Washington, D.C.: National Association of State Budget Officers, September 1990.

    General deterioration in the state and local fiscal position, as measured on a national income and products accounts (NIPA) basis, has been noted since 1984. This according to David F. Sullivan in "State and Local Government Fiscal Position in 1989," *Survey of Current Business,* Washington, D.C.: U.S. Bureau of Economic Analysis, January 1990.

2. There are a number of other purposes for which unreserved fund balance resources can be designated, including: capital improvements, self-insurance and debt service. More will be said about "designations" in the next section.

3. Fund balance is also directly affected by other financing sources and uses (e.g., operating transfers), as well as by residual equity transfers. For additional information on fund balance, see *Governmental Accounting, Auditing and Financial Reporting,* Chicago: Government Finance Officers Association, June 1988.

4. It should be noted that unreserved fund balance may not represent "specific assets" of the fund (e.g., cash or a particular investment instrument). Because of this, some governments

may find their access to unreserved fund balance resources limited, at least in the short term.

5. The American Institute of Certified Public Accountants' (AICPA) audit and accounting guide, *Audits of State and Local Governmental Units,* provides that "such designations should be supported by definitive plans and approved by the government's chief executive officer or the legislature." It should also be noted, however, that section 1800.124 of the Governmental Accounting Standards Board's 1990 *Codification of Governmental Accounting and Financial Reporting Standards* states, "such plans or intent are subject to change and may never be legally authorized or result in expenditures. Designated portions of fund balance represent financial resources available to finance expenditures other than those tentatively planned."

6. It is important to note that (a) unreserved fund balance resources "designated for contingencies" can be made available for self-insurance purposes, although they would not be restricted to that use; and (b) governments may have some flexibility in transferring resources between some of the reserved fund balance accounts and the unreserved fund balance account, although resources assigned to legally restricted reserve accounts could not be utilized in this manner (legal restrictions on transfers between reserve accounts vary from state to state). This flexibility may improve the ability of governments to respond to a fiscal crisis, although movements of this type may constitute an abuse of the fund balance reserve account structure.

7. For more information on State Budget Stabilization Funds, see Corina Eckl, "Planning Ahead with Budget Stabilization Funds," in *The Fiscal Letter,* Denver, Colo.: National Conference of State Legislatures, March/April 1990; and, *Budgeting Amid Fiscal Uncertainty,* Washington, D.C.: National Association of State Budget Officers and National Governors Association's Center for Policy Research, June 1985.

8. In computing this ratio, information from the same fiscal year is obtained from the latest available Comprehensive Annual Financial Report (CAFR).

9. It should be noted that the rating agencies sometimes use the term "fund balance" in discussions related to the issue of a government maintaining adequate financial resources for contingencies. This is imprecise language because not all of fund balance would be available for contingencies and this has led to confusion on the part of finance officers, elected officials, and other interested parties. Finance officers should assume that when the rating agencies use this term they may be referring to the level of financial resources that a government has available for contingencies. In this section, the term "fund balance" will be used, but only to avoid misrepresenting the credit rating agencies' positions regarding this subject.

10. Summarized from *Moody's on Municipals: An Introduction to Issuing Debt,* New York: Moody's Investors Service, 1989; and "Moody's Rating Process: Frequently Asked Questions," New York: Moody's Investors Service, 1990.

11. Summarized from *S&P's Municipal Finance Criteria,* New York: Standard & Poor's Corporation, 1989. Additional information on S&P's analysis was obtained in a telephone conversation with Hyman Grossman, Managing Director of S&P's Municipal Department.

12. Correspondence with Richard Raphael, Senior Vice President of Fitch Investors Service, Inc. (October 9, 1990).

13. From a conversation with Paul E. Glick, Director of the Financial Management Program at the University of Georgia, and a veteran reviewer of Comprehensive Annual Financial Reports (CAFRs).

14. The City of Minneapolis, for example, has decided that it will not maintain an unreserved fund balance in excess of 10 percent of annual expenditures so as to avoid "banking" the taxpayer's money. See Mark Wetmore, "Minneapolis Productivity Investment Fund: Looking at the Rate of Return on Projects Funded," *Government Finance Review,* October 1989. Auditors in the Office of the State Comptroller of New York also use the 10 percent figure as an informal standard for determining excessive levels of unreserved fund balance, although it is not a hard and fast rule. See *Financial Management Guide for Local Governments,* Albany, N.Y.: Office of the State Comptroller, July 1985.

15. While size is of some importance, the rating agencies' primary concern will be the trend in the size of fund balance, with sharp drops in size possibly indicating fiscal weakness.

16. The payment of principal and interest on a government's outstanding debt obligations, of course, could not be deferred. At the same time, deferral of payments for other items, such as actuarially required pension contributions, may create or contribute to long-term financial problems. Given this, it is important that governments examine the ramifications of fiscal strategies involving the deferral of purchases/expenditures very carefully.

48 Understanding Local Government Financial Statements

PREFACE

One important information source available to citizens attempting to determine how their local government is managing its financial affairs is the government's annual financial report. Although the reports are public information and can be extremely enlightening, they have not been generally utilized by private citizens because they are considered complex and confusing to those with little or no governmental accounting background. Even someone who is adept at reading the balance sheets and income statements of commercial enterprises may have difficulty with government financial reports because of differences in terminology, format, and types of statements encountered.

Accounting has been called the language of business. It is also the language of government and, like any language, it can reveal much to those who understand it. This guide has been written to help you, the concerned citizen, understand and analyze the language of your local government's financial statements. The discussion will not make you an expert on government financial reporting, but after a brief study you should have a sense of what the financial statements can tell you. This guide will also enable you to ask informed questions of appropriate government officials.

Accounting principles or standards for local governments are established by the National Council on Governmental Accounting (NCGA), an organization formed under the sponsorship of the Municipal Finance Officers Association (MFOA).* MFOA membership is comprised principally of finance directors of state and local governments. NCGA principles are included in a publication entitled *Governmental Accounting, Auditing and Financial Reporting,* also known under the acronym GAAFR. The principles in GAAFR have been recognized by the American Institute of CPAs as representing generally accepted (most preferred) accounting principles (GAAP) for local governments. However, largely because state governments have the right to establish accounting standards to be followed by their constituent governments, compliance with NCGA principles, while increasing, has often been discouraged by existing state laws or regulations.

The most frequently encountered exception to GAAP basis financial statements is "cash basis" reporting which presents only receipts and disbursements. In contrast, GAAP for government involves reporting "revenues" and "expenditures" under the modified accrual basis and "income" and "costs" under the full accrual basis of accounting. The latter two bases will be described in greater detail in the

---

Adapted by permission of Price Waterhouse & Co. This article appeared in *Casebook in Public Budgeting and Financial Management,* edited by Carol W. Lewis and A. Grayson Walker III (N.J.: Prentice-Hall, Inc., 1984), 80-95.

*At the time of this writing a "Government Accounting Standards Board" (GASB) will take over the work of NCGA and is expected to operate similar to, and in concert with, the Financial Accounting Standards Board (FASB), which sets accounting principles for the private sector.

following discussion. Generally speaking the "cash basis" of accounting is *not* considered to fairly present the results of operations or financial position of an entity, in either the commercial or governmental environment. Its principal advantage is viewed by some as its inherent simplicity.

The financial statements and accounting principles described and discussed in this guide are based upon NCGA pronouncements; however, because the guide is intended to increase understanding of the contents of governmental reporting, we have taken considerable liberty in presenting the format of the sample financial statements to which our comments will apply.

The following presentation emphasizes the two aspects of local government financial reporting considered most significant by finance officers and government managers—results of operations as represented by comparison of budget to actual revenues and expenditures, and financial position as represented by a summary of the government's assets and liabilities in a balance sheet.

THE FINANCIAL REPORTING ENTITY

Commercial accounting usually presents the results of transactions for a "single economic entity" such as a corporation (including all of its subsidiaries and divisions), a partnership, or a sole proprietorship. Identification of what constitutes the commercial economic entity is usually based on "investment" or "ownership" criteria.

Government accounting usually presents the results of the transactions of the organization's various projects and activities in "funds," i.e., groups of related accounts. Separate funds are usually established for specific types of activities. Determination of what constitutes all of the funds of the governmental entity is usually based on "control" criteria, i.e., the extent to which the city controls an activity through budgets, personnel policies, etc.

THE BASIC FUNDS

Funds are divided into three broad categories:

1. *Governmental funds:* The resources in these funds are intended to be expended within a specific period of time, usually a budget year. These funds are accounted for on the modified accrual basis of accounting and accordingly, as further described later, allocation of costs, such as depreciation among accounting periods, is not practiced in these funds. Rather, the funds generally measure the flow of resources (revenues and expenditures) into and out of the funds.

2. *Proprietary funds:* The resources in these funds are not meant to be exhausted within a specific time period. Their activities more closely resemble ongoing businesses in which the purpose is to conserve and add to basic resources while meeting operating expenses from current revenues. For this reason, proprietary fund financial statements are concerned with measuring costs (e.g., depreciation) and operating results. Therefore, they apply commercial accrual accounting principles, and their reports closely resemble commercial financial statements. Usually the intent of the proprietary activity is to break even or recover the cost of operations.

3. *Fiduciary funds:* These funds are used to account for those activities in which a governmental unit is acting as a trustee or agent for other individuals, or governments. They are used to demonstrate how the governmental unit carried out its fiduciary responsibilities with regard to the assets entrusted to it.

These broad categories are further broken down into fund *types*.

Governmental Funds

1. *General fund:* Includes all general government financial operations which are not accounted for by any other fund type. Revenues in this fund would be derived from taxes, fees, and other sources which are not designated for any specific purposes (e.g., income and property taxes, license fees). These revenues are utilized for general ongoing government services such as administration, maintenance, and police and fire protection.

2. *Special revenue funds:* Account for the expenditure of revenues which have been provided to the government for specific programs or projects (excluding expenditures for building programs and major equipment purchases or any other similar undertakings, usually classified as a capital project). An example of a special revenue fund activity would be the accounting for revenues and ex-

penditures under a federal grant for a research or training program.
3. *Capital projects funds:* Account for the collection and disbursement of revenues from a variety of sources (bond proceeds, loans, or grants) for the purposes of building or purchasing major capital assets, such as schools, public buildings, or recreational facilities.
4. *Debt service funds:* Account for resources set aside to make interest and principal payments on long-term debt.

Proprietary Funds

5. *Enterprise funds:* Account for activities which are usually self-sustaining principally through user charges for services rendered. Such activities include the operation of water supply and sewerage plants, hospitals, and transportation systems.
6. *Internal service funds:* Account for services performed by one local government organization or department for another. Often such services include maintenance and repair of vehicles by a centralized garage or operation of a data processing center.

Fiduciary Funds

7. *Trust and agency funds:* Account for collection and disbursement of assets held in trust by a government for another individual or group of individuals, or another government agency. Typical examples of trust and agency funds include pension funds in which the city is administering retirement plans on behalf of its employees, and scholarship funds in which the city awards scholarships to specified individuals in accordance with the terms of a scholarship trust agreement entered into with a donor.

In practice, a local government, although maintaining only one general fund, may establish any number of special revenue, capital project, special assessment, debt service, enterprise, internal service, and trust and agency funds to account for its many separate projects and activities.

One of the most significant recent reporting changes introduced by NCGA was to require the combining of similar fund *type* activities (e.g., all special revenue, enterprise, capital projects, etc.) in general purpose financial reporting. Previously, combining of individual funds was not considered appropriate.

NONFUND ACCOUNT GROUPS

In addition to the previously described funds, local governments also maintain separate memorandum accountability for general government fixed assets and long-term liabilities, known technically as account groups.

In the accounting for governmental funds fixed asset acquisitions are recorded as expenditures and borrowings as revenues. Accordingly, the commercial accounting procedure of recording them as assets and liabilities is not practiced. However, to establish accountability these transactions are recorded in memorandum form in account groups known as the *General Fixed Assets Group of Accounts* and the *General Long-Term Debt Group of Accounts.* As depicted later in the sample financial statements presented herein, fixed assets and long-term debt are recorded in these account groups by means of contra account posting in account group balance sheets, the offset to fixed assets being the "investment in fixed assets" and the offset to long-term liabilities being the "amount to be provided from future revenues for payment of principal on bonds." While a summary of account group changes should be presented in statement or footnote form, an operating statement has no applicability to account groups.

FOOTNOTES

Most government financial reports contain extensive footnotes which include further explanatory information about specific areas of the financial statement. For example, the footnotes will usually indicate the type of funds established by the government and a brief description of the basis of accounting for each fund type and other significant accounting policies. Footnotes usually also include information on loan covenants, commitments, and contingencies. It is a good idea to read the footnotes in conjunction with the financial statements in order to obtain a more complete understanding of your government's financial position and results of operations.

THE MEASUREMENT FOCUS

If you are a stockholder in a corporation, you are entitled to receive its annual report containing financial statements, which will tell you how well the company has accomplished its primary objective—making a profit. The income statement will reveal the size of the profit or loss. The balance sheet will tell you the composition of the company's assets and liabilities, as well as the amount of the stockholders' equity or accumulated worth.

Although you may not receive them as a matter of course, as a stockholder, that is, "taxpayer," in your local government, you should read its financial statements. If you do, you will find that they are more detailed and cumbersome than typical corporate financial statements. You will also learn that because the purpose of government reporting differs from that of a commercial enterprise, the information required to judge how well a government is accomplishing its objectives also differs.

Government operations are not intended to make a profit. Instead, its primary financial function is to use the funds it acquires from a variety of sources (e.g., income and other taxes, bond proceeds, state and federal grants) to provide services to its citizens according to a predetermined plan and within approved budgetary constraints. There is no single figure or amount which provides a measure of overall government performance. However, a government's general financial operations can be evaluated through a detailed comparison of actual performance with its adopted budget. Government financial statements are intended to facilitate such a detailed comparison.

In addition to the distinction which exists between the "profit" and "budgetary" bases of reporting, it should be recognized that, as previously noted, government operations are reported on either the "modified accrual" (general government activities) or "accrual" (business-like activities of government) bases of accounting. Alternatively, commercial accounting employs only the accrual basis of accounting. The following discussion describes the unique attributes of the "modified accrual" basis, an understanding of which is essential to proper interpretation of government financial statements.

THE UNIQUENESS OF "MODIFIED ACCRUAL" GOVERNMENT FUND ACCOUNTING

The modified accrual basis of accounting used to account for activities of governmental funds has as its primary purpose the measurement of the flow of funds into and out of the governmental unit. It is *not*, however, cash basis accounting. To understand the implications of modified accrual accounting, it is best to relate it to the more frequently encountered accrual accounting applied to commercial entities. The following is a discussion of the principal modifications which are made to accrual accounting principles to arrive at governmental fund "modified accrual" principles.

Accounting for "Expenditures" Rather Than "Costs"

In commercial accounting, the determination of costs for a particular year is important because profit, of course, is measured by income earned less costs incurred. In governmental fund accounting it is the *expenditure* of funds within a particular year rather than *cost* which is important because government operations and related budgets are usually based on expenditures or use of resources.

A good example of the distinction between *costs* used in commercial accounting and *expenditures* used in governmental accounting is provided by the accounting for fixed assets acquisitions.

Since fixed assets acquired by a commercial entity are used to generate products or services and thus income, *cost* is spread out, or depreciated, over the years during which the assets are expected to be revenue producing. Depreciation as a *cost* is not particularly useful in government accounting, because assets are not typically revenue producing. The primary focus of government is on the *expenditure* for the asset, and whether the current budget for asset purchases was exceeded. Accordingly, the acquisition price is reflected as an *expenditure* in governmental funds in the year of purchase.

Accounting for "Encumbrances" and "Available Revenues"

Encumbrances

Encumbrances are commitments for expenditures for which goods or services have not been received at the time financial statements are prepared. They may be in the form of purchase orders or contracts for goods and services. In budget to actual comparisons, expenditures are often adjusted for encumbrances because budgets are usually approved on an encumbrance or obligation basis rather than a pure expenditure or disbursement basis.

Another of the recent accounting changes promulgated by NCGA prohibits showing encumbrances as though they were expenditures, except in budget-actual comparison statements. Because of many years of use in the preparation of governmental budgets, total disappearance of encumbrance accounting from government accounting is not expected to be rapid.

Available Revenues

The character of governmental revenues is different from that of commercial income. For example, income, sales, and real estate taxes are not earned by producing goods or providing services. Rather, these revenues are usually assessed on an annual basis. Because of the flow-of-funds focus of government accounting there is a tendency to report revenues conservatively by only recognizing in the operating statement that portion of revenues which will be collected within the fiscal year, or soon enough thereafter (usually 60 days), to meet expenditures of the fiscal year just ended. Such revenues are commonly referred to as "available" (to meet expenditures) revenues. For example, property taxes which may have been levied but are not expected to be collected in time to pay current bills are recorded as "deferred revenue" in the government's balance sheet and as revenues in the period in which they meet the "available" test.

Accounting for Only Current Expenditures

Because governmental accounting focuses on changes in spendable financial resources, only those expenses that will be paid currently are recorded in governmental funds, i.e., expenses that have been incurred in the operation of the government that will be paid within the fiscal year or shortly thereafter. Those expenses that will be paid at a later time are considered long-term in nature and in the past, only disclosed in notes to the financial statements. In keeping with this expenditure philosophy, the cost related to unfunded (unpaid) pension liabilities, as well as for unpaid sick and vacation pay, are recorded in the period when cash payment or funding is required rather than the period in which benefits are earned. The amounts of earned but unpaid or unfunded pension, sick leave, and vacation benefits usually aggregate very material unrecorded liabilities for most government entities. The NCGA has under consideration a proposed change in its standards which would require recording such long-term liabilities in the general long-term debt group of accounts.

Recording Debt Proceeds as Operating Revenues

Since governmental accounting is concerned primarily with the flow of funds into and out of the government, the proceeds of *long-term debt* raised for construction and other purposes is recorded as revenue in governmental funds. The long-term liabilities are recorded only in memorandum form in the general long-term debt group of accounts. However, *short-term* debt of governmental funds, usually in the form of notes secured by a pledge of current revenues to be received, are not recorded as revenues but rather are recorded as liabilities, as is the practice in commercial accounting. Accordingly, the reader of governmental financial statements should be aware that the fund balance of governmental funds has been increased by the amount of long-term debt proceeds which require repayment in subsequent years.

The characteristics described above are the major distinctions between the so-called "modified accrual" basis of accounting used to record general government operations and the "accrual" basis used in commercial accounting and by governments to record their commercial or business-like proprietary fund activities.

AUDITOR'S REPORT

Your government's financial statements may be accompanied by a report of an independent public accountant or other auditor. This report should state whether the financial statements are presented in accordance with generally accepted accounting principles. Any significant deviations from generally accepted accounting principles should be discussed in the auditor's report and amplified where appropriate in the notes to the financial statements. In addition, the auditors should identify any limitations imposed upon their ability to perform generally accepted auditing procedures and the impact of those limitations or any other unusual factors on their opinion on the fairness of the financial statements.

Keep in mind that it is the primary role of the independent public accountant to express an opinion on whether the financial statements *present fairly the entity's results of operations and financial position in accordance with generally accepted accounting principles.*

A MODEL PRESENTATION

Now that we have discussed briefly the theory and general concepts of governmental accounting, let's look at an example of its practical application.

Annual financial reports of governments usually contain a substantial volume of financial presentations, including statistical data, individual fund, combining, and combined fund type financial statements and footnotes. We will concentrate on only two of the most frequently encountered financial statements in local government annual financial reports—(1) the Combined Balance Sheet for All Fund Types and Account Groups; and (2) the Statement of Revenues, Expenditures, and Encumbrances and Changes in Fund Balance—Budget and Actual.

The example statements illustrated in exhibits 1 and 2 may not look exactly like those produced by your local government. Jurisdictions often employ variations in terminology and format. However, after examining the exhibits and studying the referenced explanations of terms and classifications (many of which have been described in the preceding pages), you will know what to look for in your government's statements and have a basis for recognizing and understanding any differences.

Once you know how to interpret and use your local government's financial statements, they can represent a concise and readily accessible method of evaluating your government's financial condition and detecting potential problems. This introduction to the language of government accounting should assist you in becoming an informed and active participant in your local government's financial affairs.

STATEMENT OF REVENUES, EXPENDITURES, AND ENCUMBRANCES AND CHANGES IN FUND BALANCE—BUDGET AND ACTUAL (EXHIBIT 1)

The most frequently analyzed financial statement in local government is the Statement of Revenues, Expenditures, and Encumbrances and Changes in Fund Balance—Budget and Actual, which provides four important measurements:

1. revenues actually received against budgeted revenues
2. actual expenditures and encumbrances against the budgeted expenditures and encumbrances
3. total actual expenditures and encumbrances against total actual revenues
4. the changes in fund balance available for expenditure in future years

This statement (Exhibit 1) can provide a wealth of information if it is correctly interpreted. A discussion of what it reveals about your government's financial operations follows. Examine the statement and identify the following symbols:

(A) *General fund:* This statement is for the general fund which accounts for administrative and typically recurring government services (e.g., police, fire, welfare, etc.).

(B) *For the year ended December 31, 19X2:* Since this is an annual statement, it presents summary figures for the total fiscal year's operations.

(C) *Revenues:* All significant sources from which the government's general fund received revenue during the year are identified.

(D) *Expenditures and encumbrances:* Since local governments are typically organized by function, financial statements are usually organized to summarize expenditures and encumbrances, both actual and budgetary, by major functional activity.

(E) *Budget:* This column shows the estimated revenues which were expected to be collected by source and the amount of estimated expenditures and encumbrances allocated to operations by function. Ideally these two estimated figures should agree since the objective is usually a perfectly balanced budget.

(F) *Expenditures:* These figures represent, for each function, the amounts actually expended for goods and services received during the year.

(G) *Encumbrances:* These amounts represent the contractual commitments to acquire goods or services which were *not* received at year end. These amounts are included in the budget—actual financial statements as though they were expenditures if, as is customary, the government's budget is approved on an encumbrances or obligation basis.

(H) *Total actual:* Under "revenues," the amounts in this column represent revenues collected or currently receivable from each source, which is compared with budgeted revenues. For the items

Exhibit 1:

Ⓐ General Fund: Statement of Revenues, Expenditures, and Encumbrances and Changes in Fund Balance—Budget and Actual,
Ⓑ For year ended December 31, 19X2

	Ⓔ	**Ⓕ**	**Ⓖ**	**Ⓗ**	**Ⓘ**
		Actual			Budget Variance
	Budget	Expenditures	Encumbrances	Total Actual	Favorable (Unfavorable)
Ⓒ Revenues					
Property taxes	$2,633,000			$2,572,600	$ (60,400)
License and permit fees	230,000			212,500	(17,500)
Intergovernmental revenues	750,000			736,000	(14,000)
Service charges	66,000			67,250	1,250
Fines and forfeitures	80,000			80,850	850
Miscellaneous	41,000			40,120	(880)
Total revenues	$3,800,000			$3,709,320	$ (90,680)
Ⓓ Expenditures and encumbrances					
General government	$ 861,000	$ 478,260	$393,820	$ 872,080	$ (11,080)
Public safety (police and fire)	445,500	382,380	67,250	449,630	(4,130)
Highways and streets	186,000	162,200	21,170	183,370	2,630
Building inspection and maintenance	85,350	72,920	11,450	84,370	980
Sanitation	84,000	80,200	3,180	83,380	620
Culture	92,000	81,300	17,800	99,100	(7,100)
Health	101,000	111,800	6,720	118,520	(17,520)
Welfare	106,000	136,300	3,850	140,150	(34,150)
Recreation	64,150	59,920	3,580	63,500	650
Education	775,000	712,000	64,800	776,800	(1,800)
Debt service	1,000,000	1,000,000	—	1,000,000	—
Total expenditures and encumbrances	$3,800,000	$3,277,280	$593,620	$3,870,900	$ (70,900)
Ⓙ Excess (deficiency) of revenues over expenditures and encumbrances	—			(161,580)	$(161,580)
Ⓚ Unreserved fund balance, beginning of year	306,180			306,180	
Ⓚ Unreserved fund balance, end of year	$ 306,180			$ 144,600	

Note: See text for explanation of letter symbols.

under "expenditures and encumbrances" **Ⓓ**, this column contains the total of the "expenditures" and "encumbrances" columns, which is compared with the budgeted amounts for each function.

Ⓘ *Budget variance—favorable (unfavorable):* This column compares actual and estimated revenues and actual and budgeted operating expenditures and encumbrances.

Ⓙ *Excess (deficiency) of revenues over expenditures and encumbrances:* Under Column **Ⓔ** (Budget), there is no excess or deficiency of revenues over expenditures and encumbrances because the budget was prepared on the basis that "revenues" and "expenditures and encumbrances" would be balanced.

Under Column **Ⓗ** (Total actual), the figure on this line indicates that revenues fell short of operating expenditures by $161,580. This figure was computed by subtracting total "expenditures and encumbrances" from total "revenues."

Under Column (I), the identical figure is arrived at by adding the net amounts under total revenues and total expenditures and encumbrances. It can be seen that the overall operating deficit is composed of a *net* $90,680 shortfall in expected revenues and a *net* $70,900 overexpenditure of budgeted operating expenditures and encumbrances. A line-by-line analysis of this column, of course, will pinpoint the causes of these differences.

(K) *Unreserved fund balances, beginning and end of year:* The unreserved fund balance is usually comprised of the government's inception to date excess of revenues over operating expenditures and encumbrances. It has been built up over the years. Annual surpluses (i.e., more revenues than expenditures and encumbrances) increase its size. Conversely, the fund balance will be decreased by operating deficits (i.e., more expenditures and encumbrances than revenues). Deficits may even completely eliminate the balance. A series of deficits may produce a negative fund balance. When this happens, it should signal you that liabilities exceed assets, a condition usually associated with insolvency.

WHAT THE STATEMENT OF REVENUES, EXPENDITURES, AND ENCUMBRANCES AND CHANGES IN FUND BALANCE—BUDGET AND ACTUAL—CAN TELL YOU

The major point to remember when reading this or any other financial statement is not to jump to conclusions.

These statements provide summary fund information about 365 days of complex operations and financial transactions, by a variety of government departments and functions. They can alert you to potential trouble spots which you could not otherwise identify except by wading through a myriad of vouchers, invoices, memoranda, journals and ledgers.

Consider an example from the statement on Exhibit 1. From reading the statement you can see that this year the general fund had an operating deficit of $161,580. Further analysis shows that the deficit is attributable to two factors: (1) a shortfall in revenues, primarily in the area of property taxes, and (2) overexpenditures in certain areas, especially welfare and health.

The statement indicates that in spite of the current year's deficit the fund has a $142,000 balance of resources available at the end of the year. However, should the government incur another deficit in the following year the fund balance could be eliminated, or, worse yet, a deficit fund balance could be created, in which case fund liabilities would exceed assets.

Questions such as the following may occur to you now:

Are the overexpenditures and the shortfall in revenues unusual or significantly large?

Has there been an increase in government spending this year?

If so, is it a new phenomenon or has the increase in spending been a trend in recent years?

You may find answers to these questions by comparing this year's statement with statements for past years, which should be available in previously issued annual reports.

Assume that your review of prior years' statements indicates that (1) the revenue shortfall and the overexpenditures this year were indeed unusual and by comparison relatively large, and (2) government spending has been increasing significantly over the past five years.

It will now be necessary to search for causes and explanations from a variety of sources: city officials, newspapers, citizen groups, published reports of the various government departments. Was the revenue shortfall caused by a high delinquency rate, poor collection procedures, or a faulty estimate of expected revenues? Is the problem expected to recur, and is there a solution? Are the overexpenditures attributable to wasteful spending, poor estimates of the city's needs in certain areas, inflation, market conditions, or special situations? If the latter, has the situation passed, or will it continue? Will government spending keep rising and can the city handle the increasing financial burden?

You have already developed a great number and variety of questions about your government's financial condition. You might never have become concerned had you not taken a few moments to read the Statement of Revenues, Expenditures, and Encumbrances and Changes in Fund Balance—Budget and Actual.

COMBINED BALANCE SHEET (EXHIBIT 2)

Every local government's annual financial report should include a combined balance sheet (illustrated in Exhibit 2) showing the year-end financial position of governmental, proprietary, and fiduciary fund types, and account groups. This combined balance sheet may be supported by many other statements and schedules detailing the operations of individual funds. But the balance sheet by itself gives you a "snapshot" of your government's overall financial condition.

While the numerous columns and categories under "Assets" and "Liabilities and Fund Equity" make the statement look formidable, it is not nearly as complicated as it seems at first glance. Each column usually represents the financial position of numerous funds combined by fund types. In our illustration, the balance sheet reflects only one fund of each fund type.

The columns have been arranged so that all governmental funds are grouped together, as are all proprietary funds, fiduciary funds, and the two nonfund account groups. A discussion of what the balance sheet can tell you about your government's overall financial position follows the description of the references in Exhibit 2.

Ⓐ *Cash and investments:* Most governments pool or combine idle cash of different funds to the extent permitted by law in order to obtain maximum earnings on investment and minimize the number of separate disbursement bank accounts. Investments can be made by all fund types. They represent the placement of otherwise idle cash into an earnings capacity.

Ⓑ *Accounts receivable:* In commercial accounting, the term describes amounts yet to be collected from customers who have purchased goods and services on credit. In this example, the amount applies only to the Municipal Water Utility, which bills customers for services just as a commercial entity does. Accordingly, these accounts receivable represent an asset of the water utility.

Ⓒ *Taxes and assessments receivable:* Taxes and assessments receivable are monies that various property owners owe to the local government for property taxes and property assessments. If they are not expected to be received in time to pay current liabilities, i.e., their due dates are beyond 60 days after the end of the fiscal year, the revenues are recorded in the balance sheet in an account called "deferred revenue." The reader is thereby advised that receivable amounts are outstanding which will be collected at some point in the future, but they will not be considered "revenue" until the year in which collected.

Ⓓ *Due from other funds or to other funds:* Although each fund is a separate and distinct accountability unit, transfers of monies between funds sometimes occur. Rather than net (offset) the amounts due to and from other funds, amounts are shown separately in order to maintain the integrity of each fund. For example, although the amounts shown as due to and due from other funds by the general fund are equal, the funds that are due amounts from the general fund are different from those which owe amounts to the general fund. A close inspection indicates that the general fund has amounts due from the special revenue and enterprise funds and has amounts due to the internal service fund.

Ⓔ *Due from state or federal government:* Because these items often represent a major receivable, they are generally classified separately on the balance sheet. The receivables typically represent amounts due under grant or entitlement programs.

Ⓕ *Inventories/reserved for inventories:* As you may have noted, all previously discussed assets either represent cash or are convertible into cash which will be available for future operations. Inventories, however, constitute supplies and other materials which will be consumed in future operations and do not comprise a spendable or appropriable revenue. To highlight that fact, a portion of the fund balance is reserved to identify that it has already been dedicated to a specific end use.

Ⓖ *Fixed assets, at cost less accumulated depreciation:* As discussed previously, the purchase of fixed assets by governmental and proprietary funds is accounted for differently. Fixed assets which are acquired in general government operations are recorded as expenditures in governmental funds, and memorandum accountability recordkeeping is established in the general fixed assets group of accounts. The enterprise and internal service funds, on the other hand, capi-

Exhibit 2: *Combined Balance Sheet, All Fund Types and Account Groups, December 31, 19X2*

		GOVERNMENTAL FUNDS				PROPRIETARY FUNDS			FIDUCIARY FUND	ACCOUNT GROUPS	
							Internal Service Fund		Trust and Agency Fund		
Assets	General Fund	Special Revenue Fund — City Parks Fund	Capital Projects Fund — Civic Center	Debt Service Fund		Enterprise Fund — Municipal Water Utility	Central Purchasing Agency		Scholar-ship Fund	General Fixed Assets	General Long-Term Debt
Ⓐ Cash and investments	$2,376,000	$ 80,000	$40,000,000	$1,000,000		$ 115,000	$ 83,000		$3,544,000		
Ⓑ Accounts receivable	395,000					77,000					
Ⓒ Taxes receivable	16,500										
Ⓒ Assessments receivable	16,000										
Ⓓ Due from other funds							16,000				
Ⓔ Due from state government	374,000	55,000									
Ⓔ Due from federal government	200,000	450,000									
Ⓕ Inventories	45,000						214,000				
Ⓖ Fixed assets at cost						1,240,000	240,000			$47,580,000	
less accumulated depreciation						(450,000)	(28,000)				
Ⓗ Amount to be provided from future revenues for payment of principal on bonds											$38,420,000
Ⓘ Amount available in debt service fund for payment of principal and interest											1,000,000
Total assets	$3,422,500	$585,000	$40,000,000	$1,000,000		$982,000	$525,000		$3,544,000	$47,580,000	$39,420,000
Liabilities and Fund Equity											
Liabilities:											
Ⓙ Accounts payable	$1,219,000		$ 1,120,000			$ 10,000	$ 23,000				
Ⓚ Notes payable						2,000					
Ⓚ Bonds payable						36,000					$39,420,000
Ⓓ Due to other funds	16,000	$ 12,000				4,000					
Ⓛ Other liabilities	38,000										
Ⓒ Deferred revenue	411,500										
Total liabilities	1,684,500	12,000	1,120,000			52,000	23,000				39,420,000
Fund equity:											
Ⓜ Investment in general fixed assets										$47,580,000	
Ⓝ Retained earnings						930,000	502,000				
Fund balances:											
Ⓞ Reserved for encumbrances	1,548,400	520,000	2,500,000								
Ⓕ Reserved for inventories	45,000										
Ⓟ Unreserved	144,600	53,000	36,380,000	$1,000,000					$3,544,000		
Total fund equity	1,738,000	573,000	38,880,000	1,000,000		930,000	502,000		3,544,000	47,580,000	
Total liabilities & fund equity	$3,422,500	$585,000	$40,000,000	$1,000,000		$982,000	$525,000		$3,544,000	$47,580,000	$39,420,000

Note: See text for explanation of letter symbols.

talize fixed assets, depreciate them, and consider their net value as a component of fund equity. Typically a breakdown of the nature of the assets, e.g., property, plant, and equipment, will be provided either in the financial statements or footnotes.

Ⓗ Ⓘ Ⓚ *Amounts to be provided or available:* These accounts provide information on the size of the city's long-term debt, how much has been set aside to retire the debt, and how much remains to be provided from future years' revenues. Reference to item Ⓚ , "notes payable" and "bonds payable" indicates a total bonds payable liability of governmental funds (exclusive of proprietary fund amounts) of $39,420,000. Item Ⓘ indicates by memorandum entry that $1,000,000 has already been set aside in the debt service fund (see separate debt service fund). However, $38,420,000 needs to be raised in the future to service the debt.

Refer back to "Debt Service" expenditures on the Statement of Revenues, Expenditures, and Encumbrances and Changes in Fund Balance—Budget and Actual, which shows a large appropriation ($1,000,000 in column Ⓗ), which is the annual transfer to the debt service fund for debt retirement. A large annual appropriation like this will likely continue until the bond issue has been retired.

Ⓙ *Accounts payable:* These are outstanding bills which the various funds have incurred for goods or services received but have not yet paid. They will usually be paid within 60 days after the year end.

Ⓚ *Notes and bonds payable:* While the government's general long-term debt is accounted for in the general long-term debt group of accounts previously discussed, enterprise and internal service funds account for their long-term debt in the conventional commercial accounting manner as direct fund liabilities in the balance sheet.

Ⓛ *Other liabilities:* These represent miscellaneous liabilities of the respective funds for such items as payroll withholding, deposits, etc.

Ⓜ *Investment in general fixed assets:* This amount represents the aggregate original or estimated cost of fixed assets acquired and in use in general government operations.

While some would contend that this amount represents a significant factor in evaluating the entity's equity, it should be remembered that it is usually stated at original (undepreciated) cost or estimated value.

Ⓝ *Retained earnings:* This term is used in commercial accounting to denote the entity's cumulative excess of income over expenses since the date of inception of operations, net of any dividends or distributions to owners. It has the same connotation in enterprise and internal service fund accounting.

Because of their very nature, municipally owned proprietary activities do not usually have outside investors and as such they do not issue stock. Any investment required by the general government at inception or during the operation of the activity would be recorded in a "contributed capital" account within the equity section of the balance sheet as would any capital contribution received from senior governments in the form of capital grants or assistance.

Ⓞ *Reserved for encumbrances:* As previously described, encumbrances represent commitments for anticipated expenditures. (Refer to Ⓖ in Exhibit 1 for an explanation of the reason for their inclusion in that statement.) However, since they do not represent incurred liabilities at the balance sheet date (goods and services not received), they are reflected in the balance sheet as a reservation of fund balance rather than as a liability.

Ⓟ *Unreserved fund balance:* The aggregate fund balance which represents the excess of assets over liabilities (or vice versa if an accumulated deficit) can be broken down into several components. A segment may be "reserved" as a means of identifying portions of the balance set aside to meet other operational restrictions such as in the example, the reserves for encumbrances Ⓞ and inventories Ⓕ. The remainder is identified as unreserved, and is intended to identify the net assets or resources available for use in future operations. The unreserved fund balance is usually used to meet unexpected expenditure requirements (supplemental budget amendments) or to reduce future years' budget requirements.

However, a word of caution is in order. As previously discussed, long-term loan proceeds requiring future repayment are recorded as revenues when received, and accordingly, have increased the unreserved fund balance. Likewise, long-term liabilities for items such as vacation, pension, and self-insurance, which represent a claim on the government, are not recorded in governmental funds. A reference back to the asset side of the balance sheet and consideration of any "amounts *to be* provided," and a reference to the footnotes to the financial statements for other outstanding commitments may be prudent in any evaluation of the unreserved fund balances and future financing requirements.

WHAT THE COMBINED BALANCE SHEET CAN TELL YOU

You can learn a great deal about your government's financial condition from the combined balance sheet if you examine it systematically with an inquisitive mind. You might raise some of these questions:

How financially "healthy" are the various funds?

Is my government's financial position better, the same, or worse than it was a year ago?

How much of a financial burden has this year's operations placed on future years, and is that burden manageable?

First, glance at the fund balance for each fund to see whether it is positive or negative. The fact that all of the fund balances are positive may be superficially reassuring, but you should not stop there. While positive, the fund balance may have decreased from last year, an indication of potential problems.

Additionally, you should look closely at the composition of the assets of each fund type. Remember that assets within a fund are usually restricted to use in that fund. Also, assets in governmental funds should be relatively liquid or available and readily convertible into cash. If they are not liquid or available you should expect to find an offsetting reserve or deferred revenue such as is illustrated in items Ⓒ, Ⓞ and Ⓕ in Exhibit 2. (Only liquid or available assets of governmental funds should be included in the unreserved fund balance.)

Next you can look to the fund liabilities to determine whether assets are sufficient to pay liabilities or whether additional revenues must be generated for this purpose. A positive unreserved fund balance usually indicates sufficient assets to meet liabilities.

Also, most funds have "interfund receivables" (item Ⓓ, Exhibit 2). Those receivables are only available assets if the debtor fund has the ability to currently pay the creditor fund. You should make inquiries about large amounts of interfund receivables and payables that appear to remain unpaid from year to year.

Next, look at the proprietary fund balance sheets. They should include long-term assets, such as fixed assets, and all long-term liabilities of those funds, such as bonds and notes payable. Since proprietary funds are accounted for like commercial entities, their balance sheets should reflect all assets and liabilities both short- and long-term, in order to present a total picture of the fund's financial position. In our example, Exhibit 2, the proprietary funds show equity (retained earnings) which appear to represent a healthy financial position of those funds. However, it might be appropriate to inquire about the intended future use of the resources (assets) represented by the large retained earnings.

Fiduciary fund balance sheets present assets held in trust on behalf of others. Accordingly, there should rarely be deficit fund balances in these funds.

Finally, remember that the account groups represent memorandum accounts only; they are not funds. They should be evaluated together with the governmental funds to which they are related.

For example, by itself the size of the government's general long-term debt cannot be considered either a positive or negative indicator. It must be judged in terms of what led to its incurrence, whether the debt was necessary, and whether it can be repaid without placing an undue strain on operations or the taxpayers.

The annual contribution of approximately $1,000,000 to the debt service fund to repay the debt comes from general fund revenues, that is, from your taxes. Given the condition of the general fund, the annual contribution is likely to be a heavy financial burden on you as a taxpayer. Although there is little you can do about a previous bond issue, you can closely monitor your government's future borrowing activity and judge each prospective bond issue on its individual merits. What is the intended use of the bond proceeds? What is the repayment period? Are revenues available to meet debt repayment without appreciably increasing future tax rates?

Answers to these and other similar inquiries do not come easily, but hopefully this discussion has at least helped you identify the important questions—a formidable beginning in the quest to improve the accountability of your government.

The 10-Point Test of Financial Condition: Toward an Easy-to-Use Assessment Tool for Smaller Cities

Ken W. Brown

A thorough financial-condition assessment that involves a large number of factors and related indicators can be very time consuming for a municipality. As a result, analysis of financial condition may not be a regular part of financial management. When these comprehensive financial-condition assessments are conducted, the large amounts of data involved can make it difficult to communicate the results to a city's management, governing board, and citizenry.

This article describes a short test of financial condition that municipal finance officers can conduct for cities with populations under 100,000. Called the 10-Point Test, the exercise suggested in this article allows finance officers to compare 10 key financial ratios for their city to similar ratios calculated for 750 smaller cities across the nation. The 10-Point Test includes a scoring procedure by which a municipal finance officer can grade his/her city and provide some evidence of the city's financial-condition. The test was developed because of (1) the need for a quick and effective financial-condition assessment tool and (2) the improved availability of comparative city data provided by the Financial Indicators Database published in 1992 by the Government Finance Officers Association (GFOA).[1]

The 10-Point Test of financial condition provides a concise and easy-to-use vehicle for the communication of financial condition to a city government's constituents. It is based on 10 ratios, listed in Exhibit 1, that are considered useful for assessing four basic financial factors for a city: revenues (ratios 1-3), expenditures (ratio 4), operating position (ratios 5-7) and debt structure (ratios 8-10).[2] The test consists of three steps, which will be described in detail in this article: (1) calculation of 10 key financial ratios based on data contained in the city's current annual financial report, (2) comparison of the city's ratios to ratios of similar-sized cities reported in this article, and (3) grading the city's financial condition based on the comparisons in step 2.

A city has a limited ability to interpret its financial condition other than through comparisons with similar-sized cities. The GFOA's Financial Indicators Database, therefore, is valuable as a source of data for determining the 10 key ratios for cities across the nation. The database contains FY89, FY90, and FY91 financial data for all cities that were awarded the GFOA's Certificate of Achievement for Excellence in Financial Reporting in those fiscal years. All of the data have been presented in conformity with generally accepted accounting principles (GAAP) and most of the data have been subjected to independent audit. In using these data, however, one must recognize that the cities receiving this award do not represent a random sample of the nation's cities.

Without financial information such as ratios, informed decisions about financial condition are not possible. Even with financial information, the assessment of financial condition usually remains subjective. While city finance officers, city managers, and governing board members may reach conclusions

---

Reprinted from *Government Finance Review* 9, no. 6 (1993): 21-26. By permission of Government Finance Officers Association (GFOA).

Exhibit 1: *Ten Key Ratios of Financial Condition*

Ratio	Clarification of Ratio Components
1. $\dfrac{\text{Total revenues}}{\text{Population}}$	*Total revenues* is the total revenues for all governmental funds.
2. $\dfrac{\text{Total general fund revenues from own sources}}{\text{Total general fund revenues}}$	*Total general fund revenues from own sources* is the difference between total general fund revenues and amounts classified in the general fund as intergovernmental revenues.
3. $\dfrac{\text{General fund sources from other funds}}{\text{Total general fund sources}}$	*General fund sources from other funds* is general fund operating transfers in. *Total general fund sources* is the total of general fund revenues and operating transfers in.
4. $\dfrac{\text{Operating expenditures}}{\text{Total expenditures}}$	*Operating expenditures* is the total expenditures for the general, special revenues and debt service funds. *Total expenditures* is the total expenditures for all governmental funds.
5. $\dfrac{\text{Total revenues}}{\text{Total expenditures}}$	*Total revenues* is the total revenues for all governmental funds. *Total expenditures* is the total expenditures for all governmental funds.
6. $\dfrac{\text{Unreserved general fund balance}}{\text{Total general fund revenues}}$	*Unreserved general fund balance* is the total of both unreserved designated and unreserved undesignated fund balance for the general fund.
7. $\dfrac{\text{Total general fund cash and investments}}{\text{Total general fund liabilities}}$	(The components are self-explanatory.)
8. $\dfrac{\text{Total general fund liabilities}}{\text{Total general fund revenues}}$	(The components are self-explanatory.)
9. $\dfrac{\text{Direct long-term debt}}{\text{Population}}$	*Direct debt* is general obligation debt to be repaid from property tax revenues.
10. $\dfrac{\text{Debt service}}{\text{Total revenues}}$	*Debt service* is the total expenditures in the debt service fund. *Total revenues* is the total revenues of all governmental funds.

about their city's financial condition, their conclusions may be based on a few key indicators of their choice. On the other hand, some may obtain a perception of the city's financial condition and not be able to identify the basis for that perception. The 10-Point Test, however, attempts to provide an objective scoring technique to help bring closure to financial-condition decisions.

Step 1: Calculation of Ratios

The first step of the test consists of calculating the 10 ratios for one's city, using the definitions in Exhibit 1. All data required for the ratios usually are available in the city's comprehensive annual financial report and current general purpose financial statements.

A financial-condition worksheet that can be used to summarize the city's ratios and determine the city's financial-condition score is provided in Exhibit 2. After the city's ratios are calculated, they are entered in section B on the worksheet. Sections C and D are to be completed in accordance with instructions presented in step 3.

Step 2: City Comparisons

Using the definitions in Exhibit 1, the author calculated the FY89 ratios for all 750 cities in the Financial Indicators Database with a population of 100,000 or less.[3] Because of economies of scale and other differing characteristics between large and small cities, comparative ratio analysis will be more meaningful if ratio comparisons are made for similar-sized cities. To aid in that analysis, the ratios of the 750 cities were partitioned into four population groups: (1) cities between 50,000 and 100,000, (2) cities between 30,000 and 50,000, (3) cities between 15,000 and 30,000, and (4) cities under 15,000. Exhibit 3 shows the ratios,

Exhibit 2: *Financial-Condition Worksheet*

	(A)	(B)	(C) Points Assigned to Each Quartile (Circle the quartile in which your city's ratio falls.)				(D) City's Score
	Ratio	Your City's Ratio	Quartile 1 (0 to 25 percentile)	Quartile 2 (25 to 50 percentile)	Quartile 3 (50 to 75 percentile)	Quartile 4 (75 to 100 percentile)	(Enter your score circled on the left.)
1.	$\dfrac{\text{Total revenues}}{\text{Population}}$	1. _____	−1	0	+1	+2	_____
2.	$\dfrac{\text{Total general fund revenues from own sources}}{\text{Total general fund revenues}}$	2. _____	−1	0	+1	+2	_____
3.	$\dfrac{\text{General fund sources from other funds}}{\text{Total general fund sources}}$	3. _____	−1	0	+1	+2	_____
4.	$\dfrac{\text{Operating expenditures}}{\text{Total expenditures}}$	4. _____	−1	0	+1	+2	_____
5.	$\dfrac{\text{Total revenues}}{\text{Total expenditures}}$	5. _____	−1	0	+1	+2	_____
6.	$\dfrac{\text{Unreserved general fund balance}}{\text{Total general fund revenues}}$	6. _____	−1	0	+1	+2	_____
7.	$\dfrac{\text{Total general fund cash and investments}}{\text{Total general fund liabilities}}$	7. _____	−1	0	+1	+2	_____
8.	$\dfrac{\text{Total general fund liabilities}}{\text{Total general fund revenues}}$	8. _____	−1	0	+1	+2	_____
9.	$\dfrac{\text{Direct long-term debt}}{\text{Population}}$	9. _____	−1	0	+1	+2	_____
10.	$\dfrac{\text{Debt service}}{\text{Total revenues}}$	10. _____	−1	0	+1	+2	_____
						Your city's financial condition score:	_____

reported in quartiles, for the cities in each of these population categories. A quartile contains 25 percent of the cities in a given population group. Thus, in Exhibit 3, quartile 1 shows the ratios of that 25 percent of the cities in a particular population group that have the worst ratios; the 25 percent of the cities with the next best ratios are placed in quartile 2; and those with better ratios are included in quartile 3 or 4, according to their rank. As shown in Exhibit 3, the ratio of total revenues to population (ratio 1) for cities in the 50,000 to 100,000 population group was $714 or more for the cities in quartile 1. For quartile 2 cities, the ratios ranged between $714 and $532. Quartile 3 cities had ratios ranging from $532 to $429, and quartile 4 cities had the best ratios amounting to $429 or less.

Providing the ratios in quartiles enables finance officers to make definitive statements about the relationship of their city's ratio to the ranges of ratios for the database cities. For example, if a city with a population between 50,000 and 100,000 has a ratio of total revenues to population that is $500, its ratio is in quartile 3 (see Exhibit 3); thus, the finance officer can say that his/her city's ratio is better than 50 percent of the cities in the Financial Indicators Database and that his/her city is in a favorable position among this group of the nation's cities.

As Exhibit 3 shows, some ratios are favorable if they are low, while other ratios are favorable if they are high. For 6 of the 10 ratios (i.e., ratios 1, 3, 4, 8, 9, 10), low values are favorable. The other 4 ratios (i.e., ratios 2, 5, 6, 7) are favorable only if they have high values. This fact can be observed in either quartiles 1 or 4 where the ranges are described as more than or less than a given value. The generally accepted interpretations of favorable ratios are listed below.

Ratio 1: A *low ratio* suggests a greater ability to acquire additional revenue.

Ratio 2: A *high ratio* suggests the city is not reliant on external governmental organizations.

Ratio 3: A *low ratio* suggests the city does not have to rely on operating transfers to finance general government operations in the general fund.

Ratio 4: A *low ratio* suggests the infrastructure is being maintained adequately.

Ratio 5: A *high ratio* suggests the city experienced a positive interperiod equity.

Ratio 6: A *high ratio* suggests the presence of resources that can be used to overcome a temporary shortfall of revenues.

Ratio 7: A *high ratio* suggests sufficient cash with which to pay short-term obligations.

Ratio 8: A *low ratio* suggests short-term obligations can be easily serviced by the normal flow of annual revenues.

Ratio 9: A *low ratio* suggests the city has the ability to repay its general long-term debt.

Ratio 10: A *low ratio* suggests the city is able to pay its debt service requirements when due.

Exhibit 3: *FY 1989 Quartile Ranges for 750 Cities from the Financial Indicators Database*

	Ratio	Population 50,000–100,000 (162 cities) Quartile				Population 30,000–50,000 (167 cities) Quartile			
		1 (Worst) 0-25%	2 25-50%	3 50-75%	4 (Best) 75-100%	1 (Worst) 0-25%	2 25-50%	3 50-75%	4 (Best) 75-100%
1.	Total revenues / Population	$714 or more	$714 to $532	$532 to $429	$429 or less	$631 or more	$631 to $493	$493 to $399	$399 or less
2.	Total general fund revenues from own sources / Total general fund revenues	80.2% or less	80.2% to 87.7%	87.7% to 96.8%	96.8% or more	77.5% or less	77.5% to 87.4%	87.4% to 96.4%	96.4% or more
3.	General fund sources from other funds / Total general fund sources	7.285% or more	7.285% to 2.083%	2.083% to 0.003%	0.003% or less	6.598% or more	6.598% to 2.438%	2.438% to 0.001%	0.001% or less
4.	Operating expenditures / Total expenditures	95.8% or more	95.8% to 88.9%	88.9% to 81.6%	81.6% or less	94.4% or more	94.4% to 86.5%	86.5% to 77.4%	77.4% or less
5.	Total revenues / Total expenditures	0.878 or less	0.878 to 0.964	0.964 to 1.038	1.038 or more	0.864 or less	0.864 to 0.952	0.952 to 1.034	1.034 or more
6.	Unreserved general fund balance / Total general fund revenues	0.086 or less	0.086 to 0.180	0.180 to 0.300	0.300 or more	0.133 or less	0.133 to 0.211	0.211 to 0.338	0.338 or more
7.	Total general fund cash and investments / Total general fund liabilities	0.622 or less	0.622 to 1.539	1.539 to 3.372	3.372 or more	0.916 or less	0.916 to 1.909	1.909 to 3.525	3.525 or more
8.	Total general fund liabilities / Total general fund revenues	0.254 or more	0.254 to 0.101	0.101 to 0.069	0.069 or less	0.193 or more	0.193 to 0.099	0.099 to 0.063	0.063 or less
9.	Direct long-term debt / Population	$413 or more	$413 to $201	$201 to $21	$21 or less	$416 or more	$416 to $141	$141 to $15	$15 or less
10.	Debt service / Total revenues	0.134 or more	0.134 to 0.074	0.074 to 0.041	0.041 or less	0.146 or more	0.146 to 0.080	0.080 to 0.025	0.025 or less

Notes: Each quartile represents 25 percent of the cities in the population group.
The dollar ratios reported represent 1989 dollars inflated to 1992 dollars using the growth in the Municipal Cost Index.

Before proceeding to the next step, one should refer to the part of Exhibit 3 that relates to the population of his/her city and identify the quartile in which each of the city's ratios falls. This comparison will be used to help determine the overall financial condition of the city in step 3.

Step 3: Grading City Condition

The 10-Point Test's scoring technique is arbitrary and based on certain assumptions about the importance of 10 ratios. As a result, some users of this methodology may prefer to complete the analysis with the ratio comparisons in step 2 and forego the grading process suggested in step 3.

To obtain the 10-Point Test's grading of a city's financial condition, one should complete the worksheet (Exhibit 2) that contains the ratios computed for his/her city. Section C of the worksheet assigns points to each of the ratios according to the quartile in which the city's ratio falls; it can be completed by circling the quartiles in which each ratio falls.

Each quartile is assigned a score that ranges from −1 to +2. This scale is designed to allow only cities with ratios above the 50th percentile (quartile 3 or above) to obtain a positive overall score. A city with all of its ratios in quartile 3 would be above the 50th percentile among all cities and would receive an overall score of 10 points under the 10-Point Test. A city with all ratios in quartile 2 (25th to 50th percentile) would receive an overall score of 0, whereas a city with all ratios in quartile 1 (less than 25th percentile) would receive a negative overall score of −10 points.

Exhibit 3: *Continued*

	Ratio	Population 15,000–30,000 (213 cities) Quartile				Population less than 15,000 (208 cities) Quartile			
		1 (Worst) 0-25%	2 25-50%	3 50-75%	4 (Best) 75-100%	1 (Worst) 0-25%	2 25-50%	3 50-75%	4 (Best) 75-100%
1.	Total revenues / Population	$666 or more	$666 to $481	$481 to $326	$326 or less	$736 or more	$736 to $465	$465 to $368	$368 or less
2.	Total general fund revenues from own sources / Total general fund revenues	77.7% or less	77.7% to 88.6%	88.6% to 98.3%	98.3% or more	76.4% or less	76.4% to 89.2%	89.2% to 96.7%	96.7% or more
3.	General fund sources from other funds / Total general fund sources	5.987% or more	5.987% to 1.157%	1.157% to 0.001%	0.001% or less	8.089% or more	8.089% to 1.270%	1.270% to 0.001%	0.001% or less
4.	Operating expenditures / Total expenditures	97.9% or more	97.9% to 91.1%	91.1% to 81.9%	81.9% or less	99.0% or more	99.0% to 92.2%	92.2% to 80.3%	80.3% or less
5.	Total revenues / Total expenditures	0.876 or less	0.876 to 0.954	0.954 to 1.034	1.034 or more	0.868 or less	0.868 to 0.962	0.962 to 1.038	1.038 or more
6.	Unreserved general fund balance / Total general fund revenues	0.104 or less	0.104 to 0.218	0.218 to 0.386	0.386 or more	0.173 or less	0.173 to 0.278	0.278 to 0.444	0.444 or more
7.	Total general fund cash and investments / Total general fund liabilities	0.819 or less	0.819 to 1.865	1.865 to 4.719	4.719 or more	1.162 or less	1.162 to 2.522	2.522 to 5.761	5.761 or more
8.	Total general fund liabilities / Total general fund revenues	0.208 or more	0.208 to 0.104	0.104 to 0.061	0.061 or less	0.189 or more	0.189 to 0.102	0.102 to 0.057	0.057 or less
9.	Direct long-term debt / Population	$326 or more	$326 to $133	$133 to $8	$8 or less	$329 or more	$329 to $87	$87 to $1	$1 or less
10.	Debt service / Total revenues	0.133 or more	0.133 to 0.063	0.063 to 0.011	0.011 or less	0.105 or more	0.105 to 0.039	0.039 to 0.001	0.001 or less

To determine the city's overall score, one should transfer the circled points for each ratio in section C to the corresponding blanks in section D and then sum the column. Exhibit 4 shows a worksheet completed for a city with a population between 30,000 and 50,000. This Midwestern city reported one ratio in quartile 4 (better than 75 percent of the other cities), five ratios in quartile 3, two ratios in quartile 2 and two ratios in quartile 1. Because a majority of its ratios were better than 50 percent of the other cities, the city obtained a positive score of 5. The remaining task for the city in Exhibit 4, and for finance officers using the worksheet, is to interpret the final score.

Because little is known about the relative importance of the municipal finance ratios, the scoring technique of the 10-Point Test assumes that each of the 10 ratios has equal importance in the assessment of financial condition. A city with a majority of its ratios above the 50th percentile would be in better financial condition than a city with a majority of its ratios below the 50th percentile.

Cities in better financial condition will have favorable values in most of the 10 ratios. The following grading scale suggested by the author nets the favorable and unfavorable ratios to obtain an overall "grade" for a city relative to the cities in the database. To determine a city's financial condition relative to the condition of the database cities, its overall score determined in the Exhibit 2 worksheet is compared with the grading scale.

Overall Score	Overall Grade Relative to Database Cities
10 or more	Among the *best*
5 to 9	*Better* than most
1 to 4	About *average*
0 to –4	*Worse* than most
–5 or less	Among the *worst*

The database cities do not provide a random sample of all the nation's cities. Thus, the grading scale includes only relative interpretations (i.e., better or worse) instead of absolute terms, such as good or bad financial condition. While it can be said that a city with a low score from the 10-Point Test is in *poorer* condition than most of the database cities, the city may not be in *poor* financial condition. Even so, a city receiving negative scores might do well to engage in a more comprehensive study of its financial condition.

The interpretations suggested in the above scoring technique are based on the author's assumption that all 10 ratios have equal importance. Since certain ratios are probably more important than others, a city's overall grade could be biased where unfavorable but important ratios are outnumbered by favorable but less important ratios. Publications of financial ratios, however, such as the International City/County Management Association's book, *Evaluating Financial Condition: A Handbook for Local Government,* do not highlight some ratios as being more important than others. Thus, until additional research is conducted and more is known about the relative importance of ratios, the suggested scoring technique is a reasonable first stage in the development of a more refined financial-condition test.

Because of the uncertainty about ratio importance, it would be appropriate for finance officers completing the 10-Point Test to modify the scoring technique to reflect the finance officer's perceptions of the most and least important indicators. For example, the finance officer of the Midwestern city whose ratios are depicted in Exhibit 4 might feel that two of the ratios depicting operating position (i.e., ratio 5—total revenues to total expenditures—and ratio 6—unreserved general fund balance to total general fund revenues) are more important to the assessment of financial condition than the other eight ratios. To reflect this increased importance, the city's score for ratios 5 and 6 could be multiplied by two as a way to indicate that the two ratios are more important than the others. While this modification would cause the Midwestern city's score to increase from +5 to +8, its overall score could have been lowered had the two important ratios been unfavorable.

Despite the limitations just discussed, the comparisons of a city's ratios with those of the cities in the Financial Indicators Database provide new information about a city's relative financial condition that has not been available previously. The author, who is interested in further research and study of the best indicators of municipal financial condition, would like to obtain any feedback from finance officers and other analysts who complete the 10-Point Test regarding their experiences with and/or impressions of the test. The 10-Point Test is intended to provide a *conversation piece* around which finance officers and others can discuss and develop better financial-condition assessment tools.

Exhibit 4: *Sample Financial-Condition Worksheet Completed by a City with a Population between 30,000 and 50,000*

	(A) Ratio	(B) Your City's Ratio	(C) Points Assigned to Each Quartile (Circle the quartile in which your city's ratio falls.)				(D) City's Score (Enter your score circled on the left.)
			Quartile 1 (0 to 25 percentile)	Quartile 2 (25 to 50 percentile)	Quartile 3 (50 to 75 percentile)	Quartile 4 (75 to 100 percentile)	
1.	Total revenues / Population	1. $445	−1	0	(+1)	+2	+1
2.	Total general fund revenues from own sources / Total general fund revenues	2. 89.9%	−1	0	(+1)	+2	+1
3.	General fund sources from other funds / Total general fund sources	3. 6.598%	(−1)	0	+1	+2	−1
4.	Operating expenditures / Total expenditures	4. 80.5%	−1	0	(+1)	+2	+1
5.	Total revenues / Total expenditures	5. 1.048	−1	0	+1	(+2)	+2
6.	Unreserved general fund balance / Total general fund revenues	6. .268	−1	0	(+1)	+2	+1
7.	Total general fund cash and investments / Total general fund liabilities	7. 1.972	−1	0	(+1)	+2	+1
8.	Total general fund liabilities / Total general fund revenues	8. .157	−1	(0)	+1	+2	0
9.	Direct long-term debt / Population	9. $182	−1	(0)	+1	+2	0
10.	Debt service / Total revenues	10. .173	(−1)	0	+1	+2	−1
						Your city's financial condition score:	+5

Additional improvements in the test can be made in the near future because of the recent release of GFOA's Financial Indicators Database for FY90 and FY91. This provides the opportunity to integrate trend analysis into subsequent versions of the test. The test could be improved also with the development of a method for incorporating the financial condition of proprietary funds activities into the 10-Point Test. Financial-condition assessment of businesslike enterprises, however, requires techniques that are unique to each industry. Even so, a finance officer should determine the financial condition of these enterprises and consider this assessment with the results of the 10-Point Test.

Conclusion

Because of the difficult environment in which all the nation's cities now operate, finance officers need to assess their city's financial condition on a continuing basis. The test described in this article provides a quick and effective tool for officials of smaller cities to assess their city's financial condition without the use of analytical techniques that are costly, time-consuming or so complex that final assessments become difficult if not impossible. While more comprehensive tests are available, the strength of the 10-Point Test lies in the extensive set of ratios that were determined for cities from the Financial Indicators Database. Tests such as the one suggested here provide a case for continued and expanded exchange of financial information by cities so that they can make better-informed judgments about the state of their financial affairs.

Notes

1. For a description of the contents and products of the Financial Indicators Database, see "Using the Financial Indicators Database for Policy Analysis," in this issue and "A New Data Source for Comparative Analysis," in the February 1992 issue of *Government Finance Review.*

2. Except for the third ratio, the ratios used in this article were adapted from the 36 indicators included in the International City/County Management Association's *Evaluating Financial Condition: A Handbook for Local Government,* written by S.M. Groves and M.G. Valente in 1986. Ratio 3, which tests a city's reliance on proprietary funds transfers to finance general government operations, was developed by the author specifically for the 10-Point Test. Ratio selection, definitions, and interpretations of the ratios were aided by a discussion of financial condition assessment contained in *Governmental and Nonprofit Accounting* (forthcoming edition), written by Leon Hay and Earl Wilson.

3. FY89 data are used because data for only that fiscal year were available in the database when the author began preparation of this article.

Proposed Financial Ratios for Use in Analysis of Municipal Annual Financial Reports

Karl M. Zehms

INTRODUCTION

Financial reports of municipal governments are legendary for their complexity and length. Annual financial reports of major municipalities sometimes are in excess of 100 pages. Academics and accounting practitioners have struggled for years attempting to discover an approach to make these statements more user friendly. However, so long as accounting by fund type is followed for municipal operations, there is almost no way of materially shortening the length of the annual financial report.

The purpose of this article is to suggest the use of a technique widely and productively utilized in the private sector of our economy as an approach to providing summary information regarding a municipality's operations and financial condition. The technique being proposed is that of ratio analysis.

Specifically, the author is proposing the development of a series of financial ratios for use by municipalities to provide users with some easily understood broad indicators of municipal operating results and financial condition.

The author of this article has taught both governmental accounting and financial statement analysis at the college level for the past 20 years. It seems inconsistent that for profit-oriented business firms there are, and have been for decades, widely accepted and widely publicized financial ratios. Dozens of such ratios exist and some, like the "current" ratio or the "inventory turnover" ratio and "debt to equity" ratio are so well known they are virtual institutions. Yet, for some unknown reason, in the arena of municipal accounting the development of similar financial ratios has simply not taken place. Why such development has not taken place is a matter of conjecture and not really significant so far as this article is concerned.

The fact that an accepted group of financial ratios for municipalities (or state, counties, etc.) does not exist creates a serious obstacle when someone attempts to perform an analysis of the financial statements of a municipality. When a person analyzes the financial statements of a business corporation, one important step, of many, is the calculation of numerous financial ratios. Typically, these ratios are grouped into various categories such as (1) short-term liquidity, (2) long-term solvency, (3) return on investment, (4) asset utilization, (5) operating performance,[1] and (6) funds flow. Then the analyst can examine how these ratios have changed over a period of time. Additionally, the analyst can compare these ratios with external industry norms. Because a group of widely accepted financial ratios for business corporations has existed for many years, norms for these ratios by industry exist and are widely disseminated. In particular, Robert Morris and Associates publish their *Annual Statement Studies* which contains financial ratios and other data for over 350 different industries. When an analyst is performing a financial statement analysis of a business firm, an important step in the analysis process is the comparison of the results of the financial ratio computations for the firm being

---

Reprinted from *The Government Accountants Journal* 40, no.3 (1991): 79-85. By permission of Association of Government Accountants.

analyzed with the industry norms found in the Robert Morris and Associates publication.

A barrier to successfully analyzing the financial statements of municipal governments is clearly the lack of widely accepted financial ratios. A second barrier to performing such analyses is the fact that since such ratios do not exist neither are there nationwide norms against which to compare the ratios for a particular municipality. This is amazing considering the similarities of functions that a municipality provides to its citizens. In the long run it seems clear that generating norms could be done by some national organization interested in such matters, but in the shorter run the first step is to identify and eventually get agreement on what constitutes a useful group of financial ratios for municipalities. The major purpose of this article is to identify a list of potentially useful financial ratios for use in the analysis of municipal financial statements.

USERS OF MUNICIPAL FINANCIAL REPORTS

The starting point in the development of a series of financial ratios is a determination of who are the users of municipal annual financial reports. This is a subject that has been extensively researched over the past 20 years. In his authoritative study, *The Needs of Users of Governmental Financial Reports,*[2] David B. Jones summarizes the findings of no less than 16 studies which have focused on the issue of who are the users of governmental financial reports and what information do they need. Since this issue has been studied so extensively, the author relied on the Jones study for providing the starting point in identifying what groups of users should be considered when attempting to develop specific financial ratios.

Since many readers have probably not read the Jones study, a brief summary of some of his conclusions in this area is worthwhile.[3] First, Jones and several other researchers concluded that the number of user groups must be brief to be useful. Only the most predominate user groups are considered since it is not feasible nor cost-effective to try to satisfy every need of every user. Second, external financial reports and their specific content should meet the needs of users who have limited access to internal financial reports or the books and records of the municipality itself. As a result of the above comments, internal management is excluded from being viewed as one of the primary user groups. After sifting through the results of the 16 research studies alluded to earlier, Jones settled on three broad groups as constituting the primary users of government financial reports. These three groups are (1) citizen groups, (2) legislative and oversight officials, and (3) investors and creditors.[4] In this paper, the above three groups are accepted as being the primary users of external reports and accordingly the financial ratios identified later in this paper were developed with the specific "needs" of these three groups in mind.

More specifically, what are the "needs" of these three broad groups of users?

Citizen Groups

The major uses that *citizen groups*[5] make of external financial reports, and presumably for which financial ratios could be usefully developed are as follows:

1. *To evaluate efficiency and effectiveness.* Jones defines efficiency as "...producing an effect with a minimal use of resources," while he defines effectiveness as "producing a desired effect." Jones goes on to point out that to evaluate both efficiency and effectiveness "...comparability is useful. Evaluations may be based on comparisons with other governments of the same level and that have similar population characteristics."

2. *To compare results of the current year with those of previous year.* Jones states that "...citizen groups use governmental financial reports to make comparisons...of operations over time....They use historical trend data to forecast revenues needed in the future, potential expenditure levels, possible increases in taxes and so forth."

3. *To assess financial operations and financial condition.* This is clearly an important use. This use includes "...evaluating resources obtained and spent." Assessment of operations also includes "...comparing public priorities among jurisdictions." So far as evaluating financial condition is concerned Jones states that citizen groups "...evaluate the amount of a government's debt, since it is a call on future resources. They are interested in deferral of payments for obligations such as pensions because those deferrals may indicate a relatively higher tax burden for future taxpayers."

4. *To determine compliance with the budget.* This is a high priority use for citizen groups. These groups want to "...ensure that money is used in accordance with the allocations made. Over-expenditures point to the possibility of poor financial management. Under-expenditures may indicate that services could have increased...or budgetary savings could have been attained." Finally, "...citizen groups need comparisons of budgeted revenues and expenditures to actual revenues and expenditures."

5. *To advocate certain programs or actions.* Examples of this use would include citizen lobbying efforts on behalf of a new school building, books, computers, etc. Or, employee unions are concerned with the government's ability to adequately compensate employees. Jones accurately states that "...information most useful for lobbying purposes is data on available resources. For instance, a caption in the balance sheet that gives fund balance available for appropriation would be valuable." Developing financial ratios to provide this information is clearly a possibility.

Legislative and Oversight Officials

The major uses identified for *legislative and oversight officials*[6] are summarized as follows:

1. *To evaluate executive branch funding and spending proposals*
   a. by comparing current year with previous year results and
   b. by making comparisons with other governmental units.

Jones notes that these officials "...are directly involved in evaluating executive proposals for funding and spending. Anticipated revenues from the existing revenue structure usually provide a framework for evaluating the aggregate of the spending proposals. Therefore, trend data are needed to assist in the revenue forecasting procedure." This last point is important because it emphasizes the fact that while financial ratios can be important information sources, a wide variety of data are needed to satisfy fully all user needs. Regarding the matter of making comparisons with other governmental units, Jones says that legislators must make "...comparisons with other governments when making resource allocation decisions. A city council member may wish to compare the amount of money allocated to public safety in one city with that of similar cities." Certainly, legislators would find their job easier to execute if information of this type were in fact readily available for governments as it is for business corporations via the Robert Morris and Associates studies. The need for a national clearinghouse to assemble this type of data for municipalities seems compelling.

2. *To determine compliance with the budget and other finance-related requirements.* Specifically, what Jones was addressing here was the need for legislators to determine compliance with laws, regulations, and statutes. For example, comparison of budgeted to actual revenues and expenditures is used to demonstrate compliance.

3. *To monitor fund activity and financial position and to analyze fund balances.* This specific user classification is directed towards developing "...budget and program recommendations." While trend data are useful, "...the previous year's financial data may be the best indicator if conditions have been changing rapidly." Jones states that so far as evaluating financial position is concerned "...a review of the government's funds available for appropriation and its debt structure" would be most useful.

Investors and Creditors

Jones is very straightforward regarding the needs of this class, investors and creditors,[7] when he states that they need financial reports "...for one primary purpose: to ascertain the ability of a government to repay its debt." Obviously, this group shares some of the needs of citizen groups and legislative and oversight bodies. For example, Jones indicates this group needs statements of revenues and expenditures as well as the statement of financial condition and a statement of general long-term debt. There is no question that besides these basic financial statements a variety of financial ratios could be developed to assist investors and creditors in evaluating the debt-paying capacity of a municipality on both an absolute and relative basis.

IDENTIFICATION OF SPECIFIC RATIOS

Based on the user needs identified in the previous section, this paper provides 13 financial ratios organized in three broad categories that provide information which would aid in meeting the specific user needs identified earlier. The three broad categories referred to are operating ratios, debt ratios, and capital expenditure ratios. Obviously, users of governmental reports need more than these ratios. The financial statements and the attached footnotes still provide the user's most fundamental financial information needs. These ratios are merely an additional tool for users and would presumably appear as supplementary information in the annual financial report.

Development of the ratios was largely a judgmental matter. A ratio is nothing more than the mathematical relationship between one quantity and another. To develop a ratio all one needs is a numerator and a denominator. Obviously, thousands of ratios could be developed for governmental units. To be useful, however, "...the ratio must express a relationship that has significance."[8] That is, there must be a direct causal relationship between the two quantities being measured.

In developing the ratios the needs of all three user groups discussed earlier (citizen groups, legislative and oversight officials, and investors and creditors) were considered. Since in many cases the needs of the user groups were similar, the individual ratios would be of use to more than one user group. Thus, the 13 ratios developed are presented in three broad categories (operating ratios, debt ratios, capital expenditure ratios) rather than being specifically identified as being oriented towards the needs of any one user group.

Operating Ratios

Ratio I

$$\frac{\text{Unreserved Fund Balance of General and Special Revenue Funds}}{\text{Total Assets of Those Funds}}$$

This ratio is proposed because the unreserved fund balances of general and special revenue funds is an indicator of the political climate of the governmental unit. Clearly, the unreserved fund balance represents dollars extracted from taxpayers in excess of amounts expended on services. A large unreserved fund balance relative to assets would be of concern to citizen groups, taxpayers, and oversight bodies. Too low of an unreserved fund balance could also be cause for concern because it could cause expensive short-term borrowing if cash shortages develop. Citizen groups in particular would seem to be interested in examining the trend of this ratio.

Ratio II

$$\frac{\text{General Fund Revenues/Actual/Current Year}}{\text{General Fund Revenues/Actual/Previous Year}}$$

Ratio III

$$\frac{\text{General Fund Expenditures/Actual/Current Year}}{\text{General Fund Expenditures/Actual/Previous Year}}$$

The need for Ratios II and III is largely self-evident. Jones's study of user needs indicated a great deal of interest in the *trend* of both spending by governmental units as well as in the growth of revenue generation by governmental units. A direct means of measuring the growth of both revenue generation and spending is by comparing the current year actual results with the results of the previous year. This can be done in total as well as by specific type of revenue (taxes, service charges, fines and forfeits, etc.). Once these ratios have been computed for several years, the results would provide an excellent insight to the longer term financial administration policy of the governmental unit. These ratios are restricted to focus only on General Fund revenues and expenditures because it is through that fund that expenditures related to the annual operating budget of the governmental unit flow. Similar ratios could easily be developed for Special Revenue or Debt Service funds. This line of reasoning was not pursued at this time because it was felt that it would be best to keep the original number of ratios proposed at a fairly small number.

Ratio IV

$$\frac{\text{General Fund Actual Revenues}}{\text{General Fund Budgeted Revenues}}$$

Ratio V

$$\frac{\text{General Fund Actual Expenditures}}{\text{General Fund Budgeted Expenditures}}$$

Both citizen groups and legislative bodies were identified in the Jones study as having substantial interest in determining compliance with the budget. It is assumed that such groups would also have an interest in similar data regarding revenue generation, hence Ratio IV was postulated. Clearly, the formal "Statement of Actual versus Expected Revenues" and the "Statement of Actual versus Expected Expenditures" required by Generally Accepted Accounting Principles to be included in the Comprehensive Annual Financial Report would also provide users with information on budget compliance. These ratios should compare the original budget to actual results or, if not materially different, the final approved budget. Comparing actual results to the budget after all budget modifications are approved would be pointless because budgets tend to mirror actual results after modification. The above ratios would simply provide a quick overview of what is contained in those lengthy formal financial statements. Once these ratios were computed over a several year period, valuable trend data would become available to interested users. Obviously, if national norms became available, comparing the results of these ratios with national averages would provide users with important benchmark data.

Ratio VI

$$\frac{\text{Net Income (Loss) All Enterprise Funds}}{\text{Total Enterprise Fund Revenues}}$$

Ratio VII

$$\frac{\text{Net Income (Loss) All Enterprise Funds}}{\text{Total Enterprise Fund Assets}}$$

Enterprise fund activities are so significant in terms of dollars involved in the overall operations of municipal governments that developing some ratios dealing with the operating results and financial condition of these funds as a whole is necessary. Many ratios are widely used to evaluate the operating results and financial conditions of profit-oriented business firms.[9] These same ratios would be appropriate in evaluating *individual* enterprise funds. The author assumes that citizen groups, oversight bodies, and the like would be more interested in generalistic ratios for all enterprise activities taken as a whole.

Regarding evaluating enterprise operations, the overall goal of administering enterprise activities must be considered. That goal is to operate as near to a break-even level as possible. User charges are normally set at a level to, in the long run, recover the operating expenses of the enterprise including depreciation. Setting rates too high results in excessive resources being extracted from users. Setting rates too low would eventually bankrupt the enterprise. By comparing net income to enterprise revenues for all enterprise activities as a whole (Ratio VI), and by comparing net income to enterprise assets for all enterprise activities (Ratio VII), users can make a judgment as to how successful the municipality has been in establishing user charges for enterprise activities in general.

Debt Ratios

The second broad category of ratios being presented focuses on the long-term debt status of the municipality. Users of municipal financial information generally have a high interest in the long-term debt position of municipalities.

Ratio VIII

$$\frac{\text{Total Debt All Enterprise Funds}}{\text{Total Equity All Enterprise Funds}}$$

This ratio focuses on the debt position of municipal enterprise activities rather than on the "general long-term debt" of the municipality. This ratio is designed to provide an easily understood measure of the general manner in which the financial structure of the enterprise activities as a whole is established. Users would logically be interested in the degree to which the enterprises are relying on debt financing versus using equity financing. Comparing total enterprise debt with total enterprise equity provides an excellent measure of the degree to which debt financing is being utilized. Changes in this ratio over time as well as comparisons of this ratio with national norms (if they existed) would provide users with considerable insight as to the direction in which the financing of enterprise activities is moving.

Ratio IX

$$\frac{\text{Net General Long-Term Debt}}{\text{Population}}$$

Users of financial information frequently relate well to per capita data. The numerator in this ratio is computed by reducing total general long-term debt by the amount available for debt retirement in the various debt service funds. The resulting figure, net general long-term debt per capita, would be an interesting figure when examined either on a trend basis (say past five years) or in comparison with national norms. This ratio would provide useful data for all three user groups identified by Jones.

Ratio X

$$\frac{\text{Legal Debt Margin}}{\text{Legal Debt Limit}}$$

Legal debt margin is calculated by first determining the legal debt limit (usually a specified percentage of assessed valuation) and then subtracting from the debt limit the net general long-term debt. For example, a municipality with a debt limit of $500,000,000 and a debt margin of $50,000,000 would by computation have a ratio of .10 which would indicate that significant additional issuances of general long-term debt would not only be expensive but very quickly might become legally impossible. A municipality with a ratio of .80 would be viewed in a much different fashion by user groups. The need for developing national norms in this area seems evident.

Ratio XI

$$\frac{\text{Debt Service Payments}}{\text{Total Expenditures of General/Special Revenue/Debt Service Funds}}$$

All of the user groups cited earlier expressed considerable interest in the general subject of municipal debt and debt service requirements. Ratios IX and X provide insight into the absolute level of general long-term debt. Ratio XI focuses on the magnitude of general long-term debt in terms of overall annual operations of the municipality. The general and special revenue funds expend dollars to provide what are generally viewed as the "normal" operations of the municipality. By adding to those expenditure totals the annual expenditures for all debt service (interest and principal) accounted for in the debt service funds and then dividing that into the debt service expenditures, one can obtain a clearer picture as to what the true magnitude of debt service payments are on the general governmental activities of the municipality.

Capital Expenditures Ratios

The third broad category of ratios presented focuses on the magnitudes of spending for capital expenditures. Information on capital expenditures is especially important because capital expenditures are frequently funded with long-term debt which in turn is serviced by future property tax levies.

Ratio XII

$$\frac{\text{Annual Capital Project Fund Expenditures}}{\text{Population}}$$

Ratio XIII

$$\frac{\text{Capital Project Fund Expenditures}}{\text{General Fund Expenditures}}$$

Developing ratios appropriate for capital project fund activities is difficult since their activities are so "project specific." Still, the absolute dollar significance of this class of funds is so great that to simply ignore them seemed inappropriate. Since the future health of any municipality rests to an extent on maintaining and replacing its capital assets, it stands to reason that capital project expenditures per capita would be a reasonable indicator of a municipality's concern about updating its capital assets and infrastructure.

The second ratio presented in this category would provide the user with an easily understood measure of the magnitude of capital project outlays in comparison with the dollars being expended through the general fund of the municipality. Users of municipal financial information often focus their attention mainly on general fund expenditures and related activities. This ratio would encourage that more attention be focused on the often massive sums expended on capital project activities.

OTHER POTENTIALLY USEFUL DISCLOSURES

The preceding section of this article has been devoted to the identification of a series of 13 ratios organized in three categories that would provide insights for use by a variety of users regarding the operations and financial condition of municipalities. There is no doubt that other similar ratios could be developed. One could easily develop 30 or 40 ratios that would have some utility to user groups. In this article an attempt has been made to identify a relatively small number of ratios for starters. If the use of ratios for analyzing municipal financial statements does become a reality, additional ratios would probably evolve as more people become aware of the value ratios provide in analyzing municipal financial statements.

While the focus of this article has been on the use of ratios in analyzing municipal financial statements, it must be pointed out that another financial statement analysis technique used widely and effectively in the analysis of business corporations' financial statements could be effectively used in the analysis of municipal financial statements. That technique is referred to as a "common size" analysis. Simply stated, it means expressing financial statements (operating statements or financial condition statements) in terms of a percentage of 100. Thus, in a balance sheet, total assets are assigned a value of 100 percent and each individual asset is expressed in terms of a percentage of 100. This technique is especially useful when examining a display of a five-year trend of balance sheets. For income statements, sales is assigned a value of 100 percent and each other component of the income statement like "cost of sales," "operating expenses," "tax expense" is assigned a percentage of 100. While a mathematically simple technique, common size analysis results are extremely useful in performing a comprehensive financial statement analysis project.

In municipal financial statements the use of "common size" reporting would be particularly useful for "enterprise fund" or "internal service fund" activities. However, this technique could be effectively used, on a selected basis, for "governmental fund" activities as well. Without going into great detail on this subject it does seem worthwhile to identify one set of "common size" data that would be particularly useful for the three user groups identified earlier in this article.

All three user groups seem to have a substantial concern about the manner in which both "general governmental" expenditures are occurring and the manner in which "general governmental" revenues are being generated. Thus, in addition to the 13 ratios identified earlier the author suggests that the following two "common size" financial statements be presented in the municipal annual financial report along with the ratios discussed earlier. (See Exhibits 1 and 2.)

These "common size" displays provide the user at a glance if any significant changes have occurred in the pattern of general governmental expenditures

Exhibit 1: *Common Size Statement I: General Fund Expenditures, by Function,[10] for Years Ending 12-31-90 and 12-31-89*

Function	1990 Percent Expended	1989 Percent Expended
General Government	13	11
Public Safety	43	45
Highways and Streets	12	14
Sanitation	12	10
Culture/Recreation	19	18
Debt Service	1	2
Total	100	100

Exhibit 2: *Common Size Statement II: General Fund Revenues, by Source,[11] for Years Ending 12-31-90 and 12-31-89*

Source	1990 Percent Generated	1989 Percent Generated
Taxes	68	63
Licenses/Permits	5	6
Intergovernmental	16	18
Charges for Services	6	5
Fines	2	3
Interest	2	3
Miscellaneous	1	2
Total	100	100

or revenue generation. Obviously, similar "common size" presentations could be provided for any or all of the fund financial statements included in the comprehensive annual financial report. For the sake of brevity, only these two "common size" statements are proposed at this time. They are included in the article primarily to generate thought in the minds of the readers as to whether additional displays of this type might make the comprehensive annual financial report of municipalities more useful to users who in many cases may be hesitant to examine a financial report of substantial length.

SUMMARY

The purpose of this article was to point out that while the use of financial ratios is widely accepted in the analysis of financial reports of profit-oriented business concerns, the use of financial ratios in the analysis of financial reports of municipalities seems nonexistent. Ratios for use in the analysis of municipal financial statements do not exist. This is particularly troublesome because municipal annual financial reports often are lengthy enough to discourage careful reading. Given the above, it seemed logical that it would be worthwhile to develop a set of financial ratios appropriate for aiding in the analysis of municipal annual financial reports. If this idea takes hold, national norms could be established for the various ratios so that users of these reports could easily compare the ratios for a particular municipality with national standards for the various ratios. National norms for many standard ratios by industry do presently exist for profit-oriented firms, and these norms are used heavily by people analyzing business corporations' financial statements.

The author then examined the needs of three classes of users of municipal financial reports: citizen groups, legislative and oversight officials, and investors and creditors. Taking the needs of these users into account, the author identified a series of 13 ratios in three categories that provide useful information to the three broad classes of users of municipal financial reports. Each of these ratios was displayed and a brief rationale for each ratio was provided.

It is hoped that this discussion will stimulate thought amongst readers who are concerned about the overall usefulness of municipal financial reports. Readers should critique this article and suggest additional ratios or modifications to some of the ratios proposed herein. It is hoped that some day a list of ratios for use in the analysis of municipal financial statements will exist and be accepted for use as a normal part of the analysis of municipal financial reports. Clearly, for these ratios to have maximum utility they will have to be widely used for a period of time so that national norms can be created against which the results of ratio analysis for any individual municipality can be compared.

Notes

1. Leopold A. Bernstein, *Financial Statement Analysis: Theory Application and Interpretation,* 4th ed. (Burr Ridge, Ill.: Irwin Publishing Company, 1988), 91.
2. David B. Jones, *The Needs of Users of Governmental Financial Reports* (Norwalk, Conn.: Governmental Accounting Standards Board, 1985), 11-24.
3. Ibid, 25.
4. Ibid, 25.
5. Ibid, 26-28.
6. Ibid, 28-29.
7. Ibid, 30-31.
8. Bernstein, 82.
9. See any standard Financial Statement Analysis textbook.
10. This is the functional classification used in *Governmental Accounting, Auditing and Financial Reporting* (Chicago: Government Finance Officers Association, 1988), 275. The percentages illustrated are based on the illustrative example depicted on p. 275 of the 1988 *G.A.A.F.R.*
11. Ibid, 275.

Accountability

Government Auditing Standards

INTRODUCTION

(Chapter 1)

PURPOSE

1.1 This document contains standards for audits of government organizations, programs, activities, and functions, and of government assistance received by contractors, nonprofit organizations, and other nongovernment organizations. These standards, often referred to as generally accepted government auditing standards (GAGAS), are to be followed by auditors and audit organizations when required by law, regulation, agreement, contract, or policy. The standards pertain to auditors' professional qualifications, the quality of audit effort, and the characteristics of professional and meaningful audit reports.

APPLICABILITY

1.5 The Single Audit Act of 1984 requires that these standards be followed in audits of state and local governments which receive federal financial assistance.[1]

1.6 Other federal policies and regulations, such as OMB Circular A-133, require that these standards be followed in audits of institutions of higher education and other nonprofit organizations that receive federal financial assistance.[2]

1.7 Auditors conducting audits under agreement or contract also may be required to comply with these standards under the terms of the agreement or contract.

1.8 The standards in this document are generally relevant to and recommended for use by state and local government auditors and public accountants in audits of state and local government organizations, programs, activities, and functions. Several state and local audit organizations, as well as several nations, have officially adopted these standards.

1.9 The American Institute of Certified Public Accountants (AICPA) has issued auditing and attestation standards that apply in financial audits, as discussed in chapters 4 and 5 [chapter 4 is not reprinted here]. The Institute of Internal Auditors and the American Evaluation Association (formerly the Evaluation Research Society) have issued related standards.[3]

ACCOUNTABILITY

1.10 Our system of managing public programs today rests on an elaborate structure of relationships among all levels of government. Officials and employees who manage these programs need to render an account of their activities to the public. While not always specified by law, this accountability concept is inherent in the governing processes of this nation.

Excerpted from Comptroller General of the United States, *Government Auditing Standards: 1994 Revision* (Washington, D.C.: U.S. General Accounting Office, June 1994), chaps. 1, 2, 3, and 5. (Notes have been renumbered.)

1.11 The need for accountability has caused a demand for more information about government programs and services. Public officials, legislators, and citizens want and need to know whether government funds are handled properly and in compliance with laws and regulations. They also want and need to know whether government organizations, programs, and services are achieving their purposes and whether these organizations, programs, and services are operating economically and efficiently.

1.12 This document provides auditing standards to help provide accountability and to assist public officials and employees in carrying out their responsibilities. These standards are more than the codification of current practices. They include concepts and audit areas that are still evolving and are vital to the accountability objectives sought in auditing governments and their programs and services.

BASIC PREMISES

1.13 The following premises underlie these standards and were considered in their development.

   a. The term "audit" includes both financial and performance audits.

   b. Public officials and others entrusted with handling public resources (for example, managers of a not-for-profit organization that receives federal assistance) are responsible for applying those resources efficiently, economically, and effectively to achieve the purposes for which the resources were furnished. This responsibility applies to all resources, whether entrusted to public officials or others by their own constituencies or by other levels of government.

   c. Public officials and others entrusted with public resources are responsible for complying with applicable laws and regulations. That responsibility encompasses identifying the requirements with which the entity and the official must comply and implementing systems designed to achieve that compliance.

   d. Public officials and others entrusted with public resources are responsible for establishing and maintaining effective controls to ensure that appropriate goals and objectives are met; resources are safeguarded; laws and regulations are followed; and reliable data are obtained, maintained, and fairly disclosed.

   e. Public officials and others entrusted with public resources are accountable both to the public and to other levels and branches of government for the resources provided to carry out government programs and services. Consequently, they should provide appropriate reports to those to whom they are accountable.

   f. Audit of government reporting is an essential element of public control and accountability. Auditing provides credibility to the information reported by or obtained from management through objectively acquiring and evaluating evidence. The importance and comprehensive nature of auditing place a special responsibility on public officials or others entrusted with public resources who authorize or arrange audits to be done in accordance with these standards. This responsibility is to provide audit coverage that is broad enough to help fulfill the reasonable needs of potential users of the audit report. Auditors can assist public officials and others in understanding the auditors' responsibilities under GAGAS and other audit coverage required by law or regulation. This comprehensive nature of auditing also highlights the importance of auditors clearly understanding the audit objectives, the scope of the work to be conducted, and the reporting requirements.

   g. Financial auditing contributes to providing accountability since it provides independent reports on whether an entity's financial information is presented fairly and/or on its internal controls and compliance with laws and regulations.

   h. Performance auditing contributes to providing accountability because it provides an independent assessment of the performance of a government organization, program, activity, or function in order to provide information to improve public accountability and facilitate decision-making by parties with responsibility to oversee or initiate corrective action.

i. To realize governmental accountability, the citizens, their elected representatives, and program managers need information to assess the integrity, performance, and stewardship of the government's activities. Thus, unless legal restrictions or ethical considerations prevent it, audit reports should be available to the public and to other levels of government that have supplied resources.[4]

AUDITORS' RESPONSIBILITIES

1.14 The comprehensive nature of auditing done in accordance with these standards places on the audit organization the responsibility for ensuring that (1) the audit is conducted by personnel who collectively have the necessary skills, (2) independence is maintained, (3) applicable standards are followed in planning and conducting audits and reporting the results, (4) the organization has an appropriate internal quality control system in place, and (5) the organization undergoes an external quality control review.

PROCUREMENT OF AUDIT SERVICES

1.15 While not an audit standard, it is important that a sound procurement practice be followed when contracting for audit services. Sound contract award and approval procedures, including the monitoring of contract performance, should be in place. The objectives and scope of the audit should be made clear. In addition to price, other factors to be considered include the responsiveness of the bidder to the request for proposal; the experience of the bidder; availability of bidder staff with professional qualifications and technical abilities; and the results of the bidders' external quality control reviews.[5]

TYPES OF GOVERNMENT AUDITS

(Chapter 2)

PURPOSE

2.1 This chapter describes the types of audits that government and nongovernment audit organizations conduct and that organizations arrange to have conducted, of government organizations, programs, activities, functions, and funds. This description is not intended to limit or require the types of audits that may be conducted or arranged. In conducting these types of audits, auditors should follow the applicable standards included and incorporated in the chapters which follow.

2.2 All audits begin with objectives, and those objectives determine the type of audit to be conducted and the audit standards to be followed. The types of audits, as defined by their objectives, are classified in these standards as financial audits or performance audits.

2.3 Audits may have a combination of financial and performance audit objectives or may have objectives limited to only some aspects of one audit type. For example, auditors conduct audits of government contracts and grants with private sector organizations, as well as government and nonprofit organizations, that often include both financial and performance objectives. These are commonly referred to as "contract audits" or "grant audits." Other examples of such audits include audits of specific internal controls, compliance issues, and computer-based systems. Auditors should follow the standards that are applicable to the individual objectives of the audit.

FINANCIAL AUDITS

2.4 Financial audits include financial statement and financial related audits.

a. Financial statement audits provide reasonable assurance about whether the financial statements of an audited entity present fairly the financial position, results of operations, and cash flows in conformity with generally accepted accounting principles.[1] Financial statement audits also include audits of financial statements prepared in conformity with any of several other bases of accounting discussed in auditing standards issued by the American Institute of Certified Public Accountants (AICPA).

b. Financial related audits include determining whether (1) financial information is presented in accordance with established or stated criteria, (2) the entity has adhered to specific financial compliance requirements, or (3) the entity's internal control structure over financial reporting and/or safeguarding assets is suitably designed and implemented to achieve the control objectives.

2.5 Financial related audits may, for example, include audits of the following items:

a. Segments of financial statements; financial information (for example, statement of revenue and expenses, statement of cash receipts and disbursements, statement of fixed assets); budget requests; and variances between estimated and actual financial performance.

b. Internal controls over compliance with laws and regulations, such as those governing the (1) bidding for, (2) accounting for, and (3) reporting on grants and contracts (including proposals, amounts billed, amounts due on termination claims, and so forth).

c. Internal controls over financial reporting and/or safeguarding assets, including controls using computer-based systems.

d. Compliance with laws and regulations and allegations of fraud.

PERFORMANCE AUDITS

2.6 A performance audit is an objective and systematic examination of evidence for the purpose of providing an independent assessment of the performance of a government organization, program, activity, or function in order to provide information to improve public accountability and facilitate decision-making by parties with responsibility to oversee or initiate corrective action.

2.7 Performance audits include economy and efficiency and program audits.

a. Economy and efficiency audits include determining (1) whether the entity is acquiring, protecting, and using its resources (such as personnel, property, and space) economically and efficiently, (2) the causes of inefficiencies or uneconomical practices, and (3) whether the entity has complied with laws and regulations on matters of economy and efficiency.

b. Program audits include determining (1) the extent to which the desired results or benefits established by the legislature or other authorizing body are being achieved, (2) the effectiveness of organizations, programs, activities, or functions, and (3) whether the entity has complied with significant laws and regulations applicable to the program.

2.8 Economy and efficiency audits may, for example, consider whether the entity

a. is following sound procurement practices;

b. is acquiring the appropriate type, quality, and amount of resources at an appropriate cost;

c. is properly protecting and maintaining its resources;

d. is avoiding duplication of effort by employees and work that serves little or no purpose;

e. is avoiding idleness and overstaffing;

f. is using efficient operating procedures;

g. is using the optimum amount of resources (staff, equipment, and facilities) in producing or delivering the appropriate quantity and quality of goods or services in a timely manner;

h. is complying with requirements of laws and regulations that could significantly affect the acquisition, protection, and use of the entity's resources;

i. has an adequate management control system for measuring, reporting, and monitoring a program's economy and efficiency; and

j. has reported measures of economy and efficiency that are valid and reliable.

2.9 Program audits[2] may, for example

a. assess whether the objectives of a new, or ongoing program are proper, suitable, or relevant;

b. determine the extent to which a program achieves a desired level of program results;

c. assess the effectiveness of the program and/or of individual program components;

d. identify factors inhibiting satisfactory performance;

e. determine whether management has considered alternatives for carrying out the program that might yield desired results more effectively or at a lower cost;

f. determine whether the program complements, duplicates, overlaps, or conflicts with other related programs;

g. identify ways of making programs work better;

h. assess compliance with laws and regulations applicable to the program;

i. assess the adequacy of the management control system for measuring, reporting, and monitoring a program's effectiveness; and

j. determine whether management has reported measures of program effectiveness that are valid and reliable.

OTHER ACTIVITIES OF AN AUDIT ORGANIZATION

2.10 Auditors may perform services other than audits. For example, some auditors may

a. assist a legislative body by developing questions for use at hearings,

b. develop methods and approaches to be applied in evaluating a new or a proposed program,

c. forecast potential program outcomes under various assumptions without evaluating current operations, and

d. perform investigative work.

2.11 The head of the audit organization may wish to establish policies applying standards in this statement to its employees performing these and other types of nonaudit work.

GENERAL STANDARDS

(Chapter 3)

PURPOSE

3.1 This chapter prescribes general standards for conducting financial and performance audits. These general standards relate to the qualifications of the staff, the audit organization's and the individual auditor's independence, the exercise of due professional care in conducting the audit and in preparing related reports, and the presence of quality controls. General standards are distinct from those standards that relate to conducting field work and preparing related reports.

3.2 These general standards apply to all audit organizations, both government and nongovernment (for example, public accounting firms and consulting firms), conducting audits of government organizations, programs, activities, and functions and of government assistance received by nongovernment organizations.

QUALIFICATIONS

3.3 The first general standard is—

The staff assigned to conduct the audit should collectively possess adequate professional proficiency for the tasks required.

3.4 This standard places responsibility on the audit organization to ensure that each audit is conducted by staff who collectively have the knowledge and skills necessary for that audit. They should also have a thorough knowledge of government auditing and of the specific or unique environment in which the audited entity operates, relative to the nature of the audit being conducted.

3.5 The qualifications mentioned here apply to the knowledge and skills of the audit organization as a whole and not necessarily to each individual auditor. An organization may need to employ personnel or hire outside consultants knowledgeable in such areas as accounting, statistics, law, engineering, audit design and methodology, automated data processing, public administration, economics, social sciences, or actuarial science.

INDEPENDENCE

3.11 The second general standard is—

In all matters relating to the audit work, the audit organization and the individual auditors, whether government or public, should be free from personal and external impairments to independence, should be organizationally independent, and should maintain an independent attitude and appearance.

3.12 This standard places responsibility on each auditor and the audit organization to maintain independence so that opinions, conclusions, judgments, and recommendations will be impartial and will be viewed as impartial by knowledgeable third parties.

3.13 Auditors should consider not only whether they are independent and their attitudes and beliefs permit them to be independent but also whether there is anything about their situations that might lead others to question their independence. All situations deserve consideration because it is essential not only that auditors are, in fact, independent and impartial, but also that knowledgeable third parties consider them so.

3.14 Government auditors, including hired consultants and internal experts and specialists, need to consider three general classes of impairments to independence—personal, external, and organizational. If one or more of these impairments affects an auditor's ability to do the work and report findings impartially, that auditor should either decline to perform the audit, or in those situations where that auditor cannot decline to perform the audit, the impairment(s) should be reported in the scope section of the audit report. Also, when auditors are employees of the audited entity, that fact should be reflected in a prominent place in the audit report.

3.15 Nongovernment auditors also need to consider those personal and external impairments that might affect their ability to do their work and report their findings impartially. If their ability is adversely affected, they should decline to perform the audit. Public accountants should also follow the American Institute of Certified Public Accountants (AICPA) code of professional conduct, the code of professional conduct of the state board with jurisdiction over the practice of the public accountant and the audit organization, and the guidance on personal and external impairments in these standards.

Organizational Independence

3.18 Government auditors' independence can be affected by their place within the structure of the government entity to which they are assigned and also by whether they are auditing internally or auditing other entities.

Internal Auditors

3.19 A federal, state, or local government audit organization, or an audit organization within other government entities, such as a public college, university, or hospital, may be subject to administrative direction from persons involved in the government management process. To help achieve organizational independence, audit organizations should report the results of their audits and be accountable to the head or deputy head of the government entity and should be organizationally located outside the staff or line management function of the unit under audit. The audit organization's independence is enhanced when it also reports regularly to the entity's independent audit committee and/or the appropriate government oversight body.

3.20 Auditors should also be sufficiently removed from political pressures to ensure that they can conduct their audits objectively and can report their findings, opinions, and conclusions objectively without fear of political repercussion. Whenever feasible, they should be under a personnel system in which compensation, training, job tenure, and advancement are based on merit.

3.21 If the above conditions are met, and no personal or external impairments exist, the audit staff should be considered organizationally independent to audit internally and free to report objectively to top management.

3.22 When organizationally independent internal auditors conduct audits external to the government entity to which they are directly assigned, they may be considered independent of the audited entity and free to report objectively to the head or deputy head of the government entity to which assigned.

External Auditors

3.23 Government auditors employed by audit organizations whose heads are elected and legislative auditors auditing executive entities may be considered free of organizational impairments when auditing outside the government entity to which they are assigned.

3.24 Government auditors may be presumed to be independent of the audited entity, assuming no personal or external impairments exist, if the entity is

a. a level of government other than the one to which they are assigned (federal, state, or local) or

b. a different branch of government within the level of government to which they are assigned (legislative, executive, or judicial).

3.25 Government auditors may also be presumed to be independent, assuming no personal or external impairments exist, if the audit organization's head is

a. elected by the citizens of their jurisdiction,

b. elected or appointed by a legislative body of the level of government to which they are assigned and report the results of audits to, and are accountable to the legislative body, or

c. appointed by the chief executive but confirmed by, report the results of audits to, and are accountable to a legislative body of the level of government to which they are assigned.

DUE PROFESSIONAL CARE

3.26 The third general standard is—

Due professional care should be used in conducting the audit and in preparing related reports.

3.27 This standard requires auditors to work with due professional care. Due care imposes a responsibility upon each auditor within the audit organization to observe generally accepted government auditing standards.

QUALITY CONTROL

3.31 The fourth general standard is—

Each audit organization conducting audits in accordance with these standards should have an appropriate internal quality control system in place and undergo an external quality control review.

3.32 The internal quality control system established by the audit organization should provide reasonable assurance that it (1) has adopted, and is following, applicable auditing standards and (2) has established, and is following, adequate audit policies and procedures. The nature and extent of an organization's internal quality control system depend on a number of factors, such as its size, the degree of operating autonomy allowed its personnel and its audit offices, the nature of its work, its organizational structure, and appropriate cost-benefit considerations. Thus, the systems established by individual organizations will vary, as will the extent of their documentation.

3.33 Organizations conducting audits in accordance with these standards should have an external quality control review at least once every 3 years by an organization not affiliated with the organization being reviewed.[1] The external quality control review should determine whether the organization's internal quality control system is in place and operating effectively to provide reasonable assurance that established policies and procedures and applicable auditing standards are being followed.

REPORTING STANDARDS FOR FINANCIAL AUDITS

(Chapter 5)

PURPOSE

5.1 This chapter prescribes standards of reporting for financial audits, which include financial statement audits and financial related audits.

RELATION TO AICPA STANDARDS

5.2 For financial statement audits, generally accepted government auditing standards (GASAS) incorporate the American Institute of Certified Public Accountants' (AICPA) four generally accepted standards of reporting, which are:

a. The report shall state whether the financial statements are presented in accordance with generally accepted accounting principles.

b. The report shall identify those circumstances in which such principles have not been consistently observed in the current period in relation to the preceding period.

c. Informative disclosures in the financial statements are to be regarded as reasonably adequate unless otherwise stated in the report.

d. The report shall either contain an expression of opinion regarding the financial statements, taken as a whole, or an assertion to the effect that an opinion cannot be expressed. When an overall opinion cannot be expressed, the reasons therefor should be stated. In all cases where an auditor's name is associated with financial statements, the report should contain clear-cut indication of the character of the auditor's work, if any, and the degree of responsibility the auditor is taking.

5.3 The AICPA has issued statements on auditing standards (SAS) that interpret its standards of reporting.[1] This chapter incorporates these SASs and prescribes additional standards on:

a. communication with audit committees or other responsible individuals (see paragraphs 5.5 through 5.10),

b. reporting compliance with GAGAS (see paragraphs 5.11 through 5.14),

c. reporting on compliance with laws and regulations and on internal controls (see paragraphs 5.15 through 5.28),

d. privileged and confidential information (see paragraphs 5.29 through 5.31), and

e. report distribution. (See paragraphs 5.32 through 5.35.)

5.4 This chapter concludes by explaining which standards auditors should follow in reporting the results of financial related audits.

COMMUNICATION WITH AUDIT COMMITTEES OR OTHER RESPONSIBLE INDIVIDUALS

5.5 The first additional reporting standard for financial statement audits is—

Auditors should communicate certain information related to the conduct and reporting of the audit to the audit committee or to the individuals with whom they have contracted for the audit.

5.6 This standard applies in all situations where either the auditee has an audit committee or the audit is performed under contract. In other situations, auditors may still find it useful to communicate with management or other officials of the auditee.

5.7 Auditors should communicate the following information to the audit committee or to individuals with whom they contract to perform the audit:

a. the auditors' responsibilities in a financial statement audit, including their responsibilities for testing and reporting on internal controls and compliance with laws and regulations and

b. the nature of any additional testing of internal controls and compliance required by laws and regulations.

5.8 Auditors should use their professional judgment to determine the form and content of the communication. The communication may be oral or written. If the information is communicated orally, the auditors should document the communication in the working papers. Auditors may use an engagement letter to communicate the information described in paragraph 5.7. To help audit committees and other responsible parties understand the limitations of auditors' responsibilities for testing and reporting on internal controls and compliance, auditors should contrast those responsibilities with other financial related audits of controls and compliance. The discussion in paragraphs 5.9 and 5.10 may be helpful to auditors in preparing to explain those responsibilities.

5.9 Tests of internal controls and compliance with laws and regulations in a financial statement audit contribute to the evidence supporting the auditors' opinion on the financial statements. However, they do not provide a basis for opining on internal controls or compliance. The limited purpose of these tests in a financial statement audit may not meet the needs of some users of auditors' reports who require additional information on internal controls and on compliance with laws and regulations.

5.10 To meet certain audit report users' needs, laws and regulations often prescribe testing and reporting on internal controls and compliance to supplement the financial statement audit's coverage of these areas.[2] Nevertheless, even after auditors perform, and report the results of, additional tests of internal controls and compliance required by laws and regulations, some reasonable needs of report users still may be unmet. Auditors may meet these needs by performing further tests of internal controls and compliance with laws and regulations in either of two ways:

a. supplemental (or agreed-upon) procedures or
b. examination, resulting in an opinion.

REPORTING COMPLIANCE WITH GENERALLY ACCEPTED GOVERNMENT AUDITING STANDARDS

5.11 The second additional reporting standard for financial statement audits is—

Audit reports should state that the audit was made in accordance with generally accepted government auditing standards.

5.12 The above statement refers to all the applicable standards that the auditors should have followed during their audit. The statement should be qualified in situations where the auditors did not follow an applicable standard. In these situations, the auditors should disclose the applicable standard that was not followed, the reasons therefor, and how not following the standard affected the results of the audit.

5.13 When the report on the financial statements is submitted to comply with a legal, regulatory, or contractual requirement for a GAGAS audit, it should specifically cite GAGAS. The report on the financial statements may cite AICPA standards as well as GAGAS.

5.14 The auditee may need a financial statement audit for purposes other than to comply with requirements calling for a GAGAS audit. For example, it may need a financial statement audit to issue bonds. GAGAS do not prohibit auditors from issuing a separate report on the financial statements conforming only to the requirements of AICPA standards. However, it may be advantageous to use a report issued in accordance with GAGAS for these other purposes because it provides information on compliance with laws and regulations and internal controls (as discussed below) that is not contained in a report issued in accordance with AICPA standards.

REPORTING ON COMPLIANCE WITH LAWS AND REGULATIONS AND ON INTERNAL CONTROLS

5.15 The third additional reporting standard for financial statement audits is—

The report on the financial statements should either (1) describe the scope of the auditors' testing of compliance with laws and regulations and internal controls and present the results of those tests or (2) refer to separate reports containing that information. In presenting the results of those tests, auditors should report irregularities, illegal acts, other material noncompliance, and reportable conditions in internal controls.[3] In some circumstances, auditors should report irregularities and illegal acts directly to parties external to the audited entity.

5.16 Auditors may report on compliance with laws and regulations and internal controls in the report on the financial statements or in separate reports. When auditors report on compliance and controls in the report on the financial statements, they should include an introduction summarizing key findings in the audit of the financial statements and the related compliance and internal controls work. Auditors should not issue this introduction as a stand-alone report. When auditors report separately on compliance and controls, the report on the financial statements should state that they are issuing those additional reports.

Scope of Compliance and Internal Controls Work

5.17 Auditors should report the scope of their testing of compliance with laws and regulations and of internal controls. If the tests they performed did not exceed those the auditors considered necessary for a financial statement audit, then a statement that the auditors tested compliance with certain laws and regulations, obtained an understanding of internal controls, and assessed control risk would be sufficient to satisfy this requirement. Auditors should also report whether or not the tests they performed provided sufficient evidence to support an opinion on compliance or internal controls.

Irregularities, Illegal Acts, and Other Noncompliance

5.18 When auditors conclude, based on evidence obtained, that an irregularity or illegal act either has occurred or is likely to have occurred,[4] they should report relevant information. Auditors need not report information about an irregularity or illegal act that is clearly inconsequential. Thus, auditors should present in a report the same irregularities and illegal acts that they report to audit committees under AICPA standards. Auditors should also report other noncompliance (for example, a violation of a contract provision) that is material to the financial statements.

5.19 In reporting material irregularities, illegal acts, or other noncompliance, the auditors should place their findings in proper perspective. To give the reader a basis for judging the prevalence and consequences of these conditions, the instances identified should be related to the universe or the number of cases examined and be quantified in terms of dollar value, if appropriate.[5] In presenting material irregularities, illegal acts, or other noncompliance, auditors should follow chapter 7's report contents standards [not included here] for objectives, scope, and methodology; audit results; views of responsible officials; and its report presentation standards, as appropriate. Auditors may provide less extensive disclosure of irregularities and illegal acts that are not material in either a quantitative or qualitative sense.[6]

5.20 When auditors detect irregularities, illegal acts, or other noncompliance that do not meet paragraph 5.18's criteria for reporting, they should communicate those findings to the auditee, preferably in writing. If auditors have communicated those findings in a management letter to top management, they should refer to that management letter when they report on compliance. Auditors should document in their working papers all communications to the auditee about irregularities, illegal acts, and other noncompliance.

Direct Reporting of Irregularities and Illegal Acts

5.21 GAGAS require auditors to report irregularities or illegal acts directly to parties outside the auditee in two circumstances, as discussed below. These requirements are in addition to any legal requirements for direct reporting of irregularities or illegal acts. Auditors should meet these requirements even if they have resigned or been dismissed from the audit.[7]

5.22 The auditee may be required by law or regulation to report certain irregularities or illegal acts to specified external parties (for example, to a federal inspector general or a state attorney general). If auditors have communicated such irregularities or illegal acts to the auditee, and it fails to report them, then the auditors should communicate their awareness of that failure to the auditee's governing body. If the auditee does not make the required report as soon as practicable after the auditors' communication with its governing body, then the auditors should report the irregularities or illegal acts directly to the external party specified in the law or regulation.

5.23 Management is responsible for taking timely and appropriate steps to remedy irregularities or illegal acts that auditors report to it. When an irregularity or illegal act involves assistance received directly or indirectly from a government agency, auditors may have a duty to report it directly if management fails to take remedial steps. If auditors conclude that such failure is likely to cause them to depart from the standard report on the financial statements or resign from the audit, then they should communicate that conclusion to the auditee's governing body. Then, if the auditee does not report the irregularity or illegal act as soon as practicable to the entity that provided the government assistance, the auditors should report the irregularity or illegal act directly to that entity.

5.24 In both of these situations, auditors should obtain sufficient, competent, and relevant evidence (for example, by confirmation with outside parties) to corroborate assertions by management that it has reported irregularities or illegal acts. If they are unable to do so, then the auditors should report the irregularities or illegal acts directly as discussed above.

Deficiencies in Internal Controls

5.26 Auditors should report deficiencies in internal controls that they consider to be "reportable conditions" as defined in AICPA standards. The following are examples of matters that may be reportable conditions:

    a. absence of appropriate segregation of duties consistent with appropriate control objectives;

    b. absence of appropriate reviews and approvals of transactions, accounting entries, or systems output;

    c. inadequate provisions for the safeguarding of assets;

    d. evidence of failure to safeguard assets from loss, damage, or misappropriation;

    e. evidence that a system fails to provide complete and accurate output consistent with the auditee's control objectives because of the misapplication of control procedures;

    f. evidence of intentional override of internal controls by those in authority to the detriment of the overall objectives of the system;

    g. evidence of failure to perform tasks that are part of internal controls, such as reconciliations not prepared or not timely prepared;

    h. absence of a sufficient level of control consciousness within the organization;

    i. significant deficiencies in the design or operation of internal controls that could result in violations of laws and regulations having a direct and material effect on the financial statements; and

    j. failure to follow up and correct previously identified deficiencies in internal controls.[8]

5.27 In reporting reportable conditions, auditors should identify those that are individually or cumulatively material weaknesses.[9] Auditors should follow chapter 7's [not reprinted here] report contents standards for objectives, scope, and methodology; audit results; and views of responsible officials; and its report presentation standards, as appropriate.

5.28 When auditors detect deficiencies in internal controls that are not reportable conditions, they should communicate those deficiencies to the auditee, preferably in writing. If the auditors have communicated other deficiencies in internal controls in a management letter to top management, they should refer to that management letter when they report on controls. All communications to the auditee about deficiencies in internal controls should be documented in the working papers.

PRIVILEGED AND CONFIDENTIAL INFORMATION

5.29 The fourth additional reporting standard for financial statement audits is—

If certain information is prohibited from general disclosure, the audit report should state the nature of the information omitted and the requirement that makes the omission necessary.

5.30 Certain information may be prohibited from general disclosure by federal, state, or local laws or regulations. Such information may be provided on a need-to-know basis only to persons authorized by law or regulation to receive it.

5.31 If such requirements prohibit auditors from including pertinent data in the report, they should state the nature of the information omitted and the requirement that makes the omission necessary. The auditors should obtain assurance that a valid requirement for the omission exists and, when appropriate, consult with legal counsel.

REPORT DISTRIBUTION

5.32 The fifth additional reporting standard for financial statement audits is—

Written audit reports are to be submitted by the audit organization to the appropriate officials of the auditee and to the appropriate officials of the organizations requiring or arranging for the audits, including external funding organizations, unless legal restrictions prevent it. Copies of the reports should also be sent to other officials who have legal oversight authority or who may be responsible for acting on audit findings and recommendations and to others authorized to receive such reports. Unless restricted by law or regulation, copies should be made available for public inspection.[10]

5.33 Audit reports should be distributed in a timely manner to officials interested in the results. Such officials include those designated by law or regulation to receive such reports, those responsible for acting on the findings and recommendations, those of other levels of government that have provided assistance to the auditee, and legislators. However, if the subject of the audit involves material that is classified for security purposes or not releasable to particular parties or the public for other valid reasons, auditors may limit the report distribution.

5.34 When public accountants are engaged, the engaging organization should ensure that the report is distributed appropriately. If the public accountants are to make the distribution, the engagement agreement should indicate what officials or organizations should receive the report.

5.35 Internal auditors should follow their entity's own arrangements and statutory requirements for distribution. Usually, they report to their entity's top managers, who are responsible for distribution of the report.

Notes

Chapter 1

1. The Single Audit Act of 1984 (31 U.S.C. 7501-7507).
2. OMB Circular A-133, "Audits of Institutions of Higher Education and Other Nonprofit Institutions."
3. *Codification of the Standards for the Professional Practice of Internal Auditing*, The Institute of Internal Auditors, Inc., copyright 1993; and *New Directions for Program Evaluation: Standards for Evaluation Practice*, no. 15 (San Francisco: Jossey-Bass, September 1982.
4. The Single Audit Act (31 U.S.C. 7502(f)) requires that the report on single audits be made available for public inspection.
5. See *How to Avoid a Substandard Audit: Suggestions for Procuring an Audit*, National Intergovernmental Audit Forum, May 1988.

Chapter 2

1. Three authoritative bodies for generally accepted accounting principles are the Governmental Accounting Standards Board (GASB), the Financial Accounting Standards Board (FASB), and the sponsors of the Federal Accounting Standards Advisory Board (FASAB). GASB establishes accounting principles and financial reporting standards for state and local government entities. FASB establishes accounting principles and financial reporting standards for nongovernment entities. The sponsors of FASAB—the Secretary of the Treasury, the Director of the Office of Management and Budget, and the Comptroller General—jointly establish accounting principles and financial reporting standards for the federal government, based on recommendations from FASAB.
2. These audits may apply to services, activities, and functions as well as programs.

Chapter 3

1. Audit organizations should have an external quality control review completed (that is, report issued) within 3 years from the date they start their first audit in accordance with these standards. Subsequent external quality control reviews should be completed within 3 years after the issuance of the prior review.

Chapter 5

1. GAGAS incorporate any new AICPA standards relevant to financial statement audits unless the General Accounting Office (GAO) excludes them by formal announcement.
2. For example, when auditing state and local government entities that receive federal financial assistance, auditors should be familiar with the Single Audit Act of 1984 and Office of Management and Budget (OMB) Circular A-128. The act and circular include specific audit requirements, mainly in the areas of internal controls and compliance with laws and regulations, that exceed the minimum audit requirements in the standards in chapters 4 and 5 of this document. Audits of nonprofit organizations under OMB Circular A-133 and audits conducted under the Chief Financial Officers Act of 1990 also have specific audit requirements in the areas of internal controls and compliance. Many state and local governments have similar requirements.
3. These responsibilities are in addition to and do not modify auditors' responsibilities under AICPA standards to (1) address the effect irregularities or illegal acts may have on the report on the financial statements and (2) determine that the audit committee or others with equivalent authority and responsibility are adequately informed about irregularities, illegal acts, and reportable conditions.
4. Whether a particular act is, in fact, illegal may have to await final determination by a court of law. Thus, when auditors disclose matters that have led them to conclude that an illegal act is likely to have occurred, they should take care not to imply that they have made a determination of illegality.
5. Audit findings have often been regarded as containing the elements of criteria, condition, and effect, plus cause when problems are found. However, the elements needed for a finding depend entirely on the objectives of the audit. Reportable conditions and noncompliance found by the auditor may not always have all of these elements fully developed, given the scope and objectives of the specific financial audit. However, auditors should identify at least the condition, criteria, and possible asserted effect to provide sufficient information to federal, state, and local officials to permit them to determine the effect and cause in order to take prompt and proper corrective action.
6. Chapter 4 provides guidance on factors that may influence auditors' materiality judgments in audits of government entities or entities receiving government assistance. AICPA

standards provide guidance on the interaction of quantitative and qualitative considerations in materiality judgments.
7. Internal auditors auditing within the entity that employs them do not have a duty to report outside that entity.
8. Chapter 4's audit follow-up standard requires auditors to report the status of uncorrected material findings and recommendations from prior audits that affect the financial statement audit.
9. See footnote 5.
10. See the Single Audit Act of 1984 and OMB Circular A-128 for the distribution of reports on single audits of state and local governments.

The Municipal Audit: Choice and Opportunity

WHAT IS THE PURPOSE OF MUNICIPAL AUDITS?

Municipal audits are a valuable management tool in evaluating the performance of cities and towns. If municipal officials are to use this tool to maximum advantage, however, they must understand what audits are and must participate actively in the process. The purpose of this [article] is to help municipal officials understand auditing and the audit process so they may effectively use independent audits to the maximum advantage of the community and its citizens.

The [article] also aims to help local officials plan and organize the auditor selection process. An audit can only yield its maximum benefits if the municipality's non-financial officials, both elected and appointed, are involved in and understand the audit process, and are not inhibited from asking important questions. This [discussion] is designed to enhance their understanding.

WHAT IS AN AUDIT?

An audit is an examination—of systems, procedures, programs, and financial data. The product, or result, of an audit is a report; the most common example of

---

Reprinted from "Summary of the Audit Process," in *The Municipal Audit: Choice and Opportunity,* prepared jointly by the accounting firm of Coopers & Lybrand and the Massachusetts Department of Community Affairs, Office of Local Assistance. By permission of the Massachusetts Executive Office of Communities and Development.

which is the report rendered by an independent auditor of how appropriately an organization's financial statements depict its financial condition and results of its operations. To be able to render a report in which the public, investors, local officials and other users may be confident, the auditor must gain a full understanding of the municipality being examined. An *independent* audit is one performed by persons not affiliated with the organization being audited—the relevant example here being the independent, or "outside," auditor engaged to audit a municipality's financial statements.

WHY IS AN AUDIT REQUIRED?

In this era, there is increased scrutiny of all levels of government spending. Citizens are demanding better explanations of how government spends tax money. Audit requirements are increasing for all levels of government. One example is federal revenue sharing regulations, which require every recipient of $25,000 or more of revenue sharing funds to have an independent audit of its annual financial statements (including *all* funds) at least once every three years....

WHO MAY PERFORM FINANCIAL AUDITS?

Financial audits may be performed by certified public accountants [or others as provided by state or local laws].... Compliance audits for federal revenue sharing purposes must conform to the formally established professional standards known as *Generally Accepted Auditing Standards.*

WHY SHOULDN'T MUNICIPAL FINANCIAL OFFICIALS SELECT AUDITORS?

The audit focuses on the municipality's financial systems, and so is necessarily an evaluation of those responsible for the systems' operation. This includes not only the financial officials but all the municipality's departments, because they are all engaged in financial activities. To date, the selection of auditors has often been delegated to financial officials (collectors, treasurers, auditors, and accountants).

WHY SHOULD ELECTED OFFICIALS GET INVOLVED IN THE AUDIT PROCESS?

Elected officials should get involved in the audit process because their involvement significantly benefits them and their communities. Governing a municipality requires management of its financial affairs; and so it is vital that municipal decisionmakers participate in the audit process, which is a key ingredient in overall management. This involvement is important because:

1. The municipality's financial operations and internal controls may be substantially improved as a result of an audit, since auditors are required to report in writing any significant control weaknesses they find, and would normally make recommendations for needed improvements—particularly if their attention is directed to areas of concern by municipal officials at the outset.

2. Precisely because the public's demand for understandable financial information is growing, it is highly desirable—for both the public *and* municipal officials—that this information is supported by the credibility of the professional opinion of an independent auditor intelligently chosen.

3. By participating in the audit process and gaining insight into the financial operations of the municipality, the municipal officials render an important public service, and enhance their ability—and visibility—as public servants.

Financial auditing is an evaluative process performed in accordance with well-developed professional standards. To accomplish an audit, trained auditors must obtain a thorough understanding of the municipality's operations. This in-depth, objective evaluation may result in positive recommendations for revenue increases and expenditure reductions which may save the municipality substantial sums. For example, as a result of audits, Massachusetts municipalities have achieved significant savings from recommendations for improved cash management, centralized purchasing and reductions in fringe benefit costs.

Any in-depth evaluation of a municipality's activities has political implications. For example, if an independent auditor concluded that the municipality's financial records were in such disarray that they could not be audited, people might question what had been happening to public funds over the years, and be concerned with a possible loss in federal or state aid. Even a benefit such as the savings mentioned previously may have political implications because the public might then ask why financial officials hadn't saved money on their own.

Public officials who do not involve themselves in this process will miss an opportunity to gain additional insight into their government's operations and to effect constructive change.

The selection of an auditor can be a challenge. Auditors' capabilities vary, and their differences can be important to the municipality and its officials. As municipal officials who have involved themselves in the selection process have discovered, perceiving these distinctions may be difficult. However, if the municipality is going to realize the maximum benefit of the audit, they must be perceived and evaluated in terms of the municipality's needs.

WHO SHOULD SELECT THE AUDITORS?

It is recommended that the auditors be selected by an audit committee of elected officials who have overall responsibility to the public for the departments to be audited. In addition, it is advisable to include ...the chief administrative officer and informed citizens as well.

The audit committee should seek the advice of anyone it believes can help—particularly individuals knowledgeable about audits and auditors.

WHAT'S INVOLVED IN DETERMINING THE MUNICIPALITY'S AUDIT NEEDS?

Once the committee has been established, it should determine the municipality's particular needs. The needs may include the financial and compliance audit for revenue sharing requirements, any other grant programs which require financial and compliance audits and any specific evaluations the municipality may require.

The committee should also consider other factors in assessing their municipality's needs such as:

- The need for accounting and financial advice.
- The adequacy of controls exercised by the municipality's computer service bureau.
- The need for technical assistance in planning computer applications.

HOW SPECIFIC SHOULD THE REQUEST FOR PROPOSAL BE?

All too often, proposal requests include terms calling for "operational," "performance," "economy or efficiency" audits or combinations of them. If such requests are made, they must specifically identify the types of audits sought and the areas they will cover. Otherwise, the proposing auditors' responses to these requests may be general or lack comparability, thus making it difficult to evaluate them. If the municipality cannot define its requirements for such specialized audits, it may be best not to include them in the initial request for proposal, but rather to discuss the potential for these types of audits with the auditors after they have completed the initial financial and compliance audit and issued their report of comments and recommendations.

SHOULD THE COMMITTEE ESTABLISH SELECTION CRITERIA?

Once the committee has determined the audit requirements, it should determine the procedures it will follow in soliciting and evaluating the proposals. Comprehensive definitive selection criteria should be established, and their relative importance assigned by the committee. The criteria are:

- Skill, experience and the amount of time of the specific persons committed to perform the services requested.
- Auditor's demonstrated understanding of the municipality's requirements and plan for meeting them.
- Prior experience and reputation of the auditor in auditing municipalities.
- Price.

Once the municipality's needs—commonly called the scope of the examination—and the selection criteria have been established, the committee should then write its request for proposal and send it to prospective auditors. The proposing auditors' written proposals, oral presentations and references should be judged against the criteria. Checking references is particularly important.

Each committee member's evaluation of the prospective auditors will necessarily be subjective. This should not be of concern. Once the selection has been made, the reasons should be documented and communicated to the appropriate municipal body that has the legal authority to authorize the contract. All the auditors that proposed should be notified who has been selected and the reasons for the selection.

SHOULD THE COMMITTEE CONTINUE TO BE INVOLVED AFTER AN AUDITOR HAS BEEN SELECTED?

Once the selection has been made, the audit committee should stay involved. It should oversee the preparation and signing of the contract or other agreement, and it should review drafts of the audit reports prior to issuance. A member of the committee or its representative should be designated to maintain day-to-day liaison with the auditors. If the audit is not properly planned and coordinated, it may disrupt the municipality's operations and its benefits will not be realized. At the conclusion of the audit, the committee should determine if another audit should be performed, if so, what type, when, and who should perform it (the current auditor or one newly selected by starting the process outlined here again).

WHAT WILL THE AUDITOR EXPECT?

Generally, auditors will expect the following unless stipulated otherwise:

- An organized, timely and well-documented closing of the municipality's books, including

- adequate supporting documentation and reconciliations of accounts.
- Clerical assistance in typing requests for confirmation and obtaining documents from the files.
- Availability of key personnel to obtain an understanding of the municipality's operations and systems.
- Professional treatment of their staff.
- Adequate working conditions.

WHAT SHOULD THE MUNICIPALITY REASONABLY EXPECT OF THE AUDITORS?

The municipality should expect the following from its auditors (whose ability to fulfill these expectations should have been established by the selection process):

- They should communicate what they are going to do and what they have done.
- The individuals involved in the audit should be trained and well-supervised.
- They should plan the timing of the audit procedures to minimize any disruption of the municipality's activities and ensure timely completion of the audit.
- They should immediately communicate any problems they encounter. (The audit committee would be an appropriate recipient of such communications.)
- They should issue a report of comments and recommendations in which weaknesses in financial controls and opportunities to reduce costs and enhance revenues are identified, and suggestions for improvements are made.

The atmosphere in which the audit is conducted should be positive. This is possible only if the auditors and municipal officials fully understand one another's expectations and communicate often and freely.

SHOULD WE HAVE AN AUDIT EVERY YEAR?

Because of its benefits, many municipalities which have had an audit [not required by law] intend to continue the audit process on an annual basis. Some of the benefits cited are:

- Auditors' recommendations to improve financial systems have resulted in significant savings through revenue increases and expenditure reductions.
- Recommendations for improvements from an objective, independent auditor are easier to sell and implement.
- The independent audit is a way of evaluating the performance of key elected and appointed public officials.
- The auditor is a resource which may be used throughout the year to provide advice and help you solve problems.
- An audit and the presentation of financial statements with an auditor's report enhances the municipality's credibility in the investment community. It may increase the number of bidders for municipal securities and affect the interest rates which must be paid.

53 Local Government Accountability and the Need for Audit Follow-Up

Richard C. Brooks and David B. Pariser

INTRODUCTION

Greater attention is being directed toward improving accountability at all levels of government. At the local level, accountability has become increasingly important as dwindling federal and state funds force local governments to pay for more of the services they provide. Citizens—who pay the taxes and user fees for these services—hold local government officials accountable for the spending of public monies.

Accountability encompasses the notion that public officials and employees must account for all of their activities taken on behalf of the citizenry. According to the Governmental Accounting Standards Board (GASB), accountability is the cornerstone of *all* governmental financial reporting.[1] The concept of accountability also plays an important role in governmental auditing. The *U.S. Government Auditing Standards* (commonly called the *Yellow Book*) defines the scope of accountability as follows:

> The need for accountability has caused a demand for more information about government programs and services. Public officials, legislators, and citizens want and need to know whether government funds are handled properly and in compliance with laws and regulations. They also want and need to know whether government organizations, programs, and services are achieving their purposes and whether these organizations, programs, and services are operating economically and efficiently.[2]

The requirement of accountability in financial reporting brings into sharper focus the role of auditing in local government financial management and thus the need for local governments to follow up on audit recommendations. As an appraisal function, auditing provides to the public an independent opinion regarding the extent to which local government officials carry out their responsibilities in accordance with applicable laws and regulations. The *Yellow Book* requires auditors to communicate their findings to management and to provide recommendations that may improve government operations and programs. In addition to rendering an opinion on the financial statements, auditors also provide a "management letter" to local government officials. In the management letter, auditors communicate recommendations regarding operational issues such as the protection, use, and disposal of fixed assets; internal accounting and administrative controls; organizational arrangements; bonding and insurance practices; cash management; and other matters learned during the audit.[3] Hence, the management letter is the vehicle used to communicate audit recommendations to local government officials.

The real benefit of audit recommendations comes from the implementation of recommendations that lead to improvements in government operations. Consequently, a process for ensuring the implementation of audit recommendations is essential. The Single Audit Act of 1984 requires independent auditors to

---

Richard C. Brooks is assistant professor of accounting and David B. Pariser, professor of accounting, College of Business and Economics, West Virginia University.

describe the status of unresolved recommendations included in prior audit reports.[4] In addition, the *Yellow Book* requires auditors to follow up on findings and recommendations made in previous audits to determine whether government officials have taken prompt and appropriate corrective actions.

Local government managers are ultimately responsible for implementing audit recommendations. To properly carry out this responsibility, managers must have a system to monitor the status of audit recommendation implementation. When such a system is not in place, it is not uncommon for auditors to make the same recommendations year after year because the government entity has failed to implement the recommendations. Also, the lack of an audit follow-up system makes it difficult to measure the impact of audit recommendations.

A discussion of audit follow-up is presented here in five sections. The first addresses the need for audit recommendation follow-up. The second discusses how audit recommendation follow-up can improve accountability in local government operations. The characteristics of an audit recommendation follow-up system are presented in the third section; a model of such a system makes up the fourth. The article concludes with a brief summary.

THE NEED FOR AUDIT RECOMMENDATION FOLLOW-UP

Following up on audit recommendations is vital to local governments subject to the requirements of the Single Audit Act. This law requires all governmental entities receiving more than $100,000 in federal financial assistance to have an audit of their general-purpose financial statements and all federally funded programs. The Single Audit Act also requires local government officials to take prompt corrective action on all instances of material noncompliance with applicable laws and regulations that govern federal financial assistance.

In the event that a material noncompliance occurs, the Single Audit Act requires local government officials to submit to the appropriate federal agencies a corrective action plan or a statement explaining why corrective action is not necessary. Local government entities that fail to comply with the provisions of the Single Audit Act risk having their federal financial assistance reduced or suspended.

Recommendations arise not only from financial statement audits; they can evolve from performance audits and compliance audits as well. A performance audit assesses the effectiveness and efficiency of government procedures and programs. Compliance audits determine whether a governmental entity is complying with applicable laws and regulations.

Performance Audits. Performance audit recommendations attempt to improve the management of government operations and make government programs run more effectively and efficiently. Following up on performance audit recommendations enables the entity to measure the impact of these audits on government operations and programs. In addition, follow-up enables various oversight bodies such as federal and state funding agencies and city councils to be aware of the status of performance audit recommendations made to a particular government entity. The state of Florida, for example, requires each agency head to provide a status report regarding performance audit recommendations to the Legislative Auditing Committee within six months of the audit report.[5] Audit recommendation follow-up procedures established for state agencies can provide guidance to local governments interested in establishing a system designed to follow up on performance audit recommendations.

Compliance Audits. Compliance audit recommendations suggest ways that governmental entities can achieve compliance with laws and regulations. By following up on compliance audit recommendations, an entity demonstrates that it has taken corrective action to resolve such recommendations. Several states have laws that require following up on compliance audit recommendations. For example, Tennessee requires the administrative head of each agency to file an action report describing the actions taken on each compliance audit recommendation.[6] Again, local governments can establish requirements similar to those employed at the state level to ensure the implementation of compliance audit recommendations.

IMPROVING ACCOUNTABILITY IN LOCAL GOVERNMENT THROUGH AUDIT FOLLOW-UP

Local government managers and city councils can enhance accountability by using audit recommendation follow-up. Three potential uses of such follow-up are

- monitoring the status of audit recommendations,
- determining budget appropriations, and
- monitoring compliance with laws and regulations.

Monitoring Recommendations. Monitoring the status of audit recommendations is an important aspect of accountability. Because taxpayers pay for audits through their taxes, they expect local government officials to implement recommendations made as a result of governmental audits or to explain why corrective actions are not necessary. An audit recommendation follow-up system enables management to report on the status of audit recommendations to various constituencies, including federal and state oversight bodies, members of the city council, and taxpayers.

Budgeting. The purpose of governmental auditing is to improve programs and operations, provide better service to the public, and save tax dollars.[7] Audit recommendations are the means to these ends, and their follow-up can play a valuable role in the budgeting process. For example, budget committees might require evidence that prior audit recommendations have been implemented before approving a department's budget request.

Monitoring Compliance. The Single Audit Act of 1984 requires auditors to report on compliance with laws and regulations materially affecting major federal assistance programs. The Single Audit Act also requires local governments to resolve audit recommendations within six months of the audit report date.[8] Audit follow-up allows local governments to monitor and report their progress as they take corrective actions designed to bring them into compliance with laws and regulations.

CHARACTERISTICS OF AN AUDIT RECOMMENDATION FOLLOW-UP SYSTEM

A follow-up system can help local governments achieve the benefits of audit recommendations. To be effective, this system will be characterized by a number of actions:

- evaluation of recommendations including budgetary and organizational impact
- special attention to key recommendations
- preparation of corrective action plans
- periodic review to evaluate the adequacy of actions taken on recommendations
- preparation and distribution of periodic status reports

Management must evaluate each recommendation in terms of its potential impact on budgetary resources and the operation of the affected department. An evaluation should also consider whether the potential benefits of a recommendation exceed the cost of implementing and maintaining the recommended procedure. Audit recommendations requiring a substantial increase in resources should be reported to the appropriate oversight committees. In the event that adequate funding is unavailable, the manager of the affected department and the appropriate oversight committees can explore alternative methods for achieving the same goals.

All recommendations should provide a clear and obvious benefit upon implementation. However, certain "key" recommendations require special attention because of their potential impact. These include recommendations that could (1) prevent the loss of significant amounts of money, (2) prevent the loss of life, (3) prevent substantial bodily injury, or (4) prevent environmental damage.[9] An audit recommendation follow-up system should call attention to key audit recommendations. Furthermore, governmental entities should aggressively pursue the implementation of all key audit recommendations.

Corrective action plans outline the specific steps necessary to implement an audit recommendation. Such plans are essential because they facilitate follow-up and oversight activities. City managers, city councils, oversight bodies, and auditors can use corrective action plans to monitor the progress of a department during the implementation of audit recommendations. A department failing to implement a recommendation according to a corrective action plan may forego cost savings. This savings loss may be considered during budget hearings as the budget committee reviews a department's funding request.

Several states have laws governing the preparation and dissemination of corrective action plans. For example, Nevada requires executive agencies to submit a corrective action plan to the director of the Department of Administration within 60 days of an audit report. The director must then submit a report to the legislative auditor specifying the status of audit recommendations within six months of the corrective action plan. The legislative auditor then reviews the report submitted by the director and presents a summary to the legislative audit committee.[10]

A periodic review of actions taken on each recommendation is an essential part of a follow-up system, because such a review makes it possible to assess the status of each recommendation. A review might categorize the status of each recommendation as either fully implemented, partially implemented, or not yet implemented. A review might highlight the fact that a recommendation appeared in several previous audit reports. Additional information might include, for example, a note explaining that a recommendation is no longer applicable because of a change in circumstances or a change in public policy.

Finally, periodic status reports should be prepared and distributed to the appropriate local government officials and oversight committees. According to the *Miller Single Audit Guide*, the minimum level of documentation for following up on audit recommendations should include a spreadsheet or other document listing recommendations made, corrective actions taken, the date those corrective actions were taken, and the auditor's comments regarding the appropriateness of the actions taken.[11] Exhibit 1 provides a format that can effectively convey the status of individual audit recommendations. Exhibit 2 presents a form that can serve as an executive summary of the status of all outstanding recommendations. Potential uses of periodic status reports include budget oversight, program review, management evaluation, single audit planning, compliance monitoring, and performance audit planning.

A MODEL AUDIT RECOMMENDATION FOLLOW-UP SYSTEM FOR LOCAL GOVERNMENT

This section presents a three-phase audit recommendation follow-up system that can be used effectively at the local government level. It is an adaptation of

Exhibit 1: *Audit Recommendation Status Report*

Recommendation No.: _____ Date of Recommendation: _____

Recommendation Made by: _____

Recommendation:
_____
_____
_____

Corrective Actions Taken (include date of each corrective action):
_____
_____
_____

Auditor Comments on Appropriateness of Actions Taken:
_____
_____
_____

Exhibit 2: *Executive Summary of Audit Recommendation Status*

Recommendation Number	Recommendation Date	Corrective Action Date	Auditor Sign-Off
_____	_____	_____	_____
_____	_____	_____	_____
_____	_____	_____	_____
_____	_____	_____	_____

the follow-up system used in the state of Nevada, where the Nevada Revised Statutes require the state to follow up on audit recommendations made by the legislative auditor.[12] Although adaptable to both city and county governments, this model refers to a *city* audit follow-up.

Conceptual Overview. Local governments are audited by independent auditors. These independent auditors prepare written audit reports that often include recommendations to improve the efficiency and effectiveness of government operations. Local governments are governed by a city council or commission composed of representatives from the community. Independent auditors report their findings to the council or commission, director of finance, and the head of the audited department. The director of finance, with the cooperation of the head of the audited department, follows up on the implementation of the independent auditor's recommendations. Exhibit 3 summarizes the model audit recommendation follow-up system described in this section.

Reporting the Results of Audit Work. Upon completion of an audit, the auditor submits a preliminary draft report to the director of finance and head of the audited department. The preliminary draft addresses findings and recommendations of the current audit and assesses the actions taken on findings and recommendations made in prior audits. The auditor determines if management has corrected the conditions causing prior audit findings and implemented prior audit recommendations. Before a final audit report is issued, the auditor meets with the director of finance and head of the audited department for an exit conference. The exit conference provides the finance director and the audited department an opportunity to comment on the auditor's findings and recommendations. These comments may be reflected in the final audit report.

The department and the finance director then typically has a set time frame (such as 10 or 30 days) in which to respond to the preliminary audit report in writing. The response should indicate their assessment of each recommendation. Recommendations may be assessed as (1) acceptable with implementation forthcoming, (2) acceptable with implementation deferred, (3) rejected with no plans of implementation in the foreseeable future, or (4) deferred until proper statutory changes are made. The auditor may include the responses in the final audit report. In the event that they reject a recommendation, intend to defer implementation, or suggest that a statutory change is required before implementation is possible, the auditor may make a comment in the final audit report. The auditor then submits the final audit report to the city council, the director of finance, and the head of the audited department.

Implementing Audit Recommendations. After the director of finance and the city council receive the final audit report, the audited department develops a corrective action plan within a specified time frame (e.g., 60 days from the date of the audit report). The corrective action plan is then submitted to the director of finance, the city council, and the auditor. The finance director reviews the corrective action plan to assess its impact on program administration and budgets. If a department fails to develop and submit a corrective action plan within the prescribed time limit, the director of finance may withhold funding from the department. The city council reviews the corrective action plan and may conduct oversight hearings. The auditor reviews the corrective action plan to determine if it meets the intent of the recommendation.

Reviewing Implementing Actions. After the audited department submits a corrective action plan, the director of finance assesses the implementation status of each audit recommendation. The director of finance bases this assessment on inquiries and examination of written procedures as well as other means. The director then submits a report within a specified time frame (e.g., six months after submission of the corrective action plan) to the city council and the auditor, detailing the implementation status of audit recommendations.

City councilmembers review the implementation status report. The city council may request additional information regarding outstanding recommendations. For key audit recommendations, the city council may request the department to report on the progress of implementation on a periodic basis. During subsequent audits, the auditor should verify the implementation status of recommendations made in the prior audit. This completes the cycle of audit follow-up activities.

SUMMARY

This article has discussed the need for audit follow-up, explained how audit follow-up can enhance local government accountability, presented the characteristics of an effective follow-up system, and described a model for local government audit recommendation follow-up systems. The need for audit follow-up stems primarily from federal and state laws that require governmental entities to establish systems and procedures to monitor the status of audit recommendations. Audit follow-up provides a tool with which to measure the impact of audit recommendations on government operations and programs.

Audit recommendation follow-up is an integral part of governmental accountability. Citizens—as taxpayers funding local programs—expect local government officials to comply with laws and regulations and to take corrective actions when governmental audits make such recommendations. A follow-up system allows local government managers and city councilmembers to monitor the status of audit recommendations and be more responsive to the needs of oversight bodies and citizens. An effective follow-up system requires management to evaluate the expected costs and benefits of a recommendation, prepare a corrective action plan, and prepare and distribute periodic reports that summarize the status of audit recommendations.

Exhibit 3: *Three-Phase Audit Recommendation Follow-Up System for Local Governments*

Phase I
Reporting the Results of Audit Work

- Auditor prepares preliminary (draft) report which includes an assessment of actions taken on findings and recommendations made in prior audits. Auditor should determine if management has corrected the conditions causing those findings and implemented those recommendations. The preliminary report is submitted to the head of the audit department.
- An exit conference is attended by the auditor and the head of the audited department.
- The audited department responds to preliminary report in writing.
- Auditor issues final audit report to (1) the city council, (2) the director of finance, and (3) the head of the audited department.

Phase II
Implementing Audit Recommendations

- Department prepares a corrective action plan for each audit recommendation and submits those plans to the director of finance, the city council, and the auditor.
- Director of finance determines if the corrective action plans are appropriate. The director of finance also reviews the corrective action plans for their impact on program administration and budgeting.
- The city council reviews the corrective action plans and conducts oversight hearings.

Phase III
Reviewing Implementation Actions

- Director of finance monitors the implementation status of each recommendation and determines if corrective action is appropriate. Director of finance submits a status report to the city council with a copy to the auditor.
- City council reviews the implementation status of audit recommendations and conducts oversight activities.
- The above steps are repeated periodically to ensure that audit recommendations are being implemented as intended and that the public is receiving the benefits of audit work.

Notes

1. Governmental Accounting Standards Board, *Concepts Statement No. 1*, "Objectives of Financial Reporting" (Norwalk, Conn.: GASB, 1987), 20.
2. Comptroller General of the United States, *Government Auditing Standards,* 1994 Revision (Washington, D.C.: GPO, 1994), 8.
3. R. Freeman and C. Shoulders, *Governmental and Nonprofit Accounting Theory and Practice* (Englewood Cliffs, N.J.: Prentice Hall, 1993), 786.
4. Single Audit Act of 1984 Pub. L. No. 98-502, 98 Stat. 2327, October 19, 1984.
5. 1991 Fla. Laws ch. 429, p. 9.
6. Tennessee Code Ann. §8-4-109.
7. U.S. General Accounting Office, *How to Get Action on Audit Recommendations*, OP-9.2.1 (Washington, D.C.: GAO, July 1991).
8. Executive Office of the President, Office of Management and Budget, "Audits of State and Local Governments," Circular No. A-128 (Washington, D.C.: OMB, April 12, 1985), sec. 906.
9. GAO, *How to Get Action on Audit Recommendations*, 25.
10. The monitoring and follow-up system employed by the state of Nevada can serve as a model for local governments interested in setting up a formal audit recommendation follow-up system. The Nevada follow-up system is outlined in GAO, *How to Get Action on Audit Recommendations*, 59-71.
11. Rhett D. Harrell, *Miller Single Audit Guide: 1994* (New York: Harcourt Brace & Co., 1994), 3.22.
12. The three-phase audit recommendation follow-up system described in this section is an adaptation of the follow-up system used by the legislative auditor of the state of Nevada. A summary of the Nevada monitoring and follow-up system is presented in GAO, *How to Get Action on Audit Recommendations,* 59-71.